Beyond Contributory Pensions

DIRECTIONS IN DEVELOPMENT
Human Development

Beyond Contributory Pensions

Fourteen Experiences with Coverage Expansion in Latin America

Rafael Rofman, Ignacio Apella, and Evelyn Vezza, Editors

WORLD BANK GROUP

1 2 3 4 17 16 15 14

ISBN (paper): 978-1-4648-0390-1
ISBN (electronic): 978-1-4648-0391-8
DOI: 10.1596/978-1-4648-0390-1

Cover photo: Joaquín Torres García. *América Invertida.* © Museo Torres García. www.torresgarcia.org.uy. Used with permission. Further permission required for reuse.
Cover design: Debra Naylor, Naylor Design, Inc.

Library of Congress Cataloging-in-Publication Data

Beyond contributory pensions : fourteen experiences with coverage expansion in Latin America / Rafael Rofman, Ignacio Apella, and Evelyn Vezza, editors.
pages cm. — (Directions in development)
Includes bibliographical references.
ISBN 978-1-4648-0390-1 (alk. paper) — ISBN 978-1-4648-0391-8 (ebk)
1. Old age pensions—Government policy—Latin America. 2. Pensions—Government policy—Latin America. 3. Social security—Latin America. I. Rofman, Rafael. II. World Bank.
HD7105.35.L29B49 2014
331.25′2098—dc23 2014030072

Contents

Boxes

Figures

Maps

Tables

Preface

This book was written as part of a World Bank Project and coordinated by the editors and coauthors of the introductory chapter, Rafael Rofman, Ignacio Apella, and Evelyn Vezza. The authors of the country case studies are Vicente Albornoz (Ecuador), Ignacio Apella (Argentina), Javier Bronfman (Panama and Trinidad and Tobago), Ricardo Córdova Macías (El Salvador), Eduardo Fajnzylber (Chile), Roberto Laserna (Bolivia), Rafael Liberal Ferreira de Santana (Brazil), Sebastián Martínez (Bolivia), Juliana Martínez Franzoni (Costa Rica), Juan Martín Moreno (Paraguay), Daniela Oleas (Ecuador), Javier Olivera Angulo (Peru), Jorge Papadópulos (Uruguay), Guillermo Paraje (Chile), Gabriel Darío Ramírez (Mexico), Gonzalo Reyes (Panama and Trinidad and Tobago), Rafael Rofman (Argentina and Colombia), Helmut Schwarzer (Brazil), and F. Alejandro Villagómez (Mexico). Evelyn Vezza was also responsible for editing the original version in Spanish and supervising the English translation, which was prepared by Nicholas Wolf. David Anderson edited the English version of this volume.

Valuable input and comments were received during a presentation workshop held in Washington, DC, on April 30, 2013, from Javier Bronfman, Fernando Filgueira, Ariel Fiszbein, Michele Gragnolati, Margaret Grosh, David Kaplan, Leonardo Lucchetti, Andrew Mason, Angel Melguizo, Robert Palacios, Montserrat Pallares, William Price, Jamele Rigolini, Roberto Rocha, Carolina Romero, Heinz Rudolph, Anita Schwarz, Oleksiy Sluchynsky, and Asta Sviniene.

Special thanks to Augusto de la Torre (Chief Economist for Latin America and the Caribbean, World Bank) and Mansoora Rashid (Social Protection Sector Manager for Latin America and the Caribbean, World Bank) for their guidance during the preparation of this document.

The book includes 15 chapters, which discuss and analyze the different public policy initiatives aimed at expanding pension coverage beyond the traditional contributory schemes in 14 of the region's countries. The first chapter discusses tendencies in the region's social protection policies for the elderly over the last few decades, characterizing the reforms implemented and identifying some common aspects between different national initiatives. The following 14 chapters correspond to each of the countries analyzed, discussing the specific characteristics of each experience and, within the limits of available information, the demographic context; the traditional pension system's development; the contributive system performance—particularly in terms of coverage and financing; the design and implementation of new coverage expansion programs; and their impact in different relevant dimensions.

Abbreviations

AFAP	Administradora de Fondos de Ahorro Previsional
AFJP	Administradora de Fondos de Jubilaciones y Pensiones
AFORE	Administradora de Fondos para el Retiro
AFP	Administradora de Fondos de Pensiones
ANSES	Administración Nacional de la Seguridad Social
APS	Aporte Previsional Solidario
APV	Ahorro Previsional Voluntario
APVC	Ahorro Previsional Voluntario Colectivo
ASSE	Administración de los Servicios de Salud del Estado
AUGE	Acceso Universal con Garantías Explícitas
BDH	Bono de Desarrollo Humano
BEP	beneficio económico periódico
BPC	Base de Prestaciones y Contribuciones
BPCs	Beneficios de Prestación Continuada
bpd	Barrels per day
BPS	Banco de Previsión Social
CAGED	Catastro General de Empleados y Desempleados
CAJANAL	Caja Nacional de Previsión Social
CAM	Centro del Adulto Mayor
CARPAM	Centros de Atención Residencial para Personas Adultas Mayores
CASEN	Encuesta de Caracterízación Socioeconómica Nacional
CBTT	Central Bank of Trinidad and Tobago
CCSS	Caja Costarricense del Seguro Social
CDAP	Chronic Disease Assistance Programme
CEDIF	Centros de Desarrollo Integral de la Familia
CEDLAS	Centro de Estudios Distributivos Laborales y Sociales
CELADE	Centro Latinoamericano y Caribeño de Demografía
CEPAL	Comision Económica para America Latina y el Caribe
CFE	Comisión Federal de Electricidad
CIAM	Centros Integrales de Atención al Adulto Mayor

CIP	Certificados de Inversión Previsional
CIRAM	Los Círculos del Adulto Mayor
CMCs	Comités Municipales de Coordinación
CONADIS	Consejo Nacional de Igualdad de Discapacidades
CONAPAM	Consejo Nacional de la Persona Adulta Mayor
CONAPO	Consejo Nacional de Población
CONASA	Consejo Nacional de Salud
CONEVAL	Consejo Nacional de Evaluación de la Política de Desarrollo Social
CONPES	El Consejo Nacional de Política Económica y Social
CONSAR	Comisión Nacional de los Sistemas de Ahorro para el Retiro
CSS	Caja de Seguro Social
CURP	Clave Única de Registro de Población
DANE	Departamento Administrativo Nacional de Estadística
DF	Distrito Federal
DIPAM	Dirección de Personas Adultas Mayores
EAP	Economically active population
ECLAC	Economic Commission for Latin America and the Caribbean
ECH	Encuesta Continua de Hogares
ECV	Encuesta de Condiciones de Vida
EHPM	Encuesta de Hogares de Propósitos Múltiples
ENAHO	Encuesta Nacional de Hogares
ENEMDU	Encuesta Nacional de Empleo, Desempleo y Subempleo
ENIGH	Encuesta Nacional de Ingresos y Gastos de los Hogares
ENV	Encuesta de Nivel de Vida
EPH	Encuesta Permanente de Hogares
EPIs	Entidades Proveedores de Información
ESSALUD	Seguro Social de Salud
FCC	Fondo de Capitalización Colectiva
FCI	Fondo de Capitalización Individual
FISDL	Fondo de Inversión Social para el Desarrollo Local
FODESAF	Fondo de Bienestar Social y Asignaciones Familiares
FONASA	Fondo Nacional de Salud
FOP	Fideicomiso de Obligaciones Previsionales
FRUV	Fondo de la Renta Universal de Vejez
FSP	Fondo de Solidaridad Pensional
FSTSE	Federación de Sindicatos de Trabajadores al Servicio del Estado
GDP	Gross domestic product
IAMC	Institucione de Atención Médica Colectiva
ICSS	Instituto Colombiano de Seguros Sociales

ICV	Índice de Calidad de Vida
IDB	Inter-American Development Bank
IEEC	Instituto Ecuatoriano de Estadísticas y Censos
IESS	Instituto Ecuatoriano de Seguridad Social
IETS	Instituto de Estudos do Trabalho e Sociedade
IGBE	Instituto Brasileiro de Geografia e Estatística
ILO	International Labour Organization
IMAS	Instituto Mixto de Ayuda Social
IMF	International Monetary Fund
IMSS	Instituto Mexicano del Seguro Social
INAPAM	Instituto Nacional de las Personas Adultas Mayores
INDEC	Instituto Nacional de Estadística y Censos
INE	Instituto de Estadística
INEC	Instituto Nacional de Estadística y Censo
INEGI	Instituto Nacional de Estadística y Geografía
INEI	Instituto Nacional de Estadísticas e Informática
INFONAVIT	Instituto Nacional de Fomento a la Vivienda de los Trabajadores
INPC	Índice nacional de precios al consumidor
INPEP	Instituto Nacional de Pensiones de los Empleados Públicos
INPS	Instituto Nacional de Previsión Social
INSS	Instituto Nacional del Seguro Social
INSSJyP	Instituto Nacional de Servicios Sociales para Jubilados y Pensionados
IPEA	Instituto de Pesquisa Económica Aplicada
IPS	Instituto de Previsión Social
IPSFA	Instituto de Previsión Social de la Fuerza Armada
IRPF	Impuesto a la Renta de las Personas Físicas
ISAPRE	Instituciones de Salud Previsional
ISS	Instituto de Seguros Sociales
ISSFA	Instituto de Seguridad Social de las Fuerzas Armadas
ISSFAM	Instituto de Seguridad Social de las Fuerzas Armadas Mexicanas
ISSPOL	Instituto de Seguridad Social de la Policía
ISSS	Instituto Salvadoreño del Seguro Social
ISSSTE	Instituto de Seguridad y Servicios Sociales de los Trabajadores del Estado
IV	Invalidez y Vida
IVM	Invalidez, Vejez y Muerte
IVS	Invalidez, Vejez, y Sobrevivencia
JPS	Junta de Protección Social
LOAS	Ley Orgánica de Asistencia Social

LSS	Ley de Seguro Social
MDS	Ministerio de Desarrollo Social
MEF	Ministerio de Economía y Finanzas
MEI	Micro-emprendedor Individual
MIDES	Ministerio de Desarrollo Social
MIDIS	Ministerio de Desarrollo e Inclusión Social
MIES	Ministerio de Inclusión Económica y Social
MIMDES	Ministerio de la Mujer y Poblaciones Vulnerables
MPS	Ministerio de Previsión Social
MS	Minimum salary
MSP	Ministerio de Salud Pública
MTE	Ministerio de Trabajo y Empleo
MTEySS	Ministerio de Trabajo, Empleo y Seguridad Social
MVOTMA	Ministerio de Vivienda, Ordenamiento Territorial y Medioambiente
NCP	Noncontributory pension
NIB	National Insurance Board
NIBTT	National Insurance Board of Trinidad and Tobago
NPS	Nuevo Pilar Solidario
OECD	Organisation for Economic Co-operation and Development
OSNs	Obras Sociales Nacionales
PAI	Population Aging Index
PAIAM	Programa de Asistencia Integral para los Adultos Mayores
PAMI	Integral Medical Care Program
PAN	Partido de Acción Nacional
PANES	Plan Nacional de Atención a la Emergencia Social
PASIS	Pensiones Asistenciales
PBS	Pensión Básica Solidaria
PBU	Pensión Básica Universal
PEMEX	Petróleos Mexicanos
PEN	Programa Estado de la Nación
PGH	Padrón General de Hogares
PIT-CNT	Plenario Intersindical de Trabajadores–Convención Nacional de Trabajadores
PMG	Pensión Mínima Garantizada
PNAAM	Programa Nacional de Alimentación Complementaria al Adulto Mayor
PNAD	Pesquisa Nacional Per Amorstra Domicilios
PNBV	Plan Nacional de Buen Vivir

PNC	Pensiones No Contributivas
PPP	Purchasing Power Parity
PPS	Programa de Protección Social
PPSAM	Programa de Protección Social al Adulto Mayor
PRD	Partido de la Revolución Democrática
PRI	Partido Revolucionario Institucional
RAIS	Régimen de Ahorro Individual
RCV	Retiro, Cesantía en Edad Avanzada y Vejez
RGPS	Régimen General de Previsión Social
RJP	Régimen de Jubilación y Pensión
RMV	Renta Mensual Vitalicia
RNC	Régimen No Contributivo de Pensiones
RPM	Régimen de Prima Media
RT	Riesgos de Trabajo
SAP	Sistema de Ahorro para Pensiones
SAR	Sistema de Ahorro para el Retiro
SAS	Secretaría de Acción Social
SBC	Salario Base de Contribución
SBS	Superintendent of Banking, Insurance, and AFP
SEDESOLs	Secretarías de Desarrollo Social
SENPLADES	Secretaría Nacional de Planificación y Desarrollo
SIACAP	Sistema de Ahorro y Capitalización de Pensiones de los Servidores Públicos
SIEFOREs	Sociedades de Inversión Especializada en Fondos de Retiro
SIISE	El Sistema Integrado de Indicadores Sociales
SIJP	Sistema Integrado de Jubilaciones y Pensiones
SIMPLES	Sistema Integrado de Pago de Impuestos y Contribuciones de las Microempresas y de las Empresas de Pequeño Porte
SIS	Seguro de Invalidez y Sobrevivencia
SIS	Seguro Integral de Salud
SISBEN	Sistema de Identificación de Potenciales Beneficiarios de Programas Sociales
SISFOH	Sistema de Focalización de Hogares
SMN	Salario Mínimo Nacional
SNIS	Sistema Nacional Integrado de Salud
SNP	Sistema Nacional de Pensiones
SNS	Servicio Nacional de Salud
SNSS	Sistema Nacional de Servicios de Salud
SPP	Sistema Privado de Pensiones

SPS	Sistema de Pensiones Solidarias
SPSU	Sistema de Protección Social Universal
SUAS	Sistema Único de Asistencia Social
SUPEN	Superintendencia de Pensiones
SUS	Sistema Único de Salud
TFR	Total fertility rate
TMC	Transferencias Monetarias con Corresponsabilidad
UR	Unidad Reajustable

CHAPTER 1

Introduction and Overview

Rafael Rofman, Ignacio Apella, and Evelyn Vezza

Expanding Income Protection for the Elderly in Latin America

Since the beginning of the 21st century, income protection systems for the elderly in Latin America have been subject to a series of profound reforms. In contrast to the majority of reforms that were implemented during the second half of the 20th century, these reforms were not aimed at improving fiscal sustainability, incorporating new parties in management, modifying financial management rules, or adjusting the various criteria of existing contribution schemes. Instead, these reforms focused on the goal of inclusion, expanding the systems' coverage beyond the traditionally covered population of workers in the formal sector of the economy.

Although noncontributory schemes have existed in the region (and the world) for decades, the observed trend in the last few years is unprecedented in terms of the intensity and speed with which these systems have expanded. Between 2000 and 2013 at least 18 countries in the region introduced inclusive reforms, which sought to increase coverage of the elderly (figure 1.1).

This rapid succession of reforms begs the question as to the motives behind this trend. As we discuss in greater detail later in this introduction, the recent changes appear to have originated as the result of the combination of several factors, including (1) the exhaustion of the model of normative coverage expansion developed during the second half of the past century; (2) improvements in the fiscal situation of the countries in the region, due in part to policy decisions and also the result of an economic boom generated by a sudden increase in the demand for primary products; and (3) social pressure demanding more active social protection policies, with a focus on vulnerable groups.

The reforms implemented in recent years have enabled the inclusion of important groups of the elderly in social protection systems—groups that until these reforms had no access to such systems. The inclusion strategies were based

Rafael Rofman, Lead Specialist in Social Protection, Ignacio Apella, Specialist in Social Protection, both in the Social Protection Unit, Human Development Department, Regional Office for Latin America of the World Bank, and Evelyn Vezza, Associate Researcher, Center for Distributive, Labor and Social Studies.

Figure 1.1 Timeline of Reforms Aimed at Expanding Coverage for the Elderly, Selected Countries, 2000–14

2000	2001	2002	2003	2004	2005	2006	2007	2008	2009	2010	2011	2012	2013	2014
								BO						
								CL		BO				
						BR		BR		PE				ES?
			AR	AR		EC	UY	PE	ES	PY				EC?
CR	MX		MX	CO	UY	MX	MX	UY	PA	T&T	PE		CO	MX?

Source: Based on information from chapters 2 to 15 of this book and information from social security agencies in the region.
Note: AR = Argentina; BO = Bolivia; BR = Brazil; CL = Chile; CO = Colombia; CR = Costa Rica; EC = Ecuador; ES = El Salvador; MX = Mexico; PA = Panama; PE = Peru; PY = Paraguay; T&T = Trinidad and Tobago; UY = Uruguay.

on two different models: the expansion of traditional contributory social protection systems or the development of poverty reduction programs targeted at the elderly. Differences emerged between the models with respect to the legal and institutional tools used, benefit adequacy, and the fiscal and economic sustainability of the new programs. The models also showed a variety of impacts and interactions with other areas of public policy such as links to the job market, traditional social protection systems, and social assistance programs.[1] This plethora of differences offers a copious range of elements for the analysis and evaluation of coverage-related policies.

This book presents a description of the reforms implemented in Latin America, covering the experiences of 14 countries in the region. The analysis shows that the most common factor among the reforms analyzed is the search for ways to increase coverage. Nonetheless, the differences observed among the reforms are important due to the initial conditions in which they were designed, their main goals, and the implementation capacity that exists in each country. Consequently, the results are not homogenous, and it is possible to identify some aspects where policy decisions can result in better or worse outcomes.

This introduction presents a summary of the main points revealed in the analyses of each of the 14 countries included in the book. Although this work is not a complete catalog of income protection policies in the 41 countries and territories of Latin America and the Caribbean, the group of cases analyzed allows for a clear vision of the direction and characteristics of the policies considered. In the next section, we discuss in greater detail the reasons why we think this book represents a significant contribution to the debate about income protection policies for the elderly in the region, even though it does not offer a normative or prescriptive discussion in terms of the policies analyzed, but rather a description of the significant developments that have occurred in the region in recent years. The following section develops the principal elements of an analytical framework that guides the later discussion. Next, we describe the regional demographic context and its relevance to the social protection systems analyzed in this study, as well as the initial conditions that produced such reforms from the previous social protection systems and the coverage challenges they faced. In this context, the following sections begin a tour of the reforms in the region. Starting with their motives, we identify with greater precision the traditional systems' coverage problems and the recently implemented reforms, and we then propose a system of classification for them that highlights the principal characteristics and factors that define the systems. As a next step, we use this taxonomy to discuss the fiscal implications of the implemented reforms. Finally, as a conclusion, the last section of this chapter points out some of the main challenges observed in the implementation processes of these policies in the short and medium term. We discuss the chief preconditions necessary to ensure the implemented reforms' durability over time and their future prospects.

Rationale

Income protection policies for the elderly in Latin America have been the center of intense political and academic debates in recent decades. Since the adoption of an individual contribution scheme in Chile at the beginning of the 1980s, different actors have focused on evaluating the operation of traditional contribution-based and pay-as-you-go social protection systems that have existed in the majority of countries in the region, proposing different reforms aimed at improving their operations. During most of the 1990s, the policy focus turned toward improving the fiscal sustainability of the programs, reducing state exposure by introducing individual contribution schemes, and changes to eligibility criteria. This trend aroused interest among analysts, and multiple individuals and institutions prepared reports to identify the key elements of these policies and propose models for the design and management of these systems. A quick review of the activities of major international organizations during this period includes a book published by the World Bank in 1994, now recognized as central to the policy debate, which called the new schemes that began to spread across the region "multipillar" (World Bank 1994). Other authors and institutions continued the debate and analysis. The International Labour Organization's (ILO) 2001 report stood out because it highlighted the necessity of expanding social security protection to excluded workers and families through a combination of greater coverage under contributory schemes, promotion of micro-insurance, development of universal coverage schemes, and the provision of targeted benefits (ILO 2001).

At the beginning of the 21st century, many of the countries in the region and various countries in other regions had implemented reform. Discussion then slowly turned toward measuring the impacts of these reforms on the three main aspects of any income protection system for the elderly: coverage, benefit adequacy, and sustainability. Even though in many cases the reforms appear to have contributed to improving the medium-term sustainability of the systems, the impact on benefit adequacy and coverage appeared to be less or even negative. The World Bank published a regional report in 2005 discussing the effectiveness of the new systems in responding to social demands (Gill, Packard, and Yermo 2005). As an institution, the bank also reopened the debate in 2005, with the publication of *Old Age Income Support in the 21st Century*, which suggests the adoption of a scheme based on five pillars that, together, result in universal coverage (Holzmann and Hinz 2005). Similarly, other institutions weighed in on the same debate. In 2006 the Economic

Commission for Latin America and the Caribbean (ECLAC) published its report for the 31st period of sessions, suggesting that the central policy objective should be coverage under a rights-based framework. The framework would argue that benefits should not be linked to the existence of previous contributions, but rather should be a condition of citizenship (ECLAC 2006). The same citizenship rights would relate not just to elderly social protection programs, but also to health and cash transfers to families with children. The ILO, using similar reasoning, introduced in 2011 the concept of a "Social Protection Floor" that promoted the adoption of social protection systems that, through a combination of tools, permitted the development of a universal coverage model (ILO 2011). For its part, the Inter-American Development Bank (IDB) also contributed to the discussion with a recent publication (IDB 2013) that analyzes the regional situation. IDB proposes a model based on a universal coverage scheme, financed by taxes supplemented by subsidized contribution schemes. In academic circles, the discussion in recent years has also focused on the topics of coverage and social inclusion. The works of Barr (2001), Hanlon, Barrientos, and Hulme (2010), and Barr and Diamond (2009) are clear examples of this.

Within this context, this book does not attempt to present a normative vision or offer a prescriptive discussion about how to advance toward new reforms. The intention is to summarize the initiatives adopted by a significant group of countries in the region. These countries, at the same time the aforementioned debates have been occurring, in recent years have moved decisively toward schemes that all possess a more inclusive focus, and have also increased coverage of older adults under income protection systems. As you will see throughout the 14 country case studies presented, the starting points, political visions, tools used, and results in each case demonstrate important differences. Given this context, the goal of this book is to document these initiatives using the same analytical criteria, with the goal of filling what we believe is an important void in the literature. In doing so, we hope to contribute to informing policy makers and analysts about what has occurred in this area in recent years.

Analytical Framework

The main objectives of social security systems are to smooth income levels during individuals' lifetimes, beginning with replacing their work income after retirement, and reducing the incidence of poverty among older adults. An intermediate vision of these goals also proposes using them to improve intragenerational wealth distribution. A person's general capacity to possess goods constitutes a main element of the quality of life in old age. Diverse studies show that, along with lifetime risks, old age is a clear factor in the characterization of poverty (Sánchez 2000). In other words, old age contributes to a condition of fragility, in which individuals can quickly fall from subsistence-level survival to poverty more easily than in other stages of their lives (Wolf 1989).

According to Huenchuan and Guzmán (2006), the transitions to retirement and widowhood reduce income (already tightened by necessity) and increase the probability of poverty in homes with older adults. Additionally, the economic situation of individuals during old age is determined partially in the period prior to retirement from the job market, because during this period of economic activity people generate savings (compulsory and/or voluntary) that reduce the negative effects of their personal income drop during retirement.

In this context, retirement savings clearly evince characteristics of merit goods, inasmuch as there can exist a certain "shortsightedness" among economic agents, who maintain a discount rate too high to evaluate future consumption. This means that, on their own, they are not incentivized to generate savings to supplement income drops during old age. Normally it is argued that judging the well-being of each individual according to his or her own decisions—as occurs with the principle of efficiency in Pareto terms—is an unsuitable standard, given that consumers can make "bad" decisions (Stiglitz 1986).

As a result of the potential reduction in their work income, the risk of falling below the poverty line and its effects increase, ceteris paribus, to the extent that a group's age increases and the probability increases that group members will retire from the job market. In many cases, the income reduction does not occur in reality, because of the existence of individuals' other income-generating mechanisms, or because older adults that live with other family members are able to maintain their household income at levels above the poverty line.[2] This situation, along with low savings availability, and in many cases low capacity to save, causes the majority of countries to implement some type of public policy to protect older adults' income levels. In general, these public policies, designed, implemented, and/or regulated by the state, can take one of two forms depending on their primary goal, affecting their design in terms of financing schemes and beneficiary selection.

On one hand, programs whose main goal is to smooth workers' income levels during their lifetime are usually conceived as contributory schemes. Their financing comes from contributions based on gross salaries, which give workers rights to receive benefits after retiring from the labor market. This type of program is usually referred to generically as a social security system or a contributory pension.

The logic behind the creation of these systems is that retirement savings can be considered a merit good, due to the fact that during their active work lives workers tend to estimate a very low future discount factor (i.e., a very high discount rate), and for this reason they are not incentivized to save for their retirement. In other words, given that retirement saving is viewed as postponed consumption—competing with multiple alternatives of present consumption—there is less interest in evaluating it periodically. As a result, the state, playing a paternalistic role, introduces compulsory savings mechanisms during a worker's economically active periods with the goal of using these resources to pay benefits to replace work income during retirement.

In general, these systems establish minimum requirements for retirement age and the number of years contributing to the system, especially if they include minimum benefit clauses in their design. Although financing this model in its pure version depends exclusively on collections, its effectiveness in accomplishing its objectives depends on labor market conditions, which limits its expansion of coverage beyond the sector of formal workers. In other words, a person's work history—especially the amount contributed—defines their benefit eligibility.

On the other hand, the majority of labor markets in the region register significant proportions of the population working informally or in unpaid jobs (especially among women). The high turnover observed, where workers frequently move between formal, informal, and unpaid jobs and unemployment and inactivity, has pushed many countries to focus their efforts on poverty prevention. As a result, they have tried to prioritize systems supported through general revenues, with eligibility not conditioned upon work history. These schemes, usually called noncontributory or social pensions, grant cash transfers during old age intended to mitigate the risk of falling below the poverty line during periods in a worker's lifetime when it is not possible to obtain sufficient income from the labor market.

The policies and programs directed toward poverty alleviation among older adults obviously have points in common with those directed to other groups, whether they are families with children or the general population. Upon consideration of these programs, several reasonable doubts present themselves: Why should the state be any more or less concerned with poverty among older adults than with poverty in general? If the motivation is the same for all age groups, should age-specific programs exist, or should the focus be on the most vulnerable? Arguments in favor of supporting older adults in particular exist (they face greater difficulties in obtaining resources from nonpublic sources such as the labor market, and they are more vulnerable because of age-associated factors), but the debate remains unresolved.

Both types of programs of income transfer to the retired population are called social protection systems, and they are further divided into contributory and noncontributory, respectively. Together, they form the foundation of the system of income protection for older adults. Although different design options exist, the social protection systems (or, more broadly, income protection systems for older adults) have in common that they are public policies through which the state pursues the objectives of sustaining income during old age. These policies are implemented in a restrictive environment, where labor market characteristics, the availability of fiscal resources, and political conditions typically make up the main factors that affect the state's capacity to achieve the stated objectives.

In general, the performance of social protection systems, both contributory and noncontributory, is evaluated based on three criteria: (1) coverage, understood as older adults' access to benefits—especially the most economically vulnerable groups—and in the case of contributory schemes of the workers that should be generating rights to future benefits; (2) benefit adequacy, that is, that the value of the transfers beneficiaries receive should be sufficient to achieve the stated goals; and (3) sustainability, actuarial, fiscal, and economic, that is, that society in general and the state in particular in relation to the responsibilities that it assumes by managing the system are able to fulfill the financial commitments created by the system in the short, medium, and long term.

These three criteria are in competition, in the sense that it is not possible to increase coverage or raise benefits without affecting the financial needs of income protection schemes. The central challenge for policy makers and system implementers is to find politically and socially acceptable equilibria. This is expressed with programs that respond to policy goals through defining beneficiary selection, the calculation of monetary benefits, the institutional framework for administering fiscal resources and expenses, and the type of financing and sustainability.

Coverage

The reach or coverage of social protection systems is determined by the particular goal pursued, which simultaneously allows one to limit the range of possible tools for identifying and selecting beneficiaries. Faced with the goal of replacing income from work, traditional social protection systems are based on contributory schemes that use collection mechanisms among active workers intended to pay for retirement benefits, administered through pay-as-you-go or funded schemes. These schemes are similar to insurance, in which active workers pay a monthly premium to insure themselves against the risk of losing work income during old age. All workers that have paid the insurance premium during their working years are entitled to receive a pension when the loss, the reduction of work income, occurs. Given the stated objective, beneficiary eligibility is usually defined as a function of the minimum legal retirement age and the accumulation of contributions throughout a worker's economically active years. Workers' contribution density, measured as the quotient of the number of months or years contributing and the total months or years potentially active, determines their access to benefits and the amount they receive.

Alternatively, it is possible to make the goal of the system reducing the incidence of poverty among older adults. In this case, beneficiary eligibility should be determined based on some measure that identifies the population with the highest level of vulnerability. In general, the selection mechanisms vary among countries, depending on available records, technical capacity, and policy preference. Targeting eligibility based on poverty level always presents difficulties associated with making inclusion errors (including beneficiaries that are not vulnerable) and exclusion errors (excluding vulnerable older adults). Targeting options include verifying income levels through surveys, administrative records, and categorical or geographic targeting, among others.

The process of defining goals and the selection of mechanisms for identifying beneficiaries determine, at least partially, which institution will be responsible for administering and implementing noncontributory income transfer programs. In that sense, given the objective of coverage expansion, it could be reasonable to assign this task to the institution that typically administers the contributory social protection program. On the other hand, faced with the goal of poverty reduction among the most vulnerable groups, it could be more logical to use a different institution, especially if there is already an agency tasked with managing income transfers to households via targeted mechanisms.

Benefit Adequacy

Once policy makers have defined a system's goals and the tools it will use to achieve a certain level of coverage, a second important aspect in social protection system performance is setting benefit levels, that is, the amount received by beneficiaries sufficient to accomplish the goals set by the system. Again, a performance evaluation of systems along this dimension requires one to specify the desired policy goal. If the goal is to replace salary income with a contributory system, then a good performance indicator could be the replacement rate, that is, the ratio of benefits to salary. In general, contributory pay-as-you-go systems tend to define benefits as a percentage of workers' historical income, individually or collectively, whereas individually funded schemes offer, by definition, a benefit linked to the historical contributions (and therefore the salaries) of each worker. By this logic, it is reasonable to evaluate the suitability of benefits of these programs by comparing the value of benefits received with the salaries or incomes of active workers.

In the case of programs principally designed to prevent poverty, it makes more sense for benefit levels to be tied to the value of consumer price indices or poverty lines. In many cases benefits in these types of programs are set using mechanisms similar to poverty reduction programs for other segments of the population. Thus, it appears more justifiable for these types of programs to examine the relationship between poverty lines and benefit levels to evaluate their adequacy.

Sustainability

In a context of budget limitations a clear dilemma between programs' benefit levels and coverage exists because both variables affect the level of required funding in the same way, creating risks for program sustainability. This is particularly important in traditional contributory social protection systems based on pure pay-as-you-go financial regimes, in which actuarial sustainability (i.e., the capacity to sustain a sufficient flow of contributed resources to cover the expected expenditures for a reasonably long period of time) is of utmost importance. However, sustainability is not just important for pure pay-as-you-go systems, but also affects any funding scheme for income protection programs for older adults.

In general terms, fiscal sustainability is also apt for consideration, specifically the state's capacity to generate enough income to cover expenditure obligations. This aspect is relevant when the state assumes a financial commitment to sustain the system beyond the resources it collects, as is the case in the majority of contributory systems in Latin America. In these systems, through additional funding, minimum pension guarantees, or other schemes, the state commits to pay for a portion of benefits from its general revenues.[3] This same definition of fiscal sustainability is also suitable for evaluating noncontributory social protection systems or coverage expansion because their funding comes completely from tax collections.

Finally, a broader concept of sustainability of income protection programs for older adults is called economic sustainability. This concept deals with an entire society's capacity to earmark a certain percentage of its wealth to transfers to the older adult population, regardless of the funding source. This concept becomes more relevant in countries like those in Latin America that are undergoing a process of demographic aging. This process has potential impacts not just on the quantity of the population dependent on income from third parties in the future, but also on the economy's capacity to maintain the rate of capital accumulation, productivity increases, and economic growth sufficient to assign a portion of these resources to the older adult population.

Although the discussions about sustainability in this chapter focus on the costs of recent initiatives to increase coverage, it is important to recognize that in many cases income protection programs for older adults can be viewed as comprehensive policies. In this context, the fiscal space to introduce a noncontributory scheme is not just determined by the cost of the proposed program, but also by the impact that traditional social protection programs have on public accounts and the economy in general. If existing systems produce severe deficits that must be covered by general revenues, then it is likely that they will create a crowding out effect. This crowding out means that a program that on its own may not produce very high costs could be judged as an addition to a sector or set of programs that is already too costly.

The discussion of the reforms implemented in the region in recent years that is presented in the following sections is organized around this analytical framework. We identify the different characteristics of the initiatives considered in this analysis through the taxonomy developed in the "Procoverage Reforms: Why Now?" section, and we examine how these initiatives impact coverage, appropriateness of benefits, and system sustainability in the different countries. At the same time, we recognize that important difference exist in each country's initial conditions and economic, political, and social context.

The Demographic Context in Latin America

Latin American and Caribbean countries are engaged in a process of demographic transition characterized by sustained growth in the dependency ratio of the older adult population. The aging of the population creates concerns, in the medium and long term, related to the job market, the health care system, and especially the social protection system. Social protection systems in particular are vulnerable to the effects of population aging on their actuarial and fiscal sustainability. This topic has been the subject of a wide range of literature and has provoked multiple reforms to contributory pay-as-you-go schemes over the years. Even in systems based on an individually funded model, the effects of aging impact their economic sustainability as we discussed in the previous section.

The aging phenomenon starts with clearly declining mortality and fertility rate trends across the region. In 1950 life expectancy was on average just 52 years, but by 2010 had reached 74 and by 2100 it is expected to exceed 85 years. In just 150 years, the region's population will have extended the average lifespan by more than 60 percent. In terms of fertility, the total fertility rate, which was around six children per woman in 1950, has dropped to two children per women currently and is expected to remain stable around this level in the future.

These trends, which undoubtedly represent important social and quality of life improvements for the population, will have a major impact on the overall age structure, which is especially important for income protection policies for older adults. Figure 1.2 shows the median age for the Latin American population from 1950 to 2100, an indicator generally used to observe the population aging process. The region's median age, which was less than 20 years in 1950, is currently about 28 years and will continue increasing to about 47 years by the end of the century. As a result, the dependency ratio of older adults (defined as the ratio between the population over 65 and the population from 15 to 65 years old) will increase from approximately six older adults per 100 economically active adults in 1950 and 10 older adults in 2010 to more than 50 in 2100.

The overall trend hides significant heterogeneity among countries in the region. Figure 1.3 shows, for each country, the dependency ratio observed in

Figure 1.2 Median Age and Dependency Ratio of the Elderly, Latin America, 1950–2100

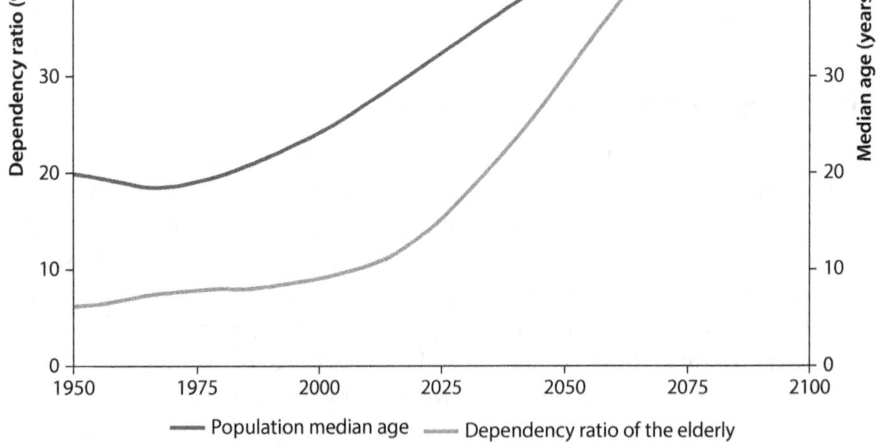

Source: Centro Latinoamericano y Caribeño de Demografía—Economic Commission for Latin America and the Caribbean (CELADE-ECLAC).

Figure 1.3 Dependency Ratio of the Elderly, Selected Countries, 2010 and 2100

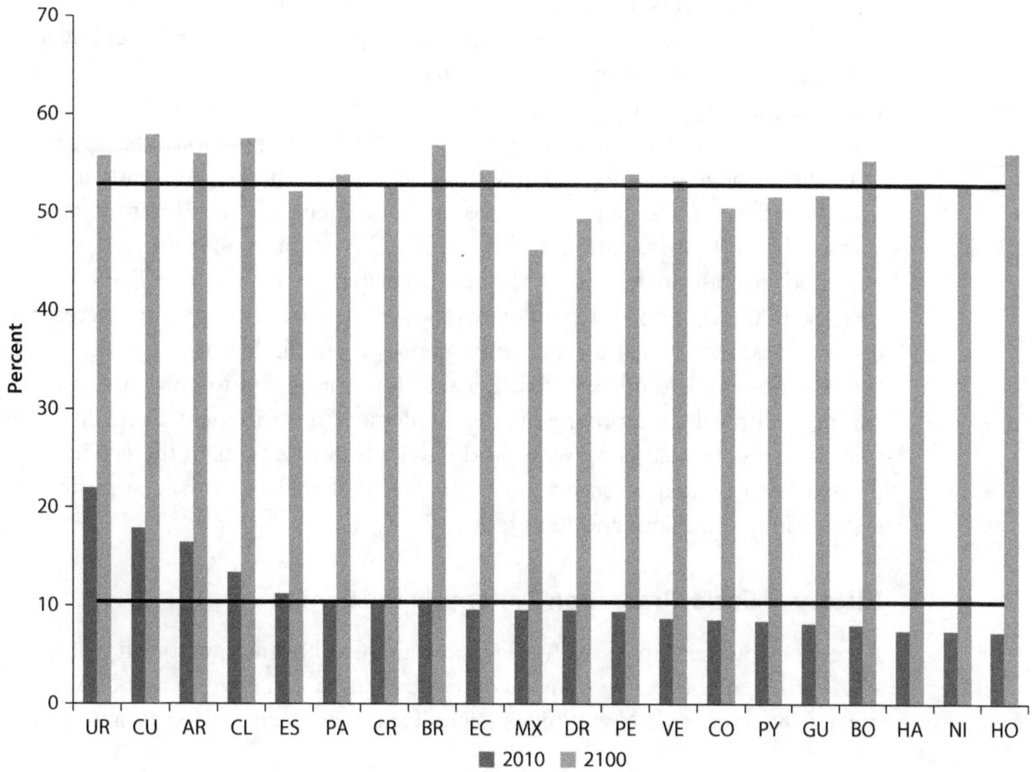

Source: Based on information from Centro Latinoamericano y Caribeño de Demografía—Economic Commission for Latin America and the Caribbean (CELADE-ECLAC).

Note: AR = Argentina; BO = Bolivia; BR = Brazil; CL = Chile; CO = Colombia; CR = Costa Rica; CU = Cuba; DR = Dominican Republic; EC = Ecuador; ES = El Salvador; GU = Guyana; HA = Haiti; HO = Honduras; MX = Mexico; NI = Nicaragua; PA = Panama; PE = Peru; PY = Paraguay; UR = Uruguay; VE = Venezuela, RB.

2010 and the expected value for 2100. Four countries in Latin America stood out in 2010 for having dependency ratios that were significantly higher than the average: Uruguay (22 percent), Cuba (20.1 percent), Argentina (17.3 percent), and Chile (15.2 percent). At the other extreme, during the same period Nicaragua (7.4 percent), Honduras (7.6 percent), and Haiti (7.6 percent) had dependency ratios that were 33 percent or more below the regional average. These results demonstrate the heterogeneity of the aging process among countries, with sharp differences of up to 14.6 percentage points. Even though projections assume convergence for the principal demographic variables in the long term, it is clear that these differences will persist for many years. By 2100 Cuba is expected to have the highest dependency ratio in the region (57.9 percent), whereas Mexico will have the lowest (46.3 percent), reflecting the different transition processes taking place in each country.

Although the demographic situation is a direct constraint on the performance of social protection systems, both as a determinant of the potential beneficiary population and as it affects the systems' actuarial sustainability, other processes, such as changes in labor market participation, can significantly dampen or increase these effects. In general, the demographic dependency ratio is defined statically at certain cutoff ages, considering the population under 15 and over 65 as inactive. But the average ages for entering and leaving the workforce change over time, making an analysis of the economic dependency ratio (defined as the ratio between the inactive population and the active population) more relevant than the demographic dependency ratio. Figure 1.4 shows the trends in these activity ratios for the population around retirement age and for middle-aged women (20–60 years) gathered from ECLAC's estimates and projections. The expected increase in female workforce participation should be reflected as an increase in the economic dependency ratio. For its part, the expected increase in economic activity ratios for the retirement-age population appears to indicate that the observed trend in recent decades (and projected to continue into the future) will result in a progressive postponement of retirement from the labor market. These trends, along with productivity improvements in the economy in general, are essential to ensure the economic sustainability of social protection systems in the medium and long term.

History of Social Protection Systems in the Region

All of the countries in Latin America and the Caribbean have social protection systems designed to achieve the income substitution and poverty reduction goals previously discussed. Nonetheless, significant heterogeneity exists among the

Figure 1.4 Activity Ratios for Adults from 55 to 75 Years Old and Women from 20 to 60 Years Old, Latin America, 1980–2050

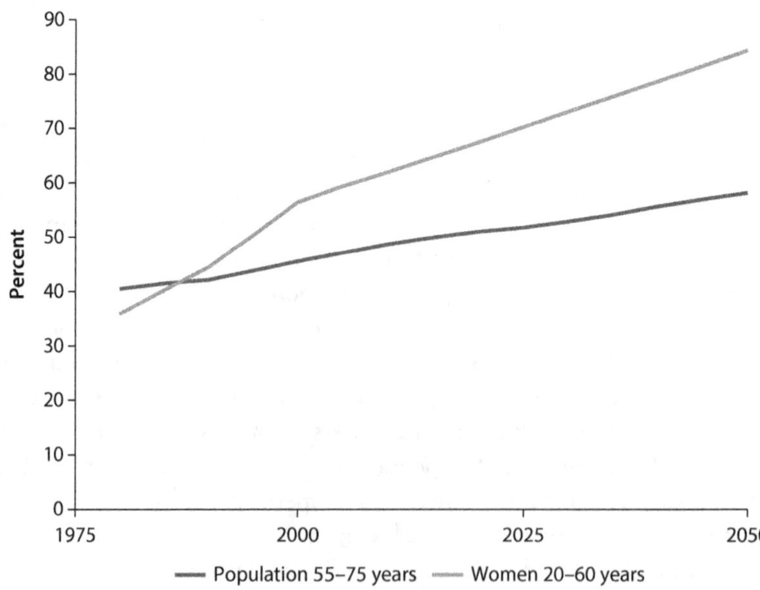

Source: Based on information from Centro Latinoamericano y Caribeño de Demografía—Economic Commission for Latin America and the Caribbean (CELADE-ECLAC).

systems, in terms of both their historical development and their current characteristics and functioning. According to Mesa-Lago (1978), the countries of the region can be classified in three groups according to the origin and level of development of their social security systems: pioneers, intermediate, and latecomers.

The group of pioneers is composed of those countries that introduced their systems during the first three decades of the 20th century: Argentina, Brazil, Chile, Cuba, and Uruguay. During this period social protection systems began by protecting occupations or labor force groups that were more organized, generally related to unions, and linked to the state. Later, larger and less powerful sectors were incorporated into the systems. One of the characteristics of these systems was the gradual and fragmented expansion of coverage through the creation of specific funds for different occupations (Mesa-Lago and Bertranou 1998). The absence of coordination among subsystems in terms of coverage and eligibility criteria for acquiring rights and benefits caused these countries to maintain the most stratified systems in the region.

The intermediate group of countries introduced their first social protection systems in the 1940s and 1950s. This group is composed of Bolivia, Colombia, Costa Rica, Ecuador, Mexico, Panama, Paraguay, Peru, and República Bolivariana de Venezuela. The social security systems of this group of countries began with a lower level of stratification compared with the pioneer countries because their systems were not the products of worker demands from different sectors, but rather government initiatives that sought to build a model of the Welfare State by replicating institutions that existed in the countries of Western Europe.

Finally, the latecomer group of countries is made up of El Salvador, Haiti, Honduras, Guatemala, Nicaragua, and the Dominican Republic. In these countries, social security programs began in the 1960s and 1970s. In general these systems are limited in terms of coverage and funding, with significant levels of exclusion for workers outside the public sector or the most dynamic economic sectors. It is also possible to include the non–Latin Caribbean countries, given that they achieved independence in the 1970s and 1980s and were the last to introduce social security systems. In general terms, this group maintains the most unified and uniform systems in the region.

The majority of the region's social protection systems grew out of contribution-based funding schemes. This type of funding system sets up contribution mechanisms for the economically active population that pay for benefits upon retirement, whether through immediate transfers (pay-as-you-go schemes) or a savings plan (funded schemes). For this reason, eligibility requirements are tied to workers' contribution histories, such that those individuals that contribute earn the right to receive benefits. As such, the contributory mechanism operates not just as a funding system, but also as a targeting tool that helps identify potential beneficiaries of the program among those who have received income during the periods when they were economically active that should be replaced with pension income upon retirement. This funding system, and therefore targeting mechanism, is unavoidably subject to the risks associated with labor market limitations that affect workers' job histories, and that can produce budget and coverage problems if the system is not designed for the real labor market in a context of high labor informality.

Contribution-based systems are associated with—even if only theoretically—the idea that the need to receive retirement benefits arises from people's inability to continue working and earning a salary after a certain age. Thus it is necessary to find a way to replace this lost income. Following Rofman and Oliveri's (2012) logic, there would be no need to provide retirement benefits to people who did not receive wages before retirement age, given that upon retirement they would not face any lost income that would need to be replaced. Therefore, retirement benefits would represent a form of providing continuity to salary income, and they could even be considered to be part of a worker's salary paid as deferred wages. Consequently, social protection systems can be classified as contributory as much from a funding perspective as from a beneficiary selection perspective.

However, in reality the connection between beneficiary selection and funding models does not always function perfectly. In many cases, contribution-based schemes (in terms of funding) have redistributive components in terms of access to benefits. And, conversely, it is common to find programs in which only those who have contributed have access to benefits, even though their funding is at least partially from noncontributory sources (and where access is more difficult for groups with the greatest vulnerability in terms of entry into the job market, such as people with lower educational achievement, low-income groups, and women) (Rofman and Oliveri 2012).

For most of their history, Latin American social protection systems have been based on a pay-as-you-go funding system. Thus, their financial sustainability (income/expenses) depends on two factors: the level of contributions (dependent on salary and the share set aside for contributions) and the ratio between active contributing workers and retired beneficiaries (dependent on the economic activity ratio and the demographic situation of the society in question). The existing pay-as-you-go systems in the majority of pioneer and intermediate countries were designed using very optimistic estimates of functional dependency ratios (i.e., how many contributing workers per beneficiary). As a result, they showed their first symptoms of crisis as they matured and the number of beneficiaries increased. The history of social protection systems in each of these countries is the story of gradual increases in contributions, reductions in expected benefits,[4] and eligibility restrictions, all used to improve the their financial sustainability in the short and medium term. These restrictive reforms have almost always been difficult in political terms, and in some cases in social aspects as well, because as a consequence of the restrictions some workers were excluded from the system.

In the final decades of the last century fiscal concerns increased significantly. On the one hand, demographic trends indicated that in the majority of the countries in the region the process of demographic aging was accelerating. At the same time, the systems were becoming so mature that it was no longer viable to expand the pool of contributing workers as a means of improving the financial situation of the programs. Finally, the budget situation of countries in the region was complex for most of the 1980s and 1990s, which limited the ability of governments to finance their social protection systems' temporary or structural deficits. As can be seen in panel a of figure 1.5, the available estimates of implied pension obligations at the beginning of the 1990s showed very high levels of fiscal commitments, above 100 percent of gross domestic product (GDP) in almost all of the countries analyzed and above 200 percent in several.

Figure 1.5 Implied Pension Obligations, Selected Countries, 2000–50

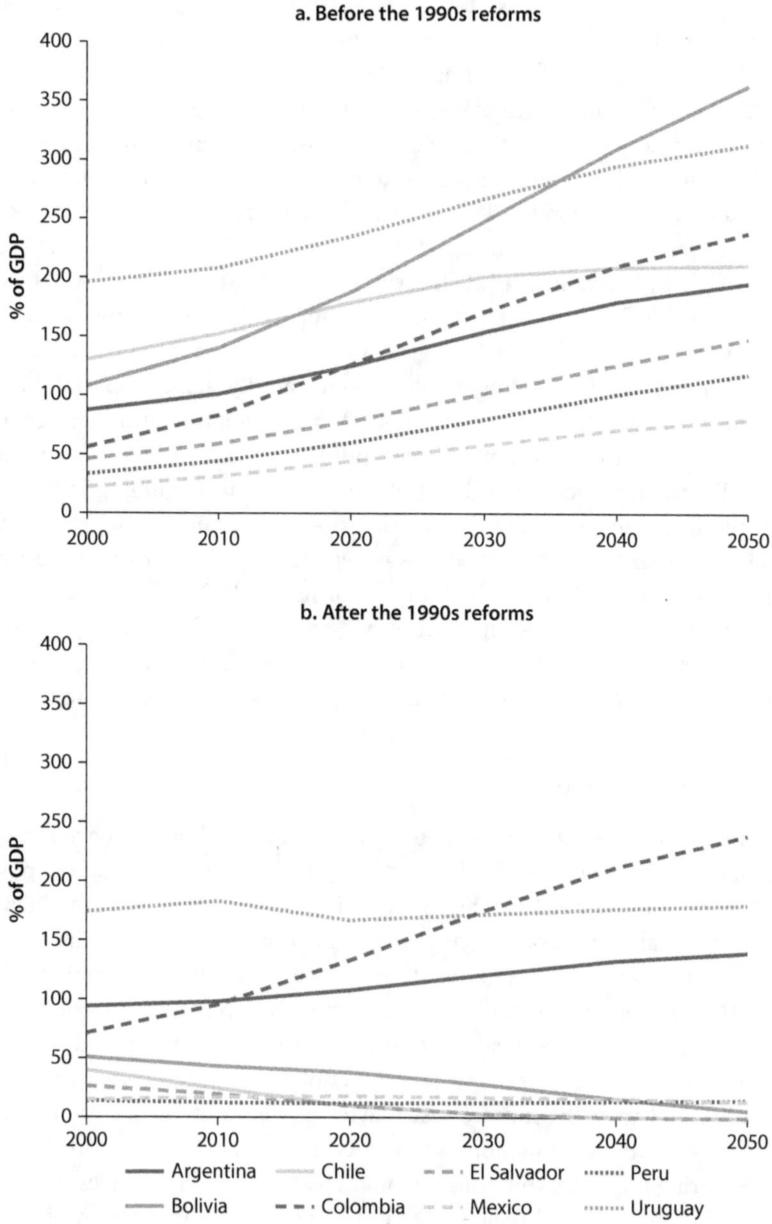

Source: Zviniene and Packard 2004.

This situation was the primary motive behind a new series of reforms, which began in Chile in 1981 and after 1993 expanded to various countries in the region. These reforms incorporated new restrictions on benefit eligibility, such as increases in the minimum retirement age and the required number of years of contributions or work to gain benefits. They also introduced individually funded components in the programs that resulted in a reduction of expected benefits and a transfer of financial market and volatility risk from the state to the individual. The impact of these reforms was important for the medium- and long-term sustainability of these systems. Panel b of figure 1.5 shows the implied pension obligation levels after implementing the reforms, clearly demonstrating a reduction in the state's future financial commitments.

Chile exchanged its traditional system of pay-as-you-go social protection for one of individually funded accounts to pay for retirement, while disability and death benefits are funded under a mixed individual savings and collective insurance system. Beginning in the 1990s, Peru (1993), Argentina (1994),[5] Colombia (1994), Uruguay (1996), Bolivia (1997), Mexico (1997), El Salvador (1998), Ecuador (2001),[6] Costa Rica (2001), the Dominican Republic (2003–05), and Panama (2005–07) introduced structural reforms. These reforms had distinct aspects and characteristics, but they all shared a common objective: to make their social protection systems viable among rapidly aging populations, or in other words to ensure that they are funded in the medium and long term. Just a few countries in the region maintained public pay-as-you-go social protection systems. Brazil introduced significant eligibility reforms beginning in the 1990s, and República Bolivariana de Venezuela approved a new model to substitute for the old system, but this model was rejected by the current government, which in turn also adopted eligibility reforms. In 1999 Nicaragua approved an individually funded system, but it was never implemented. Guatemala, Honduras, and Paraguay have also considered structural or eligibility reforms, but no public discussion of reforms have taken place in Cuba or Haiti.

The Coverage Problem

From their beginnings, social protection systems in Latin America have faced serious challenges in including the greatest proportion of the population possible, both workers and older adults. The root of this problem is related to the high level of labor informality present in Latin American countries, added to the contributory nature that social protection systems in the region have maintained during most of their history. The various eligibility reforms implemented throughout the 20th century, as well as those adopted in the 1980s and 1990s, aimed to improve the financial sustainability of the social protection systems, but in many cases these reforms brought with them more restrictive eligibility criteria and, consequently, less coverage. Some analysts hoped that the introduction of individually funded schemes during the last two decades would create a set of incentives for workers that would drive increased registration and compliance with pension obligations, but this does not appear to have been the case, at least not in any significant way.

Given that social protection systems exist to protect the population of older adults who cannot continue to earn a living in the labor market, low levels of coverage are a serious signal of the systems' lack of effectiveness. This problem is usually attributed to high levels of labor informality. This argument is technically correct, but it does not answer a basic question: In the public policy framework, what role does a social protection system that does not smooth consumption nor offer protection from poverty for the majority of older adults in a society have? Given that these systems are contribution-based, it makes sense to check the economically active population's level of participation in them. Figure 1.6 shows the percentage of the economically active population that contributed to pension systems at the beginning of the 1990s, in the early 2000s, and, currently, in 18 countries in the region.

The coverage rate for the economically active population was less than 30 percent in eight of the 18 countries for which information was available at the end of the first decade of the 21st century. These countries' relative position compared with the rest of the region is not very different from their position at

Figure 1.6 Economically Active Population That Contributes to the Social Protection System, Selected Countries, 1990, 2000, and 2010

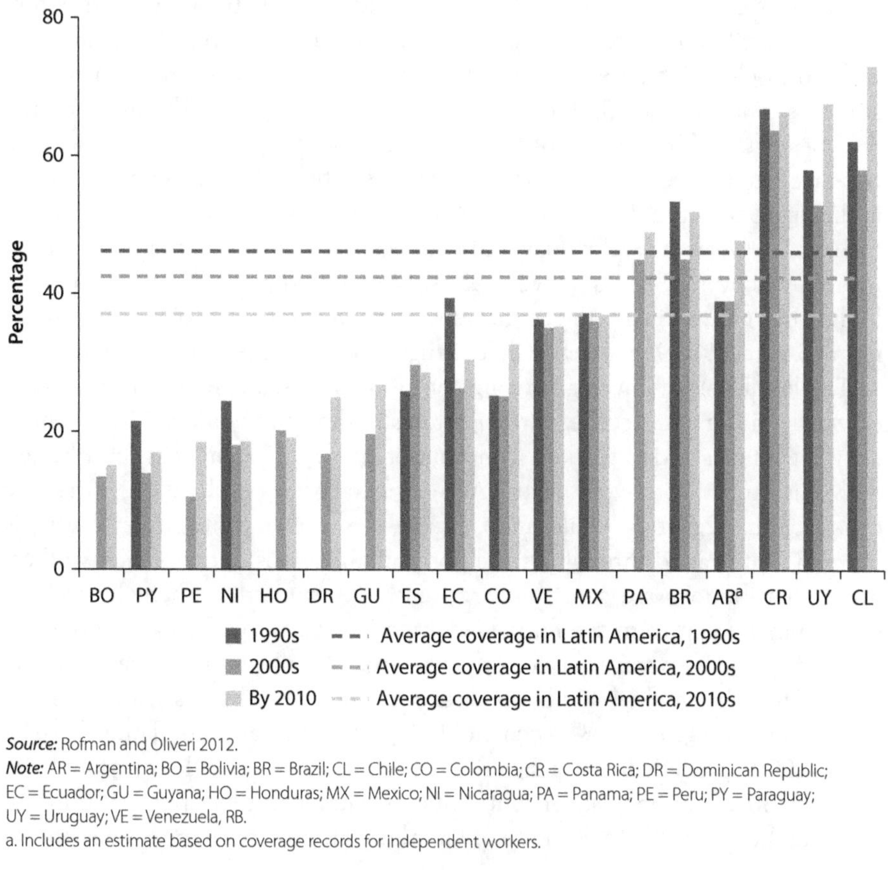

Source: Rofman and Oliveri 2012.
Note: AR = Argentina; BO = Bolivia; BR = Brazil; CL = Chile; CO = Colombia; CR = Costa Rica; DR = Dominican Republic; EC = Ecuador; GU = Guyana; HO = Honduras; MX = Mexico; NI = Nicaragua; PA = Panama; PE = Peru; PY = Paraguay; UY = Uruguay; VE = Venezuela, RB.
a. Includes an estimate based on coverage records for independent workers.

the beginning of the decade. Some countries, such as Peru and the Dominican Republic, have shown significant improvements, but they still exhibit very low coverage levels. At the other extreme, only Chile, Uruguay, Costa Rica, Argentina, and Brazil demonstrate active population coverage levels above 50 percent.

Between the beginning of the 1990s and the beginning of the 2000s coverage decreased in almost all the countries in the region. The main causes of this phenomenon include labor market difficulties that resulted from the successive financial crises that occurred during the decade, the privatization of state enterprises that employed significant numbers of workers, technological changes, market openings and liberalization, and a trend toward more flexible labor regulations, all processes that increased unemployment and labor informality. The majority of the countries in the region were in recession or experiencing very low economic growth, although the situation reversed itself in the following years, driving an increase in pension coverage.

This pattern is observed primarily in those countries with the highest levels of coverage among active workers. As a result of these trends, coverage of the economically active population, measured at a regional level, fell from around 46 percent at the beginning of the 1990s to near 37 percent 10 years later, and recovered to 42 percent by the end of the last decade.[7]

In terms of coverage of the inactive population, figure 1.7 shows the percentage of adults over 65 that receive retirement benefits, divided between contributory and noncontributory systems. According to Rofman and Oliveri (2012), the coverage of the older adult population is extremely low in many countries. On average, at the beginning of the 1990s coverage was 59.7 percent, a decade later it neared 58.5 percent, and by the end of the first decade of the 21st century the average coverage rate was 60.7 percent. In six of the 18 Latin American countries shown in the figure coverage is less than 19 percent: Honduras, the Dominican Republic, El Salvador, Guatemala, Paraguay, and Nicaragua. A second group of seven countries shows coverage levels between 22 percent and 60 percent, with Costa Rica leading this group. Finally, the countries with the highest levels of coverage range from 83 percent to 91 percent (Chile, Uruguay, Brazil, Argentina, and Bolivia).

The low levels of coverage among contribution-based systems in the region, especially in the past decade, mirror patterns in the labor market, where beneficiary eligibility is tied to workers' contribution history, meaning that contribution density is a function of work history. According to Forteza et al. (2009), in a study conducted in Argentina, Chile, and Uruguay, the average contribution density is low and quite varied throughout the population. Periods during which workers make contributions are short and frequently interrupted, with high levels of entry into and exit from the formal labor market. These results explain the low levels of pension coverage, particularly when many countries in the region made changes to pension eligibility by increasing the number of years with contributions required to gain access to benefits. Using a Monte Carlo simulation, Forteza et al. (2009) predicted that a significant portion of the population would not reach the 20, 30, or 35 years of contribution (required in the three countries) by the time they were 65 years old to obtain the minimum retirement pension.

Figure 1.7 Coverage of the Older Adult Population, Selected Countries, 1990, 2000, and 2010

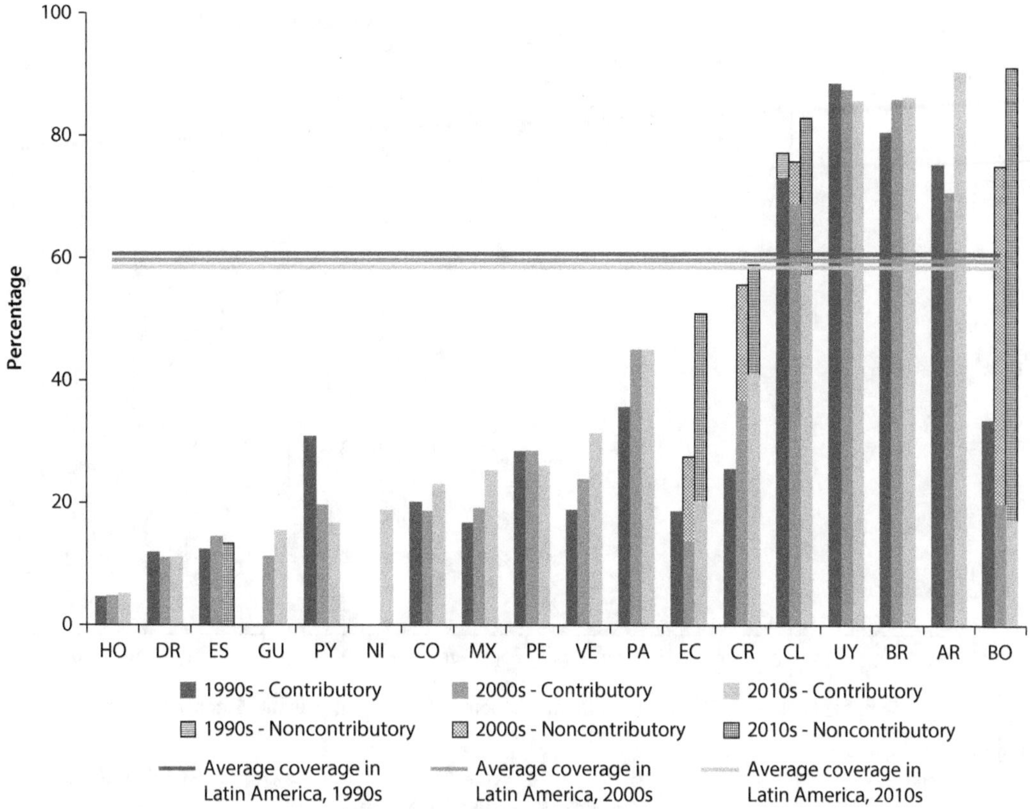

Source: Rofman and Oliveri 2012.
Note: NC = noncontributory; AR = Argentina; BO = Bolivia; BR = Brazil; CL = Chile; CO = Colombia; CR = Costa Rica; DR = Dominican Republic; EC = Ecuador; ES = El Salvador; GU = Guyana; HO = Honduras; MX = Mexico; NI = Nicaragua; PA = Panama; PE = Peru; PY = Paraguay; UY = Uruguay; VE = Venezuela, RB.

By introducing individually funded schemes, the reforms of the 1980s and 1990s allowed workers with low contribution densities to gain access to retirement benefits because the individual account system did not have a minimum contribution requirement. Nonetheless, low contribution densities result in very low balances in the accounts upon retirement, which means that benefits, if they exist, are very limited in terms of the amount available (or the length of time they are available, depending on rules specific to each country). As such, some of these workers could be counted as beneficiaries of the contribution-based social protection system, although the pension they receive is not sufficient.

One characteristic of the coverage of the older adult population is the system's bias in favor of the individuals that make up the highest income percentiles in almost every country in the region (figure 1.8). Two countries feature coverage rates below 20 percent among the richest quintile, but in the majority of countries coverage is above 50 percent for this group. Meanwhile, in 12 of the 18 countries with information available, the contributory social protection system's coverage rate among adults over 65 that belong to the poorest quintile was less

Figure 1.8 Older Adult Pension Coverage, by Income Quintile, around 2010

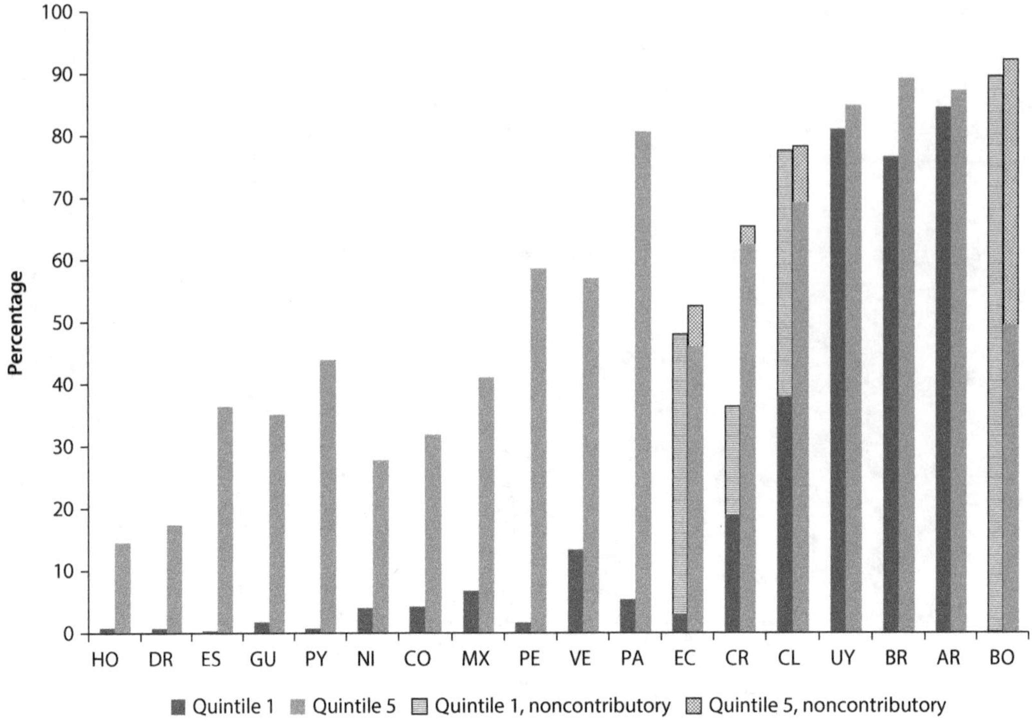

Source: Rofman and Oliveri 2012.
Note: NC = noncontributory; AR = Argentina; BO = Bolivia; BR = Brazil; CL = Chile; CO = Colombia; CR = Costa Rica; DR = Dominican Republic; EC = Ecuador; ES = El Salvador; GU = Guyana; HO = Honduras; MX = Mexico; NI = Nicaragua; PA = Panama; PE = Peru; PY = Paraguay; UY = Uruguay; VE = Venezuela, RB.

than 10 percent. Only República Bolivariana de Venezuela, Costa Rica, Chile, Uruguay, Brazil, and Argentina had higher levels. The situation improves in several countries, especially Ecuador and Bolivia, when we include noncontribution-based social protection systems.

The existence of significant coverage differences between high- and low-income populations seriously affects the role of traditional social protection systems in reducing poverty. In some countries it is possible to observe that traditional retirement benefits and pensions create a strong reduction in poverty among older adults, but in others the impact is less. In a static comparison exercise, Cotlear (2010) simulated the impact of social protection systems on poverty among older adults[8] midway through the last decade. Figure 1.9 shows the percentage of adults over 65 living in poor households before and after pension transfers. The results support the importance of pensions as a tool to reduce the rate of poverty among the elderly, especially in countries such as Argentina, Chile, and Uruguay that have high levels of coverage. In these countries the poverty level among adults over 65 is less than 3.5 percent and would increase on average to above 37 percent. At the other extreme, the impact of the social protection system in countries such as Mexico, El Salvador, Peru, Ecuador, and

Figure 1.9 Extreme Poverty Rate for Adults over 65, with and without Pension Income, Selected Countries, around 2006

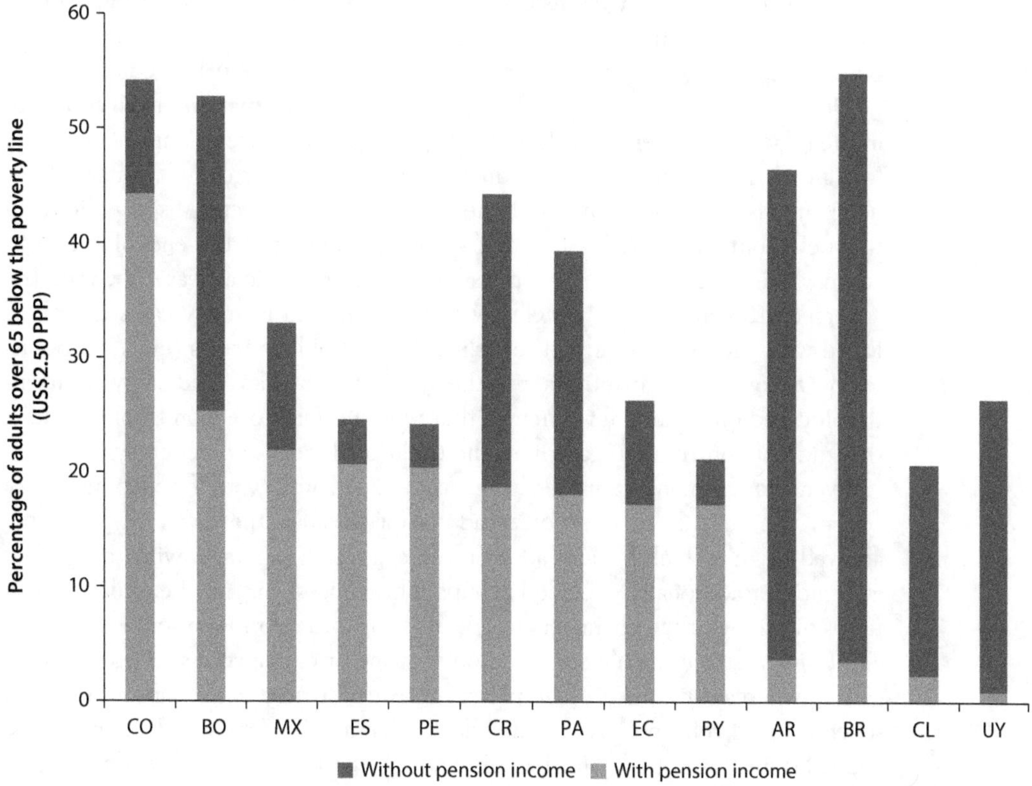

Source: Cotlear 2010.
Note: AR = Argentina; BO = Bolivia; BR = Brazil; CL = Chile; CO = Colombia; CR = Costa Rica; EC = Ecuador; ES = El Salvador; MX = Mexico; PA = Panama; PE = Peru; PY = Paraguay; UY = Uruguay.

Paraguay was low, due to the almost zero coverage of the poorest older adults. On average in the region, the percentage of adults over 65 in poverty was 20.1 percent, and that rate would increase to 35.8 percent without social protection systems.

Procoverage Reforms: Why Now?

The coverage problems of traditional social protection systems in the region are not new. Throughout the history of social protection policy in Latin America, the contributory systems never managed to cover more than half of active workers, with few exceptions. Throughout the 20th century, the majority of countries sought to increase coverage by including new groups of workers in the system. In many cases these countries achieved models that, from a legal standpoint, offered coverage to practically all salaried workers and, in several countries, independent workers as well. This tendency to include new groups of workers not only improved the social profile of the programs, but also contributed to their financial situation because adding new workers increased the overall salary base upon which contributions were paid in exchange for the payment of future benefits. However, as this strategy ran its course (due to the fact that fewer groups of new workers remained outside the system, and they had less capacity to make contributions), the focus switched to the financial context, as we discussed earlier.

During the early years of the 21st century the fiscal situation of the countries in the region underwent a profound change, in part because of improvements in foreign markets (especially for countries that were exporters of primary products) and also because of the implementation of more effective fiscal policies. In this new context, in contrast to the focus on funding at the end of the 20th century, the regional debate over pensions began to shift to a clearer focus on the coverage problem, which was clearly insufficient, and in many cases declining. Faced with the impossibility of recycling decades-old strategies (i.e., incorporating new groups of contributors into the system), politicians' and analysts' attention focused on looking for schemes that would offer protection to older adults that did not contribute regularly to the traditional social protection system.

Even though many countries have maintained some type of noncontributory system targeting the poorest older adults for decades, the focus on this topic allowed them to look for and adopt more aggressive programs with the goal of integrating traditionally excluded groups. This process has not been uniform in terms of timing or the characteristics of the proposed reforms. In some cases policies to increase coverage were based on growing or easing access to existing programs, whereas in others new programs were created or contribution-based schemes were reformed. As we discuss in chapters 3, 4, 5, and 7 of this book, countries such as Bolivia, Brazil, Chile, and Costa Rica had already adopted measures to increase coverage during the 1980s and 1990s. Other countries moved forward more clearly in recent years; in almost all cases, the proposed changes were subject to multiple revisions and adjustments with the goal of increasing the process of inclusion even more. Considering the measures adopted since 2000, one can observe that until 2004 significant initiatives were underway in Costa Rica, Mexico, Argentina, and Colombia. In Mexico, new reforms continued in the following years. After 2005, many more reforms were implemented. Bolivia, Brazil, Chile, Ecuador, El Salvador, Panama, and Uruguay undertook new actions in this area. More recently, Bolivia, Paraguay, Peru, and Trinidad and Tobago implemented reforms in 2010. Finally, Colombia launched the "Colombia Mayor" program in 2013, and Mexico, Ecuador, and El Salvador are considering new reforms.[9]

For some countries the reforms meant continuing a process they began in the 1990s to grow existing programs. Indeed, Costa Rica was the pioneer at the beginning of the 2000s in expanding coverage that already existed under the Noncontributory Regime (Régimen No Contributivo) with the approval of the Worker Protection Law (Ley de Protección al Trabajador). The new law expanded coverage for the active population, creating a social protection system for independent workers, while also extending the reach of noncontributory pensions to include older adults in poverty. Meanwhile, Mexico spent the 1990s expanding assistance programs, which it then used to target the elderly in poverty and without pension coverage in the new millennium. A first step for noncontributory programs was the "Food Assistance for Adults" (Pensión Alimentaria para Adultos) implemented in Mexico City in 2001, which later in 2003 was implemented nationally with a focus on older adults in rural areas and eventually became the "70 and over" ("70 y más") pension in 2007.[10]

Argentina (in the first stage), Bolivia, and Trinidad and Tobago approached the expansion of coverage through the expansion of their preexisting noncontributory pension plans. Thus, in Bolivia, the noncontributory pension "Bonosol" established in 1997 was the precursor to the larger "Dignity Income" (Renta Dignidad) program in 2008. In 2003 Argentina eased access requirements for the traditional noncontributory disability and elderly pensions. In Trinidad and Tobago, where noncontributory pensions for the elderly were developed at the same time as their contributory counterparts, the "Senior Citizens' Grant" was relaunched in 2010, as is discussed in chapter 14 of this book.

Other pushes for reform demonstrated less continuity with the reforms from the previous decade. Moreover, several countries implemented measures that required profound changes to the previous model. A clear example is Chile's 2008 reform, which created the Basic Solidarity Pension (Pensión Básica Solidaria), a benefit that is fully integrated with the contribution-based social protection system. Another example is the unification of the contributory and noncontributory systems in Bolivia in 2010 with the implementation of the solidarity pension.

Alternatively, other countries created new noncontributory programs for the elderly without access to the traditional social security system. Clear examples of this focus are the "Elderly Social Protection Program" (Programa de Protección Social al Adulto Mayor [PPSAM]) in Colombia in 2004 (replaced by "Colombia Mayor" in 2013); the "Human Development Voucher" (Bono de Desarrollo Humano) in Ecuador in 2006; the noncontributory pensions in the Fairness Plan (Plan de Equidad) in 2006 and the subsidies for elderly persons in poverty set out in law in 2008 in Uruguay; "100 to 70" (100 a los 70) in Panama; the "Universal Basic Pension" (Pensión Básica Universal) in El Salvador in 2009; the "Nutritional Pension for the Elderly" (Pensión Alimentaria para Adultos Mayores) in Paraguay; and the "Gratitude Voucher" (Bono Gratitud) and "Pension 65" in Peru in 2010 and 2011 respectively.

Finally, some countries opted for a hybrid focus compared with the previously mentioned examples, extending coverage through the contributory social protection system and easing access in some cases to the noncontributory system. As we show in chapter 2, this is the case in Argentina, which implemented a special incentive regime known as "Social Security Moratorium" (Moratoria Previsional) for the inclusion of autonomous workers in 2005. Under this regime workers that did not meet the requirement for years of contributions received a subsidy to enter the system. The incentives for inclusion of independent, domestic, and temporary rural workers in Brazil in 2006–08 represent similar cases, as do the terms provided to workers in small businesses in Peru in 2008, and the easing of access requirements for domestic workers and other groups in Uruguay in 2008.

It is important to emphasize that the initiatives developed by the countries in Latin America and the Caribbean are in line with many of the efforts undertaken by many other countries in the world. Even though the reforms discussed in this document represent significant innovations in terms of public policy design and implementation, it is important to note that they are a part of a framework of similar policies and programs that is being developed in other regions as well. Box 1.1 provides more detail.

Box 1.1 Social Pensions in the Rest of the World

"Social pensions," defined as the different types of programs of pension income that seek to guarantee a minimum income during old age and prevent poverty (Robalino and Holzmann 2009), have existed in the richest countries for decades, complementing contribution-based systems. Social pensions also exist in medium- and low-income countries, where the authorities have realized that the contributory systems do not offer a minimum level of economic security to older adults.

Among the 30 high-income countries that belong to the Organisation for Economic Co-operation and Development (OECD), 17 offer targeted noncontributory pensions, 13 universal basic pensions, and 17 some type of minimum pension within a contribution-based system (which for societies with high coverage rates for their contribution-based systems can be considered equivalent to a universal minimum pension). As is evident in figure B1.1.1, in several cases there is more than one type of program, reflecting the complexity of these policies.

Figure B1.1.1 Typology of Social Pension Programs in OECD Countries, 2007

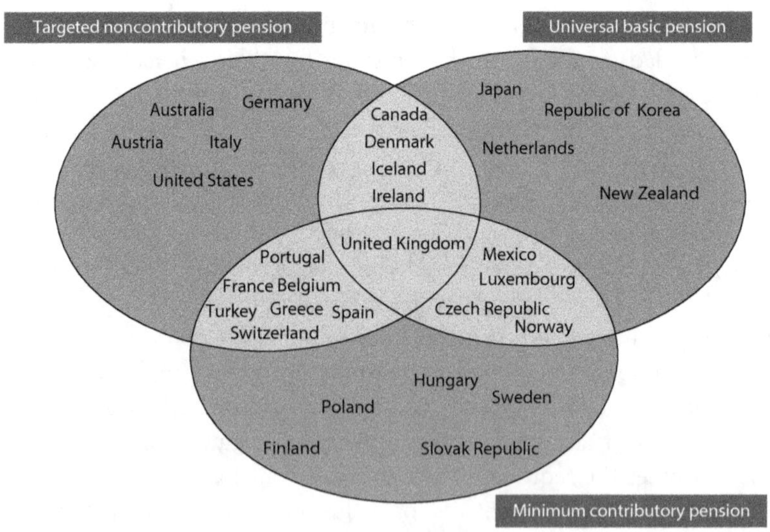

Source: Based on Pearson and Whitehouse 2009.

box continues next page

Box 1.1 Social Pensions in the Rest of the World *(continued)*

On average, these social pension programs offer benefits of about 29 percent of workers' average income, although the range is significant, from 16 percent in Japan to 40 percent in New Zealand and Portugal. Coverage under these programs also varies widely. In countries with universal basic pensions, coverage of older adults is by definition 100 percent of the population. On the other hand, the targeted schemes have varying levels, ranging from Austria and Switzerland, which cover less than 15 percent of older adults, to Denmark and Australia, where coverage is between 70 percent and 80 percent of the population.

Beyond the group of the most developed countries, the information about these types of programs around the world is not completely organized. HelpAge International has built a database with the main characteristics of social pension programs in 99 countries. Sixty percent of these programs are from medium-high and high-income countries. Almost half of the programs are targeted, approximately one-third can be classified as "targeted to achieve universality" according to the taxonomy presented in this chapter, and the rest are universal, although they do not always have national coverage.[a]

Among medium- and low-income countries (except those in Latin America), HelpAge identified 29 new social pension systems between 1990 and 2011, where there had only been six systems before 1990. South Africa and Mauritius are the most remarkable examples, because both have a decades-long history with well consolidated systems. In the case of South Africa, in theory the system is targeted, but in practice it offers universal coverage. In Mauritius, every citizen has a right to receive an income equivalent to 20 percent of the per capita income, after reaching 60 years of age (Palacios and Sluchynksy 2006). The basic characteristics of these schemes differentiate them from the systems studied in Latin America, in terms of both the level of coverage and the relative generosity of the benefits. In this sense the country that is most similar to South Africa and Mauritius is Trinidad and Tobago, with its Senior Citizens' Grant. On a lesser scale, other medium- and low-income countries have implemented some initiatives in this direction. In North Africa, Algeria and Egypt have noncontributory systems that could be considered similar to an assistance pension, with characteristics similar to the intermediate countries in Latin America; in India and Bangladesh subnational systems also exist that, although they are small in relation to the overall population, offer basic incomes to a significant number of older adults (Robalino and Holzmann 2009).

a. Social Pensions Database, HelpAge International (2012), http://www.pension-watch.net.

Toward a Taxonomy of the Noncontributory Reforms in Latin America

Each country's starting point in terms of its income protection programs for older adults is an important determinant of the strategies utilized to expand coverage. Table 1.1 presents the main characteristics for each country, including the level of coverage of the traditional contribution-based social protection system, the fiscal or economic cost of the system (and, therefore, the space available to expand the program), the existence of a noncontributory social protection scheme upon which an expanded model could be built, and the primary goal proposed in policy discussions. As you can see, the initial conditions are very heterogeneous, which inevitably resulted in different proposals from each government.

Table 1.1 Initial Conditions before Inclusive Reforms

Country	*Coverage level of the contributory system*	*Fiscal/economic cost*	*Existence of noncontributory system*	*Primary policy objective*
Argentina	High	High	Yes	Universal inclusion in the contributory system
Brazil	High	High	Yes	Universal inclusion in the contributory system
Chile	High	Medium	Yes	Universal inclusion in the contributory system
Trinidad and Tobago	High	Medium	Yes	Poverty prevention
Uruguay	High	High	Yes	Universal inclusion in the contributory system
Colombia	Medium	Low	Yes	Poverty prevention
Costa Rica	Medium	Low	Yes	Poverty prevention
Ecuador	Medium	Medium	No	Poverty prevention
Mexico	Medium	Low	Yes	Poverty prevention
Panama	Medium	Low	No	Poverty prevention
Peru	Medium	Low	No	Poverty prevention
Bolivia	Low	Medium	No	Poverty prevention
El Salvador	Low	Low	No	Poverty prevention
Paraguay	Low	Medium	No	Poverty prevention

Source: Based on information from chapters 2 to 15 of this book and information from social security agencies in the region.

Using the analytical framework presented earlier, we will present a taxonomy of the noncontributory social protection programs implemented in 14 countries in the region, with the goal of identifying the strategies used in each one to reduce social protection coverage gaps in the new millennium. This classification attempts to illustrate both the diversity and the depth of the reforms undertaken, revealing the "patterns" that have emerged in the region and pointing out some aspects of particular interest to analysts and policy makers who would like to identify lessons applicable in their own countries.

The 14 countries covered in this study have witnessed initiatives to expand coverage to the elderly population via different types of tools applied for different purposes. Inclusion has been based mainly on noncontributory programs that have operated concurrently with the traditional system or have even eased access to the existing contributory social protection system.

After identifying the most illustrative and representative reforms, we define a taxonomy of interventions based on their design and implementation criteria, respectively. From a design standpoint, the reforms can be classified according to the target population, the strength of their relationship with the existing social protection system, and their time horizon. From an implementation point of view, the programs can be grouped according to the speed of their application and their links with existing social security management institutions.

Design: Universal, Targeted to Achieve Universality, or Targeted

The countries in this study have adopted three different strategies in terms of the target population set forth in their new noncontributory programs or components. In some cases, universality was the standard, creating a system where all citizens that meet a minimum requirement, such as retirement age, can access the social protection system. This is the case in Bolivia and Trinidad and Tobago, which give all citizens access to the programs, regardless of their eligibility for the contributory social protection system, as we discuss in depth in chapters 3 and 14. In other cases, policy makers chose to focus on the population that for one reason or another could not access the contributory social protection systems, for which we can assume that the goal of this focus was to achieve universal protection. This group of countries includes the reforms undertaken in Argentina, Brazil, Chile, Mexico, Panama, and Uruguay. In Argentina, the Social Security Moratorium allowed elderly adults that had not satisfied the requirement for contribution years to retire with benefits in the contributory system (chapter 2 presents a detailed discussion of the design and operation of this program). In Brazil the rural pension included the entire population with a work history in the sector, even subsistence farmers, and the Continuous Compensation Benefit (Beneficio de Prestación Continua) complemented this system to include the most vulnerable urban sectors. In its 2008 reform, Chile established that the poorest 60 percent of the elderly population that did not have retirement benefits or access to a minimum pension would receive a solidarity pension. Given that the coverage of the contributory system was well above 50 percent, the reform actually converted the system to a universal coverage scheme. In Mexico's case, access to the "70 and over" program was not universal in the beginning because it was targeted at rural areas. But the system was slowly opened to small urban centers, and eventually the residency qualification was eliminated. In Panama, the law that created the "100 to 70" program did not set targeting criteria, but a reform in late 2010 stated that beneficiaries should be in "a situation of poverty, extreme poverty, or social vulnerability or risk," and in Uruguay the combination of the expansion of access to the elderly pension and the easing of eligibility criteria for benefits in the contributory system resulted in a de facto universalization of pension benefits.

In contrast, other programs have defined the target population as those older adults at risk of or already living in poverty. Their eligibility should be verified via a means test. Colombia, Costa Rica, Ecuador, El Salvador, Panama (since 2011), Paraguay, and Peru belong to this group. In almost all cases governments use the same means test that they utilize to determine eligibility for other social programs (such as conditional cash transfers to support children or nutrition programs), but in some cases this has created implementation difficulties.

Design: Integrated with or Independent of the Existing Social Protection System

Coverage expansion initiatives emerged differently in relation to the existing social security systems in different countries. Some countries implemented reforms using the traditional social protection system framework, opening up access to these systems with changes to rules that had previously created access problems for potential beneficiaries. By contrast, other countries designed coverage expansion programs independent of the traditional social security system, linking the new programs with preexisting social assistance programs and poverty reduction policies.

In Argentina the Social Security Moratorium established flexible criteria for workers to regularize their social protection situation, thus extending the coverage of the contributory system. In Brazil, the recognition of newly insured rural workers was based on the state accepting responsibility for conditions like the seasonality of agricultural work that had pushed these workers to the margins of the formal labor market and social protection system, while also developing the Continuous Compensation Benefit (Beneficio de Prestación Continua) at the same time. Chile's reform established a New Solidarity Pillar (Nuevo Pilar Solidario) within the social protection system that replaced the existing noncontributory programs—Assistance Pensions (Pensiones Asistenciales [PASIS]) and the Guaranteed Minimum Pension (Pensión Mínima Garantizada [PMG])—with a single plan, the Basic Solidarity Pension (Pensión Básica Solidaria). Similarly, Trinidad and Tobago integrated its Senior Citizens' Grant with the traditional social security system. For its part, Uruguay sought inclusion for the elderly without coverage through changes to eligibility requirements for the existing contribution-based and noncontribution-based social protection systems.

In contrast to the previous model, Bolivia, Colombia, Costa Rica, Ecuador, El Salvador, Mexico, Panama, Paraguay, and Peru expanded social security coverage independent of the traditional social protection system. They designed new social assistance programs that had little or no interaction with existing social protection systems. In these cases, it is interesting to examine the operation of these programs directed at older adults and their connection with other social assistance programs, which are generally focused on families with children. In some cases we find significant integration (as is the case in Ecuador, Panama, Paraguay, and Peru), with the same institutions managing the new programs, using the same tools to select beneficiaries, and employing similar or identical database and payment systems as the programs targeting children. In other cases, the connection is much weaker.

The different strategies observed among the countries in the region appear to respond, as can be expected, to the goals set forth in the early design of the reform. Countries that sought to expand the coverage of their existing systems searched for models that were more integrated with their existing systems. In contrast, countries that wanted to shift from a poverty reduction policy that targeted households with children via cash transfers to a broader policy that also included older adults focused on independent models or programs integrated with social protection agencies. Bolivia appears to be the exception to this pattern: From the beginning coverage expansion was linked to the 1996 social protection reform; however, the expansion was never integrated with the social protection system on a programmatic level.

Design: Permanent or Temporary Programs

Policy makers can introduce reforms as permanent changes that deal with structural conditions of the labor market, or as temporary measures designed to respond to an economic situation that they expect to overcome in time. In the first situation, the initiative is not time-limited, but rather becomes a part of the policy framework for protection of the elderly. In the second situation, the reform has an expiration date, which also implies a limited period for it to create the desired effects. It makes sense that implicit in the decision to propose a permanent or temporary reform is a judgment on the causes behind low coverage levels. In countries with structural problems that limit the ability of traditional systems to offer protection to the entire target population as a result of inconsistencies between program design and the characteristics of the local labor market, it is logical to propose permanent reforms. On the other hand, if the problem is cyclical, resulting from temporary problems in the labor market or from a system design flaw that was corrected for the future, then it is more reasonable to approach it as a temporary tool.

Except for the Social Security Moratorium in Argentina, coverage expansion policies do not have limited periods of applicability. In Argentina, a 2004 law established a payment plan for independent workers that allowed them to make up for missing contributions up to 1994 by paying them over time, including if they were already receiving a pension because they had met the minimum age requirement. In this way, the program made it easier for workers who could prove they had worked independently until 1994 to access the social protection system. However, the limited time horizon also excluded from the program younger generations of workers who, because of their age, had not worked regularly before this date.

Implementation: Gradual or Immediate

The sequence of implementation of these initiatives is divided between those that established a gradual timeline to achieve full implementation of the proposed reform and those that guaranteed immediate access to the eligible groups. Reforms were implemented gradually in Chile, Colombia, El Salvador, Mexico, Paraguay, Peru, and Uruguay (in the case of Old Age Retirement) to ease operational changes and avoid abrupt increases in funding needs. In contrast, the rest of the reforms examined here were implemented immediately, including in Argentina, Bolivia, Brazil, Costa Rica, Ecuador, Panama, Trinidad and Tobago, and Uruguay.

In Chile, El Salvador, Mexico, Colombia, and Peru the rate of implementation of the programs was determined by the guidelines regarding inclusion of the target population. The Basic Solidarity Pension in Chile was first restricted to the poorest 40 percent of the population in 2008, increased to 45 percent in 2009, and to 60 percent after 2012. The 2010–14 Five Year Development Plan for the Universal Basic Pension in El Salvador outlined the inclusion of municipalities according to the level of social risk, beginning with municipalities with severely extreme poverty in 2009–10, continuing with those with high extreme poverty in 2011–12, and finally increasing the number of beneficiaries in these municipalities in 2013 and maintaining them in 2014. In Mexico, the "70 and over" program began in rural areas in 2007 and grew to cover larger municipalities in 2012 after policy makers eliminated the geographic targeting component. Colombia implemented PPSAM gradually by limiting the number of possible beneficiaries in order to avoid excessive budget pressures. However, since the creation of the Elderly Colombia (Colombia Mayor) program, these restrictions have been removed. Finally, in Peru the Pension 65 program began in five municipalities and progressively expanded until it included the entire eligible population in the country.

Implementation: Working with Existing Institutions or Creating New Institutions

The agency or institution in charge of administering these programs is one relevant aspect that differentiates the implementation strategy for one initiative from another. Management of these new programs can fall to existing social security institutions, new institutions, or existing institutions unrelated to the administration of social security programs.

Several countries have placed responsibility for their coverage expansion programs with the same institution that manages the contributory social protection system. These include the following: Argentina—National Social Security Administration; Bolivia—Collective Capitalization Fund; Brazil—National Social Security Institute; Chile—Social Security Institute; Costa Rica—Costa Rican Social Security Bank; and Uruguay—Social Security Bank.

In the remaining countries, noncontributory social protection programs are usually administered by the same institutions responsible for development or social assistance programs. Examples include: the Social Development Secretariat in Mexico, the Social Development Coordinating Ministry in Ecuador, the Social Development Ministry in Panama, and the Social Development and Inclusion Ministry in Peru. Alternatively, in Colombia the Labor Ministry takes the lead, while the Social Investment for Local Development Fund is in charge in El Salvador. Paraguay is a unique case; the new program is administered by the Noncontributory Pensions Directorate, which is part of the Treasury Ministry.

As with decisions about autonomous versus integrated program design, decisions about which institutions will administer the new programs appear to depend on existing management capacity. In countries where the new systems are targeted at specific populations, policy makers tend to take advantage of the existence of agencies that already have the ability to implement targeting processes effectively, relying on these agencies to manage the new program. In contrast, when new programs are not highly targeted, but instead require strong financial management and payment systems capacity, traditional social security institutions have responded well to the challenge.

Table 1.2 provides a summary of the main reforms covered according to the taxonomy developed in this section for each of the countries included in this study.

Table 1.2 Coverage Expansion Programs, Design Characteristics

Country	*Program*	*Beneficiary population*	*Integration with contributory system*	*Duration*	*Gradualism in implementation*	*Responsible institution*
Colombia	Elderly Colombia	Targeted	Independent	Permanent	Gradual	Labor Ministry
Costa Rica	Noncontributory pension	Targeted	Independent	Permanent	Immediate	Costa Rican Social Security Fund
Ecuador	Human Development	Targeted	Independent	Permanent	Immediate	Social Development Coordinating Ministry
El Salvador	Universal Basic Pension	Targeted	Independent	Permanent	Gradual	Social Investment for Local Development Fund
Paraguay	Nutritional Pension for the Elderly	Targeted	Independent	Permanent	Gradual	Treasury Ministry
Peru	Pension 65	Targeted	Independent	Permanent	Gradual	Social Development and Inclusion Ministry
Mexico	70 and over	Targeted to achieve universality	Independent	Permanent	Gradual	Social Development Secretariat
Panama	100 to 70	Targeted to achieve universality	Independent	Permanent	Immediate	Social Development Ministry
Argentina	Social Security Moratorium	Targeted to achieve universality	Integrated	Temporary	Immediate	National Social Security Administration
Brazil	Rural Pension; Continuous Compensation Benefit	Targeted to achieve universality	Integrated	Permanent	Immediate	National Social Security Institute
Chile	Basic Solidarity Pension	Targeted to achieve universality	Integrated	Permanent	Gradual	Social Security Institute
Uruguay	Contributory system relaxation/ Elderly Pension Reform	Targeted to achieve universality	Integrated	Permanent	Gradual	Social Security Bank
Bolivia	Dignity Income	Universal	Independent	Permanent	Immediate	Collective Capitalization Fund
Trinidad and Tobago	Senior Citizens' Grant	Universal	Integrated	Permanent	Immediate	Popular Power and Social Development Ministry

Source: Based on the information available in chapters 2 to 15 of this book and data from social security agencies in the region.

Different Needs and Financial Sacrifices

The initiatives put forth by countries in the region differ not just in terms of design and implementation tools, but also in their scope, the adequacy of benefits, and the fiscal resources required to pay for them. The new programs offer coverage to about one-third of the older adult population in the region. This average figure hides significant differences, with coverage ranging from above 90 percent in Bolivia and Trinidad and Tobago to less than 15 percent in El Salvador, Paraguay, Peru, and Uruguay (figure 1.10).[11]

Nonetheless, it is important to examine the coverage gap in the contributory system that these programs have managed to close. Bolivia and Trinidad and Tobago cover nearly all their older adult population via their noncontributory social protection systems, whereas new cash transfer programs in Argentina, Brazil, Chile, Panama, and Uruguay have significantly covered the gaps in the contribution-based social protection system. Finally, Colombia, Costa Rica, Ecuador, El Salvador, Mexico, and Peru need to make additional efforts.

Figure 1.10 Coverage of New Social Protection Systems, 2012

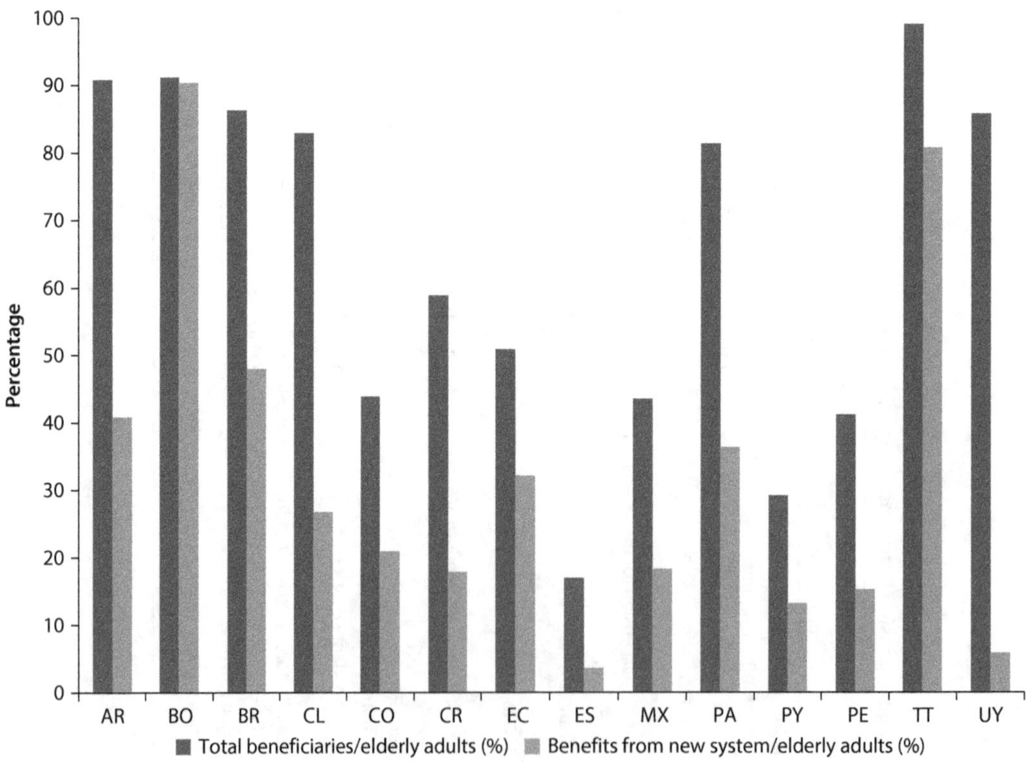

Source: Based on information from chapters 2–15 of this book and data from social security agencies in the region.
Note: The information presented in this figure combines registration and household survey data and refers to covered persons, not paid beneficiaries, to avoid double counting persons who receive more than one benefit. AR = Argentina; BO = Bolivia; BR = Brazil; CL = Chile; CO = Colombia; CR = Costa Rica; EC = Ecuador; ES = El Salvador; MX = Mexico; PA = Panama; PY = Paraguay; PE = Peru; TT = Trinidad and Tobago; UY = Uruguay.

Figure 1.11 shows the average benefit level of the new systems, expressed in terms of the poverty line,[12] relative to the average benefit paid under the contributory social protection system, and as a percentage of national per capita GDP. As with other aspects of the new systems, the benefit amount varies widely among the countries studied. Trinidad and Tobago, Argentina, Costa Rica, and Uruguay are the most generous countries relative to the benefits paid to participants in the contributory social protection systems. In contrast, when comparing benefits relative to per capita GDP, Argentina continues to rank among the most generous countries (paying benefits equivalent to nearly 40 percent of per capita GDP), followed by Trinidad and Tobago. Interestingly, Paraguay jumps into third place, and appears to be paying much higher benefits in terms of the size of its economy relative to other countries with similar programs. As we discussed earlier, in several countries the poverty line appears to be the main determinant of the benefit amount. Brazil, Chile, Panama, and Paraguay all offer benefits at or around this level. Meanwhile, some countries (Argentina and Trinidad and Tobago) pay relatively high amounts compared to the poverty line (between 3.5

Figure 1.11 Average Benefit of New Social Protection Systems, 2012

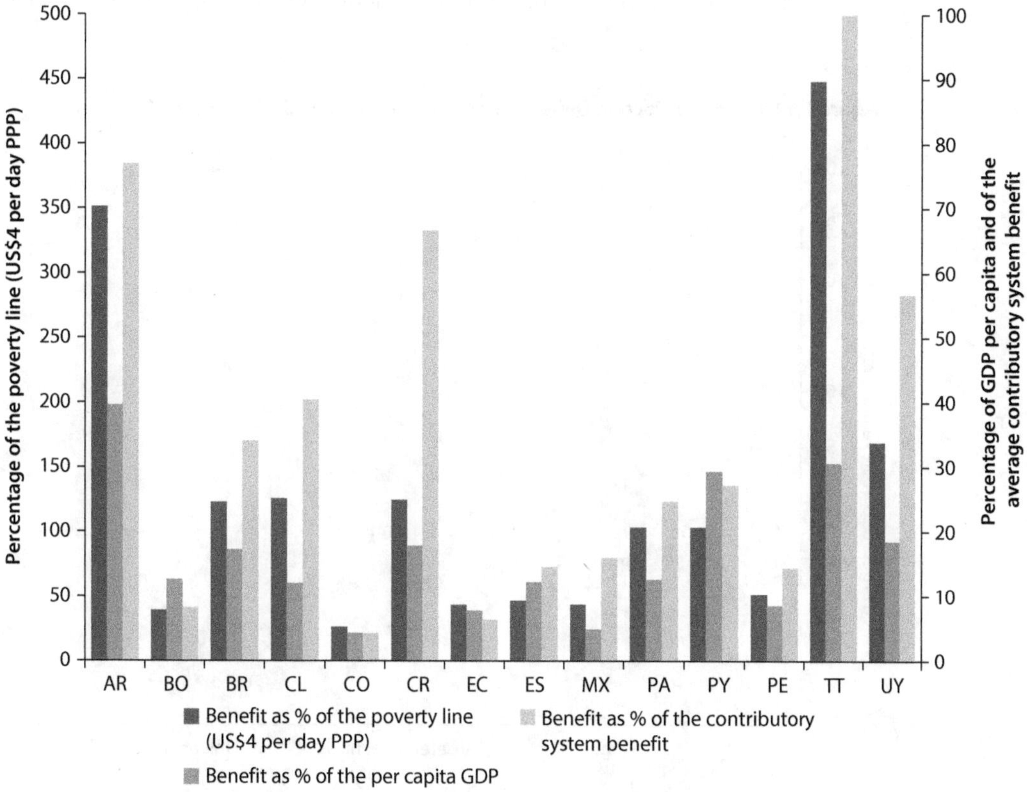

Source: Based on information from chapters 2 to 15 of this book and data from social security agencies in the region.
Note: GDP = gross domestic product; PPP = purchasing power parity; AR = Argentina; BO = Bolivia; BR = Brazil; CL = Chile; CO = Colombia; CR = Costa Rica; EC = Ecuador; ES = El Salvador; MX = Mexico; PA = Panama; PY = Paraguay; PE = Peru; TT = Trinidad and Tobago; UY = Uruguay.

and 4.5 times), whereas other countries, such as Bolivia, Colombia, Ecuador, El Salvador, and Mexico, do not reach even 50 percent of the poverty line.

With the goal of understanding the differences between benefits from noncontributory systems as a percentage of the contributory systems' benefits, the countries are grouped into three categories according to the way they determine beneficiary eligibility: those with social pensions targeted at vulnerable populations, those that adopted "targeted to achieve universality" schemes, and those that use a universal model. Using this classification, figure 1.12 shows the distribution of countries relative to the social benefit as a percentage of the contributory system benefit.

The results show a clear correlation between the target population and the benefit amount as a percentage of the contributory system benefit. The countries with more universal models tend to offer better benefits, which makes sense given that their focus is more on income substitution instead of poverty reduction. At the same time, programs with universal access or targeted to achieve universality face fewer risks in terms of incentives to contribute than countries with targeted programs, which allows them to offer better benefits relative to the contribution-based system. Argentina, Brazil, Chile, and Uruguay target their noncontributory programs at the excluded population with the goal of achieving universal coverage. In these systems, the noncontributory benefit is greater than that in targeted

Figure 1.12 Form of Selecting Beneficiaries and the Noncontributory Benefit

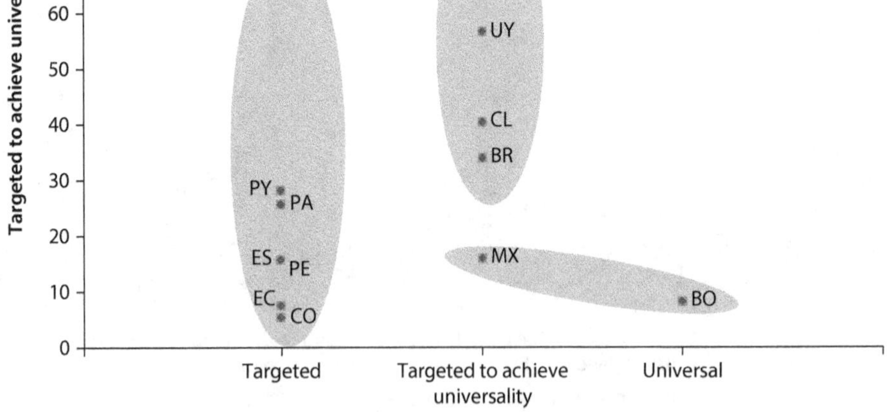

Source: Based on information from chapters 2–15 of this book and data from social security agencies in the region.
Note: AR = Argentina; BO = Bolivia; BR = Brazil; CL = Chile; CO = Colombia; CR = Costa Rica; EC = Ecuador; ES = El Salvador; MX = Mexico; PA = Panama; PY = Paraguay; PE = Peru; TT = Trinidad and Tobago; UY = Uruguay.

programs, but less than the contributory system benefit, eliminating potential incentives for labor informality. Finally, Mexico and Bolivia are outliers in this analysis. Both countries have contributory social protection systems with low coverage levels and social pension schemes that were initially introduced as part of their poverty reduction policies. However, they did not design beneficiary identification systems that targeted beneficiaries based on income, unlike other countries in the same situation. In Bolivia this difference is due in part to the political context in which the new program was introduced in 1996 (during the privatization of the major state-owned enterprises which established the "Bonsol" pension as a means of distributing the benefits gained from this process). In Mexico, the explanation is also connected to the political process: The initiative began as a geographically targeted program (which was limited to older adults residing in towns with up to 30,000 inhabitants), but was expanded to include the rest of the population and became a universal coverage scheme.

Additionally, the degree of complementarity that exists between noncontributory and contributory benefits is significantly correlated with the adequacy of said benefits. Figure 1.13 shows the correlation between the noncontributory

Figure 1.13 Noncontributory Benefit Relative to the Contributory Benefit and the Poverty Line

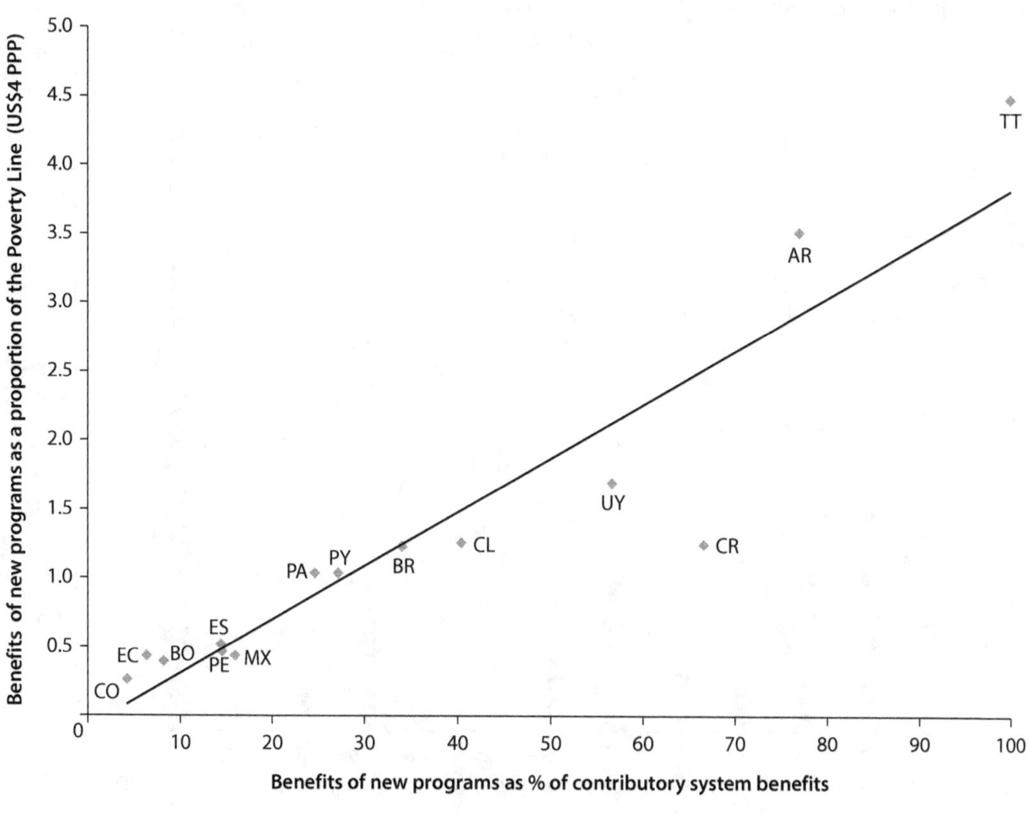

Source: Based on information from chapters 2–15 of this book and data from social security agencies in the region.
Note: AR = Argentina; BO = Bolivia; BR = Brazil; CL = Chile; CO = Colombia; CR = Costa Rica; EC = Ecuador; ES = El Salvador; MX = Mexico; PA = Panama; PY = Paraguay; PE = Peru; TT = Trinidad and Tobago; UY = Uruguay.

benefit expressed as a percentage of the contributory benefit and as a proportion of the poverty line (US$4 daily PPP adjusted) as a proxy for adequacy.

The level of financial resources demanded by each of these initiatives also varies widely among countries. Figure 1.14 shows the total spending of the coverage expansion programs, expressed as a percentage of spending on traditional social protection systems and as a percentage of GDP. Of the countries studied, Trinidad and Tobago spends the most on its inclusion program relative to the contributory social protection system, with the noncontributory system receiving 80 percent of the amount spent on traditional programs. Argentina also spends a significant amount on coverage expansion (nearly 50 percent of spending on contributory benefits). At the other extreme, countries like Colombia, El Salvador, Uruguay, and Peru spend less as a proportion of their traditional social protection system spending. Uruguay poses an interesting case because the relatively low amount it spends on noncontributory pensions is due to the broad coverage offered by its contributory social protection system, which means that the noncontributory system needs to cover only 5 percent of older adults.

Figure 1.14 Spending on New Social Protection Systems as a Percentage of GDP and of Spending on Contributory Pensions, 2012

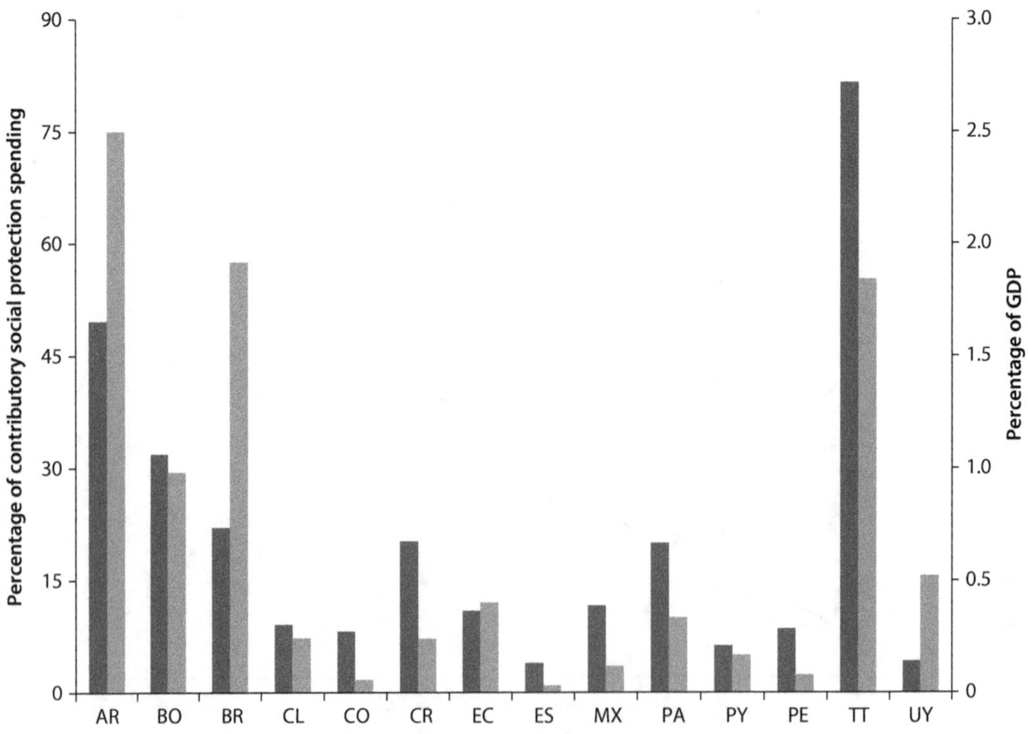

Source: Based on information from chapters 2–15 of this book and data from social security agencies in the region.
Note: GDP = gross domestic product; AR = Argentina; BO = Bolivia; BR = Brazil; CL = Chile; CO = Colombia; CR = Costa Rica; EC = Ecuador; ES = El Salvador; MX = Mexico; PA = Panama; PY = Paraguay; PE = Peru; TT = Trinidad and Tobago; UY = Uruguay.

Considering spending as a proportion of GDP, Argentina and Brazil spend the most on their new programs, followed by Trinidad and Tobago, Bolivia, and, to a lesser extent, Uruguay. The rest of the countries in this analysis spend less than 0.5 percent of GDP on their noncontributory social protection systems. These data clearly show that some countries (in particular Argentina, Brazil, Trinidad and Tobago, and Bolivia) are taking on significant fiscal commitments with their implementation of new, inclusive programs. Argentina's case appears to be the most serious, with 2.5 percent of GDP directed to this program, although it is important to point out that this is due to the program's temporary nature, which should cause spending to decline in the future (unless, of course, the program is renewed periodically). In contrast, Brazil's and Trinidad and Tobago's fiscal commitment is near 2 percent of GDP, a value that will probably increase with time as the population ages.

These major differences can be partially attributed to the scope of each initiative. Figure 1.15 shows the correlation between the spending on new programs as a percentage of GDP relative to the number of new beneficiaries and the

Figure 1.15 Relationship between Coverage Increase and Financial Commitment, 2012

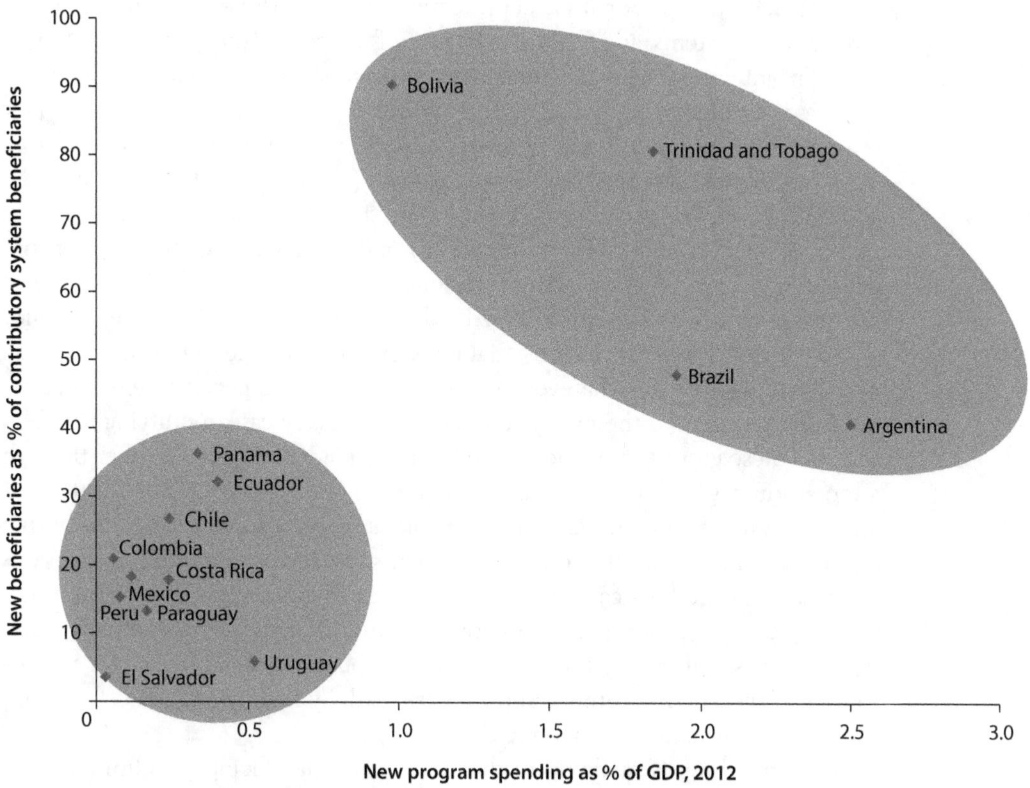

Source: Based on information from chapters 2 to 15 of this book and data from social security agencies in the region.
Note: GDP = gross domestic product.

population over 65 years of age. Two clearly defined groups of countries emerge. The first is composed of Argentina, Bolivia, Brazil, and Trinidad and Tobago, which spend between 1 percent and 2.5 percent of GDP to cover between 40 percent and 90 percent of older adults. The rest of the countries make up the second group, spending less than 0.5 percent of GDP and covering between 4 percent and 36.4 percent of the population over 65 years.

Conclusion: Policy Options, Challenges, Preconditions, and Prospects for Income Protection Systems for Older Adults

The discussion in the previous sections shows how, facing a common problem (the limited coverage of existing social security systems), the countries in this analysis adopted different policies. Many of these differences reflect the divergent initial conditions each country faced upon implementing reforms, the main reform goals, and implementation capacity. In general, it does not appear possible to declare certain policy options superior to others a priori, but it is reasonable to analyze the consistency between the context and the goals, on one hand, and the tools used, on the other.

The differences in initial conditions can be divided into essentially four categories: (1) the policy objectives set forth upon proposing the reform, (2) the coverage level of traditional social protection systems, (3) the fiscal and economic cost of these systems, and (4) the existence of noncontributory social protection programs integrated with the contributory social protection system. Using these criteria, it is possible to identify three groups of countries based on the policy option chosen. The first group consists of countries with traditional contributory social protection systems with wide coverage (more than 50 percent of older adults) that require significant resource flows (whether fiscal resources or from the labor market and privately managed) and with well-functioning noncontributory social protection systems despite low coverage levels. This group of countries, including Argentina, Brazil, Chile, and Uruguay, clearly set a policy goal of "social security inclusion," that is, extending coverage to the small portion of older adults that for whatever reason had not received pension benefits previously. In this context, the policy response was, in every case, modifying the rules to allow these groups to be incorporated in the general system, whether through a moratorium (Argentina), a special scheme for rural workers (Brazil), the creation of a New Solidarity Pillar as a part of the general social protection system (Chile), or the easing of access requirements for regular and elderly pensions (Uruguay). In the four cases the new schemes are an integral part of the traditional systems, are managed by existing institutions, and offer benefits that are less than those offered by the traditional contributory system, but closer to contributory levels than in other countries (particularly in Argentina and Uruguay) and at a similar fiscal or economic cost.

A second group is made up of those countries that, facing medium coverage levels in their contributory systems (between 20 percent and 50 percent of the elderly population) and low fiscal costs associated with these systems, proposed strategies mainly designed to reduce poverty among older adults. These countries (Colombia, Costa Rica, Ecuador, Mexico, Panama, and Peru) designed targeted programs, but with the intention of expanding coverage beyond the vulnerable population. Mexico and Panama are the best examples of the tendency toward universal coverage, although recent advances and proposals currently under discussion in Colombia, Ecuador, and Peru also point in this direction. It is interesting to note that Costa Rica, which in many aspects was a pioneer in the development of social policy in the region, has not advanced as much toward universal coverage compared with other countries.

Finally, the third group is made up of those countries that began the process from a very low coverage level and with little institutional development of social protection systems. As a result, their steps toward inclusion were made within targeted poverty reduction programs that were already in the process of being implemented. El Salvador and Paraguay are the best examples of countries in this group.

Bolivia and Trinidad and Tobago are two unusual cases that do not fit easily into any of the three categories mentioned above. In Bolivia, the initial conditions most closely resemble the third group of countries; however, it has created a universal noncontributory social protection system, with a reduced benefit and, until recently, autonomous from the traditional pension system. Trinidad and Tobago's different approach appears to be more linked to its institutional history and connection to the British model than to financial or policy effectiveness considerations. In the annex to this chapter we present the principal system performance indicators for each country in simplified form.

The reforms and expansions undertaken in the countries in this analysis show a clear paradigm shift in the social protection models in Latin America, shifting from systems firmly based on the contributory model to mixed systems that combine noncontributory components at a level never before seen in the history of these programs. As we have pointed out, the initiatives undertaken in each country are not homogenous in their design or impact, in terms of the types of protection offered, and in their fiscal requirements.

The information we have gathered appears to demonstrate that countries that had stronger traditional social protection systems (i.e., with greater coverage, resources, and administrative capacity), such as Argentina, Brazil, Chile, Trinidad and Tobago, and Uruguay, have tended in general to seek to expand existing programs, incorporating the social sectors that were previously excluded from them. In this context, it is more efficient to manage the new initiatives within the institutions that already coordinate the traditional contributory social protection systems, thereby taking advantage of their preexisting abilities (in terms of scale) to implement massive benefit payment systems.

In contrast, countries with contributory systems with limited scale and resources have sought to respond to the challenge of coverage expansion through targeted programs and with limited resources, following the model of the conditional cash transfer schemes that they were already using to support families with children. Bolivia appears to be an exception to this pattern in terms of coverage because it sought universal coverage from a starting point of very low coverage in the contributory system. However, it fits the pattern in terms of funding because it offers benefits that are much lower than the contributory system (which is reasonable because the goal of the system is to prevent poverty, not match the benefits paid by the traditional social protection system). In these countries, the administration of noncontributory systems is usually the responsibility of the same institutions that manage social assistance programs. This appears to be consistent with their strategy of targeting because they seek to use the experience and resources available in these institutions to identify and evaluate potential beneficiaries.

Noncontributory initiatives designed to offer protection against the risk of falling below the poverty line in old age are closely linked in terms of design and implementation to social protection and income transfer programs for other age groups. If the main objective is to reduce poverty, then it is clear that income transfer programs for older adults, as well as those directed to other age groups, should have similar designs and implementation strategies.

One debate frequently presented in the literature concerns the existence (or creation) of incentives in favor of labor informality as a result of these types of noncontributory transfer programs (Amarante et al. 2011; Camacho, Conover, and Hoyos 2009; Grosh, Emil, and Ouerghi 2008; among others). The central argument in these analyses is that the existence of noncontributory benefits reduces the willingness of workers to contribute to traditional schemes. However, given that the goal of these programs is to improve the quality of life of the elderly population, and that these expected incentives are linked to that goal, the more relevant debate considers both sides of the cost-benefit equation, not just the costs in isolation. Any discussion of this relationship should consider the positive social impacts that come from the quality of life improvements for beneficiaries as well as the possible negative effects that a noncontributory social protection program could have on the labor market by incentivizing labor informality. Even though this is not easy to evaluate in quantitative terms, it is still pertinent to the debate. Some analyses demonstrate a reduced impact on labor informality. Amarante et al. (2011) estimate an impact on incentives in favor of informality among men that can be attributed to income transfer programs in Uruguay in 2006–07, although the effect does not exist among women. In a study on the effects of a program of universal health insurance coverage in Colombia, Camacho, Conover, and Hoyos (2009) estimated an impact between 1.9 percent and 3.2 percent on labor informality as a result of the Subsidized System (Régimen Subsidiado), which expanded health coverage to more than 50 percent of Colombians.

The magnitude of the impact on incentives could depend on factors related to the social security system, such as the design and coordination of the contributory and noncontributory systems, as well as other factors exogenous to the social security system, such as workers' preferences and budget limitations or decisions made by third parties like employers in the case of salaried workers. As we pointed out in the previous section, the benefits offered by noncontributory pensions are usually lower than their contributory counterparts. Among the countries in this analysis, only Argentina, Costa Rica, Trinidad and Tobago, and Uruguay offered noncontributory benefits that exceeded 50 percent of their contributory counterparts, and in the other 10 countries in the study the average amount varied from 4 percent to 40 percent of the benefits paid by contribution-based pensions. In the majority of the countries in the region contribution obligations apply only to salaried workers, who, in many cases, do not have the ability to make decisions regarding compliance with social security obligations because of the asymmetrical power relationship they have with their employers.[13]

In an analysis of the effects of conditional cash transfer programs, Grosh, Emil, and Ouerghi (2008, p. 127) found that the impact of these programs on the labor market was minor, noting that "Participation in safety net programs has only small or moderate effects on employment or hours worked in developed countries and even smaller effects in developing countries." Even in cases where the impact could be more significant, the authors identify different tools to mitigate the effects that allow conditional cash transfer programs to achieve their objectives without significant impacts on the labor market. In any case, given the potential effect that any income transfer policy, whether to families with children, workers, or older adults, could have on their decisions in the labor market, it is clear that these impacts should be carefully considered when designing and implementing programs such as those discussed in this chapter.

Finally, an important challenge for many of the programs and reforms analyzed here is sustainability, both fiscal and economic as well as political. On one hand, these programs have been created under good macroeconomic and fiscal conditions, given the international economic situation during the first decade of this century, which begs the question of what attitude the different governments will adopt in the event that economic conditions deteriorate in the future. At the same time, the regulatory framework of these programs is in many cases significantly more flexible than that of the traditional contributory social protection system, as can be witnessed in the ease with which authorities have made reform after reform to the same programs in relatively little time. In this context, a politically adverse situation could result in the reversal of some of these initiatives, something that should be considered in the future with the goal of consolidating the gains made in recent years toward coverage of the most vulnerable sectors of older adults in the region.

Based on this study of the design and implementation aspects of the income protection programs for older adults (beyond just traditional contributory social protection systems) in 14 countries in the region, we can conclude that there is not a single prescription for all of the countries in the region, as long as distinct exogenous factors exist that limit the effectiveness of the stated goals. The main difference that one can note among the various initiatives in this study is related to their divergent focuses and policy objectives, even when dealing with the same policy tools. Even though the heterogeneity of initial conditions makes a strict discussion of best and worst practices nearly irrelevant, it does appear possible to propose some general guidelines that would allow us to organize a debate related to future policy proposals, keeping in mind their stated goals.

On one hand, in many of the countries studied here we have seen situations where the older adult coverage of the contributory social protection system is moderately high and funded with contributions from active workers, but also significant transfers from general revenues. This creates a problem of horizontal inequality where the excluded population finances the contributory benefits through their tax payments. Faced with the goal of expanding coverage to achieve universal coverage and reduce inequality, one possible option is to provide a monetary benefit to the excluded population. The benefit should be similar to the contributory benefit, but a lesser amount to limit undesired effects on the job market, and should be administered by the institutions that manage contributory pensions. This benefit could function both as a social inclusion program and as a form of compensation (although not exact) for the existing transfers between nonbeneficiaries and beneficiaries through the noncontributory funding of the traditional pension programs.

On the other hand, from a starting point of low coverage of the contributory social protection system, and as a result lower expenditures and impact on horizontal equality, the goal is usually to reduce the most vulnerable older adults' risk of falling into poverty. Consequently, the most viable option is to transfer income to the target population, adapting the design and implementation of transfer programs designed for other age groups. This option relies on clear poverty targeting tools and is managed by institutions with the ability and experience to implement these programs effectively.

However, even at this broad level, there are some doubts that should be considered in the design and implementation of both new noncontributory social protection programs and the expansion of existing programs. First, how financially sustainable can these programs be, given the demographic transition that is underway in the region? In other words, as the population ages, the financial resources needed to address this process will increase. In general, noncontributory pensions are based on a more flexible legal framework than their contributory counterparts, which means that faced with budgetary restrictions, their value could be adjusted. However, international experience suggests that other dimensions such as political and social forces make tightening the program difficult.

Finally, it is clear that in any system many decisions related to the political, social, economic, and management capacity context in different countries must be made. Given the variety of implementation tools used to expand social security coverage to older adults in the region, a more detailed analysis of the characteristics of each implementation process would be a fundamental contribution toward achieving better informed and more effective policy-making processes. Because resources are always limited, it is crucial to understand the dynamics among the different components of the social security system, including contributory and noncontributory social protection systems, social assistance programs, and the advantages and disadvantages of adopting universal versus targeted schemes. For social protection programs that benefit the most vulnerable populations, monitoring targeting mechanisms is an important step toward improving and reducing exclusion and inclusion errors. Additionally, it is important to evaluate the complementarity of noncontributory social protection programs and other income transfer programs designed for other vulnerable age groups with the goal of reducing household poverty. Criteria to prioritize among the various vulnerable groups are not always explicit and competition for scarce resources can result in significant social inefficiencies.

These are some of the debates that we have seen open up in recent years with the emergence of new coverage expansion programs for older adults. The diversity of responses that we have observed in the region appears to indicate that there are not unambiguous answers or universal solutions to these problems. However, it is clear that tracking the processes begun in recent years will help identify some ideas that deserve to be replicated and others that should be avoided in the future. This book offers a first step in that direction, and we believe that further efforts to delve into this field are necessary in the future.

Annex 1A Coverage Expansion Programs

Table 1A.1 Coverage Expansion Programs, Performance Indicators, 2012
Percent

					Average benefit as a percentage of		
Country	*Program*	*Total beneficiaries/ population 65+*	*New beneficiaries/ population 65+*	*Program spending/ GDP*	*Contributory benefit*	*Poverty line*[a]	*GDP per capita*
Argentina	Social Security Moratorium	91	41	2.5	77	351	39.6
Bolivia	Dignity Income	91	90	1.0	8	39	12.6
Brazil	Rural Pension	86	48	1.9	34	123	17.2
Chile	Basic Solidarity Pension	83	27	0.2	40	126	12.0
Colombia	Elderly Colombia	44	21	0.1	4	26	4.3
Costa Rica	Noncontributory pension	59	18	0.2	67	124	17.8
Ecuador	Human Development Voucher	51	32	0.4	6	43	4.9
El Salvador	Universal Basic Pension	17	4	0.0	15	46	12.2
Mexico	70 and over	44	18	0.1	16	43	4.9
Panama	100 to 70	81	36	0.3	25	104	12.6
Paraguay	Nutritional Pension for the Elderly	29	13	0.2	27	103	29.3
Peru	Pension 65	41	15	0.1	14	52	8.6
Trinidad and Tobago	Senior Citizens' Grant	99	81	1.8	100	448	30.5
Uruguay	Contributory system relaxation	86	6	0.5	57	169	18.4

Source: Based on information from chapters 2 to 15 of this book and information from social security agencies in the region.
a. Defined as the value in national currency equivalent to US$4 per day (PPP).

Notes

1. This chapter focuses on the policies of income transfer to the elderly. However, it is important to note that the demographic and social processes discussed also have a significant impact on other areas of social policy, such as the provision of health services or long-term care, that are not the subject of the present analysis.
2. For a detailed discussion of the processes of workforce retirement and the financing mechanisms for consumption during this stage, see Murrugarra (2011).
3. Of course, it is possible that these external resources could be used to pay for benefits for all participants based on proportionality. Therefore, for those sectors with fewer resources or for those that start from privileged positions, the impact of the system will not be neutral in terms of equity.
4. By expected benefit, we mean the replacement ratio that future retirees can expect.
5. In 2008, Argentina implemented a counterreform of its system, eliminating private administration of individually funded accounts and returning to a pay-as-you-go scheme administered by the state.
6. The individually funded scheme in Ecuador was approved in 2001, but it was never implemented.
7. Using coverage indicators for occupied workers and salaried workers we observe the same trend.
8. The exercise is a static comparison given the poverty rate (US$2.50 purchasing power parity [PPP]) including and not including household pension income, ignoring the possibility that individuals could obtain other sources of income if they did not have access to pensions.
9. For a detailed description of each of these schemes, see the corresponding chapters in this book.
10. This program was replaced by the "Pension for Older Adults" (Pensión para Adultos Mayores), which expanded coverage to adults over 65 years of age.
11. In some cases, such as Colombia, Paraguay, and Peru, the low percentage is the result of the gradual implementation of programs, and coverage is expected to increase significantly in the near future.
12. The poverty line is defined as US$4 daily PPP converted to the national currency using an average monthly exchange rate.
13. Apella and Casanova (2008) showed, based on household surveys, that in the Argentine context the ability to make contributions or budget limitation is the primary factor affecting labor formality, leaving very little space for individual decisions.

Bibliography

Amarante, V., M. Manacorda, A. Vigorito, and M. Zerpa. 2011. "Social Assistance and Labor Market Outcomes: Evidence from the Uruguayan PANES." IBD Publications 79,879, IDB, Washington, DC.

Apella, I., and L. Casanova. 2008. "Los Trabajadores Independientes y el Sistema de Seguridad Social. El Caso del Gran Buenos Aires." In *Aportes a Una Nueva Visión de la Informalidad Laboral en la Argentina*. Buenos Aires, Argentina: World Bank—Ministerio de Trabajo, Empleo y Seguridad Social.

Barr, N. 2001. *The Welfare State as Piggy Bank*. New York: Oxford University Press.

Barr, N., and P. Diamond. 2009. "Reforming Pensions: Principles, Analytical Errors, and Policy Directions." *International Social Security Review* 62 (2): 5–29.

Camacho, A., E. Conover, and A. Hoyos. 2009. "Effects of Colombia's Social Protection System on Workers' Choice between Formal and Informal Employment." Documentos CEDE 006003. Universidad de los Andes, CEDE, Bogotá.

Cotlear, D. 2010. *Population Aging: Is Latin America Ready?* Washington, DC: World Bank.

ECLAC (Economic Commission for Latin America and the Caribbean). 2006. *Shaping the Future of Social Protection: Access, Financing and Solidarity*. Report for the thirty-first session, ECLAC, Montevideo.

Forteza, A., I. Apella, E. Fajnzylber, C. Grushka, I. Rossi, and G. Sanroman. 2009. "Work Histories and Pension Entitlements in Argentina, Chile and Uruguay." Social Protection Discussion Paper 926, World Bank, Washington, DC.

Gill, I., T. Packard, and J. Yermo. 2005. *Keeping the Promise of Social Security in Latin America*. Washington, DC: World Bank and Stanford University Press.

Grosh, M., C. Emil, and A. Ouerghi. 2008. *For Protection and Promotion: The Design and Implementation of Effective Safety Nets*. Washington, DC: World Bank.

Hanlon, J., A. Barrientos, and D. Hulme. 2010. *Just Give Money to the Poor*. Sterling, VA: Kumarian Press.

Holzmann, R., and R. Hinz. 2005. *Old Age Income Support in the 21st Century*. Washington, DC: World Bank.

Huenchuan, S., and J. Guzmán. 2006. "Seguridad Económica y Pobreza en la Vejez: Tensiones, Expresiones y Desafíos para Políticas." Reunión de Expertos sobre Población y Pobreza en América Latina y el Caribe, Santiago, Chile.

IDB (Inter-American Development Bank). 2013. "Mejores pensiones, Mejores trabajos: Hacia la Cobertura Universal en América Latina y el Caribe." IDB, Washington, DC.

ILO (International Labour Organization). 2001. *Social Security: A New Consensus*. Geneva, Switzerland: ILO.

———. 2011. *Social Protection Floor for a Fair and Inclusive Globalization*. Geneva, Switzerland: ILO.

Mesa-Lago, C. 1978. *Social Security in Latin America: Pressure Groups, Stratification and Inequality*. Pittsburgh, PA: University of Pittsburgh Press.

Mesa-Lago, C., and F. Bertanou. 1998. "Manual de Economía de la Seguridad Social." Centro Latinoamericano de Economía Humana (CLAEH), Montevideo, Uruguay.

Murrugarra, E. 2011. "Employability and Productivity among Older Workers: A Policy Framework and Evidence from Latin America." Social Protection Discussion Paper 1113, World Bank, Washington, DC.

Palacios, R., and O. Sluchynsky. 2006. "Social Pensions Part I: Their Role in the Overall Pension System." Social Protection Discussion Paper 0601, World Bank, Washington, DC.

Pearson, M., and E. Whitehouse. 2009. "Social Pensions in High-Income Countries." In *Closing the Coverage Gap: The Role of Social Pensions and Other Retirement Income Transfers*, edited by R. Holzmann, D. Robalino, and N. Takayama. Washington, DC: World Bank.

Robalino, D., and R. Holzmann. 2009. "Overview and Preliminary Policy Guidance." In *Closing the Coverage Gap: The Role of Social Pensions and Other Retirement Income*

Transfers, edited by R. Holzmann, D. Robalino, and N. Takayama. Washington, DC: World Bank.

Rofman, R., and L. Oliveri. 2012. "La Cobertura de los Sistemas Previsionales en América Latina: Conceptos e Indicadores." Serie de Documentos de Trabajo sobre Políticas Sociales 7. World Bank, Buenos Aires.

Sánchez, P. 2000. "Sociología de la Vejez versus Economía de la Vejez." *Papers Revista de Sociología*, Vol. 61, pp. 39–88, Universitat Autònoma de Barcelona, Spain.

Stiglitz, J. 1986. *La Economía del Sector Público.* Barcelona, Spain: Antoni Bosch.

Zviniene, A., and T. Packard. 2004. "A Simulation of Social Security Reforms in Latin America: What Has Been Gained?" Background document, Oficina del Economista Jefe para América Latina, World Bank, Washington, DC.

Wolf, S. 1989. *Los Pobres en la Europa Moderna*. Barcelona, Spain: Ed. Crítica.

World Bank. 1994. *Averting the Old Age Crisis*. Washington, DC: World Bank.

CHAPTER 2

Argentina

Rafael Rofman and Ignacio Apella

Background

The Argentine social security system is one of the oldest in Latin America and the world, with a history spanning over more than 100 years. It began as a diverse set of income protection programs for the elderly, which were created and managed independently for each industry or sector, and expanded and integrated throughout the 20th century. The regulatory and institutional structure, as in other countries, underwent several changes over those decades, and its maturation came about in a context of reform and great debate. At the beginning of the 1990s a major structural reform was introduced with two main characteristics. First, it completed the consolidation of most previously autonomous schemes into one system, centrally managed. Second, it also implied a revision of system parameters and participation conditions, to contain what was perceived as a worrying growing tendency in social security expenditures. These reforms, within the context of a deteriorating labor market, resulted in a declining trend in coverage of active workers as well as the elderly. The existence of a noncontributory scheme (introduced in 1948) was not sufficient to compensate this decline, which motivated an increasing concern among specialists and policy makers.

The negative trend began to improve after the 2002 crisis. First, the proportion of the active population participating in the contributory social security system increased as unemployment and informality decreased. Approaching 2010, the percentage of workers contributing to the system reached a level similar to that of 20 years before. However, coverage of the elderly did not change as quickly. The percentage of this population with social security benefits had fallen to less than 70 percent by 2002 after a 12-year decline and showed no signs of recovery until 2006.

The Demographic Transition

As in other countries in the region, Argentina is in a process of demographic transition characterized by sustained growth of the old age dependency rate. Figure 2.1 shows the percentage of persons over age 65 in Argentina, compared with the regional average. The figure shows the increasing weight of this group

Figure 2.1 Population Older than 65 Years, Argentina and Latin America, 1950–2100

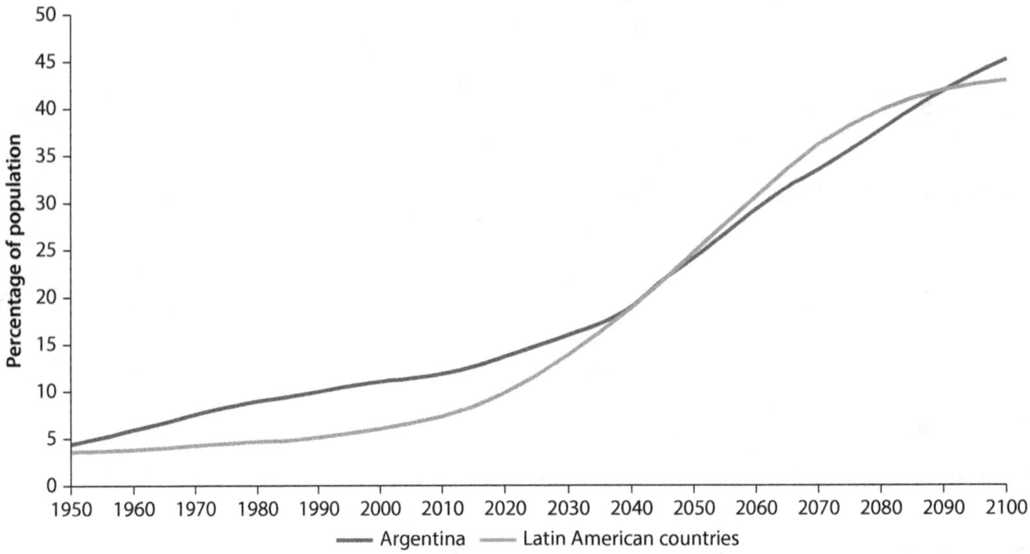

Source: Centro Latinoamericano y Caribeño de Demografía—Comisión Económica para América Latina (CELADE-CEPAL).

in the total population, as it grew by 7.5 percentage points between 1950 and 2010, to reach 11.9 percent. Further growth is expected in coming decades, and by 2100 45.2 percent of the population should be older than 65 years.

This demographic trend is caused, as in other countries, by a decline in death and birth rates. Life expectancy at birth has experienced a sustained growth, from 62 to 76 years between 1950 and 2010, with a projected level of 85 years by the end of this century. The improvement is particularly fast among the elderly, as life expectancy at 60 years old increased from 16.4 to 21.6 years over the last few decades, and it is expected to rise to 28.4 years by 2100. Looking at birth rates, the total fertility rate decreased from 3.15 in the middle of the last century to close to replacement level in 2010 (2.17 children per mother), and it should reach 1.7 children per woman as we approach the year 2100.

Population aging has long-term impacts on the labor market, as well as the health and pension systems. In particular, traditional pay-as-you-go schemes based on defined contributions are particularly vulnerable to the effects of aging, because it produces sustained increases in dependency rates. However, this impact has been exaggerated in some discussions, and some mitigating effects should be considered. Bertranou et al. (2012) note that the aging process in Argentina tends to be slow, gradual, and predictable, which facilitates long-term adjustments of the pension system. The increase in the old age dependency rage is usually compensated by a decrease in the child dependency rate, freeing resources that can be reallocated over time. Participation in economic activity (especially among women) has also grown over time, and this in part compensates the reduction in the number of young adults. Additionally, sustained growth in labor productivity tends to compensate the reduction in the number of young adults, generating additional resources to finance elderly consumption.

Historic Background

Argentina is considered a pioneer in the development of social security policies in the region (Mesa-Lago 1978). The earliest regulation associated with pensions was Law no. 870, from 1877, granting retirement benefits to magistrates, in a tax-financed scheme. In 1886, Law no. 1090 introduced a system for teachers, and in 1887 Law no. 2219 also included national government staff who had served for at least 35 years, in all cases financed with general revenues.

The first modern pension scheme was created in 1904. Law no. 4349 introduced the first social security fund financed through contributions from the participant population. Between 1904 and 1944 workers from different sectors were included as new pension funds were created (railways, public utilities, banks, journalists, merchant navy, and insurance and retail workers, among others). In all these cases, pension funds were autonomous and were financed with the sector's employers' and employees' contributions and administered independently, with active workers' total or partial control.

The creation of the National Social Security Institute (Instituto Nacional de Previsión Social [INPS]) in 1944 can be considered as the beginning of the reversal of this fragmentation process, since the state became involved in the management of social security. In this period a gradual expansion to the entire working population began, including independent and salaried workers. This expansion was unplanned and uncoordinated, and, as a result, in the mid-1960s the system had a wide normative coverage (from 7 percent of the labor force in 1944 to 55.2 percent in 1960), but it was fragmented, and eligibility requirements, contribution, financing, and benefit rules were heterogeneous (Isuani and San Martino 1995a, 1995b).

In 1967 the National Social Security System (Sistema Nacional de Previsión Social) was created, reorganizing the existing pension funds into three schemes: (1) private sector employees, (2) civil servants, and (3) independent workers. Law no. 18037 established a defined benefit scheme for salaried workers (public or private), defining the pension as a percentage of the average of the best three salaries in the last 10 years of employment. For independent workers, regulated by Law no. 18038, the benefit was determined as a percentage of the presumed income of currently active independent workers. Eligibility requirements included a minimum age of 55 for men and 50 for women, and 20 years of contributions in all cases. This reform did not affect the system's contributory nature, or its direct link with formal employment, because only formal workers (or registered independent workers) who contributed had a right to receive benefits, and financing was sustained mainly by employees and employers contributions.

Between 1975 and 1993 several parametric reforms were introduced, mostly affecting employer contributions, which were eliminated in 1980 (and replaced by an increase in value-added tax rates), and then reinstated in 1984. During the 1980s and the early 1990s the pension system began to show financial sustainability issues for several reasons. On one hand, real salaries in the formal labor market showed a declining trend, while unemployment and informality grew, resulting in a loss of revenue. On the other hand, the coverage expansion of previous decades lost momentum as the system maturated, and the population aging process also had a growing negative impact on the financial performance of the system.

In the midst of a financing crisis, in 1993 a structural reform was introduced, incorporating a funded pillar, managed by for-profit firms. Law no. 24241 instituted the Integrated Retirement and Pensions System (Sistema Integrado de Jubilaciones y Pensiones [SIJP]) to cover old age, disability, and death contingencies. This system would have two schemes: a public system financed through a pay-as-you-go scheme and administered by the National Social Security Administration (Administración Nacional de la Seguridad Social [ANSES]), and a funded scheme based on individual accounts, managed by independent Pension Fund Administrators (Administradoras de Fondos de Jubilaciones y Pensiones [AFJP]). At the same time, several important changes were introduced in the system's parameters: The minimum legal retirement age was increased by five years (to 65 years for men and 60 for women), the number of required years of service went from 20 to 30, and the employees' contributions were increased from 10 percent to 11 percent of salaries.

All workers were moved to the new system. Participation in a first pillar was compulsory, which offered a flat benefit to all retirees, financed by employers' contributions and managed by ANSES, as part of the public pension scheme. At the same time, workers had to join a second pillar, which offered benefits linked to past employee contributions. They had to choose between the public scheme, which offered a defined benefit scheme financed with employees' contributions, or the funded scheme, which offered contribution defined benefits and was managed by an AFJP selected by the worker. If workers did not make this choice, they were assigned to the funded scheme. This scheme grew consistently following its introduction, and, by 2006, 82 percent of workers registered by the SIJP had joined it (Apella 2008). The pension system as a whole was financed from workers' and employers' contributions (11 and 16 percent of wages). On top of contributions revenue, several tax resources have been used to finance it, including 15 percent of tax revenues that the federal government distributes among provinces.

Since its implementation, the design and function of the SIJP has been the subject of debate. On the one hand, different observers have pointed out several market failures resulting in a less efficient than expected funded scheme. Also, the fiscal pressures originating by the transition process was considered as a relevant factor in the economic crisis of 2001–02 in Argentina, and some of the public scheme regulations did not respond to the system's or its beneficiaries' needs. As a result, and since its introduction in 1994, the system has been the subject of multiple modifications and adjustments, including more than 40 laws modifying its original text. Among these, the most relevant are Law no. 26222 which, in February 2007, allowed workers in the funded pillar to switch back to the pay-as-you-go scheme, and Law no. 26425, which, at the end of 2008, permanently eliminated the funded scheme, directing all contributions to the public pay-as-you-go system. This last reform, however, did not eliminate other reforms introduced in 1993, such as the increased contribution rate, the minimum retirement age, or the number of years of contributions required to retire.

Although Argentina has had some types of pension schemes financed with taxes since the 19th century, the first formal, noncontributory pension model (Pensiones No Contributivas [PNC]) for low-income sectors was implemented in 1948. This scheme, which established a minimum pension for all citizens over 60 who were not already included in a social security scheme, did not have any access restrictions, and so could be considered to be a universal coverage program. However, in practice the program had limited access for several decades because of budgetary restrictions. When the social security system was reformed in 1994, the PNC scheme was separated from contributory programs, and its administration was shifted to the Social Development Secretariat, which by 1999 had become the Ministry of Social Development.

The Pension System Performance

Pension Coverage

The Argentine social security system was created as a contributory scheme, which broadened its coverage of active workers as new activities were incorporated throughout most of the 20th century. Following the 1980s, as a result of changes in the labor market and the deterioration of macroeconomic conditions, this growing coverage trend began to show signs of stagnation and decline (Rofman, Fajnzylber, and Herrera 2010).

The system's structural reform in 1993 was accompanied by two important parametric changes: an increase in the legal retirement age by five years and an increase in the number of years of service required for retirement, from 20 to 30 years. These changes made access conditions more rigid, as greater stability in formal employment was required. Figure 2.2 shows the contribution density function for the period 1994–2001. As shown, it is bimodal, concentrated on values close to zero and one. In other words, in this period 20 percent of workers had very high contribution densities (over 80 percent), and at the same time almost half of workers had densities lower than 50 percent, which implies that over time it would be difficult for them to accumulate the number of years with contributions required by the system to obtain a pension benefit.

Figure 2.3 shows coverage of the labor force population and unemployment rates for the period between 1992 and 2011. There is a constant decline in coverage during the 1990s until the year 2003. The percentage of contributors in relation to employed workers showed a similar tendency, decreasing from 49.7 percent in 1992 to 38.7 percent in 2003. This tendency reversed after the

Figure 2.2 Distribution of Contribution Density, 1994–2001

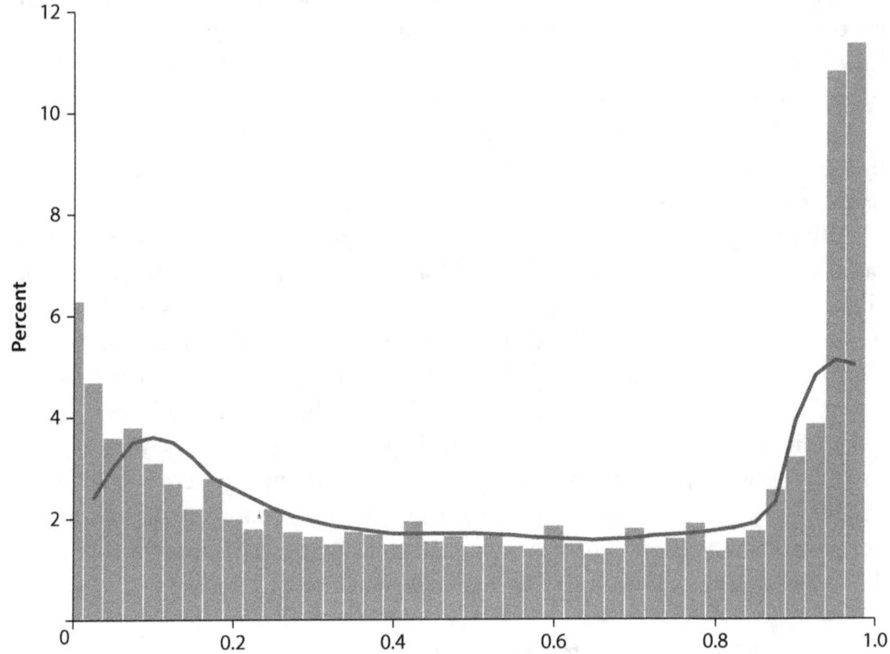

Source: Based on Sistema Integrado de Jubilaciones y Pensiones (SIJP).

Figure 2.3 Pension System Coverage for the Economically Active and Employed Population, 1992–2010

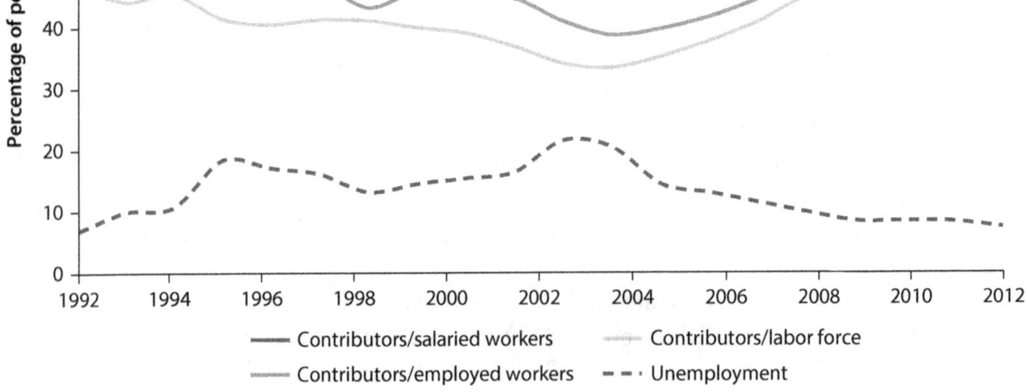

Source: Rofman and Oliveri 2012; calculations based on data from the Encuesta Permanente de Hogares (EPH) and Instituto Nacional de Estadística y Censos (INDEC).

second semester of 2003, as the percentage of contributing salaried workers increased to 59.2 percent in 2006, whereas the contributors/labor force rate reached 44.7 percent.

The decrease in coverage observed during the 1990s could be attributed in part to a rise in unemployment, which remained very high during this period. Also, a more open approach to international trade and currency appreciation in those years had a significant influence on employment patterns, because they resulted in changes in production profile and promoted the substitution of labor by capital in production. Hence, the low employment-product elasticity in that period reflects a weak labor demand and the labor market's lack of dynamism (Apella 2007). This process was reversed after convertibility was abandoned, and peso was devaluated, in 2002.

However, unemployment explains part of this evolution. In fact, coverage of employed and salaried workers showed tendencies similar to that of the labor force. Labor informality was an even stronger factor to explain the growing coverage gap, particularly among the employed and salaried workers.

In terms of coverage of the elderly, figure 2.4 shows the percentage of those over age 65 that received pension income, from 1992 to 2011. During these years, coverage was as high as 78 percent in 1993 and as low as 68 percent 11 years later, showing a dangerously declining trend.

From a gender perspective, coverage was higher for males than females during the period, essentially because of differences in work histories (figure 2.5). Traditionally, women were not part of the labor force, because of their role as housewives. This limited their contribution to the social security system during contributory age and therefore their access to benefits granted by the system.

Figure 2.4 Population over Age 65 Receiving a Social Security Benefit, 1992–2011

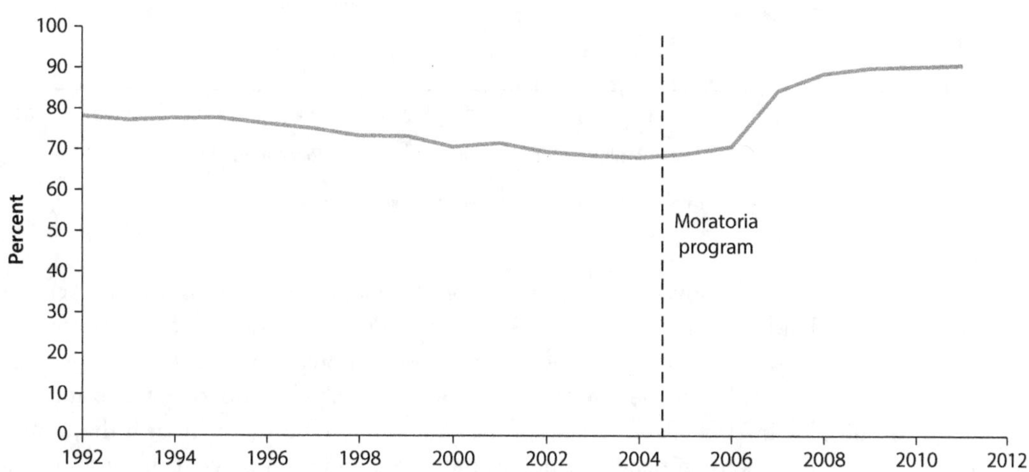

Source: Rofman and Oliveri 2012; calculations based on data from the Encuesta Permanente de Hogares (EPH).

Figure 2.5 Population over Age 65 Receiving a Social Security Benefit, by Gender, 1992–2011

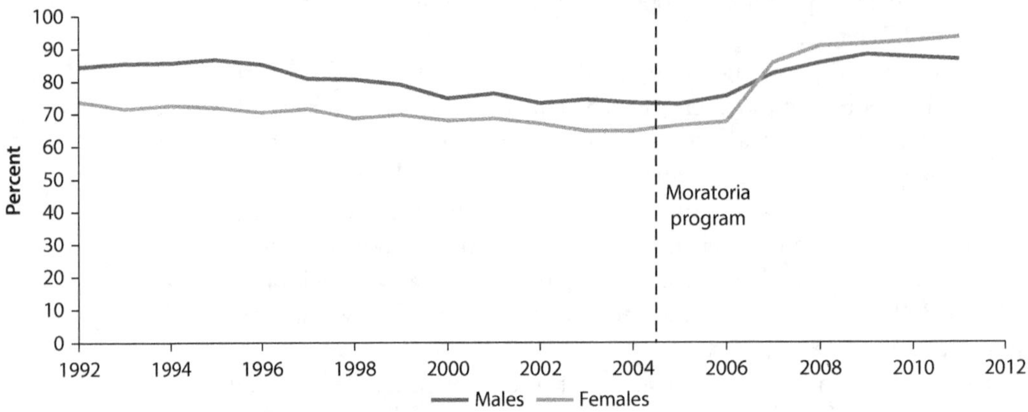

Source: Rofman and Oliveri 2012; calculations based on data from the Encuesta Permanente de Hogares (EPH).

Figure 2.6 Population over Age 65 Receiving a Welfare Benefit, by Income Quintile, 1992–2011

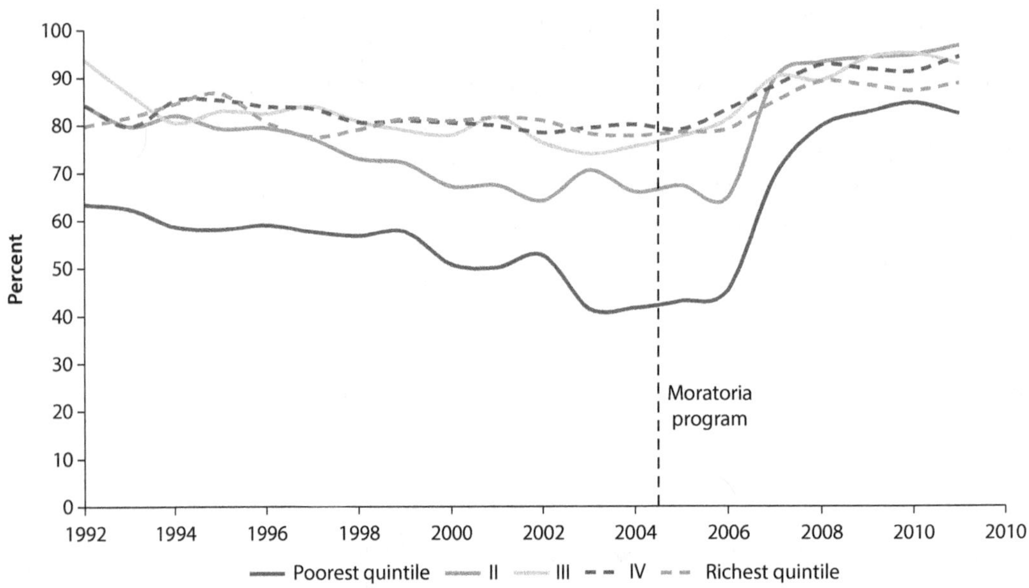

Source: Rofman and Oliveri 2012; calculations based on data from the Encuesta Permanente de Hogares (EPH).

Figure 2.6 shows coverage rates for the elderly, by quintiles of per capita household income.[1] Between 1992 and 2006 there was a clear bias toward greater coverage of higher income groups. Although for this period coverage shows a steady decline, the trend is more noticeable in the lowest two income quintiles. In 2006, 81.1 percent of the elderly in the third, fourth or fifth quintile received a pension benefit, whereas only 45.3 and 64.8 percent of those in the first and second quintiles were covered.

Coverage of Noncontributory Pension Programs

The PNC program offers six types of benefits: (1) old age, (2) disability, (3) "ex gratia," assigned by the National Congress, (4) mothers of seven or more children, (5) Malvinas war veterans, and (6) others through special laws (including families of those "desaparecidos" during the military dictatorship, Nobel Prize laureates, former bishops, and Olympic medalists). Among these programs, the first three could be seen as equivalent to a pension system (although in the case of ex gratia pensions there are no explicit age limits for access). PNC constitutes a relevant program, given the number of beneficiaries as well as the volume of resources it distributes (figure 2.7). In general, the program could be characterized as social assistance by nature, as it and aims to alleviate poverty, although some of the benefits do not reach this objective. Despite this, the PNC program seems to be targeted enough to have a positive impact on poverty reduction on covered households.

PNC coverage remained stable during the 1990s and until 2003, with a slow decline in ex gratia pensions (as rules were made more transparent) and a small increase in disability pensions. In practice, authorities capped the number of old age or disability pensions, so that once an applicant was confirmed to qualify to receive a benefit, it was granted only "if a space became available" in the program. From 2003 an expansion process began as budgets increased, allowing for more old age and disability pensions. Disability pensions grew rapidly, increasing more than five times in seven years. Old age pensions also increased at first, but the possibility of accessing an ordinary pension from 2006 onwards diverted demand toward that program.

Figure 2.7 Noncontributory Pension Benefits, 1996–2011

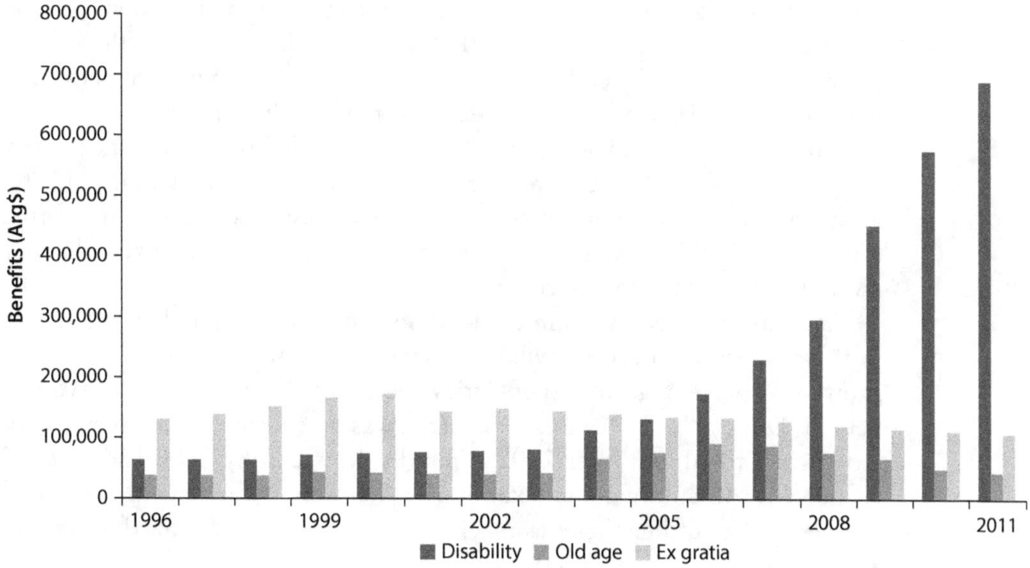

Source: Boletín de la Seguridad Social, Ministerio de Trabajo, Empleo y Seguridad Social (MTEySS).

Benefit Adequacy

An important aspect to consider when discussing the performance of the pension system in Argentina is the benefit adequacy. The purchasing power of pension benefits received by beneficiaries during the 1990s remained approximately constant, because there were no adjustments and inflation was very low. The minimum benefit was AR$150 (US$150), and the average was approximately AR$331 (US$331), so the average amount was 2.2 times the minimum value. Between 1994 and 2001, the average benefit increased by 22 percent. This recovery was not due to generalized increases, but to a composition effect: New retirees received higher benefits than those who had been retired for longer, because of the effect of incomplete indexation of benefits and reference salaries before 1992.

Starting in 2002, authorities began to increase benefits, with a particular focus on the minimum benefit. The gap between minimum and the average benefit declined as a result of this approach. Decree 1275/02 established a subsidy to ensure that all retirees received at least AR$200 (US$57.30). Successive increases brought the minimum pension to AR$240 by the end of 2003, AR$308 in 2004, AR$390 in 2005, AR$470 in 2006, AR$596 in 2007, and AR$690 in 2008 in a context of limited price inflation. As a consequence, the real value of this benefit grew by 100 percent in seven years. These increases were applied discretionally through presidential decrees, without any regulation regarding amount or frequency. Since the increases had a strong focus on the minimum pension, they caused a significant flattening in the scale of benefits. Figure 2.8 shows the minimum and average benefits and the ratio of these values from 1995 to 2011. In 2001 the average retirement benefit was 2.4 times the minimum benefit, whereas in 2011 this ratio reduced to 1.3.

These increases resulted in an effective protection of the minimum pension purchasing power during the early 2000s crisis and the recovery of the average pension to the 1990s levels by 2007. Figure 2.9 shows the minimum pension in relation with the poverty line and extreme poverty line in Argentina. During most of the 1990s the minimum pension was equivalent to 2.5 times the poverty line and very similar to the extreme poverty line, but this ratio declined in 2002 as the crisis disproportionately affected prices of basic goods. Recovery started soon, and by 2007 the minimum benefit was equivalent to two poverty lines or more than four extreme poverty lines.

The faster increase of minimum benefits until 2006 resulted in an increase in the proportion of retirees who receive the minimum benefit. Figure 2.10 shows the percentage of beneficiaries receiving the minimum by type of benefit. During the 1990s this percentage was on average 28.6 percent, with a declining trend, but after 2002 it rapidly grew and by 2006 had reached 63 percent. An automatic indexation rule was adopted by law in 2008, and the percentage of beneficiaries receiving the minimum stabilized at around 70 percent.

Figure 2.8 Average and Minimum Pensions, and Ratio between Them, 1995–2011

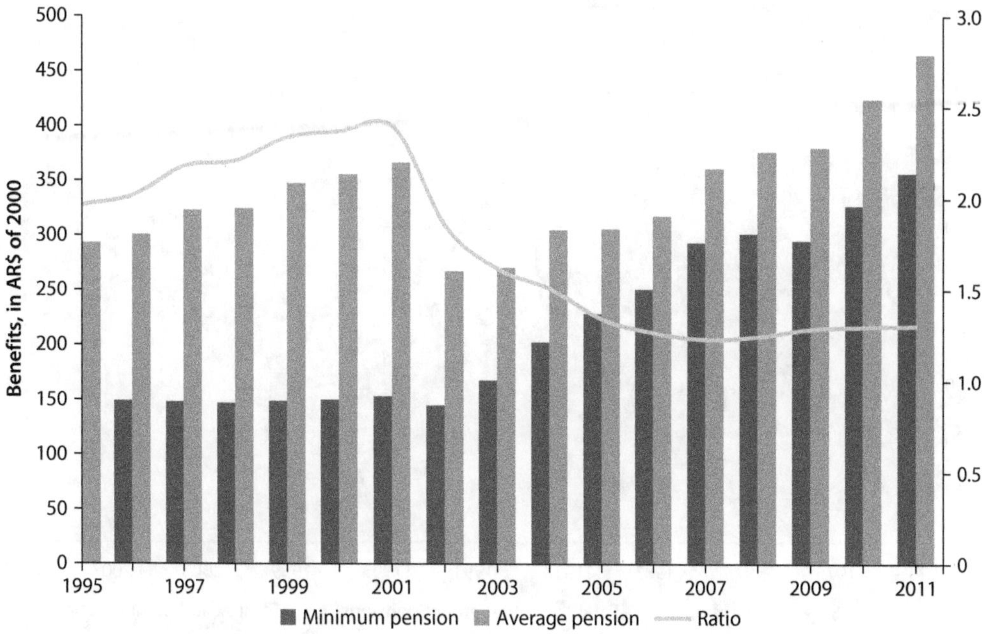

Source: Based on Ministerio de Trabajo, Empleo y Seguridad Social (MTEySS).
Note: Real values were calculated using INDEC CPI data until 2007 and Santa Fe Province consumer price index since then.

Figure 2.9 Minimum Pensions as a Proportion of Poverty and Extreme Poverty Lines, 1995–2011

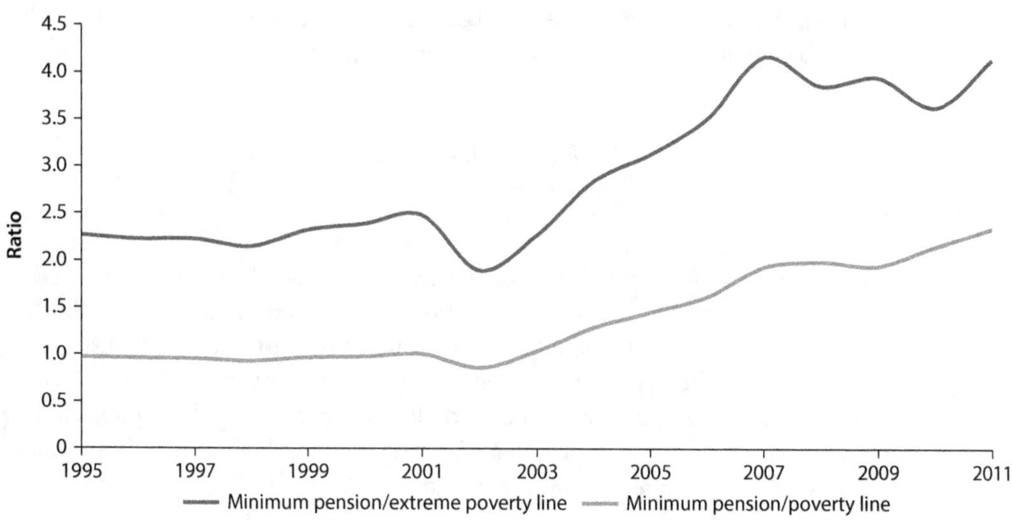

Source: Based on Ministerio de Trabajo, Empleo y Seguridad Social (MTEySS) and Instituto Nacional de Estadística y Censos (INDEC).

Figure 2.10 Percentage of Beneficiaries Receiving the Minimum, by Type of Benefit, 1991–2011

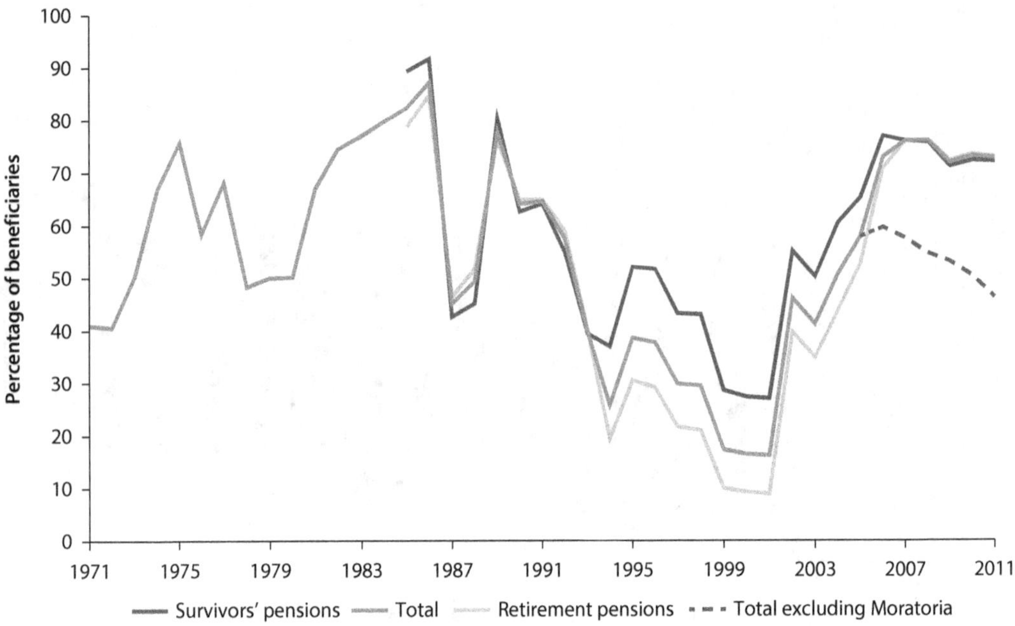

Source: Based on Ministerio de Trabajo, Empleo y Seguridad Social (MTEySS) and Instituto Nacional de Estadística y Censos (INDEC).

Law no. 26417, sanctioned in 2008, established a new indexation scheme for benefits and all other relevant variables in the pension system, based on the evolution of wages, contributions, and tax collection. A two-tiered formula applies depending on which of the two alternative calculations results in higher benefit increases:

$$m = \begin{cases} a = 0.5 \times RT + 0.5 \times w \\ b = 1.03 \times r \end{cases} \quad if \begin{cases} a \le b \\ a > b \end{cases}$$

where m is the semiannual increase; RT is the variation of an index of earmarked tax revenues per benefit; w is the variation of the general salary index, published by the National Statistics and Census Institute (Instituto Nacional de Estadística y Censos [INDEC]), or the variation of Workers' Average Taxable Income (Remuneración Imponible Promedio de los Trabajadores Estables, published by the Social Security Secretariat, depending on which is higher; and r is the variation of ANSES' total resources per benefit paid (including contributions and earmarked taxes).

The mechanism was subject to a heated debate in Congress, and its approval resulted in an increase in the system's performance predictability. The law also established that this formula would not apply if it resulted in a decrease in nominal values. All benefits in the contributory system, including old age, disability, and survivor pensions, as well as reference salaries used to calculate benefits at the time of retirement, are now adjusted according to this index.

Financial Performance

The Argentine pension system's financial performance has evolved throughout its history, depending on maturation, regulatory changes, and the labor market. The evolution of the social security financial result depends on two large groups of variables. The first includes those variables that directly affect the system's revenues, such as the number of contributors, salary levels, and contribution rates; the second group includes variables that affect the level of expenditures, such as the number of benefits (which in turn depends on retirement age and required contributions) and the level of benefits. Both groups of variables have evolved diversely, affecting the social security financial result in different ways.

Figure 2.11 shows the balance between contribution revenue and benefits in the public system, as a percentage of total resources. There are three clearly defined periods. The first begins in 1944 and ends in 1966, with positive results (initial surplus); a second period shows relative balance between income and expenditures between 1966 and 1980; and the third period was characterized by strong financial imbalances between 1980 and 2010.

Figure 2.11 Contribution Revenues–Benefit Expenditures Balance, Argentina's Pension System, 1944–2010

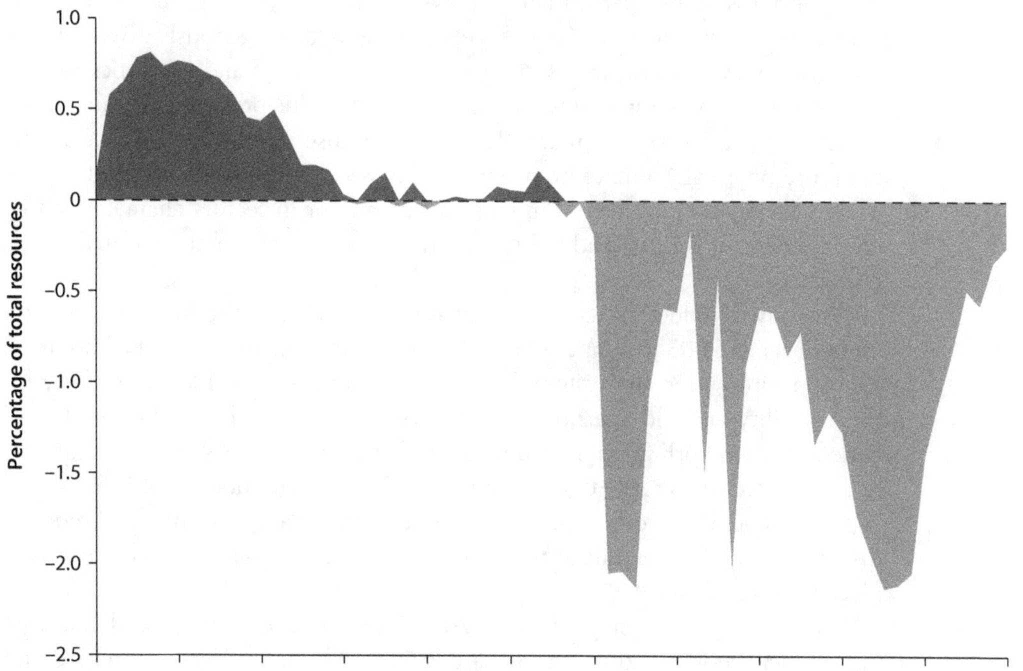

Source: Centrángolo and Grushka 2004 and Bertranou et al. 2012.

During the first period a substantial surplus was accumulated, because of the rapid increase in the number of contributors as new groups of workers joined the system. This process became more balanced, and from the mid-1960s it began to show balanced results. Starting in the 1980s, the combination of policy reforms and labor market trends resulted in growing negative results.

The system's deficit, which began in the 1980s and has remained to this day, is the result of several different factors: On one hand, the natural maturation of the demographic profile of participants exhausted the positive results of the early years. At the same time, the labor market faced growing informality and rising unemployment, which worsened the system dependency rates; the overall demographic context grew smaller as population aged; different institutional weaknesses resulted in poor management of reserves and granting of benefits to individuals not complying with minimum requirements; and other macroeconomic factors (such as inflation) and the use of welfare policy instruments for macroeconomic policy purposes contributed to this process.

The 1993 reform had a moderating effect on pension spending (which had grown steadily since the 1980s) but also on contribution revenue, because part of the employee contributions began to finance the funded scheme, and employer contributions were reduced to soften labor costs and promote formalization.

Expansion of Coverage beyond Labor Formality

The pension system's performance shows one of the typical problems affecting contributory schemes: Coverage levels are defined exogenously to the social security policy, because the labor market's performance and dynamics are the determinant forces for inclusion or exclusion in the programs. Contributory coverage reproduces labor market patterns, because middle-aged workers, who are more physically able to be productive, have a higher level of education, are often in salaried employment in large companies or in sectors characterized by employment stability, and have greater chances of paying contributions (Apella 2007).

As a way to reduce the coverage gap among the elderly, the Argentine government began in 2003 to adopt policy initiatives to include those who had not been able to retire within the system. PNCs became more accessible, particularly for the disability and old age programs. Between 2003 and 2006, the number of beneficiaries in both programs doubled, and, in the case of PNCs for disability, it has continued to increase, to reach, by 2011, 750 percent more beneficiaries than eight years before. These increases were not due to changes in rules and requirements for beneficiaries, but to the elimination of the capping system that was in place until then.

On the other hand, in December 2004 Law no. 25994 was passed, allowing independent workers to pay overdue past contributions under a simplified and very generous scheme, known as the Moratoria[2] program. This regulation, together with other decrees and resolutions, meant that any citizen that fulfilled the minimum age requirements but not the required years of service could claim those years under the independent workers' scheme, retire immediately, and pay the debt in installments while collecting a pension benefit. In addition, this scheme was also available to those who could claim survivors' benefits. The voluntary debt regularization scheme created by this regulation is open for any individual, although it recognizes only years contributed before 1994, so its use will gradually wind down.

ANSES is responsible for management of this program; it calculates applicants' debt, processes retirement applications, and pays benefits. Individuals are considered as qualifying for benefits as soon as they enter the Moratoria, and so payments of past debt are made at the same time benefits are collected (Arza 2009). Workers who were old enough to retire but did not reach the minimum contribution requirement could then begin to receive a benefit immediately, with a deduction to pay the debt in as many as of 60 monthly installments.

The Moratoria resulted in a significant increase in the number of beneficiaries, and it broadened the program's scope to include the entire elderly population, without specifying requirements in terms of employment history. However, this did not equate to a substantive reform, because it was an exceptional measure, so it could be considered as the result of a combination of contributory and universal noncontributory approaches. The system shows continuity with the traditional model, because beneficiaries are still considered to be former workers, who state in their application that they had worked independently and neglected to pay their social security contributions (although these statements were not verified). For example, many women who were housewives during their younger years had to define themselves as independent workers to access the benefit. There were no other eligibility requirements, such as vulnerability or poverty, which meant that this policy granted universal access to the social security system, with no direct links to poverty reduction criteria.

The design of the policy instrument analyzed here is different from the traditional contributory systems, as well as from welfare mechanisms designed to offer protection to those who did not participate regularly in the formal labor market. Given that those retiring under Moratoria received benefits higher than those from the PNC program, the number of old age PNC beneficiaries began to decline in 2006, when many gave up this benefit to join the new scheme. A similar effect could be observed among participants in subsidy programs for the elderly managed by provincial or municipal governments.

The Moratoria and Its Impact

The Moratoria represents an access to pension benefits for many that did not meet the eligibility requirements. Between 2005 and the end of 2011, a total of 2.7 million elderly adults gained access to a pension benefit. The inclusion of beneficiaries was slow at first, but it rapidly accelerated, and in a six-month period between September 2006 and March 2007, a record of 980,959 new pensioners joined the system. By the end of 2011, the total number of

Figure 2.12 Social Security Beneficiaries, by System, 1999–2011

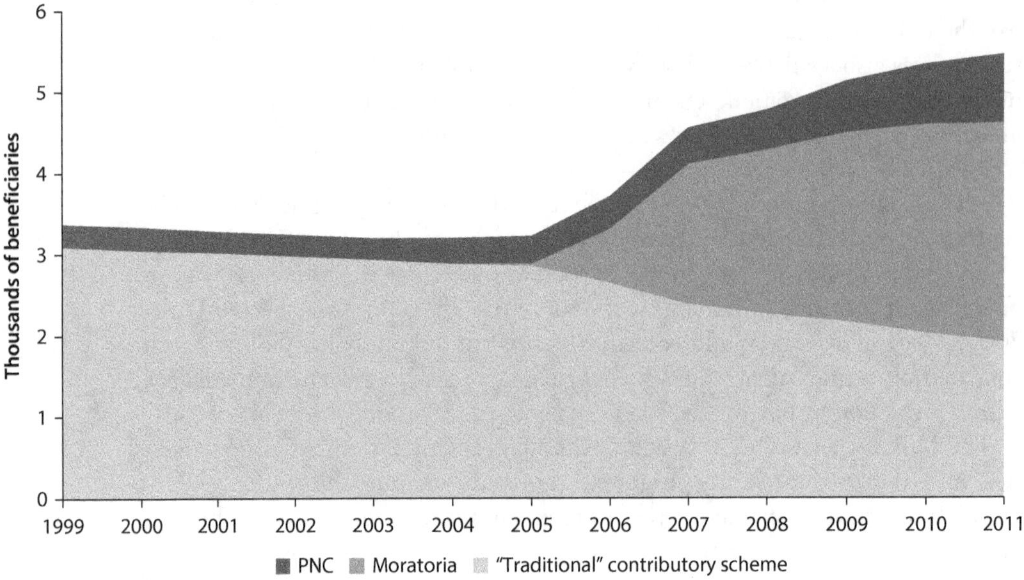

Source: Ministerio de Trabajo, Empleo y Seguridad Social (MTEySS) 2003.
Note: PNC = Pensiones No Contributivas.

beneficiaries in the national system had risen to 4.6 million, and almost 1 million received noncontributory pensions for disability, old age, or ex gratia (figure 2.12).

The changes implemented over the last few years have distanced the system from a traditional contributory model. Although the contributory nature of the traditional scheme could be questioned in terms of the financial scheme and beneficiaries' contribution records, more than 90 percent of beneficiaries who retired before 2005 had accessed benefits following the contributory system's rules. With the expansion of PNCs and the Moratoria, by the end of 2011 this percentage had fallen to nearly 35 percent. These changes, together with a high level of complexity in rules regarding financing, made it very difficult to assess the system's horizontal equity, because the ANSES is partly financed through earmarked taxes and general revenue. During the 2000–10 period revenues from contributions were on average 47 percent of ANSES total revenues, and income from other taxes represented 53 percent (figure 2.13).

Although in the last few years the relevance of contribution revenue has increased, the percentage that is financed with other resources is still substantial. Thus, it is possible to consider the Moratoria as giving access to the contributory system for beneficiaries who did not make enough contributions in the past, but indirectly financed the social security system through other taxes.

The Moratoria has had a significant impact on coverage levels since 2006, when the declining trend was reversed. Coverage of the elderly rapidly recovered

Figure 2.13 ANSES' Own Resources and Taxes, 1994–2010

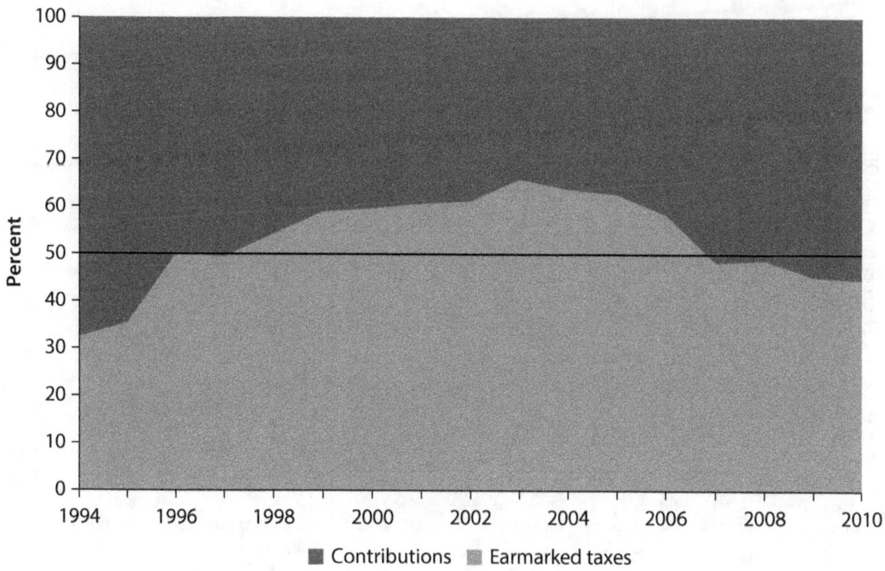

Source: Informe de la Seguridad Social, Administración Nacional de la Seguridad Social (ANSES).

between 2005 and 2006, when it reached 84.3 percent, and continued to grow gradually until it reached 90.8 percent in 2011 (figure 2.5). This rapid growth in meant that the coverage rate in Argentina became the highest in the region, overtaking Brazil by 3 percentage points and Uruguay by 4 percentage points in the year 2009, the last year with comparable data available among those countries (Rofman and Oliveri 2012).

The decrease in coverage until 2005 affected the poorest elderly, because those who were in the richest per capita household income quintile not only lost coverage but also increased their chances of retirement; the coverage among those in the poorest quintile went from 63.4 percent in 1992 to 42.9 percent in 2005 (figure 2.6). Symmetrically, when this trend was reversed in 2006, this was the group that benefited the most, reaching 84 percent by 2010. The same effect was observed among women, who historically had lower rates of coverage, and in 2007 reached a rate higher than that of men, for the first time in history (figure 2.5).

From a financial perspective, the Moratoria meant an increase in benefit spending for ANSES. Figure 2.14 shows ANSES expenditures as a percentage of GDP. Stagnation of elderly coverage during the 1990s meant stable spending, around 5 percent of GDP until 2002. After the reduction in spending from 2003 to 2005 (because of the fall in the real value of benefits), recovery meant a sustained increase, until it reached 6.12 percent of GDP in 2010.

In 2007 benefit payments linked to Moratoria reached 1.4 percent of GDP, equivalent to 28 percent of total social security benefits (figure 2.15).

Figure 2.14 ANSES Expenditures on Benefits, 1994–2010

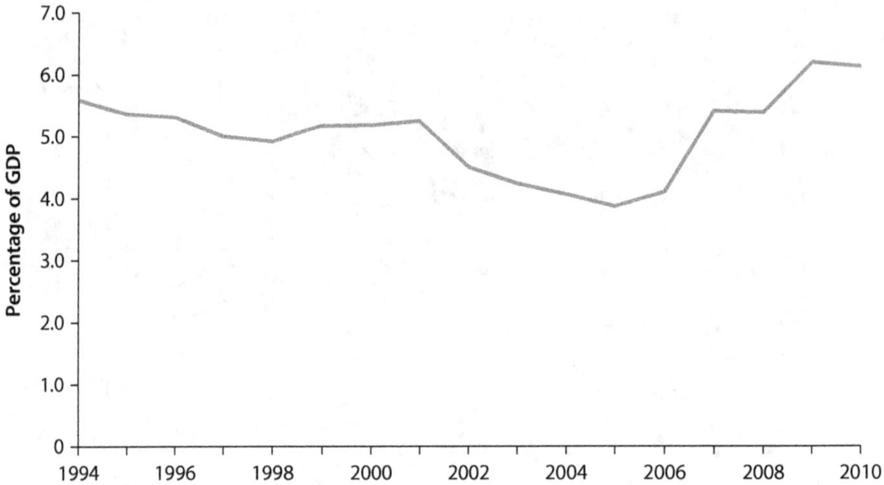

Source: Based on data from Administración Nacional de la Seguridad Social (ANSES) and Instituto Nacional de Estadística y Censos (INDEC).

Figure 2.15 ANSES Spending on Pension Benefits, by Type of Benefit, 2007–11

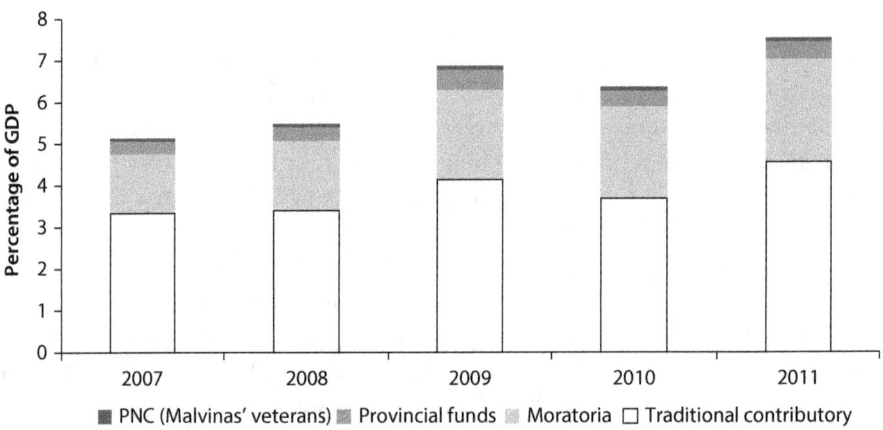

Source: Based on D'Elia et al. 2010, Instituto Nacional de Estadística y Censos (INDEC), and Ministry of Economy and Public Finance.

These expenditures continued to grow, because of increases in the number of beneficiaries (particularly, until early 2009) and indexation of benefits. By 2010, 35 percent of the pension benefits paid by ANSES, equivalent to 2.5 percent of GDP, corresponded to the Moratoria.

Although it is not possible to rigorously assess the program's impact on income distribution because of the lack of detailed data, Rofman and Oliveri (2011) estimated that the increase in coverage may have had a positive impact on income distribution among the elderly. Their estimations show that the difference between the Gini coefficient of per capita income distribution with or without pensions has increased from 2007, after the Moratoria was implemented.

In this context, the proportion of beneficiaries receiving the minimum benefit grew 16 percent between 2006 and 2010. Until 2006, this increase was the result of the discretional nature of indexation, which focused on the minimum benefit. From 2006 onwards, the increase in in the proportion of beneficiaries receiving the minimum benefit was a consequence of the incorporation of beneficiaries through the Moratoria, who entered the system with the minimum benefit in most cases. As observed in figure 2.10, 73.1 percent of pensioners in 2010 received the minimum payment, but among those who did not have a Moratoria benefit, the percentage was only 50 percent.

The Political Economy of the Reforms

In any policy reform process there are different stakeholders, who are involved to protect their respective interests. Each of them has objectives relevant to the sector, which shape their strategy accordingly. These strategies are not unambiguous but consist of different actions implemented autonomously or in response to actions developed by other participants. Hence, these objectives and strategies define an expected result, in monetary and nonmonetary terms.

A sector reform implies changes in the rules of the game that defines its dynamics. Such changes have potential effects on each participant's compensation and generate strategic reactions. Social security policies are not exempt from this type of strategic interaction among stakeholders. However, the objectives of these policies—income protection during old age, income redistribution, fostering national savings, and the like—are generally long term. For this reason, the successful implementation of any reform initiative, structural or parametric, depends on intense discussions and the adoption of cooperation mechanisms among all decision makers.

According to Spiller, Stein, and Tommasi (2003), the institutional configuration of Argentina has been frequently seen as unfavorable and adverse for attaining and sustaining cooperative political behaviors, because political actors usually respond to short-term objectives, inadequate incentives, or both.

The Moratoria was established through several laws and decrees that led to a de facto universalization of the system. The underlying institutional process to the reform began in 2004 with the approval of the law in Congress with no debate among legislators, because the project that included the article allowing the Moratoria was voted *in camera* during the final session of the year. One year later, the law was regulated by the Executive and implemented. However, even though the reform was defined behind closed doors with only a few political actors defining its components, the proposal presented to society was positively received by the majority of stakeholders.

This natural consensus was favored by the importance given by many policy makers and relevant actors to the declining coverage as an indicator of the pension system performance. Since the mid-1990s pension coverage has been a relevant study topic in terms of determinants and characterization, and different analysts noted its worrying declining tendency (e.g., Grushka 2001; Rofman 2005). In 2002 and 2003 a number of diagnostic and reform proposals were prepared, involving both the national government and social actors such as academics and trade unions. As a result of this process, a shared concern regarding the low level of coverage among the elderly was voiced, as well as the need to find a strategy to expand it.

In this context, the approval of Law no. 25994 meant an opportunity for the national government to promote the inclusion of elderly who had no pension coverage. In a context of economic growth and greater fiscal space, authorities considered this to be an opportunity to reverse the declining tendency in coverage and implemented the Moratoria. Provincial governments also benefited with this reform from a fiscal point of view. This is because the Moratoria does not affect their revenues and lowered spending in local noncontributory pensions and public health services for the elderly, since the new retirees had access to the national health insurance for pensioners.

Trade union representatives and formal workers were a group that could potentially disagree with the Moratoria implementation, because they had traditionally defended the system's contributory nature, in the face of a possibly unfair treatment of those who contributed during their working lives but would receive similar benefit to those who did not. However, the Moratoria did not imply a redistribution of resources among these groups, but the allocation of additional funds. Also, seeing that a significant proportion of the contributory pension scheme was already funded with earmarked general taxes, the Moratoria improved the distribution of resources between those who contributed and those who do not.

Under these conditions, the reform received ample political and social support. However, an important aspect that needs to be considered is its social and political sustainability. As with any new social policy, its implementation could be reversed or suffer cutbacks in the future if fiscal constraints grow or it does not continue to sustain a strong level of political and social consensus. The challenge is particularly important in relation to the Moratoria, because it is not a permanent policy, and its future application will depend on the authorities' decisions.

Health Coverage for the Elderly

The Argentine health system can be described as broad in terms of coverage, segmented in terms of the number of participants, and with a marked separation between financing and service provision. Coverage of health services is shared between the public sector (national, provincial, and municipal); the social security sector (health insurance for active workers and their families); the National Institute for Pensioners' Social Services (Instituto Nacional de Servicios Sociales para Jubilados y Pensionados [INSSJyP]) or PAMI (Integral Medical Care Program), as it is known by its main program's acronym, for

Figure 2.16 Health Insurance Coverage, by Type, 2010
Percent

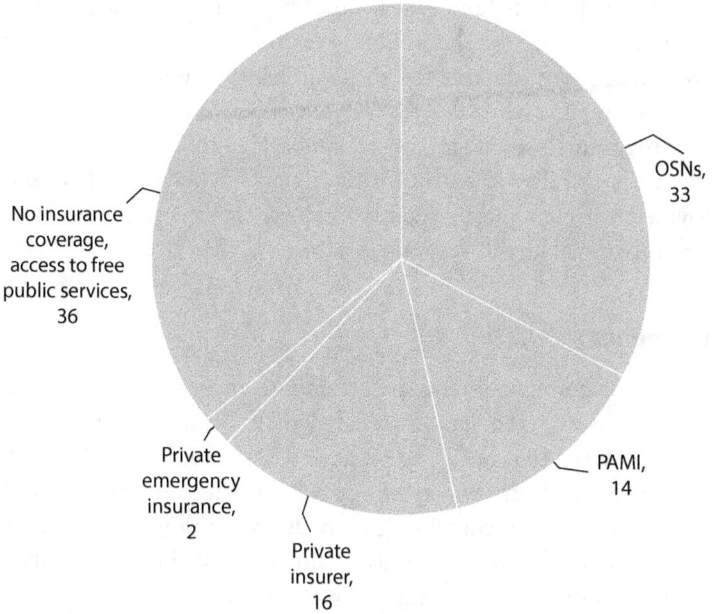

Source: Based on Instituto Nacional de Estadística y Censos (INDEC).
Note: PAMI coverage was estimated from census data related to population and type of health insurance and age. PAMI = Integral Medical Care Program. OSNs = National Health Insurance providers (Obras Sociales Nacionales).

retirees from the national system; and the private sector, with strong interrelation in provision and financing. The broad public health insurance system (including national and provincial health insurances, plus free services offered by public institutions) covers 82 percent of the population, and the remaining 18 percent receive health coverage from private, prepaid medical insurance companies, or private emergency companies (figure 2.16).

National Health Insurance providers (Obras Sociales Nacionales [OSNs]) include approximately 300 institutions that offer health insurance to active workers and their families, segmented by industry. Until 1998 membership in OSNs was compulsory associated with the member's occupation, but a reform implemented that year allowed workers to switch OSNs. Financing comes from employees (3 percent of the salary) and employers (5 percent). For the elderly, the main provider is the INSSJyP, commonly known as PAMI, which insures all national pensioners and their dependents. Beneficiaries in the national social security system are automatically included in PAMI, except that for those who choose to continue with coverage from the OSN they had until retirement; in some cases, there is double coverage. PAMI is financed with contributions from active workers (3 percent of their salary) and employers (2 percent); contributions from pensioners, which varies between 3 and 6 percent of their income, depending on their benefit level; and contributions from the national treasury.

Beneficiaries of the national social security system who obtained their pension through the Moratoria have the same health coverage as those who accredited their years of contributions, and so it was not necessary to design an independent health insurance scheme for them. PNC beneficiaries are not covered by PAMI but by an independent scheme, the Federal Health Program (Programa Federal de Salud), which offers health care services financed by the National Public Health Ministry and provincial governments. Health care for beneficiaries of PNC is the responsibility of each of the provinces where they live, and in most cases provided through public health services, so that the funds are used to finance the provincial health systems.

Final Comments

The objectives of pension systems are to smooth income and consumption during the life cycle and reduce the incidence of poverty for the elderly. The Argentine pension system has been organized since its origins on the basis of a contributory scheme from two perspectives. On the one hand it is financed, although partially, through contributions made by employers and employees. On the other hand, beneficiaries' eligibility is directly linked to the number of years of contribution to the system during their active period.

This type of financial arrangement is affected by the performance of the labor market, in terms of employment levels and formality, because they limit coverage expansion beyond those formally employed during their working years. Given the prevailing conditions in Argentina's labor market, coverage of the elderly was as low as 68.1 percent in 2004, even though legislation established universal coverage (for those with formal employment).

These results suggest design failures in the pension program. The number of years of contribution required to access the pension benefit is attainable for only part of the population, at least under the current conditions of the labor market. There is a high risk of reaching retirement age with an incomplete contributions history, hence failing to satisfy the years with contributions requirement, particularly when dealing with dual labor markets.

With the aim of reducing the coverage gap for the retired population, Argentina implemented a special program for independent workers, which would be known later as the Pension Inclusion Plan or *Moratoria*. This program became the main instrument to rapidly expand coverage and include those elderly adults previously excluded from the social security system. The strategy consisted of making requirements more flexible, allowing workers of retirement age who did not have the required number of years of contribution to access benefits, and discounting a percentage of the benefit as payment of the overdue contributions. As a result, almost 2.7 million people joined the system as beneficiaries and coverage of the elderly rose to over 90 percent by 2011.

However, the Moratoria is a short-term solution with two basic characteristics. First, the coverage expansion came about while still maintaining a contributory principle. Second, this initiative was adopted as an exceptional response to what was considered an exceptional situation, but no structural changes in the rules of the system regarding retirement requirements were adopted. In this sense, the Moratoria suspended the contributory system rules to expand coverage, allowing workers who contributed only for a few years or even never to access the benefit, but this softening of requirements has only temporary effects and will lose relevance as time goes on. For this reason, and under the current contributory system, if formality rates in the active population do not increase rapidly, coverage will become a problem again in the medium and long term.

This situation suggests the need to consider alternative strategies to guarantee universal coverage of the elderly in the medium and long term and advance toward a system that recognizes informal workers' rights and permanently incorporates them into the social protection system. Hence, a more predictable system that provides a social protection floor for all of the elderly should to be adopted, eventually including health insurance coverage. One proposal worth considering is the establishment of a minimum coverage floor for all elderly, regardless of their employment history, with a range of additional benefits linked to contributions. In this way, the individuals' participation in the productive system during the working years would be recognized independently of their employment history, and at the same financial contributions would be compensated after retirement. Such a system would be more predictable, for both the population and a fiscal perspective. The alternative is to maintain a formally contributory system with strict requirements, but with exceptions implemented periodically and discretionally. This could lead to similar results, but in the process it would probably generate serious problems of inequity across generations, as well as unpredictability regarding fiscal spending, with the social and economic costs that this would imply.

Notes

1. Family income includes the sum of all sources of income of the individual's household, such as labor, rent, pensions, family support transfers, and so forth.
2. This program was later called the "Pension Inclusion Plan" (Programa de Inclusion Previsional) in documents published by ANSES and other entities, although this name was never used in any legal documents.

Bibliography

Apella, I. 2007. "Determinantes de la Cobertura del Sistema de Pensiones Argentino. Un Enfoque desde los Microdatos." *Documentos de Trabajo CEDES 36, Buenos Aires.*

———. 2008. "Discrete Choice Model in a Market with Product Differentiation. The Argentine Pension Fund System." *Journal of Pension Economics and Finance* 7 (2): 179–97.

Arza, C. 2009. "La política provisional argentina: de la estratificación ocupacional a la individualización de los beneficios." mimeo.

Bertranou, F., O. Centrángolo, C. Grushka, and L. Casanova. 2012. *Encrucijadas en la Seguridad Social Argentina: Reformas, Cobertura y Desafíos para el Sistema de Pensiones*. Buenos Aires: CEPAL y Oficina Internacional del Trabajo.

Centrángolo, O., and C. Grushka. 2004. "Sistema Previsional Argentino: Crisis, Reforma y Crisis de la Reforma." Serie Financiamiento del Desarrollo 151, CEPAL, Santiago de Chile.

D'Elia, V., S. Rottenschweiler, A. Calabria, A. Calero, and J. Gaiada. 2010. "Análisis de la Cobertura Previsional del SIPA: Protección, Inclusión e Igualdad." Serie Estudios Especiales, ANSES.

Grushka, C. 2001. "La Cobertura Previsional en Argentina a Fines del Siglo XX." *Sociales* 4, Rosario, Argentina.

Isuani, E., and J. San Martino. 1995a. "El Nuevo Sistema Previsional Argentino. ¿Punto Final a Una Larga Crisis?" *Boletín Informativo Techint* 281, January–March, Organización Techint, Buenos Aires.

———. 1995b. "El Nuevo Sistema Previsional Argentino. ¿Punto Final a Una Larga Crisis? Segunda Parte." *Boletín Informativo Techint* 282, April–June, Organización Techint, Buenos Aires.

Mesa-Lago, C. 1978. *Social Security in Latin America: Pressure Groups, Stratification and Inequality*. Pittsburgh, PA: University of Pittsburgh Press.

MTEySS. 2003. "Libro Blanco de la Previsión Social." Ministerio de Trabajo, Empleo y Seguridad Social, Secretaría de Seguridad Social, Buenos Aires.

Rofman, R. 2005. "Social Security Coverage in Latin America." Social Protection Discussion Paper Series 523, World Bank, Washington, DC.

Rofman, R., E. Fajnzylber, and G. Herrera. 2010. "Reformando las Reformas Previsionales en La Argentina y en Chile." *Revista CEPAL* 101: 85–109.

Rofman, R., and L. Oliveri. 2011. "Las Políticas de Protección Social y su Impacto en la Distribución del Ingreso en Argentina." Serie de Documentos de Trabajo sobre Políticas Sociales 6, World Bank, Buenos Aires.

———. 2012. "La Cobertura de los Sistemas Previsionales en América Latina: Conceptos e Indicadores." Serie de Documentos de Trabajo sobre Políticas Sociales 7, World Bank, Buenos Aires.

Sánchez, P. 2000. "Sociología de la Vejez versus Economía de la Vejez." *Papers Revista de Sociología*, Vol. 61, 39–88, Universitat Autònoma de Barcelona, Barcelona, Spain.

Spiller, P., E. Stein, and M. Tommasi. 2003. "Political Institutions, Policymaking Processes, and Policy Outcomes. An Intertemporal Transactions Framework." Inter-American Development Bank, Washington, DC.

Woolf, S. 1989. *Los Pobres en la Europa Moderna*. Barcelona, Spain: Ed. Crítica.

CHAPTER 3

Bolivia

Roberto Laserna and Sebastián Martínez

Background

Bolivia is part of a group of Latin American countries that are starting to age. A large proportion of the elderly population participates in the labor market, particularly in rural areas. Also, many of these elderly are socially vulnerable, and their poverty incidence is high. Their participation in the labor market is characterized by instability, with 87 percent of the older population informally employed. In this context, pension system coverage is low, reaching 16 percent of the elderly, which makes the universal noncontributory pension scheme a substantial instrument of income support for the elderly.

Income and Social Protection Policies for the Elderly

Bolivia is still a demographically young country, although the onset of a maturing process can be observed on the age pyramids. The pyramid basis, which expanded notably between 1950 and 1990, has started to get narrower and will continue to do so, as shown in figure 3.1.

According to data from the 2009 household survey by Bolivia's Institute of Statistics (Instituto de Estadística [INE]), adults over 60 years old represent 8 percent of the Bolivian population (figure 3.2). This elderly population was born before 1952, the year when the national revolution produced an important boost in public education, especially in rural areas, among other things. The difference in educational profile of the generation born before 1952 is significant, with almost 35 percent of the elderly population classified as illiterate. When this aspect is analyzed among all heads of household,[1] illiteracy affects only 10 percent (figure 3.3).[2]

The elderly in Bolivia play an important role in the household economy. In fact, 64.2 percent of over-60s are heads of household. Among all elderly, whether or not they are heads of household, almost 60 percent are involved in economic activity (figure 3.4). Table 3.1 shows that among the elderly population, this percentage is even greater for those living in rural areas, where 79 percent are

The authors would like to thank Santiago Laserna and Enrique Araníbar.

Figure 3.1 Population Pyramids, 1950–2100

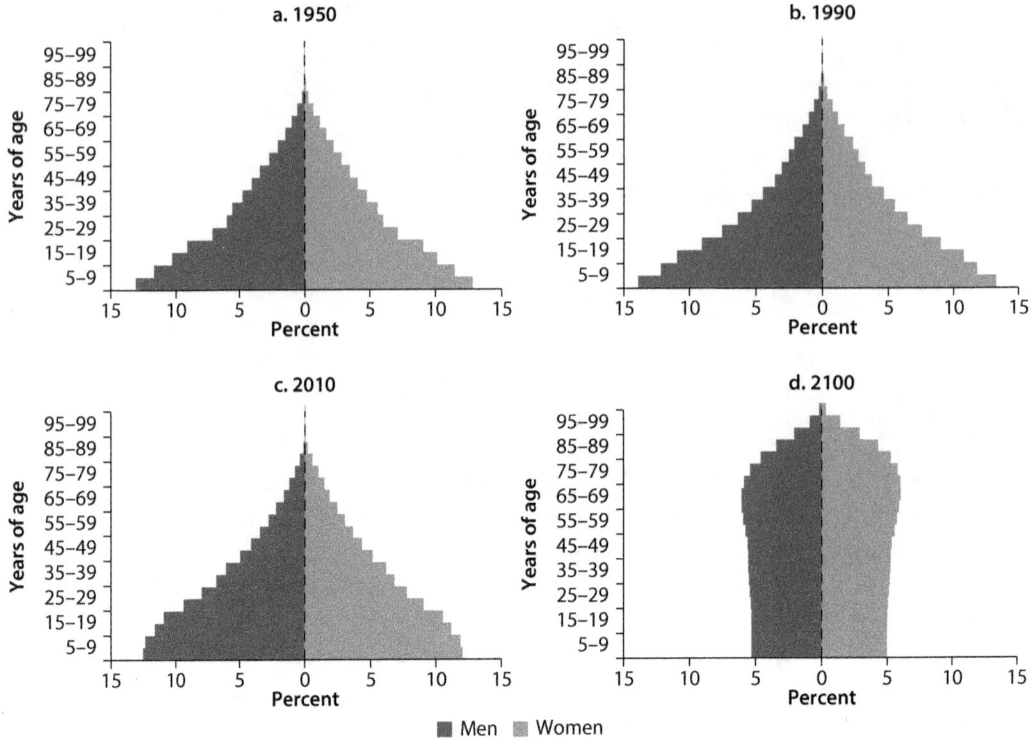

Source: Centro Latinoamericano y Caribeño de Demografía (CELADE).

Figure 3.2 Population, by Age Group, 2009
Percent

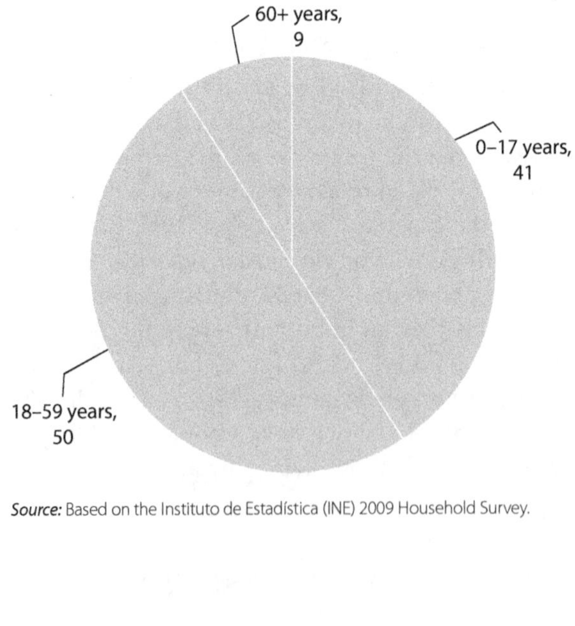

Source: Based on the Instituto de Estadística (INE) 2009 Household Survey.

Figure 3.3 Literacy Rates, 2009

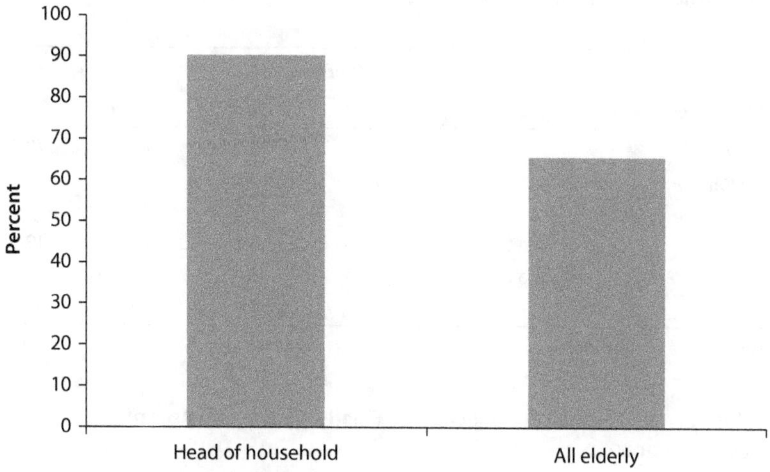

Source: Based on the Instituto de Estadística (INE) 2009 Household Survey.

Figure 3.4 Employed Population, 2009

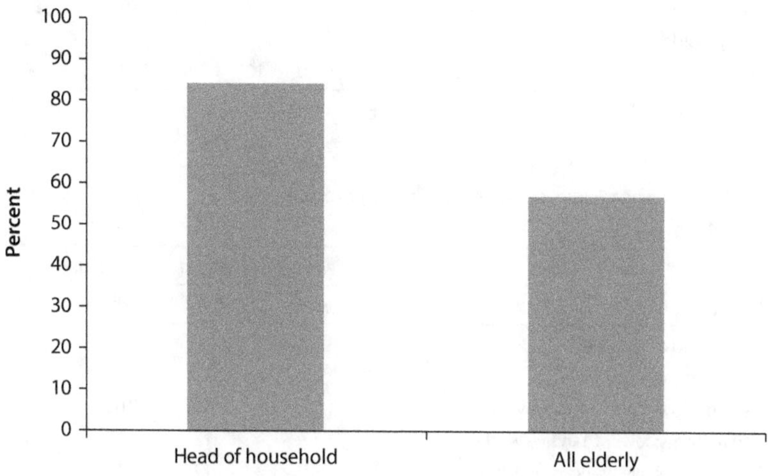

Source: Based on the Instituto de Estadística (INE) 2009 Household Survey.

active, whereas in urban areas this drops to 43 percent, because nearly 55 percent of the elderly are inactive. Data from the survey show that as a result working life in Bolivia goes beyond 60 years of age and that the majority of elderly people remain active for as long as they are in good health, particularly in rural areas.

Intense labor activity in the over-60s is mainly found in the informal employment sector. Although informality affects 66 percent of the employed population younger than 60 years old, the incidence grows to 87 percent among the elderly (and as much as 95 percent of those in rural areas, as shown in table 3.2). A look at the over-60s' labor market (table 3.3) shows that 63 percent of the elderly in

Table 3.1 Labor Activity of the Elderly: Heads of Household and Total Population, by Area of Residence, 2009
Percent

		Heads of household		Total elderly	
Labor activity		*Urban*	*Rural*	*Urban*	*Rural*
Employed		83.9	94.2	43.4	79.2
Unemployed	Lost a job	2.2	0.3	2.2	0
	Never had a job	0.2	0	0	0
Inactive	Had a job in the past	11.5	5.1	42.8	19.1
	Never had a job	2.2	0.4	11.6	1.7
Total		100	100	100	100

Source: Based on the Instituto de Estadística (INE) 2009 Household Survey.

Table 3.2 Employment Formality of the Elderly, by Age and Area of Residence, 2009
Percent

		60 years and more		
Labor formality	*Younger than 60*	*Total*	*Urban*	*Rural*
Formal	31	11	20	5
Informal	66	87	76	95
Households	3	2	4	0
Total	100	100	100	100

Source: Based on the Instituto de Estadística (INE) 2009 Household Survey.

Table 3.3 Labor Force, by Sector of Employment, 2009
Percent

	Heads of household		Elderly	
Sector	*Urban*	*Rural*	*Urban*	*Rural*
Household employees	2	0	4	0
Government	13	7	8	1
Self-employed and family-owned	37	69	63	87
Private firms: fewer than five workers	17	12	13	8
Private firms: five workers or more	31	12	12	4
Total	100	100	100	100

Source: Based on the Instituto de Estadística (INE) 2009 Household Survey.

urban areas are self-employed or work for a family member without pay. This rises to 87 percent in rural areas.

Pensions reach only 16 percent of the elderly in Bolivia. Within this coverage, the difference between the urban and rural situation is sharp: Whereas 25 percent of those over 60 years old living in cities receive a pension, less than 5 percent of those in rural areas are in this situation (figure 3.5).

Finally, even with other social protection policies, such as the noncontributory pension schemes Bonosol and Renta Dignidad, the elderly are overrepresented in

Figure 3.5 Elderly Population Receiving a Pension, 2009

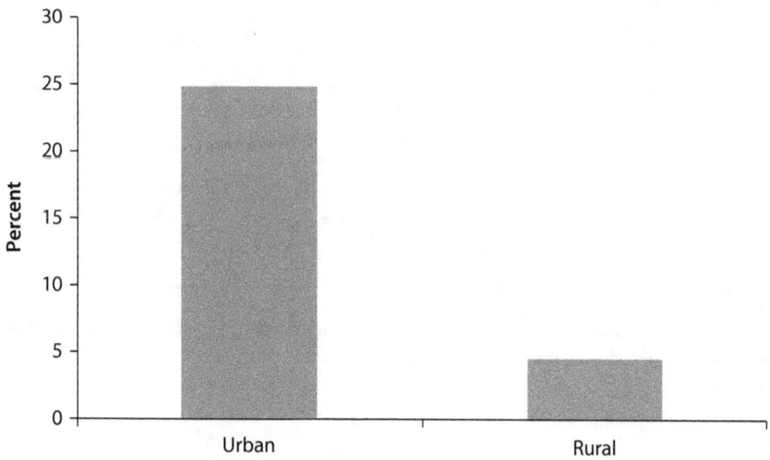

Source: Based on the Instituto de Estadística (INE) 2009 Household Survey.

Table 3.4 Per Capita Family Income per Month, by Age of Head of Household and Participation in Renta Dignidad Program, 2009
Bolivianos

Head of household age	*Receiving Renta Dignidad*	*Not receiving Renta Dignidad*	*Total*
Less than 60	1,045.9	804.4	805.6
60 and older	957.7	757.9	838.8
Total	958.9	804.2	818.3

Source: Based on the Instituto de Estadística (INE) 2009 Household Survey.

the poorest households in the country. The per capita income of households with heads over 60 is lower than that of households with heads under 60 (table 3.4). Considering the population distribution for the over-60s by income quintile, it is important to note that even after receiving Renta Dignidad, 54 percent of over-60s are in the lower two income quintiles (table 3.5).

Income sources of the elderly in Bolivia show that this group has some difficulties to survive independently. According to the 2009 Household Survey, among the 870,000 elderly in Bolivia less than 16 percent received a pension, equivalent to approximately US$300 per month on average. Disability, survivors, and war pensions reached only 0.5 percent of the elderly (table 3.6). An extremely low percentage receives income for dividends, returns, or interest, which portrays the weakness of the economic system in allowing the participation of individuals in the formation of productive capital. Foreign remittances are relevant, and 7 percent of the elderly receive them, as well as rent, which rises to 5.1 percent. These data show that real estate is used much more as a protection strategy in old age than investment in economic activity or monetary capital. In this context, the Renta Dignidad program is identified as a source of income for

Table 3.5 Distribution of Over-60s, by Quintile of Per Capita Household Income, 2009

Per capita household income quintile	*Average income within the quintile (Bs)*	*Percentage of elderly within the quintile*
1	144.2	34
2	405.7	20
3	604.5	14
4	889.8	15
5	1,866.7	17
Total	782.8	100

Source: Based on the Instituto de Estadística (INE) 2009 Household Survey.
Note: The poverty line in Bolivia is estimated between Bs 185 and Bs 385 per month depending on whether it is a rural or an urban area and there are notable differences between departments. See UDAPE (2006). These data are pre-2005.

Table 3.6 Income Sources of Nonlabor Income Recipients among the Elderly, 2009

Income source	*Individuals*	*Average benefit (Bs)*	*Percentage*
Pension	138,542	2,131	15.9
War veterans	4,248	850	0.5
Survivors	2,377	1,397	0.3
Disability	4,461	1,487	0.5
Renta Dignidad	787,799	180	90.5
Remittances	60,669	n.a.	7.0
Dividends	562	n.a.	0.1
Real estate rent	44,800	1,723	5.1
Interest	6,347	635	0.7
Total elderly[a]	870,228		

Source: Based on the Instituto de Estadística (INE) 2009 Household Survey.
Note: n.a. = not available.
a. The total is more than the sum of the different income sources because one person may have more than one source.

more than 90 percent of over-60s. The data clearly show the need to establish effective protection systems for the elderly and to improve the existing ones, a task that will require optimization of regulations and adjustment of financing mechanisms to the current economic conditions and employment structure.

Origin of the Elderly's Protection Systems

The social protection system in Bolivia was formally launched with the Social Security Code on December 14, 1956, and was regulated through a Supreme Decree issued three years later. The social security system was established in the context of state institutional transformation, which accompanied the National Revolution of 1952 and included nationalization of large mining companies, an agricultural reform that dissolved large estates and distributed land in high plateau and valleys, voting rights universalization, and an educational reform.

The social security system was introduced as part of an emergency process, at a time of rapid political change. The first years of the revolution were difficult because of the replacement of the oligarchic elite by a nationalist professional middle class that had links with both farming and manufacturing unions. Disorganization in production and in fiscal spending caused high inflation, and, by 1956, a new government was elected from the same political party, but with a clear mandate to establish order. President Siles Zuazo implemented a stabilization plan designed by Professor George Eder, who presided over an international support mission, and faced reactions from social groups that were affected by fiscal spending cuts and the elimination of subsidies, as well as other privileges and exceptional measures. The president himself had to declare a hunger strike within the presidential palace to counterbalance social pressures. It was in this context that several measures were launched to demonstrate social sensitivity, and among them was the Social Security Code, which was to regulate the system over the next four decades.

The 1956 Social Security Code was aimed at providing health, maternity, work-related sickness, disability, and old age and death benefits, based on workers' and employers' contributions and administered by the National Social Security Fund. A key aspect of the code was to regulate social security contributions, which in some cases had risen to 37 percent of payroll, a rate that could not be afforded by many companies. During this period, pressures from unions resulted in reductions of workers' contributions or, in some cases, even eliminated them, while miners demanded that social security should be financed with a specific tax on tin (Eder 1968). The code reduced employers' contributions to 4 percent and raised employees' to 7.5 percent, adding a state contribution that in some ways compensated the mining sector's demands.

By design, the system would be financed by employers' and employees' contributions and subject to fiscal control. In reality, because the state was the main employer, governments and national companies frequently failed to deposit contributions. The lack of resources in the system, especially due to chronic delays in state entities' contributions, led unions and corporate groups to create supplementary funds that allowed them to keep part of the contributions and improve pensions and services for their members. However, this led in turn to a proliferation of entities, which resulted in a growing heterogeneity of pension schemes, labor protection mechanisms, and different privileges (including the creation of taxes earmarked to finance benefits of specific groups), depending on the pressure capacity of each union.

The creation of the Bolivian Social Security Institute in 1973 was an attempt to legislate to harmonize and reorganize the system, and in 1987 a new reform separated the short-term insurance (focused on health services) from the long-term pension (retirement, disability, and death) programs. The long-term schemes would be managed by the Fondo Nacional de Reserva (Reserve National Fund), which would be replaced three years later by the Fondo de Pensiones Básicas (Basic Pension Fund). There were also 36 additional funds that had been created by union and corporate initiatives. Of those 36 funds, 17 were for public sector employees, five combined contributors from the public and private sector, and five exclusively for the private sector. The remaining nine were integral, meaning that they also covered short-term risks, such as health care (Mercado 1998).

During this period, the pension system operated as a pay-as-you-go scheme. The pension amount was calculated considering the salaries received just before retirement and was financed with contributions from active workers and their employers. In this system, a worker could retire with the equivalent of 70 percent of the average of their last two years of salaries if he had been contributing to the system for at least 15 years.[3] Forty percent of payments were financed with resources from the Basic Pension Fund, and 30 percent came from each sector's supplementary fund. For each year of contributions, the pension amount increased 2 percent, so that a person who had 30 years of contributions could retire with 100 percent of his last salary (averaged over the last two years of employment).

This system was regulated by a complex legislation that included more than 17 laws (including decrees issued by de facto governments) and 250 supreme decrees. Widely varying requirements, benefits, exceptions, and rules were accumulated in a system that lacked unity and allowed the creation of independent pension systems for groups with stronger certain economic or political capacity, such as the military or bank employees. The social protection system had been introduced in Bolivia as part of labor laws and regulations, sometimes with state financing commitments that were difficult to maintain given the fiscal restrictions. However, as the system evolved, inequalities and privileges consolidated in response to political pressures.

A fundamental challenge for the pension system during this period was its low coverage. Just 12 percent of the economically active population (EAP), or 23 percent of the urban EAP, contributed to the system. Most workers in small firms or family businesses did not have access to this system, and, in practice, the informal and rural sector were excluded. The system also lent itself to manipulation. Workers that had contributed minimum amounts achieved high pensions using temporary salaries or even falsifying wage reports, in collusion with employers. The active contributing population included only 340,000 workers who supposedly contributed 9 percent of salaries, but those receiving partial or full retirement pensions were 115,000. Supplementary contributions should include an additional 4.5 percent of payroll, but the total percentage rarely added up, since contributions from state institutions were not always paid.[4] The simple relationship between active contributors and retirees indicated that the system was not sustainable. Between eight and ten contributors were needed to cover a retiree's income, but the system had only an average of three.[5]

This fragmented and unsustainable pension system created unmanageable fiscal pressures and was deemed to be on the brink of collapse by the mid-1990s. The ratio of contributors to retirees had decreased, actuarial reserves were depleted, and the deficit seriously threatened fiscal resources. In 1996 a radical reform of the system was inevitable given that it could drag the state into collapse, leaving thousands of elderly without any source of income, even though most of them had contributed during their active lifetime.

The 1996 reform took place in a broader context of institutional change, although without the political mobilization and economic instability that surrounded the system's creation in 1956. The country adopted the Chilean model of individual capitalization and took on the challenge of making the tax burden explicit in the hope that resources captured by administrators would channel capital to the productive sector and promote economic growth in such a way as to lower the tax burden over time.

The privatization of state companies, also deficitary, opened up an additional opportunity. The capitalization model adopted implied that, instead of selling the companies, interested parties would be invited to invest in them, acquiring 51 percent of the stocks. These new partners would be selected considering their strategic proposals that would increase the companies' value, with the promise that they would assume the firms' administration. To guarantee that this would be the case, and that the state would not intervene in their management, a newly created Fondo de Capitalización Colectiva (Collective Capitalization Fund) received the remaining 49 percent of shares, with the obligation of distributing the dividends from the fund among all citizens older than 65 years, through a program that was called Bono Solidario or "Bonosol."

Organization of the Contributory System

The 1996 reform implemented an individual capitalization system instead of the pay-as-you-go system. The transition to the new system was immediate, and the state assumed the majority of the reform's costs, pooling all funds and guaranteeing payment to existing pensioners through the Basic Pension Fund. Those who had contributed to the pay-as-you-go system in the past would have their contributions recognized at the time of retirement in the new system, and a transitional benefit called "contribution compensation" would be paid together with benefits from the new system. Hence, retirees who contributed to both systems would have two sources of income: the debt that the state recognized, and what came from their accumulated individual contributions. For these contributors, and those that entered the labor force after the reform, individual accounts would be created to accumulate contributions and the returns generated by investments of the balance. Contributors paid 10 percent of their salaries or declared income and received regular information about their accounts, specifying commissions paid for fund administration and returns earned. Retirement age was set at 65 years old, but contributors could take early retirement if their accumulated contributions were enough to finance a benefit of at least 70 percent of their preretirement income. In this way, the new system established a direct link between contributions and benefits and became a mechanism for encouraging long-term saving.

The government gave the responsibility of managing the new system to two Pension Fund Administrators (Administradoras de Fondos de Pensiones [AFPs]) who combined international companies with experience in the field and some

Bolivian shareholders.[6] At the onset of the new system, the contributing population was randomly distributed between the two AFPs so that they were of a similar size. The administrative fee, a key aspect in the selection of AFPs, was 0.5 percent of wages, paid by the contributor. Contributions would go to the Individual Capitalization Fund (Fondo de Capitalización Individual [FCI]), which was invested in a low-risk portfolio. After the first five years, contributors were able to choose which AFP they preferred: changing over if they were already assigned or choosing one if they were joining the labor force for the first time.

The new contributory pension system performed well compared to the previous system. Coverage expanded (although slowly in the case of independent workers), and resources accumulated in the individual capitalization funds. Over the first 15 years, the FCI accumulated nearly US$6 billion. Returns during the first decade were, on average, 8.7 percent, and passive interest rates in the country reached an average of 4.7 percent (Ferrufino 2008). System administration costs were also considerably lower than in the previous system. Returns reached higher levels than bank deposits, although their investment potential was partially restricted because of the obligation imposed on administrators to buy treasury bonds. These represented slightly more than half of the investment portfolio, and, although they are low risk, they also have limited returns.[7] However, investment in bonds was essential to finance the obligations taken on by the state with contributors and pensioners in the previous system. Hence, in practice this system was similar to a pay-as-you-go scheme, with active workers directly financing pensions of those who were already retired. The fundamental difference was that the state mediated in the process, and the debt to retirees from the previous system was formalized and made explicit. In effect, this allowed the state to gradually recognize the implicit debt to pensioners from the pay-as-you-go system, financed by the new contributors but with administrative mediation from AFPs and the management guarantees that they implied.

Despite the new system's achievements, it was subject to social pressure that resulted in increased costs. During Banzer's government (1997–2001) pensioners and those who were nearing retirement age at the time of the reform took part in demonstrations and hunger strikes until they gained two significant increases in the minimum retirement pension, which created an incentive for early retirement and significantly raised the number of retirees. Additionally, the time limit for contributors to the old system to take early retirement under that system's rules was extended, which also increased the number of pensioners. At the time of the reform's design it had been projected that only 3,000 people would take the early retirement benefit. However, 49,000 workers retired under this scheme, and this multiplied the cost of the pension system transition by 15. Since then, pensioner's organizations have regularly been involved in lobbying activities to increase state-financed basic pensions. In fact, although in 2007 around 12,000 people qualified to receive a retirement pension, the number increased to 20,000 in 2008 and 25,000 in 2009 (Pensions and Insurance Authority 2010).

By October 2012, almost 50,000 people were receiving retirement payments in the new system for a monthly sum of over Bs 113 million (US$16.4 million), corresponding to a monthly average of Bs 2,280 (US$327). It is estimated that around 80,000 people were receiving pensions in the old system at that time.[8]

Organization of the Noncontributory System

Until the pension system was reformed and the capitalization of state companies approved in 1996, there was no noncontributory pension system in Bolivia, and much less one that aspired to universal coverage. The first noncontributory pension program in the country, Bono Solidario or "Bonosol," (Solidarity Bond) was created by Sánchez de Lozada's government as part of the privatization process of large state businesses.

As previously mentioned, through capitalization of state companies private shareholders injected new capital and acquired 51 percent of the shares, with the remaining left in the state's hands. These state shares, whose value had been determined by bids from interested investors, were transferred to the adult population through the Collective Capitalization Fund (Fondo de Capitalización Colectiva [FCC]). With the capitalization of the first companies, the FCC began with a capital of over US$1.6 billion. The government assigned this fund to finance a universal noncontributory pension for the population over 65 years old. Considering the small size of the market, the administration of the FCC was also given to the AFPs.

The first Bonosol payment was made in 1997 with the sale of part of the FCC's shares, but it was decided that this process would come into play only if the companies' profits were not enough to cover the cost of the benefits in the future. In its first year, Bonosol benefits were established at almost US$250, to be paid in one annual transfer. The benefit was distributed directly to 364,000 people, with the only requirement being a national identity document to prove Bolivian citizenship and that the beneficiary was over the age of 65.[9] Bonosol represented an important amount for poor households in the country, equivalent to 27 percent of per capita national income, 50 percent of annual income for the poor, and 85 percent of annual income for the extreme poor (von Gersdorff 1997).

The creation of Bonosol was surrounded by great controversy. For the political opposition, it was an electoral bribery tactic and was considered to be a waste of resources, to the point that one candidate promised to remove it and use the resources for education, considering that children have a future and it was not worth spending money on the elderly. When Banzer's government took office in 1998, Bonosol payments were suspended. However, social pressure, and program evaluations that found it had a positive impact, determined its reinstatement in 2000, although under a new name (Bolivida) and limited to the distribution of the FCC returns retroactively. At the end of the year 2000 and during the first months of 2001, Bolivida payments were made for a yearly sum equivalent to US$120. Similarly, Bolivida was paid retroactively for the years 2000 and 2001 in 2002.[10] In the same year Sánchez de Lozada returned to office and Bonosol was reinstated through a law that fixed the minimum amount at Bs 1,800 (around US$230) and authorized the AFPs to tender FCC shares if returns did not cover the amount required. Finally, in 2006 the FCC was expropriated by President Morales, and shares in oil companies became property of the national oil company, Bolivian National Oilfields (Yacimientos Petrolíferos Fiscales Bolivianos). Since February 2008 the government has continued to pay the noncontributory pension under the name Universal Old Age Pension (Renta Universal de la Vejez or "Renta Dignidad"),[11] mainly financed through a hydrocarbon tax. Table 3.7 shows the evolution of the noncontributory pension in terms of amounts and coverage.

From the beginning, this noncontributory pension program has been universal. Beneficiaries needed to prove only that they were citizens and their age. Of course, this posed a challenge for the identification system since many elderly people lacked proper documentation. However, as these issues were resolved, an integrated database was created that allowed the banking system to detect and report anomalies straight away, forcing pension fund administrators to meet the demands of the elderly. Initially, payments were made annually, and the date of payment was associated to the beneficiary's date of birth, establishing a simple mechanism for distribution over time. When Bonosol became Renta Dignidad, coverage was expanded and transactions also multiplied,

Table 3.7 Noncontributory Pension (Bonosol, Bolivida, Renta Dignidad): Amounts and Beneficiaries, 1997–2012

	Benefit amount			*Total*		
Year	*Bs*	*US$*	*Payments made*	*Bs*	*US$*	*Number of beneficiaries*
1997	1,300	247.21	364,261	473,539,300	90,047,739	364,261
1998	395	71.62	318,529	125,818,955	22,812,851	—
1999	395	67.83	340,403	134,459,185	23,089,068	—
2000	420	67.81	334,371	140,435,820	22,675,290	—
2001	420	63.47	351,166	147,489,720	22,289,796	—
2002	—	—	—	—	—	—
2003	1,800	234.71	448,864	807,955,200	105,350,649	445,371
2004	1,800	226.70	458,914	826,045,200	104,035,919	442,018
2005	1,800	223.05	482,002	867,603,600	107,509,740	440,904
2006	1,800	224.72	487,832	878,097,600	109,625,169	487,832
2007	1,800	229.30	493,437	888,186,600	113,144,790	493,437
2008	2,153[a]	297.38	8,429,004	1,614,278,850	222,966,692	749,774
2009	2,159[a]	307.55	8,490,972	1,624,637,600	231,429,858	780,378
2010	2,170[a]	311.39	9,170,277	1,741,781,400	249,896,901	802,520
2011	2,190[a]	314.65	9,373,225	1,777,131,750	255,335,021	811,433
2012	2,244[a]	322.50	9,568,382	1,831,046,450	263,081,386	815,755

Source: Based on data from the Superintendence for Pensions, the Pension Authority, and the Ministry of Economy.
Note: — = not available.
a. Weighted average. If the beneficiary is also eligible for a contributory benefit and receives another pension, the amount is Bs 1,800 (16.8 percent of total beneficiaries). If the beneficiary does not receive another pension, the amount is Bs 2,400 per year.

because beneficiaries could now receive payments once a month, once every three months, or annually.

Coverage Extension Reforms

In December 2010, the government passed Law no. 065, the new pension law, aimed at a system reform. This implied a partial return to the pay-as-you-go system, including a contributory and noncontributory old age pension and a semicontributory "solidarity pension" with minimum pensions that have no direct relationship to contributions made by beneficiaries in the past. The new pension system also includes the elimination of private pension fund administrators and the establishment of a unique public agent. The law reduced the retirement age to 58, even lower in the case of miners (56), workers in unhealthy environments (51), and women (one year per child until 55 years of age). It also reduced the minimum contribution period from 15 to 10 years for the solidarity pension and the reference period for calculation of retirement benefits from the last 60 to the last 24 contributions.

Reforms and New Programs

The new integrated pension system was created by merging the contributory system based on individual capitalization, the noncontributory system, and the semicontributory system (which provides a solidarity pension to workers whose contributions were not enough to guarantee them a minimum wage when they reached retirement age). This reform has brought into effect the solidarity pension, financed with additional contributions made by workers for a minimum 0.5 percent of contributable income that increases if this income exceeds 13,000 bolivianos (US$1,854). Labor costs have also increased for companies by introducing a 3 percent contribution to finance the solidarity pension. The AFPs have begun negotiations with the government to transfer accounts and responsibilities to the public sector. One particular issue with the transfer of system administration is the collection of overdue contributions from employers, including firms or government entities that no longer exist, since the law does not allow for a monetary fine for accumulated late payments. As a result of these difficulties, as of December 2012 complete transfer of the pension system had not yet taken place.

In the context of the latest reforms, in 2009 the noncontributory Universal Old Age Pension or Renta Dignidad has been instituted in the new political constitution,[12] where article 67 states: "All elderly adults have the right to a decent standard of living in old age, with quality and human warmth. The state will provide a lifetime old age pension, within the integral social security system, according to the law."

Under the new system, the noncontributory pension is financed through the Universal Old Age Pension Fund (Fondo de la Renta Universal de Vejez [FRUV]), which receives resources from the hydrocarbon tax (30 percent of the total) and dividends from public capitalized companies.[13] In 2011 total FRUV revenue was US$382.7 million, equivalent to 1.6 percent of GDP (Escobar, Martínez, and Mendizábel 2013).

The Political Economy Behind the Reforms

The establishment of the current pension system is contextualized in the political and economic reforms initiated in the country toward the end of 2003, including the nationalization of hydrocarbon companies and the Morales's government approach to social security based on principles of solidarity and universality.[14] As part of the social policy, welfare for the most vulnerable population groups was made a priority, including for the elderly.

The 2010 pension system reform created a hybrid system that combines simple pay-as-you-go to guarantee the minimum pension with individual capitalization. The favorable prices of hydrocarbons over the last few years and the accumulation of reserves have allowed the system to be sustainable so far. However, the system is vulnerable to changes in oil and mineral price trends, and if fiscal revenues contract, the system financial health would depend on Capitalization Fund reserves.

The 1997 reform had been resisted by trade unions, comprising mainly state workers, because they trusted that financing problems would be resolved in a traditional way, with government subsidies assigned to avoid system bankruptcy, depending on each group's capacity to pressure for these subsidies. For union leaders, who have always held a privileged position, the reform also implied losing the perspective of pensions based on high salaries from the last period, which could be real or nominal. Union conflicts had hardly ever dealt with system management or sustainability, except for demands regarding participation of union leaders in pension fund boards or subsidies and special allocations financed by public resources. This resistance was condensed in the "sandwich generation" composed of those who were already contributing to the old system and were close to retirement but had to switch to the new scheme. Ultimately this group's protests were the result of not being able to access the same privileges that those before them had received. Occasionally resistant groups were supported by workers who had already retired and who sought improvements to their pensions based on political decisions and not merely on financial and actuarial calculations or solvency of funds.

The pension system change promoted by President Morales's government has considered some of these vindications but not all, and has responded more to the need to fulfill the vague promise of changing what the "neoliberals" did than actually solving specific problems. For this reason, the government's proposal has not been fully backed by trade union organizations, who hoped for a full return to the pay-as-you-go system and the exclusion of pension fund administrators. This first point is not contemplated in the law, and the second has not been put into practice.

Intended and Observed Impacts on Coverage and Level of Benefits

As part of the changes made to the noncontributory pension Renta Dignidad, the government lowered the eligibility age to 60, increasing coverage by more than 50 percent as compared with the previous Bonosol program. The average transfer increased to approximately US$300 annually, differentiated by whether or not the person also had a contributory retirement pension.[15] The Renta Dignidad beneficiaries should be registered in the program beneficiaries' database, which was created on the basis of Bonosol and information provided by the electoral body, which oversees the civil registry and the General Identification System. The database uses a unique beneficiary number,[16] and beginning in 2009 a biometric identification system was introduced based on beneficiaries' fingerprints, to reduce the number of undue payments and identity errors. However, with the sudden rise in the number of beneficiaries and in the number of transactions, the risk of fraud has increased, and some cases were detected and reported.[17]

By the year 2012, the annual Renta Dignidad benefit was 2,400 bolivianos (approximately US$350) for nonpensioners) and 75 percent of this sum was for pensioners. The frequency of payment was also changed, from annual to 12 monthly payments. Under this scheme, beneficiaries could collect their benefit on a monthly basis or accumulate payments and withdraw them less frequently. On average, 57 percent of payments are made immediately in the month that corresponds to the payment, 37 percent in the first trimester after it is due, and only 6 percent of payments are made in later periods (Escobar, Martínez, and Mendizábel 2013).

The Pensions and Insurance Supervision Authority (Autoridad de Fiscalización y Control de Pensiones y Seguros) is responsible for regulating Renta Dignidad, and the administration and management is the responsibility of a Managing Body.[18] For benefit payment, the Managing Body subcontracts with bank services, mutual funds, and other institutions and financial cooperatives or channels them through Information Provider Entities (Entidades Proveedores de Información [EPIs]).[19] Of the approximately 815,000 beneficiaries who received at least one payment in 2012, 83.2 percent were eligible for 100 percent of Renta Dignidad and 16.8 percent were eligible for 75 percent of that amount due to their status as a pensioner. Around 55 percent of beneficiaries are women. The majority of payments are made through the banking system (83 percent). The rest of the payments are made by the EPI (15 percent) or the military (2 percent) (Escobar, Martínez, and Mendizábel 2013).

According to data from the 2009 Household Survey, 92 percent of the population over 60 years old received Renta Dignidad, at the national level, with slightly lower coverage in rural areas (89 percent) (table 3.8). Given the estimated population of 870,000 citizen older than 60 years, the estimated number of beneficiaries from the household survey is consistent with the number of beneficiaries registered, with a 2.5 percent difference. Among the elderly who reported not having received Renta Dignidad, the average income is less (table 3.9), which reflects in part the effect of the same monetary transfer, as well as that these elderly may come from poorer households and have difficulty accessing information, processing documentation, or traveling to payment points. As shown in the table, Renta Dignidad contributes to significantly improving household incomes when the impact of the per capita income of each member of the household is measured.

Table 3.8 Elderly Population Receiving Renta Dignidad, by Residential Area, 2009
Percent

Receives Renta Dignidad?	*Urban*	*Rural*
No	8	11
Yes	92	89
Total	100	100

Source: Based on the Instituto de Estadística (INE) 2009 Household Survey.

Table 3.9 Total and Per Capita Income in Households with Heads Older than 60 Years
Bolivianos

Receives Renta Dignidad?	*Household average*	*Per capita average*
No	2.749,55	757,91
Yes	2.925,84	957,74
Total	2.909,12	938,78

Source: Based on the Instituto de Estadística (INE) 2009 Household Survey.

Fiscal Sustainability and Expected and Observed Impacts on the Labor Market

The impact of noncontributory pensions has been evaluated from different perspectives, highlighting its diverse aspects and concluding, in general, that they have been positive for the well-being of the elderly and the national economy (Aponte et al. 2006). For example, from the point of view of the elderly, their place in the family has been highlighted and revaluated, and they have experienced a subsequent improvement in their quality of life. In terms of where resources are spent, improvements in nutrition and health in recipients have been noted, as well as in the family as a whole, particularly in rural areas where money is normally used to improve agricultural productive capacity through the purchase of animals, tools, and seeds. From a broader point of view, transfers have expanded the internal market and stimulated investment, boosting economic growth, which substantially improves income distribution and reduces poverty.[20]

The pension system may encourage long-term saving and establish a source of financing for investment, boosting the stock market and economic growth, and having an indirect impact on poverty reduction. But more directly, pensions contribute to preventing poverty in adult life, and improve the consequences for families that need to support elderly family members without insurance or pensions. Although it is not their specific objective, noncontributory pension programs can be considered policy tools for poverty reduction, by supporting the income of the elderly who are overrepresented in low-income households in the country.

With the objective of fighting poverty, it can be observed that the cash transfers to the elderly through Bonosol and Renta Dignidad have had a very relevant impact on income and consumption in beneficiary households. The elderly have helped to improve nutrition levels in their homes and have used part of their noncontributory pensions to improve productive capacity in their families by purchasing tools, supplies, seeds, or credit guarantees. Impact analysis of Bonosol has found important effects on household consumption, with increases of around 6.3 percent in food purchases, particularly in rural areas. Beneficiaries' homes in rural areas have shown a positive impact in household consumption of around 165 percent of the amount that they receive, in part because of the multiplying effect on investment in agricultural production activities. In urban areas, not much evidence has been found of a change in food consumption, but an increase in nonfood items and medical expenses is seen (Aponte et al. 2006). More recently, in the context of Renta Dignidad, the impact study has found significant effects of the pensions on per capita income and household consumption, with beneficiary households increasing per capita consumption by 14.5 percentage points and reducing the probability that a beneficiary household would be classified as poor (Escobar, Martínez, and Mendizábel 2013).

As previously mentioned, the reform of the pension system in the 1990s was inevitable because it lacked financial viability. The contributors were not able to cover retirees' pensions, and poor administration had exhausted most of the invested funds. The individual capitalization system does not have these problems because each retiree receives what corresponded to his or her contributions and the returns obtained with them. This may not guarantee a substantial pension, but it does avoid contributions being appropriated by others and mismanagement becoming a fiscal liability.[21] During Banzer's government (1997–2001) this reform suffered from social pressure, which increased costs, accentuating the fiscal deficit, but in the long term, it seemed that the future was secure.

The last reform, which introduced a minimum pension, broadened coverage for noncontributors, and reduced the minimum retirement age independently of the amount of contributions, may have introduced some vulnerabilities in the system.[22] The creation of liabilities and expenses so that contributors and employees can contribute to solidarity pensions, as well as the imposition of upper limits to retirement pensions, have been decided with short-term criteria, trying to ensure immediate financing of the new benefits. Studies showing 10- or 20-year projections have not been disseminated.

The noncontributory pension now called Renta Dignidad did not have financing problems at its conception, because it was based on stock returns from former state-owned companies, which were deposited in the FCC, as well as an eventual auction of these stocks. It had been estimated that the funds would suffice to finance the system until 2052, when it was calculated that practically all beneficiaries would have left the system because of natural causes. As the source of financing was changed and the age for access to the benefit was reduced, the financial viability of this pension now depends on the performance of hydrocarbon exports.[23] The price level for the last five years has impeded visualizing problems that emerge when the drop in gas reserves and loss of export markets are taken into account. A significant drop in prices would jeopardize the financing of Renta Dignidad, because the elderly would have to compete with powerful groups and trade unions, and with levels of government that have much greater capacity to exert pressure than they do.

Other Services for the Elderly

As well as their pensions, the elderly population can also access several different social and economic support mechanisms. Those include economic preferential treatment for some services, as well as healthcare services.

Preferential Treatment of the Elderly

Law no. 1886 for Rights and Privileges of the Elderly, passed in 1998, states that special treatment should be given to adults over age 60 in transportation, financial, water provision, drainage, and power services. The law granted a 20 percent discount in electric power fees for those consuming between 0 and 100 kilowatts per month, in drinking water for those consuming between 0 and 15 square meters per month, and similar discounts in land, air, railroad, and river/sea transportation. A reduction of 20 percent was also established for property taxes, and the elderly have the right to preferential attention in public and private entities that provide services, creating special counters or not requiring the elderly to make appointments, so that any errands can be carried out more comfortably. The discounts are subject to the presentation of bills and property deeds in the name of the elderly, and although preferential treatment also depends on the process being personal, in practice it is really based on perception and the willingness of officials and others.[24]

In practice, this seems to have created a small niche of work opportunities for some elderly who run errands for other people because of this preferential treatment, paying for services and making bank deposits.[25] In many cases, it is just additional help that the elderly can provide for other members of their household, but in some cases they have been paid by offices and firms. In any case, the preference is not just a mark of respect for this population, but it is also a way of allowing them to negotiate a better position in their relationships with those around them.

Encouraged by this policy, some companies offer special facilities to the elderly. For example, the airline Aerosur reduced its prices on tickets for over-60s and created a special program of free tickets for the over-80s, even on international trips. These passengers had to only pay taxes and prove that they had someone to receive them at their destination.[26] The new state airline, Boliviana de Aviación, although it does not actively promote it, has a third-off discount for over-60s purchasing tickets.

Health Care

The Rights and Privileges Law also provides free old age medical insurance to anyone without health insurance. This law was complemented by Supreme Decree 25.186 of September 30, 1998. It rules that the National Health Office must provide free services for sickness, preventive medicine, and nonwork-related accidents for all over-60s who are not covered by other health insurance.

This means that the national and municipal governments pay 60 percent and 40 percent, respectively, of an annual premium equivalent to US$56 per elderly person insured, for which they must register their affiliation based on certification of age and residence in the country.

In the year 2006, this Law was replaced with Law no. 3323 (January 16, 2006) and regulated through Supreme Decree 28968 (December 13, 2006), which specifies the types of services included in health insurance (dental treatment, hospitalization, diagnosis, surgeries, medicines) and includes departmental governments among the financers.

Conclusions and Future Challenges

Although Bolivia is going through a boom period because of the export of primary goods, it is still one of the continent's smallest and most vulnerable economies, and a large proportion of the elderly population is living in poverty. In this context, protection of the elderly in Bolivia has significantly expanded over the last two decades. This age group has access to a universal noncontributory pension, Renta Dignidad, has preferential treatment in several public services, has health coverage that is better than the average for the country, and receives indirect subsidies through power, water, and sewage services. Quality of service and the magnitude of these subsidies could naturally be a controversial subject, but these demonstrate unquestionable progress in terms of social policies for the low-income elderly population, both in comparison to previous periods and when the degree of the country's relative development is taken into consideration.

The increase in fiscal revenue that the country has observed since 2005 has allowed for a large expansion of the main noncontributory protection mechanisms. At the same time, the dependence of the noncontributory pension finances on the export of hydrocarbon raises concerns about its sustainability, given that expansion periods based on the external market have been volatile in the past. However, it is important to highlight that the majority of these programs were initiated before the boom, and even when the fiscal accounts had a strong deficit, showing that with political will and creativity it would be possible to maintain them even if exports decrease. At the same time, it can be politically difficult to reverse benefits that the population considers to be acquired rights, although if problems are resolved through social pressures, the elderly could be at a disadvantage.

On the other hand, the reform of the contributory pension system has generated strong expectations with the guarantee of a pension on more favorable terms and at an earlier retirement age. Fiscal burdens could rise quickly because most retirees are part of the group that began working before 1996 and, for this reason, receive adjustment compensations that are financed with fiscal resources. Experience shows that the individual capitalization system could be sustainable and profitable, basically because each pensioner receives what they accumulated through their working life. Additionally, this system has the potential to transform the contributions into productive capital, through the financial markets. If these channels worked better, entrepreneurs could access capital, which would result in business expansion, employment growth, salary improvements, and the corresponding growth of the tax base. With a hybrid contributory and semicontributory pension system, the main risk of returning to a pension system administered by the state is to expose it to the same political and social pressures that pension systems have previously experienced in the country.

The demographic trends in the medium and long term indicate that the elderly will continue to grow as a proportion of the total population, and so the importance of the social protection system for the elderly will increase in the future. The challenge then will still be to finance these services and support mechanisms as well as improve their quality and extend their scope to those elderly people who most need them. One of the largest limitations for universal legal coverage to become a reality is the physical barriers that some of these services impose. If water provision does not reach the rural population, the subsidy is useless to the elderly living in that area. Also, if the elderly are still lacking proper identification, they cannot request their noncontributory pension. Some services, such as those providing health care, are provided through institutions and organizations that are already overburdened and require improvements to their facilities.

In terms of social impact of the protection programs for the elderly, the fact that these also affect their households and families, thereby reducing the burden that the elderly bring to them, must be highlighted. Studies show that by improving the position of the elderly in the family, they can then negotiate a better arrangement and prolong their contribution, which is particularly important in the poorest sectors. This last observation highlights, finally, the fact that protection mechanisms in Bolivia have had a perceivable and positive impact on poverty reduction and in the mitigation of its worst effects, so that the elderly can aspire to an old age with greater dignity and economic security.

Notes

1. Heads of household include those identified as such in the 2009 Household Survey, independently of their age. According to that survey, 21 percent of heads of household are over 60 years of age.
2. As a comparison, we contrasted adults over 60 with the heads of household (which includes part of the elderly group), because it concerns the most dominant family group. The "over-60s," because of age and experience, are also in a socially relevant position. Comparisons with other groups would show more marked differences.
3. The minimum statutory retirement age in 1956 was 60 years for men and 55 for women. Political pressures resulted in a reduction to 55 and 50, respectively, so that the average retiree could enjoy a 25-year income having contributed for 15 years.
4. Of the 9 percent contribution for basic pensions, 1.5 points should have been paid by the state, which rarely complied.
5. The supplementary funds had actuarial reserves that had to be invested to increase availability of resources, but they had poor investment strategies and did not achieve the necessary returns, and in general suffered real losses as a result of corruption and favoritism. At the time of the 1996 reform, reserves from the group of supplementary funds reached US$150 million, barely 5 percent of their accumulated liabilities.

6. An international bidding process was launched to transfer management to private administrators under strict supervision mechanisms and control.
7. This obligation restricts the possibility of AFPs intervening more actively in the capital market in Bolivia, whose stock market usually settles more fixed rate bonds than company shares.
8. This information has been inferred from the Household Survey (INE 2009), which registers sources of personal income and includes the category "pensions." It was not possible to obtain more reliable data from the entities that administer the pension system.
9. This excluded the nondocumented population, which provided strong motivation for the elderly to acquire their identity documents.
10. Eligibility criteria for 65 year olds in 2001, and only those aged 66 and over received it in 2002.
11. Established and regulated through Law no. 3791 of November 28, 2007, and Supreme Decree 29400 of December 29, 2007.
12. Passed through a referendum on the January 29, 2009, and made law on February 9 that year.
13. Resources not used for benefit payments or administrative costs are invested in the stock market, generating income for the FRUV.
14. Plan Nacional de Desarrollo—Bolivia Digna Soberana, Productiva y Democrática para Vivir Bien (National Development Plan—Bolivia Dign, Sovereign, Productive and Democratic for the Welfare).
15. Eligibility for 100 percent of Renta Dignidad is conditioned on not receiving a benefit from the contributory pension system, a war veteran pension, or a special pension from the government. It is also required that the beneficiary is not receiving a salary funded by the national general budget and that he or she had not been suspended from the Bolivida or Bonosol programs.
16. In Bolivia, there was a period in which the National Unique Record (Registros Únicos Nacionales) was issued by a decentralized public entity, instead of the identity card (Cédula de Identidad) provided by the Bolivian police.
17. In April 2010, a criminal network was found to have appropriated around US$10 million from Renta Dignidad through fraudulent payments that, in some cases, resulted in actual beneficiaries not being able to collect their payments. Police investigations found that staff from the electoral court and some banks were involved.
18. Since 2009 this function has been contracted though public tender. Seventy-five percent corresponds to a temporary association made up of the insurance company La Vitalicia de Seguros and Reaseguros S.A. as well as the Sociedad Administradora de Fondos de Inversión BISA-SAFI S.A., both part of Grupo Financiero BISA, and the remaining 25 percent to the company Provida, formed by the Insurers Illimani and Credinform.
19. EPIs include the National Pension System Service (Servicio Nacional del Sistema de Reparto), the Military Social Insurance Corporation (Corporación del Seguro Social Militar), the Pension Fund Administrators (Administradoras de Fondos de Pensiones), insurance entities who pay lifetime pensions, and the Ministry of Defense in charge of the armed forces.
20. Some studies have been carried out based on econometric models and following different methods. Some discrepancies are seen in the size of the figures but coincidences are found in terms of tendencies: cash transfers reduce inequality and reduce poverty (Laserna 2007; Morales 2009; Barja 2009.

21. See the set of papers included in Aponte et al. (2008).
22. There is no evidence of actuarial studies used to support the formulation and approval process of the last reform.
23. See the complete study of the Bolivian political economy by Morales (2012).
24. Companies recover the discounts by billing to the National General Treasury, which actually constitutes a differential subsidy that benefits the elderly, who have access to public services through their property ownership.
25. Personal observations and communications obtained in the field.
26. The company is currently bankrupt and ceased operations at the beginning of 2012.

Bibliography

Aponte, G., R. Ferrufino, L. C. Jemio, and J. C. Urioste. 2008. "Pensiones y Jubilación en Bolivia." Fundación Milenio, La Paz.

Aponte, G., L. Jemio, R. Laserna, S. Martinez, F. Molina, E. Schulze, and E. Skinner. 2006. "La Inversión Prudente." Fundación Milenio, La Paz.

Autoridad de Pensiones y Seguros. 2010. "Compendio Estadístico." La Paz. https://www.aps.gob.bo/estadisticas/Paginas/Boletines-y-Documentos-Estadísticos.aspx.

Barja, M. 2009. "Ejercicio exploratorio sobre el impacto macroeconómico de la distribución de una renta personal universal." Manuscript, Fundación Milenio, La Paz.

Eder, G. 1968. *Inflation and Development in Latin America. A Case History of Inflation and Stabilization in Bolivia.* Ann Arbor: University of Michigan.

Escobar, F., S. Martínez, and J. Mendizábal. 2013. "Renta Dignidad: Política de Redistribución del Ingreso, Consumo y Reducción de la Pobreza en Hogares con Personas Adultas Mayores. Informe de Evaluación de Impacto de la Renta Dignidad." Unpublished manuscript, Unidad de Análisis de Políticas Sociales y Económicas, La Paz.

Ferrufino, R. 2008. "Los logros y desafíos de la reforma de pensiones a once años de su aplicación." In *Pensiones y Jubilación en Bolivia,* edited by G. Aponte, R. Ferrufino, L. Jemio and J. Urioste. La Paz: Fundación Milenio. http://www.fundacion-milenio.org/pensiones-y-jubilacion-en-bolivia.

Laserna, R. 2007. *Entre el ch'enko y el rentismo: "riqueza nacional para la ciudadanía", una opción para la democracia y el desarrollo en Bolivia.* Boletín económico análisis de coyuntura; no. 6. La Paz: Fundación Milenio.

Mercado, M. 1998. "La reforma del sistema de pensiones de la seguridad social." In *Las reformas estructurales en Bolivia,* edited by J. Cháves Corrales. La Paz: Fundación Milenio. http://biblioteca2012.hegoa.efaber.net/registros/7703.

Morales, J. 2012. *La política económica boliviana 1982–2010.* La Paz: Plural Editores.

Morales, R. 2009. "Modelo de simulación para evaluar el impacto de transferencias directas a la población entre 18 y 60 años de edad." Unpublished manuscript, La Paz.

UDAPE (Unidad de Análisis de Política Económica). 2006. "Pobreza y desigualdad en municipios de Bolivia." La Paz. http://www.udape.gob.bo/portales_html/.../pobrezaydesigualdad%202006.pdf.

Von Gersdorff, H. 1997. "The Bolivian Pension Reform Innovative Solutions to Common Problems." Mimeo, World Bank, Washington, DC.

CHAPTER 4

Brazil

Helmut Schwarzer and Rafael Liberal Ferreira de Santana

History

There is a general consensus that Brazil is currently experiencing a relatively generous demographic period, during which the participation of the population in the economically active age range is increasing. The so-called demographic dividend, however, is temporary and points to challenges in a scenario in which the proportion of the elderly relative to the total population will reach higher and higher levels.

The Demographic Pattern

According to the Brazilian Institute of Geography and Statistics (Instituto Brasileiro de Geografia e Estatística [IBGE]), in the last 10 years there was a drop in the population of children and youth under 14 years of age of four percentage points, with the subsequent increase in the adult and elderly populations. These changes are associated with the sustained fall in the fertility rate and the increase in life expectancy. In 2010 the total fertility rate was 1.76. This decrease in births will have an impact on the percentage of the elderly in the overall population. As it stands, 22.7 percent of the Brazilian population will be over age 65 in 2050, compared to 5.4 percent in 2000. In 2050 there will also be 13.7 million adults over age 80. This population segment was only 1.6 million people in 2000.

The projections also indicate that life expectancy will continue growing in the coming years. By 2050, women will have gained an additional year of life expectancy for each decade since 1980 (figure 4.1). In 1980, life expectancy for women aged 60 was 77.6 years. In 2050 that same measure will be 87 years. Life expectancy for men followed a similar pattern during the same period. On average, they live less than women, but the growth trend is similar, increasing for men aged 60 from 75.2 years in 1980 to 82.7 years in 2050.

As life expectancy increases, the fertility rate is falling. According to projections, this rate, which in the past has been more than enough to replace the population, in a short time will be at the same level as the fertility rates in the demographically

Figure 4.1 Projection of Life Expectancy at 60 Years of Age, 1980–2050

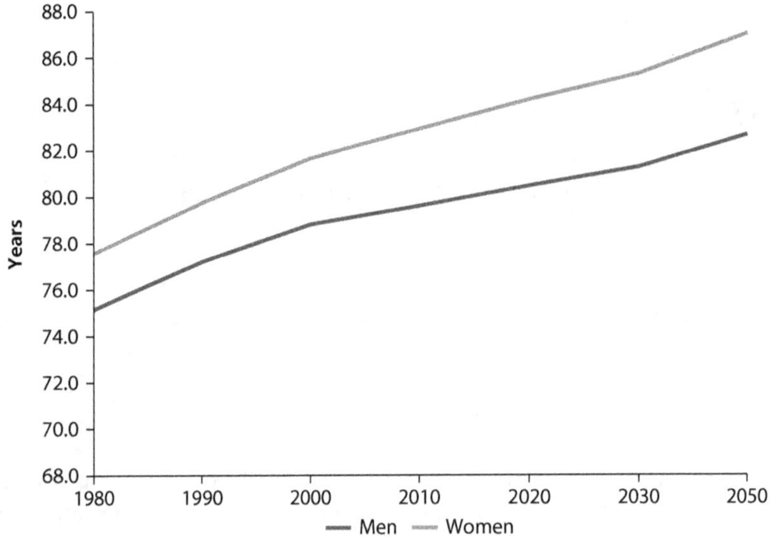

Source: Instituto Brasileiro de Geografia e Estatística (IBGE) 2008.

Figure 4.2 Projection of the Total Fertility Rate, 1980–2050

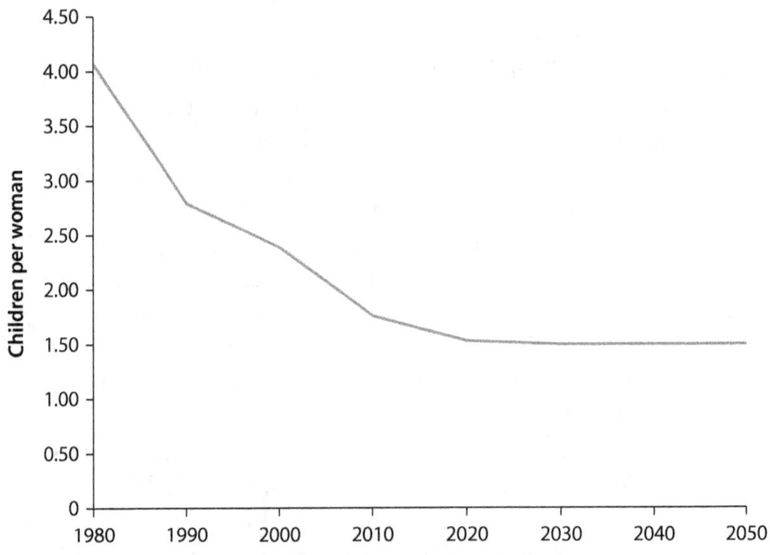

Source: Instituto Brasileiro de Geografia e Estatística (IBGE) 2008.

mature European countries (figure 4.2). The result of fewer children being born and adults living longer is the gradual aging of the population.

It is important to point out that population aging is the result of a constellation of factors and policies, and represents the success of the country and its citizens because it means that the country is achieving various objectives.

People want to live longer, and, judging by the increase in life expectancy among various age groups, Brazilian society has had great success in meeting this goal (figure 4.3). Furthermore, the reduction in the number of children per woman, the second component that explains the aging of the population, is also a reflection of profound social changes, such as changes in women's roles, which have increased their participation in the labor market and in the creation and distribution of income with greater equality between the genders (figure 4.4).

The country is facing, therefore, a new situation created by social gains that have produced new challenges for public policies in many fields. With this scenario in mind, it is important to decide which models of development of social protection are desirable in the future, as well as how to pay for them. Along the same lines, Brazil must decide which social justice components should be incorporated into this system with the goal of avoiding the pitfalls that have historically affected Latin America in these sectors, such as institutional fragmentation and lack of coordination, inequality, the absence of guidelines for sustainability, and the shortsightedness of policies.

In Brazil, the economically active population (EAP) is the predominant group in the population structure, and according to official projections this group will continue growing until the end of the 2020s (2029 to be precise). This demographic development has favored the increase of the segment of the population involved in economic activities in the labor market, which supports efforts to improve employment levels and reduce unemployment and favors economic growth policies. However, if public policies in general and social protection policies in particular are to be sustainable, a major investment in workers'

Figure 4.3 Projection of the Elderly Population, 1980–2050

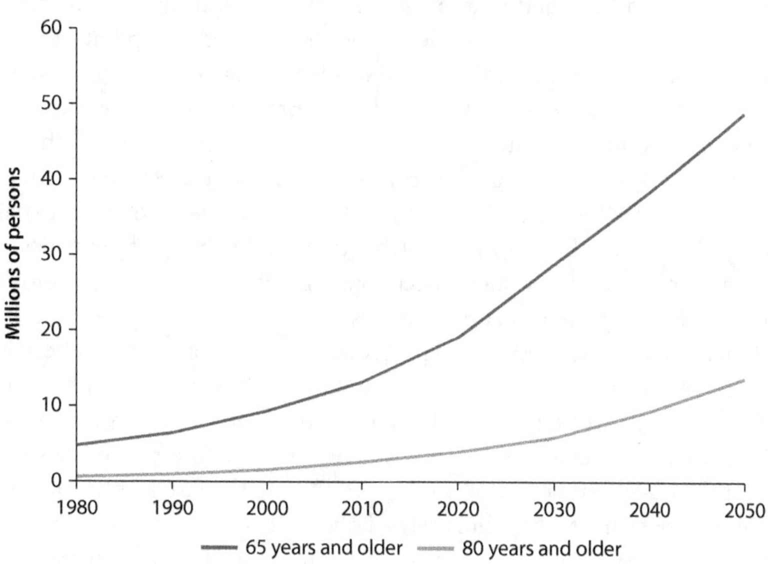

Source: Instituto Brasileiro de Geografia e Estatística (IBGE) 2008.

Figure 4.4 Projection of the Elderly as a Proportion of the Total Population, 1980–2050

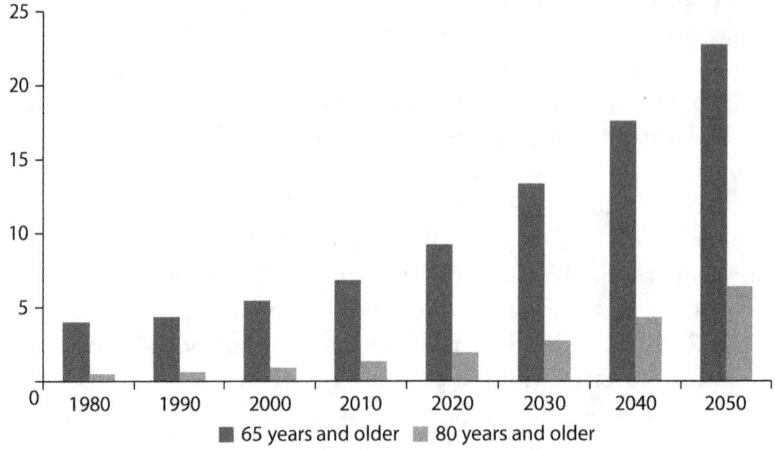

Source: Instituto Brasileiro de Geografia e Estatística (IBGE) 2008.

professional qualifications and a significant increase in productivity will be necessary in the coming decades, to create the fiscal space necessary to fund the model in the future.

Recent Dynamics of the Labor Market

Among the policies that make up the Brazilian social protection system, social security remains strongly connected to the dynamics of the labor market. The degree of labor market formalization is important for various reasons, among them because workers' and employers' mandatory contributions constitute the first requirement to access entitlements and, from a financial point of view, sustain the system. Increasing the coverage levels of their social security systems is a challenge for developing countries, including Brazil, especially among informal workers that are at the margin of the social protection system. In the case of groups that are less able to contribute, it is necessary to develop innovative entry points to overcome the barriers to formalization and achieve coverage expansion. At the same time, the fiscal space available to pay for subsequent expansions will surely be correlated with sustained economic growth that impacts positively on the funding bases of the respective models.

In Brazil the ratio between social protection contributors and beneficiaries was around 2:1 in 2011, which means that for each beneficiary there were approximately two active workers.[1] Low inflation, along with an environment of economic growth in recent years, means that, at a minimum, the system will maintain the current ratio, if not improve it. During the last 10 years (2002–12), according to data from the Ministry of Labor and Employment (Ministerio de Trabajo y Empleo [MTE]) almost 18 million net formal jobs were created.[2]

Between 2004 and 2011, the proportion of employed workers with a signed employment contract increased from 30.1 percent to 38.5 percent of total employed persons in the labor market, and this movement was seen in all regions of the country (figure 4.5). The average salary also shows an increase, with real gains above the rate of inflation, which also contributes to the improvement in social protection collections.

At the same time that the participation of workers with signed employment contracts in the formal labor market was increasing, the average salary for workers in the labor market was also evolving. From 2003 to 2011, data from the General Registry of Employed and Unemployed Persons (Catastro General de Empleados y Desempleados [CAGED]) show a real increase of 39.3 percent in the average hiring salary of workers (figure 4.6), increasing from R$726.30 (US$237) to R$1,011.77 (US$516).[3]

The process of formalization of the labor market has been important in explaining the increase in urban areas' coverage in a demographically favorable context that is expected to continue until 2020. However, as this cycle of formalization progresses it will result in new requests for benefits, and the topic of long-term sustainable funding for Brazilian social protection will surely need new public policy measures.[4]

Figure 4.5 Formal Employed in Total Employed, by Region, 2004–11

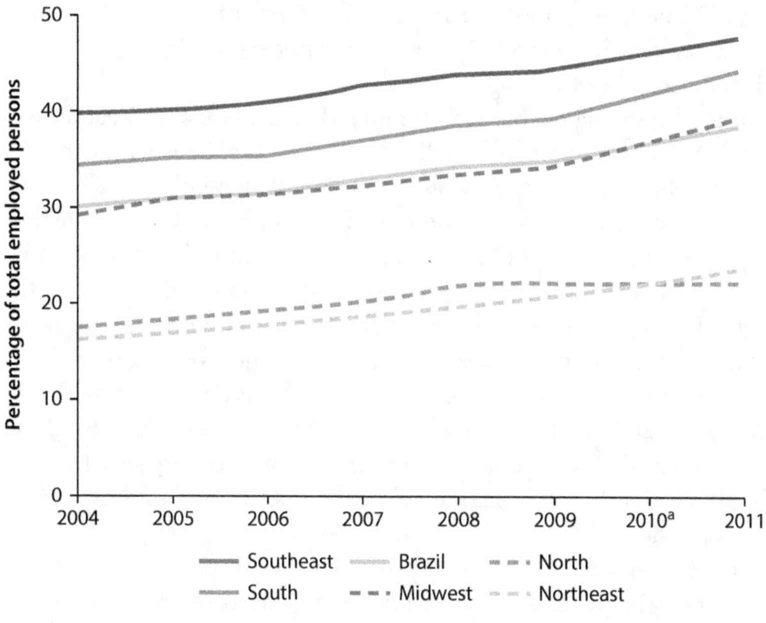

Source: Instituto de Estudos do Trabalho e Sociedade (IETS) 2012, based on the National Household Survey (Pesquisa Nacional per Amorstra Domicilios [PNAD]).
Note: The PNAD was not carried out in 2010. For this year a simple interpolation was performed based on the data for employed persons with signed employment contracts.

Figure 4.6 Average Hiring Salary, 2003–12

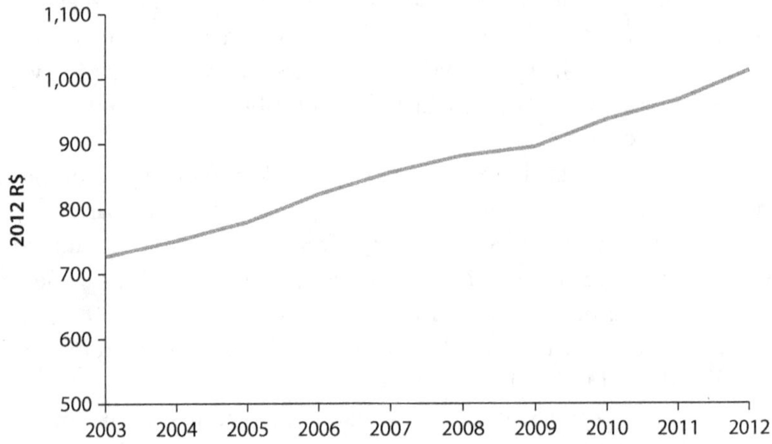

Source: Catastro General de Empleados y Desempleados (CAGED), Ministerio de Trabajo y Empleo (MTE).
Note: Values deflated by the average INPC from the period January–December 2012.

Origin and Development of Social Protection for the Elderly

Through the historical process of development of social protection policies in Brazil it is possible to identify different types of government intervention, which each contributed to the current setup, with its wide and varied group of social programs. Nonetheless, until the 1988 constitution was put in place, the strategies were not closely connected with an overall perspective that dealt with the population's social risks.

Until the beginning of the 20th century, Brazilian social protection was characterized by the payment of benefits funded by the Treasury to small groups from the public sector, such as public servants and members of the armed forces, and by works of charity, such as the Holy Homes (Santas Casas), which offered health care services. As the country's agricultural export-based economy transitioned to the growth of the urban economy based on salaried labor in the 20th century, following a process similar to several other countries in Latin America, Brazil introduced contributory social security regimes for urban workers. Their creation began with laws related to occupational hazard insurance in the first two decades of the 20th century, followed by the Eloy Chaves Law (1923), which is officially recognized as the initial framework for contributory social security, and which presaged the authorization of benefits such as disability, elderly, and survivor's pensions.

During most of the 20th century Brazilian social policy was based on the contributory principle and on payroll contributions as the main funding source for public social protection mechanisms. One important exception was the introduction of rural benefits funded by a tax on agricultural production since the 1970s. As in other Latin American countries, the contributory system has increased its coverage, especially in the formal sector in urban areas. The pattern of economic growth and the concentration of revenues, which accompanied import-substitution industrialization, have created obstacles to access for the poorest Brazilians in the contributory social security model. Moreover, the crisis in the 1980s that halted the growth previously seen during the "Brazilian miracle" period in the 1970s had a very negative impact on the creation of formal jobs and on real salaries in the economy, which led to a deterioration of the funding pillars for the social protection systems.

The federal constitution of 1988 has formed the legal basis of the social protection system in recent decades. The discussions regarding creating a new constitution involved important participation from social movements, including the unions. The constitution contains a broad chapter on social security policies and regulations and presents several guiding principles, such as the quest for universal coverage, nondiscrimination against rural populations in terms of social protection, the protection of the real value of benefits, the formation of a mixed funding base that combines payroll contributions with general taxes, and the participation of society as a whole in the development of social policies.

Social security was redefined as a set of social policies, made up of contributory social security and universal social protection and health care systems, organized by the government and funded by society as a whole. The gradual introduction of the principles defined in the 1988 constitution during the 1990s and the subsequent institutional reforms have given form to the current social protection regimes in Brazil. Medical attention was completely transferred to the Ministry of Health (Ministerio de Salud), and implementation was decentralized mainly to the states and municipalities, giving rise to the Single Health Care System (Sistema Único de Salud [SUS]) in 1990. Before this development, health care was the responsibility of the National Institute of Social Security Health Care (Instituto Nacional de Asistencia Médica de la Previsión Social) and was directed to those who contributed to social security. After the creation of the SUS, all people, regardless of their social class or employment situation, were entitled to medical attention via a broad network that encompassed all levels of care, from health centers to highly complex hospitals.

Social security was administratively restructured and modernized at several points during the 1990s and 2000s, with especially positive impacts on the elderly population. Benefits with modern social protection characteristics, such as the Continued Compensation Benefits (Beneficios de Prestación Continuada [BPCs]), were introduced in the mid-1990s in the Social Protection Framework Law (Ley Orgánica de Asistencia Social [LOAS]). Also in the 1990s, the National Policy for the Elderly (Política Nacional del Adulto Mayor) and, during the following decade, the Elderly Statute (Estatuto del Adulto Mayor) contributed to the creation of a set of support and protection policies for the elderly in situations of poverty through contributory benefits (retirement and pension benefits, etc.) and noncontributory programs.

The environment of low inflation following the success of the Plan Real in 1994 allowed the government to halt the benefits' and the minimum salary's continuous loss of value, whose value in real terms has increased markedly since 1995. In addition, macroeconomic stability dispelled high inflation as a perverse instrument that had been used in the previous period to adjust public finances by delaying spending and the deterioration of the real value of the payments to be made—a mechanism that had also been used in the field of social protection—and demonstrated the need for changes and modernization to be dealt with in a series of constitutional and administrative reforms to social security during the 1990s and 2000s.

In both health care and social protection, mechanisms to coordinate activities have been created at the federal level. The beginning of the social dialogue was introduced through participatory councils in each sector of social policy as well as sectorial conferences on social dialogue policies, especially in the 2000s. With this in mind, Brazil's ratification of the International Labour Organization's Convention no. 102 on Minimum Standards for Social Security stands out.

As the previously unused concept of "social security" gained prominence in Brazil, it fostered notable advances in contributory schemes and the formation of the SUS, as well as the inclusion of many organizational details. At the same time, the 1988 constitution had not foreseen the conditional cash transfer programs that spread throughout the 1990s. In contrast to the social safety nets of the 1980s that reacted to the most difficult social impacts of structural adjustment policies, these programs combined income transfers that alleviated poverty with health and education requirements that the beneficiaries had to fulfill. Their objective is to alleviate extreme poverty in the short term and, with a view toward the long term, overcome the lack of access to human capital that individuals need to benefit from development, which constitutes one of the structural causes of poverty and inequality.

The first municipalities to adopt these conditional transfer policies were Campinas, Ribeirão Preto, and Brasilia in 1995, and they were later expanded to almost the entire country. In 2001 the federal government introduced the School Scholarship (Bolsa Escola) nationally, as well as other similar programs linked to health and energy, for example. At the end of 2003, all of the transfer programs were merged, resulting in the current Family Grant Program ("rograma Bolsa Familia), which is funded from taxes connected to social security. Currently the Family Grant covers almost 14 million families, the first time that a social protection program in Brazil has achieved this scale.

Recent Panorama of Social Protection and Its Coverage

The current set of social policies in Brazil represents a complex network of social protection and promotion through cash transfers and providing public goods and services to families and individuals. The evolution of social spending in the last 16 years demonstrates an increasing trend. Between 1995 and 2011, spending as a proportion of GDP grew from 11.2 percent to 16.2 percent; the figure becomes more important given the significant proportion of the elderly that are beneficiaries of these policies.[5]

The monetary benefits directed to the Brazilian elderly currently come mostly from the social security and social protection systems. These regimes offer coverage to private sector workers. and their benefits can be from the contributory social security regime (semicontributory, in the case of rural beneficiaries), or noncontributory social protection. The elderly retired from public service (civilian or military) are also covered under special regimes specifically directed to these groups of workers.

In contrast to other countries in Latin America that opted for structural reforms to their social protection systems in the 1980s and 90s—especially their partial or complete privatization—since the 1990s Brazil has invested in parametric reforms (especially through constitutional amendments no. 20 of 1998 and no. 41 of 2003) within the current social protection system that prolong the period during which workers make contributions and expand coverage. Although the system faces comparatively high costs and it has been impacted by the changes underway in the population's demographic profile, the social protection that the Brazilian system provides to active workers and the elderly is very significant.

According to the PNAD, in 2011 social protection covered 60.47 million people aged 16–59,[6] which represented coverage of 70.7 percent of the 85.55 million Brazilians in this age group that stated they were employed (figure 4.7). This level of coverage in 2011, seven of every 10 workers, was the historical highest. Since 2002, when the coverage level clearly reversed its downward trend, coverage has increased almost nine percentage points, especially because pf the creation of formal jobs and specific actions on coverage policies for independent

Figure 4.7 Social Protection Coverage among the Employed Population Age 16–59 Years, 1992–2011

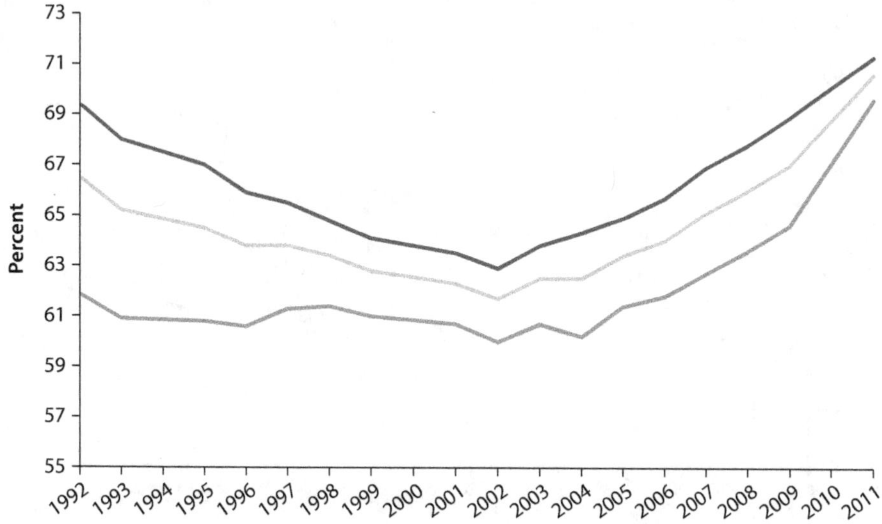

Source: Brasil: Ministério da Previdência Social 2012b.
Note: The PNAD was not carried out in 1994, 2000, and 2010. For these years we performed a simple interpolation of the data for social protection coverage.

workers and for small and medium enterprises. The strengthening of the tax supervision, labor inspection, and social protection systems has also contributed to the improvement in coverage indicators. It should also be mentioned that 7.8 percentage points of the 2011 coverage level correspond to rural workers, who are protected by a special scheme that we will describe in detail later in this chapter.

The increase in social protection coverage for active workers also represents, in addition to protection from risks resulting from work in the present, a future entitlement to income and social protection. The impacts of income transfers to beneficiaries of the system, especially the elderly, are recognized as one of the main poverty reduction mechanisms in the government's social policy toolkit, as we will see later in this chapter.

Coverage of the elderly, considered here to be persons aged 60 and older that receive some type of benefit, whether social security or protection, reached 82.2 percent of the total in 2011 (figure 4.8). The indicator for that year also represents the highest level of coverage seen since the beginning of the data series in 1992, according to a study from the Ministry of Social Protection based on the PNAD. The breakdown of coverage by gender shows that the expansion is largely due to coverage of elderly women, given that coverage for elderly men has remained relatively stable since 1993. This movement is related to the greater participation of women in the workforce witnessed in recent decades and, as long as the trend remains constant, will be seen in the reduction of the differences in social protection between elderly men and women.

Figure 4.8 Social Protection Coverage for the Elderly Aged 60 and Older, 1992–2011

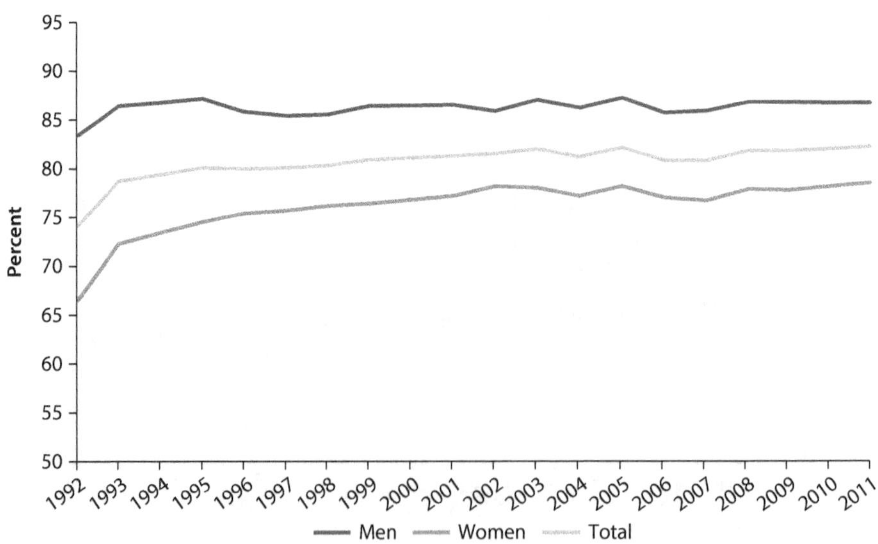

Source: Brasil: Ministério da Previdência Social 2012b.
Note: The PNAD was not carried out in 1994, 2000, and 2010. For these years we performed a simple interpolation of the data for social protection coverage.

Protection via Basic Social Security

In recent years, social protection has demonstrated significant activity incorporating new groups of workers to its programs. The magnitude of the numbers, on its own, evidences the importance of this public policy. In terms of the General Regime of Social Protection (Régimen General de Previsión Social [RGPS]), the number of beneficiaries grew by 48 percent, increasing from 17.5 million to 26 million between 2000 and 2012, especially in the following programs: retirement benefits and survivor's pensions, assistance for illnesses, and assistance for on-the-job accidents (figure 4.9).

Currently more than two-thirds of the beneficiaries (20 million people) receive pension benefits worth one minimum salary, especially workers in the family economy regime in rural areas (figure 4.10). This figure also includes assistance benefits for the elderly and individuals with disabilities. This situation reflects the distributive character of social protection policy in Brazil, in line with the 1988 constitution, which specified that social policies should be organized based on the principles of selectivity and distributiveness in making benefits and services available. At the same time, it also highlights the importance of the real valuation of the minimum salary in the last decade because it functions as a baseline for the benefits of two-thirds of the workers currently included among the beneficiaries of social protection.

The increase in coverage, along with the increase in the real value of benefits, resulted in the rise of the regime's total spending, which has increased from 5.6 percent of GDP in 2000 to 7.2 percent in 2012 (R$316.6 billion in benefit spending, equal to US$162 billion). The majority of this increase occurred between 2000 and 2006, subsequently stabilizing and remaining steady up to the present (figure 4.11).

Figure 4.9 Benefits of Social Protection, 2000–12

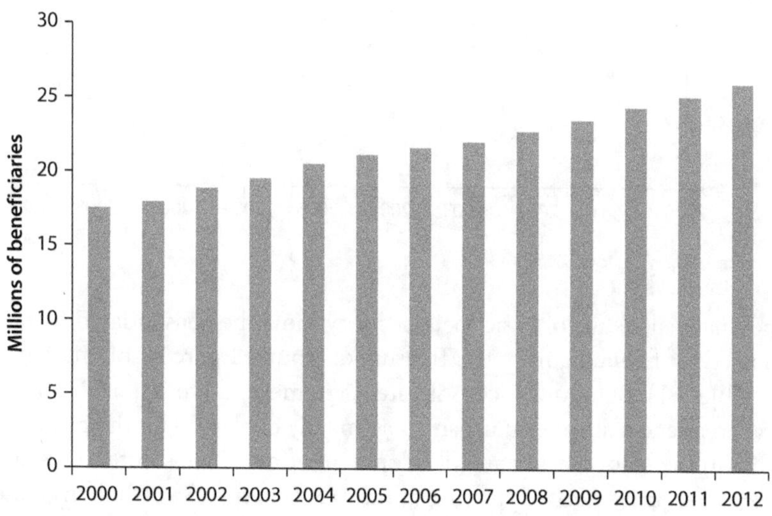

Source: Brasil: Ministério da Saúde 2013a.
Note: Includes benefits from social security and occupational hazards.

Figure 4.10 Distribution of Benefits Paid by Social Security Based on the Amount Received, December 2012
Percent

Source: Brasil: Ministério da Previdência Social 2012c.

Figure 4.11 Spending in Social Security Benefits in Terms of GDP, 2000–09

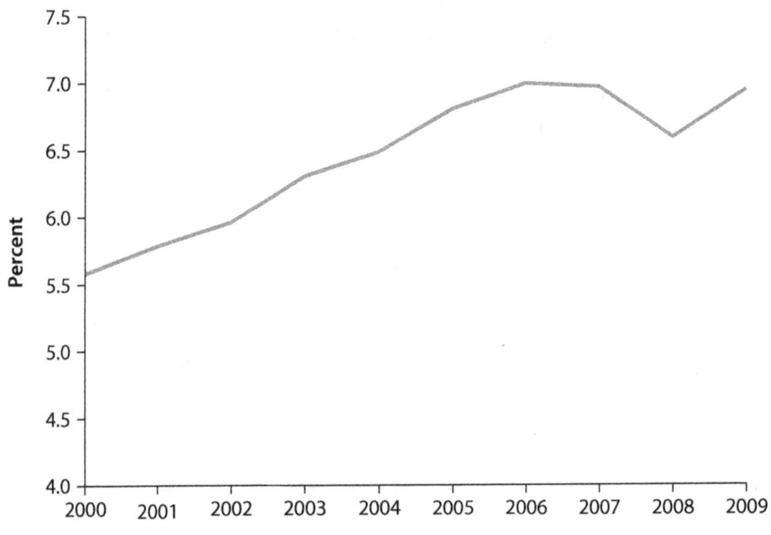

Source: Brasil: Ministério da Saúde 2013a, 2013b.

The financial results of basic social security show the consolidated (urban plus rural) need for financing from the Treasury of around 1 percent of GDP in recent years (table 4.1). Behind this consolidated statement, there is a need for funding in rural areas and a surplus in urban areas, mainly explained by the positive environment in the labor market and development efforts. In absolute terms, in 2012 basic social security needed funding of R$40.8 billion (US$21 billion), based on a deficit from rural areas of R$65.3 billion (US$33 billion) and a surplus of R$24.5 billion (US$13 billion) in urban areas.

Table 4.1 Results from the Urban and Rural RGPS, 2011–12
Billions of R$

	2011	*Percent GDP*	*2012*	*Percent GDP*
Net collections	245.9	5.9	275.8	6.3
Urban	240.5	5.8	270.0	6.1
Rural	5.4	0.1	5.8	0.1
Benefit spending	281.4	6.8	316.6	7.2
Urban	220.0	5.3	245.5	5.6
Rural	61.4	1.5	71.1	1.6
Social security results	−35.5	0.9	−40.8	0.9
Urban	20.5	0.5	24.5	0.6
Rural	−56.0	1.4	−65.3	1.5

Source: Brasil: Ministério da Previdência Social 2012a; Brasil: Ministério da Saúde 2013b.

The Rural Protection Regime

Within the RGPS there is a protection program with special rules for rural workers in the family economy regime (the rural insured). Brazilian Rural Social Security was first designed in the 1970s (interestingly under the military regime), and with the 1988 constitution it was expanded in the 1990s. The distinct treatment of rural insured persons includes a contribution based on the production sold (collected by the buyer), verification of the amount of time worked in family agriculture instead of the time making individual contributions, and age and access requirements slightly different from urban insured persons. The differences are justified because farmers in the family economy regime do not receive income in the same way that urban workers do (who can contribute based on a regular monthly salary). The differentiation is a conceptual innovation that has allowed the social inclusion of poor rural working families and has a favorable impact on the social fabric in rural areas.

Various studies have measured and demonstrated the income redistribution effects of social security in Brazil, principally in rural areas. In 1998 Delgado and Cardoso (1999) evaluated the social and economic impact of the income provided by rural social security to families living in the Northeast and Southern regions of Brazil, interviewing more than 3,000 beneficiary households in each of the two regions. One of the study's findings is that the retirement benefit from one of the members of the family was the principal source of family income in 22 percent of households in the Northeast and 11 percent of households in the South of the country. Another observation resulting from this work is that the families that received income from social security benefits could use it to acquire tools for work and inputs (such as seeds) to invest in the cycle of work on their farms and absorb the impacts from contingencies during which it was not possible to obtain income from agricultural production.

At the same time, in a case study performed in the state of Para, Schwarzer (2000a) confirmed that in almost 90 percent of the rural beneficiary households interviewed, rural social security provided at least 50 percent of monetary income.

The studies performed have shown that in 1995 the rural social security system injected a volume of resources approximately three times greater than the value of the payroll of all formal workers within a particular municipality in the small municipalities studied in Para state, which is an amount equal to one-fifth of the value of the region's agricultural production.

Including rural workers in social security has been an important step in terms of social inclusion. Before the 1988 constitution, special insured persons received a basic assistance benefit, equal to 50 percent of the current minimum salary, and faced more restrictive access conditions. The rural benefit was given only to the head of the household (man or woman) upon turning 65 years old. The required contribution was 2.1 percent of agricultural production sold, to be collected by the buyer. By including rural workers (men and women) in social security in the category of special insured persons, they immediately obtained higher incomes. The value of the benefit was doubled, women gained an entitlement to retirement benefits, and the minimum retirement age was reduced by five years. In rural areas, men can retire at age 60 and women at age 55. In 2012, 8.8 million direct beneficiaries (without counting their families) received a monthly benefit equal to the minimum salary (figure 4.12).

The studies mentioned above were able to confirm the relationship between rural social security and the reduction of rural-urban migration and the development of family farming, which represents a contribution to food security because family farming produces the majority of foodstuffs consumed in Brazil, in addition to greater solidarity among rural working families that have retirees and pensioners. Obviously, this policy, which operates within a broader concept of social security (and not within social security in a strict sense), represents a cost for the Treasury. However, it is a recognized fact that a social security policy for

Figure 4.12 Rural Benefits Paid by Social Security, 1993–2011

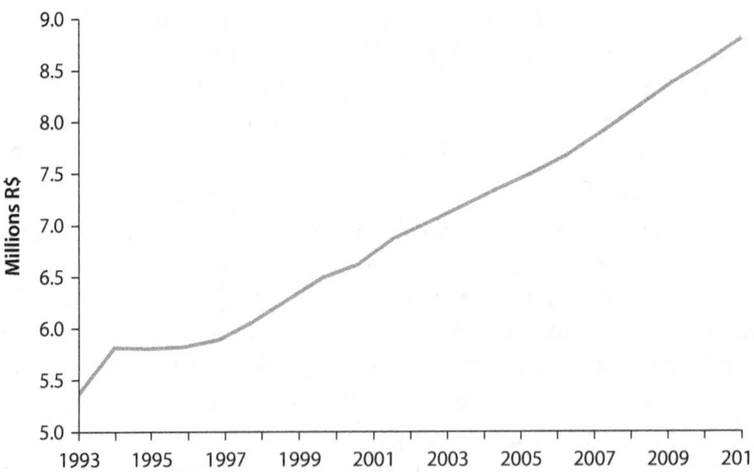

Source: Brasil: Ministério da Saúde 2013a.

rural areas in any country in the world spends in rural areas more resources than those collected. This is a consequence of a process of socioeconomic development that tends to create a stronger urban sector in oppose to the family farming sector, and this urban sector is more capable of taking advantage of economic growth. The contributions made by the rural sector to finance the retirement and pension system were 0.1 percent of GDP in 2012, and the cost of benefits for this sector reached 1.5 percent during the same year (figure 4.13).

The critical analyses of the fiscal impact of rural social security in Brazil in general lack the concept that, as a result of reproducing the Beveridgian (William Beveridge) model, the rural social security subsystem does not have a means to exist if it is not financed, in large part, by taxes. Precisely for this reason, the 1988 constitution foresaw that the social security system would be financed by a series of taxes on different bases of funding. These cross-subsidies are necessary to guarantee social security for rural workers that work in the family economy regime without taxing them with contributions that are actuarially equivalent to the benefits they will receive, which they would not have the capacity to contribute.

It is important to highlight that as the country urbanizes, as has occurred during recent decades, the proportion of rural workers decreases relative to the total population. In this way, although approximately four million families still work in subsistence agriculture in a reasonably stable manner according to estimates from the Ministry of Agricultural Development (Ministerio de Desarrollo Agrario), the decreasing trend as a proportion of the total insured population will continue while the urban labor force keeps growing. Thus, the arguments about the negative fiscal impacts of rural social security are weakened because the tendency is toward a gradual decrease in this sector's weight as Brazilian society transforms itself.

Figure 4.13 Collections, Benefit Spending, and Results of Rural Social Security in Terms of GDP, 2008–12

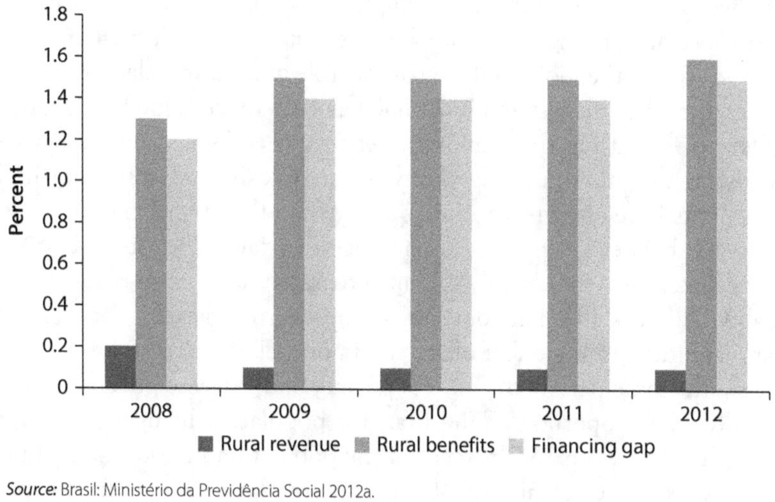

Source: Brasil: Ministério da Previdência Social 2012a.

The Public Servants' Regime

For the public servants' regime, a series of reforms in the 1990s and 2000s (constitutional amendments 20 of 1998, 41 of 2003, and 47 of 2005) sought, in general terms, to strengthen the contributory nature of the system and make it more equal from the point of view of its guiding rules and principles as compared with the General Regime, which covers private sector workers. It is important to highlight the recent creation of complementary social security for public workers, which has been debated since the 1990s and anticipated in constitutional amendment 41 of 2003, but not legislated until 2012. With the approval of the creation of a complementary social security fund, which is mandatory for new public employees since its creation, the system adopted limits in contributions and benefits equivalent to the ones under the General Regime (currently R$4,159.00 equal to US$2,122). Membership in the complementary pension fund and its retirement and pension benefit limit is optional for those public employees that were already employed when the fund began operating.

The social security coverage guaranteed for civil public servants and federal members of the military represents a significant component of public spending if we analyze it based on the number of beneficiaries in the regime. In 2012, spending on the regimes for civilian and military federal public employees was R$81 billion (US$41 billion, equivalent with 2 percent of GDP) to cover 966,300 beneficiaries (retirement and pension) (Brasil: Ministério da Previdência Social 2012d).

Impact of Transfers on Inequality and Poverty Levels

The payment of RGPS benefits—as well as assistance pensions (continued compensation benefits) and conditional transfers such as family grants—have contributed to the decrease in income inequality in Brazil during the 2000s according to the PNAD. The Gini index fell from 0.596 in 2001 to 0.543 in 2009, mainly as a result of three factors.

First, the recent period of economic growth has created 11.8 million formal jobs between 2002 and 2009, according to the CAGED, and has increased real salaries, especially among the poorest workers, in both the formal and informal markets. Second, the policy of increasing the minimum salary had multiple effects on the labor market and functioned as a reference value for the assistance benefits and for setting the minimum benefits in the social protection system. Thus, just as the minimum salary grew more quickly than inflation, the minimum benefits have also grown more quickly than the other benefits, decreasing the distance between the average and the least favored groups. Third, social transfers, including the Family Grant Program, have also reduced income inequality (figure 4.14). The joint impact of income transfers appears to be of similar magnitude to the effect of the minimum salary increase.

During the same period, the rates of poverty and extreme poverty (indigence) fell rapidly. The proportion of the Brazilian population living in a situation of poverty decreased from 35.2 percent of the population in 2001 to 21.4 percent in 2009, a reduction of almost 40 percent. In the case of extreme poverty,

Figure 4.14 Poverty and Extreme Poverty Rates, and Gini Index, 1992–2009

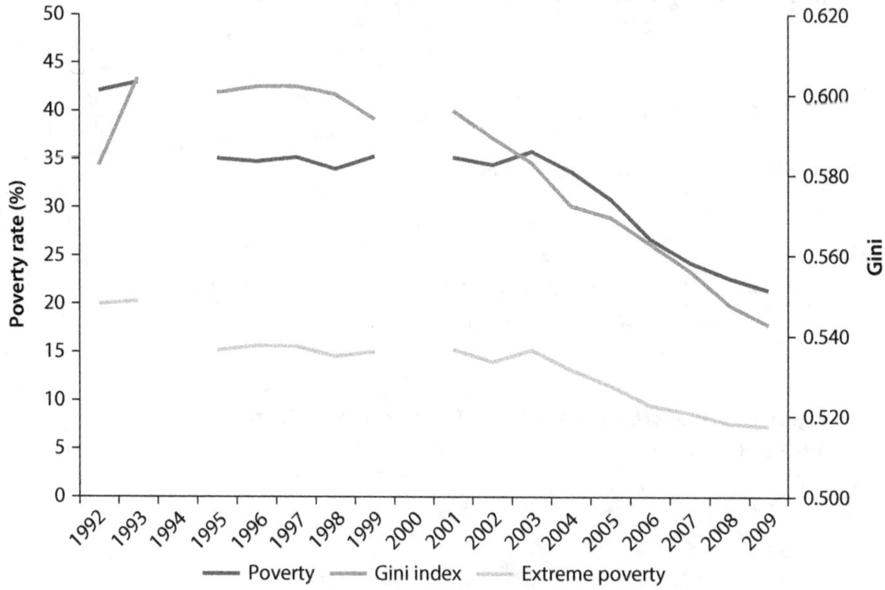

Source: Instituto de Pesquisa Econômica Aplicada (IPEA) 2013, based on the PNADs.
Note: The extreme poverty line used is an estimate of the value of a basket of foods with the minimum number of calories necessary to adequately feed a person, based on recommendations from the FAO and the WHO. The poverty line used doubles the extreme poverty line.

the reduction recorded was even greater, 52 percent in the same period (from 15.3 percent of the population in 2001 to 7.3 percent in 2009). Thus, the combination of inclusive economic growth with income transfers has helped Brazil to reduce extreme poverty by half, achieving Goal no. 1 of the Millennium Development Goals in advance.

Using a different methodology, but finding similar results, the Ministry of Social Protection (Ministerio de Previsión Social [MPS]) also monitors the impacts of social protection on poverty reduction in Brazil. Basing its definition of poverty on the existence of per capita household income below the average minimum salary, the MPS estimated that 51.2 million people were living in conditions of poverty in 2011 (considering income from all sources). If income from social protection and assistance pension benefits were excluded, the number of people living in conditions of poverty would be 75 million, which demonstrates that the payment of social security benefits rescued around 23.7 million individuals from poverty—a reduction of 12.8 percentage points in the poverty rate (table 4.2).

For the elderly specifically, the income transfer policies of recent years have resulted in a clear reduction in the levels of poverty among this group in comparative terms. A recent Instituto de Pesquisa Econômica Aplicada (IPEA) study indicates that the percentage of elderly living in poverty fell more than 20 percentage points between 1992 and 2011 (figure 4.15). For men, the drop

Table 4.2 Persons with Per Capita Household Income Less than Half the Minimum Salary (R$272.50 Equal to US$139), Including and Excluding Social Security Benefits, 2011

Description		*Number of people (millions)*	*Percent of total*
Population		184.56	100
Persons with income less than R$272.50	Including income from social security	51.27	27.8
	Excluding income from social security	74.97	40.6
Impact of benefits on the "number of poor persons"		23.71	12.8

Source: Brasil: Ministério da Previdência Social 2012b.

Figure 4.15 Proportion of the Elderly That Live in Poor Households, 1992 and 2011

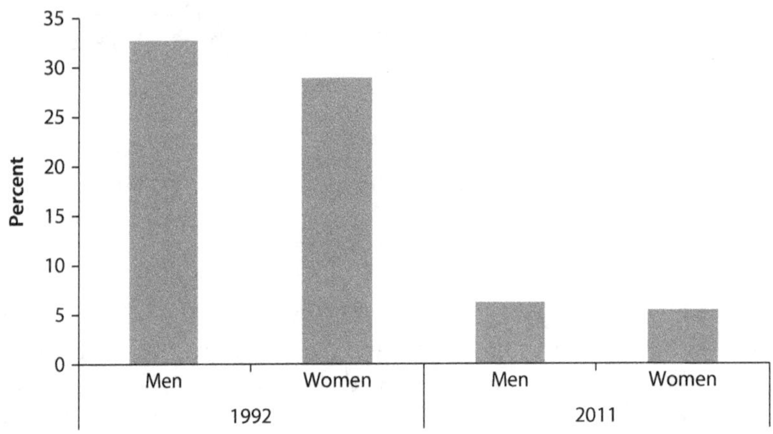

Source: Instituto de Pesquisa Económica Aplicada (IPEA) 2012a.

was from 32.7 percent to 6.2 percent, and poverty among elderly women fell from 28.9 percent to 5.4 percent in this period (IPEA 2012a).

It is worth remembering that it is difficult to perfectly isolate the effects of social security policy from other effects, such as those from the expansion and diversification of social protection policy and employment since the beginning of the 1990s, as well as the improvement in the Brazilian labor market since the beginning of the 2000s.

Protection via Social Assistance

Social assistance has shown significant activity in incorporating new population groups to its programs. We can reference two factors to explain this phenomenon. On the one hand, the restructuring of the field under the new constitution is marked by the implementation of the LOAS and the payment of the BPCs—assistance pension—for the elderly and individuals with disabilities in conditions of extreme poverty. On the other, conditional cash transfer programs stand out as a factor.

The BPC assistance pensions are equal to the monthly minimum salary for persons aged 65 and older and for individuals with disabilities who cannot work or live independently. In both cases, authorities must verify that the monthly per capita income of the family unit is less than one-fourth of the current minimum salary. The assistance benefit can be paid to more than one family member once the aforementioned conditions have been met. In this case the value of the first benefit entitled is included in the calculation of overall family income. The benefit ceases when the conditions that created the need for the benefit have been overcome or when the beneficiary dies, with no survivor's benefits for dependents.

This assistance benefit was set out in the 1988 constitution and put into law in 1996 to replace the old Monthly Annuity Income (Renta Mensual Vitalicia [RMV]) program, a benefit that required at least 12 contributions to the social security system to gain access to the benefit. Since its creation in 1996 it has incorporated 3.77 million people, including 1.75 million elderly and 2.02 million individuals with disabilities, both groups that had not been taken into much account by the old RMV (figure 4.16). Through collaboration between social security and assistance policies, the program is implemented by the National Social Security Institute (Instituto Nacional del Seguro Social [INSS]), which performs, under delegation from the Ministry of Social Development

Figure 4.16 Evolution of BPCs, 2000–12

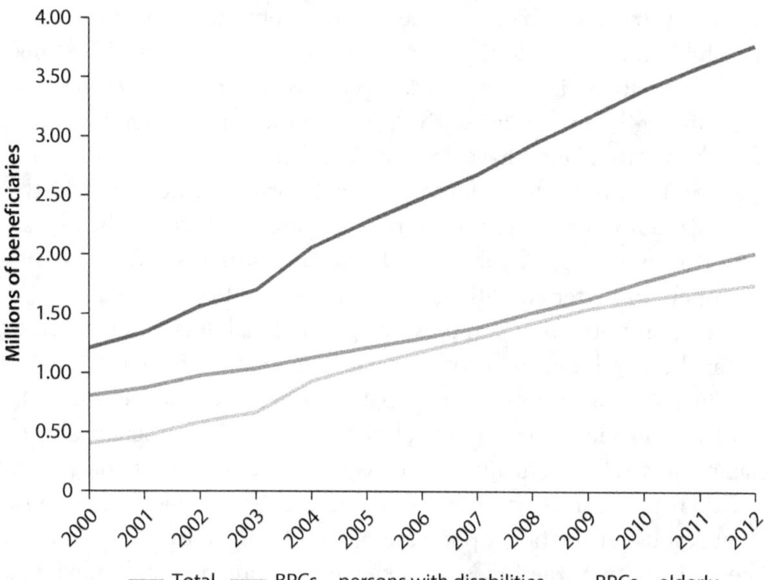

Source: Brasil: Ministério da Saúde 2013a.
Note: Only includes assistance benefits from the LOAS. The RMV and the Monthly Annuity Pension are not included. BPCs = Beneficios de Prestación Continuada.

(Ministerio de Desarrollo Social [MDS]), the evaluations of disabilities and income requirements and makes payments through its normal channels.

After the BPCs' implementation, policies were focused on the inclusion of families in situations of poverty through a series of direct and conditional income transfer programs. Since 2000, authorities have implemented programs such as the School Scholarship, the Food Grant (Bolsa Alimentación), the Gas Voucher (Vale-Gás), and the Family Grant Program, the last being the result of the merger and expansion of the former programs undertaken at the end of 2003. These programs allowed the government to extend social assistance protection from a little less than 5 million families in 2001 to 13.9 million families in 2012. The cost of the program in 2012 was R$21.2 billion (US$11 billion), equivalent to just 0.5 percent of GDP.

The Family Grant Program supplements income among the poorest families. The value of the benefit was between R$32 (US$11) and R$306 (US$156) per month in 2012, based on the socioeconomic conditions of each family. The main requirement to enter the program is that the family receive a per capita monthly income less than R$70 (US$36), and the transfer is preferentially directed toward women. The program's funds contribute to alleviating the beneficiaries' poverty in the short term, and the conditionalities and support services improve access to health care and education for the families. This combination is aimed at creating conditions to reduce poverty in the long term. The program establishes three principal conditionalities: (1) for children aged 6–17, families must show proof of school attendance (between 75 percent and 85 percent), (2) pregnant women and children must comply with a health care program (vaccination, prenatal exams), and (3) there must be no child labor among family members. Families without children can also receive a basic income of R$70 from the Family Grant, and families with children receive additional amounts based on the number of children.

Various evaluations indicate that the program has reduced extreme poverty and inequality with low administrative costs. Analysts have also observed that the rates of school attendance have increased and improvements in the nutrition levels of beneficiary families. Moreover, beneficiaries' participation in the labor market tends to improve after they join the program, which can be explained by their access to services and by facilitating small investments and necessary spending to compete in better conditions for job opportunities.

The operation of the program uses a single, national data registry, whose information can be compared with other social programs, which facilitates greater precision in targeting benefits. Municipalities offer social services and have an important role in identifying potential beneficiaries. The program also sets out financial incentives for municipalities to keep the databases up to date (table 4.3).

The expansion and diversification of the assistance benefits have produced significant results for the target population as determined by vulnerability indicators. The availability of the BPCs for the elderly population and individuals with disabilities living in extreme poverty, as well as the provision of a set of direct income transfers, have contributed to a decrease in the rates of poverty and extreme poverty during recent years.

Table 4.3 Families Covered by Conditional Cash Transfers, 2001–12

Year	*Family grant*	*School scholarship*	*Food grant*	*Gas voucher*	*Food card*
2001	0	4,794,405	30,137	0	0
2002	0	5,106,509	966,553	8,556,785	0
2003	3,615,596	3,771,199	369,463	8,229,144	349,905
2004	6,571,839	3,042,779	53,507	5,356,207	107,907
2005	8,700,445	1,783,917	24,175	3,401,097	83,524
2006	10,965,810	36,481	2,474	641,644	32,136
2007	11,043,076	5,860	229	293,920	22,193
2008	10,557,996	179	2	226,131	14,686
2009	12,370,915	6	0	0	9,138
2010	12,778,220	0	0	0	6,934
2011	13,352,306	0	0	0	1,537
2012	13,902,155	0	0	0	0

Source: Brasil: Ministério do Desenvolvimento Social e Combate à Fome 2013.

Thus, the ability of the social security and social assistance programs to reduce poverty and inequality was related to the constitution's stipulation that benefits would be homogenous throughout the country (free of distinctions that could harm rural areas or less economically developed regions). It was also associated with the constitutional stipulation that the main social security and assistance benefits would have a baseline value linked to the national minimum salary.[7]

Recent Measures Focused on Coverage

The Brazil without Misery Plan and the Fight against Extreme Poverty

In mid-2011 the government launched the Brazil without Misery Plan. The plan's principal strategy is to identify the population geographically that still lives in extreme poverty and expand the programs and services appropriately to all local realities. The plan starts by recognizing that, despite the availability of social protection programs, in 2010 16 million people still were living in a situation of extreme poverty. These are people whose per capita income is less than R$70 per month and probably face features in their social contexts that do not allow them to overcome the barrier to inclusion via the existing programs.

The plan describes an "Active Search" ("Búsqueda Activa"), in which placing the Poverty Map on top of the Opportunities Map shows what type of geographic and institutional targeting the government should perform to provide the resources and services to the most vulnerable population. In rural areas, the government seeks to create more opportunities to increase production and guarantee the purchase of foodstuffs by the government for food security programs. In addition, access to potable water is still not universal, and authorities have considered expanding existing cistern construction programs. In the cities the focus is on creating employment and income for the poorest individuals, between 18 and 65 years old, through professional training courses, job placement services, expansion of microcredit policy, and incentives for the social and solidary economy.

The plan's Active Search applies to all families and persons in extreme poverty that could access the network of existing social programs but have never requested them or were never reached by them for a variety of reasons. This process also includes the elderly not covered by the BPCs who meet the eligibility requirements. In short, the idea is that government should take a different approach to move from poverty reduction to poverty eradication, reaching excluded persons in order to help them overcome social, economic, cultural, and geographic barriers that inhibit their access to the transfers and essential social protection services. According to the MDS, since Brazil without Misery began in June 2011, 791,000 families have been identified, registered, and included in the Family Grant program, and it is estimated that another 700,000 are still outside the registry.

Measures for Inclusion in Social Protection

In recent years, the Brazilian experience with social security coverage expansion has been translated into specific actions directed to groups of people that have not been able to benefit from the strengthening of the formal labor market. They are unemployed workers; workers without labor contracts, whether in urban or rural areas; and independent and domestic workers who, because of the weakness of their labor market insertion, are not covered by the social security model based on formal employment relationships.

To offer the necessary social protection to these groups both during their active period as well as during their retirement, the government has created new rules that have resulted in important inclusive actions. Some of these actions go beyond the formal labor relationship and have presented numerically significant results. The following sections describe some of the main inclusive actions for social security adopted in Brazil in recent years.[8]

SIMPLES Law (Law no. 9,317 of 1996)

Between 1996 and 1997, the Microenterprise and Small Business Integrated Tax and Contribution Payment System (Sistema Integrado de Pago de Impuestos y Contribuciones de las Microempresas y de las Empresas de Pequeño Porte [SIMPLES]) was instituted. This program's objective was to simplify tax payments for micro- and small enterprises by unifying the payment of various federal taxes (single payment) and using a single collections form. The employer's contribution to social security stands out among these taxes, which changed from being calculated as a percentage of payroll to being defined as a percentage of the monthly gross receipts of a business.

According to Delgado et al. (2007), the implementation of this law can be linked to the net creation of approximately 500,000 new establishments and at least 2 million new formal employment relationships between 2000 and 2005, related to SIMPLES. The study also shows that the combination of the inclusion of old informal establishments with the enrollment of new establishments that emerged as a result of the system's conditions has generated more revenues for social security. This effect is more significant than the loss derived from the change of the tax regime for microenterprises that were already in the formal sector. SIMPLES was expanded in 2006 with Supplementary Law no. 123, which created the National SIMPLES (or Super SIMPLES) and replaced Law no. 9,317.

Simplified Plan for Social Security Inclusion and the Individual Microentrepreneur

In 2006 the Simplified Plan for Social Security Inclusion (Plan Simplificado de Inclusión de Previsión Social) was created through Supplementary Law no. 123. The plan starts from the principle that self-employed workers have generally low incomes, and, as a result, the Simplified Plan establishes a contribution quota of 11 percent of the minimum salary (R$74.58 in 2013, equal to US$38) as an alternative to the 20 percent required by the standard rules. With this contribution, workers receive an age-based retirement entitlement in addition to access to the other benefits of the General Regime, except for retirement based on the amount of time making contributions (which is awarded for 35 years of contributions for men and 30 for women).

The monthly payment of the reduced contribution quota entitles the worker to a benefit equal to the current minimum salary. Self-employed (independent) contributors can join the Simplified Plan, as long as they do not have a formal employment relationship; small businesspersons and partners in businesses—whose prior year annual gross income was less than R$36,000 (US$18,000)—are also eligible, as well as optional contributors (housewives and individuals over age 16, without income). Since this plan took effect in August 2012, nearly 1.4 million new contributors have joined the simplified scheme.

The Individual Microentrepreneur (Micro-emprendedor Individual [MEI]) program was an expansion of the Simplified Plan for Social Security Inclusion. Set up under Supplementary Law no. 128 of 2008, it seeks to incentivize the formalization of small businesses through the simplification and debureacratization of the traditional processes of formalizing a business. The program focuses on enterprises whose annual receipts are less than R$60,000 (US$31,000). In addition to the reduced social security contribution quota—5 percent of the minimum salary (R$33.90 in January 2013, or US$17)—the formalized small enterprises do not pay any other federal taxes and only minimal amounts in provincial and municipal taxes.[9]

The MEI's target population includes, for example, low-productivity small sellers and service providers. Some advantages that the MEI offers these groups are registration in the National Registry of Legal Entities (Catastro Nacional de Personas Jurídicas), which facilitates their access to banking and credit, and the ability to issue fiscal documents that allow the formalization of service provision, increasing the incentive for greater investment and resulting in greater competitiveness.

Another important advantage is the ability for MEIs to employ one person whose salary does not exceed the minimum salary or the salary baseline for the respective category. In this situation, the MEI must pay 3 percent of the employee's salary as the employer contribution to social security, using the single collections form, in addition to the contribution discounted from the worker's pay.

The results of the MEI program have been very positive. From its beginning in 2009 until 2012, nearly 2.6 million individual entrepreneurs have formalized their activities by enrolling in the program.[10] Through its actions, the MEI program has also shed light on a large universe of informal workers, allowing the government to formulate more adequate policies for support and productive inclusion in the future.

Formalization of Temporary Workers in Rural Areas

The challenges of expanding coverage in rural areas that have emerged in recent years have been principally related to two issues. The first concerns a better definition of the concept of "special insured persons," as a way to reduce tensions between social protection and the movement of rural workers in its interpretation to make decisions regarding granting benefits. The agreed-upon diagnosis was that throughout the 1990s and the beginning of the 2000s many transformations occurred in rural areas, changing family farming. The concept of special insured person from the 1991 law was out of step with the new reality, and it was necessary to update the definition of who constitutes a special insured person in rural areas in the family economy regime. Second, issues emerged related to registering rural workers and enrolling them in social security, given that in this segment informal hiring of workers occurred at a greater scale.

With Law no. 11,718 of 2008, many new situations for special insured persons in family farming as well as the already identified ones from the past became legally recognized. Thus, an old distortion was corrected, in which special insured persons had informally hired other rural workers to help them with their agricultural activities, mostly during harvest periods. The main change was the option to hire temporary workers for up to 120 worker-days per year (for example, during the harvest period or when there was high demand for extra labor), without losing one's status as a special insured person in terms of social security. Before the aforementioned law, family farmers did not pay contributions and those of temporary helpers to avoid losing their status as special insured in the social security system because paying these contributions would have obligated them to transfer to the "urban regime" and comply with its requirements.

The impacts of this measure have not yet been evaluated; however, it is clear that it has made an advance in updating to requirements for rural social protection. According to the *2011 Social Protection Statistical Yearbook* (*Anuario Estadístico de la Previsión Social de 2011*), the number of contributing employees basically stalled in agricultural activities between 2009 and 2011 (1.504 million and 1.554 million, respectively) (Ministerio da Previdencia Social 2011).

Inclusion of Domestic Workers and Individuals without Personal Income from Poor Families

In the category of domestic employees, the change in the legislation was made through fiscal incentives to increase the degree of formalization. Law no. 11,324 of 2006 allowed domestic employers to deduct the amounts paid each year corresponding to the employer contribution to social protection for domestic employees (12 percent of the salary; the domestic employee pays the remaining 8 percent) from their personal income tax (Imposto de Renda de Pessoa Física [IRPF]). This fiscal incentive is limited to one employee per employer.

The impact of the measure is still little known. A study from the MPS signals that the law might not have had all of the desired effects. It is possible that some employers that had already registered their domestic employees have received the fiscal benefits, but the impact in terms of newly formalized domestic workers is not known (Dantas, Barbosa, and Ferreira 2012). Household surveys indicate that Brazil has seen a slow and steady increase in the degree of formalization of domestic workers since the 1990s (approximately 15 percent). This could be explained in part by the demographic changes on the labor market that have caused the labor supply in this segment to decrease.

Individuals without personal income that only perform domestic labor and belong to low-income families (monthly family income less than two minimum salaries) are another vulnerable group that has also been the target of inclusive actions. Law no. 12,470 of 2011 established a special contribution rate for this category of optional insured. The standard 20 percent rate for optional insured persons was reduced to 5 percent for this group, limited to one minimum salary. Enrollment in the Federal Government's Single Registry for Social Programs (Catastro Único para Programa Sociales del Gobierno Federal) is necessary to verify the insured's family income meets the requirements, which reinforces coordination mechanisms between social security and social assistance. According to the MPS, between October 2011 and August 2012 the number of new low-income optional insured persons reached 325,000 enrollments.

The Benefit Readjustment Policy

The retirement, pension, and assistance policy requires a concurrent and consistent rule regarding benefit readjustment. This rule ensures that entitled benefits maintain their purchasing power over time. Without a readjustment policy, the value of benefits could be diminished by inflation in a short amount of time, in which case retirees, mostly elderly, and beneficiaries of assistance programs would face the risk of poverty.

In Brazil, the law establishes as a general rule that the annual readjustment of social security benefits should be performed such that the benefits' purchasing power is preserved. A consumer price index is used to this effect, normally the *índice nacional de precios al consumidor* (INPC). The readjustment of benefits is carried out once per year, accounting for the inflation that has occurred during the prior 12 months.

Regarding the guarantee of a minimum social security benefit and the BPCs, the 1988 constitution defined that this level should be equal to the country's official minimum salary. Therefore, the policy in recent years of real readjustments to the minimum salary has had a significant fiscal impact on social security.

As the salaries paid to active workers are increased, the adjustment automatically pulls up the minimum social security benefits. In recent years there has been a significant increase in the real value of the minimum social security benefit (table 4.4). The cumulative real increase between 1995 and 2011 was 122.59 percent.

It is worth remembering that, as we pointed out earlier, 69 percent of social security beneficiaries receive a benefit equivalent to the social security minimum guarantee. In urban areas nearly 47 percent of the benefits paid are less than or equal to one minimum salary (Brasil: Ministério da Previdência Social 2012c). In rural areas this percentage is practically 100 percent.

For social security benefits above the minimum, the law establishes that the readjustment should be sufficient to guarantee purchasing power. Law no. 8,213 of 1991, which set up the Social Security Benefits Plan, established the INPC as the readjustment index. In some periods, especially in the 1990s, other indices have been used as part of economic stabilization plans that the country has adopted to control inflation. Nonetheless, the INPC has been the reference index for annual readjustments once again since 2000.

The guarantee of periodic benefit readjustments occurs on the same dates and with the same frequency as the minimum salary. During the period 1995–2011, benefits with values above the minimum salary had a real increase of 15.83 percent—because of the different indices used for these benefits compared to the INPC (table 4.5).

Because of the readjustments, the average value of the retirement and pension benefits paid by social security is growing over time, increasing from R$778.78 (US$397) to R$934.77 (US$477) between 2005 and 2012, which is equivalent to an increase of 20 percent during this period (figure 4.17).

Service Provision for the Elderly

Health Care Services

The SUS, set forth in the 1988 constitution and created in 1990, offers universal access to its services regardless of citizens' payment capacity, that is, without a

Table 4.4 Social Security Minimum Benefit Readjustments, 1995–2011
Percent

Period	*Minimum social security benefit readjustment*	*INPC*	*Real increase*
1995–98	85.71	55.18	19.68
1999–2002	53.85	27.61	20.56
2003–06	75.00	39.64	25.32
2007–10	45.71	18.81	22.65
2011	6.86	6.47	0.37
1995–2011	678.57	249.78	122.59

Source: Ansiliero 2011.

Table 4.5 Readjustments of Social Security Benefits with Values above the Minimum Benefit Level, 1995–2011
Percent

Period	*Benefit readjustment (>MS)*	*INPC*	*Real increase*
1995–98	85.55	71.52	8.18
1999–2002	30.13	27.67	1.92
2003–06	40.00	38.58	0.85
2007–10	23.76	18.81	4.16
2011	6.47	6.47	0
1995–2011	344.63	283.85	15.83

Source: Ansiliero 2011.

Figure 4.17 Average Real Amount for Paid Social Security Benefits, 2005–12

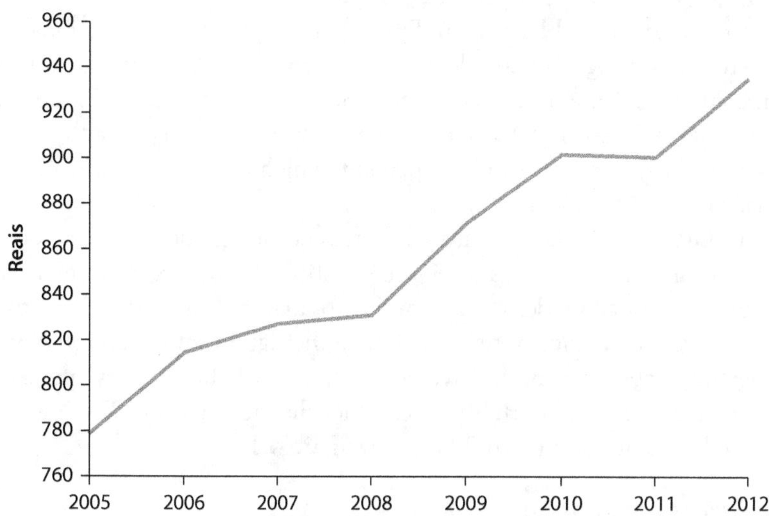

Source: Brasil: Ministério da Previdência Social 2012a.
Note: Values deflated by the average INPC from January to December 2012 and only include social protection and accident benefits.

requirement for prior contributions. The system is funded by taxes directed to social security, defined in the constitution, in addition to federal, state, and municipal tax revenues. Its management is carried out on a regional level and is hierarchical, requiring close coordination between the subnational governments and the federal government.

Until the SUS was created, the paradigm for health care in Brazil was the contributory social security system. The 1988 constitution's restructuring of this area, based on the principle of universality, resulted in a significant increase in the availability of health care services for the entire Brazilian population, not just the segment linked to the urban formal labor market. Concurrently, this increase was conceptually aimed at a "preventive" perception of health care, essentially primary care, which required investment in other types of services beyond ambulatory and hospital care. Nonetheless, secondary care and tertiary care continue to make up a significant proportion of health care spending.

One example of primary preventive care was the expansion of the Family Health (Salud de la Familia) program that has existed since the 1990s, which had 24,562 teams covering 43.97 percent of the population in 2005 and increased to 33,404 teams and a coverage level of 54.84 percent of the Brazilian population in 2012 (table 4.6). Similarly, the teams of Community Health Workers (Agentes Comunitarios de Salud) were increased to 257,262 workers in 2012, covering 65.59 percent of the population. The Oral Health (Salud Bucal) program increased its teams from 12,602 to 22,203 during the period 2005–12.

In terms of spending, the budgets assigned to the Basic Health Care (Family Health Program and Basic Care Basis) and Medium and High Complexity Care programs grew in terms of GDP in the last 10 years, increasing from 0.63 percent of GDP in 2002 to 1.03 percent in 2012 (figure 4.18).

In addition to the public system, Brazil has a supplementary optional health care system. Coverage by supplementary contributory health care plans has shown continuous growth in recent years. Between 2005 and 2012, the proportion of Brazilians covered by some type of supplementary health care plan increased from 19.2 percent to 24.7 percent, which represents nearly 47 million Brazilians (table 4.7).

The results from the health care sector reflect the restructuring that occurred in the programs and activities after the constitution, which have made health care protection for a broader portion of the population viable, as well as coverage of a more diversified range of risks (including the significant expansion of universal programs focused on preventive actions). One of the primary indicators in the sector is the infant mortality rate, which has fallen from 27.4 deaths per 1,000 live births in 2000 to 16.0 in 2010 (figure 4.19).

Social Policy Coordination

Modern social assistance policies in Brazil are the result of continuous institutional development guided by the passage of the Framework Law of Social

Table 4.6 Coverage of the Main Primary Health Care Programs, 2005–12

	Family health		*Community health workers*		*Oral health teams*	
Year	*Coverage (%)*	*Teams*	*Coverage (%)*	*Workers*	*Coverage (%)*	*Teams*
2005	43.97	24,562	58.14	208,094	34.71	12,602
2006	46.33	26,729	59.01	219,492	39.85	15,086
2007	46.75	27,324	56.77	210,964	40.87	15,694
2008	49.51	29,300	60.04	230,196	39.20	17,801
2009	50.69	30,328	60.87	234,767	47.50	18,982
2010	52.75	31,660	62.58	244,883	34.10	20,424
2011	53.41	32,295	64.06	250,602	35.71	21,425
2012	54.84	33,404	65.59	257,262	37.04	22,303

Source: Brasil: Ministério da Saúde 2013b.
Note: Other programs also make up Basic Health Care (Atención Básica a la Salud), but the data are either not available or the programs do not track coverage indicators.

Figure 4.18 Spending on Basic Health Care and Medium and High Complexity Care Programs in GDP Terms, 2002–12

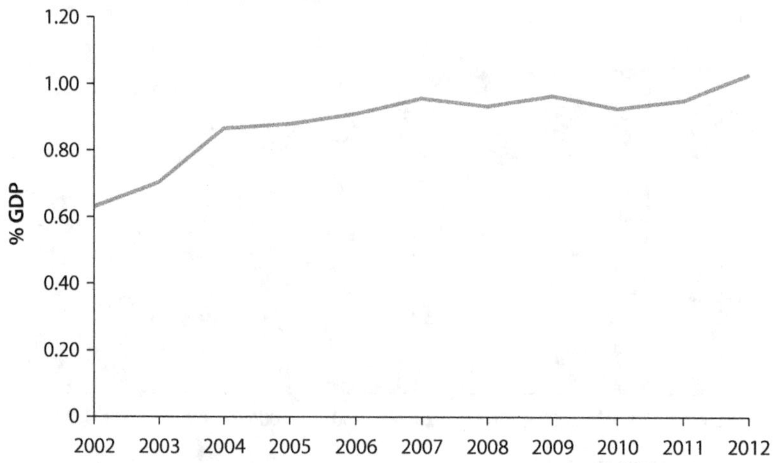

Source: Brasil: Ministério da Saúde 2013b.
Note: Basic Health Care includes the Family Health Program, community health workers, oral health teams, and minimum basic care, among others. GDP = gross domestic product.

Table 4.7 Private Health Care Plan Coverage, 2005–12
Percent

Year	*Coverage of private health care plans*
2005	19.2
2006	19.9
2007	20.8
2008	21.8
2009	22.2
2010	23.8
2011	24.4
2012	24.7

Source: Brasil: Ministério da Saúde 2013b.

Assistance in 1993 and the gradual administrative and budget institutionalization that resulted from the creation of the State Secretariat of Social Assistance (Secretaría de Estado de Asistencia Social) in 1999 and the MDS in 2003.

Based on the National Social Assistance Policy (Política Nacional de Asistencia Social), approved in 2004 by the National Social Assistance Council (Consejo Nacional de Asistencia Social), the Single Social Assistance System (Sistema Único de Asistencia Social [SUAS]) was created in 2005. The SUAS organizes assistance services in Brazil in a decentralized manner. With a participatory management model, it coordinates efforts and funds from the three levels of government to implement and finance the National Social Assistance Policy, directly involving national, state, municipal, and Federal District regulatory structures and frameworks.

Figure 4.19 Infant Mortality Rate for Children Less than One Year Old, 2000–10

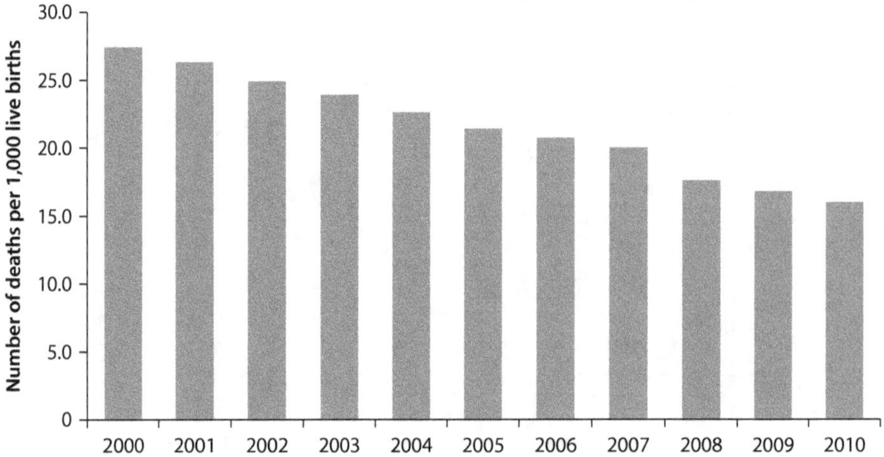

Source: Brasil: Ministério da Saúde 2013b.

In order for the SUAS to begin operating in 2004, a new National Social Assistance Policy was created and in 2005 the SUAS' Basic Operational Guidelines (NOB/SUAS) were issued, which described the responsibilities of each federal agency, the axes of implementation, and the standards for services. The states and municipalities underwent a training process to administer and implement the assistance policies as set forth by the NOB/SUAS. As of July 2010, 99.7 percent of Brazilian municipalities were certified to one of the SUAS management levels. The SUAS also has social assistance councils at national, state, and municipal levels that supervise the implementation of the policies. During 2011 the SUAS was reinforced with a specialized law, strengthening its institutional environment.

Final Considerations and Future Challenges

In Brazil the social protection system has advanced significantly in recent decades. Since the 1988 constitution, various socioeconomic indicators have improved because of the coverage expansion of transfers and social services.

Regarding social security, the increase in formality in the labor market, coupled with economic growth witnessed in recent years, has positively impacted coverage of workers. Additionally, significant changes were made to the enrollment rules for independent workers and employees in small and medium enterprises, which have contributed to the expansion of social security. The existence of a robust social security education program also stands out, operating in the INSS since the late 1990s, which informs citizens of their rights and obligations in terms of social security and social assistance.

In the social assistance sector, the government has succeeded in moving away the assistance model and gradually implementing an income transfer and service provision model based on specific legislation. As a result, we have witnessed relative stability in the main social programs in recent years, irrespective of the changes in government. The administrative structure of the social assistance programs has benefited from the experiences gained throughout the last two decades. They have also incorporated new information, communication, and management technologies, which have resulted in greater efficiency in the programs.

Another significant advance was the expansion of the health care system's coverage through the creation of the SUS. Programs such as Family Health and Oral Health have contributed to the expansion of coverage, as well as various collective programs, focused on prevention and based on public health principles.

Despite the advances in all of these areas, various challenges are pending. Funding the health care and social security systems in the long term constitutes a significant challenge. The approach of diversifying the sources of funding is, in principle, correct. However, the complete exoneration of employer payroll contributions, adopted in 2011 for some economic sectors, does not fit with this diversification strategy and introduces elements of uncertainty about sources of funding in the long term, especially for social security. The loss of income from the Provisional Contribution on Financial Transactions (Contribución Provisoria sobre Movimientos Financieros), eliminated in the 2000s with a parliamentary vote against the administration, did not create more "fiscal space" for social protection policies either, especially in terms of health care and combating poverty.

A second challenge is presented by the demographic and social transformations. These will likely necessitate adjustments and reforms to the social protection system's rules in the future to adapt it and allow it to continue fulfilling its role of maintaining income in the face of social risks. This challenge does not just refer to increases to the retirement age, but also to changes in other social policies. The process of population aging also places special attention on the issue of eldercare.

In the health care sector, epidemiological transformations require continuous monitoring to make changes to the SUS. Another important challenge deals with maintaining constant control of health care costs, especially at the secondary and tertiary levels. Progress is also necessary on service quality and accessibility issues, as well as fighting tropical illnesses.

The challenge of coordinating policies among different bodies and at different levels of administration is very important. The government has achieved significant advances with the introduction of coordination tools for the health care systems, with the creation of the SUS, and in the social assistance sector, though the SUAS, as well as the consolidation of the principle of social dialogue in the various sectors of social policy. However, opportunity still exists for greater synergy among the different sectors. On this point, the Brazil without Misery Plan, whose objective is to eradicate extreme poverty before 2014, seeks a higher level of coordination of policy, transfers, and services, both conceptually and geographically.

The current social policy setup in Brazil has contributed, therefore, to protecting the socioeconomic progress and the higher levels of well-being achieved in recent decades. Nonetheless, observers have noted an accelerated process of demographic and social changes that will place new challenges on the agendas of all social policies. Thus, the current success in implementing various social policies will demand continuous efforts in the future to guarantee that the coverage achieved will be maintained and expanded, increasing the impacts on poverty reduction over time.

Notes

1. Figures from December 2011. The monthly average of contributors is 47,465,918 contributors, and the number of active beneficiaries of the Régimen General de Previsión Social (RGPS) is 23,286,550 (Brasil: Ministério da Previdência Social 2011).
2. The net balance of employment is the result of the hires made by businesses minus dismissals, recorded by the General Registry of Employed and Unemployed Persons (Catastro General de Empleados y Desempleados), administered by the MTE. All Brazilian companies are required to inform the ministry of all hires and dismissals of workers monthly (Law no. 4,923/65).
3. For 2003, the average 2003 exchange rate (US$1.00 = R$3.07). For all other values mentioned in dollars in this chapter the conversion was made using the 2012 average exchange rate (US$1.00 = R$1.96), in accordance with the Focus Report (Informe Focus) from January 4, 2013 (Central Bank).
4. For example, discussions in recent years have included possible changes in the rules for survivor's pensions, incentives to delay the effective retirement age, and a reduction in the number of contributors lost due to work-related accidents and illnesses.
5. According to the methodology developed by the Institute of Applied Economic Research (Instituto de Pesquisa Económica Aplicada [IPEA]) based on the concept of area of action (which seeks to overcome the institutional focus by reorganizing spending programs that are sometimes distributed across various organizations; see Castro et al. 2009). The set of policies considered are those that make up social security—health care, social protection, and pensions—in addition to the benefits directed to federal public servants (civilian and military), especially retirement and pension benefits. Policies related to education, labor and income, housing and urbanization, food and nutrition, basic sanitation, agricultural development, and culture are also considered to be social policies.
6. We use the Ministry of Social Protection's definition of coverage, which considers the entire employed population between 16 and 59 years old. The definition of coverage includes contributors to the General Regime, contributors to the public servants' regimes (civilian and military), and rural workers (special insured persons), which also form part of the General Regime but have different contribution rules. For greater detail, see Brasil: Ministério da Previdência Social (2012b).
7. Although we do recognize that the link between the value of the minimum salary and the guarantee of a minimum pension could create coordination problems in the long term between social security policy and labor policy.
8. For more details, see Dantas, Barbosa, and Ferreira (2012).
9. For the Goods and Services Circulation Tax (Impuesto sobre Circulación de Mercancias y Servicios), these payments are limited to R$1.00 (US$0.50) for small

businesses engaged in commerce, and for the Services Tax (Impuesto Sobre Servicios), it is limited to R$5.00 (US$2.60) for entrepreneurs in the service sector.

10. See the Entrepreneur's Portal (Portal del Emprendedor), www.portaldoempreendedor.gov.br.

Bibliography

Ansiliero, G. 2011. "Regras de Indexação dos Benefícios Previdenciários: Evolução Recente e Implicações para o Regime geral de Previdência social." *Informe de Previdência Social* 23 (8), MPS, Brasilia, August.

Brasil: Ministério da Previdência Social. 2011. "Anuário Estatístico da Previdência Social." Ministério da Previdência Social, Brasilia.

———. 2012a. *Resultado do Regime Geral de Previdência Social—RGPS 2012*. Ministério da Previdência Social, Brasilia.

———. 2012b. "Evolução Recente da Proteção Previdenciária e seus Impactos sobre o Nível de Probreza." *Informe de Previdência Social* 24 (10), Ministério da Previdência Social, Brasília.

———. 2012c. "Boletim Estatístico da Previdência Social." Ministério da Previdência Social, Brasília.

———. 2012d. "Boletim Estatístico de Pessoal." 17 (200), December, Ministério da Previdência Social, Brasilia.

Brasil: Ministério do Desenvolvimento Social e Combate à Fome. 2013. "Matriz de Informação Social." http://aplicacoes.mds.gov.br/sagi/mi2007/tabelas/mi_social.php.

Brasil: Ministério da Saúde. 2013a. "Sala de Apoio à Gestão Estratégica." Ministério da Saúde, Brasila. http://189.28.128.178/sage/.

———. 2013b. "Informações de Saúde DATASUS." Ministério da Saúde, Brasila. http://www.datasus.gov.br.

Castro, J., A. Ribeiro, A. G. Campos, and M. Matijascic. 2009. "A CF/88 e as políticas sociais brasileiras." In *Constituição brasileira de 1988 revisitada*, vol. 1, ed. J. Cardoso, Jr. Brasilia: IPEA.

Dantas, E., E. Barbosa, and A. Ferreira. 2012. "Medidas de Inclusão Previdenciária no Brasil." *Informe de Previdência Social* 24 (9), September, MPS, Brasilia.

Delgado, G., and J. Cardoso, Jr. 1999. "O idoso e a previdência rural no Brasil: a experiência recente de universalização." Discussion Paper, IPEA, Brasilia.

Delgado, G., A. Querino, A. Campos, F. Vaz, L. Rangel, and M. Stivali. 2007. "Avaliação do Simples: implicações à formalização previdenciária." Discussion Papers 01/2007, IPEA, Brasilia.

IBGE (Instituto Brasileiro de Geografia e Estatística). 2008. "Projeção da População do Brasil por Sexo e Idade: 1980–2050, Revisão 2008." Estudos e Pesquisa—Informação Demográfica e Socioeconômica no. 24, IBGE, Rio de Janeiro.

IETS (Instituto de Estudos do Trabalho e Sociedade). 2012. "Retrato Socioeconômico Brasileiro: a Década de 2000." IETS, Rio de Janeiro.

IPEA (Instituto de Pesquisa Económica Aplicada). 2012a. "Boletim Políticas Sociais: Acompanhamento e Análise." No. 20, IPEA, Brasilia.

———. 2012b. "Tendências Demográficas Mostradas pela PNAD 2011." Comunicados do IPEA, 157, IPEA, Brasilia.

———. 2013. *Social Dados e Indicadores*. Brasilia: IPEA. http://www.ipeadata.gov.br.

Ministerio da Previdencia Social. 2011. *Anuario Estadistico da Previdencia Social*. Brasilia.

Schwarzer, H. 2000a. "Impactos Sócio-Econômicos do Sistema de Aposentadorias Rurais no Brasil—Evidências Empíricas de um Estudo de Caso no Pará." Discussion text 729, IPEA, Rio de Janeiro.

———. 2000b. "Paradigmas de previdência social rural: um panorama da experiência internacional." Discussion text 767, IPEA, Brasilia.

Schwarzer, H., and A. Querino. 2002. "Benefícios sociais e pobreza: programas não contributivos da seguridade social brasileira." Discussion text 929, IPEA, Brasilia.

CHAPTER 5

Chile

Eduardo Fajnzylber and Guillermo Paraje

History

Chile is one of the countries in Latin America that has most advanced through the process of demographic transition. This transition has generally been most evident in a significant reduction in the total fertility rate and a major increase in life expectancy at birth. Projections signal a sustained increase in the dependency ratio in the coming decades. A pattern of active labor market participation has persisted among a significant segment of the elderly between 65 and 75 years of age.

Demographic and Labor Profile of the Elderly Population

The fertility rate for women from 15 to 49 years old moved from 4.95 during the five-year period 1950–55 to 2.67 in 1980–85, and down to 2 from 2000 to 2005. Estimates predict that by 2050 the rate will be just 1.85. Life expectancy during the five-year period 1950–55 was 54.8 years, increasing to 70 years during 1980–85, and to 78.4 during 2005–10. Adult, child, and maternal mortality rates also fell drastically during this period. These factors produced notable changes in the population structure, resulting in population aging that is expected to become more acute over time (figure 5.1).

Chile's aging index (defined as the population 60 years and older per child aged 0–14 years) has increased significantly since the 1970s and is expected to continue growing until 2080 (figure 5.2). During the period from 1950 to 2100 Chile's index is well above the Latin American average, demonstrating how much more advanced the general aging process is in Chile as compared with the rest of the region.

Table 5.1 shows a series of demographic indicators covering the last 60 years and the next 40. All the indicators show an acceleration of population aging beginning in the final years of the 20th century and the first years of the 21st. The last indicator, "Parent support ratio," is particularly interesting, because it shows the dependency ratio of adults over 80 on adults aged 50–64 years. This ratio essentially demonstrates the economic burden that the over 80 age group places on the age group closest to retirement (presumably affecting their decisions regarding work and savings during this period).

Figure 5.1 Population Distribution Forecast, by Gender and Five-Year Age Cohort, 2002 and 2050

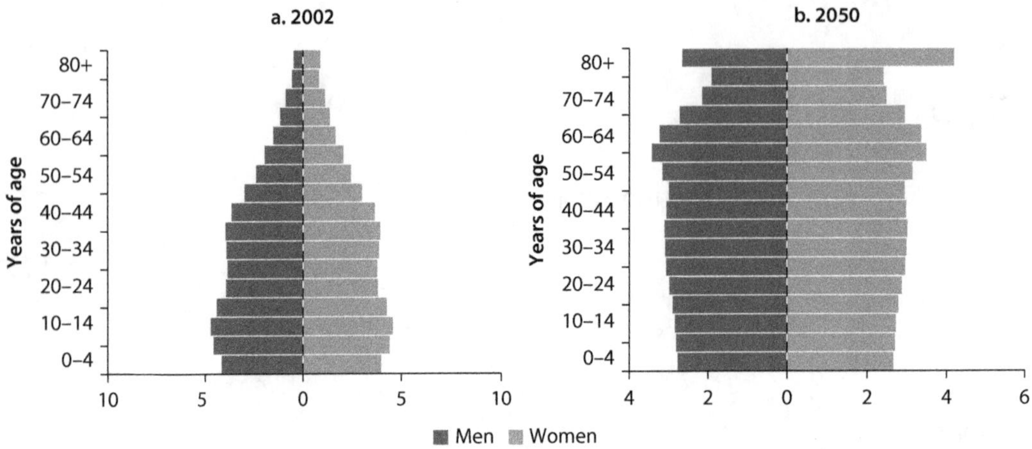

Source: National Ecology Institute—Economic Commission for Latin America and the Caribbean (INE-ECLAC).

Figure 5.2 Aging Index in Latin America and Chile, 1950–2100

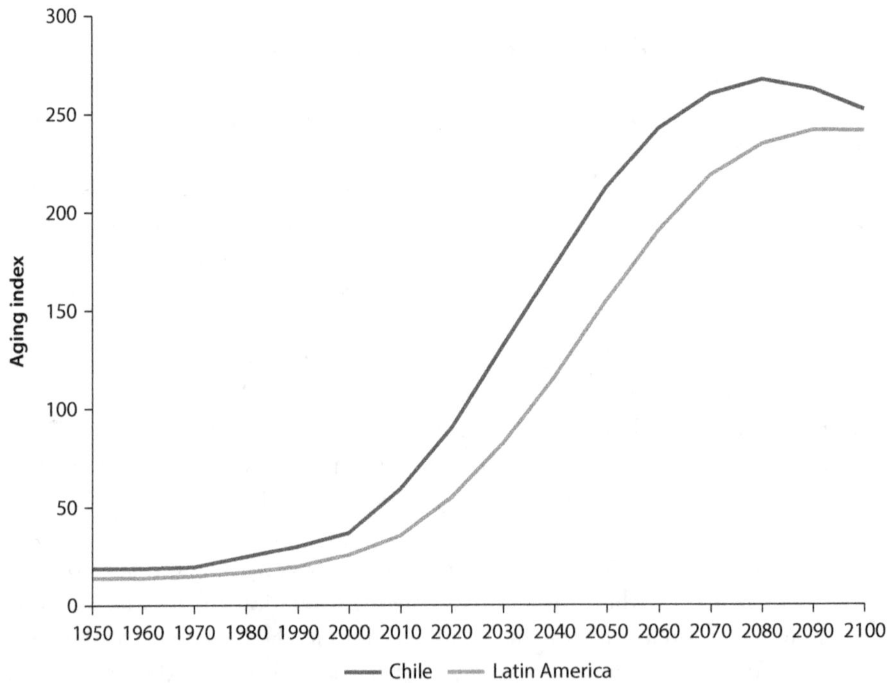

Source: Economic Commission for Latin America and the Caribbean (ECLAC) 2011.

Table 5.1 Population Aging Indicators, 1950–2050

Indicators	*1950*	*1970*	*1990*	*2010*	*2030*	*2050*
Total population (thousands)	6,082	9,579	13,214	17,149	19,430	19,589
Percentage of population						
0–14 years	36.7	39.7	30.0	22.1	17.4	14.4
15–59 years	56.4	52.6	61.1	64.8	59.5	55.0
60–74 years	5.7	6.0	6.7	9.3	16.0	17.7
75 and over	1.2	1.7	2.3	3.8	7.0	12.8
Dependency ratio 60 and over[a]	12.1	14.7	14.7	20.2	38.7	55.5
Potential support ratio[b]	8.2	6.8	6.8	4.9	2.6	1.8
Parent support ratio[c]	4.5	8.0	11.3	13.8	22.2	40.1

Source: Economic Commission for Latin America and the Caribbean (ECLAC) 2011.
a. Population 60+/population 15–59 years.
b. Population 15–59 years/population 60+.
c. Population 80+/population 50–64 years.

In recent years, this age group has been relatively active in the labor market. Table 5.2 shows the economic activity and unemployment rates, as well as the distribution of adults over age 65 by job sector, broken down into adults aged 65–75 years and those over 75. These indicators are formulated based on the National Socioeconomic Profile (Caracterízación Socioeconómica Nacional [CASEN]) surveys taken in 2000, 2003, 2006, and 2009. The economic activity rate for adults over 65 hovered around 16–18 percent between 2000 and 2006, falling to 15 percent in 2009. Within this group the 65–75 age group was more active, with at least one in five adults working during the survey years (and with nearly one in four working in 2006). Naturally this situation exposes the failings of a pension system (in terms of coverage and benefits) that essentially does not allow adults over 65 to retire from the job market. As might be expected, this group's unemployment rate is low: The elderly that wish to continue working after age 65 find work probably because they cannot allow themselves to consider too many options in the job market.

In employment terms, the distribution of economically active older adults by economic sector has varied over time, although not in any notable way. First, the elderly reduced their participation in the primary sector between 2000 and 2009, although their participation in this sector is still above the average for the general population. In the construction and services sectors their participation is just below average, although it has increased over time. In industry the elderly participate on par with the average population. Overall, the service sector provides the most jobs to the three age groups studied, followed by the primary sector.

The Origin of Social Protection Systems for the Elderly

The initial structure of the social protection system was characterized by a high level of fragmentation. The process of consolidation was driven through an individually funded scheme that, although it did correct imbalances, maintained inequalities in terms of benefit access, which were the result of the contribution

Table 5.2 Economic Activity Indicators for the Elderly, 2000–09
Percent

Indicators	*2000*	*2003*	*2006*	*2009*
Economic activity rate				
Over 65 years	16.8	16.2	17.9	14.9
65–75 years	22.7	21.6	24.6	21.5
Over 70 years	6.6	7.7	8.3	6.1
Unemployment rate				
Over 65 years	0.8	0.7	0.5	0.5
65–75 years	1.3	1.1	0.8	0.8
Over 70 years	0.1	0.2	0.2	0.1
Economic sector over 65 years				
Primary	23.7	21.0	19.7	18.1
Industry	12.1	13.8	11.2	10.7
Construction	6.0	6.5	7.8	7.9
Services	58.1	58.5	60.6	62.5
Economic sector 65–75 years				
Primary	22.0	20.4	19.5	17.5
Industry	12.6	13.3	10.6	9.4
Construction	6.2	6.9	8.9	9.0
Services	59.0	59.3	60.3	63.6
Economic sector over 75 years				
Primary	33.9	24.0	20.5	20.8
Industry	8.6	16.2	13.6	16.9
Construction	4.6	4.9	3.0	2.9
Services	52.9	55.0	62.2	57.4

Source: Based on Encuesta de Caracterízación Socioeconómica Nacional (CASEN) surveys from 2000, 2003, 2006, and 2009.

history of workers affiliated with the system. To compensate for these inequalities, the system included a minimum pension in the contributory system and a noncontributory social pension scheme, both of which were replaced by the New Solidarity Pillar (Nuevo Pilar Solidario) in 2008.

Government policy toward income protection for the elderly was first established in 1924, with the creation of the Compulsory Insurance Bank (Caja de Seguro Obligatorio) and the Private Employees' Pension Bank (Caja de Previsión de Empleados Particulares).[1] Also, in 1925 the government created the National Public Employees' Bank. These three institutions formed the foundation of the system of income transfer to the elderly until a reform in 1980 created a system of individual accounts that still exists today.

From 1925 to 1980 the provision of social security to the elderly was complicated by the creation of a series of parallel systems for different groups of workers, with broad heterogeneity of eligibility rules and benefits. This diversity was the product of the negotiation processes between the government and interest groups, which received concessions from the government in the form of special benefits (such as early retirement, benefit indexation, and access to preferential nonreadjustable/fixed interest loans) in proportion to their political and social power (Godoy and Valdés 1994). As a result, when the military regime established the 1980 reform, there were 32 social security institutions in charge of more than 100 distinct regimes (Cheyre 1991). The structure of the system translated into serious sectoral fragmentation problems, inequality resulting from the different negotiating positions, and high administrative costs due to the redundancy of functions in the different pension banks.[2] Additionally the demographic shift, accompanied by poor administration of the reserve funds at the state banks, translated into growing deficits at the pension systems, which were absorbed by increased government spending.

In 1980 the variety of pension regimes was replaced by a single national scheme based on individually funded accounts.[3] Under these schemes, each worker has a single account in his or her name, independent of the job or employer. Each dependent worker (including public employees) automatically contributes 10 percent of taxable income to the individually funded account. This account is administered by a Pension Fund Administrator (Administradora de Fondos de Pensiones [AFP]) that the worker has selected to manage and invest these savings in financial instruments. Upon meeting the requirements to retire, the individual savings can be used to acquire an annuity offered by an insurance company or transferred to the worker in monthly payments from the individual account.

Aside from benefits for the elderly, the system also delivers disability and survivor benefits. Disability benefits are pensions awarded to qualified individuals subject to the determination of a medical commission run by the pension system. Survivor benefits are paid to the direct beneficiaries (spouses, children, and parents in some cases) of a deceased worker. Both types of benefits are paid for by the savings in the individual account of the worker and can be supplemented by an insurance payout if the worker was still active in the labor force at the time of death or disability in order to achieve a benefit level proportional to the salary of the covered worker.

The scheme introduced in 1980 was compulsory for all workers who joined the labor force for the first time. Workers that had made contributions to one of the previous schemes under the old system could choose to remain under the previous regime or transfer (irrevocably) to the new scheme. In this case the previous contributions could be turned into financial resources upon retirement through a system of Recognition Bonds (Bonos de Reconocimiento) issued by the government.

The AFPs are free to set a management fee for the services they offer, and workers can change AFPs at any time. In addition, the operations of AFPs are closely regulated by series of laws and rules. The Superintendent of Pensions is in charge of the regulation and supervision of these institutions.[4] Regulations detail the services each AFP can and must offer, a system of controls on the financial instruments in which workers' funds can be invested, and capital requirements calculated based on the amount of funds under management, as well as a set of penalties for administrators that demonstrate financial returns much lower than their peers.

Originally, each administrator could offer only a single fund for all of its clients. In 2002 a second fund (lower risk than the original) was allowed, and in 2004 the AFPs began to offer five different funds, differentiated based on the level of exposure to variable income instruments. If a client does not specify which type of fund his or her savings are to be invested in, regulations stipulate a dynamic system of investment throughout the account's lifecycle (with greater exposure to risk in earlier years, reducing exposure as the individual nears retirement age).

It is important to stress that under the Chilean system, normally classified as a defined contribution system, the amount of benefits an elderly person receives is directly dependent upon the amount contributed during the individual's working years and any increases resulting from the investment of the funds in the individual's account.[5] This means that existing differences in the labor market in terms of formal employability, compensation levels, or gender discrimination are transferred directly to pension system distributions. Additionally, upon calculating benefits actuarially, we see that early retirement is proportionally penalized (because of lower savings and longer survival periods). This affects women significantly because they usually have less savings, can choose to retire at a younger age (60 years in contrast to 65 years for men), and live longer.

The existing pay-as-you-go schemes before the 1980 reform included minimum pension schemes that established a floor for benefits paid to eligible workers. However, the access requirements (usually expressed as a minimum number of monthly or weekly contributions throughout a worker's lifetime) and the informality associated with certain types of economic activities (such as agriculture) resulted in some sectors of the population being left out of traditional schemes, without access to benefits for the elderly.

The 1980 reform included in its design a minimum pension scheme with characteristics similar to the previous scheme. Elderly retirees in the new system that had exhausted their pension savings and that had contributed at least 20 years (240 months) to the system were guaranteed a minimum pension (Minimum Guaranteed Pension; Pensión Mínima Garantizada [PMG]), paid for by the government.[6] This scheme was not subject to a means test, except that the beneficiary could not receive other pensions for amounts greater than the minimum pension.

In terms of noncontributory benefits, in 1975 the government created the Social Pensions (Pensiones Asistenciales [PASIS]) scheme with elderly and disability benefits. Assistance pensions for the mentally impaired were later included in the system. The scheme belonged to a system of noncontributory benefits awarded to individuals living in poverty ("lacking resources") and paid for from the government's general revenues. The system's reach was relatively limited (only those living in poverty), its availability was subject to the annual budget assigned to the program (it was not characterized as an individual right), and the amount was initially defined as 50 percent of the current minimum pension (less than the poverty line in some cases). This scheme continued functioning until the 2008 reform, which replaced the assistance pensions and minimum guaranteed pension benefits with the New Solidarity Pillar.

Reforms Aimed at Improving the Coverage of Transfer Programs in Recent Years

A series of reforms were adopted to expand coverage and reduce the inequalities inside the system. The government established a system of solidarity pensions called the "New Solidarity Pillar" (Nuevo Pilar Solidario [NPS]) that absorbed the noncontributory programs, while also expanding the compulsory nature of the system and introducing changes to the contributory regime.

Reforms and Programs

According to the analysis performed during the reform, one of the principal challenges the system faced was to improve coverage through interventions along three pillars: the poverty prevention pillar, the compulsory contribution pillar, and the voluntary contribution pillar. For each of these pillars we have identified some elements of the analysis and the corresponding policy measures that were adopted.

First, the poverty prevention programs that existed before the reform (PASIS and PMG) were by their nature limited in reach and barely integrated with the contributory system, which meant they were not effective tools for the universalization of coverage. For this reason, they were replaced by the Solidarity Pension System (Sistema de Pensiones Solidarias).

Second, the compulsory contribution pillar was not going to be capable of delivering adequate pensions based on personal incomes. This was mainly a product of the low density of workers' contributions. In the case of men, the low density was explained by the relatively high proportion of time dedicated to independent or informal labor, both of which were excluded from compulsory contributions to the contributory scheme. In the case of women, the low density was the result of childcare responsibilities and caring for other relatives. Additionally, young workers also had low contribution densities, which was particularly significant for a pay-as-you-go scheme that relied on contributions from young workers to fund a significant portion of the pension budget. As a result of this diagnostic, the government opted to expand compulsory contributions to include independent workers that provided services covered by the tax system through "honoraria bills" (boletas de honorarios). The government also established a bonus for each living child they gave birth to, payable to women upon turning 65 years old and equivalent to the amount of 18 contributions based on the minimum wage. To foment the formalization of young workers, the government created a subsidy scheme for hiring young workers.

Third, the voluntary contribution pillar, consisting of tax incentives for savings in certain types of instruments, was an especially regressive system because it benefited only workers with a high marginal tax rate. For this reason the government created an alternative tax regime accompanied by a state subsidy for voluntary retirement savings. Additionally, policy makers created the legal structure of Collective Voluntary Retirement Savings (Ahorro Previsional Voluntario Colectivo) in the spirit of including employers in the effort to increase workers' savings levels.

Finally, the actuarial nature of the benefits awarded by the system meant that women, who tend to have lower incomes, lower contribution density, earlier retirement, and greater longevity, received pensions that were systematically lower than those of men, even at the same level of retirement savings. To partially correct this difference, policy makers separated buying disability and survivor's insurance between men and women, charging everyone the higher premium (the premium for men), and depositing the difference between the two premiums in women's individual accounts. This means that women overcontribute (around 0.4 percent of taxable income), without creating a difference in the salary cost for men and women.

In the next section we present the different measures adopted to increase the system's coverage in greater detail.[7]

The New Solidarity Pillar

The 2008 reform replaced the existing programs (PASIS and PMG) with a single scheme that guarantees all individuals over 65 years of age that belong to the poorest 60 percent of the population access to a basic guaranteed pension independent of their contribution history. This new program offers subsidies for the elderly and disabled paid for by the state.

The new solidarity pension scheme was rolled out gradually. In the first year, beginning in July 2008, the Basic Solidarity Pension (Pensión Básica Solidaria [PBS]) was equivalent to US$137 and was restricted to the poorest 40 percent of the population. This benefit increased to approximately US$172 in July 2009, covering the poorest 45 percent of the population. The final benefit scheme came into effect in July 2012 and currently covers the poorest 60 percent of the population.

Benefits are granted according to the following scheme. Individuals that have not made any contributions can receive a pension for the elderly if they are older than 65 and they meet income and residency requirements. Individuals that have made contributions, but that would only receive a pension below a predetermined threshold, can receive a Solidarity Retirement Contribution (Aporte Previsional Solidario [APS]), with the same income and residency requirements.[8] The disability program grants benefits based on similar conditions, but its target population is individuals between 18 and 64 years old. Once disabled individuals turn 65 years old they are eligible for solidarity benefits for the elderly.

The affluence test is a type of income test applied to ensure that an individual does not belong to the richest 40 percent of the population (60 percent in the first year). The initial implementation, during the first two years, was based on the Social Protection Profile (Ficha de Protección Social), the main targeting tool used for social programs in Chile. Currently the system uses a Pension Targeting Score (Puntaje de Focalización Previsional), which takes the family structure component of the Social Protection Profile and combines it with an administrative history of labor, financial, and retirement income. The residency test requires that individuals live a minimum of 20 years in Chile after turning 20 years old, and at least three of the five years before applying for the pension.

Figure 5.3 Final Subsidies and Pensions under the New Solidarity Pillar

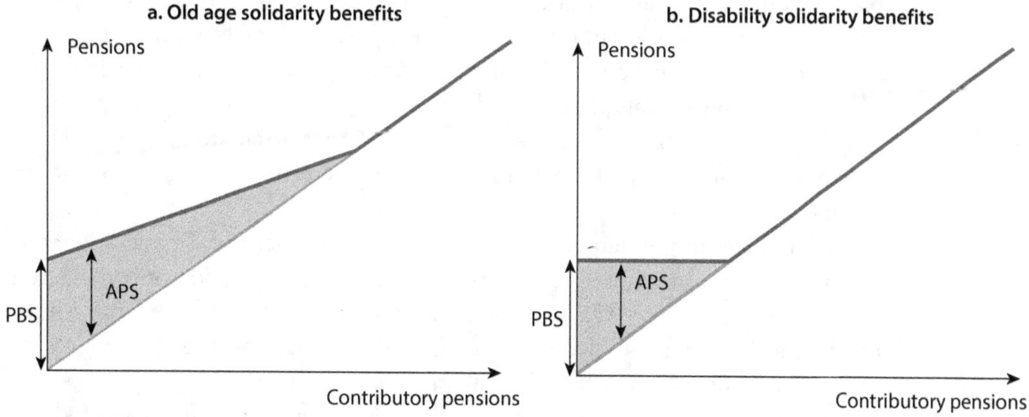

Source: Rofman, Fajnzylber, and Herrera 2008.
Note: APS = Aporte Previsional Solidario; PBS = Pensión Básica Solidaria.

Figure 5.3 describes the subsidy scheme, presenting solidarity subsidies and total pensions as a function of contributory pensions.

It is important to highlight two elements of this design: the integration between the contributory system and the solidarity pillar and the worries about incentives for contribution that this integration generates. The integration guarantees that the first three quintiles will receive a pension at least equal to the PBS. If the benefit had been established with a ceiling (as is the case for disability pensions), it would have created disincentives toward contributions by low-income individuals because their pension would not increase with the number or amount of their contributions. With the chosen design, total pensions are steadily increasing as individually funded savings increase—each peso saved always increases the pension, although the ratio is not one to one.

Compulsory Contributions for Independent Workers

To be consistent with the coverage expansion brought about by the introduction of the NPS, the reform requires all independent workers that receive taxable income to make social security contributions based on their annual income. The introduction of this requirement is gradual, beginning with an informative period of three years, followed by another three-year period during which contributions will be discounted from independent workers unless they expressly opt out (the default option is to participate in the system). During this transition period the portion of taxable income subject to this requirement will increase from 40 percent in the first year to 70 percent in the second, and finally 100 percent in the third year. After 2015 compulsory participation will be fully implemented.

Collective Voluntary Retirement Savings Plans (Ahorro Previsional Voluntario Colectivo) and Incentives for Medium- and Low-Income Workers

In Chile, as in many other countries, voluntary retirement savings can benefit from tax exemptions. This type of saving is known as Voluntary Retirement

Savings (Ahorro Previsional Voluntario [APV]). Workers can participate in APV plans through a special account at an AFP, special mutual funds offered by banks and other financial institutions, and life insurance contracts with savings. As a result of its design, this type of exemption mainly attracts voluntary savings from high-income individuals that are subject to higher marginal income tax rates. Regular tax exemptions do not offer incentives to participate in these plans to the majority of low- and medium-income workers because they do not pay income tax.

The reform implemented two mechanisms to increase salaried workers' voluntary savings in general, especially of those workers who do not benefit from regular tax exemptions. On the one hand, the government created the Ahorro Previsional Voluntario Colectivo (APVC) plans, a scheme that provides fiscal incentives to firms that offer their workers savings plans with supplementary contributions from the employer.[9] On the other hand, the reform created two additional incentives for voluntary individual savings: (1) workers can choose if the tax exemption is applied when making the contributions or upon withdrawal, and (2) workers can benefit from a government-funded bonus of 15 percent of their voluntary contributions (individual or collective) that is intended to increase the pension amount or prepare for retirement, subject to an annual limit.

Subsidies for Young Workers' Retirement Contributions

One unique aspect of defined contribution systems is that, as a result of the effect of compounding over a long period of time, early contributions can have a significant impact on the final benefit. For this reason, and to reduce youth unemployment, the government created a special subsidy to pay a portion of the pension contributions of employers that hire workers aged between 18 and 35 years. Specifically the government subsidizes employers by paying 50 percent of the pension cost (contribution plus commission) of a minimum wage worker, during the first 24 contributions for young workers whose compensation is equal to or less than 1.5 times the monthly minimum salary.

Additionally, these workers will receive a government-funded bonus equivalent to the hiring subsidy, which will be deposited directly in their individual account. This bonus is valid for the first 24 contributions between 18 and 35 years of age for a salary less than 1.5 times the minimum salary.

Government-Funded Grant to Mothers for Each Live Birth or Adoption

The reform introduced a grant for each live birth or adoption. The subsidy is equivalent to the full-time minimum salary contribution during 18 months and is increased by an annual rate of return (equal to the average net return of type C funds in the AFP system) from the day of birth until the mother turns 65. This benefit is subject to residency requirements but not to the income test.

Because Chile is among the countries in the region that experiences the longest periods of maternity leave (18 weeks) and at the same time has one of the lowest female labor participation rates, the introduction of this grant is important to achieve adequate levels of retirement benefits, particularly among low-income female workers. Beyond the financial benefit, the measure is valued as a kind of social recognition of the act (noncompensated) of giving birth and caring for children during their first months of life.

Separation of Disability Insurance Contracts between Men and Women and Transfer of the Premium Difference to the Individual Accounts of the Lower Cost Group

Before the reform, the premium charged by the Disability and Survivor's Insurance (Seguro de Invalidez y Sobrevivencia [SIS]) to participants in the AFP system was the same for men and women, despite the fact that it is less likely that women will become disabled and that they generate survivor's benefits for their husbands. To avoid this cross-subsidy, the reform required AFPs to contract separate insurance for men and women, to charge participants the higher of the new premiums (most likely the premium from the men's contract), and to deposit the difference in the savings accounts of the lower risk group (most likely women). As a result, women's final contribution to their pension funds will be slightly higher than the 10 percent required by law. This program is a way of maintaining a single-price insurance program for all participants while also increasing the amount of savings available to women upon retirement.

Contributory Pension System Performance before and after the 2008 Reform

Approximately 84 percent of the elderly population is covered by elderly pensions. The 2008 reform has noticeably impacted pension coverage for women, mostly of the noncontributory variety. The fiscal opening to fund this reform has been generated through the gradual reduction of the pension system deficit that remained as a result of the unification of the old system in individual accounts.

Coverage

The level of coverage provided through the contributory pension schemes directly depends on the capacity of workers to make frequent contributions. This is the case in both pay-as-you-go systems as well as their individually funded counterparts. In the first case, the benefit rules include minimum contribution requirements, and the agreed-upon replacement rates increase with the number of contributions (although usually with a maximum). In the funded systems, the pension depends on the accumulated balance at retirement, which comes from individual contributions and the financial rate of return they have accumulated.

For this reason a common coverage indicator is the so-called occupational coverage indicator, or the portion of occupied workers contributing to the pension system at a given time. Figure 5.4 shows this measure of coverage for the period 1975–2009, broken down among the pay-as-you-go regimes of the old system, Social Security Institute (Instituto de Previsión Social [IPS]) groups, and the AFP scheme. First, it is notable that aggregate occupational coverage was not significantly affected by the introduction of the new system. In the second place, this indicator of coverage appears to respond more readily to changes in the

Figure 5.4 Occupational Coverage, 1975–2009

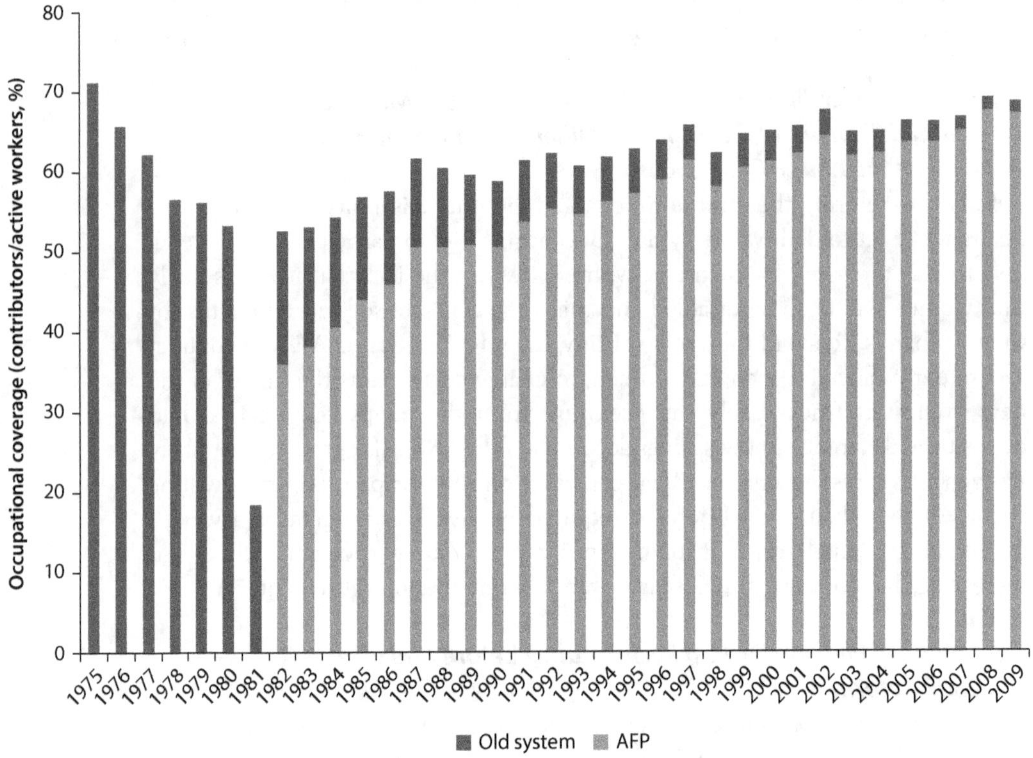

Source: 1975–99: Based on box 5 in Arenas de Mesa 2000. 2000–09: Based on the National Employment Survey (employed), statistics of total contributors from the Superintendent of Pensions (AFP contributors), and 2009 *IPS Statistical Yearbook* (contributors to the old system).
Note: The information for the AFP system in 1981 is not available.

macroeconomic environment, particularly the 1982 crisis. In the third place, one can appreciate the rapid transition from the pay-as-you-go scheme to the individually funded scheme; already in 1982 contributors to the new scheme represented 68 percent of the total and by 1999 they were 93 percent. The speed with which workers transitioned to the new system was at first due to the difference in the contribution ratio of the old system (above 20 percent) and the new system (initially around 13 percent, including the AFPs' commission). This difference was an important incentive for workers or their employers to change systems and increase their liquid income. Finally, by 2009 nearly 69 percent of employed workers were contributing to the pension system.

A more direct form of measuring pension system coverage consists of measuring the proportion of the elderly that receive pension income (contributory or noncontributory) or some type of occupational income. Table 5.3 presents the proportions of adults over 65 years that receive income from different sources, separated by gender, for the years 2006 (before the 2008 reform) and 2009–11 (postreform). Pension income consists of all income from any pension system and includes elderly, disability, widow, and orphan pensions.

Table 5.3 Proportion of Adults over 65 with Different Types of Income, 2006, 2009, and 2011
Percent

		Contributory pension income	Noncontributory pension income	Labor income	Any income
CASEN 2006	Women	54	19	3	77
	Men	69	14	10	93
	Total	61	17	6	84
CASEN 2009	Women	52	32	2	86
	Men	64	20	9	93
	Total	57	27	5	89
CASEN 2011	Women	56	26	2	84
	Men	67	17	8	92
	Total	61	22	5	88

Source: Based on Encuesta de Caracterización Socioeconómica Nacional (CASEN) 2006, 2009, and 2011.

In the aggregate, 84 percent of adults over 65 received some type of income in 2006. This figure increased to 89 percent in 2009 and fell slightly to 88 percent in 2011. The gender numbers show an important difference in favor of men. Ninety-three percent of them received some type of income in both periods, compared with 77 percent of women in 2006. The figure for women increased to 86 percent in 2009, which is basically explained by the increase in coverage via noncontributory pensions (the PASIS from 2006 that were replaced with the PBS in 2008). This measure fell slightly in 2011. Additionally, a significant portion of the gender difference comes from work income, where men display nearly 7 percentage points more than women in the three periods.

It is worth mentioning that the previous analysis was undertaken based on individual data, without considering indirect coverage that men and women can have through their spouses. This can be seen more clearly in figures 5.5, 5.6, and 5.7, which show the details for different age groups (men between 65 and 69, 70 and 74, 75 and 79, and 80 and older, followed by women in the same age groups) for the years 2006, 2009, and 2011. From the 2006 analysis, we can observe in the case of the men a significant percentage of individuals with income from their primary occupation (19 percent) in the 65–69 age group. The percentage is partially substituted by income from contributory pensions in the 70–74 age group but remains relatively stable in the subsequent groups (with a gradual decline in labor income). In the female case, on the other hand, we observe a persistent increase in the proportion of women with income from contributory pensions, explained by the greater propensity to receive widow pensions.

The outlook for 2009 and 2011 is qualitatively similar, except for the increased participation in noncontributory pensions (PBSs), especially among women. Finally, the figures for both years suggest that nearly 84 percent of adults over 65 receive some type of pension, although among women these pensions tend to be noncontributory, and, as a result, in lower amounts.[10]

Figure 5.5 Income by Type of Pension among the Elderly, by Gender, 2006

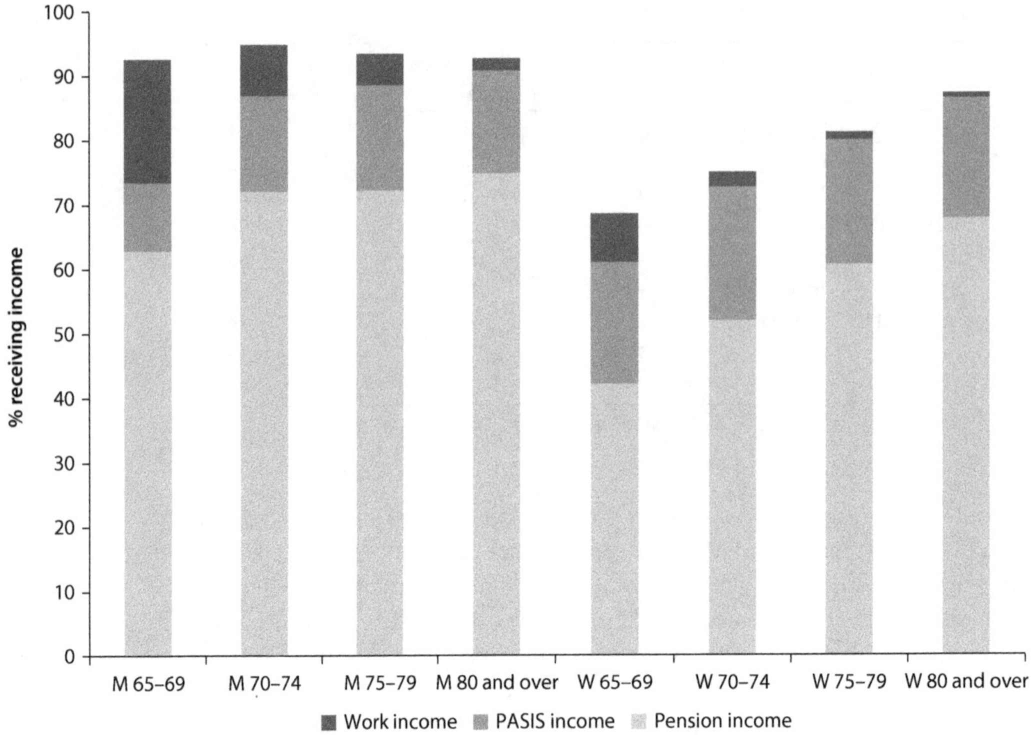

Source: Encuesta de Caracterízación Socioeconómica Nacional (CASEN) 2006.
Note: M signifies men and W signifies women. PASIS = Pensiones Asistenciales.

Benefit Adequacy

The analysis of coverage in the previous section focuses on income that the elderly receive, independent of the amount received. The adequacy of benefits refers to the level at which the benefits received allow for the appropriate replacement of income received while workers were actively employed. The best measure of this concept is the replacement rate, defined as the portion of preretirement taxable income that is received via the pension.

Although official statistics for this measure do not exist, it is possible to make an estimate based on the system's aggregate statistics. First, the existing statistics for benefits currently being paid for elderly pensions are in table 5.4. In April 2012 the government paid nearly one million elderly pensions in Chile, of which 63 percent were paid using funds from the AFP system. The average contributory pension was US$386. Pensions paid by the AFP system are divided approximately equally between scheduled withdrawals and annuity payments.[11] In general, early retirements (which were known as seniority retirements under the old system) feature much higher payouts than the pensions of retirees who retire at the minimum legal age. As a result, in the AFP system regulations require that

Figure 5.6 Income by Type of Pension among the Elderly, by Gender, 2009

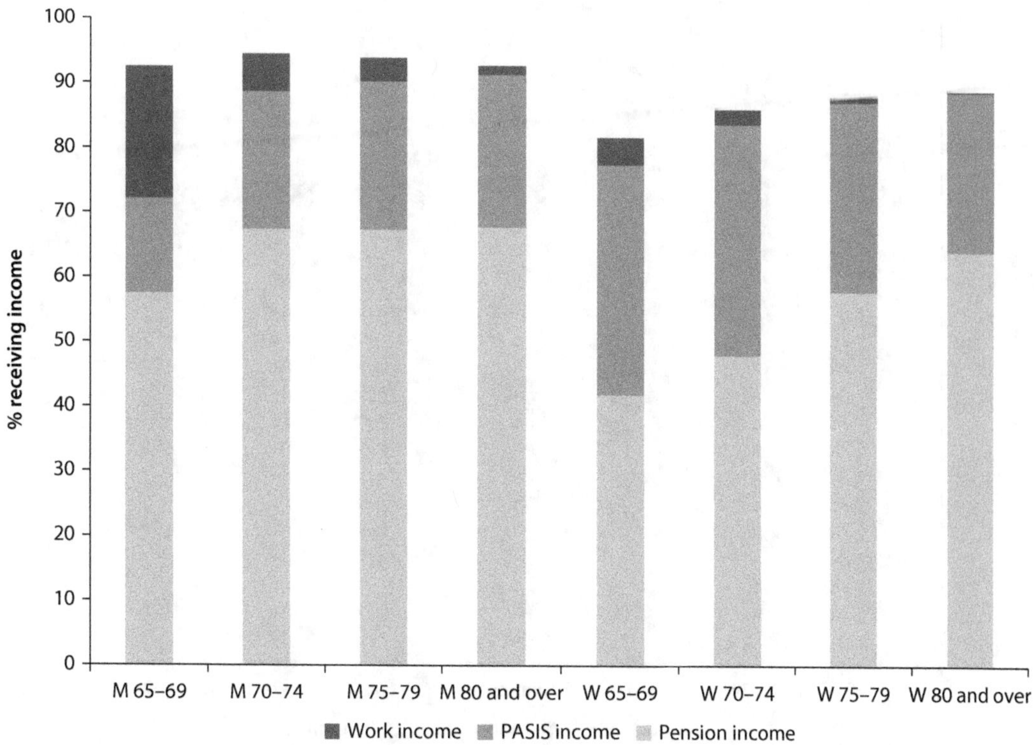

Source: Encuesta de Caracterízación Socioeconómica Nacional (CASEN) 2009.
Note: M signifies men and W signifies women. PASIS = Pensiones Asistenciales.

pension payments be more than 150 percent of the minimum pension to qualify for early retirement. For the regimes managed by the Social Security Institute (Instituto de Previsión Social [IPS]), the required surplus is even higher, creating a similar situation whereby the system requires a relatively high number of contributions in the case of seniority retirements.

It is striking that the pensions granted once the minimum age was reached under the private regimes administered by the IPS are virtually identical (on average) to those of the AFP system. Seniority retirements from this group are higher than their counterpart in the individually funded system, possibly as a result of the penalties for early retirements in the latter. Retirees from the public sector regimes managed by the IPS stand out because of the high payouts they receive (although they are small in relative terms) on average of US$1,172, or almost four times the average pension in the system. This difference is explained by the formulas used to calculate benefits: In these regimes, the pension is defined based on the retiree's final salary, in contrast to five-year average income in the social security regimes or the complete income history in the funded system.

Figure 5.7 Income by Type of Pension among the Elderly, by Gender, 2011

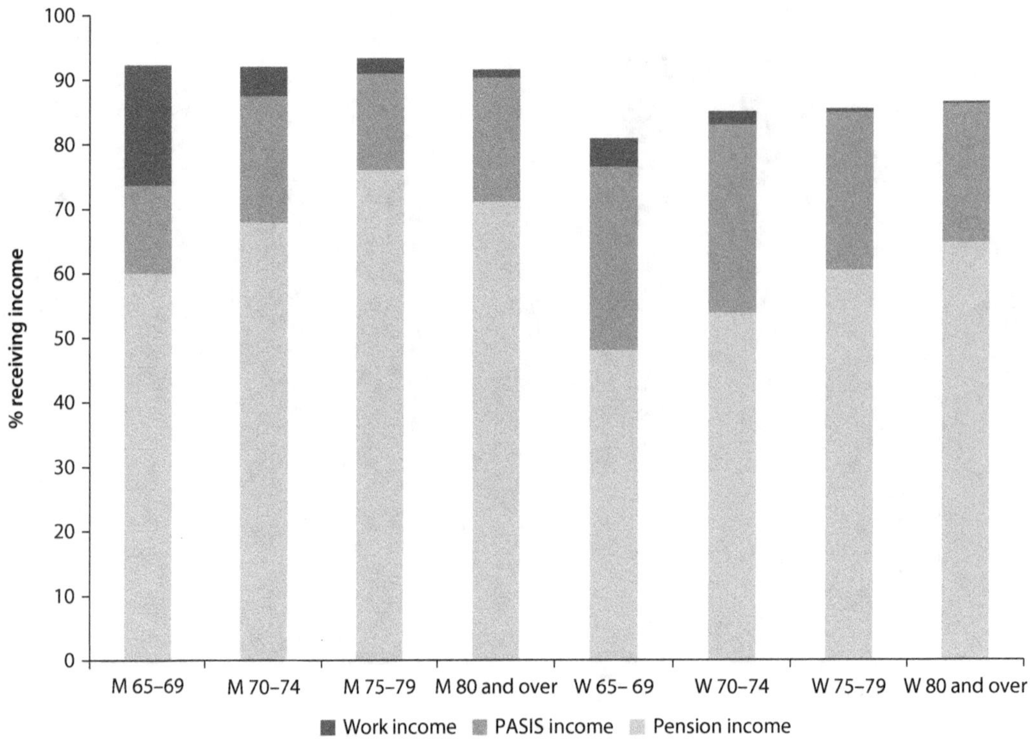

Source: Encuesta de Caracterízación Socioeconómica Nacional (CASEN) 2011.
Note: M signifies men and W signifies women. PASIS = Pensiones Asistenciales.

To express these figures as replacement rates, it is necessary to estimate the taxable income upon which current pensioners made their contributions. By calculating the average income of individuals close to retirement, we can approximate this value. Estimates show that, on average, men aged 55–60 years in March 2012 contributed based on an income equivalent to US$1,172 (table 5.4). Women from the same age group contributed based on an average income of US$1,096. As a result, the average worker paid into the pension system based on an income of US$1,145, which signifies a 33 percent replacement rate based on a worker's final salary for the AFP system.

Financial Sustainability

One of the principal challenges of a reform like the one implemented in Chile in 1980 is the significant fiscal cost associated with the transition from a pay-as-you-go scheme to a funded system. The state must continue to pay pension obligations made to contributors to the old system, without receiving the contributions of future participants in the system (because once the reform is in place these contributions will be invested in financial instruments). This is known as

Table 5.4 Elderly Pensions Paid in April (AFP) and January 2012 (IPS)

		Elderly at legal minimum age	*Early retirement*[a]	*Total*
Scheduled withdrawals	Number	281,111	25,967	307,078
	Average amount[b]	US$223	US$666	US$261
Annuity[c]	Number	96,788	216,912	313,700
	Average amount	US$509	US$480	US$489
AFP total	Number	377,899	242,879	620,778
	Average amount	US$296	US$500	US$376
IPS private sector	Number	290,782	18,979	309,761
	Average amount	US$292	US$732	US$319
IPS public sector	Number	24,755	23,626	48,381
	Average amount	US$1,172	US$688	US$936
IPS total	Number	315,537	42,605	358,142
	Average amount	US$361	US$708	US$402
System total	Number	693,436	285,484	978,920
	Average amount	US$326	US$531	US$386

Source: Based on statistics available at http://www.spensiones.cl.
a. Early retirement pensions correspond to, in the case of IPS-administered benefits, Seniority Retirement, which in general are equivalent to pensions paid before legal retirement age.
b. The amounts in U.S. dollars were obtained based on values reported on "Unidades de Fomento," (UF), a price indexed unit used in Chile, considering the value for the UF and the dollar observed on June 13, 2012, available at http://www.bcentral.cl; $22,627 per UF, $504.03 per U.S. dollar.
c. Only scheduled withdrawals and annuities were included in this analysis, excluding the temporary income option (9,093 pensions paid per month).

the transition cost of a substitutional reform. In Chile's case, this cost can be divided in two parts. The first is the difference between the pensions paid to the beneficiaries of the old system and the contributions of workers who decided to remain in the old system. This component is known as the IPS operational deficit. In the second component, those individuals that opted to change to the funded system will receive, subject to certain conditions, a recognition bonus from the state equal to the current value of the contributions they have made, payable once they reach the legal retirement age. This is the recognition bonds cost. At the same time, the government must fund the noncontributory pension programs. Before the 2008 reform, this spending was focused on the assistance pension program and the state-guaranteed minimum pension. Finally, the state must finance the deficit resulting from the armed forces and security services retirement systems, which were excluded from the 1980 reform.

Figure 5.8 shows the evolution of these components of fiscal spending for the period 1981–2004 and projected until 2025, according to information presented to the Presidential Advisory Committee (Consejo Asesor Presidencial) created before the 2008 reform. In aggregate terms, between 1981 and 2004 the civil social protection system added up to an average cost equivalent to 4.3 percent of annual GDP. The main component of this spending is the operational deficit, although its size has gradually shrunk as a result of the lower number of pensioners relative to GDP. Second, the recognition bonds grew consistently until

Figure 5.8 Estimated (1981–2004) and Forecasted (2005–25) Civil Pension Deficit

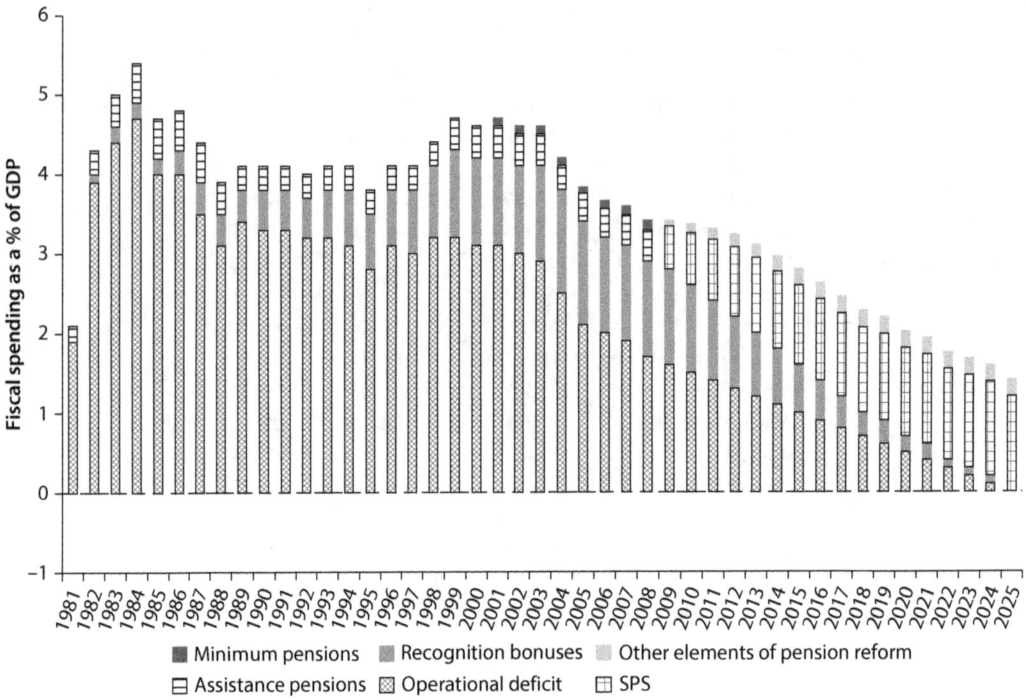

Source: Based on Arenas de Mesa 2006, Arenas de Mesa et al. 2008, and Arenas de Mesa and Ganas 2005.
Note: The period 1981–2004 is estimated in box 3 of Arenas de Mesa 2006. The 2005–10 forecast is in appendix box 2 in Arenas de Mesa 2006. The 2011–25 forecast of pension reform (SPS and others) is in box 9 in Arenas de Mesa et al. 2008. The 2011–25 forecast of recognition bonuses is based on box 7 in Arenas de Mesa and Ganas 2005. We assume a linear decrease for the IPS operational deficit from 2011 to 2025. SPS = Sistema de Pensiones Solidarias.

peaking in 2004 (at 1.3 percent of GDP). After this point their relative size has begun to gradually decrease. Assistance pensions have remained constant relative to GDP. In summary, the transition cost required a significant fiscal effort during the first 25 years of the reform although after 2003 it began to decrease. This was one of the key aspects that led policy makers to contemplate the creation of an NPS that granted noncontributory benefits higher than the PASIS to a large portion of the population.

This can be verified by the fiscal cost projections associated with the 2008 pension reform, which were divided into two components: the Solidarity Pension System (Sistema de Pensiones Solidarias [SPS]) and the other components of the reform (child bonus, young workers' subsidy, etc.).[12] The gradual reduction of the transition cost of the original reform opened up fiscal space for the introduction of a noncontributory pillar that cost more than the PASIS and the minimum guaranteed pension programs combined. According to the projections in Arenas et al. (2008), by 2025 the SPS will require increased spending of 0.8 percent of GDP, relative to the cost projections for PASIS or PMG without the reform.

Ultimately, the contingent liabilities associated with the structural imbalance of the pay-as-you-go systems were exposed with the 1980 reform, requiring the state to generate significant fiscal savings during the first 25 years of the reform. The gradual reduction in these liabilities allowed the government to later focus its effort on the noncontributory pillar of poverty prevention. By 2025 this effort will cost about 1.2 percent of GDP per year.

The Political Economy behind the Reforms

The previous reforms to extend the coverage of other social benefits contributed to the introduction of the noncontributory pillar in an environment of broad political consensus. This unified position also allowed policy makers to introduce changes to promote competition among plan administrators in the contributory regime.

In Arenas de Mesa (2010), the author explains that the 2008 Pension Reform began to develop in the mid-1990s as the result of growing dissatisfaction with the expected coverage levels of the existing system. The centrist coalition governments that governed Chile from the return to democracy until 2010 (the Concertación de Partidos por la Democracia, or Concertación) implemented in its first three administrations significant social structural reforms in the fields of education (Complete School Day), justice (Criminal Procedure Reform), labor market (introduction of Unemployment Insurance), and health (creation of the Universal Access with Explicit Guarantees).

Additionally, at the beginning of the 2000s, the government created microlevel databases that allowed it to produce more accurate projections of expected coverage levels under the contributory and noncontributory pillars.[13] One example of these analyses are the works of Berstein, Larrain, and Pino (2004, 2005, and 2006), which clearly established the low contribution density of Chilean workers (especially women) and the high proportion of workers that retired in the following years with pensions below the minimum pension, but who were not able to access the state-guaranteed benefit because they did not meet minimum contribution requirements. Based on this situation, President Michelle Bachelet chose pension system reform as the central theme of her electoral campaign and later administration, keeping the AFP system as the foundation of the contributory pillar, but making significant reforms in terms of coverage and competition.

The main element in improving coverage was the reform of the noncontributory pillar, replacing the PASIS and PMG programs with the SPS. Based on direct support from the Budget Directorate (Dirección de Presupuesto) for the fiscal sustainability of this type of change, the introduction of the Solidarity Pillar enjoyed wide approval from across the political spectrum.

The policies to increase competition among AFPs, exemplified in the proposal to tender for public bids the right to enroll new participants in the system to facilitate the entrance of new players in the industry, faced pressure from the financial conglomerates in charge of the AFPs, on the one hand, and the influence of other political groups in favor of completely reforming the contributory system and returning to a pay-as-you-go scheme, on the other (Arenas de Mesa 2010).

Ultimately the key to the political negotiations was the idea that the reform was a single project that could not be subdivided. This created sufficient consensus to approve not only the popular reform to the noncontributory pillar, but also the reform to increase competition.

Expected and Observed Impacts

Approximately 500,000 elderly adults will join the ranks of those receiving solidarity pensions during the next decade. Women are expected to continue to make up the majority of this group of beneficiaries. The fiscal cost associated with this pillar is projected to reach 1.2 percent of GDP.

The new SPS began to pay benefits July 1, 2008.[14] In the beginning, only elderly and disability PBS benefits were paid, and most of these beneficiaries were transferees from the elderly and disability Assistance Pension system.[15] Starting in October 2008, the government began to pay Solidarity Pension Contributions (APS), although these represented just a small fraction of total benefits.

As table 5.5 shows, during September 2009 the government paid 623,296 solidarity subsidies, of which 95 percent were PBS elderly pensions (62 percent) and disability pensions (33 percent). Sixty-four percent of benefits were paid to women.

The limited importance of the APS relative to the PBS appears to be a temporary phenomenon arising from two causes. On the one hand, the majority of current PBS beneficiaries were previously PASIS beneficiaries. Many of these individuals are pensioners who retired, exhausted their retirement accounts, and began to receive the assistance benefit. Pensioners with low balances receive an APS benefit from the beginning. On the other hand, pensioners who were over 65 and participating in the scheduled withdrawal program can temporarily qualify for the APS benefit when they choose, and the benefit is calculated based on their balance when they make the request. This means that many individuals with low balances in their retirement accounts prefer to maintain the minimum pension (currently around US$210) until they exhaust their balance and then solicit the APS benefit (which is equal to the PBS benefit, or about US$150, because the individual no longer has a personal retirement balance).[16] This process will occur gradually, and will slowly increase the number of APS beneficiaries.

With regard to benefit amounts, the law established that in the beginning the PBS benefits would be US$120 per month. These benefits were increased to approximately US$150 per month in July 2009. Table 5.6 shows the average benefit amounts paid each month by type of benefit and beneficiary gender.[17]

It should be noted that in the beginning, average APS benefits should always be less than PBS benefits. In the preceding table, that is not the case because of the inclusion of first-time payments, which can include more than one monthly payment and as a result are usually higher. This situation should normalize itself over time.

Figure 5.9 shows the projection until 2025 prepared by the Budget Directorate (Arenas de Mesa et al. 2008). It is apparent that the APS will play a dominant role in benefits paid out by the system, exceeding PBS benefits. In the same

Table 5.5 Number of PBS and APS Paid per Month, July 2008 to September 2009

	Men				*Women*				*Total*			
	PBS elderly	*PBS disability*	*APS elderly*	*APS disability*	*PBS elderly*	*PBS disability*	*APS elderly*	*APS disability*	*PBS elderly*	*PBS disability*	*APS elderly*	*APS disability*
July 2008	101,418	84,277	—	—	189,152	108,433	—	—	290,570	192,710	—	—
Aug. 2008	101,669	84,831	—	—	190,467	109,473	—	—	292,136	194,304	—	—
Sept. 2008	108,162	84,559	—	—	221,383	108,959	—	—	329,545	193,518	—	—
Oct. 2008	110,075	84,437	955	229	230,808	108,604	2,444	217	340,883	193,041	3,399	446
Nov. 2008	111,136	84,286	1,159	294	236,178	108,404	3,067	290	347,314	192,690	4,226	584
Dec. 2008	113,630	84,823	1,234	348	244,815	109,628	3,251	352	358,445	194,451	4,485	700
Jan. 2009	114,748	85,291	1,765	481	249,383	110,901	4,434	468	364,131	196,192	6,199	949
Feb. 2009	115,183	85,481	2,132	584	251,808	111,775	5,048	596	366,991	197,256	7,180	1,180
Mar. 2009	115,759	85,609	2,584	703	254,074	112,459	5,703	787	369,833	198,068	8,287	1,490
Apr. 2009	116,177	85,787	3,131	922	255,795	113,104	6,499	1,119	371,972	198,891	9,630	2,041
May 2009	116,638	86,085	3,842	1,125	258,094	114,003	7,208	1,372	374,732	200,088	11,050	2,497
June 2009	116,982	86,441	4,373	1,346	260,086	114,983	7,817	1,674	377,068	201,424	12,190	3,020
July 2009	117,124	86,710	4,882	1,670	261,334	116,028	8,395	2,118	378,458	202,738	13,277	3,788
Aug. 2009	117,348	87,229	5,603	1,969	261,917	117,514	9,052	2,469	379,265	204,743	14,655	4,438
Sept. 2009	117,430	87,678	15,010	2,203	267,244	118,761	12,193	2,777	384,674	206,439	27,203	4,980

Source: Fajnzylber 2010, elaborated based on information available at http://www.spensiones.cl.
Note: — = Not available.

Table 5.6 Average PBS and APS Amount per Month (U.S. Dollar Equivalent), July 2008 to September 2009

	Men				*Women*				*Total*			
	PBS elderly	*PBS disability*	*APS elderly*	*APS disability*	*PBS elderly*	*PBS disability*	*APS elderly*	*APS disability*	*PBS elderly*	*PBS disability*	*APS elderly*	*APS disability*
July 2008	120	120	—	—	120	120	—	—	120	120		
Aug. 2008	120	120	—	—	120	120	—	—	120	120		
Sept. 2008	120	120	—	—	120	120	—	—	120	120		
Oct. 2008	126	121	401	314	132	120	316	326	130	121	340	320
Nov. 2008	124	121	148	134	128	121	126	142	127	121	132	138
Dec. 2008	129	125	175	116	132	129	122	120	131	127	137	118
Jan. 2009	124	125	221	182	125	130	174	163	125	128	188	172
Feb. 2009	123	124	147	150	124	129	118	158	124	127	126	154
Mar. 2009	123	124	156	135	123	129	116	157	123	127	129	147
Apr. 2009	122	125	180	173	122	129	146	195	122	127	157	185
May 2009	122	126	172	148	123	131	121	151	122	129	139	150
June 2009	122	127	140	140	123	133	113	147	123	130	122	144
July 2009	152	157	174	207	152	164	151	210	152	161	160	209
Aug. 2009	154	159	207	183	152	168	163	187	153	164	180	185
Sept. 2009	152	159	132	169	158	166	157	173	156	163	143	172

Source: Fajnzylber 2010, elaborated based on information available at http://www.spensiones.cl.
Note: To calculate the U.S. dollar equivalent we used an exchange rate of Ch$500 per US$1. — = not available.

Figure 5.9 Projection of Solidarity Pension System Beneficiaries, 2009–25

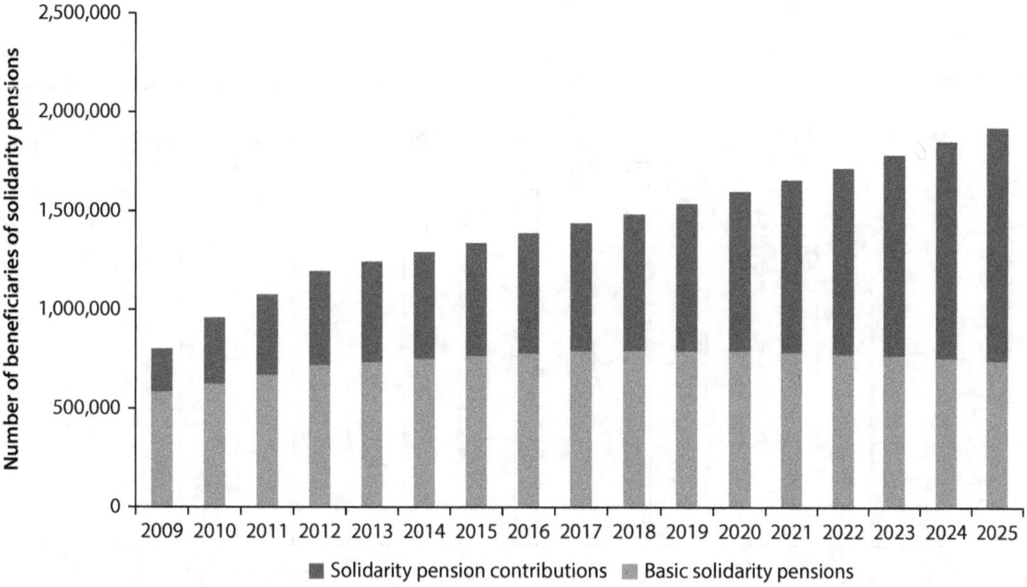

Source: Arenas de Mesa et al. 2008.

projection, policy makers estimate that the solidarity system will continue favoring women over men.

As we mentioned earlier, the government's fiscal participation in income transfers to the elderly as a result of the 1980 reform was concentrated in paying the transition cost to the funded system (the impact of which began to decline as a fraction of GDP from the mid-2000s on) and in financing the SPS. On top of these items, a series of lesser costs is added to pay for other elements of the pension reform. These are presented in figure 5.10. Although the SPS is certainly the main source of social protection spending, the youth hiring incentives and child bonuses will represent a not insignificant cost in terms of GDP in 2025.

One of the concerns associated with the introduction of the noncontributory pillar is the impact it could have, both as an income effect and a substitution effect, on the incentive to work in the formal sector and make pension contributions. The income effect comes from the increased potential earnings in the noncontributory system, while the substitution effect comes from the fact that the benefit structure signifies an implicit tax on individual savings of around 30 percent. Valdés Prieto (2007) argues that the design of a system like the SPS can offer stronger incentives in favor of individual savings than the previous PASIS and PMG programs. However, he also posits that there is a risk that political economy will favor raising the system's floor (the PBS) without necessarily accompanying such a change with an increase to the subsidy for higher-value pensions (because of the high fiscal cost that is a part of the second component).

Figure 5.10 Projected Fiscal Cost for Different Line Items as a Result of the 2008 Reform, 2009–25

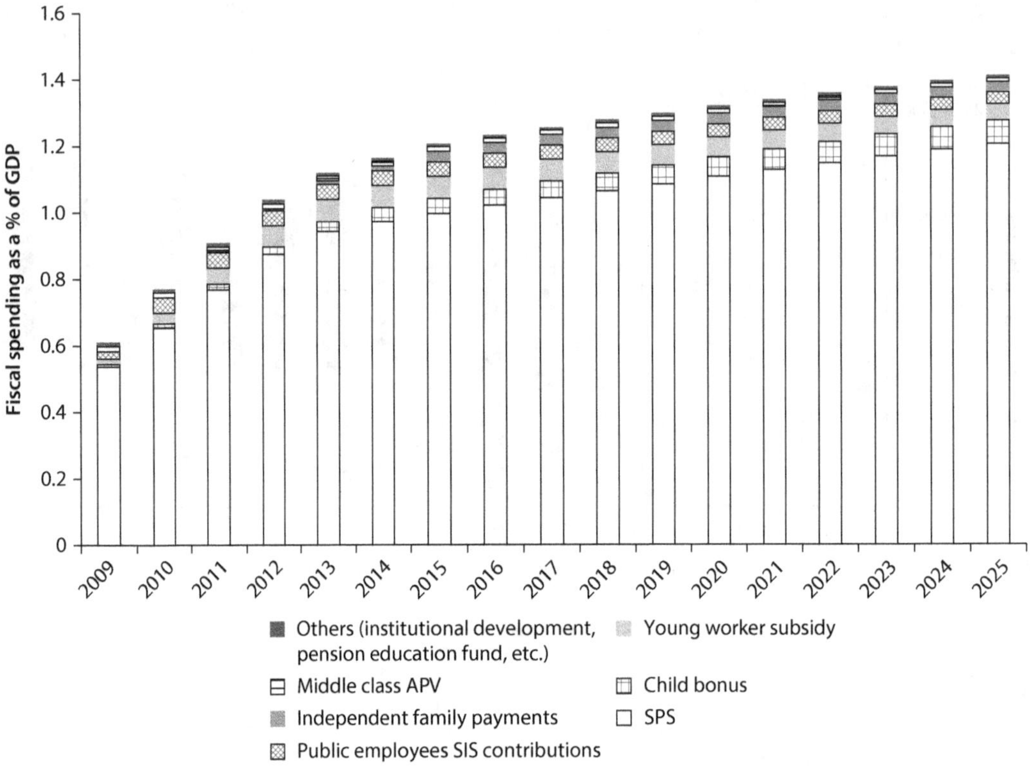

Source: Based on box 9 in Arenas de Mesa et al. 2008.
Note: APV = Voluntary Retirement Savings (Ahorro Previsional Voluntario); GDP = gross domestic product; SIS = Seguro de Invalidez y Sobrevivencia; SPS = Sistema de Pensiones Solidarias.

This would imply an increase on the implicit tax on individual savings that could have further negative effects on the incentives for formal employment. Nonetheless, there are no current studies that have estimated the reform's empirical effect on labor participation.

Challenges to Implementation

In the first two years of implementation, the targeting tool used to qualify individuals for SPS access was the preexisting tool for access to social programs, the Social Protection Profile. Once implementation was underway, policy makers designed and adjusted the income verification tool, known as the pension targeting score.

During the first years of President Bachelet's administration, the government began implementation of a new public transport plan for the capital, known as Transantiago. The plan's implementation quickly became a large-scale crisis because of serious planning and incentive problems that created major challenges for those trying to travel throughout Santiago.

This event was on policy makers' minds during the planning of the pension reform. The government took all the necessary steps to ensure that the introduction of the new system of solidarity pensions was as quick as possible. According to Délano (2010), policy makers made the following key operating decisions: (1) the state assuming responsibility for legal background, to ease access, (2) establishment of standards and indicators of the quality of service to beneficiaries, (3) use of state-of-the-art technology, (4) strengthening and diversifying in-person and remote channels, (5) development of backup systems and options in the event of failures, and (6) prioritization of the use of national and regional mass media.

One of the most complex aspects of the process of awarding solidarity pensions is determining the poverty level of the beneficiary. The concept of affluence introduced in the reform was slightly different from the concept widely used in general social programs. Faced with the possibility of operational problems while starting up the system, the reform included the option to use the Social Protection Profile system used to award other government benefits during the first two years. The current targeting system, pension targeting scoring, was introduced later. It combines elements of the Social Protection Profile with other administrative records from various government agencies.

The reform used existing IPS payment systems, utilized for paying pensions under the old system as well as other government benefits, to make payments under the new system.

Other Services for the Elderly Linked to These Programs

Health insurance and provision of health benefits is the responsibility of a public system, the National Health Fund (Fondo Nacional de Salud [FONASA]), and a private system, the Pension Health Institutions (Instituciones de Salud Previsional [ISAPRE]), in which workers are affiliated. The process of joining is conditioned on payment capacity and the private insurers' risk selection process, which lacks regulation and to the detriment of the public system, where most members with low payment capacity and higher costs are concentrated. Seventy-nine percent of elderly adults are covered by FONASA.

History of Health Services Provision

The first system of health insurance and provision of services with wide coverage was the National Health Service (Servicio Nacional de Salud [SNS]). It was implemented in 1952 and unified various public bodies that had offered health services, mainly covering workers and indigents. After 1964, the government made significant investments in assistance centers, training, and enrollment of employees (it eventually had 120,000 employees). By 1972 the number of hospitals had increased by 7.5 percent (compared to 1964), and the number of health centers and infirmaries had increased by 78 percent, covering much of the country's geographic area.

After the military coup in 1973, the SNS continued, but with notable funding reductions (Unger et al. 2008). In 1979 the SNS was dismantled, and the

National System of Health Services (Sistema Nacional de Servicios de Salud [SNSS]) was created. In the insurance sector, FONASA was created in the public sector with the mission of managing the compulsory contributions for workers that chose to be insured by this fund. FONASA was divided in four groups: group A for indigents, B for low-income individuals (who are treated for free in the public health system), and C and D for individuals with greater payment capacity (and who make copayments for health services).

Alternatively, the ISAPRE institutions were allowed to proliferate as private insurers that could compete with FONASA to insure the population. These institutions were almost completely unregulated, with the ability to choose which risks they wanted to cover. This reform signified a break with the "risk pooling" model of the previous system, leaving the ISAPRE with a portfolio biased toward young individuals, men, and individuals with relatively high purchasing power. The most costly beneficiaries were left for FONASA, which continued insuring relatively more costly individuals with fewer resources. This created a high discrepancy in the cost per beneficiary between the two systems (Unger et al. 2008).

In terms of the provision of health services, primary care was decentralized to the municipalities, with the subsequent appearance of inequalities based on funding capacity and, above all, system management. Secondary care in the public sector was fundamentally based in hospitals located in the main cities and health clinics. Additionally, significant and rapid development of private hospitals and clinics ensued to attend the beneficiaries of the ISAPRE system.

This dual system of insurance/provision still prevails today, save some changes. In terms of attention to the elderly, there has not been a specific system for this group, and they have been integrated into FONASA or ISAPRE according to their payment capacity (which depends, in most cases, on the pension they receive). However, because in general they have lower payment capacity and higher expected risk (the ISAPRE institutions have applied risk selection processes permanently), they have tended to join FONASA.

Table 5.7 shows the distribution of the general population, the elderly population (65 and over), the group from 65 to 75 years old, and the group over 75 years by type of health insurance. It is apparent that between 2000 and 2009 FONASA consistently received a proportion of the elderly population that was much higher than their proportion of the general population. Thus, for example, in 2000 FONASA covered 65 percent of the population while insuring 82 percent of the elderly and 84 percent of the elderly over 75 years. During 2009, the situation was similar (79 percent of the general population and 87 percent of the elderly). In contrast, the elderly insured by the ISAPRE institutions did not reach 6 percent, even when these institutions insured 13 percent of the population. The table shows, moreover, that the elderly are mostly in groups A and B in FONASA, and that this trend has increased markedly in 2006 and 2009. Additionally, we observe that practically all elderly adults have some type of health coverage. This trend has also grown stronger over time. By 2009, only 1.4 percent of the elderly lacked health insurance.

Table 5.7 Distribution of the Elderly by Type of Health Insurance, 2000, 2003, 2006, and 2009

	FONASA A	FONASA B	FONASA C	FONASA D	Total FONASA	ISAPRE	Other	None	Unknown
2000									
Total population	24.0	20.5	8.9	10.9	65.5	20.8	3.5	9.7	0.6
Over 65	23.8	41.6	5.9	9.0	82.0	6.5	5.9	5.2	0.4
65–75 years	22.3	40.5	6.4	9.9	80.6	8.2	5.3	5.3	0.6
Over 75	26.3	43.5	5.1	7.5	84.2	3.5	7.0	5.1	0.2
2003									
Total population	27.9	23.1	11.7	8.0	71.7	16.7	3.3	7.3	1.1
Over 65	25.5	43.0	5.9	7.7	83.5	6.2	5.7	3.7	0.9
65–75	24.8	41.8	6.4	8.7	83.0	7.1	5.1	4.0	0.8
Over 75	26.5	44.7	5.0	6.1	84.3	4.8	6.6	3.2	1.1
2006									
Total population	29.4	24.2	12.8	8.8	76.9	13.5	3.2	5.1	1.4
Over 65	35.4	38.4	5.4	7.0	88.3	4.3	4.8	1.8	0.7
65–75	34.6	37.5	5.8	8.2	88.1	4.9	4.5	1.9	0.6
Over 75	36.6	39.6	4.7	5.2	88.7	3.4	5.4	1.7	0.9
2009									
Total population	31.5	24.3	11.5	6.8	78.8	13.1	2.9	3.5	1.8
Over 65	43.3	30.6	3.7	5.0	87.5	5.6	4.1	1.4	1.4
65–75	43.7	30.0	4.2	5.6	87.7	6.3	3.4	1.4	1.2
Over 75	42.7	31.6	3.1	4.3	87.2	4.7	5.1	1.4	1.7

Source: Based on Encuesta de Caracterízación Socioeconómica Nacional (CASEN) 2000, 2003, 2006, and 2009.

Inclusive Health Insurance Reform

With the objective of dealing with the inequalities of access to system benefits, in 2005 the Universal Access with Explicit Guarantees (Acceso Universal con Garantías Explícitas [AUGE]) reform was introduced. This reform defined a floor of minimum benefits for which medical attention was guaranteed through a set of established protocols. The elderly were particularly impacted by the greater use of medical services because they have obtained greater coverage given the type of sicknesses and illnesses included in the minimum benefits. The projections for health spending for the elderly predict a substantial increase in the near future.

The Chilean health system has undergone constant reforms, none of which have significantly changed its underlying duality. However, in 2005 the government implemented perhaps the most ambitious reform since 1979. The so-called AUGE reform did not seek to change how the system worked through structural changes, but instead by empowering the system's users. The reform sought to reduce the access and quality gaps between users of the public and private systems, while financially protecting the beneficiaries of both systems (Infante and Paraje 2010).

The reform's political process was, as is almost always the case with this type of initiative, tortuous (Lenz 2007). The government's original idea was not just to improve access for the most disadvantaged societal groups, but also to change some structural factors of the Chilean health system that had been present since 1980. Specifically, the government proposed financing the reform with contributions from the beneficiaries of the private ISAPRES system and to create a risk Compensation Fund between FONASA and the ISAPRES institutions. In practice, this fund would transfer resources from the private system to the public system (due to the lower relative risk in the private portfolio), although it would also incentivize the ISAPRE institutions to compete for high-risk individuals (by receiving resources from this fund that would, in theory, be sufficient to cover the higher risk). This idea, nonetheless, was rejected after facing threats from various sectors (among them the ISAPRE institutions) to boycott the reform.

The reform created a list of conditions based on an algorithm designed according to certain predetermined criteria (sickness burden, cost effectiveness, socioeconomic access differences, high cost, etc.). In practice, however, just a couple criteria explained the vast majority of the diseases selected: high sickness burden and social preferences (Vargas and Poblete 2008). In total, 25 sicknesses were selected initially, although this group quickly increased to the 69 that are currently included. For these sicknesses, the government defined protocols that guaranteed timely medical attention once the disease was detected. These protocols ensured a basic level of quality, at least from a medical point of view. Additionally, the reform offered financial protection: If the annual spending on AUGE diseases exceeded a predetermined level (as a function of the insured's income), then the insured was no longer liable to pay according to the type of insurance carried.

Some of the diseases selected among the group to be guaranteed directly affect the elderly and treatment of these conditions can improve their quality of life. This is the case with hip replacement for persons over 65 with osteoarthritis of the hip with severe functional limitations, acquired pneumonia outpatient treatment in persons over 65, refraction defects in persons over 65, orthopedics (or technical aids) for persons over 65, bilateral hypoacusis (hearing loss) in persons over 65 that requires use of a hearing aid, and integral dental health for adults 60 and over. Nonetheless, other ailments have a relatively high prevalence among the elderly even when their treatment is not restricted to a certain age group. For example, this is the case with cataract operations or medical treatment in persons 55 years and older with mild or moderate osteoarthritis of the hip and/or knee.

AUGE has covered a little more than 14 million cases, from its beginning through December 2011. Of these, 9.5 percent (some 1.3 million cases) belong to pathologies exclusive to the elderly. Among these cases, a little more than 51 percent are treatment for refraction defects, 18 percent provision of orthopedics, 1.6 percent walking pneumonia, and 9.7 percent integral dental health treatments, and the rest is divided almost equally among hip replacement and bilateral hearing loss. In almost 99 percent of the cases, the FONASA beneficiaries were the users of AUGE for these ailments/treatments.

A comprehensive impact study of the AUGE reform has not been performed. Nonetheless, information and some studies on user evaluations, epidemiological results, and post-AUGE changes in inequalities exist. For example, Bitrán, Escobar, and Gassibe (2010) find that for hypertension, type I and II diabetes, and depression access was increased. Survival rates also increased for these ailments, as well as for epilepsy and HIV/AIDS. This study does not examine the rest of the guaranteed conditions, but focuses only on these six.

In terms of changes in inequality and equity, Paraje and Vásquez (2012) analyze the use of health services (e.g., general practitioners, specialists, emergency rooms, or days of hospitalization) pre- and postreform. Comparing service utilization from 2003 to 2009, the authors find a minor change or no change in the most commonly used indicators of inequality. In this sense, the reform was successful in increasing the usage of services, but not as much in diminishing the socioeconomic gaps related to health service utilization. In terms of financial protection, information does not exist either, although there are indications that the AUGE reform has had a minor effect, given the health care costs that households in Chile are still paying postreform.

In terms of the elderly population, no comprehensive studies exist on the financial burden that sicknesses impose on this group. As in the majority of countries, this group would be linked with greater morbidity and treatments that on average cost more. There are some estimates for the copayments incurred by the elderly (60 years and over) in the ISAPRE system. As was mentioned earlier, this group's participation in the private insurance system is relatively low. Nonetheless, by examining this partial data, we can gain an idea of the level of effective insurance in this group.

Figure 5.11, taken from Cid, Muñoz, and Pezoa (2008), shows the evolution of average copayments for outpatient and in-patient services for elderly adults (60 and over) and for the entire population. Several facts stand out. In the first place, the copayment made by the elderly exceeds the general population average in both cases because the ISAPRE plans set copayments for different conditions and an upper limit. This means that these plans cover 70 percent of the cost of treatment up to a determined limit, for example. In the case of relatively expensive treatments, patients reach the plan's limit quickly, and their effective copayment ends up being much higher than what their insurance plan contributes.

In the second place, the figure shows that the copayments for the elderly (and for the whole population) are relatively high, although they have decreased since 2005 (presumably as a result of the AUGE reform). In the case of outpatient attention, for example, the minimum copayment observed is from June 2008 and is a little more than 38 percent. In the case of in-patient hospital attention (which has a lower copayment, but is usually more expensive) the minimum copayment exceeds 28 percent. In both cases, the copayments are relatively high and indicate that the insurance system has low effective coverage. Knaul et al. (2011) arrive at similar conclusions.

Figure 5.11 Copayments in ISAPRE as a Percentage of the Billed Cost per Beneficiary, by Type of Attention and Age, 2001–08

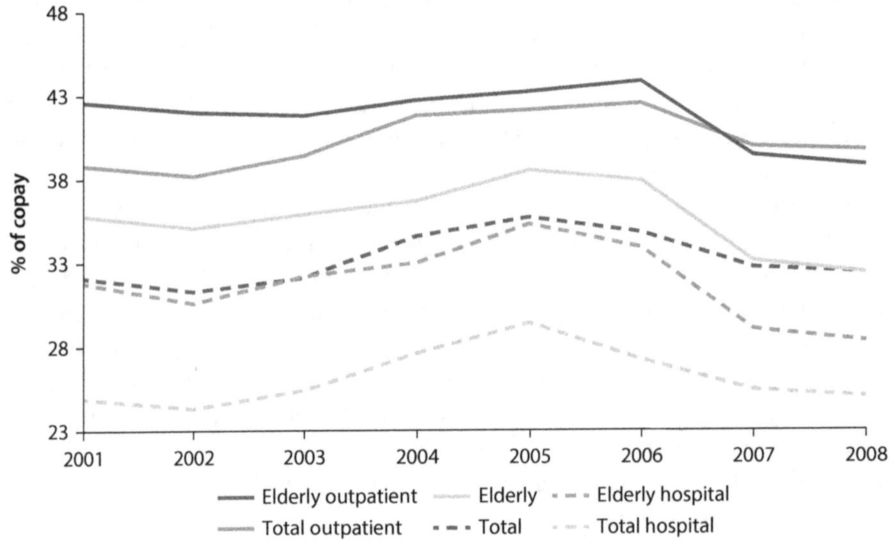

Source: Cid, Muñoz, and Pezoa 2008.

Spending on medicines must be added to the previously mentioned costs. The cost of medicines is not covered under ISAPRE plans, nor by FONASA for the majority of ailments. According to Olivares-Tirado and Salazar (2006), by 2000 spending on medicines represented a little more than half of the out-of-pocket health costs for FONASA beneficiaries and about 30 percent for ISAPRE beneficiaries. The same study found that, on average, the elderly take seven or more medicines daily, highlighting them as the group for which this kind of spending is relatively more significant.

Based on population projections, which show population aging occurring, and using current utilization rates for in-patient and outpatient procedures, Olivares-Tirado and Salazar (2006) forecast health spending up to 2020 (figure 5.12). According to this estimate, total health spending will increase a little more than 120 percent between 2010 and 2020, with hospitalization costs and outpatient medical attention accounting for the majority of total costs.

Conclusions and Future Challenges

Chile's rapid completion of the demographic transition means that social protection systems for the elderly are becoming more important in economic terms. This has two clear areas of influence. On the one hand, there is the fiscal or public area, in which the government should increase resources for this age group. This is particularly important from the health system perspective where, because of the existing segmentation in which the public insurance program

Figure 5.12 Projection of Health Costs for the Elderly, 2002–20

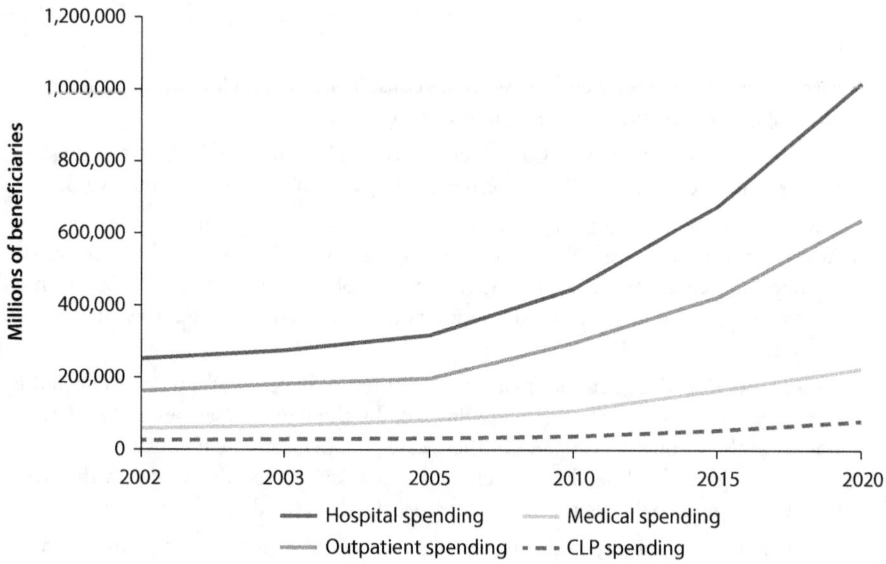

Source: Olivares-Tirado and Salazar 2006.
Note: CLP = Cuidados de Largo Plazo (long-term care).

covers the majority of the elderly, it is expected that an increasing proportion of total public spending on health will go to this age group. This phenomenon will also be accompanied by a displacement of medical attention to other groups because of the congestion in the use of health resources (doctors, hospital beds, equipment, etc.). Alternatively, a greater part of the new investment in the health sector will serve the needs of the elderly. From the pension system perspective, the 2008 reform signifies greater public sector participation in the financing of income after retirement.

On the other hand, there is a private or market environment, where the greater number and longer lifespans of the elderly will have greater effects on the labor market by requiring more savings effort during workers' economically active periods. Additionally, it is possible that retirement may have to be postponed and that the labor market will be transformed for this age group.

As much for the pensions sector as for the health sector, the recent reforms have been designed to expand coverage while offering a minimum standard of quality (the basic solidarity pension in the case of pension reform and a number of guaranteed pathologies in the case of health reform). The changes in recent years, although they have implied significant fiscal effort, represent important advances in the context of social security in Latin America. In both reforms, however, the guarantees are minimal (for example, US$160 for the PBS). To further advance in improving the quality of coverage, individuals will have to put forth more effort (through greater savings, higher out-of-pocket health spending, etc.), or the public sector will have to increase its involvement.

Notes

1. Simultaneously the government issued a series of labor regulations. See Arellano (1985).
2. Part of this redundancy was fixed with the consolidation of regimes under the Pension Normalization Institute, created one year before the 1980 reform.
3. It is important to mention that the armed forces and security services pension systems were not included in the 1980 reform, and they continue to operate independently.
4. This institution was originally created as the Superintendent of Pension Fund Administrators. Its area of responsibility was expanded with the 2008 reform to include supervision of the public entity in charge of administering the New System of Solidarity Pensions. With this expansion, its name changed to the Superintendent of Pensions.
5. As was mentioned earlier, the disability and survivor benefits of a worker covered by disability and survivor's insurance are financed by the worker's savings and a contribution from the insurance company. In these cases the pensions are expressed similarly to pay-as-you-go and defined benefit schemes: a portion (replacement rate) of the worker's average income during the 10 years before death or the disability eligibility request.
6. Beneficiaries of disability and survivor pensions could also receive benefits from the minimum guaranteed pension subject to other minimum contribution requirements.
7. This section is based on Rofman, Fajnzylber, and Herrera (2010).
8. The APS was first paid to those individuals whose contributory pensions were less than US$161 and belonged to the poorest 40 percent of the population in July 2008. This range was progressively increased until 2012, when the benefit included those that received less than US$586 through their contributory pensions and belonged to the poorest 60 percent of the population.
9. The Ahorro Previsional Voluntario Colectivo plans follow the same principle as 401K plans in the United States and other defined contribution occupational plans applied in other countries. Employers can establish savings contracts with any institution that offers individual APV plans (AFP, banks, mutual funds, and insurance companies), supplement contributions made by workers, and establish a minimum number of years of contributions to gain access to the contributions made by the employer. The conditions must be the same for all workers, and employers cannot, under any circumstances, restrict benefits to certain groups.
10. For a detailed discussion of the analysis in terms of coverage before the 2008 reform see Berstein et al. (2009), chapter 2.
11. It is important to note that not only individuals with pensions above the PBS can opt to receive annuity payments. In practice, among individuals that can choose, the portion that opts for annuity payments is much higher than 50 percent.
12. For greater detail on the projected fiscal costs associated with the pension reform, see Arenas de Mesa et al. (2008).
13. In particular, in 2001 the government organized a sample of around 24,000 system participants, which was used to create an administrative database of the individuals in the sample; the database is known as the Participant Pension Histories (Historias Previsionales de los Afiliados). The same sample was later used for the Social Protection Survey in 2002, 2004, 2006, and 2009.
14. A significant portion of this section was extracted from Fajnzylber (2010).

15. From January to June 2008, an average of 228,065 elderly Assistance Pensions and 212,327 disability pensions (PASIS) were paid (www.suseso.cl). Note that some of the disability pensions (PASIS) were paid to persons over age 65, meaning that the figures are not directly comparable with the PBS elderly and disability pensions that were paid beginning in July 2008.
16. As an example, a person whose pension is based on scheduled withdrawals of US$60 could opt to request the APS benefit, in which case he or she would receive US$190 for the rest of her life; or opt to remain adjusted to the minimum pension (US$210) until his or her balance is exhausted (which would occur in about four years) and receive the PBS pension from then on (US$150).
17. It is worthwhile to point out that the average amounts include payments made retroactively from the moment the application was received. For example, if a person requested an APS benefit July 1, 2008, and his or her first payment was made in October 2008, then that payment would be equivalent to four payments. This explains why the averages are higher than the maximum benefit (US$120 before July 2009 and US$139 after then that date) and why in the first months of APS payments, the amounts recorded are higher than the maximum benefit.

Bibliography

Arellano, J. P. 1985. "Políticas Sociales y Desarrollo 1924–1984." Estrategias de Desarrollo y Economía, Políticas Públicas, Cieplan.

Arenas de Mesa, A. 2000. "Cobertura previsional en Chile: Lecciones y desafíos del sistema de pensiones administrado por el sector privado." Serie Financiamiento del Desarrollo 105, CEPAL, Santiago.

———. 2006. "Informe de Diagnóstico para el Consejo Asesor para la Reforma Previsional. Tema 5: Los Compromisos Fiscales." Presentation at the Consejo Asesor Presidencial para la Reforma Previsional, March.

———. 2010. *Historia de la Reforma Previsional Chilena: Una Experiencia Exitosa de Política Pública en Democracia.* Santiago: International Labour Organization.

Arenas de Mesa, A., and P. Benavides. 2003. *Protección social en Chile. Financiamiento, cobertura y desempeño, 1990–2000.* Santiago: International Labour Organization.

Arenas de Mesa, A., P. Benavides, J. González, and L. Castillo. 2008. "La Reforma Previsional Chilena: Proyecciones Fiscales 2009–2025." Estudios de Finanzas Públicas, Dirección de Presupuesto, December.

Arenas de Mesa, A., and P. Ganas. 2005. "Proyecciones del Gasto Fiscal Previsional en Chile, Bonos de Reconocimiento: 2005–2038." Estudios de Finanzas Públicas, Dirección de Presupuesto, December.

Berstein, S., P. Castañeda, E. Fajnzylber, and G. Reyes. 2009. "Chile 2008: Una Reforma Previsional de Segunda Generación." Superintendencia de Pensiones de Chile, Santiago. http://www.spensiones.cl/573/article-6102.html.

Berstein, S., G. Larrain, and F. Pino. 2004. "Cobertura, densidad y pensiones en Chile: Proyecciones a 30 años plazo." Presented at the seminar "Competencia y Cobertura," Centro de Estudios Públicos y la Superintendencia de AFP, November 11–12, Santiago.

———. 2005. "Cobertura, densidad y pensiones en Chile: Proyecciones a 20 años plazo." Working paper 12, Serie Documentos de Trabajo Superintendencia de Administradoras de Fondos de Pensiones de Chile, November.

———. 2006. "Chilean Pension Reform: Coverage Facts and Policy Alternatives." *Economia* 6 (2): 227–79.

Bitrán, R., L. Escobar, and P. Gassibe. 2010. "After Chile's Health Reform: Increase in Coverage and Access, Decline in Hospitalization and Death Rates." *Health Affairs* 29 (12): 2161–69.

Cheyre, H. 1991. *La Previsión en Chile Ayer y Hoy.* 2nd ed. Santiago: CEP.

Cid, C., A. Muñoz, and M. Pezoa. 2008. "Evaluación de la Reforma de Salud en el Sistema Isapres y su Impacto en los Beneficiarios: Informe Final 2008." http://www.supersalud.cl/documentacion/569/article-5408.html.

Délano, M. 2010. "Reforma Previsional en Chile. Protección Social para Todos." International Labour Organization, Santiago.

Fajnzylber, E. 2010. *Marco Metodológico para el Análisis del Sistema de Pensiones Solidarias.* Consultancy Report, Inter-American Development Bank, January.

Godoy, O., and S. Valdés. 1994. "Democracia y Previsión en Chile: Experiencia con dos Sistemas." Cuadernos de Economía 93, Pontificia Universidad Católica de Chile, August.

Infante, A., and G. Paraje. 2010. "Reforma de Salud: Garantías Exigibles como Derecho Ciudadano." In *Las Nuevas Políticas de Protección Social en Chile*, edited by O. Larrañaga and D. Contreras. Santiago, Chile: Uqbar Editores.

Knaul, F., R. Wong, H. Arreola-Ornelas, and H. Méndez. 2011. "Household Catastrophic Health Expenditures: A Comparative Analysis of Twelve Latin American and Caribbean Countries." *Salud Pública de México* 53 (Supp 2): S85–95.

Lenz, R. 2007. "Proceso político de la reforma AUGE de salud en Chile: algunas lecciones para América Latina. Una Mirada desde la Economía Política." Serie Estudios Socio Económicos 38, CIEPLAN.

Olivares-Tirado, P., and E. Salazar. 2006. "Impacto Del Envejecimiento En El Gasto En Salud: Chile 2002–2020." Working paper, Superintendencia de Salud. http://www.supersalud.gob.cl/documentacion/569/w3-article-4021.html.

Paraje, G., and F. Vásquez. 2012. "Equity within the Chilean Health System: What Was the Impact of the AUGE Reform?" Draft manuscript, Santiago.

Rofman, R., E. Fajnzylber, and G. Herrera. 2008. "Reforming the Pension Reforms: The Recent Initiatives and Actions on Pensions in Argentina and Chile." Social Protection Discussion Paper 0831, World Bank, Washington, DC, May.

———. 2010. "Reformando las Reformas Previsionales en la Argentina y en Chile." Revista CEPAL 101, Chile, 85–109.

Unger, J., P. De Paepe, G. Solimano, and O. Arteaga. 2008. "Chile Neoliberal Health Reform: An Assessment and a Critique." *PLoS Medicine* 5 (4): e79.

Valdés Prieto, S. 2007. "Pensión solidaria: ventajas, defectos y propuestas." Temas de la Agenda Pública, Pontificia Universidad Católica de Chile, year 2, no. 13, December.

Vargas, V., and S. Poblete. 2008. "Health Prioritization: The Case of Chile." *Health Affairs* 27: 782–92.

CHAPTER 6

Colombia

Rafael Rofman

History

Although the history of social protection in Colombia began briefly at the end of the 19th century and the beginning of the 20th, the formation of a full-fledged pension system, with managing institutions and a more recent goal of broader coverage, began in earnest in the mid-1940s. During this period the National Social Protection Bank (Caja Nacional de Previsión Social [CAJANAL]) and the Colombian Institute of Social Security (Instituto Colombiano de Seguros Sociales [ICSS]) were created, which covered public and private sector workers, respectively. This system had very limited coverage and suffered serious management and financial problems from the beginning. These institutions' financial and management difficulties, the multiple reforms in operation rules, and the creation of special banks and funds for public workers (which achieved better conditions for their members according to their occupational area or region) worsened their sustainability problems. The serious financial difficulties led to a general restructuring, articulated in the 1991 constitution and Law no. 100 of 1993, which established that both the contribution salary and the minimum pension could not be less than the minimum legal salary. The restructuring set forth a mixed pension scheme that continues to this day.

The effectiveness of the contributory pension system that functioned in Colombia until 1993 was very limited in terms of the coverage offered to workers and the elderly. Only about 20 percent of active workers and a similar percentage of the elderly participated in the system as contributors or beneficiaries, while the rest of the society did not have any interaction with the system. The authors of the reform law passed in 1993 made reference to this situation in the act's preamble, stating. "The greatest fault of the current pension system is its low level of coverage" (MIDAS 2008). They attributed this problem to the high level of informality in the labor market, noting that "what a pension system reform can do to overcome the lack of coverage is ensure that the system does not have an adverse impact on economic growth and formal employment, eliminating the aspects that can promote evasion, and incentivize the participation of independent workers with savings capacity" (MIDAS 2008). In this context the reforms at the beginning of the 1990s were aimed at reducing the effect that the pension system would have on the job market, with the understanding that the main engine to promote greater coverage would be the formalization of the economy. However, as we will discuss in this chapter, this reform was not able to solve the fundamental problems in terms of coverage of the elderly population, which remained at low levels. In recent years, the authorities have adopted policies explicitly designed to protect the most vulnerable sectors of the population, as part of a reform process that they are still designing and implementing.

Demographic Trends and the Job Market

Colombia began its demographic transition somewhat later than other countries in the region. Although mortality rates began to decline in the middle of the 20th century as in other Latin American countries, Colombians' life expectancy was clearly lower than that in the leading countries in the region, such as Argentina, Chile, or Uruguay. Moreover, during the middle of the 20th century the fertility rate in Colombia was much higher than in other countries, including Brazil and the regional average, signaling that the demographic transition had not yet begun (figure 6.1). The reduction in the fertility rate accelerated at the beginning of the 1970s, when the total fertility rate (TFR) was above five children per woman. The rate registered a rapid decrease from the 1970s to the mid-1980s until the fertility rate for Colombian women resembled that of other countries in the region.

Figure 6.1 Mortality and Fertility in Colombia and Latin America, 1950–2100

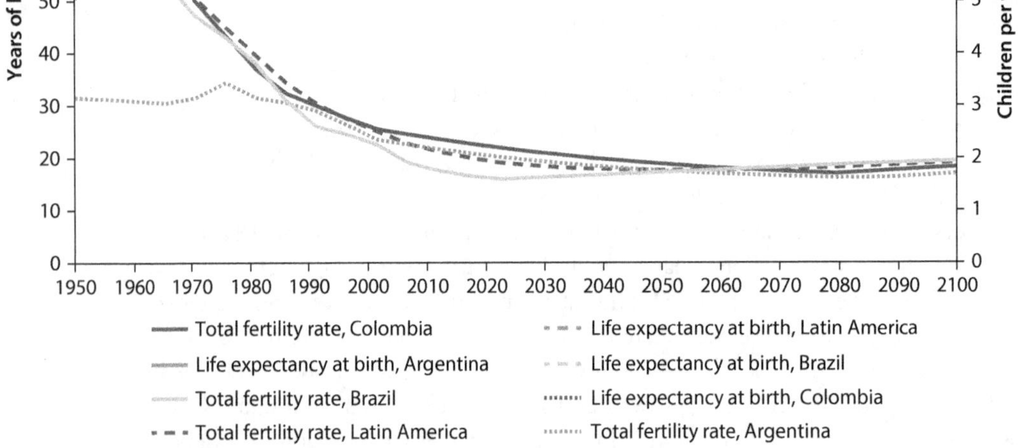

Source: Centro Latinoamericano y Caribeño de Demografía–Economic Commission for Latin America and the Caribbean (CELADE-ECLAC) 2011.

Projections from the Centro Latinoamericano y Caribeño de Demografía (CELADE) indicate that the trend should continue in the future, although the rate will continue to be higher than the regional average for a few more decades.

As a consequence of these trends, the population aging process in Colombia has followed a different path than in the region as a whole. Figure 6.2 shows how, in the last 60 years, the percentage of the population over 65 years in Colombia has been significantly lower than that of other large countries in the region, such as Argentina or Brazil, and even below the regional average. At the same time, and given that in Colombia the downward trend in the fertility rate will be milder than in other countries, this percentage will increase more slowly. This means that by 2100 Colombia's population will still be somewhat younger than the rest of the region.

For its part, the labor market in Colombia has behaved similarly to other countries in the region, with long-term stable activity and unemployment rates, high prevalence of self-employment, and strong job participation from small firms. Nearly 70 percent of the adult population is economically active, and unemployment in recent years has maintained a downward trend, with rates near 15 percent at the beginning of the 21st century and falling below 10 percent more recently. Not surprisingly, there are significant differences in activity rates for men and women and youth unemployment is higher than for the general population (and especially for young women, persistently around 30 percent).

Figure 6.2 Population over 65 Years, 1950–2100

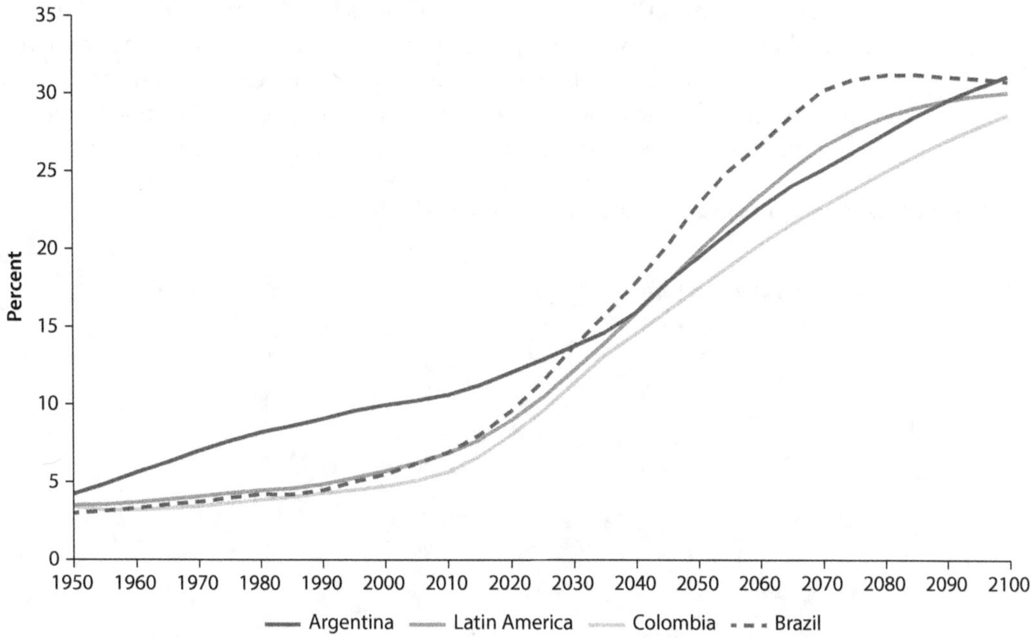

Source: Centro Latinoamericano y Caribeño de Demografía—Economic Commission for Latin America and the Caribbean (CELADE-ECLAC) 2011.

Somewhat fewer than half of workers are salaried, and 43 percent were considered self-employed in 2011. Nearly two-thirds of workers are in small enterprises in the private sector, which makes them more vulnerable to labor informality and the lack of access to social security coverage.

One aspect that differentiates Colombia from other labor markets is the low level of participation of the public sector, which accounted for just 4 percent of total employment in 2011 (figure 6.3). That value is less than half of that observed in other countries in the region such as Argentina, Brazil, Chile, and Peru, which makes Colombia the country with the lowest proportion of public employment on the continent. This also affects labor informality because, although not in every case, government employment usually means a high level of labor formality.

Development of the Pension System

Colombia formally created its pension system in the mid-1940s with the passage of the laws that created CAJANAL and ICSS. CAJANAL was to provide social security services to public sector workers, and ICSS offered the same services to the private sector. This scheme offered little protection in terms of the number of workers covered and suffered from some significant design and management problems that led to repeated financial crises during its first decades of existence.

The system's financial and management difficulties, which were the backdrop for the operations of ICSS, CAJANAL, and other small social security banks, led to the implementation of multiple reforms during those years. This included the replacement of ICSS with the Social Security Institute (Instituto de Seguros Sociales [ISS]) in 1977, and various modifications to the contribution and benefit rules of the programs. In CAJANAL's case, different groups of public sector employees left the institution over the years, creating their own banks or special funds for their occupational group or region that achieved better conditions for participants, but had serious sustainability problems.

Figure 6.3 Workers by Occupational Category, Sector, and Firm Size, 2011
Percent

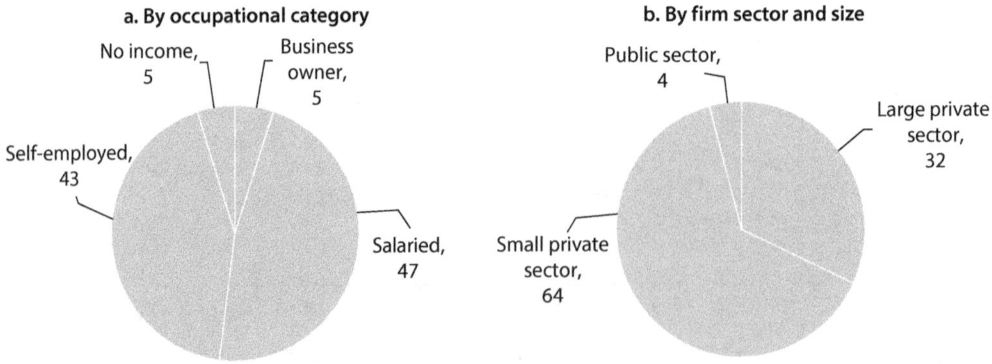

Source: Centro de Estudios Distributivos Laborales y Sociales (CEDLAS) 2011.

These banks and special funds eventually included nearly 1,000 different institutions by the beginning of the 1990s (Ayala and Acosta 2001). The continuous reforms were not able to reverse the ongoing crisis that afflicted the system, and as a result social security was extremely relevant during the constitutional reform process that ended with the approval of the 1991 constitution. The constitutional text included various definitions that have marked the debate and policies in the last two decades. For example, the constitution establishes social security as a "mandatory public service"[1] that all inhabitants have a right to. This definition, along with the one adopted in Law no. 100 of 1993, which established that both the contribution salary and the minimum pension had to be above the minimum legal salary, imposed a set of restrictions on the design of the income protection system for the elderly in Colombia that have determined how the system has evolved up until today.

Nonetheless, as we will see in the following section, the 1993 reform had a limited impact on the participation of active workers and the protection of the elderly in Colombia. This caused policy makers to implement additional initiatives fundamentally focused on providing a minimum income to the poorest elderly Colombians, but also creating alternative mechanisms to promote long-term savings among active workers.

The 1993 Reform

The parallel pension regimes were merged when the system was reformed in 1993. From the beginning there had been one system for public employees and another for private sector employees, as well as different independent social security banks that offered services to workers from specific sectors or enterprises, such as military personnel and the National Police, members of the National Social Security Fund for Educators, workers from the Colombian Petroleum Enterprise, and the regional banks and funds. The majority of these programs, including those managed by the ISS and CAJANAL, were merged in a mixed-fund, pay-as-you-go system, but some sectors were unaffected (educators, military personnel, and Ecopetrol) because they were excluded from the new system.[2]

The system approved in 1993 is a dual scheme, with a funded regime and a separate pay-as-you-go system that seeks financial sustainability in the medium term. Among other modifications, the reform increased the retirement age to 62 for men and 57 for women. The increase would be implemented over time. Additionally, the system originally required a minimum of 1,000 weeks of contributions to receive a pension, which would have gradually increased to 1,300 weeks in 2015. The system also offers a replacement rate (in the case of the pay-as-you-go regime) of 65–85 percent of a retiree's previous salary. Law no. 100 established a complex transition scheme from the multiple existing regimes to the general regime, which must be completed by 2014.

Once the law took effect, active workers were able to choose between joining a subsystem of individual savings by signing up with a Pension and Unemployment Fund Administrator (Administradora de Fondos de Pensiones y Cesantías [AFP]), or joining the pay-as-you-go subsystem (Régimen de Prima Media [RPM]), administered by the ISS. In the first case, workers' contributions are directed to a fund that they capitalize themselves and upon retirement they can purchase an annuity or choose an equivalent payout. In the second case, contributions are directed to the ISS, which manages them under a traditional pay-as-you-go system and guarantees benefit payments. In both cases workers are entitled to a minimum benefit equivalent to the prevailing minimum salary if they have met the requirement for the minimum number of weeks of contributions.

In contrast to other countries where funded and pay-as-you-go regimes were implemented in parallel, in Colombia workers kept the ability to switch between the regimes indefinitely, as long as they did not switch again for at least three years (increased to five years in 2003). This possibility provoked an intense debate over the equality (or lack thereof) between the two subsystems and the incentives for workers to choose one or the other. Different experts pointed out that the existing rules suggested that it made sense for workers to enroll in the individual savings subsystem and later switch to the pay-as-you-go subsystem, due to the differences in rates of return that workers could expect from the two regimes in the different stages of their careers.[3]

One unique aspect of the pension system in Colombia was the creation of a specific solidarity scheme, through the Pension Solidarity Fund (Fondo de Solidaridad Pensional [FSP]), which subsidizes contributions to specified groups of workers, and which was complemented in 2003 with the Minimum Pension Guarantee Fund (Fondo de Garantía de Pensión Mínima) (table 6.1). Both funds were financed with money from the contributions of high-income workers. According to Law no. 100 the FSP was designed to supplement the contributions of workers who were not able to make contributions equivalent to the minimum salary, either in the pay-as-you-go regime or the individual savings subsystem. The program was financed by a 1 percent contribution from workers that earn more than four times the minimum wage, and managed through an administrator that was assigned to workers who did not reach the minimum wage in their contributions. The subsidy could not cover 100 percent of the contribution obligation, so workers were required to continue

Table 6.1 Solidarity Pension Fund, Requirements and Benefits, by Population Group until 2003

Population group	*Age conditions*	*Subsidy time limit*	*Percentage of minimum wage contribution subsidized (%)*
Urban informal workers	Men 40–65 years Women 35–65 years	500 weeks	70
Rural informal workers	Men 35–65 years Women 30–65 years	480–600 weeks[a]	90
Workers with disabilities	20–65 years	480–800 weeks[a]	95
Community mothers (madres comunitarias)	Any age	480–600 weeks[a]	80

Source: El Consejo Nacional de Política Económica y Social (CONPES) 2002.
a. Dependent on the participation in the transition regime.

contributing to the system, although in some cases, such as for workers with disabilities, the subsidy could reach as high as 95 percent.

The requirement to make contributions, even when subsidized, to qualify for FSP benefits had a major impact on the level of coverage the program achieved. The fund began to receive contributions once the system was implemented, but it only began to pay subsidies in 1996. The rules established that participants in the program were required to keep making contributions; in the event that they did not make any over four months, they would lose eligibility for the subsidy and the funds that had been transferred to their accounts would be returned to the FSP. By 1998 the subsystem covered almost 450,000 workers, equal to about 2 percent of the workforce. However, since then the number of covered persons has fallen consistently, mainly because the beneficiaries do not meet contribution requirements and according to the rules must be dropped from the program (figure 6.4).

The FSP's low coverage caused the fund to accumulate a significant surplus in financial terms, because it did not distribute all of the funds that it received. As a result, as of December 2012 it had accumulated around Col$2.5 trillion, equal to about US$1.3 billion or 0.4 percent of GDP.

Various analysts have sharply criticized the FSP's performance, stating that the fund's low coverage, along with management problems and weak controls, resulted in a very low impact on the quality of social protection offered by the state. The main problem has been identified as the prevalence of slow or late payments among participants. According to Social 60 document of the Council for National Economic and Social Policy (El Consejo Nacional de Política

Figure 6.4 Beneficiary Population of the FSP Contribution Subsidy, 1996–2012

Source: Ministerio de la Previsión Social, various years; CONPES 2007.

Económica y Social [CONPES]), the strict application of disenrollment rules for late payers meant that in 2001 coverage dropped dramatically by half. Additionally, the report identified three main causes of the late payment problem: operational problems with payment systems (because some commercial banks have refused to participate), the low level of income for the target population, and the population's low loyalty to the program (CONPES 2002). Other analysts have pointed out significant problems related to targeting the program because of a lack of reliable information on the characteristics of program participants and a lack of control with respect to compliance with participation conditions. This is due in part to inefficiencies at the agencies in charge of managing the program because they lack a reliable beneficiary database, but serious problems have also been identified trying to access information from other agencies, such as the ISS. In 2001 an audit report recommended "that this program should be eliminated, and the FSP's resources and the 1 percent payroll tax that is charged from this point forward should be directed to pay minimum pensions" (Henao 2001, p. 18). Along the same lines, the official CONPES Social 70 document pointed out that FSP had only helped 1,500 people per year achieve pensions in the first years of the system (CONPES 2003). Additionally, the limited number of subsidies awarded had a strong bias in favor of the highest quintiles of the income distribution (figure 6.5), concentrating most of the subsidies there (Millán 2010). This is due in part to the fact that participation in the pension system in general is strongly biased toward high-income groups, but in addition it would appear that a capacity differential exists among the different groups with regard to their ability to receive these benefits.

Figure 6.5 Distribution of FSP Subsidy Beneficiaries, by Income Quintile, 2003

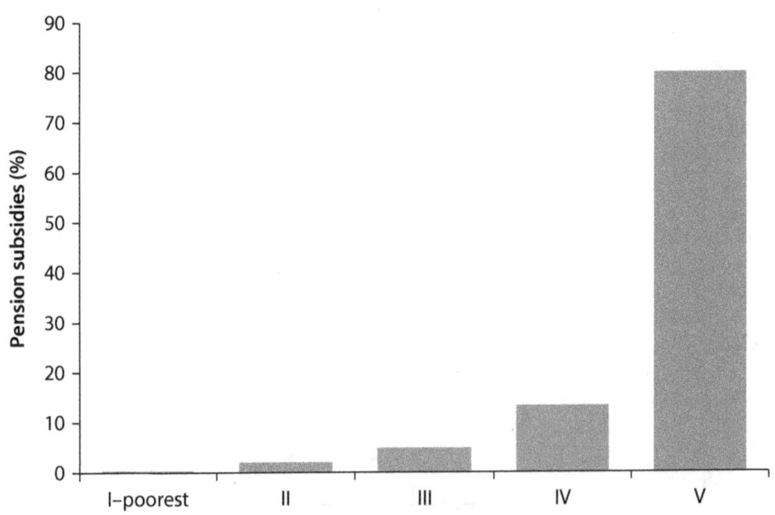

Source: Millán 2010.

Reforms to Expand Coverage

In January 2003 Congress approved Law no. 797, which introduced important reforms to the pension system. Several of these reforms dealt with the two subsystems (pay-as-you-go and individual savings), including increases in contribution rates, the creation of a Minimum Pension Guarantee Fund that would pay for minimum pensions with funds from worker contributions, and an increase in the contribution requirement to be eligible for the minimum pension guarantee (which was gradually increased to 1,300 weeks).[4] Several of these reforms, including the increase to the required number of weeks of contributions, were declared unconstitutional and were never applied.

Changes to the Contributory and Noncontributory Regimes

Law no. 797 included important reforms to the design, objectives, and operation of the FSP. First, the law put forward a restriction on the contribution subsidy system, limiting coverage to individuals over 55 (if they participate in the Individual Savings Regime; Régimen de Ahorro Individual [RAIS]) or over 58 (if they are enrolled with an AFP). This restriction significantly reduced the number of potential beneficiaries, while at the same time dividing the FSP into two subaccounts: "solidarity," which would continue financing contribution subsidies, and another called "subsistence," which would focus on supporting the elderly in situations of extreme poverty. The funding for both subaccounts would come from dividing the FSP's resources equally (i.e., 50 percent of the contributions from the 1 percent payroll tax on those who earn more than four times the minimum wage) with the subsistence subaccount receiving an additional contribution from workers earning more than 16 times the minimum wage and pensioners receiving more than 10 times the minimum wage, along with resources from the national budget. The CONPES Social 70 document established that resources from this subaccount would be used to pay for a subsidy equal to the poverty line, as measured by the National Administrative Statistics Department (Departamento Administrativo Nacional de Estadísticas [DANE]). Beneficiaries' eligibility is determined by age (they must be at least three years younger than retirement age), income (they cannot earn more than 32 percent of the minimum salary), living conditions (they should be classified in levels I or II of the SISBEN),[5] and nationality and residency requirements. The benefit consists of a transfer that brings the total income to the poverty line, with between 33 percent and 70 percent of the subsidy delivered in cash and the remaining 30 percent used to pay for complementary services that the beneficiaries receive through the Comprehensive Assistance Program for the Elderly (Programa de Asistencia Integral para los Adultos Mayores [PAIAM]).

In 2004, with the goal of unifying the operations of the different components of the FSP subsistence subaccount, the government created the Social Protection Program for the Elderly (Programa de Protección Social al Adulto Mayor [PPSAM]), which would manage both cash subsidies as well as in-kind assistance and services. This program is implemented by diverse institutions at a national level (including the Colombian Institute of Family Wellbeing; Instituto Colombiano de Bienestar Familiar; and Procesar—the trustee that administers the FSP). In addition, the program contemplates the participation of the Departmental Councils, Municipal Governments, and Territorial Entities. Given this diversity, Social Protection Ministry was established with the primary responsibility for managing the new program. The PPSAM offered protection to a growing group of the population, until reaching about 700,000 beneficiaries by the end of 2012, when it was replaced by the Elderly Colombia (Colombia Mayor) program. The coverage level of these programs was always a function of available financial resources. The national government established an annual coverage goal and authorized the Social Protection Ministry to enroll new beneficiaries according to the prioritization criteria for new applicants.

Even though the 2003–04 reforms were able to implement a system of income protection for the poorest elderly, the authorities remained concerned with the pension system's low level of coverage during workers' economically active years. They continued to seek alternatives to increase participation while also seeking to consolidate the financial sustainability of the contributory system. In July 2005, Legislative Act 01 was approved, which introduced a reform to article 48 of the constitution. This reform was aimed at guaranteeing the funding of pension benefits, reducing the transition period to the system introduced in 1993, while eliminating special pension systems (except for the Public Forces, the President of the Republic, and educators). Act 01 also prohibited the establishment of pension conditions through administrative actions other than laws, such as collective bargains, agreements, or legal judgments, that had been the mechanisms for the creation of multiple schemes in the past. This Legislative Act made clear that no pension could be less than the minimum salary, and at the same time introduced a new concept to the system, signaling that "the law will determine the cases in which the system can offer periodic economic benefits below the minimum salary, to individuals with limited resources that do not meet the requirements to be eligible for a pension" (Legislative Act 01 of 2005).

This reference to periodic economic benefits (beneficios económicos periódicos [BEPs]) began a process of analysis and debates that, in the last eight years, has consumed much of the attention of those who work in the pension system, elderly social protection, and related sectors in Colombia. Even though the Legislative Act was not explicit, the authorities interpreted that the objective of the BEPs would be to offer a long-term savings scheme that, without forming part of the general pension system, would allow low-income workers to generate resources to sustain themselves during old age. Based on this logic, the development of the regulations necessary to implement this program was built around the idea of offering appropriate incentives to promote saving among the target population, subsidizing it as necessary.

In 2009, Law no. 1328 that regulated different aspects of the financial market included an article that established who could receive BEPs. It classifies as recipients—for an amount less than the minimum pension—individuals who, having reached the minimum retirement age contemplated in the General

Pension System, had insufficient accumulated savings to fund a minimum pension. The state could offer incentives in the form of savings subsidies that could not exceed 50 percent of the amount saved by the participants. Even though the law established some basic criteria for BEP operations, they were not implemented until 2012.

Pension System Performance

Pension Coverage

The traditional contributory pension system in Colombia has featured a low level of coverage, reflecting the high level of informality in the labor market. Since the introduction of the multipillar system with Law no. 100 in 1993, the percentage of the economically active population that makes regular contributions has hovered around 25 percent, with small fluctuations and, apparently, a slight upward trend in recent years (figure 6.6). This data, obtained from the Colombian Household Surveys that correspond to the period of analysis, show that various efforts undertaken since the 1990s to increase coverage of workers have had a limited impact. Coverage is evidently somewhat higher considering active workers (although the difference is minor, due to the fact that unemployment rates in Colombia have never been very high) and much higher among salaried workers, whose participation rate neared 60 percent in the previous decade. In contrast, the system never managed to effectively attract self-employed workers, whose coverage level never exceeded 10 percent during the observed period.

Active workers' low participation is directly reflected in the situation of the elderly. Taking as a reference the population 65 years and older,[6] the pension

Figure 6.6 Pension System Coverage of the Economically Active Population and the Employed, 1996–2009

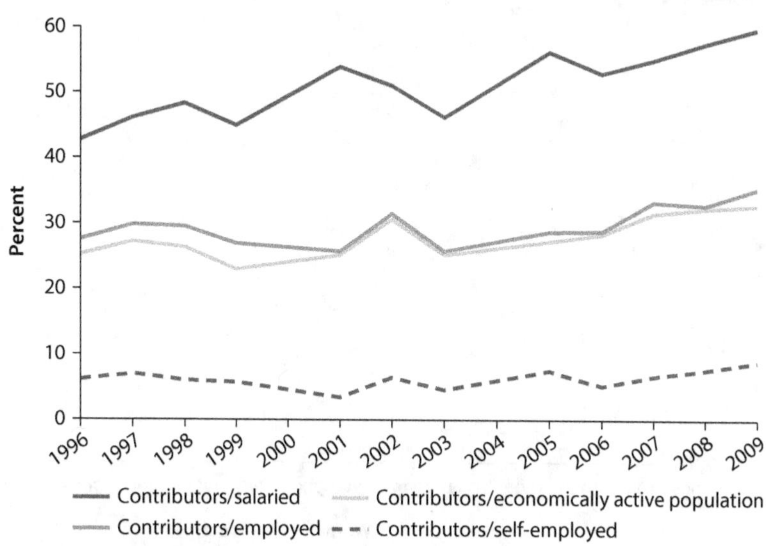

Source: Rofman and Oliveri 2012.

system coverage level has fluctuated around 15–20 percent in recent decades, although in recent years it appears to have improved slightly, with nearly 25 percent of elderly receiving a pension benefit in 2009 (figure 6.7). This figure reflects the percentage of the population of this age group that claimed in surveys to receive pension benefit income. Throughout the period we observe a strong gender bias, with men maintaining a coverage level that exceeded women's level by 10–15 percentage points. This difference should be attributed to existing labor market disparities between the sexes as well as their current activity rates. It also reflects rates in past decades, when today's elderly were economically active and making contributions that would eventually allow them to qualify for pensions. Upon verifying the notably lower economic participation rates for women in this period, it is inevitable that these rates would affect the current coverage of the elderly, given the contributory nature of the system.

Noncontributory Pension Program Coverage

Even though it is not possible to obtain data series with information as detailed as it is for contributory pensions, the noncontributory schemes (principally the PPSAM since 2003) have demonstrated increasing coverage that has been linked to the availability of budget resources, as was mentioned earlier. Starting from very low coverage when the program was started in 2003, the number of beneficiaries has increased continuously until reaching about 700,000 (equal to about 25 percent of the 65 years and older population), according to registration data published by various official sources.[7]

One alternative source of registration data is the Quality of Life Survey (Encuesta de Calidad de Vida [ECV]), which has been conducted by DANE

Figure 6.7 Pension Coverage of the over 65 Population, Total and by Sex, 1986–2009

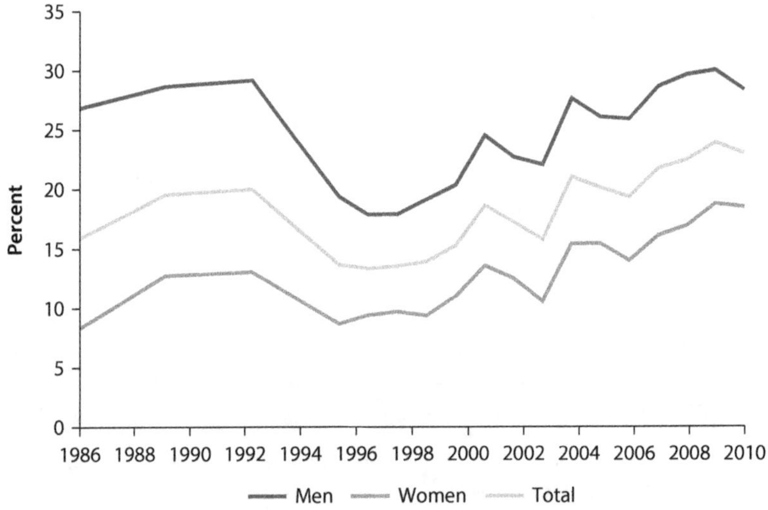

Source: Rofman and Oliveri 2012.

annually since 2010. This survey inquires about the perception of the PPSAM benefit among households, which makes it impossible to identify beneficiaries individually. However, it is possible to evaluate the characteristics of the 65 years and over population that resides in households that received at least one benefit from the program. According to this source, PPSAM's coverage would be something less than that shown in figure 6.8, because the surveys reveal that between 17 percent (2010) and 19.5 percent (2012) of adults over 65 years lived in households that received at least one PPSAM benefit. Given that, by design, it is not possible to duplicate coverage between the pension system and PPSAM, it can be estimated that in 2012 total coverage would have reached around 45 percent of the elderly population over 65 years old.

Figure 6.9 shows PPSAM program coverage by age group. It is apparent that the total coverage levels in 2010 and 2011 were very similar: 13.7 percent of adults over 60 percent and 16.9 percent of adults over 65 lived in a household that received a PPSAM benefit in 2010. These values decreased slightly to 12.6 percent and 15.6 percent, respectively, in 2011, and increased in 2012 with the launch of the Elderly Colombia program. During these three years strong growth of coverage as age increases is apparent. Although the population aged 60–64 years has coverage rates around 8 percent, the 80 and over population exceeds 20 percent (in 2012, it reached 25 percent). This difference is the logical consequence of the program's prioritization strategy that

Figure 6.8 PPSAM Program Beneficiaries, 2003–12: Total and Percentage of the Population 65 Years and over

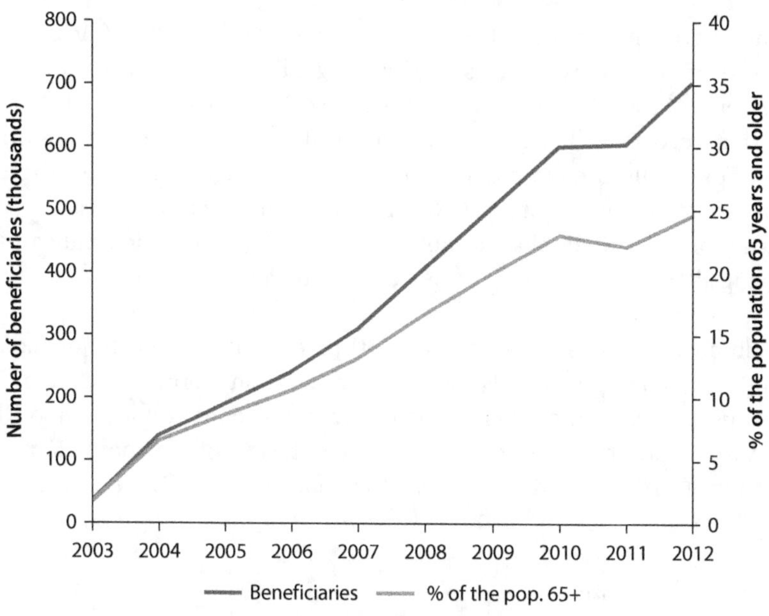

Source: El Consejo Nacional de Política Económica y Social (CONPES) 2007 and 2012.
Note: The data from the period 2007–10 are estimates based on CONPES projections.

Figure 6.9 Elderly Population Living in Households with PPSAM Program Beneficiaries, by Age Group, 2010–12

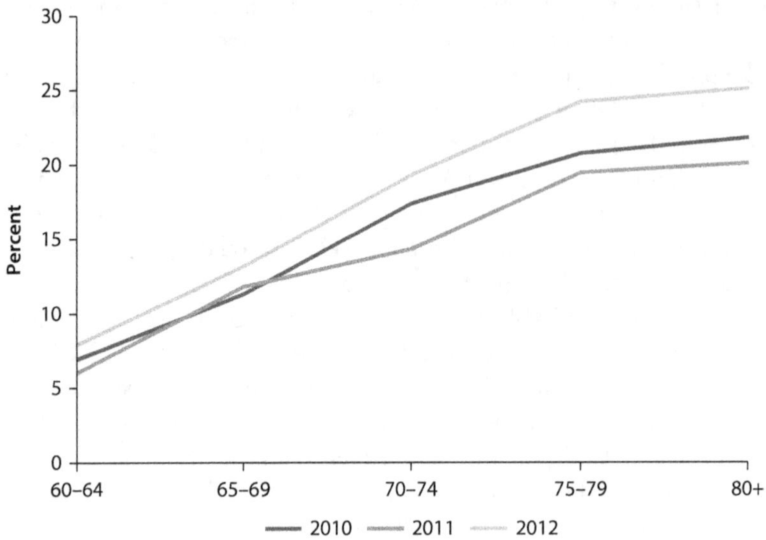

Source: Departamento Administrativo Nacional de Estadística (DANE), Encuesta de Condiciones de Vida (ECV) 2010–12.

considers age among the criteria to accept new beneficiaries. Given the greater coverage of the contributory system among men and that of PPSAM for older groups, we can estimate that both among the population 80 years and older and among men 65 years and older total coverage would reach about 50 percent of the population.

One interesting aspect of the information available in the ECV is the high rate of economic activity registered among PPSAM beneficiaries and their dependents. Around 40 percent of those over 65 years that live in a household that receives a benefit are economically active. The vast majority of these individuals are employed, and unemployment rates for these age groups are very low (figure 6.10). These economic activity rates are similar to those for individuals that do not receive the benefit, which indicates that receiving PPSAM benefits does not appear to have a major effect on labor supply.

Additionally we observe that nearly 30 percent of the directly or indirectly PPSAM-covered population did not have access to any formal education during their youth, whereas the other 60 percent reached only primary school. These levels vary significantly from those observed in the rest of the population, among whom just 14 percent did not receive any education, and 37 percent exceeded primary school.

Adequacy of Coverage

In recent decades the minimum salary has been between 50 percent and 70 percent of the economy's median salary, and between 30 percent and

Figure 6.10 Distribution of the Population 65 and Older, by Economic Activity and Education and by Residency in Households Covered by the PPSAM Program, Average, 2010–12

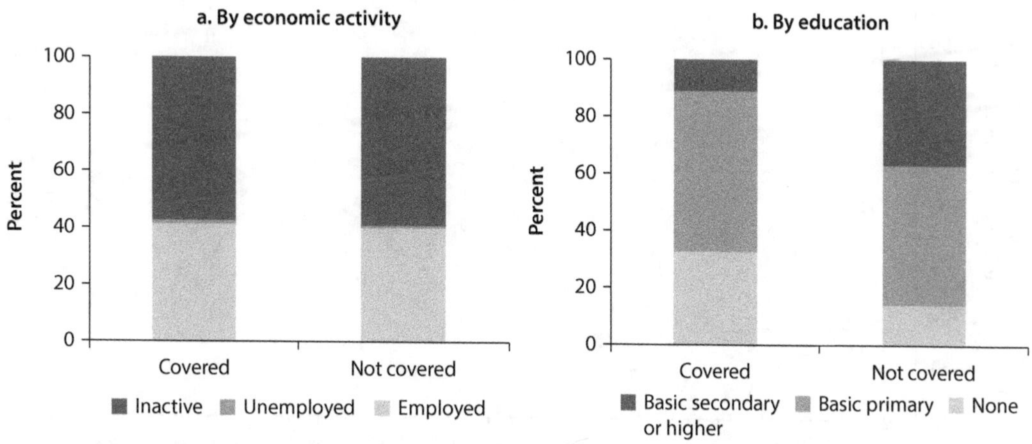

Source: Departamento Administrativo Nacional de Estadística (DANE), Encuesta de Condiciones de Vida (ECV) 2010–12.

40 percent of workers report income below the minimum salary (Millán 2010). The rules of operation of the general pension system allow workers only to make contributions (whether to the RPM or to the RAIS) based on a salary that is equal to or greater than the minimum salary. In addition, as discussed in previous sections, current legislation in Colombia establishes that the minimum pension cannot be less than the economy's minimum salary. The combination of these two rules means that the distribution of pension amounts tends to be concentrated around the minimum value, with few variations; unfortunately, statistical reports that would allow us to evaluate the magnitude of the concentration of this distribution and its evolution over time are not available. According to the latest Activity Report (Informe de Actividades) presented to Congress by the Ministerio de la Protección Social (2004), the value of the average pension was approximately 1.8 times the minimum, demonstrating the significant compression of income distribution among beneficiaries.

Because the minimum pension in Colombia is equal to the minimum salary, it guarantees a reasonable level of adequacy for those that are able to access it. During the last two decades of the 20th century the minimum pension remained stable, around US$100–150, but since 2004 it began to increase and exceeded US$300 in 2012 (figure 6.11). At the same time, if we consider the relationship between the minimum pension and the urban poverty line, we notice that since the 1990s both have increased continuously. Although the minimum pension represented 150 percent of the poverty line in 1994, that value neared 250 percent two decades later.

For their part, PPSAM benefits (and currently Elderly Colombia) are determined normatively based on the extreme poverty line in each region. Given that the objective of the program is to avoid that the elderly live in poverty, the

Figure 6.11 Minimum Salaries and Pensions, 1984–2013

Source: Labor Ministry, World Bank databank, and Economic Commission for Latin America and the Caribbean (ECLAC).

program seeks to supplement their income so that they can reach this level. As a result, the benefit amount is significantly lower than the minimum pension.

Financial Performance

The financial cost of the RPM has been a main topic of debate in Colombia since the approval of Law no. 100 in 1993. Although some analysts believed the law would contribute to stabilizing the fiscal sustainability of the system, others expressed their concern about the situation in the medium and long term. The available information shows that between the implementation of the reform in 1993 and the approval of Legislative Act 01 of 2005, the budget for the pension system more than tripled (figure 6.12). Thus, the fiscal cost, defined as the transfers that the public sector must make to pension programs, was around 1 percent of GDP in 2004, and reached 3.4 percent in 2005. The situation would appear to have stabilized after the sudden increase registered that year, and the cost reached about 3.7 percent by 2011. The Treasury Ministry's official projections indicate that this level would be near the maximum expected level and that the fiscal cost would begin to decrease in the coming years to converge at a level between 0.5 percent and 1 percent of GDP in the long term.

In terms of the cost of the noncontributory and subsidy schemes, the CONPES Social 156 document estimated that it would represent just 0.25 percent of GDP in 2013 (CONPES 2012). The largest share of this spending is from the Elderly Colombia program, paid for by the FSP, but the BEPs and contribution subsidies also play a role, and they are paid for from the national treasury. According to projections from the National Planning Directorate

Figure 6.12 Pension System Deficit, 1994–2062

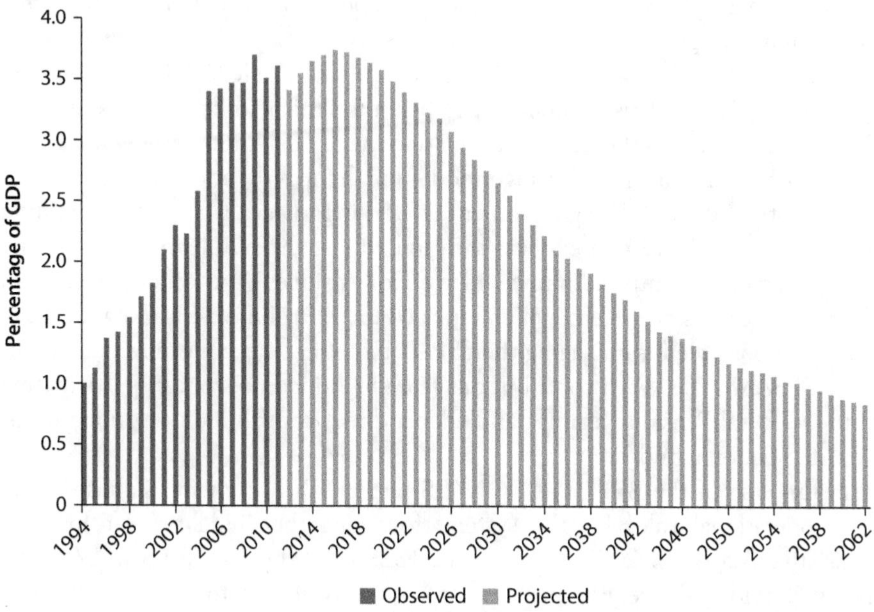

Source: Ministerio de Trabajo 2013.

(Dirección Nacional de Planeamiento) the cost of serving the elderly that participate in these programs will vary between Col$1.7 and Col$2 trillion in the next five years, or around 0.25 percent of GDP. The cost could increase in the coming decades, as the coverage of BEPs and Elderly Colombia is expanded, but it is not expected to exceed the equivalent of 8.5 percent of current GDP in the next four decades (until 2050). Slightly more than half of these funds will be paid by the FSP, while the rest will require transfers from the national treasury.

The Reform Process Begun in 2012

President Juan Manuel Santos's administration gave a new push to the pension system and elderly social protection reform discussion, in the framework of the National Development Plan 2010–14 "Prosperity for All" (Plan Nacional de Desarrollo 2010–14, "Prosperidad para Todos"). This plan sets universality, equality, sustainability, and solidarity goals and proposes the combination of reforms to the General Pension Regime and the PPSAM program as a model, as well as the effective implementation of the BEPs first set out in Legislative Act 01 of 2005.

As part of the institutional reforms created as a result of the plan, the Labor Ministry was created in 2011, with the functions of planning and executing policies regarding pensions, economic benefits, and other benefits. To that end, the Vice-ministry of Employment and Pensions was created, with a Directorate of Pensions and Other Benefits, which quickly made advances on aspects relevant to the pension system and noncontributory programs. In this setting, during 2012 reforms to PPSAM were approved, and rules were laid out for operation of the BEPs, and in 2013 a comprehensive reform proposal for the elderly social protection system was presented.

In 2012 PPSAM was substituted by a new program called "Elderly Colombia" (Colombia Mayor). This program offers benefits similar to its predecessor's, but the main difference is the goal of eliminating the annual limits on new beneficiaries to achieve a universal coverage model for the elderly population in levels I and II of the SISBEN. The government is working toward a goal of one million beneficiaries for 2013 and expects to reach almost three million by 2030. The new program is jointly administered by ColPensiones (the official agency in charge of the pension system, which replaced the ISS) and Elderly Colombia, the trustee responsible for managing the FSP. The funding mechanism remains similar to PPSAM's (i.e., with contributions from high-income workers participating in the General Pension Regime) and adds a direct contribution of public funds from the national budget.

In the case of the BEPs, the CONPES Social 156 document established the basic operational rules for the system, following the guidelines set forth in Legislative Act 01 of 2005 and Law no. 1328 of 2009 (CONPES 2012, p. 5). Included among the requirements to access the benefit is that applicants must have reached the retirement age set by the RPM in the General Pension System. An additional requirement is that the saved funds plus the value of mandatory and voluntary contributions to the Mandatory Pension Fund and others authorized by the national government for the same purpose must not be sufficient to obtain a minimum pension. Moreover, the worker's annual savings amount must be less than the minimum annual contribution set by the General Pension System.

The document points out that the target population for BEPs is workers who upon retirement are not able to fund a pension from the contributory system and belong to SISBEN level I, II, or III. The program functions in the following manner: Eligible workers make contributions to an individual account administered by ColPensiones, which will accept contributions up to a maximum amount each year (for 2012 individual savings could not exceed Col$885,000, equal to approximately US$500). Upon retirement, if workers meet the conditions set forth in the previous paragraph, the state will make an additional contribution of 20 percent of the account balance. Based on the resulting amount, which can also include compensation to substitute any contributions made to the General Pension System, a monthly distribution amount is calculated. The distribution cannot exceed 85 percent of the minimum salary and includes survivor's benefits in the event of the beneficiary's death. If for any reason the participant becomes eligible to receive a pension under the General Pension System framework, he or she can use the balance accumulated and its investment earnings to fund this pension, although the government will not make the additional 20 percent contribution.

The third proposed reform deals with the general pension regime. Since its creation in 1993 and successive reforms, the system has maintained the existence of two parallel regimes as the foundation of its design: the RPM that awards defined benefit pensions via a pay-as-you-go scheme administered by the state;

and the individual savings scheme (RAIS) run by private administrators that uses a funded and defined contribution model. Workers can opt for either subsystem and can even switch between them periodically, which has created controversy with respect to the equality between the systems and the fiscal and social impacts of these changes. In its "New Model for Social Protection of the Elderly" ("Nuevo Modelo de Protección para la Vejez") proposal, the Labor Ministry has suggested that in addition to the introduction of the Elderly Colombia program and BEPs, the General Pension System should be modified to make the two subsystems more complementary instead of competitive (Ministerio de Trabajo 2013). This proposal outlines a shift to a model in which all workers are obligated to contribute to the pay-as-you-go regime on the basis of the minimum salary, while their income that exceeds the minimum can be used as the basis for contributions to the individual savings regime.

Figure 6.13 presents a diagram of the proposed model. It shows that in the current system the poorest segment of the population is covered by the PPSAM, but the higher-income sectors have access to the General Pension System, choosing voluntarily between the RAIS, RPM, and other contributory schemes (which only some groups, such as the public forces and educators, can access). Meanwhile, a large segment of the population does not have access to any social protection system. In the new proposal, the coverage offered by Elderly Colombia would be much wider in order to cover all indigents, the BEP scheme would protect those who have slightly more income (and therefore

Figure 6.13 Design of the Elderly Social Protection System in Colombia

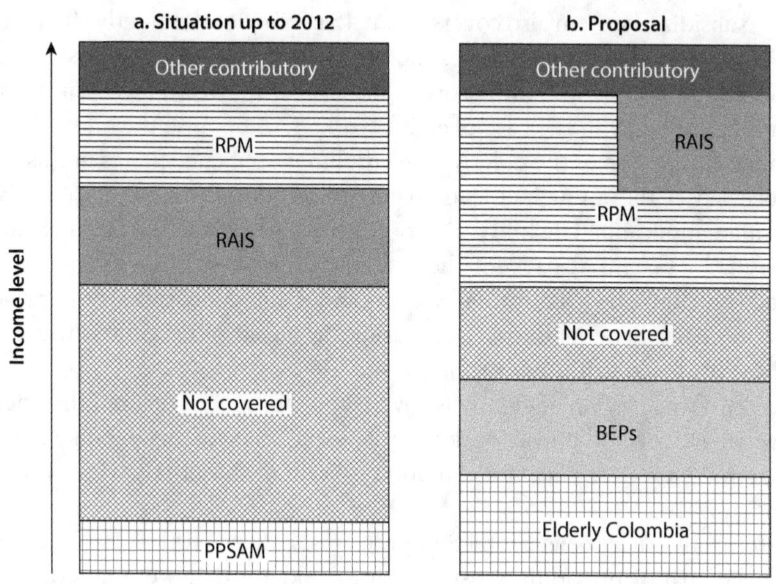

Source: Based on El Consejo Nacional de Política Económica y Social (CONPES) 2012 and Ministerio de Trabajo 2013.
Note: BEP = Beneficio Económico Periódico; PPSAM = Programa de Protección Social al Adulto Mayor; RAIS = Régimen de Ahorro Individual; RPM = Régimen de Prima Media.

savings capacity) but who do not exceed the minimum salary, and the group of workers with formal employment and income above the minimum salary would contribute the amount corresponding to the minimum salary to the RPM, and any amount above that level to the RAIS. Thus, the RPM would become a single benefit scheme for all participants, and differences in contribution capacity would be reflected in the RAIS individual accounts. In addition, the special contributory schemes would remain untouched by this reform proposal.

The Ministry of Labor has estimated that once this scheme is implemented, the total coverage of elderly at retirement age would increase from 43 percent currently (31 percent by the General Pension System and 12 percent by Elderly Colombia) to 80 percent in 2030 (distributed with 34.3 percent covered by the General Pension System, 30 percent by Elderly Colombia, and 10.6 percent by BEPs, with the remaining 5 percent covered by other small-scale systems).

Health Coverage and Other Services for the Elderly

Health coverage for the elderly is no different than for the rest of the population. There are two main coverage schemes (the contributory regime and the subsidized regime) and other smaller schemes that are less relevant in terms of their effective coverage. Almost 45 percent of elderly that continue working in the formal economy or receive a pension participate in the contributory system. In this system, in exchange for a compulsory monthly contribution, the participants have access to health services for themselves and their dependents (who are also considered covered). The services are provided by a Health Promotion Entity (Entidad Promotora de Salud) that receives the contributions through the social security system.

The subsidized system also covers about 45 percent of the elderly (figure 6.14). This group includes people who cannot access the social security system, either because they do not work, they work informally, or they earn less than two times the minimum salary in the case of active workers, or because they do not receive a pension in the case of the elderly. The enrollment of beneficiaries in this system is processed at the municipal level, where local authorities use the SISBEN to determine applicants' eligibility. The Solidarity and Guarantee Fund (Fondo de Solidaridad y Garantía) pays for the system. The fund receives its funding from payroll contributions from formal workers and the national treasury. In principle, access to health benefits for participants in the subsidized regime is the same as for those in the contributory regime.

Finally, a small group of elderly is covered by the "special regime" that includes those that are covered by one of the special social security regimes, like members of the armed forces or educators. About 3 percent of the elderly were part of this regime in 2010.

In terms of other social protection programs, Law no. 100 of 1993 also established the goal of providing assistance to the elderly that were in situations of extreme poverty. The first program implemented as a response to this legal mandate was the REVIVIR program that operated between 1994 and 1998 as part of the Social Solidarity Network (Red de Solidaridad Social). It covered 70,000

Figure 6.14 Health Coverage of the Elderly, 2010
Percent

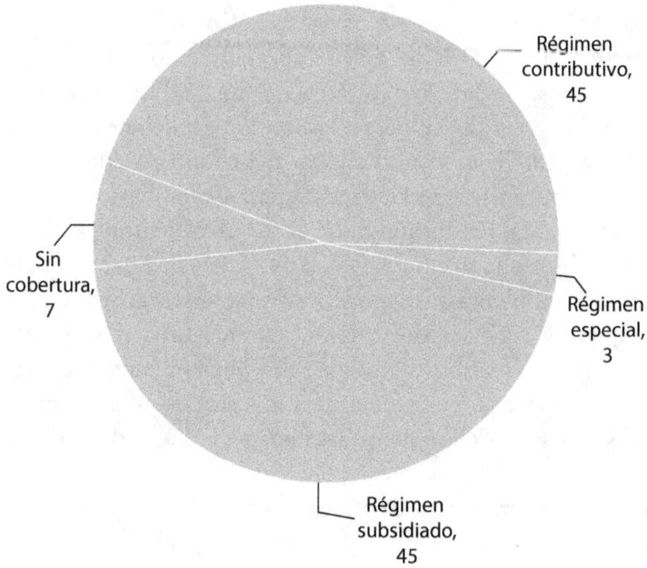

Source: Profamilia 2010.

beneficiaries and was later replaced by the PAIAM. Both programs focused on the provision of basic foodstuffs, distributing through markets and offering rations or prepared food to participants, although they also delivered some cash benefits. These programs offered protection to the indigent population older than 65 years (or 50 in the case of indigenous and people with disabilities), with subsidies between 24 percent and 37 percent of the minimum salary.

A 2002 evaluation of PAIAM highlighted that the program faced difficulties expanding coverage because of funding restrictions imposed by the national government. Nonetheless, even faced with these limitations, the evaluation found that "PAIAM has had a significant positive impact on nutrition services, health attention, medicine, housing, entertainment, and productive free time" (CONPES 2003).

In 2003, at the same time it implemented the PPSAM, the government began the National Complementary Elderly Nutrition Program "Juan Luis Londoño de la Cuesta" (Programa Nacional de Alimentación Complementaria al Adulto Mayor "Juan Luis Londoño de la Cuesta" [PNAAM]), which replaced the PAIAM. This program provided a nutritional supplement to the elderly in urban and rural areas. Around 400,000 beneficiaries have received support from this program each year, with financing coming from the FSP Subsistence subaccount. The program's participation requirements are similar to those of the PPSAM, but because the available spaces are different the beneficiary populations are not identical. The benefits, which can be delivered as prepared rations or rations to be prepared, are administered by the Colombian Institute of Family Wellbeing.

Final Reflections

Despite being a country with a medium development level compared to the region, the traditional social security system in Colombia is one of the weakest in Latin America in terms of coverage, especially among the elderly, where it protects just one in five citizens. Authorities and analysts have recognized this situation, and it has been the subject of wide-ranging debates and initiatives that sought to improve the living conditions for the country's elderly.

Even though it began as a centralized system, Colombia's pension system suffered serious fragmentation during much of the 20th century, as different groups of workers (usually from the public sector) achieved the enactment of special schemes that offered benefits on more generous terms than the general regime, which subsequently suffered the loss of resources and management capacity. The 1993 reform was an effort to mitigate this phenomenon, seeking to integrate all of the schemes (with a few exceptions) in a single system, while introducing an individual savings-funded regime that endeavored to reduce the state's financial liabilities.

Moreover, this reform sought to increase the relationship between the contributions made and the expected benefits, with the goal of aligning incentives to increase worker participation in the system. However, this effect does not appear to have had a major impact, given that the percentage of workers that participate in the system did not change significantly. There are several possible explanations for this,[8] but in any case it is clear that Colombia's General Pension System did not achieve the goal of offering an acceptable level of income protection to the elderly during its seven decades of existence.

As in other countries in the region, at the beginning of the last decade the state adopted a program to provide basic economic resources to the most vulnerable groups among the elderly as a response to the problems that had been observed. Thus, the PPSAM represented the first attempt to expand the reach of social protection beyond the traditional pension system. Even though it offered minimal benefits and its coverage was limited by budget restrictions, its implementation marked the first step in the search for alternatives to the traditional contributory system.

Throughout the last decade the search for policy options has continued, and in recent years Colombia has again taken up the goal of elderly inclusion as a central policy point. The coverage expansion of PPSAM (and its replacement Elderly Colombia), the launch of the BEP program, included in legislation since the middle of the previous decade but recently implemented as of 2012, and the government's proposal of a comprehensive reform that aims at reaching near universal coverage by 2030 show that the subject has taken a central position in the social policy arena in Colombia. The challenge, of course, will be to ensure that the debate expands to include all of society with the goal of promoting the adoption of a new policy whose objective is the universalization of an income protection system for the elderly, based on sustainability, equality, and efficient management.

Notes

1. Article 48 of the Political Constitution of Colombia, 1991.
2. According to article 279 of Law no. 100 of 1993.
3. See, for example, Santa María et al. (2010, p. 12) or Ayala and Acosta (2001, p. 30).
4. The Minimum Pension Guarantee Fund did not signify a change for system participants because they already had access to this guarantee, but it did modify the guarantee's financing mechanism and imposed somewhat more restrictive conditions to access the guarantee.
5. The Identification System of the Potential Social Program Beneficiaries (Sistema de Identificación de Potenciales Beneficiarios de Programas Sociales [SISBEN]) is the system that is used in Colombia to target goods and services subsidy programs. It is built around a quantitative measurement of household quality of life indicators, with the understanding that poverty is not a purely monetary phenomenon, but rather has multidimensional characteristics. The SISBEN scores potential beneficiaries from 0 to 100 (where the higher value represents better quality of life), which is divided into five levels of vulnerability. The levels determine the potential beneficiaries' eligibility to participate in the different programs.
6. The minimum retirement ages in Colombia are less than 65 years, but the use of this age as a cutoff allows us to evaluate the impact of the system beyond the differences generated in the short term by regulation changes or retirement behavior in the labor market.
7. The statistical information published by the PPSAM and Elderly Colombia is limited, with incomplete and contradictory data. For example, one official report (Ministerio de Trabajo 2013) highlights that the number of beneficiaries for Elderly Colombia was 933,000 for 2012 (p. 25) and 627,000 (p. 39), whereas the CONPES 156 document claims the figure is 842,000 (CONPES 2012, p. 4).
8. The arguments offered include the effect of design problems with the pay-as-you-go regime, the role and level of the minimum pension, the institutional weakness of the public institutions responsible for collections and monitoring of employers' compliance with their obligations, and the existence of structural factors that influence labor informality and do not respond to worker incentives, among others.

Bibliography

Ayala, U., and O. Acosta. 2001. "Reformas Pensionales y Costos Fiscales en Colombia." Serie Financiamiento del Desarrollo 116, ECLAC, Santiago de Chile.

———. 2002. "Políticas para Promover una Ampliación de la Cobertura del Sistema de Pensiones en Colombia." Serie Financiamiento del Desarrollo 118, ECLAC, Santiago de Chile.

CONPES (Consejo Nacional de Política Económica y Social). 2002. "Fondo de Solidaridad Pensional: Pautas para un mejor desempeño 2002." CONPES, Documento 60, Departamento Nacional de Planeación, Bogotá.

———. 2003. "El Nuevo Papel del Fondo de Solidaridad Pensional." CONPES, Documento 70, Departamento Nacional de Planeación, Bogotá.

———. 2004. "Ajustes a los Requisitos del Programa de Protección Social al Adulto Mayor Subcuenta de Subsistencia, Fondo de Solidaridad Pensional." CONPES, Documento 78, Departamento Nacional de Planeación, Bogotá.

———. 2007. "Fondo de Solidaridad Pensional: Ampliación de Cobertura y Ajustes en los Requisitos y Operación." CONPES, Documento 105, Departamento Nacional de Planeación, Bogotá.

———. 2012. "Diseño e Implementación de los Beneficios Económicos Periódicos (BEPS)." CONPES, Documento 156, Departamento Nacional de Planeación, Bogotá.

Henao, M. 2001. *El Fondo de Solidaridad Previsional.* Draft report, Bogotá.

MIDAS (Mas Inversión para el Desarrollo Alternativo Sostenible). 2008. "Diseño de los Beneficios Economicos Periodicos—BEPS. Informe Final." USAID, Bogotá.

Millán, N. 2010. "El Sistema Pensional en Colombia: Retos y Alternativas para Aumentar la Cobertura." Fedesarrollo, Bogotá.

Ministerio de la Protección Social. 2004. "Programa de Protección Social al Adulto Mayor. Manual Operativo." Bogotá.

Ministerio de Trabajo. 2013. "Nuevo Modelo de Protección para la Vejez." Bogotá.

Rofman, R., and L. Oliveri. 2012. "La Cobertura de los Sistemas Previsionales en América Latina: Conceptos e Indicadores." Serie de Documentos de Trabajo sobre Políticas Sociales 7, World Bank, Buenos Aires.

Santa Maria, M., R. Steiner, J. Botero, M. Martínez, and N. Millán. 2010. "El Sistema Pensional en Colombia: Retos y Alternativas para aumentar la Cobertura." Fedesarrollo, Bogotá.

CHAPTER 7

Costa Rica

Juliana Martínez Franzoni

Profile of the Elderly Population

Costa Rica is in the process of an advanced demographic transition that is expected to end around 2050. This transition is the result of a reduction in the fertility rate—currently below the population replacement rate, improvements in the population's health and education conditions, and the pursuant increase in life expectancy at birth. Even though the elderly population's labor participation has decreased, 45 percent of pensioners were working in 2011. Labor market participation for this group is marked by weak demand, and self-employment or microenterprises are the predominant options.

Demographic Situation and the Link with the Job Market

Once the demographic transition process is completed, it is expected that the population of Costa Rica will stop growing by 2050, after reaching almost six million inhabitants. The fast pace of growth of the elderly population is reflected both in absolute numbers as well as figures relative to the population in general. According to the National Statistics and Census Institute (Instituto Nacional de Estadística y Censo [INEC]), in 2011 there were 364,333 elderly persons, or 142,576 more than in 2000 (figure 7.1). As a result of the growth of the elderly (over 65) population, it now represents almost 8 percent of the total population, after barely exceeding 5 percent in the second half of the 20th century, and is expected to reach 30 percent by 2070.

Costa Rica's population structure has aged during the past century and is expected to continue doing so in this century. Figure 7.2 shows the population pyramids for 1950, 2000, 2050, and 2100, where we can clearly see the trend of a diminishing base and a widening peak in each successive period.

Far from being homogenous, the elderly population faces heterogeneous social profiles and risks (CCP and CONAPAM 2008). The majority of elderly persons lack paid work (they are considered "inactive"). Since 2001 the elderly population's labor participation rate has fallen (figure 7.3), from 18 percent to 15 percent in 2011 (compared with a mostly stable 60 percent of the population older than 15). Unemployment among the elderly is 3.1 percent (compared with

Figure 7.1 Evolution of the Total Population and Relative Weight of the Elderly, 1950–2100

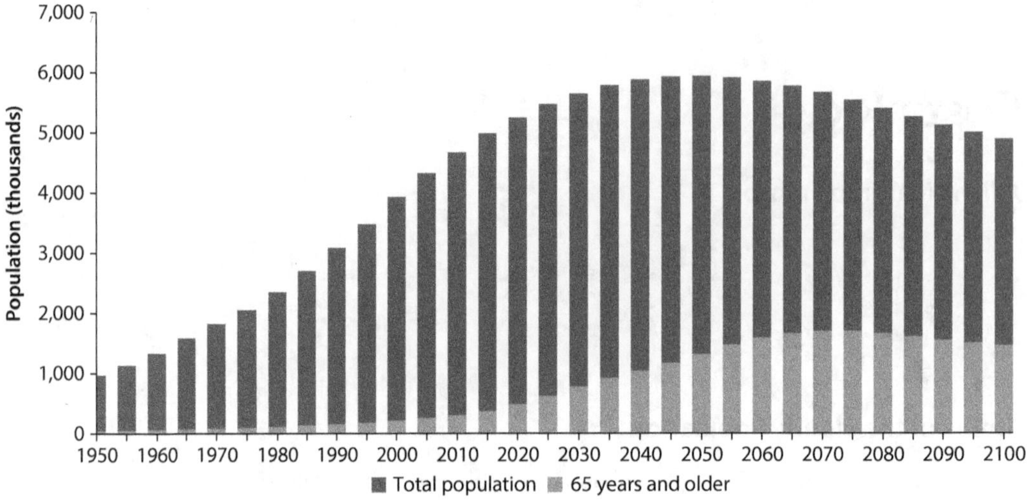

Source: Centro Latinoamericano y Caribeño de Demografía (CELADE).

Figure 7.2 Population Pyramids, by Gender and Age, 1950–2100

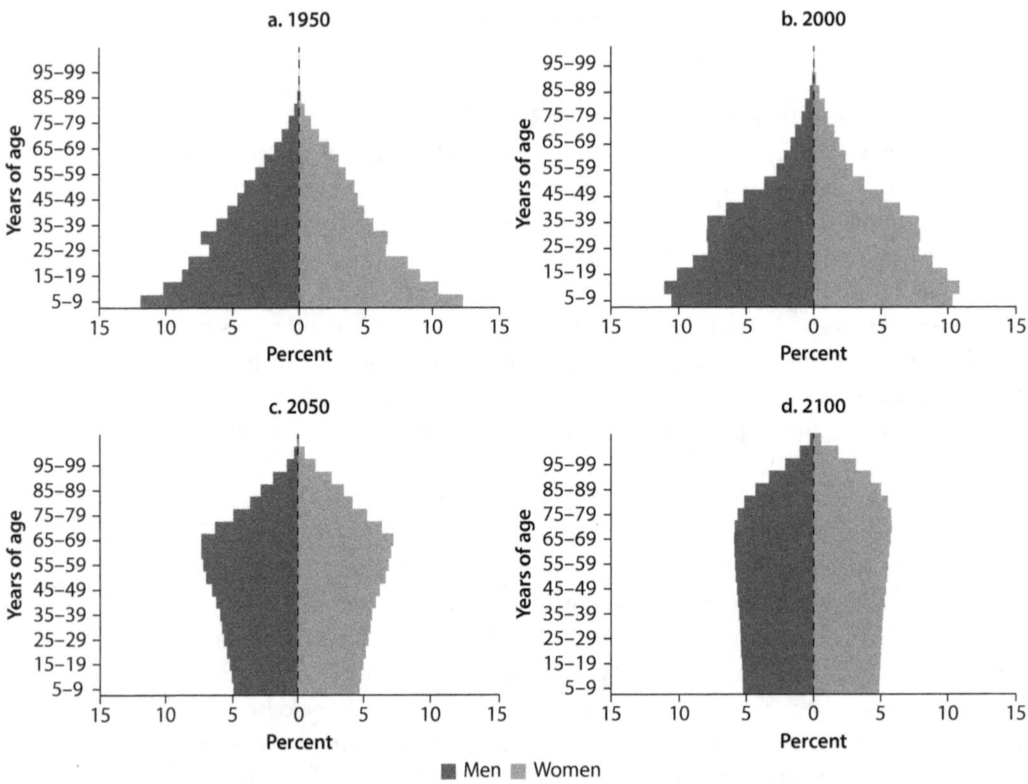

Source: Centro Latinoamericano y Caribeño de Demografía (CELADE).

Figure 7.3 Evolution of the Employed Elderly Population Receiving Pensions, Labor Force Participation, and Unemployment Rates for the Elderly and the Population 15 Years and Older, 2001–11

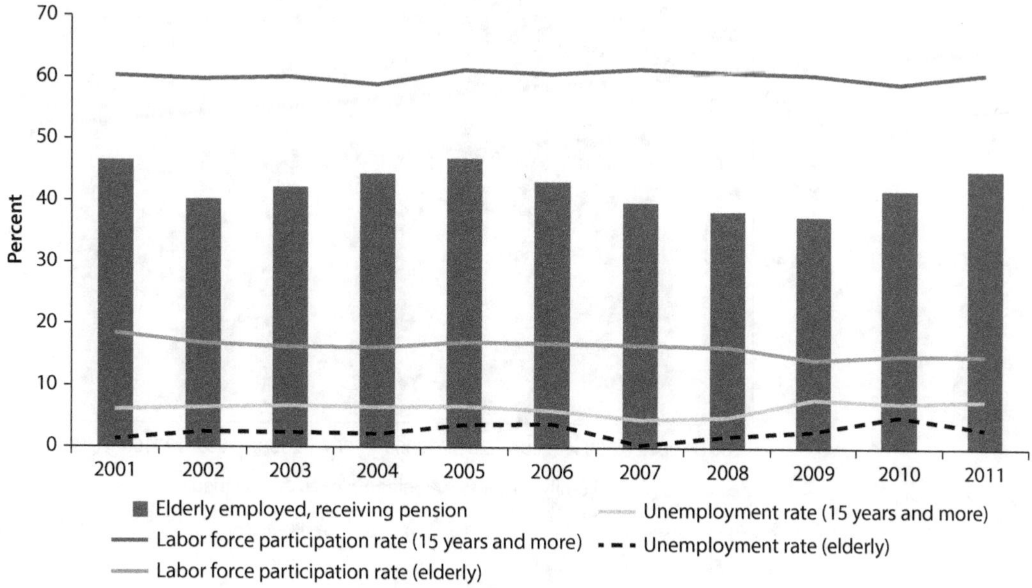

Source: Based on Household Surveys, Instituto Nacional de Estadística y Censo (INEC).

7.7 percent for the general population). Around 60,000 elderly persons work, most as self-employed workers and in microenterprises, in jobs that are not covered by the contributory pension system. More than 40 percent of the elderly that is employed is also receiving a pension.

Job placement for the elderly population is more precarious than for the general population. In terms of occupational categories, the proportion of the elderly population working independently is high (figure 7.4). In 2001, 66.7 percent of the working elderly was in this category, three times more than the total employed population (22.8 percent). Most work in microenterprises (84.5 percent in 2011), in jobs that are mainly subsistence economic activities.[1]

The precarious job placement is also associated with a high proportion of the elderly working more than 48 hours per week. During the last decade the distribution of workers among different lengths of work weeks has been relatively stable (figure 7.5). In 2011, 60 percent of employed persons in this age group worked part-time, 20 percent full-time, and 20 percent overtime.

In 2011, more than one-quarter of the employed elderly population worked in agriculture (29.8 percent) and approximately another quarter in the commercial sector (23.4 percent). The rest are distributed among manufacturing (10.6 percent), domestic labor (5.1 percent), and other activities (31 percent).

Access to Social Protection

Costa Rica is, along with Chile and Uruguay, one of the three countries with the highest pension coverage as a percentage of the economically active

Figure 7.4 Evolution of the Distribution of the Elderly Population, by Occupational Category, 2001–11

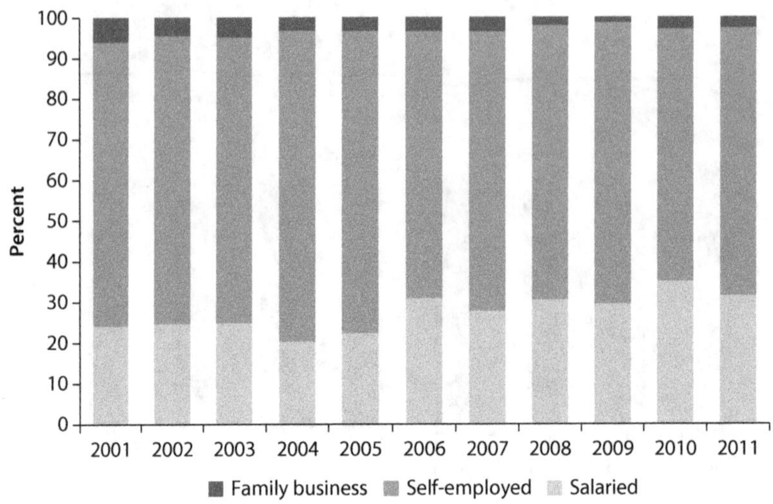

Source: Based on Household Surveys, Instituto Nacional de Estadística y Censo (INEC).

Figure 7.5 Evolution of the Elderly Population, by Length of the Work Week, 2001–11

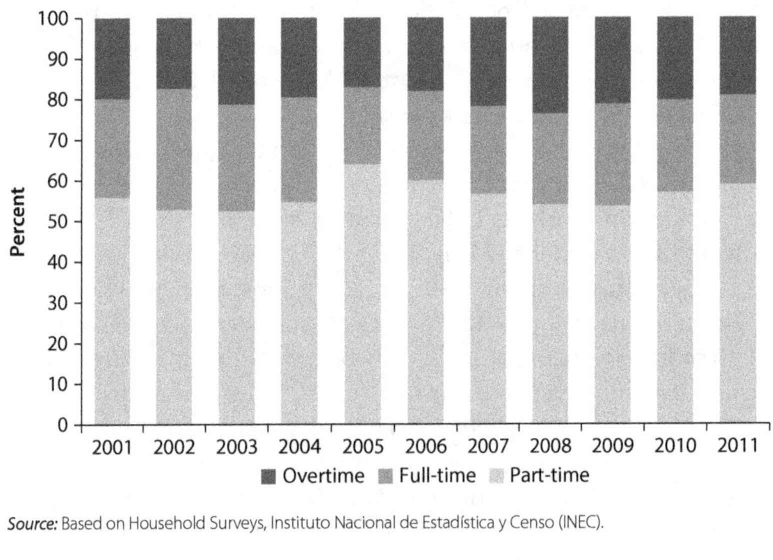

Source: Based on Household Surveys, Instituto Nacional de Estadística y Censo (INEC).

population (EAP) (Mesa-Lago 2009; Rofman and Oliveri 2011). The 2005 reform drove an increase in coverage, especially among the self-employed and women. In 2009, 70 percent of the employed population contributed to social security, 80 percent of the salaried population and somewhat less than 40 percent of self-employed or independent workers (figure 7.6). In contrast with Chile, Costa Rica reached this level of coverage through a partially funded, collective

Figure 7.6 Pension Insurance Coverage, by Type of Work, 1989–2009

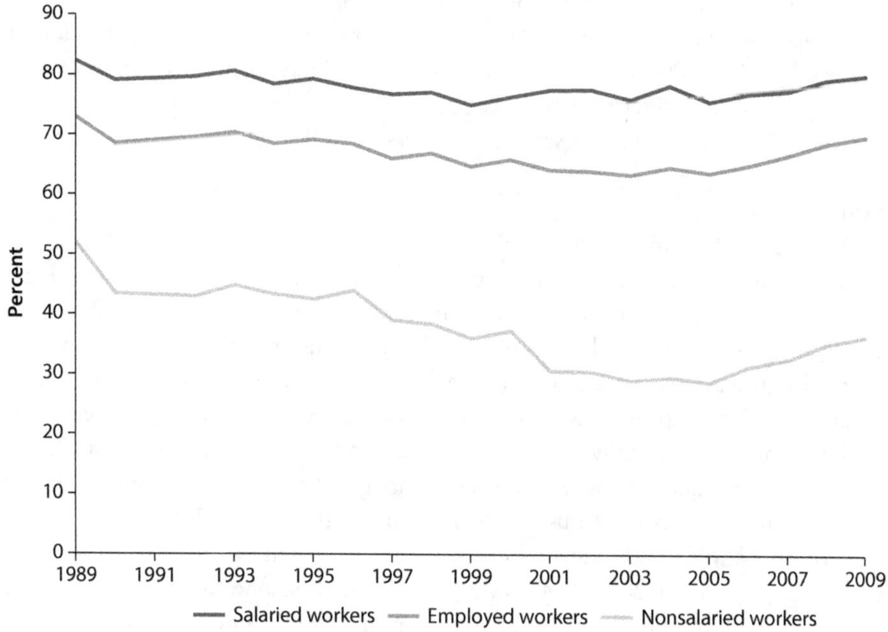

Source: Rofman and Oliveri 2011.

pension system with universal coverage and solidarity benefits, supplemented by a noncontributory pension established during the first half of the 1970s. This architecture remained intact during the wave of promarket reforms that swept across the region in the mid-1980s and 1990s. The reforms in Costa Rica added to and modified this system instead of replacing it. The changes were parametric and strengthened the solidarity and the progressiveness of the regime.

The 2005 reform had two objectives: extend coverage under a framework of pension universalization and improve access conditions for women to social security in its own right (Technical Advisory Group 2005). Specifically the reform made participation in the system compulsive for self-employed workers and introduced incentives for women. The reform improved the financial sustainability, with a positive outlook for a 50-year period, and increased progressivity in both reference salary and replacement rates. It also defined criteria for the establishment of a minimum pension in the contributory system that would in turn affect the minimum for the noncontributory pension. Finally, it created a modality for retiring with a reduced pension, aimed at incentivizing participation and increasing the coverage of the general pension regime.

Together, many of these changes should reduce the pressure on the noncontributory regime and improve the quality of the contributory regime's benefits in the medium term. The creation of a complementary individual savings regime would also have positive effects in terms of broadening coverage because it created an additional incentive for high-income workers to contribute to the collective partially funded system, making it a requirement for enrollment in the system. Figure 7.6 shows the evolution of coverage over two decades, including the implementation of the Worker Protection Law (Ley de Protección al Trabajador) in 2000. The data demonstrate the increase in insurance of self-employed workers since the approval of the 2005 reform and the increase that the reform produced among salaried workers as well.

Long-Term Care Services

As in the rest of Latin America, long-term care of the elderly for Costa Ricans has been almost exclusively the responsibility of women within families. Three main trends are driving changes to this eldercare arrangement: the reduction of average family size, the increase in households made up exclusively of elderly persons, and women's growing participation in the labor market. These trends pose new challenges for a social protection policy that is strongly supported by unpaid care within families, specifically care given by women (Martínez Franzoni 2008).

Among the main trends, we can see a change in household composition and a reduction in the size of households made up of the elderly. In 2011, 21.2 percent of households had elderly members, compared with 17.4 percent in 1990 and 18.3 percent in 2000 (see table 7.1).[2] Both households with one elderly person as well as households with two or more elderly have increased. At the same time, the average size of these households has shrunk, from 4.6 members in 1990 to 4.2 in 2000 and to 3.9 in 2009, while the number of potential caregivers for each elderly person has also decreased from 3.4 in 1990 to 2.6 in 2011 (Sauma 2011). Additionally, the number of households made up exclusively of the elderly has increased, nearly doubling from 3.4 percent of households in 1990 to 6.2 percent in 2011 (equal to 81,795 households). It is reasonable to expect that these persons have less access to caregivers from within their own families.

The proportion of people who can be full-time caregivers has also decreased. Table 7.2 shows an estimate of the presence of adults with time available for caregiving, both men and women as well as just women. We can observe a continuous reduction in the number of households that have at least one adult that

Table 7.1 Households, by Presence of the Elderly, 1990, 2000, and 2011
Percent

	1990	*2000*	*2011*
Total households	100	100	100
Without elderly	82.6	81.7	78.8
With one elderly person	12.8	13.1	15.2
With two or more elderly	4.6	5.2	6.0
Households with just one elderly person			
• As a percentage of households with elderly persons	19.4	23.4	29.1
• As a percentage of all households	3.4	4.3	6.2

Source: Based on Instituto Nacional de Estadística y Censo (INEC).

Table 7.2 Presence of Potential Caregivers in Households with at Least One Elderly Member, 1990, 2000, and 2011
Percent

	1990	*2000*	*2011*
Persons in the household between 18 and 64 years that do not study or work for pay			
None	51.5	59.2	68.2
One or more	48.5	40.8	31.8
One member	37.1	33.7	27.1
Two members	9.6	5.8	4.0
Three or more members	1.9	1.3	0.7
Women in the household between 18 and 64 years that do not study or work for pay			
None	55.8	64.1	73.3
One or more	44.2	35.9	26.7
One woman	36.1	31.8	24.3
Two women	7.1	3.6	2.3
Three or more women	1.0	0.6	0.1

Source: Based on Instituto Nacional de Estadística y Censo (INEC).

does not study or work. These households made up almost half of the total in 1990 (48.5 percent) and less than one-third in 2011 (31.8 percent). Considering just women, households with at least one woman that did not study or work for a wage fell from 44.2 percent in 1990 to 26.7 percent in 2011 (a reduction of 17.5 percent). In other words, 6.8 of every 10 households with elderly members lack at least one adult available to be a full-time caregiver, and 7.3 of every 10 lack women with this availability.

Another pattern observed is the increase in the average age of women who are potential caregivers for the elderly population. The population that needs care from third parties to perform basic daily activities receives this care almost exclusively from immediate family, from daughters in particular, whether or not they live in the same household (CCP and CONAPAM 2008, p. 83). Upon observing behavior among those who live in the same household it is possible to confirm the role played by daughters (table 7.3). The individuals called upon to care for the elderly population are women, and those that do not study or have paid work in particular. Between 1990 and 2011 the average age of these caregivers increased from 45 to 50 years old. Given the sustained trend toward more women in the labor market in the country and the region, it can be expected that this average age will continue to increase. This trend results in two new social problems: greater tension between the demands associated with paid work and demands associated with caregiving among employed women, and a greater proportion of children, young people, and especially the elderly that will have to care for themselves, even if they are not in a condition to do so.

It is estimated that three of every 10 elderly have some level of dependence or require care (Sauma 2011). Many elderly care for other people, especially children.[3] In Costa Rica, the Social Protection Committee (Junta de Protección

Table 7.3 Average Age of Individuals Identified as Caregivers to the Elderly, 1990, 2000, and 2011
Years

	1990	*2000*	*2011*
Without paid work			
• Men and women	43	44	45
• Women only	44	45	47
Without work or studies			
• Men and women	45	46	49
• Women only	45	47	50

Source: Based on Instituto Nacional de Estadística y Censo (INEC).

Social [JPS]) defines a dependent person as someone who requires the permanent support of a third party because of functional or mental health problems. More specifically, "an elderly person can be said to be dependent when he or she presents a loss of functional autonomy and needs the help of other people in order to go about daily life" (JPS 2010, p. 1). Fourteen percent of the elderly (51,000 people) have low-level dependence; that is, they require support for one or two daily activities. Eight percent (almost 30,000 people) have medium dependence, requiring support for three or four daily activities. The other 8 percent are highly dependent and require support for five or more activities each day (CCP and CONAPAM 2008; Rosero-Bixby, Fernández, and Dow 2005).[4] This is a third relevant feature for the social protection system because it highlights the limits of monetary transfers in the face of service needs, whether private, public, or family.

Funding Consumption

The pension system is the main source of income for the elderly population. Table 7.4 shows the source of income that the elderly population contributes to households. The relative importance of labor income is not only minor (18 percent overall, 26 percent among men and 4 percent among women), but it has decreased considerably compared with 1990. Half of this population's income comes from contributory pensions (48 percent overall and 51 percent in the case of women due to the combination of their own pensions and survivor benefits as widows). The relative importance of noncontributory pensions is very small (5 percent) although it is somewhat higher for women (8 percent). Since 1990 the role of contributory pensions has diminished, both for the elderly population in general (among whom it fell from 53 percent to 48 percent) and even more for women (from 60 percent to 51 percent), while the source of income that experienced the greatest increase was "other income." This source tripled for the overall elderly population (from 9 percent in 1990 to 29 percent in 2011) and more than doubled for women (from 15 percent to 37 percent). The main item included in this concept is asset income. These transfers are made up of rental income, interest income, dividends, benefits,

Table 7.4 Income Source Structure for the Elderly, by Gender, 1990, 2000, and 2010
Percent

	1990	*2000*	*2010*
Both genders	100	100	100
Labor income	33	24	18
Noncontributory regime	5	4	5
Contributory regime	53	53	48
Other income	9	19	29
Men	100	100	100
Labor income	38	32	26
Noncontributory regime	4	3	3
Contributory regime	50	49	46
Other income	7	17	24
Women	100	100	100
Labor income	17	6	4
Noncontributory regime	8	9	8
Contributory regime	60	62	51
Other income	15	23	37

Source: Based on Instituto Nacional de Estadística y Censo (INEC).

alimony payments, and foreign pensions. This data are difficult to interpret because of comparability problems stemming from changes to the formulation of the questions in the 2010 survey.[5]

Historical Trajectory and Current Architecture of Pensions

Costa Rica has maintained a stable social protection architecture in general, including the system that supports the elderly population. The pension system original design included both noncontributory and contributory components. The system was consolidated early in its development by expanding pensions beyond the occupational schemes through a collective funding model.

Before 1941 two types of pensions existed in Costa Rica, ex gratia and contributory. The first type was awarded by the Congress of the Republic and was fully funded by the national budget.[6] The second type requiring that workers contribute during their active years, as in other countries in Latin America, was created for diverse occupational groups of public employees, starting with members of the military[7] and educators,[8] to expand later to other areas[9] (Castro Méndez 2012).

In the absence of several of the conditions that normally existed during the creation of general social security (such as demand from an organized worker class), in 1941 the government created the general pension regime administered by the Costa Rican Social Security Agency (Caja Costarricense del Seguro Social [CCSS]), which was called Disability, Old Age, and Death (Invalidez, Vejez y Muerte [IVM]). As in other intermediate countries, the system was a unified regime for workers without divisions based on occupation. The creation of social security was enshrined in the chapter on Social Guarantees of the Political Constitution, which also established the CCSS's monopoly over the administration of social security.[10] Coverage expansion began with primarily urban low-wage unskilled workers and later included those with higher incomes.

The general regime was created as a collective, partially funded system and from its creation has operated with a reserve fund. In contrast with other regimes in the region, the Costa Rican system never operated as a pure pay-as-you-go regime, which in many countries in the region resulted in the adoption of structural reforms and pension privatization because of the effects of actuarial and financial crises.

Even though the general regime explicitly sought to unify the existing special regimes,[11] these not only remained, but others were also created. For example, the Treasury regime was created in 1943 and the Public Works and Transport regime in 1944. One problem with these regimes was that they lacked government contributions (neither as the employer nor as the state) and the national budget had to make up the difference between the contributions received and the cost of honoring the benefits granted (Rodríguez Herrera and Durán 1998).

Meanwhile, the general regime evolved toward universal coverage. One factor that contributed to its expansion was health insurance. At the time the CCSS was created, the preexisting special regimes lacked medical services (a marked difference from other intermediate countries in the region such as Mexico). Hospitals were managed by charity institutions, and by offering its own health services, the general regime had a strong incentive for workers to join it.

From the 1970s on, the incremental expansion of contributory pensions was accompanied by the creation of nontraditional coverage schemes, both contributory and noncontributory, with the latter directed to the underprivileged population. Specifically two regimes were created for the poor, the Noncontributory Pension Regime (Régimen No Contributivo de Pensiones [RNC]) in 1974 and the Insured at the State's Cost (Asegurados por Cuenta del Estado) in 1984 to enable access to health services. Additionally, the government established voluntary insurance for nonsalaried workers (1975). This coverage expansion relaxed the system's Bismarckian origins and created the conditions necessary to expand coverage that, in practice, gave rise to scenarios with highly stratified benefits.

Costa Rica experienced fragmentation in terms of access and benefit requirements. At the same time the general regime was consolidating, the special regimes were also expanding. By 1990 there were nearly 20 such regimes, and most were funded from the national budget. This fragmentation was successfully corrected. In 1992, the Pension Framework Law (Ley Marco de Pensiones) specified that all new civil servants would join the general pension system. The special regimes shut down but continued serving those that were contributing in July 1992 with unified retirement requirements set by the same law. The two exceptions were the staff of the judiciary and educators (Magisterio Nacional).[12] These two regimes kept special benefit and contribution requirements that differentiated them from the pensions funded by the national budget.

In 1995 a voluntary system of individually funded pensions was created by the Private Regime of Complementary Pensions law (no. 7523 of July 7, 1995). It was a long-term savings system, funded by voluntary individual or collective contributions that would be administered by public or private pension operators.

The general pension system's universalization process was reinforced in 2000 with the passage of the Worker Protection Law (Ley de Protección al Trabajador). From a coverage expansion point of view this law introduced two important changes. First, it established mandatory disability, old age, and life insurance in the general regime for all independent workers. Second, it established that all elderly individuals living in poverty and lacking a pension from another regime should receive a noncontributory pension. The law prioritized elderly housewives (Castro Méndez 2001).

Simultaneously, the Worker Protection Law introduced a second mandatory pension pillar exclusively for salaried workers. As in other countries, it was an individually funded regime with defined contributions and benefits determined by contributions and investment returns. In contrast to other countries, the 4.25 percent contribution that funds this system comes from the reassignment of preexisting payroll contributions that had been assigned to institutions other than the general pension system,[13] including a reform of the unemployment assistance (compensation for unjustified dismissal).[14] This regime is administered by privately and publicly owned corporations. Costa Rica's mixed or multipillar system is unique in that the entire insured population must contribute to the general collective regime, which awards the main portion of a worker's pension, while salaried workers must also contribute to the fully individually funded regime which finances a complementary pension (Mesa-Lago 2010).[15]

The Worker Protection Law also harmonized the voluntary individually funded regime (article 14 and subsequent articles), honoring the previously agreed-upon requirements even though it established access to elderly benefits as soon as 57 years of age (article 76 and Transitory Provision XV of the same law) (Castro Méndez 2001). The creation of a centralized collection system managed by the CCSS was a very important tool for coverage expansion and was a necessary condition for the start-up of the operators of the individually funded component.[16]

In terms of supervision, the Worker Protection Law converted the existing Pensions Superintendency (Superintendencia de Pensiones [SUPEN]) into the regulator and supervisor of the national pension system.[17] Given the administrative autonomy granted to the CCSS by the Political Constitution (article 73), the regulator's scope is mainly focused on the individually funded components of the system (Castro Méndez 2001). In the case of the CCSS general regime, the SUPEN's scope of responsibility is limited to nonbinding recommendations (Mesa-Lago 2010) based on actions that are mandatory. Specifically, the law requires SUPEN to evaluate the annual report that CCSS should submit to the IVM regime Oversight Committee;[18] supervise the investment of funds in accordance with the law; define the content, format, and frequency of the information that the CCSS should provide to SUPEN; and oversee the disability qualification system.[19] In 2005 the general pension system underwent parametric changes in matters of contribution amounts, benefit amounts and progressiveness, and the diversification of pension eligibility conditions, which complemented the structural reform from 2000.

Noncontributory Access to Social Protection for the Elderly

The RNC covers the elderly population living in conditions of poverty, with a focus toward rural communities and regions distant from the central valley (PEN 2009). Since its creation, it has not undergone substantial changes that would improve coverage, although changes have been made to the criteria regulating the assignment of available pensions and to pension amounts.

The RNC was created during the 1970s and protects nonsalaried workers in a condition of income poverty who do not qualify for access to any of the existing contributory regimes. The benefits include both a cash pension payment as well as access to health insurance provided by the CCSS. More specifically, to access this program the individual should receive income below the official poverty line established by INEC and lack economically significant assets, and, in the event he or she does owns property, it should be less than 400 square meters (urban) or 1,000 square meters (rural) (CCSS 2005, articles 4 and 5).[20]

Most beneficiaries of the noncontributory regime are 65 years and older, which is the same age limit for men accessing the contributory pension system. Persons with disabilities or in extreme poverty, widows lacking other income, and orphaned children are also entitled to receive this pension.[21] From 2000 to 2009 the makeup of the population receiving these pensions has remained mostly unchanged: The population over 65 years represented 70 percent of the beneficiary population in 2000 and 69 percent in 2009 (Trejos 2010). According to the CCSS Integrated Pension System, in recent years 60 percent of noncontributory pensions have gone to the elderly population, 35 percent to persons with disabilities, and the rest to persons in other situations (PEN 2009, p. 111). Inconsistencies in reporting are due to the different sources used (household surveys and the Integrated Pension System, respectively).

In 2008, 27 percent of the elderly population in conditions of poverty did not receive a pension (PEN 2009, p. 121). Seventeen percent of pensions were distributed to individuals living alone, 44 percent to those living in households with two or three members, and 39 percent to those in households with four or more members (PEN 2009, p. 111). In most cases (more than 90 percent) households do not receive more than one noncontributory pension. With the passage of the Worker Protection Law in 2000, the noncontributory pension amount was fixed at half the value of the lowest contributory pension. Pension amounts recently increased between 2006 and 2008 to meet this legal requirement. Noncontributory pensions increased in 2006 from US$34.20 (C 17,500) to US$64.50 (C 35,000); in mid-2007 they reached US$96.80 (C 50,000), and in March 2008 they were US$109.30 (C 57,500), equal to 183.8 percent of the cost of the basic food basket.[22]

Figure 7.7 shows the evolution of the ordinary pension in the noncontributory regime since 1999 and illustrates the considerable increase it has experienced. During 2011, increases in neither the number nor the amounts of pensions took place, and a deficit situation prevailed. In the future, the amount and the coverage will be able to increase only if the minimum contributory pension increases and if the economic recovery creates more jobs and raises real salaries and the tax take, respectively (Trejos 2010).

The impact of the RNC pensions on the population's income poverty conditions has been systematically analyzed by the State of the Nation Program (Programa Estado de la Nación) (PEN 2010). Table 7.5 illustrates these effects since 2006, when the RNC amount had not yet been increased. From this year forward, we observe a progressive increase in this regime. In 2007 the RNC

Figure 7.7 Evolution of the Real Monthly Pension, 1999–2010

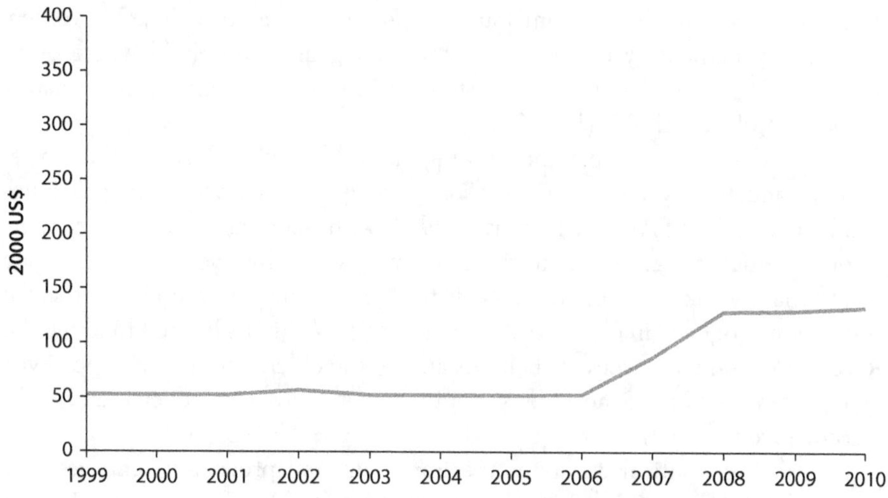

Source: Trejos 2010.

Table 7.5 Effects of the RNC on the Incidence of Poverty and Extreme Poverty, 2006–10

	Reduction as a result of the RNC (in percentage points) of the incidence in	
Year	*Poverty*	*Extreme poverty*
2006	0.5	1.0
2007	2.2	2.2
2008	1.9	2.0
2009	1.8	2.3
2010	1.7	1.9

Source: Programa Estado de la Nación (PEN) 2011.
Note: Poverty and extreme poverty correspond to the first two-tenths and the first tenth of the income distribution, respectively.

reduced the incidence of poverty by 2.2 percentage points and extreme poverty by 2.2 points. This effect of the noncontributory pensions began to diminish in 2008 in relation to the poverty level and in 2010 in relation to extreme poverty (PEN 2011).

These effects on poverty reduction are the result of appropriate targeting. In 2009, 60.5 percent of the noncontributory beneficiaries belonged to the poorest 20 percent of the population. Almost half belonged to the first decile of the income distribution, that is, they were in or nearly in extreme poverty, and 13.2 percent were in the second decile. Moreover, 9.2 percent belonged to the third decile, which is considered vulnerable persons, and the remaining 25 percent represented leakage to other income levels (PEN 2010). This percentage has not varied significantly since 2006 (Sauma 2011).

The RNC can benefit women proportionally more than men. The National Development Plan (Plan Nacional de Desarrollo) (MIDEPLAN 2010, p. 106) proposes that reinforcing the RNC pensions should "focus especially on women in a condition of economic helplessness or that, because of their family situation, cannot join the labor market in adequate conditions." In 2011 there were 23,593 male pensioners in the noncontributory regime, compared to 36,971 women. Also, a complementary benefit for women living in a household where other member receives a RNC pension existed until recently, covering approximately 10 percent of households (PEN 2009).

Given that the noncontributory regime is financed through the Social Welfare and Family Income Fund (Fondo de Bienestar Social y Asignaciones Familiares [FODESAF]), which is funded with sales and payroll taxes, its resources fluctuate according to the economic cycle. This cyclical aspect is one of the main weaknesses of the noncontributory regime, as well as other social protection programs in Costa Rica (Trejos 1995). Within its limited funding, the RNC has evened out access to benefits among the elderly population. However, a significant sector of the elderly population still lives in poverty and lacks income (Trejos 2010).

In terms of political economy, the important and progressive changes that occurred between 2006 and 2008 were implemented by the Executive Branch in the midst of an expansion of public social spending associated both with a countercyclical rationale as well as the electoral competition reflected in the first national referendum in October 2007. The government proposed the "Shield Plan" (Plan Escudo) to confront the economic crisis. Among other measures, the plan announced a 15 percent increase in RNC pensions, the fourth increase since President Arias took office in 2006 (PEN 2009). Almost 10 years after it had become law, the government was finally implementing what had been stipulated in the Worker Protection Law, which specified that the noncontributory pension amount should equal half of the minimum contributory pension.

Recent Performance and Reach of Pensions

Costa Rica is among the Latin American countries with the highest coverage of active workers and the elderly. These countries have relatively low incidence of

Table 7.6 Social Protection Coverage among the Elderly Population, 1990, 2000, and 2011
Percent

	Total			*Men*			*Women*		
Total	*1990*	*2000*	*2011*	*1990*	*2000*	*2011*	*1990*	*2000*	*2011*
Salaried	1.7	1.8	0.8	2.9	2.8	1.7	0.6	0.9	0.1
Self-employed	8.5	6.1	6.6	13.7	9.5	10.7	3.5	3.1	3.5
Pension	27.2	38.8	44.6	36.4	51.1	54.3	18.4	27.8	37.1
Noncontributory	27.2	24.0	19.9	26.0	21.4	17.8	28.3	26.3	21.5
Family	26.2	23.5	23.7	10.2	8.0	10.5	41.7	37.2	33.8
None	8.5	5.5	3.4	10.5	6.8	3.7	6.6	4.3	3.1
Others or ignored	0.6	0.3	1.1	0.4	0.4	1.3	0.9	0.4	0.9
Total	100	100	100	100	100	100	100	100	100

Source: Based on Instituto Nacional de Estadística y Censo (INEC).

labor informality and poverty among the elderly, as well as available noncontributory or social insurance mechanisms (Mesa-Lago 2010).

Table 7.6 presents data relative to the different types of coverage, total and by gender, in 1990, 2000, and 2011. The trend shows an increase in coverage. In 1990 the elderly population that lacked income was 8.5 percent of the total, whereas in 2011 it had decreased to 3.4 percent. During this period access to contributory pensions increased (from 27.2 percent in 1990 to 44.6 percent in 2011). Conversely, noncontributory access, family insurance, and the existence of labor income decreased. It is also relevant that these trends took place both among men and women.

One factor that influenced the increase in pension coverage in Costa Rica with respect to other high coverage countries is that, as in Argentina, Brazil, and Uruguay, insuring the independent or self-employed working population is mandatory. Moreover, although in terms of informality and poverty Costa Rica has performed worse than these countries, the self-employed participating in the pension system receive a tax subsidy that makes up for the absence of an employer contribution. This is one of the factors that explain why among employed workers coverage of the salaried population has remained constant, while among the self-employed population it has increased considerably. Finally, the country has also had greater relative success in insuring the rural population: 83.8 percent of the rural population and 95.8 percent of the rural elderly have some type of social insurance access (regardless of the type). Of the entire elderly population that resides in rural areas, 54.4 percent have a pension.[23]

Benefit adequacy is defined by the relationship between the benefits and the risks affecting the beneficiary population. For the elderly, the risk structure has two main components: the cost of living (food, clothing, housing) and access to health services that cover chronic conditions and catastrophic situations. Taken together, they should offer access to adequate levels of transfers and services.

In Costa Rica the retirement age is 65 years although it is possible to receive an early pension at 60 years of age for women and 62 for men, with at least

25 years of contributions (the longest period in the region, after Argentina and Uruguay, established in 2005).[24] Contributions rates are being increased, from 7.5 percent to 10.5 percent in a tiered process (0–5 percent every 5 years; CCSS 2005). Also, since 2005 the replacement rate considers salaries of the last 20 years in real terms, which favors less qualified workers whose salaries tend to decrease as they age. The replacement rate is tiered: 52 percent for those who on average have earned two minimum salaries or less, decreasing to 45 percent for those who on average have earned eight minimum salaries or more. As Mesa-Lago (2010) points out, this method exceeds the norm set by the International Labour Organization (ILO) of at least 40 percent of the reference salary.

In 2005 a reduced pension for individuals with at least 15 years of contributions was also introduced. This pension was thought to be particularly important for women, whose working years may have been reduced to raise their children. This pension is less than the minimum contributory pension, but greater than the noncontributory pension.

Contributory pensions are indexed considering the consumer price index. Using this index as a reference, between 2003 and 2009 the value of pensions increased 41.7 percent (Mesa-Lago 2010). Table 7.7 shows the more recent evolution. The annual growth rate declined in 2010, coinciding with the postelectoral period.[25]

Inequalities in Benefit Adequacy

The gap between benefit levels of the contributory and noncontributory pensions has shortened. Nonetheless, the situation is more unfavorable for women, who access the system mostly through the noncontributory regime. Between 2006 and 2008, the ratio between the highest pension and the lowest pension decreased from 7.6 to 4.5 times (Mesa-Lago 2010). Pension benefits of the contributory scheme increased 20 percent in this period, and noncontributory benefits grew 170 percent. This had a progressive impact on income distribution, although some analysts have shown concerns as it could act as a disincentive to participate in the contributory pension system. To avoid this risk, in 2009 the CCSS established that the pension amount in the noncontributory regime could

Table 7.7 Amount of the Minimum Pension of the General Regime of Disability, Old Age, and Death, and Real Growth Rates, July 2006–11

	Amount of the minimum pension		
Year	*Colones*	*US$*	*Annual growth rate (%)*
2006	60,000	117	15.0
2007	75,000	145	25.0
2008	86,625	165	15.5
2009	101,220	177	16.8
2010	107,613	205	6.3
2011	113,181	224	5.2

Source: Caja Costarricense del Seguro Social and estimates based on CCSS data.

not exceed 66.6 percent of the minimum contributory pension. Hereafter adjustments to the noncontributory pension amounts are dependent on adjustments to the IVM minimum pensions.

In terms of gender, most women receive lower benefits. Coverage of elderly women is higher than the regional average and has been increasing. However, as a reflection of the lower salaries and contribution densities, while in the labor force their contributory coverage is 20 percentage points lower than that of men (Mesa-Lago 2010). Survivor's insurance for widows and widowers is granted to spouses of deceased individuals if they were economically dependent from them. Historically it was available only for women, but it was extended to men if they can prove their economic dependency on their respective spouses. As direct coverage of women increased in recent years, the number of new survivors' benefits declined, which indicates that women's vulnerability has been declining, because they are less dependent on their spouses. Survivor's benefits are defined as a percentage of the pension received by the spouses and the decline in income due to the loss of a family member could, in some cases, lead the survivors toward poverty.

Financial Sustainability

The contributory system captures the largest part of social spending directed to the elderly. Reforms and actuarial studies point to the need for measures to ensure the financial sustainability of the system. The elderly population receives a percentage of social spending (18 percent) that is twice its weight in the total population and 2.5 times the average social spending per inhabitant (Trejos 2010). This spending includes pensions (contributory and noncontributory) and health services.

Pension spending is unequally divided between the contributory and noncontributory programs. In 2009, two-thirds of the spending corresponded to contributory pensions (which disproportionately favor the highest income quintile), 17 percent on health services, 10 percent on RNC pensions, and 6 percent on other programs for the elderly (education, housing, municipal services, recreational cultural services, and other social security programs).

The 2005 reform sought to reestablish the actuarial balance of the IVM regime through a reduction of expenditures and an increase in revenues. The goal was to avoid tapping interest income to finance benefits after 2011. Contributions plus interest income would have been insufficient in 2011 to finance all benefits, and by 2028 the reserve fund would have been drained (Technical Advisory Group 2005). Based on the results generated by the 2005 reform, the 2007 actuarial evaluation projected that the public pillar would be balanced until 2048, once the tiered contribution rate scheme established in 2005 is fully implemented (CCSS 2007).[26]

Political Economy of Changes and Continuities

Costa Rica adopted a process of discussion and production of technical evidence on the need for reforms that fostered room for agreement on parametric changes to the system. Within this process, the reform implemented in 2005 began with a government proposal to increase contributions and reduce replacement rates. The initial reaction among stakeholders was negative, mainly from unions and other organizations that disputed the actuarial scenario put forth by the CCSS. Finally, a negotiating group was formed called the Comisión Social (Social Commission), with broad membership from three sectors[27] that would diagnose the situation and propose solutions. At the beginning of 2005 a technical advisory group drew up a proposal that was approved by the Board of Directors of CCSS.

From the beginning there were two main factions: one in favor and another against the adjustment initially proposed by the CCSS' technical advisors. However, one point of agreement between both factions was the need to improve the administrative efficiency of the IVM regime, both in terms of collections as well as the granting process of pensions in general, including disability pensions. A review of the initial actuarial diagnostic proposed by the CCSS showed that greater administrative efficiency would help improve the situation, but it would not solve it.

The final proposal showed a favorable balance for increased financial sustainability along with a more progressive regime through a tiered replacement rate scheme that decreases as the salary level of contributors' increases. Also, a minimum pension was introduced. These changes were favorable for low-income individuals, such as the lengthening of the pension calculation period (from the last 48 to the last 240 contributions). On balance, the IVM regime was strengthened while maintaining payroll taxes below 10.5 percent, a limit that was considered critical by different stakeholders. Union leaders had to convince membership of the need to agree to an increase in contributions as the only way of maintaining the solidarity regime in the medium and long term. The main argument was that since the creation of the CCSS, contributions had remained stable even though the country has one of the highest life expectancies in the Americas.

In 2004, during the negotiation process that led to the IVM parametric reform adopted in 2005, the financial sector representative proposed that the administration of the collective pension fund be transferred to the private sector, but the proposal did not receive support from other participants, including the Costa Rican Union of Chambers and Associations of Private Enterprise (Unión Costarricense de Cámaras y Asociaciones de la Empresa Privada). In 2012 the financial sector was still interested in administering the collective pension fund, and the context for a reform was more favorable, for three reasons. First, the Illness and Maternity Insurance program is going through a crisis, under the management of CCSS, creating some doubts about the institutional capacity to manage the social insurance programs. This crisis, which is financial in nature and has manifested itself as insufficient liquidity, has been overcome by selling bonds from the general pension regime's reserves, a measure that was legally challenged because some considered it prejudicial to the pension fund financial situation.[28] The second reason is that, during 2010 and 2011, the CCSS office of Pension

Management was audited and the chief executive was removed from his post, an event that contributed to the public perception that the fund has serious problems. Finally, the actuarial study that the Superintendent of Pensions presented in 2010, although it was controversial and contradicted by other experts (from the ILO and the CCSS), contributed to this perception of disorder and insolvency.

Other Public Programs Aimed at the Elderly Population

Next to the pension schemes, two other programs aimed at the elderly stand out: the health program, because of its weight in total social transfers, and the long-term care services offered by the National Council of the Elderly (Consejo Nacional de la Persona Adulta Mayor [CONAPAM]) because it is an institutional innovation that coordinates with income transfer programs.

Access to Health Insurance

For the elderly population, access to health services is important and the financing mechanism (collective or individual, prepaid or out-of-pocket) is critical for dealing with chronic illnesses and catastrophic situations. In 2010, 91.9 percent of the entire population was covered by CCSS health insurance (directly, including pensioners, through a family member, or through the state). Direct coverage insurance reaches 81.7 percent of the salaried economically active population and 68.8 percent of nonsalaried workers.

The high level of coverage stands out as a positive performance indicator of the health system, with 70 percent of the economically active population paying premiums for health insurance and 92 percent of the total population covered by this insurance. This is a universal access health insurance program, with open benefits, organized as a pay-as-you-go scheme also administered by the CCSS. This insurance offers health services and cash transfers in the event of disability and pregnancy. Contributory access coexists with the noncontributory system ("por el Estado"),[29] which reached 11.9 percent of the population in 2009 and 32 percent of the direct insured. However, important coverage gaps exist among the most vulnerable population, because 62 percent of the population in the lowest income quintile was excluded in 2009.

In both insurance programs, contributory and noncontributory, there is a directly insured population, including the retired elderly population, and the population that is insured as economic dependents. The entire insured population, either direct or through a family member, has access to an open basket of services (basically the same services, except dental care) without waiting periods. Access to cash transfers on the other hand is limited to the direct insured and in the case of independent workers is subject to a waiting period.[30]

Noncontributory access for families is more important in quantitative terms than contributory access. In 2008 Costa Rica was the fourth ranked country in the region, after Uruguay, Panama, and Chile, in terms of health coverage for the economically active population, in contrast with near universal access when the participation of economically dependent family members is also considered.

Among the negative aspects, the health insurance program is undergoing a financial crisis that is the product of the organization of services and the conflicts of sectoral interests, both of a political-partisan nature as well as union-related and linked to the health care business. Costa Rica did not experience radical promarket reforms to its health care system, but rather changes to the management and patient attention models that began in the mid-1990s. During this process advances were seen in decentralization (although not in geographical terms) and in private-sector participation (although much more de facto than explicit and with clear rules).[31]

The result has been an incomplete reform that has profoundly changed the political economy inside and outside the system. Along with the administration of the general pension regime, the administration of the health care fund is an area of public policy subject to enormous promarket pressures. In terms of services, the system is going through a period of reduction in service quality, including for waiting periods.

Long-Term Care Services

In terms of coverage, public long-term-care services are currently marginal. The three main service modalities are so-called homes for the elderly (hereinafter referred to as "homes"), shelters, and day care centers.

Elderly homes provide comprehensive services to individuals that live there permanently. Beyond housing, the homes offer nursing, medical, and paramedic services, along with physical and occupational rehabilitation; nutrition; mental stimulation; recreational, occupational, and cultural activities; spiritual services; and laundry. These establishments are also expected to have trained personnel, appropriate support staff, and suitable layout of the physical installations, as well as any necessary adaptations to the facilities.

Shelters are a variation of elderly homes that were created to serve the population that lacks family support. The community takes over guardianship and provides attention to basic needs. They are open institutions, receive visitors, and members come and go in the community. There are two types of shelters: collective shelters are housing units with no more than 20 people, and they offer basic services (such as food, laundry, recreation, social, and other types of activities, and mental stimulation). Individual shelters are housing units in which a single elderly person who is capable of caring for him- or herself lives alone.

Day care centers serve the population with varied schedules and provide basic nutrition services and recreation activities. As with the previous modalities, these establishments are expected to have trained personnel, an adequate support team to offer diverse services, and a suitable layout of the facility. This service offering is a complement to living with family and seeks to maintain close relationships among the elderly, their families, and the community.

CONAPAM sets costs annually for elderly persons to stay in each of the three options. The organization undertakes a cost study periodically. The last study is from 2004 (CONAPAM 2004) and, along with annual cost-of-living increases, is used to distribute public resources (Sauma 2011). In 2010, CONAPAM set the cost of a monthly stay at US$657.60 for elderly homes and US$263.10 for day care centers (Sauma 2011).

In 2010, it was estimated that these three service offerings reached 2 percent of the elderly population (0.5 percent in homes and the rest in day care centers). The Social Protection Board of San Jose (Junta de Protección Social de San José) estimated that 6,000 elderly were residents of homes or attended day care centers in 2010. Public spending on these programs is also low, approximately 0.06 percent of GDP in 2009 (Sauma 2011). Not everyone who receives services from homes, shelters, or day care centers also benefits from government transfers, because they are assigned based on targeting criteria (Sauma 2011).

The current administration's National Development Plan aims at increasing coverage through various modalities to 2,500 people between 2011 and 2014.[32] The plan defines this goal as duplicating current coverage, which is estimated as 5,000 elderly (MIDEPLAN 2010, p. 55). However, as a proportion of the entire elderly population, this figure is very small, at just 0.001 percent.

The most recent change is the quest to organize these services as part of a network, the Caregiving Network (Red de Cuido), announced by the President of the Republic in 2010 and currently still in a design phase. Other background for this is the Equality and Gender Equity Policy (2007–17), which also focus on caregiving. The Caregiving Network includes a component aimed at the elderly population that defines the Mixed Institute of Social Aid (Instituto Mixto de Ayuda Social [IMAS]), which is responsible for dealing with extreme poverty, and CONAPAM as the responsible institutions. The estimated budget for achieving the goal set forth for 2011–14 is C 10,000 million.

The creation of caregiving services was part of the presidential campaign, promoted by an alliance of civil society organizations that were organized around the theme "Ten ways to face the crisis through social inclusion." The proposal was presented to the candidate and precandidates in 2009, including, among other measures, the formalization of existing jobs and the creation of a new environment of caregiving for different groups of the population.

The current president committed to promote the topic and as candidate launched the proposal to create the National Caregiving Network (Red Nacional de Cuido), which initially focused on the low-income population. This was part of the effort to strengthen the social protection programs that the National Liberation Party (Partido Liberación Nacional) has sought to implement since regaining the presidency in 2006. The first administration (Arias Sánchez, 2006–10) was more successful in achieving it than the 2010–14 administration of Laura Chinchilla Miranda.

In contrast to the measures promoted by Arias, which were more focused on cash transfers, the creation of the caregiving network requires transforming and supplementing existing caregiving services. This requires consulting with and organizing the social welfare institutions that provide services to the elderly population, the government institutions that are involved with this population (such as CCSS, FODESAF, and IMAS), as well as civil society organizations that work with children, whose demands could either coincide or conflict with or the agenda of those that work with the elderly population.

The National Development Plan establishes that "On the subject of public investment, the 'National Caregiving Network' Program, directed to children and elderly, the Chinchilla Miranda Administration will increase the coverage of the Education and Nutrition Centers and Children's Comprehensive Service Centers (CEN-CINAI) and strengthen the day care and recreation programs directed to the elderly." However, few advances have been made in an environment of serious financial limitations.

Funding for the few caregiving services comes from three sources: earnings from the national lottery distributed by the Social Protection Board, resources from FODESAF, and taxes on liquor, beer, and cigarettes. The CONAPAM channels the last two sources of funds (Sauma 2011). However, the existence of these funds does not guarantee that these services are a fiscal priority: in 2009, the equivalent of 0.06 percent of GDP was transferred to elderly homes and day care centers. At this time, the Treasury Ministry reported that public social spending increased to 22.3 percent of GDP of which, admittedly, one-third corresponded to pensions, whose beneficiaries are primarily the elderly population.

Challenges

Costa Rica has one of the most robust social protection systems in the region, along with those of the Southern Cone and Brazil, with a trajectory tending toward universal protection of the population (Filgueira 2005; Martínez Franzoni and Sánchez Ancochea 2012). At the same time, the country is experiencing tensions between the profound transformations that have taken place in its productive sector and the inertia of its social protection system. One of the principal links between these two sectors is the labor market, which is a determinant of pension access. A good part of these tensions comes from the conflicts over the role of the state and the role of the market in managing social risks. In contrast to other countries in the region, Costa Rica did not undergo a period of decisive market reforms, and it is not now experiencing a process of prostate counterreforms. The social protection system in general and the part that affects the elderly population in particular is a disputed area between those that promote greater market participation in risk management and those that resist that approach.

Social protection itself evidences strengths in terms of access and coverage (although pension universality is still pending) and weaknesses in terms of quality of services, which also affects the adequacy of cash transfers to prevent and manage social risks. Facing these challenges requires careful attention to several aspects of the social protection policy. First, greater clarity is required relative to the services demanded, in particular those associated with long-term care of the elderly population living in the country. Second, the system needs more and better coordination between cash transfers and services, in particular health care services and long-term care (JPS 2010). Third, more resources are required for long-term-care services, ideally originating from diverse sources that operate countercyclical with the economy trends and not tied to payrolls.[33]

Notes

1. Microenterprises and be subsistence-type or accumulation-type (simple or enlarged) (Trejos 1995). On average, however, microenterprises have the lowest levels of insurance among the employed population, around 40 percent compared to the average insurance level in the private sector is 75 percent.
2. Household surveys exclude the population living in long-term care facilities.
3. "However, it should be pointed out that the average number of children in this situation in the households considered (with elderly members) has also decreased. The average number has fallen from 0.8 to 0.6 to 0.4 respectively" (Sauma 2011, p. 12).
4. The level of dependency increases with age: the average age of those who do not require support is 72 years, while for those who need high levels of care it is 82 years (76 and 79 years, respectively, for the low and intermediate levels of dependency).
5. In 1990 the Multipurpose Household Survey (Encuesta de Hogares de Propósitos Múltiples [EHPM]) only asked if in the last month the respondent had received other cash transfers (separate from transfers from the state). The 2000 survey included a new question that recorded interest, rental income, and other asset income separately, but still limited the time frame to the past month. In 2010 the question was unbundled and included house, land, vehicle, etc., rental income; interest from fixed term deposits, loans to third parties and other; shareholder dividends; and cooperative or solidarity association benefits. The 2010 question did not ask about the last payment period, but instead if the respondent received periodic cash income from any of the above sources.
6. Law no. 44 of Retirement for inability to work and poverty of 1890; Law no. 43 of Ex-Gratia Public Pensions of 1902.
7. Military Code of 1884; Ordinance for the Military Law no. 6 of 1898; Pensions and fiscal guards Law no. 27 of 1905; Pensions for musicians of the Military Bands, Decree no. 76 of 1909; Pensions for widows, sons, and fathers of officers and soldiers that perished or were disabled by the work in the actions of Rio Coto, Decree no. 21 of 1921; Pensions participants in the Campaigns of 1856 and 1857, Decree no. 14 of 1905 and Law no. 29 of 1929; and Law no. 16 of Pensions for Guards, Police, and Soldiers of 1935.
8. Law no. 6 General of Common Education of 1886, that created the pension for graduated teachers with more than 10 years of service, as well as Law no. 182 of Retirements and Pensions for Teachers and Professors of 1923 and Law no. 23 of Retirements and Pensions of the Teaching Profession of 1926.
9. Law no. 131 of Retirements and Pensions Public Records Employees of 1925; Law no. 44 of retirements and pensions for Postal employees of 1923; Law no. 64 of Pensions Employees Public Records of Property of 1932; Law no. 23 of Elderly Insurance and retirement of the employees and workers of the National Press of 1934. In general application Law no. 16 of Pensions and Retirements of 1901 is promulgated, Law no. 33 General about Pensions of 1912, and the General Pensions Law of 1935. These are the first attempts to organize the pension regimes, both legally granted and ex gratia.
10. Article 63, Law no. 24 of 1943.
11. Law no. 17 of 1941 and article 65 of Law no. 17 constituting the Bank of 1943 that comprehensively reformed the 1941 law. Article 66 established the possibility of remaining in special regimes while also contributing to the bank.
12. The first was created by Law no. 8 of 1937 and reformed by Law no. 7333 the Fundamental Law of the Judicial Branch of 1993. The second was created via Law

no. 2248 of 1958 and is regulated by two additional laws, no. 7268 of 1991 and no. 7531 of 1995.

13. Here 1.25 percent comes from contributions made to the Popular and Community Development Bank (Banco Popular y de Desarrollo Comunitario), 1.5 percent employer contribution from a 1 percent reduction in Worker's Liability contributions (Riesgos del Trabajo), and 0.5 percent from a reduction in employer contributions to the National Institute of Learning (Instituto Nacional de Aprendizaje) (Castro Méndez 2001).
14. Financed by an employer contribution equal to 3 percent of salary costs. Annually, this fund should transfer half of the contributions to the mandatory complementary pension regime.
15. Additionally, a "third" voluntary pillar exists that supplements the pensions.
16. This system consolidates the collection of the bank's maternity and sickness insurance, the IVM regime, contributions to the labor capitalization fund, the complementary pension regime, and other social contributions made to the bank (articles 9 and 58 of the Worker Protection Law, and 31 of the Bank Formation Law, reformed by articles 85 and 87 of the Worker Protection Law) (Castro Méndez 2001).
17. Reforms to Law no. 7523 of the Private Regime of Complementary Pensions, the Stock Market Law, and the Central Bank of Costa Rica Formation Law.
18. Made up of insured persons that represent workers and employers. SUPEN should evaluate the report before the committee, which will eventually make recommendations to the Board of Directors of CCSS (Castro Méndez 2001).
19. Articles 85 and 87 that reform article 39 of the Bank Formation Law and article 79 that reforms article 37 of Law no. 7523.
20. In previous qualitative studies it has been shown that this last requirement frequently pushes the elderly population into poverty when they own land but lack monetary income (Martínez Franzoni 2008).
21. Additionally, the RNC has pensions directed to persons with cerebral palsy and assistance or help by beneficiary. This assistance was a minimum additional sum to pensioners with dependent family members. Recently these payments were eliminated and replaced with pensions paid directly to the dependent family members (Trejos, personal communication, 2010).
22. In March 2008, the basic food basket cost C 31,285 per person per month.
23. Based on the author's estimate from data in the 2011 household survey.
24. In the IVM regime regulations, transitory provision 14 defined a table that established new rules for the population under 44 years of age, gradual changes for individuals between 44 and 55 years, and the continuation of current rules for those 55 years and older (CCSS 2005).
25. Each year's measurements correspond to the month of July.
26. In Costa Rica the ILO, the CCSS, and SUPEN have prepared actuarial valuations, and their results are not in agreement (the first two are significantly more optimistic in terms of the system's sustainability than the last).
27. The CCSS, the Ministry of Labor and Social Security, and the National Institute of Women participated, along with business chambers, unions, cooperative members, and solidarity members (mutual savings and credit organizations made up of workers and employers). The Citizens' Ombudsman (Defensoría de los Habitantes) and SUPEN participated as observers, and the ILO was the technical facilitator.

28. Daniel Muñoz Correa, oficio SP-759-2012, 29th March 2012.
29. Coverage leakages of the noncontributory program reach 38.5 percent. Considering only the poorest 40 percent of the population, coverage gaps affect 66.5 percent, and leakages reach 17 percent (PEN 2009, p. 125).
30. Additionally, there is a student insurance policy that offers access to children and young students independent of their parents' insurance.
31. For a detailed analysis of the health reform and its reach almost a decade after beginning its implementation, see Martínez Franzoni and Mesa-Lago (2003).
32. In the Social Welfare chapter there is a section entitled "Care and attention for children and the elderly" (MIDEPLAN 2010, p. 55).
33. The resources available from payroll taxes, lottery income, liquor, beer, and cigarette taxes, and the resources that fund FODESAF—national budget resources and payroll taxes—depend largely on the global economic situation, which makes it difficult to foresee, at least in the short term, strong increases in their calculation bases.

Bibliography

Castro Méndez, M. 2001. "Estudio sobre el derecho del trabajo de Costa Rica. Comentarios sobre la situación de la libertad sindical." Estudio realizado para ANEP-COSI BA-FETRAL–CTRN.

———. 2012. "Derechos colectivos en el empleo público según la Sala Constitucional: Giro Jurisprudencial y Selectividad Interpretativa." Tesis de Maestría en Derecho del Trabajo y Seguridad Social, UNED, San José.

CCP and CONAPAM. 2008. "Primer Informe del Estado de Situación de la Persona Adulta Mayor en Costa Rica." Centro Centroamericano de Población (CCP) de la Universidad de Costa Rica (UCR) y Consejo Nacional de la Persona Adulta Mayor (CONAPAM), San José.

CCSS (Caja Costarricense de Seguro Social). 2005. "Reglamento del Seguro de Invalidez Vejez y Muerte (IVM)." CCSS, San José.

———. 2007. "Valuación Actuarial." CCSS, San José.

———. 2009. "Observaciones del informe elaborado por la firma Nathal Actuarios y Consultores S.A." October, CCSS, San José.

CONAPAM (Consejo Nacional de la Persona Adulta Mayor). 2004. "Estudio costos atención integral para personas adultas mayores residentes en un hogar de ancianos." Elaborated by Julia Chan Jiménez, CONAPAM, San José.

———. 2010. "Red de atención progresiva para el cuido integral de las personas adultas mayores en Costa Rica." CONAPAM, San José.

Filgueira, F. 2005. "Welfare and Democracy in Latin America: The Development, Crises and Aftermath of Universal, Dual and Exclusionary Welfare States." Working Paper, UNRISD, Geneva.

JPS (Junta de Protección Social). 2010. "Manual de criterios técnicos." *La Gaceta* 83, April 30, San José.

Martínez Franzoni, J. 2008. "Costa Rica's Pension Reform: A Decade of Negotiated Incremental Change." In *Lessons from Pension Reform in the Americas*, edited by Stephen J. Kay and Tapen Sinha, 317–39. New York: Oxford University Press.

Martínez Franzoni, J., and C. Mesa-Lago. 2003. "Las reformas inconclusas: salud y pensiones en Costa Rica." Fundación Ebert, San José.

Martínez Franzoni, J., and D. Sánchez Ancochea. 2012. *Good Jobs and Social Services: How Costa Rica Achieved the Elusive Double Incorporation*. New York: Palgrave Macmillan.

Mesa-Lago, C. 2009. "Impacto de la crisis económica mundial en la seguridad social en Costa Rica." Presentation for the 15to Informe del Estado de la Nación en Desarrollo Humano Sostenible, Programa Estado de la Nación, San José.

———. 2010. "Estudio comparativo sobre la capacidad de los sistemas de pensiones en Centroamérica para enfrentar la crisis actual y sus posibles efectos en los principios fundamentales de la seguridad social." Programa Estado de la Región, San José.

MIDEPLAN (Ministerio de Planificación Nacional y Política Económica). 2010. "Plan Nacional de Desarrollo 2011–2014 'María Teresa Obregón Zamora'." MIDEPLAN, San José.

PEN (Programa Estado de la Nación). 2009. *Decimoquinto Informe Estado de la Nación en Desarrollo Humano Sostenible*. PEN, San José.

———. 2010. *Decimosexto Informe Estado de la Nación en Desarrollo Humano Sostenible*. PEN, San José.

———. 2011. *Decimoséptimo Informe Estado de la Nación en Desarrollo Humano Sostenible*. PEN, San José.

Rodríguez Herrera, A., and F. Durán. 1998. *Reforma de Pensiones: Los Desafíos de la Vejez*. Segunda Vicepresidencia de la República y MIDEPLAN, San José.

Rofman, R., and L. Oliveri. 2011. "Las Políticas de Protección Social y su Impacto en la Distribución del Ingreso en Argentina." Serie de Documentos de Trabajo sobre Políticas Sociales 6, World Bank, Buenos Aires.

Rosero-Bixby, L., X. Fernández, and W. Dow. 2005. "Costa Rica: Estudio de Longevidad y Envejecimiento Saludable (CRELES)." Joint project of Centro Centroamericano de Población (CCP) and the Instituto de Investigaciones en Salud (INISA), San José.

Sauma, P. 2011. "Elementos para la consolidación de la Red Nacional de Cuido de las personas adultas mayores en Costa Rica." ECLAC, Ministerio de Cooperación Económica y Desarrollo, GTZ.

Technical Advisory Group. 2005. "Propuesta para la sostenibilidad del Régimen de Invalidez, Vejez y Muerte dela CCSS." Group made up of advisors from the Caja Costarricense del Seguro Social, the Instituto Nacional de las Mujeres, unions, and cooperatives. Technical Facilitation: International Labour Organization. Observer: Citizens' Ombudsman. February 28.

Trejos, J. 1995. "La Pobreza en Costa Rica: una síntesis cuantitativa." Documento de Trabajo no. 172, Instituto de Investigaciones en Ciencias Económicas, Universidad de Costa Rica, San José.

———. 2010. *Situación y perspectivas del programa de pensiones no contributivas por monto básico (RNC)*. UCR-ECLAC, San José.

CHAPTER 8

Ecuador

Vicente Albornoz and Daniela Oleas

History

Tied to the entry into a state of more advanced demographic transition, a mild but continuous process of population aging and an evolution of the epidemiological profile is taking place. The elderly population increased to 940,905 people in 2010. Approximately three in 10 elderly belong to the economically active population, and one in 10 has an occupation.

Characteristics of the Elderly Population

According to the Population and Housing Census (Censo de Población y Vivienda) of 2010, the average age in Ecuador is 28. Around 6.5 percent of the population is over 65, whereas the same group was 6.7 percent of the population in 2001 and it represented 4.3 percent in 1990. Trends show that population aged below 14 years is shrinking (table 8.1) because of the gradual reduction of the fertility rate. Moreover, an increase in the population over 40 is taking place as the offspring of generations with higher birth rates age. According to the Ecuadorian Institute of Statistics and Censuses (Instituto Ecuatoriano de Estadísticas y Censos [INEC]), this means the beginning of the aging process of the Ecuadorian population.

This aging process will accelerate in the coming years. Figure 8.1 shows the population pyramids by gender and age from 1950 to 2100. We can see that, even though the demographic change began during the second half of the last century, it is not until the 2000–50 period when the population will age more quickly.

As a result of the demographic changes, the population older than 65 has registered changes in the causes of morbidity and mortality. According to information from the Interinstitutional Action Plan (Plan de Acción Interinstitucional)

The authors thank Rafael Rofman for his suggestions and José Mieles for his help in collecting and organizing the information.

Table 8.1 Population by Age Group, 1990, 2001, and 2010

	1990	*Percent*	*2001*	*Percent*	*2010*	*Percent*
0–14 years	3,739,224	38.8	4,040,020	33.2	4,528,425	31.3
15–39 years	3,973,965	41.2	4,994,177	41.1	5,918,242	40.9
40–64 years	1,516,817	15.7	2,308,787	19.0	3,095,927	21.4
65 and older	418,183	4.3	813,624	6.7	940,905	6.5
Total	9,648,189	100.0	12,156,608	100.0	14,483,499	100.0

Source: Instituto Nacional de Estadística y Censo (INEC), Population and Housing Census 1990, 2001, and 2010.

Figure 8.1 Population Pyramids, 1950–2100

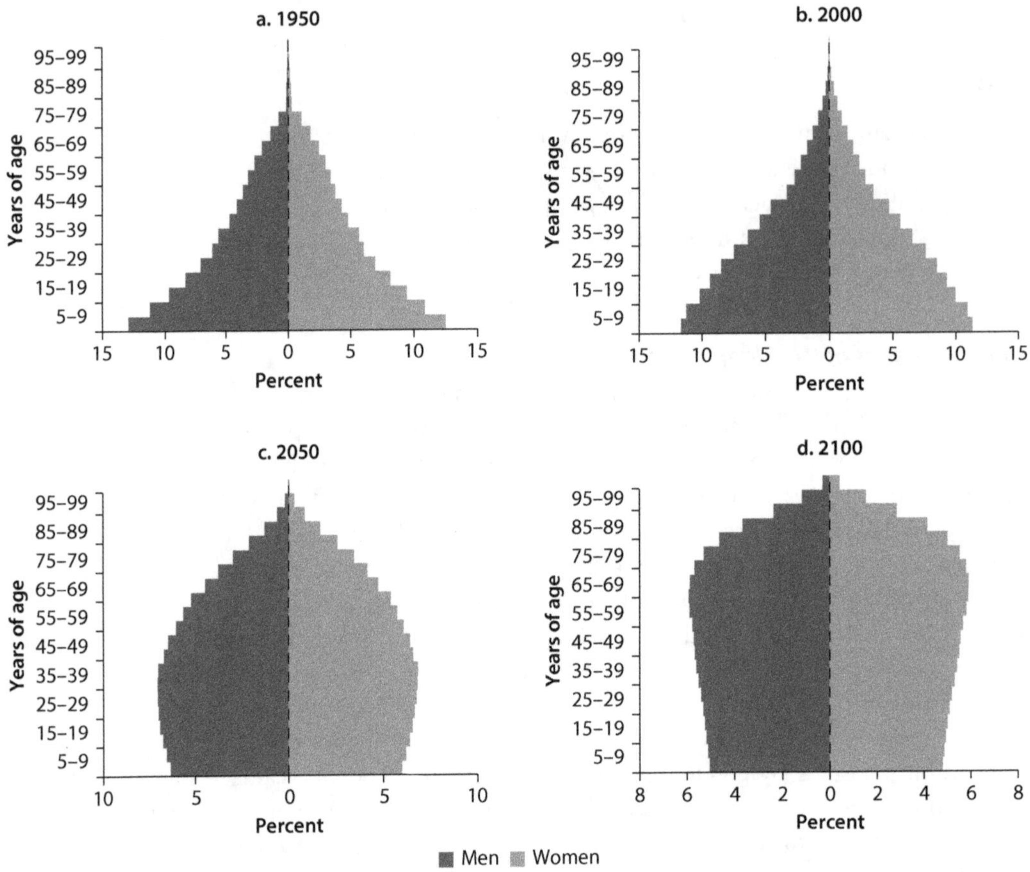

Source: Centro Latinoamericano y Caribeño de Demografía (CELADE).

for the elderly, Ecuador's epidemiological profile has changed from a traditional profile to a modern one, given that there is an overlap of two epidemiological profiles in different proportions for different population segments. The prevalence of chronic noncommunicable diseases has been observed relative to communicable diseases.

In terms of the labor market, the economically active population (EAP) over age 65 represented 38 percent of the elderly population in urban areas in 2008. This proportion decreased to 32 percent in December 2011. As can be seen in table 8.2, the over-65 unemployed population represented 62 percent of the EAP.

In geographic terms, the elderly population is concentrated in the provinces of the central Sierra, Cotopaxi and Tungurahua, Loja, and Imbabura, with Bolívar being the province with the greatest concentration of the elderly (map 8.1).

Table 8.2 Labor Profile of Elderly over 65, 2008–11

	Urban population	*EAP*	*Employed*	*EAP/Urban population (%)*	*Unemployment rate (%)*
Dec. 2008	593,426	228,087	84,847	38.4	62.8
Dec. 2009	675,421	241,436	89,811	35.7	62.8
Dec. 2010	771,418	250,683	91,664	32.5	63.4
Dec. 2011	720,900	231,236	87,705	32.1	62.1

Source: Instituto Nacional de Estadística y Censo (INEC), Urban Employment and Unemployment Survey, and Encuesta Nacional de Empleo, Desempleo y Subempleo (ENEMDU) 2008–11.

Map 8.1 Percentage of Elderly, by Province, 2010

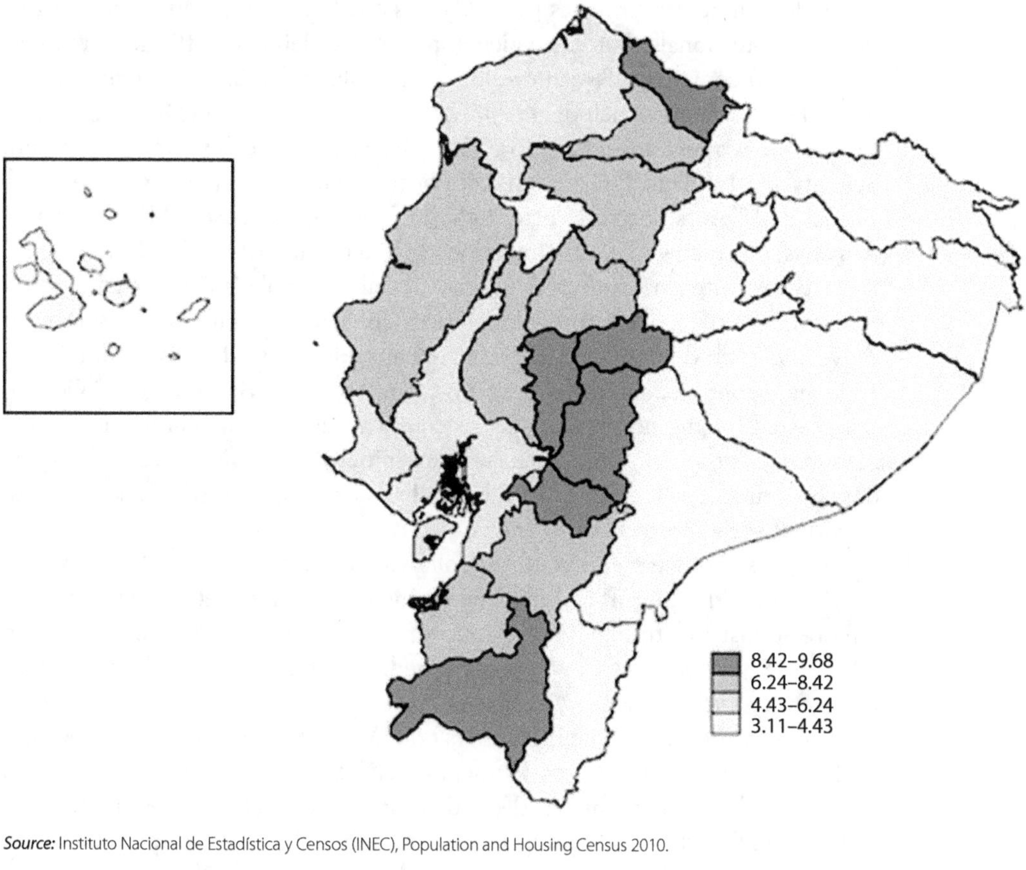

Source: Instituto Nacional de Estadística y Censos (INEC), Population and Housing Census 2010.

Origin of the Social Protection Systems for the Elderly

Old-age insurance for specific groups of workers was the first intervention to provide social protection for the elderly population. The program's extension to workers from other economic sectors or occupations and its obligatory nature were the subsequent milestones in the construction of the pension system. More recently, social programs to give coverage to a significant portion of the most vulnerable elderly population have emerged.

The origin of social protection systems for the elderly began in 1928 through the creation of the Civil Survivor and Pension Fund, Military Retirement and Survivor Pension, and Savings and Cooperative Bank (Caja de Pensiones y Montepíos Civil, Retiro y Montepío Militares, Ahorro y Cooperativa) intended for public and civil, military, and bank employees, respectively. From the beginning the benefits consisted of retirements, civil survivor pensions, and death benefits. In 1968, the Farmer's Social Security (Seguro Social Campesino) program was created, which sought to give benefits to the marginalized rural population that worked in agriculture. In 1970 the Ecuadorian Institute of Social Security (Instituto Ecuatoriano de Seguridad Social [IESS]) was created, which is currently in charge of the administration of the Mandatory General Insurance (Seguro General Obligatorio) system.

In 1992, the Armed Forces Social Security Institute (Instituto de Seguridad Social de las Fuerzas Armadas [ISSFA]) was created with the goal of protecting military professionals, their dependents and eligible claimants, officers-in-training, soldiers, and conscripts. To achieve this goal, ISSFA organized a system of benefits and social services, including (1) Retirement, Disability, and Death Insurance, (2) Unemployment Insurance, (3) Maternity and Health Insurance, (4) Death Benefits, (5) Life and On-the-Job Accident Insurance, and (6) a Reserve Fund. The Armed Forces Social Security Law (Ley de Seguridad Social de las Fuerzas Armadas) regulates the aforementioned system. In 1995 the Police Social Security Institute (Instituto de Seguridad Social de la Policía [ISSPOL]) was created with the objective of providing retirement services, help, and assistance for active and retired employees of the national police as well as their families. In 1998 an unconditional transfer program called Solidarity Bonus (Bono Solidario) was created for the poorest families as compensation for the elimination of the gas subsidy. Although the program was not initially conceived as a social protection program, it was later redirected and is currently one of Ecuador's most important social protection programs.

Two laws that were approved the following decade, the Social Security Law (Ley de Seguridad Social) and the Law for the Elderly (Ley del Anciano), created a more robust institutional framework for social protection for the elderly. In 2001 the Social Security Law was published, preserving the IESS as an autonomous entity with its own legal capacity and funding separate from general government fiscal revenues. The IESS offers both Mandatory Social Security (Seguro Social Obligatorio) as well as Farmer's Social Security to the marginal rural population that is economically dependent on agricultural activities. In 2006 the Law for the Elderly was promulgated. It established the IESS's responsibilities to this sector of the population, including to (1) undertake campaigns to promote services for the elderly in all of the country's provinces; (2) coordinate with the Social Communications Secretariat (Secretaría de Comunicación Social), Provincial Councils, and Municipal Councils on various programs of services for the elderly; (3) offer ongoing advice and training to retired and retiring individuals; (4) promote programs that allow the elderly to find work, preferably paid vocational programs, and motivate private-sector institutions to do the same; and (5) encourage the formation and supervise the operation of volunteer groups designed to protect the elderly.

At the Executive level, with the support of this law, the Ministry of Economic and Social Inclusion (Ministerio de Inclusión Económica y Social [MIES] since 2007 and previously the Ministry of Social Well-Being [Ministerio de Bienestar Social]) is responsible for managing these activities. In effect, MIES is mandated to promote comprehensive attention to the population throughout their lifetimes (childhood, adolescence, youth, adulthood, and old age), prioritizing its actions for those individuals or groups that live in situations of exclusion, discrimination, poverty, or vulnerability. In the specific case of the population over 65, the National Directorate of Gerontology (Dirección Nacional de Gerontología) manages programs, while other specific programs are managed through MIES, such as the Social Protection Program (Programa de Protección Social [PPS]). Likewise, the Law for the Elderly created the National Institute of Gerontological Research (Instituto Nacional de Investigaciones Gerontológicas), the Attorney's General Office for the Elderly (Procuraduría General del Anciano), and the National Fund for the Elderly (Fondo Nacional del Anciano) and established tax and fee exemptions[1] for individuals over 65. The Banking and Insurance Superintendent is responsible for ensuring that public and private social security goods and services are in accordance with the law.

More recently, in 2008 a constitutional reform process took place that specified rights and obligations on the subject of social protection for the elderly. From this reform a set of programs emerged that were intended to fulfill the guarantees therein established (table 8.3).

The Traditional Pension System

The traditional pension system consists of a general regime, Mandatory Social Security, and of specific regimes—Farmer's Social Security and social security for the security forces. Currently, the system is undergoing reforms as a response to the guidelines set forth in the 2008 National Constitution.

One of the characteristics of the social protection system in Ecuador is the existence of three pension systems simultaneously. On one side are the Mandatory Social Security system and the Farmer's Social Security program, divided into pensions and health benefits, and on the other the military sector and police social security programs coexist. The Mandatory Social Security pension for old age is awarded to the head of the family for a quantity equal to 75 percent of the minimum contribution salary, in 12 monthly payments per year, as long as the beneficiary is between 65 and 70 years old and has completed at least 10 years

Table 8.3 Timeline of Social Protection Systems for the Elderly in Ecuador

Year	*System*	*Beneficiaries*	*Benefits*
1928	Civil retirement and Survivor's Pension, Military Retirement and Survivor's Pension, Savings and Cooperative Banks	Public, civil, and military employees, later bank employees	Retirement, Civil Widow's Pension, and Death Benefits
1935	Mandatory Social Security, foment Voluntary Insurance, and exercise the Trusteeship of the Indigenous and Montubio		Social Security Medical Service begins
1937	Mandatory Social Security Law is reformed		
1942	Mandatory Social Security Law is issued		
1963	The Pensions Bank is merged with the Insurance Bank to form the National Social Security Bank under the supervision of the National Retirement Institute		Workers' Compensation Insurance, Artisanal Insurance, Professional Insurance, Domestic Worker Insurance, in 1966 Secular Clergy Insurance
1968	Social Security Code issued; Farmer's Social Security	Universality Farmers from marginal rural areas	
1970	Ecuadorian Institute of Social Security (IESS)		
1981	Farmer's Social Security Law extended		
1986	Mandatory Insurance for Agricultural Workers, Voluntary Insurance, and the Marginal Social Security Fund	Population with income below the minimum living salary	
1992	Armed Forces Social Security Law	Military professionals, their dependents and eligible claimants	(1) Retirement, Disability, and Death Insurance; (2) Unemployment Insurance; (3) Maternity and Health Insurance; (4) Death Benefits; (5) Life and On-the-Job Accident Insurance; and (6) a Reserve Fund
1995	National Police Social Security Law	Active duty and retired national police personnel and their families	Retirement, help, and assistance
1995	Popular referendum on bringing in the private sector to Social Security, proposal rejected		
2001	Social Security Law	(1) Salaried workers; (2) self-employed workers; (3) independent professionals; (4) business managers; (5) sole proprietors; (6) minor independent workers; and (7) all insured under the General Mandatory Insurance	Two types of insurance: Mandatory Social Security and Farmer's Social Security
2006	Law for the Elderly	Establishes rights and duties of the population over 65 years of age	Creates the National Institute of Gerontological Research (INAGER), the General Prosecutor for the Elderly, and the National Fund for the Elderly (FONAN)

Source: Ecuadorian Social Security Institute, History of Social Security in Ecuador; Social Security Law 2001; Instituto de Seguridad Social de las Fuerzas Armadas (ISSFA) Law 1993; Instituto de Seguridad Social de la Policía (ISSPOL) Law 1995.

of contributions. For each year of deferred retirement after 70 years of age, it is possible to subtract one year from the number of required years of contributions, but in no case can it be fewer than five years of contributions be allowed. In addition, the death of any member of a family affiliated with the system triggers a payment equal to 25 percent of the minimum contribution salary for funeral benefits. Survivor benefits come into effect if the active insured has made at least 60 contributions at the time of his death. The widow's pension is applicable if a couple lived together for at least two years or have a child as a result of their union.

In 2008 the constitution outlined a series of rights for the elderly population, as well as obligations for the state, that set the standard for multiple reforms on the subject of social protection that the state has the obligation to make viable. The constitution establishes an inalienable right for all people to social security and fixes it as a fundamental duty and responsibility of the state. The principles of social security are solidarity, its mandatory nature, universality, equality, efficiency, subsidiarity, sufficiency, transparency, and participation, to attend to the needs of individuals and groups. The constitution further establishes that it is the state's responsibility to guarantee the ability to exercise the right to social security, including individuals who work without pay in the home, perform subsistence activities in rural areas, or are engaged in independent work, as well as those who are unemployed (box 8.1).

Box 8.1 Social Security in the Constitutional Framework of 2008

The constitution establishes that the state should guarantee, without discrimination, the rights stipulated in the constitutional text, where the right to social protection is one of them.[a] In addition, it establishes that the state will guarantee and implement the full exercise of the right to social security, which includes individuals who work without pay at home, in subsistence activities in rural areas, and in all forms of independent work, and those who are in a situation of unemployment.[b] It specifies that the elderly are part of a priority population group[c] that will receive priority and specialized service in the public and private spheres, especially in the fields of social and economic inclusion and protection from violence. Elderly persons will be considered to be those who are at least 65 years of age.[d]

The constitution also notes that social security protection will extend gradually to unpaid work in the home, in accordance with the general conditions of the system,[e] and that it will be implemented through a public and universal social security system, which cannot be privatized and will serve the contingent needs of the population. Protection from chance events will be implemented through the universal mandatory insurance system and its special regimes.[f]

The constitution specifies that the universal mandatory insurance will cover illnesses, pregnancy, paternity, occupational hazards, termination, unemployment, old age, disability, and incapacity.

box continues next page

Box 8.1 Social Security in the Constitutional Framework of 2008 *(continued)*

Health benefits for illnesses and pregnancy will be provided through the comprehensive public health network. Moreover, the constitution establishes that the universal mandatory insurance system will expand to cover the entire urban and rural population, regardless of their employment status. Benefits for individuals who perform unpaid domestic work and offer care services will be funded through state contributions;[g] nonetheless the constitutional text stipulates that the creation of new benefits should be fully funded.

The constitution also clearly sets out how Farmer's Social Security should be treated, which forms part of the IESS as a special regime of the universal mandatory insurance system to protect the rural population and individuals who work as traditional fishermen. This regime will be funded through solidarity contributions from insured persons and employers in the national social security system, with the differentiated contribution from covered heads of families and with fiscal appropriations that guarantee its strengthening and development. The insurance will offer health benefits and protection from contingent disability, incapacity, old age, and death. Public and private insurance, without exception, must contribute to the funding of Farmer's Social Security through the IESS.[h]

The IESS began the reform process with a view toward meeting constitutional requirements in 2009. However, the process of universal coverage is laid out as gradual in the constitution and only when expansions are fully funded.

During the 1990s the Ecuadorian population enrolled in some type of insurance increased. In 2010, 28.9 percent of the economically active population was enrolled in the General Mandatory Insurance program,[i] and in 1999, 79.22 percent of the population did not have any type of insurance[j] and only 9.39 percent of the economically active population was enrolled in the General Mandatory Insurance program. This difference can be explained by several reasons, with the most important being the social security reform inaugurated in 2001 in which the system switched from a pay-as-you-go scheme to a mixed pension system, as well as the period of political and economic instability that Ecuador suffered in the 1990s, which deepened the socioeconomic inequality and increased unemployment and underemployment.

a. Constitution of the Republic of Ecuador, Art. 3.
b. Constitution of the Republic of Ecuador, Art. 34.
c. Constitution of the Republic of Ecuador, Art. 35.
d. Constitution of the Republic of Ecuador, Art. 36.
e. Constitution of the Republic of Ecuador, Art. 333.
f. Constitution of the Republic of Ecuador, Art. 367.
g. Constitution of the Republic of Ecuador, Art. 369.
h. Constitution of the Republic of Ecuador, Art. 373.
i. Instituto Nacional de Estadística y Censo (INEC), Results of the Population and Housing Census 2010.
j. Instituto Nacional de Estadística y Censo (INEC), El Sistema Integrado de Indicadores Sociales (SIISE), Quality of Life Survey.

Coverage Expansion Reforms

National Plan for Good Living 2009–13 and the Social Agenda 2009–11

As a result of the constitutional reform, both laws and programs have been transformed with the goal of adapting the country's institutional framework to the guidelines of the current constitution, including those related to social protection.

These changes were captured in the National Plan for Good Living (Plan Nacional de Buen Vivir [PNBV]), as well as in updates to laws, the formulation of sectorial planning agendas, and finally resolutions and programmatic adaptations.

The 2008 constitution positions planning and public policy as instruments to achieve the Good Living Objectives (Objetivos del Buen Vivir) and to guarantee rights. The constitution establishes that the PNBV is the instrument that should govern policies, programs, and public projects; the scheduling and execution of the state budget; as well as the investment and appropriation of government resources. It is worth mentioning that aligning with the PNBV is obligatory for the public sector and a guideline for other sectors.

The 2009–13 PNBV's first objective seeks "To Support social and territorial equality, cohesion, and integration in diversity" through a policy of "comprehensive social protection and solidary social security of the population with quality and efficiency throughout one's lifetime based on the principles of equality, justice, dignity, and multiculturalism" and sets the specific goal of reaching 40 percent of people with social security in 2013.

The Social Agenda of the Coordinating Ministry of Social Development 2009–11 establishes that the government should ensure social protection in the face of unforeseen events, reducing economic, social, and territorial inequalities, as well as guaranteeing the comprehensive social protection of the population and the promotion of comprehensive and equitable territorial development. This policy emphasizes priority service groups (children and youth, persons with disabilities, and the elderly, among others).

The document outlines that the social protection system is aimed at reducing the population's vulnerability and improving quality of life, in particular for the most unprotected. Thus, the document justifies guaranteeing access at a minimum income level for the population in situations of vulnerability and poverty, creating the basic necessary conditions to develop the skills and the income generating capacity. The Human Development Bonus (Bono de Desarrollo Humano [BDH]) is an important tool for achieving this goal. Improving coverage continues to be a challenge, above all among populations experiencing extreme poverty and those in rural areas, giving special attention to priority groups, including the elderly.

The main reform relating to the elderly is the implementation of the universalization of the noncontributory retirement pension as a change to the BDH directed to the population over 65 living in poverty. This transformation aspires to significantly improve this population's economic situation, supplementing the pension with specialized programs for the elderly, although coverage is still limited.

Implementation of Reforms

Implementation has different characteristics depending on the type of transfer. In the case of contributory transfers, the government modified the access and enrollment requirements and strengthened the IESS enrollment supervision mechanisms for salaried workers. In the case of the noncontributory transfers, the government adjusted the targeting mechanisms.

For the IESS Mandatory Social Security, the challenge is to gradually increase the affiliate base. This could be done either by adding new workers who make contributions or through the inclusion of specific groups of beneficiaries that have a constitutional right to access to the system, even though they do not have the capacity to contribute, as is the case with women who do not have a paid job. Nonetheless, the law sets forth a safeguard that conditions the gradual expansion of the system on a secure and stable funding source.

In the case of members who do not make contributions, funding can come from only two sources, through the General Budget of the state and/or through cross-subsidies as is the case with the Farmer's Social Security program, which has a significant solidary subsidy. In addition, there is a high percentage of persons who are not enrolled in social security, and these individuals belong to the group that does not have an employee-employer relationship, given that all salaried workers are required by law to be enrolled in social security under strict supervision from both the Ministry of Labor Relations (Ministerio de Relaciones Laborales) as well as the IESS. Nonetheless, according to information from the 2010 Census, 61 percent of the economically active population is not enrolled in any social security system, whether IESS, ISSFA, or ISSPOL.

Coverage improvements in the Mandatory Social Security program began with the inclusion of IESS Insurance members' sons and daughters under age six, as well as the IESS' orphan survivor pensioners as beneficiaries of comprehensive health development and promotion actions; prevention, diagnosis, and treatment of illnesses; recovery; and rehabilitation of individual health.[2] IESS reformed the voluntary enrollment requirements and eliminated the medical exams to certify disabilities for pensioners over 65 years old.[3]

Members can take advantage of the expansion of IESS's health services by paying a premium of 3.41 percent on the taxable amount in addition to the member's normal contribution, which allows them to access all the comprehensive health development and protection services. However, this does not grant members access to pregnancy and illness subsidies.[4] In contrast, persons who have made IESS, ISSFA, and/or ISSPOL contributions can access old-age pensions if they meet one of the following requirements: (1) 40 or more years of contributions, (2) more than 30 years of contributions and over 60 years old, (3) more than 15 years of contributions and older than 65, or (4) more than 10 years of contributions and older than 70.[5]

Additionally, the Labor Relations Ministry created a program called Decent Work (Trabajo Digno) that has as its principal objective ensuring that salaried workers, especially domestic workers, are enrolled with the IESS. In any case, the Executive branch proposed a popular referendum in 2011 that asked (among other questions) whether or not enrolling in social security and making contributions should be mandatory, with a view toward penalizing those who did not enroll or contribute. The regulation was accepted and now must be put into practice in the new Penal Code. So far the regulation has not entered into force, but as a result the Decent Work program urges employees that are not enrolled in social security to report their employers through campaigns and visits to the neighborhoods, offering information and performing door-to-door surveys about compliance with the law.[6] After the door-to-door survey and once compliance with the law has been verified, the visitors place a sticker on the door of the dwelling, office, or apartment as recognition that the employer has complied with the law and as a marker to avoid redundant on-site verification.

The increase in IESS' active enrolled population is complex given its direct association with the reduction of informality in the Ecuadorian economy. Thus, all policies that promote reductions in informality will also deliver greater enrollment to social security. These policies include use of the state's coercive force (public servants penalizing employers that do not enroll their workers), the creation of incentives to formalize (for example, simplified tax payment schemes), and the simplification of paperwork for companies.

In terms of the BDH program, one of the targeting characteristics of the Elderly Pension is that beneficiaries are not enrolled in social security, whether with IESS, ISSFA, and/or ISSPOL. As part of the constitutional reform, to comply with obligations established in the 2008 constitution, the government reformed the BDH targeting process. The SELBEN survey was replaced with a registry called the Social Register.

The Social Register is obtained through a living conditions survey that seeks to identify individuals, more accurately classifying them as living in extreme poverty, poverty, and out of poverty. Since 2009, BDH beneficiaries have been identified below the poverty line. The Social Register is managed by the Coordinating Ministry of Social Development and is the only authorized way to define beneficiaries. The information is turned over to the PPS, which then includes them in the payment database.

In May 2012 MIES issued a timeline for incorporating the entire over-65 population registered in the Social Register in the Elderly Pension program.[7]

In accordance with the gradual approach established in the constitution, the PPS added up to 80,000 additional elderly to the active payment database during 2009 in the Elderly Pension Subprogram, prioritizing those persons that belonged to family units that were below the cutoff line provided by the Coordinating Ministry for Social Development. At the end of 2012, 588,149 adults over 65 qualified for receiving Elderly Pension payments (table 8.4).

The transfers linked to contributions, as is the case with social protection programs mentioned, are paid via the national banking system. Members are required to register a savings or checking account from any bank or cooperative in the national financial system, and the transfers are made directly to the registered account. BDH payments are made through the national financial network, and the government has also implemented a debit card called "Fast Bonus" (Bono Rápido) that allows the subsidy beneficiary to access it through any ATM. BDH currently has 1,120 payment points throughout the country.

Table 8.4 Reforms to Improve BDH Coverage

	Reforms	*Date*	*DE/AM*
Coverage improvements for the elderly and disabled	The social pension is established for the elderly and persons with disabilities living in poverty as a subprogram of the BDH, consisting of a monthly cash transfer of US$11.50, directed to persons 65 years and older that belong to the poorest 40% of the population or with a disability equal to or greater than 70%, accredited with a CONADIS card, from the first or second quintile, in accordance with the targeting index established by the Technical Secretariat for the Social Area. IESS, ISSPOL, and ISSFA members and pensioners cannot receive this pension benefit.	Sept. 7, 2006	DE no. 351
	As of February 1, 2007, this is the social pension for the elderly and persons with disabilities living in poverty as a subprogram of the BDH, consisting of a monthly cash transfer of US$30, without any additional requirements, directed to persons 65 years and older that belong to the poorest 40% of the population or with a disability equal to or greater than 40%, accredited with a CONADIS card, from the first or second quintile, in accordance with the targeting index established by the Technical Secretariat for the Social Front.	Jan. 17, 2007	DE no. 12
	The value of the transfer is increased to US$35 per month. In addition, information from the registry of family units (with the cutoff limits established by the Coordinating Ministry for Social Development) is established as the main form of identifying beneficiary family units for cash transfers.	July 20, 2009	DE no. 1838
	It is established that program beneficiaries will be those that are living in poverty below the cutoff limit—the poverty line provided by the Coordinating Ministry for Social Development. The Elderly Pension is established as universal. However, in accordance with the gradual expansion established in the constitution, the Social Protection Program (PPS) is authorized to begin by including up to 80,000 additional elderly in its payment rolls for 2009 in the Elderly Pension Sub-program, prioritizing persons who belong to family units that are below the cutoff line provided by the Coordinating Ministry of Social Development.	July 24, 2009	AM no. 37
	The inclusion of the entire elderly population registered in the Social Register is authorized as a gradual process according to the well-being index.	May 3, 2012	AM no. 0014

Source: Social Protection Program, Executive Decrees, various years.
Note: AM = Ministerial Agreement; BDH = Bono de Desarrollo Humano; CONADIS = National Council on Disability Equality (Consejo Nacional de Igualdad de Discapacidades); DE = Executive Decree; IESS = Instituto Ecuatoriano de Seguridad Social; ISSFA = Instituto de Seguridad Social de las Fuerzas Armadas; ISSPOL = Instituto de Seguridad Social de la Policía; PPS = Social Protection Program.

The Political Economy Behind the Reforms

The reforms that begun in Ecuador in recent years have been a response to the proposals of Rafael Correa's administration (2007 to present) to strengthen the role of the state and improve the distribution of wealth based on an endogenous growth model guided by the framework set forth in the "Good Living" concept. This focus is expressed in the PNBV developed in the National Secretariat of Planning and Development (Secretaría Nacional de Planificación y Desarrollo [SENPLADES]), which proposes a paradigm shift and questions the concept of development.

The PNBV document points out that the strategy of economic accumulation and redistribution is just one aspect of an array of focuses that should make up a strategy to achieve Good Living. However, because of the high levels of unsatisfied basic needs, it is necessary to create alternatives, and the plan describes four phases to achieve this.

The first phase proposes the objective of a transition from economic dependence on primary goods to a more diversified economy and the beginning of a process of redistribution, considered to be the main focus of change in this period and of the strategy as a whole. In this setting, protecting labor-intensive sectors that create jobs will be the priority in this phase, as well as those associated with initiatives that come from the social and solidary economy, the exercise of the country's food self-sufficiency, and, in general, meeting citizens' basic needs.

In the second phase, the goal is to encourage a new national industry in addition to consolidating an energy surplus, mainly through the production and consumption of clean energy and bioenergy. In this phase the strategy of wealth creation is bolstered through community-based ecotourism and seeks to distribute the surplus through the production process by strengthening the popular, social, and solidary economy. Investment in research and development is prioritized as a strategy, because of a tripartite alliance: universities, industry (public or private), and public or technology research centers. For this goal, the consolidation of a postgraduate education system and of centers of applied research excellence will be the priority in this phase. During this period, generating revenues for the national economy will still be dependent on responsible and sustainable extraction of nonrenewable natural resources such as hydrocarbons and eventually mining.

The third phase consolidates the diversification strategy and export substitution. Domestic manufacturing is expected to satisfy internal demand and create surpluses for export. Additionally, the strategy seeks to substitute exports with higher value-added goods instead of exclusively exporting goods dependent on extractive processes. In this phase, the relative weight of national manufacturing will be equal to the relative weight of exportable primary goods in the national economy. Investment in science and technology should drive productive innovation in aspects related to industries in which the government seeks to substitute imports first.

The objective of the fourth phase is the development of bioservices and their technological applications. The knowledge services and their application that will be supported are linked to the nascent industries that are fomented in the first phase. In this context, the strategy of Ecuador's strategic and sovereign insertion in the world depends closely on the endogenous strategy to satisfy basic needs.

The current reforms are responses to the first phase of endogenous development, as proposed by SENPLADES.

Expected and Observed Impacts on Coverage

Contributory and noncontributory transfers have expanded their coverage among the elderly population in recent years. In terms of reach, social security coverage through its different modalities is less than that offered by the noncontributory BDH system. In addition, the government has seen an increase in participants in the contributory system.

According to information from IESS, and as shown in figure 8.2, there is a trend toward recovery of the percentage of the insured population that received social security pensions in recent years. Although the percentage of insured persons as a portion of the economically active population as well as the percentage of salaried workers with access to social security has not reached the levels seen at the end of the 1980s, a recovery has been seen in the number of beneficiaries relative to the population of the elderly, as well as the voluntary enrollment of independent workers.

Based on IESS statistical information from 2007, 1,486,159 active members were registered in the system. According to institutional information,[8] in September 2012, 2,425,904 individuals were registered in the system, representing a 39 percent increase during this period. This increase can be explained by the 2008 constitutional reforms, the tax incentives promoting new jobs offered by the Internal Revenue Service (Servicio de Rentas Internas), and above all the Executive branch proposal to penalize noncompliance with social security payment obligations through a popular referendum in May 2011. Moreover, the IESS began to offer mortgage loans for new home construction and remodeling as well as the purchase of land and offices to members as long as they met some requirements, including being up to date on their contributions and having made at least 36 consecutive contributions to Mandatory Social Security.

Figure 8.2 Social Security Insured and Pensioners, 1989–2009

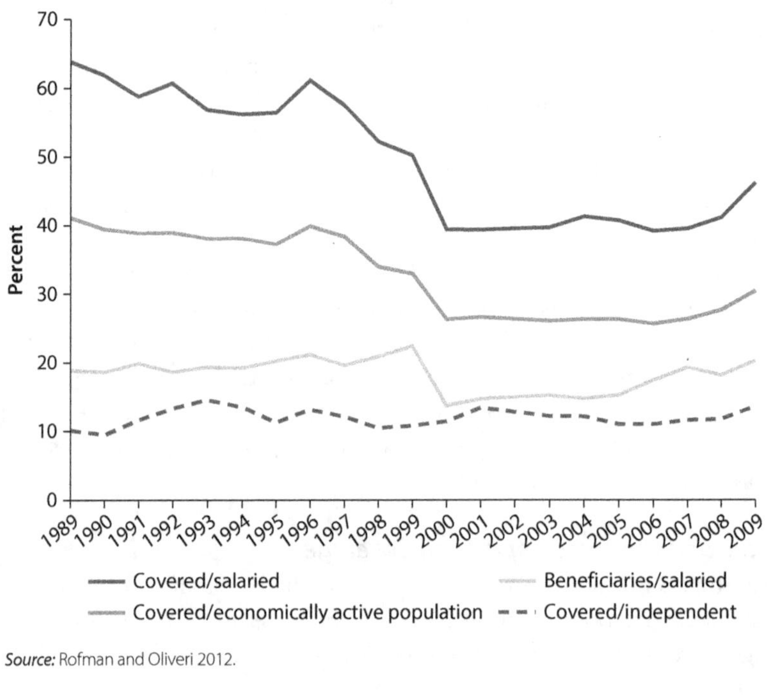

Source: Rofman and Oliveri 2012.

The trend in terms of the protected population relative to the number of members has stayed the same over time, with the exception of 2012, when the IESS included people below 18 years as a protected population, increasing coverage by 1,400,000 additional persons (figure 8.3).

According to information from the 2010 Census, the distribution of contributions by type of insurance reveals that the majority of the insured population belongs to the Mandatory Social Security program (29 percent), followed by membership in Farmer's Social Security (4 percent), Voluntary Social Security (2 percent), and ISSFA and ISSPOL (1 percent each). According to the 2010 Census, 61 percent of the population does not contribute to any type of contributory social security program (table 8.5).

Figure 8.3 Social Security Members and the Protected Population, 1990–2012

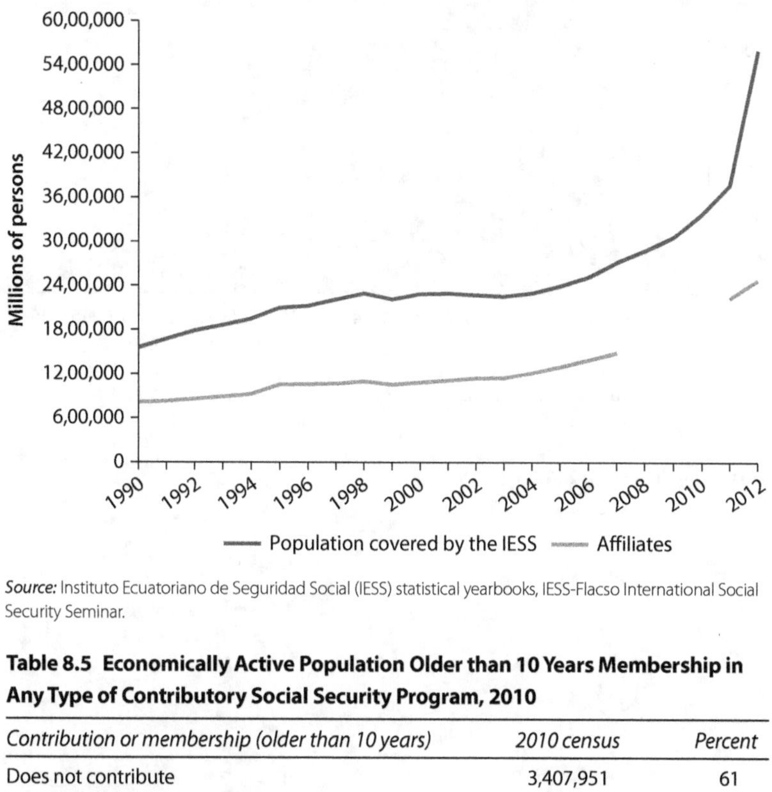

Source: Instituto Ecuatoriano de Seguridad Social (IESS) statistical yearbooks, IESS-Flacso International Social Security Seminar.

Table 8.5 Economically Active Population Older than 10 Years Membership in Any Type of Contributory Social Security Program, 2010

Contribution or membership (older than 10 years)	*2010 census*	*Percent*
Does not contribute	3,407,951	61
IESS Mandatory Social Security	1,600,529	29
IESS Farmer's Social Security	208,365	4
IESS Voluntary Social Security	85,656	2
ISSFA Insurance	59,720	1
ISSPOL Insurance	29,610	1
IESS, ISSFA, ISSPOL Retiree	42.267	1
Do not know	110,488	2
Total	5,544,586	100

Source: Population and Housing Census 2010.
Note: IESS = Institiuto Ecuatoriano de Seguridad Social. ISSFA = Instituto de Seguridad Social de las Fuerzas Armadas. ISSPOL = Institiuto de Seguridad Social de la Policía.

In terms of coverage by age group, in May 2012, 78 percent of active members were between 20 and 50 years old, 14 percent between 50 and 60 years old, and 4 percent older than 60 years. The population less than 20 years old represented 4 percent of total active members (figure 8.4).

In geographic terms, according to information from the IESS in 2012, 36 percent of members were in the province of Pichincha, followed by the province of Guayas with 25 percent of the total (figure 8.5 and map 8.2).

Figure 8.4 Active Members, by Age Group, 2012

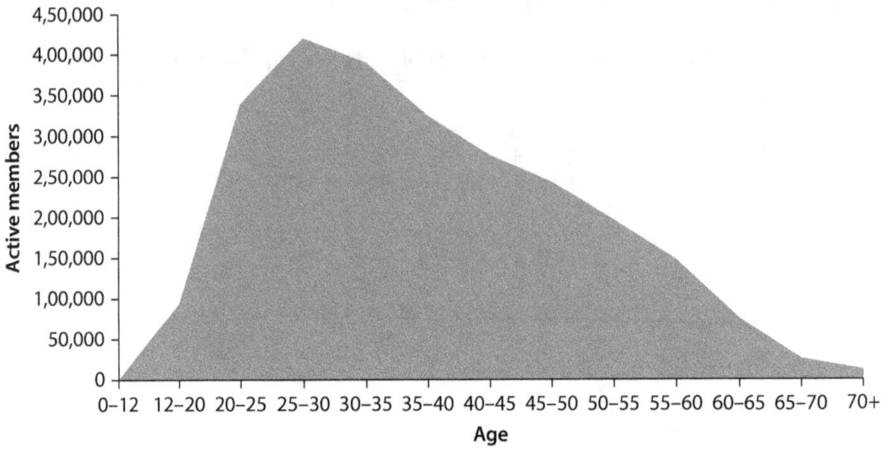

Source: Instituto Ecuatoriano de Seguridad Social (IESS), http://www.iess.gob.ec.

Figure 8.5 Active Members, by Province, 2012

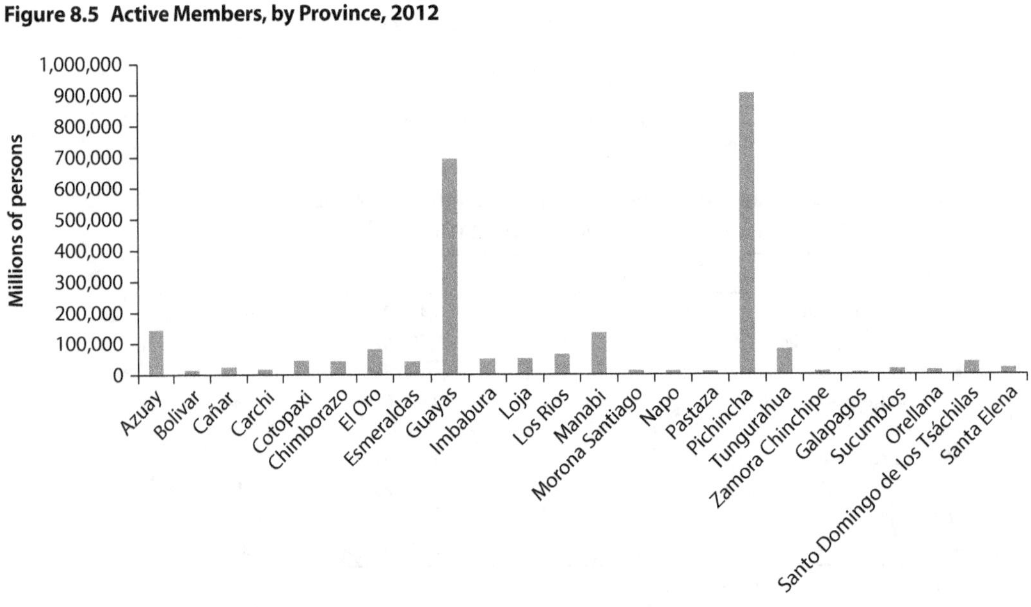

Source: Instituto Ecuatoriano de Seguridad Social (IESS), http://www.iess.gob.ec.

Map 8.2 Social Security Pensioners, by Province, 2012

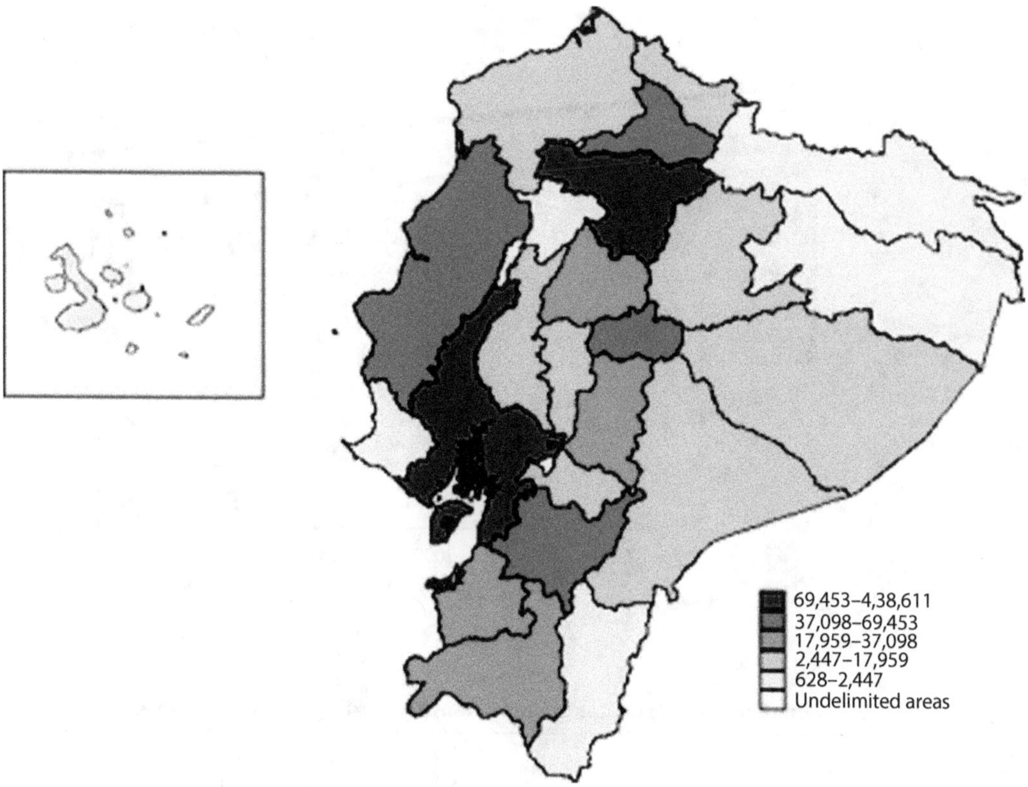

Source: Instituto Ecuatoriano de Seguridad Social (IESS), http://www.iess.gob.ec.

The other 37 percent of members were distributed among the rest of the 22 provinces.

In terms of elderly beneficiaries of the BDH, we also observe a sustained increase from 2007 to the present (figure 8.6), with the most significant increase between 2008 and 2009 on the order of 26 percent, followed by 25 percent between 2009 and 2010. According to the Urban Employment and Unemployment Survey undertaken by the INEC in 2010, 30 percent of Ecuadorian households received the BDH. In 2011 the BDH had 1,854,054 beneficiaries, of which approximately 28.9 percent received the elderly pension, or 536,185 persons. This figure is significant when compared with the number of members of the IESS Mandatory Social Security program.

Fiscal Sustainability

The highest social security membership indices have meant additional resources for the contributory system. Nonetheless, the state uses its own resources to fund 40 percent of pension costs, in addition to assuming 100 percent of the spending on BDH noncontributory transfers.

Figure 8.6 Elderly Enabled to Receive the BDH, 2007–12

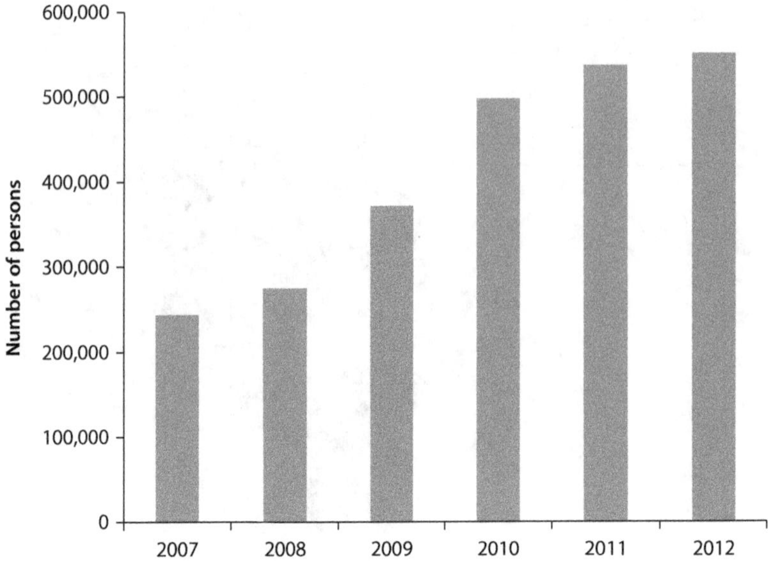

Source: Social Protection Program 2007–12.

Table 8.6 Funding for Contributory Transfers: Participants and Employers

	Personal contribution (%)	*Employer (%)*
Salaried workers	4.00	6.00
Independent workers and voluntary participants	10.00	n.a.
Employees and workers for General Disability, Old Age, and Life Insurance	5.00	3.50
Public servants for General Old Age and Life Insurance	7.00	3.50
Independent workers and voluntary participants for General Disability, Old Age, and Life Insurance	8.50	n.a.
All, cross-subsidy to Farmer's Social Security	0.35	0.35
Independent workers and voluntary participants for General Occupational Hazard Insurance	0.50	n.a.
Independent workers and voluntary participants to fund the operation of the IESS	0.80	0.80
Reserve funds	n.a.	8.33

Source: Social Security Law.
n.a. = not applicable.

The funding for contributory transfers has three main components: (1) personal contributions from participants, (2) employer contributions, and (3) mandatory financial contribution from the state (table 8.6).

The state also covers 40 percent of the pensions that the IESS pays to its retirees and eligible survivors. Moreover, it covers 0.30 percent of the taxable

Table 8.7 IESS Budget, 2010–12
US$

	2010	2011	2012
Management and General Administration	90,894,000	138.491.231	145,538,005
Termination Fund	418,540,858	564,363,559	573,186,758
Pension Insurance	1,801,160,283	2,464,549,920	2,544,282,422
Occupational Hazard Insurance	77,703,305	108,286,338	119,605,918
Farmer's Social Security	151,707,199	188,188,136	200,424,892
Individual and Family Health Insurance	1,284,472,174	1,291,440,605	1,565,489,533
Survivor Pensions	36,958,936		
Total	3,861,436,755	4,755,319,789	5,148,527,528
Increase		23%	8%

Source: Instituto Ecuatoriano de Seguridad Social (IESS), Resolution CD 299 05.01.2010, CD 343 14.01.2011, Resolution CD 402 13.01.2012.

amount of all salaried workers of the Mandatory Social Security program to fund the Farmer's Social Security program. There is also an annual contribution equal to US$288,000 to the Farmer's Social Security program.

According to information from the IESS, the budget approved during the last three years has increased 23 percent during 2010–11 and 8 percent during 2011–12 (table 8.7). The most significant categories are Pension Insurance (50 percent on average during the three years) and Individual and Family Health Insurance (30 percent on average in the three years).

The funding for the BDH comes exclusively from fiscal resources. In 2010 the BDH budget directed to the elderly was US$208.7 million, increasing to US$225.2 million in 2011. The 2012 budget was US$230.8 million.

Other Services for the Elderly Linked to These Programs, Relevance, and Performance

The expansion of transfers to the elderly has been accompanied by increases in the coverage of other services, mainly health care. In this setting, modifications to the access requirements for contributors and their families have taken place, and the government has also established specific actions and goals for expansion of the networks for health care services and eldercare.

The current constitution recognizes the elderly as rights holders for specialized priority service in the public and private spheres, protection from violence, and free and specialized health care. The elderly also have a right to free access to medicines; paid work depending on their abilities, and keeping their limitations in mind; universal retirement; discounts on public services and on private transport and performances; exemption from the tax regime and notary and registration costs, according to the law; and access to a dwelling that ensures a decent life with respect for their opinion and consent.[9] Additionally, the constitution says that the state should establish public policies and programs to serve the elderly that address specific differences between urban and rural areas, gender inequalities, ethnicity, culture and individual differences, communities, peoples, and nationalities, as well as strengthen as much as possible personal autonomy and participation in defining and implementing these policies.[10] In this setting the government until now has undertaken a set of reforms (table 8.8).

In 2007 the Ministry of Public Health issued the "Comprehensive Policies for the Health of the Elderly" ("Políticas Integrales de Salud de los Adultos Mayores"),[11] which enshrines the tenet of "Active Aging" with the objective of understanding how the determinants of aging impact on the lives of persons and populations.[12] The aforementioned policy defines three basic pillars: health, participation, and security.

In terms of health, the policy focuses on social and behavioral health risk factors, with the goal of maintaining physical functionality and mental autonomy. The state is committed to creating spaces, opportunities, and the conditions so the elderly can live in optimum conditions and continue contributing to the productive system, through paid or unpaid activities. The government will also facilitate participation of the elderly in social, cultural, sports, recreational, and spiritual activities, according to their capacities, needs, and preferences, and belonging to formal and informal groups and networks. In terms of security, the government seeks to guarantee protection and assistance. Priority will be given to cases of family abandonment, solitude, dependence, and extreme poverty through a social structure that promotes, regulates, supervises, and enables medium-term stay and long-term stay elderly daycare centers, within a continuous, assistive, and progressive model.

Based on the above, the Ministry of Public Health approved the Interinstitutional Action Plan for the Elderly, including active and healthy aging, 2011–13 (Plan de Acción Interinstitucional para Personas Adultas Mayores, incluye evejecimiento activo y salduable, 2011–13) in 2011, which establishes the strategies to implement the Comprehensive Policies for the Health of the Elderly. The main goals of the plan are summarized in table 8.9.

In 2010 the IESS approved a complementary set of rules for the elderly for specialized academic training programs[13] and development of national tourism through assisted tourism programs and through the elderly university. Funding will be available through loans without collateral via the capitalized funds of the General Individual and Family Health Insurance.

Additionally, the MIES, the guiding institution for policy on the elderly, has committed to the following lines of action.

Improving nutritional conditions. The goal of this line of work is to promote good nutritional practices as a way of maintaining a healthy lifestyle. Currently 200,000 elderly persons benefit from direct nutritional attention and receive soup and *colada* Vilcabamba as a nutritional supplement.

Direct attention to this population. This type of attention is given through 139 eldercare centers situated throughout the country, cofinanced by the Ministry of Economic and Social Inclusion. The types of attention currently offered are residency or long-term stay, day care, and family care, serving 10,316 elderly persons. The goal of the direct attention to the elderly is to help them maintain their

Table 8.8 Inclusive Reforms in Health Insurance, Contributory Insurance, Universal Access Schemes, and Aspects of Coverage and Funding, 2009–11

	Reforms	*Date*	*Resolution*
Improvements to the quality of health care	Creation of 577 positions for medial health care units, of which 472 are additional.	Jan. 13, 2009	CD 238
	Creation of 610 positions for medical health care units	Dec. 13, 2011	CD 397
Improvements to mandatory health insurance, universal access schemes	Sons and daughters of IESS members, as well as IESS orphan survivor pensioners, will be beneficiaries until they turn six years old, of comprehensive health development and promotion actions; prevention, diagnosis, and treatment of illnesses; and recovery and rehabilitation of individual health.	June 10, 2009	CD 265
	Fee schedule approved for general individual and family health insurance for medical services offered through the IESS health care units and other external service providers, whether public and/or private, qualified, accredited, and contracted by the IESS.	Sept. 7, 2009	CD 276
	Conversion factors approved for the application of the fee schedule for the general individual and family health insurance.	Sept. 24, 2009	CD 277
	Regulations for the concession of General Individual and Family Health Insurance benefits, which establishes those subject to coverage, wait times for health events, and pregnancy and sickness and coverage periods.	July 5, 2010	CD 322
	Update to the regulations for the concession of General Individual and Family Health Insurance benefits.	Oct. 27, 2010	CD 332
	Members that wish to can avail themselves of the expansion of IESS health care services by paying a premium of 3.41% of the taxable amount and in addition to the participant's other contributions. With this payment the member can access all of the comprehensive health development and protection services. However, members do not gain access to pregnancy and illness subsidies.	Oct. 20, 2010	CD 370
	Regulations for insuring and delivering benefits for Farmer's Social Security, in which health care service levels, service modalities, and pharmaceutical prescriptions for doctors, dentists, and obstetricians are established.	Feb. 2, 2011	CD 353
	Regulations for insuring and delivering benefits for Farmer's Social Security.	July 21, 2011	CD 370
	Regulations for qualifying and accreditation of individual medical offices: norms for qualifying and accrediting health care professionals that can individually or collectively offer external health care services to IESS members. To serve this population, members should accept the institutional fee schedule, prescribe medicines in accordance with the national basic medicine chart from CONASA, and meet a minimum of 95% of medical appointments including the most important. Accreditation is valid for six months and can be extended to one year after evaluation.	Aug. 9, 2011	CD 378

Source: Instituto Ecuatoriano de Seguridad Social (IESS) Board of Directors Resolutions, various years.
Note: CD = Director's Resolution; CONASA = Consejo Nacional de Salud (National Health Council).

Table 8.9 Goals of the Interinstitutional Action Plan for the Elderly, 2011–13

Priority strategies	*Goals*
I: Health and well-being of the elderly in public policy	2011: Construct a social inclusion policy and interinstitutional action plan for the elderly that includes active and healthy aging 2013: Update to the Law for the Elderly based on human rights, relating to attention to the elderly
II: Adaptation of the social and health care system to the needs and conditions of the elderly population	2013: Have a strategy to promote healthy behaviors and environments 2013: Have rules that regulate and certify the functioning of elderly daycare centers, family care centers, and long-term-care centers 2013: 50% of the chronic illness prevention and management programs will have developed specific and adequate requirements for the unique characteristics of the elderly 2013: 50% of the operating units in the country will implement the Permanent Assistance and Progressive model, with the goal of optimizing socio-health services and responding to the needs of the elderly, strengthening primary health care (Atención Primaria de la Salud [APS])
III: Training and permanent education in human resource services	2013: 30% of the human resources training institutions in health care and related areas will include the topics of aging over a lifetime and the specific needs of this population group in undergraduate curricula 2013: 20% of the Schools of Medicine, Nursing, and related areas in the country will offer postgraduate specialization courses and masters programs in geriatrics and gerontology 2013: Completion of 80% of the training for health care and social workers on the policy, interinstitutional plan, and current set of rules for attending the elderly and topics associated with aging 2013: Offer a health and social training program to the elderly and their caregivers
IV: Monitoring, evaluation, and research	2013: 50% of the related institutions in the country will use a systematic process of continuous quality improvement to monitor and evaluate comprehensive health services for the elderly 2013: 30% of the institutions that work with and for the elderly will have undergone at least one national-level research study on the health and well-being of this population group

Source: Ministry of Public Health 2011.

autonomy and live a dignified life, mainly in the protection of their families and communities. To achieve this objective, the government is strengthening attention on families and the creation of local support networks for elderly persons and their families.

Promotion and development of associativity. The goal is to create hubs of interactions among the elderly about the defense of their rights and their positioning as local actors that promote actions in favor of a dignified old age.

Conclusions and Future Challenges

Ecuador faces a problem associated with the increase in the number of elderly relative to the total population. This population segment is characterized by comorbidity (more than three illnesses at the same time), fragility, dependence, social uprooting, and poverty and requires a complex and up-to-date response in terms of attention and care to their needs.

At the same time, the supply of public services is restricted by capacity to satisfy the growing demand, keeping in mind the gradual incorporation of the elderly population. In parallel, the systematic increase of the prevalence of chronic degenerative diseases associated with the elderly directly depends on lifestyle. Decisions on public policy still favor larger, more vulnerable groups (mothers, children, and adolescents).

In this context, the reforms established in the 2008 constitution require an institutional response. And while the law calls for a gradual implementation subject to the availability of funding, it also demands greater and better quality. It should be pointed out that the government has started various reforms that although still in their early stages, entail large institutional and budgetary challenges.

The aforementioned implies significant reforms and responses in diverse fields, both at the level of benefits related to social protection as well as at the level of the health care sector. Moreover, one of the challenges has to do with the levels of institutional coordination and the development of specialized studies that support public policy and optimize resource utilization.

The importance of the Elderly Pension administered by the PPS should be pointed out relative to the proportion of the population analyzed. Based on the magnitude of the program and the associated population, any institutional reform should analyze how to incorporate the specific group served by this program within the services offered.

The Elderly Pension is a transfer that ensures a minimum level of income, but it is not enough to accomplish the task and to fulfill the rights established by the constitution.

One of the immediate challenges is related to updating the Law for the Elderly and the Intergenerational Equality Agenda that SENPLADES must develop in the coming months. All of the aforementioned implies an important challenge in the future. Furthermore, all of these reforms are necessary to adequately attend to the elderly population according to their specific needs and with a view toward fulfilling the rights established in the current constitution of the republic.

Notes

1. "Art. 14.—Tax Exemption.—All persons older than 65 years and with an estimated monthly income of maximum five unified basic remunerations or that have assets that do not exceed 500 unified basic remunerations, will be exempt from the payment of all types of fiscal and municipal taxes.

   Art. 15.—Persons older than 65 years, will enjoy an exemption of 50 percent of the cost of air, land, sea, and river transport, and of entrance fees to public, cultural, sporting, artistic, and recreational events. In order to receive this discount, it is only necessary to present an identification card or retiree's or pensioner's card from Ecuadorian Social Security. The cost of consumption is reduced by 50 percent for: the use of metered electrical energy services up to 120 kWh monthly consumption; metered potable water for consumption up to 20 cubic meters, any usage in excess of these limits will be subject to normal rates, and 50 percent of the basic residential telephone service rate in the beneficiary's home. All other meters or telephone apparatuses in the name of the beneficiary or spouse or partner will be charged at the normal rate. In order to receive this discount, it is only necessary to present an identification or citizenship card or retiree's or pensioner's card from the IESS.

This information should be verified by the companies that offer these services. Moreover, the cost of consumption is reduced by 50 percent for non-profit institutions that offer services to the elderly, such as nursing homes, shelters, dining halls, and gerontological institutions.

Art. 16.—Private clinics and hospitals will make available 5 percent of their infrastructure to the elderly in extreme poverty, whether through new construction or use of existing installations."

2. IESS Board of Directors Resolution, June 10, 2009.
3. IESS Board of Directors Resolution, October 20, 2009.
4. IESS Board of Directors Resolution, October 27, 2010.
5. IESS Board of Directors Resolution, July 15, 2011.
6. Labor Relations Ministry, Decent Work program.
7. Economic and Social Inclusion Ministry, MIES, Ministerial Agreement 00014, May 3, 2012.
8. IESS, information from September 2012.
9. Constitution of the Republic of Ecuador, Art. 36.
10. Constitution of the Republic of Ecuador, Art. 38.
11. Ministerial Accord no. 0000153, Official Register no. 398.
12. Organización Panamericana de la Salud/Organización Mundial de la Salud, Political Framework, "Active and Healthy Aging," 2002.
13. IESS Resolution CD 302, February 22, 2010.

Bibliography

Central Bank of Ecuador. 2004. *La seguridad Social en el Ecuador*. Central Bank of Ecuador, Quito.

Ministry of Public Health. 2011. *Plan de Acción Interinstitucional para Personas Adultas Mayores*. Ministry of Public Health, Quito.

Rofman, R., and L. Oliveri. 2012. "La cobertura de los sistemas previsionales en América Latina: conceptos e indicadores." Serie de Documentos de Trabajo sobre Políticas Sociales 7, World Bank, Buenos Aires.

SENPLADES (Secretaría Nacional de Planificación y Desarrollo). 2009. *Plan Nacional del Buen Vivir 2009–2013*. SENPLADES, Quito.

CHAPTER 9

El Salvador

Ricardo Córdova Macías

History

El Salvador is passing through a stage of the demographic dividend in which the active population reaches its maximum participation and the elderly population gradually increases its size as a population segment. Poor pension coverage and living conditions reveal a vulnerable situation for the elderly, and especially for elderly women. The reform to the contributory regime in the 1990s, which entailed a switch from a pay-as-you-go scheme to a funded system, did not deal with the coverage problem and presents challenges in terms of benefit adequacy and budgetary room to manage the transition between schemes.

Profile of the Elderly Population

The case of El Salvador is not isolated from the global trends of demographic changes, although its demographic transition has its own characteristics. The evolution of the population during the period 1950–2007 can be mostly explained by decreases in two key demographic indicators: the total fertility rate and the mortality rate, as well as a net negative migration rate (Córdova et al. 2010; UNPF 2010) and an increase in life expectancy.

But the most important phenomenon is the transformation that has occurred in the relative weight and the absolute number of the different age groups, among them the elderly segment of the population. According to census information, the elderly population grew from 92,650 inhabitants in 1950 to 137,897 in 1961, increasing to 190,946 in 1971, 378,527 in 1992, and reaching 542,191 elderly persons in 2007.[1] Figure 9.1 shows how the composition of the population in El Salvador has transformed significantly, and will continue doing so in the coming decades. The participation of the population 60 years and older is growing, increasing from 6.1 percent in 1950 to 8.8 percent in 2005, and is projected to reach 21.5 percent in 2050 and 34.4 percent in 2100. We also observe an increase in the percentage of persons younger than 15 years, from 42.7 percent

The authors thank María Elena Rivera and Rafael Rofman for their comments on a preliminary version of this chapter.

Figure 9.1 Percentage Distribution of the Population, by Age Group, 1950–2100

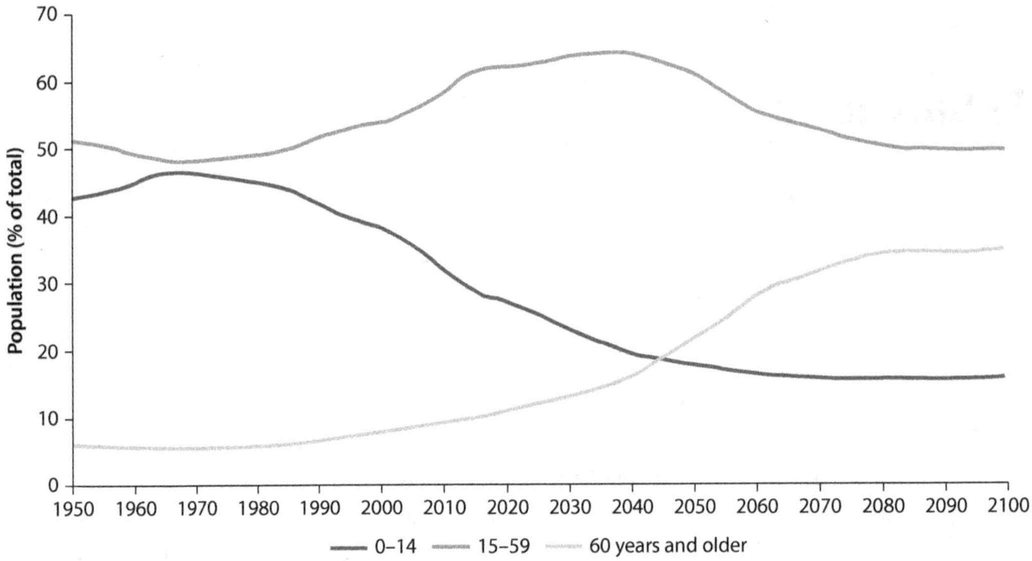

Source: Centro Latinoamericano y Caribeño de Demografía (CELADE) 2012.

in 1950 to 46.4 percent in 1970. However, after 1975 this group registered a mild decline until 1990 (41.7 percent), followed by a more accelerated reduction to 35.7 percent in 2005 and is projected to fall to 25.3 percent in 2025, 17.8 percent in 2050, and 15.9 percent in 2100. In terms of the potentially active population, we can observe a reduction during the period 1950–70, followed by the beginnings of an increase from 48.7 percent in 1970 to 55.5 percent in 2005, and is projected to reach its peak at 64.9 percent in 2040—a phenomenon known as the demographic dividend—later decreasing and projected to fall to 52.5 percent in 2070 and 49.7 percent in 2100.

Figure 9.2 presents the Population Aging Index (PAI) to show the transformation of the age structures. Since 1975 this indicator has shown a sustained increase, reaching 29.2 in 2010, and is projected to reach 121 in 2050 and 217.2 in 2100; this means that by 2100 for every 100 children and adolescents between 0 and 14 years old, Salvadoran society will have 217 elderly inhabitants.

Another indicator that reflects the changes in the population age structure is the dependency ratio, which expresses the population at potentially inactive ages relative to the population at potentially active ages (ECLAC 2008).[2] Figure 9.3 presents the total dependency ratio, which is the sum of the two dependencies (youth and elderly) relative to the economically active population (EAP) by age (15–59 years). This dependency ratio is expressed in terms of the number of young people and elderly for every 100 individuals between 15 and 59 years old. In the case of El Salvador, the total dependency ratio showed a mild rise in the period from 1950 to 1970, increasing from 95.2 to 107.8, to later decrease slightly to 101 in 1985, and it is projected to decrease rapidly until arriving at its

Figure 9.2 Population Aging Index, 1950–2100

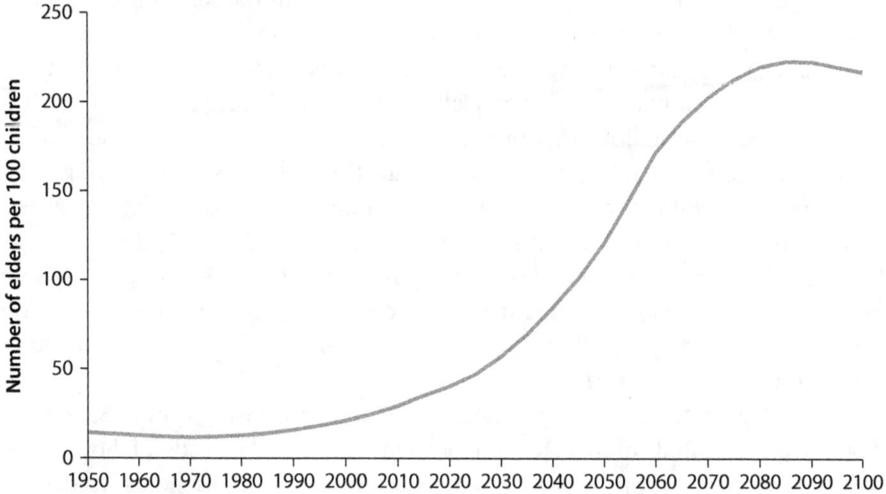

Source: Centro Latinoamericano y Caribeño de Demografía (CELADE) 2012.

Figure 9.3 Demographic Dependency Ratios, 1950–2100

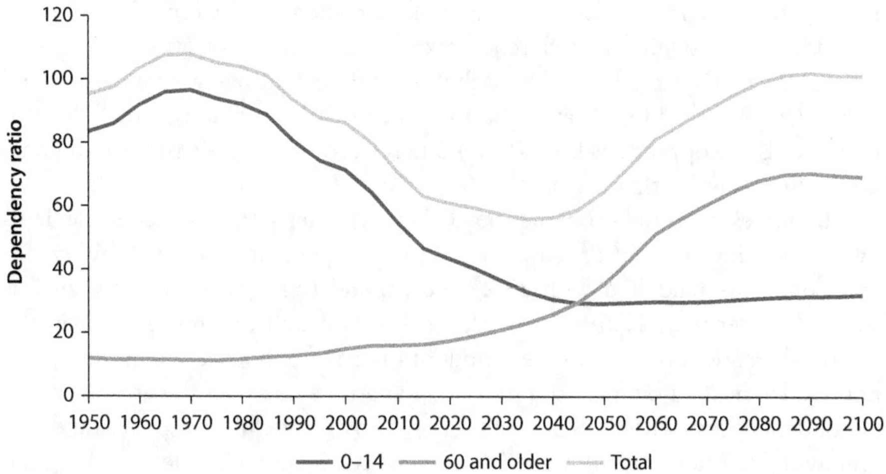

Source: Centro Latinoamericano y Caribeño de Demografía (CELADE) 2012.

low point of 55.9 in 2035. After 2035, the ratio is expected to recover and stabilize around 100 in the long term.

This demographic transition process, which is characterized by a decreasing trend in the dependency ratio (the relative weight of the population at potentially productive ages increases while the weight of those at potentially inactive ages decreases), "theoretically represents a window of opportunity for Salvadoran society to reach higher levels of production, savings, and investment due to the lower number of dependents relative to the number of people in active ages.

However, in order to take advantage of this potential it is necessary to create public policies aimed at improving the functioning and absorption capacity of the labor market to receive the growing working age population increases, and in job quality, such that jobs offer salaries and benefits related to social security; as well as invest in human capital, especially in youth" (Córdova et al. 2010, p. 40).

It has been pointed out that in the elderly segment of the population "there exists a process of feminization and urbanization. The first is occurring even more markedly among the elderly than in the population as a whole; largely as a product of women's greater longevity" (Córdova et al. 2010, p. 44). After reviewing the 2007 census data we observe that these two features have grown more prominent in the elderly segment of the population, with women making up 55.7 percent of the population, and 64.2 percent of the elderly population concentrated in urban areas.

According to the 2007 Population and Housing Census, 1,406,485 households were counted, of which 23.3 percent had elderly heads of household. Table 9.1 shows the difference between the number of households headed by men and women for the population aged 60 years and older, as well as for those younger than 60 years. Heads of household among both population segments are predominantly men. However, this predominance is lesser among the elderly population (58.4 percent) relative to the population younger than 60 years (67.2 percent), which is due to a longer life expectancy for women.

Additionally, significant differences exist in matrimonial status according to gender. In elderly male-headed households, 77.9 percent live with a partner and only 22.1 percent do not have a partner. Meanwhile, in elderly female-headed households the opposite is the case: 84.2 percent do not have a partner and only 15.8 percent live with a partner.

Among residents of households headed by the elderly, the most common family relationship is son or daughter, with 39 percent, followed by grandchild or great-grandchild with 33.2 percent, and third place in importance is spouse/partner with 17.5 percent. However, significant differences exist in the type of dependent relative to the gender of the head of household. In the case of households headed by men, the sons and daughters make up the greatest number of dependents with 39.8 percent, followed by grandchildren/great-grandchildren with 26.2 percent, and wives/partners with 25.3 percent. Meanwhile, in the case of households headed by women the largest number of dependents corresponds to grandchildren or great-grandchildren at 45.6 percent, followed by

Table 9.1 Heads of Household for the Elderly Population and the Population Younger than 60 Years, by Gender, 2007

Head of household	*Total*	*Men*	*Women*	*Men (%)*	*Women (%)*
Younger than 60 years	1,078,462	724,643	353,819	67.2	32.8
60 years and older	328,023	191,457	136,566	58.4	41.6
Total	1,406,485	916,100	490,385	65.1	34.9

Source: Based on the VI Population and Housing Census 2007.

children at 37.7 percent, and in third place sons-in-law or daughters-in-law at 4.4 percent, but husband/partner represents only 3.8 percent (Córdova et al. 2010).

Table 9.2 illustrates that women make up one-person households in a greater quantity than men (21.3 percent versus 13.4 percent), whereas the distribution of two-person households is slightly lower among men than among women (20.7 percent versus 23.3 percent). The most relevant piece of information is that in the majority of multiperson households (which make up 61.5 percent of all households), male-headed households predominate (65.9 percent versus 55.4 percent).

An analysis of the data presented in this section allows us to identify the greatest conditions of vulnerability for households headed by elderly women. On one hand, checking the matrimonial status shows that a higher proportion of elderly female heads of household do not have a partner compared with elderly male heads of household. On the other, upon analyzing the type of household, it is apparent that women-headed households are more likely to be single-person households and less likely to be multiperson households. This last point is related to the previous point about matrimonial status, in which a higher percentage of men live with a partner.

The profile of economic activity of the elderly population also highlights conditions of vulnerability. Of the total of households headed by the elderly, 38.1 percent correspond to the EAP (Córdova et al. 2010), indicating that even though they have reached retirement age, a significant segment continues to be active in the labor market. Upon analyzing the data relating to the EAP, 84.7 percent of elderly heads of household are employed and 15.3 percent are unemployed.

Upon focusing on the EAP, we observe that the elderly mainly perform domestic work (59.7 percent), followed by pensioners (20.5 percent),[3] permanently restricted from work (11.5 percent), and other reasons (7.5 percent). A recent study of elderly heads of household reported two discoveries. The first is the significant gap that exists between men and women in domestic work: the proportion of women working as homemakers is practically double that of men. These uneven allocations of reproductive work are principally the result of the social constructs that assign different roles to men and women and lead women to chiefly perform reproductive work. Second, in the category of retirees, pensioners, or individuals deriving income from personal investments, men represent 31.3 percent, but women make up just 10.8 percent, reflecting on some level the more

Table 9.2 Heads of Household among the Elderly Population, by Gender According to the Type of Household, 2007

Type of household	*Total*	*Men*	*Women*	*Total (%)*	*Men (%)*	*Women (%)*
One-person	54,644	25,577	29,067	16.7	13.4	21.3
Two-person	71,501	39,615	31,886	21.8	20.7	23.3
Multiperson	201,878	126,265	75,613	61.5	65.9	55.4
Total	328,023	191,457	136,566	100	100	100

Source: Based on the VI Population and Housing Census 2007.

limited access that women have had to the formal labor market and as a result the ability to contribute to a pension savings fund (Córdova et al. 2010).

Figure 9.4 shows that among the total of dependent persons (868,655 people) in households headed by a person aged 60 years and older, only 29.4 percent perform paid work, with son and daughter, son-in-law or daughter-in-law, standing out with 42.2 percent and 43.2 percent of paid work, respectively, whereas among partners only 17.1 percent perform paid work.

This analysis reveals that, despite having reached retirement age, a high percentage of the elderly continue working, as much out of desire as out of necessity because of the low coverage of the pension system. Additionally, we observe that a significant proportion of the elderly have dependents in their care and that in their households intergenerational dynamics are developing that deserve to be analyzed in future studies.

The Traditional Pension System

Social security in El Salvador developed late, gradually, and relatively fragmentarily. At the beginning of the 20th century

> only the armed forces and public employees had a rudimentary pension regime, and only workers in manufacturing and commerce were legally protected from

Figure 9.4 Distribution of Dependent Person in Households with an Elderly Head of Household, by Paid Work Situation, 2007

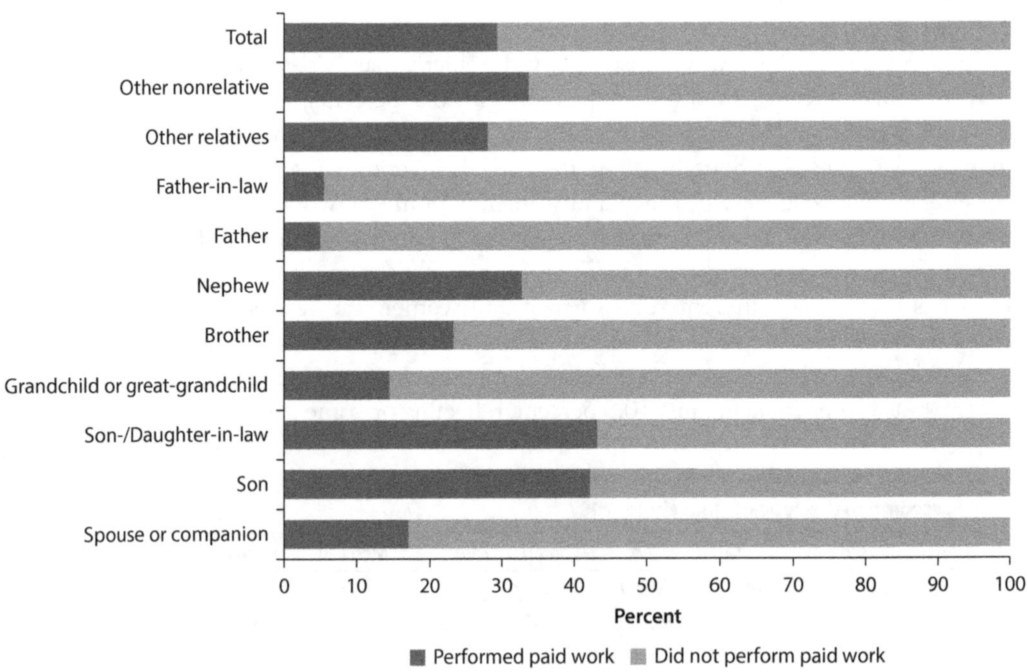

Source: Córdova et al. 2010.
Note: Only includes persons aged 10 and older, given that the census questionnaire frames the question in this way.

> occupational hazards. Between 1926 and 1942, a few groups obtained health care protection through mutual companies and it was not until 1954–55 that the [Salvadoran Social Security Institute, Instituto Salvadoreño del Seguro Social] ISSS and its health care program for some groups of workers were established. ISSS' pension program did not begin until 1969, and was the penultimate to appear in the region. … [The National Institute of Public Employee Pensions, Instituto Nacional de Pensiones de los Empleados Públicos] INPEP and its pension program were created even later, between 1975 and 1978, and the inclusion of insured individuals from the administrative branch of INPEP in a special ISSS health care regime occurred from 1978 to 1989. The [Military Social Security Institute, Instituto de Previsión Social de la Fuerza Armada] IPSFA was established in 1980–81, but the armed forces had already had a mutual company since 1974—
>
> (Córdova, López, and Mesa-Lago 1994)

The public pension system (ISSS and INPEP) was characterized by a defined benefit system (determined by law), undefined contributions (change over time), a pay-as-you-go financial regime (without copious reserves), and public administration (Mesa-Lago 2011).

In December 1996, the Legislative Assembly produced a structural reform to the pension system with the approval of the System of Pension Savings Law (known as the SAP [Sistema de Ahorro para Pensiones] Law), which took effect beginning in 1998. With this reform, the system switched from a pay-as-you-go scheme to a privately managed, individually funded system. The reform established two contributory pension systems: the Public Pension System (Sistema Público de Pensiones [SPP]), which was closed to new enrollees, but continued paying benefits to current pensioners, and the Pension Savings System (Sistema de Ahorro para Pensiones [SAP]).[4] Because of this reform, El Salvador converted from a public pay-as-you-go pension system to an individually funded system, that is, a private sector "replacement" scheme (Mesa-Lago 2004).

Moreover, as part of the transition, for those persons who were already enrolled with one of the public social protection systems (Salvadoran Institute of Social Security [ISSS] and the National Institute of Public Employee Pensions [INPEP]) the SAP Law dictated regimes for transferring from SPP to SAP (Martínez de Ayala 2008). The contributors to the public system at the time of the reform were grouped into three large segments: the group obligated to remain in SPP, made up of persons that as of April 15, 1998, were 50 years old in the case of women or 55 years old in the case of men; a group that could opt to remain enrolled in ISSS or INPEP or simply transfer to the SAP system, made up of those persons who as of April 15, 1998, were at least 36 years old, but were less than 50 or 55 years old for women and men, respectively; and a group obligated to transfer to SAP made up of persons that as of the date of the beginning of operations of SAP were less than 36 years old. From then on, workers that entered the EAP and were insurable had to join SAP.

Because of these regulations, by December 2011 SAP had 98.7 percent of the insured in the entire system. SAP is a completely funded system with individual accounts that are the property of the members, administered by private institutions known as Pension Fund Administrators (Administradores de Fondos de Pensiones [AFPs]).[5] It is a defined contribution regime in which the benefit depends on the accumulated balance in the individual pension savings account, which depends on the member's income during his or her work life and the return on investment of the account balance.

The reform modified the type of scheme, funding mechanisms, the type of administration, and the type of participation. Despite these changes, the reform did not affect two basic aspects of the system: the type of coverage and that coverage was restricted to workers from the private and public sectors. Table 9.3 compares the main characteristics of both systems.

According to Mesa-Lago (2011), retirement ages set by ISSS were not modified, remaining at 55 years old for women and 60 years old for men. The contribution required to gain access to a pension is 25 years of contributions and 10 years to estimate the base regulating salary.[6] In SAP early retirement requires that the balance in the individual account be sufficient to finance a pension equal to or greater than 160 percent of the minimum pension as well as equal to or greater than 60 percent of the base regulating salary, but without a state funding guarantee for the minimum pension. For insured members who have reached retirement age, but have less than 25 years of contributions, they can receive the accumulated balance in the individual account or can continue contributing until meeting the minimum contribution requirement. In SPP, the insured member that reaches retirement age but has not completed the required contribution period receives a lump sum.

Table 9.3 Comparison of the Characteristics of SPP and SAP

Characteristics/system	*SPP*	*SAP*
Type of coverage	Not universal	Not universal
Type of scheme	Defined benefit	Defined contribution
Financial regime or funding model	Partially funded (tiered average premium)	Completely individually funded
Type of administration	Public	Private with state supervision, for which the Superintendent of Pensions (Superintendencia de Pensiones) was created
Type of participation	Mandatory for private and public sector employees, without an option for voluntary participation of independent workers	Mandatory for employees from the private, public, and municipal sectors, with a modality for voluntary participation of independent workers
Coverage for special groups of workers	Not applicable: Coverage restricted to workers from the private and public sectors	Promotes the incorporation of agricultural and domestic workers, according to the conditions and unique characteristics of their work, for which a special regime will be created;[a] allows the enrollment of nonresident Salvadorans

Source: Taken from Argueta 2011, with some adjustments.
Note: SAP = Sistema de Ahorro para Pensiones; SPP = Sistema Público de Pensiones.
a. So far the regulations pertaining to the incorporation of these workers do not exist, nor were they set out during the operational years of SPP.

Using figures from the Superintendent on monthly elderly, disability, and survivor's pensions in SPP and SAP, Mesa-Lago (2011) estimated the general weighted average pension in each of the two systems from 2004 to 2010. From the first year, elderly and disability pensions from SAP are consistently higher than those from SPP, although they increase in both systems and the gap trends downward (table 9.4).

However, we should consider the warning that

> the SAP is a very young system in which just 40% of pensions are elderly pensions and 55% are survivor's pensions, while the SPP is a mature system in which 52% of pensions are elderly pensions and 27% are survivor's pensions. ... Survivor's pensions are calculated based on the elderly pension of the deceased and are received on average by three to four people, which makes the resulting payments much lower than elderly pension payments. These are much higher in the SAP than in the SPP even though the gap falls from 88% to 70% between 2004 and 2010; the same occurs with disability pensions, but the gap is lesser and remains around 17%.
>
> (Mesa-Lago 2011, p. 26)

The pension system reform brought along with it an increase in the contribution percentages. The ISSS Public Pension System (SPP) increased from 3.5 percent in the 1990–96 period to 8 percent in 1997, reaching 13 percent in 2001, and finally 14 percent in 2003 (7 percent from the employer and 7 percent from the enrolled employee). In terms of the regimes managed by INPEP—Administrative and Education—both, like ISSS, reached a total contribution of 14 percent in 2008, in which both parties—enrolled employees and employers—pay the same contribution percentage (7 percent each). SAP began in 1998 with a contribution rate of 9.5 percent (5 percent

Table 9.4 Monthly Average Amount of Total Contributory Pensions, Elderly, and Disability in SPP and SAP, 2001–10
US$

	Total		*Elderly*		*Disability*	
Years[a]	*SPP*	*SAP*	*SPP*	*SAP*	*SPP*	*SAP*
2001	178		222		188	
2002	197		239		140	
2003	204		245		140	
2004	222	210	270	494	154	175
2005	231	264	279	522	155	178
2006	230	265	280	513	154	181
2007	238	267	290	512	157	183
2008	241	270	293	517	160	190
2009	259	270	311	535	178	205
2010	259	279	315	537	178	208

Source: Mesa-Lago 2011.
Note: SAP = Sistema de Ahorro para Pensiones; SPP = Sistema Público de Pensiones.
a. December of each year; September in 2010.

from the employer and 4.5 percent from the enrolled employee) and reached 13 percent in 2002 (6.75 percent from the employer and 6.25 percent from the enrolled employee).

Pension System Coverage

Contrary to the argument presented by the supporters of structural reform, basically that the reform would create incentives that would increase coverage, this has not occurred. To analyze the pension system, contributors are a better indicator than enrolled members because they are both enrolled and make contribution and commission payments to the AFPs in a given month. Figure 9.5 presents the evolution of the number of effective contributors and the contribution density, which relates the number of effective contributors and the number of members, and indicates the proportion of those who made payments at a given point in time. We can observe that since 1998, contribution density has shown a consistent drop, beginning at 69.7 percent in 1998 and falling to 27.6 percent in 2011, the lowest level recorded in the period 1998–2011. This means that for 2011, for every 100 members, only 27 are making their contributions. This is an

Figure 9.5 Enrolled Members and Contributors in the Pension System and Contribution Density, 1998–2011

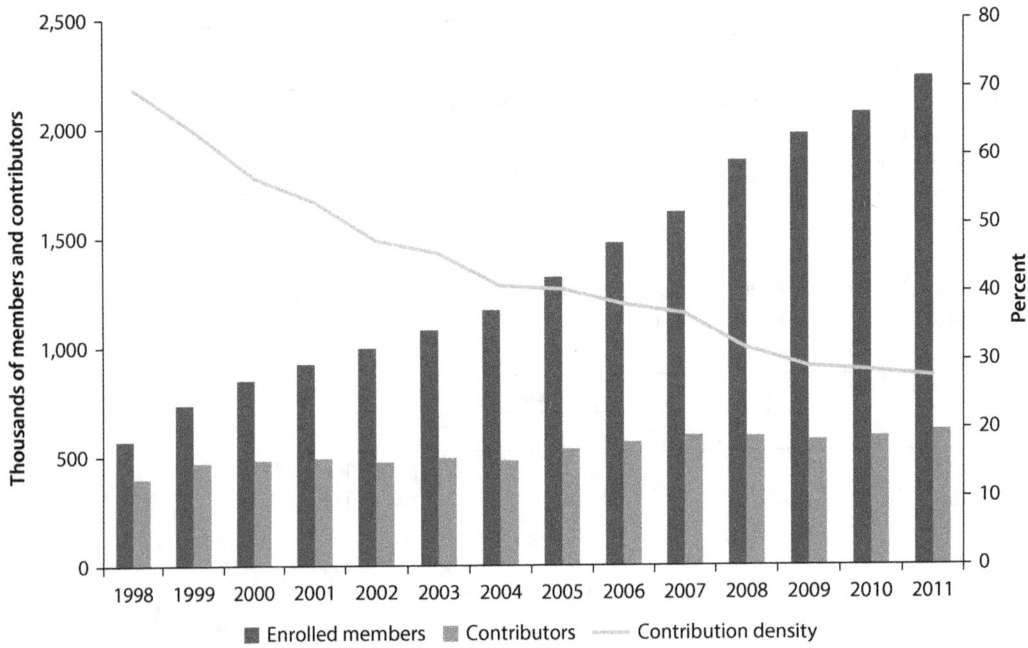

Source: Based on enrolled members from the Social Protection Statistics Magazine from the Pension System Superintendent (Superintendencia del Sistema de Pensiones), 1998–2011; SAP contributors from 1998 to 2011 from the Social Protection Statistics Magazine from the Pension System Superintendent, 1998–2011; and SPP contributors from 2005 to 2009 from Mesa-Lago (2011) and 2010 and 2011 from the Social Protection Statistics Magazine from the Pension System Superintendent, 2010–11.

Note: From 1998 to 2004 includes information only on the number of enrolled members and contributors from SAP because the authors did not have access to information on SPP enrolled members, which means that contribution density refers to SAP. From 2005 to 2011 the number of enrolled members and contributors are the total of SAP and SPP, which means that contribution density refers to SAP and SPP together.
SAP = Sistema de Ahorro para Pensiones; SPP = Sistema Público de Pensiones.

important aspect to consider, because although the number of enrolled members has been increasing, the number of effective contributors has stalled at an average of 523,563 during the period analyzed, and what matters in terms of accumulating savings in the individual account to receive a future pension is the number of months in which contributions were made.

Figure 9.6 presents the relationship that exists between the number of effective contributors to SAP and SPP and the EAP, observing that this coverage is low, around 23.6 percent during the period 1998–2011. For its part, Mesa-Lago (2011) calculates the coverage of the EAP using household surveys and reports that this methodology results in figures that are above the institutional numbers. The average in this case for the period 1998–2008 would be coverage of 30.7 percent according to surveys.

The structural reform did not substantially increase the coverage of the EAP. "based on institutional data it decreased 4.4 percentage points in the 13 years between 1998 and 2010, although it increased 3.2 percent based on surveys from 1998 to 2008, before the worst point of the crisis" (Mesa-Lago 2011, p. 21); covering an average of 23.6 percent of the EAP according to institutional statistics and 30.7 percent of the EAP according to the surveys.

Figure 9.6 Contributors, Economically Active Population, and Coverage of Contributors to the Pension System with Respect to the EAP, 1998–2011

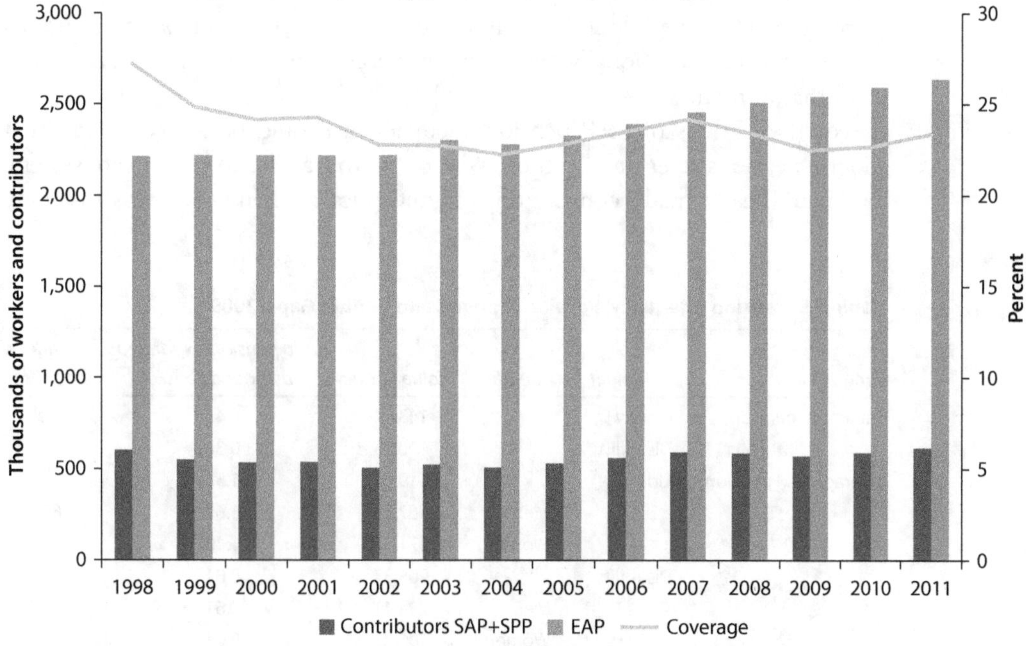

Source: Based on SAP contributors from 1998 to 2011 from the Social Protection Statistics Magazine from the Pension System Superintendent, 1998–2011; SPP contributors from 1998 to 2009 from Mesa-Lago (2011) and 2010 and 2011 from the Social Protection Statistics Magazine from the Pension System Superintendent, 2010–11; and estimates and projections of the Economically Active Population 1990–2020, updated October 2011 from the International Labour Organization.
Note: EAPs include employed persons or that are actively seeking work and aged 15 years and older. EAP = economically active population; SAP = Sistema de Ahorro para Pensiones; SPP = Sistema Público de Pensiones.

In terms of the reasons behind this low level of coverage, it had already been stated that an increase in coverage after the reform was not to be expected "due to the predominance of the informal sector, the enormous increase in workers' required contributions (especially in the private sector), and the contrary experience of other countries where structural reforms also saw a stall or fall in coverage" (Mesa-Lago 2011, p. 18). Other reasons pointed out respond to factors present in the labor market, especially the high rate of jobs in economic activities in the informal sector (Alvarenga 2002), as well as the economy's own performance. Even though these last two aspects are structural in nature, "if this situation does not improve in the next few years, it will have a greater impact both on the number of individuals that retire without a pension, as well as on the amounts of pensions" (Córdova et al. 2010, p. 118). The challenge that logically follows from this situation is to find ways of increasing pension coverage for segments of the informal sector of the economy.

Pension Adequacy

Argueta (2011) compares SAP benefits with the cost of the expanded basket of basic goods (poverty threshold) and the basic nutritional basket (extreme poverty threshold)[7] for urban sectors in the country and signals that, on average, the amount of the elderly pension covers both baskets (table 9.5). Meanwhile, the average disability pension is insufficient to cover the expanded basket of basic goods, but it does cover the basic nutritional basket. On the other hand, the minimum elderly and disability pensions do not even cover the basic nutritional basket of goods. Additionally, the elderly pension for women is 17 percent lower than that of men.

For the analysis of SAP pension adequacy, it should be kept in mind that elderly pensions refer only to those who opted to transfer to the private system, but had already made contributions in the public scheme, whereas disability

Table 9.5 Pension Adequacy, Pension Amount, and Gender Gaps, 2009

Program	*Benefit*	*Gender*	*Value (US$)*	*Ratio pension/expanded basic goods basket*	*Gender gap[a] (%)*
Minimum pension	Elderly		143.64	0.43	n.a.
	Disability		100.55	0.30	
Average SAP pension	Elderly		519.62	1.55	
		Men	567.65	1.69	83
		Women	471.58	1.40	
	Disability		205.37	0.61	
		Men	204.41	0.61	101
		Women	206.33	0.61	
Cost urban basket of basic goods	Nutritional		168.01	n.a.	n.a.
	Expanded		336.02	n.a.	

Source: Argueta 2011.
Note: n.a. = not applicable. SAP = Sistema de Ahorro para Pensiones.
a. Represents the average women's pension as a percentage of the men's pension.

pensions include both those who opted to switch and those who have been enrolled only in SAP. The system is still several years away from beginning to pay pensions to those who have been incorporated into the private system since the beginning of their work lives, and as a result it is too early to draw conclusions about the pensions that this system will pay out. However, in individually funded systems two main factors determine the benefit level that contributors will receive upon their retirement: the salary amount and the contribution density, understood as the number of months that the worker participated actively in the labor market and as a result contributed to his or her individual account, and the return on investment for the funds in the pension system. Information is available regarding this last aspect.

Two elements characterize the performance of the funds in the pension system during the period 1998–2011: The investment portfolio has not been diversified, and the pension fund's return on investment has decreased consistently. In regard to the first aspect, between 1999 and 2011 "the investment in public debt increased from 64.6% to 84.5%" (Fundación Dr. Guillermo Manuel Ungo 2011, p. 2), which shows that the investment portfolio has not been diversified, but rather has been increasingly concentrated in public debt. With regard to the second, figure 9.7 presents the gross return on investment (without subtracting the net commission), which is estimated by the Superintendent of Pensions since 1999 in two ways: the average in the previous year and the annual accumulated average from the beginning of SAP to present (Historical Series 1), adjusted for inflation. Mesa-Lago (2011) has warned that the high return on investment in the first two years could be the result of the fact that the return was still being calculated in colones, and the accumulated funds were very small, making them

Figure 9.7 SAP's Real Return in the Previous Year and since Its Creation, 1998–2010

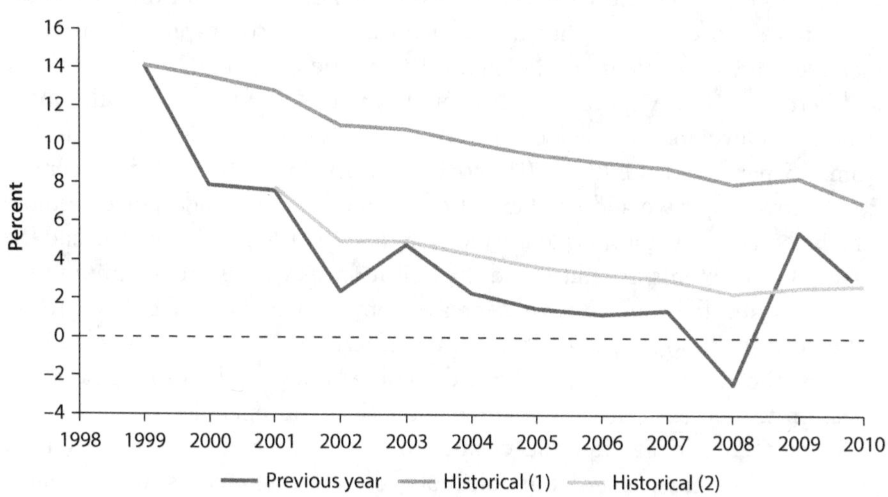

Source: Fundación Dr. Guillermo Manuel Ungo 2011.
Note: SAP = Sistema de Ahorro para Pensiones.

irrelevant for the expected cumulated returns over the lifetime of a worker. This lead the author to perform an independent calculation of the historic return on investment ignoring the first two years, shown as "historical (2)"in figure 9.7. The alternative calculation shows lower results than the Superintendent's calculation and decreases from 7.8 percent to 2.7 percent in 2010. This decrease in the pension funds' return will undoubtedly have an effect on future pensions.

Financial Sustainability

The cost of the transition from the public system to the private is paid for by the state and has three major components: "(1) the deficit that occurs in the closed public system once it has few or no contributors but still has present and future pensions to pay out; (2) the recognition bonds or transfer certificates that are given to the insured members in the private system for the contributions they made to the public system before the reform; and (3) the minimum pension for insured members of the private system—when the funds accumulated in their individual accounts are insufficient to fund at least the minimum pension, the State pays the difference" (Mesa-Lago 2011, p. 15).

After the structural reform, the ISSS reserves ran out in October 2000 and INPEP reserves were exhausted in August 2002, and the funding of the public system's obligations was covered with resources transferred from the Treasury Ministry. However, because of the growing costs for public finances, in 2006 the government approved a reform that created the Retirement Obligations Trust (Fideicomiso de Obligaciones Previsionales [FOP]), as a funding mechanism for the public system pensions. According to Argueta (2011, p. 40), "Under the trust structure, the SPP pension obligations are absorbed by the pension fund through an apparent investment mechanism, that obligates the system to transfer private funds from the SAP contributors to make payments that should be covered by the state's public institutes."

A projection from the World Bank before the 2006 reform of the Salvadoran pension system estimated that the total fiscal cost of social protection would increase from 1.4 percent of GDP in 2001 to 3.2 percent in 2020 (Gill, Packard, and Yermo 2005). A more recent report from the World Bank and the Inter-American Development Bank estimated that SPP's operating deficit will decline from 1.5 percent of GDP in 2010 to 1.1 percent in 2020 and 0.5 percent in 2030. However, if we add up the cost of the recognition bonds issued to those who had made contributions to the old system at the time of the reform, and the financial instruments issued to fund the transition, as well as the minimum pension guarantee, the total cost will decrease from 2.4 percent of GDP in 2010 to 1.8 percent in 2030 (World Bank and Inter-American Development Bank 2010).

After the reform there have been difficulties tracking the exact amount of social protection debt because there is not a clear and operational definition of social protection debt after the creation of the Retirement Obligations Trust (FOP). In this sense, "in some publications, there are references just to annual issuances of type 'A' Retirement Investment Certificates (Certificados de Inversión Previsional, CIP A); in others annual issuances of the CIP A and the type 'B'

Retirement Investment Certificates (CIP B); while in others the total balances of the CIP A, or even the total balances of the FOP" (Argueta 2011, p. 52).

According to Mesa-Lago, a Treasury Ministry projection made in March 2011 for 2016 pointed out that "the combined cost of the social protection debt financed by the state plus the CIP financed by the AFP, shows that it will increase 39 percent from $792 to $1,061 million (46 percent from the state and 54 percent from the CIP). The cost of social protection with respect to GDP will average 3.6 percent during the period, peaking in 2012 and then posting a gradual decline. … Another estimate of social protection debt, which adds information from the bonds, plus the two types of CIP, and the cost of the minimum pension, shows percentages of GDP that grow from 6.8% in 2006 to 10.6% in 2009" (Mesa-Lago 2011, p. 55).

Meanwhile, another estimate made by Argueta that considers the FOP balances as debt argues that "they reflect the accumulation of the state's obligations in terms of both types of CIP, as well as the financial costs associated with the issuance of this type of debt" and estimates that in 2010 "the social protection debt will rise a little more to US$2.6 billion dollars, approximately 12.71% of nominal GDP for that year, with a clearly upward trend" (Argueta 2011, pp. 52–53).

Considering the different components and estimates presented that are the products of the work of various authors, we can conclude that it is necessary to have an official estimate that updates this information and accounts for the fiscal effort required for the transition, which all estimates show is growing and prolonged.

The Noncontributory Scheme

The Universal Social Protection System (Sistema de Protección Social Universal [SPSU]) is a social policy strategy designed at the beginning of president Mauricio Funes' administration and is defined within the framework of the Five-Year Development Plan 2010–14 ("Plan Quinquenal de Desarrollo 2010–14"). The plan expresses that this strategy "is based on a rights-based approach, strengthens human development and territorial management, and promotes the active participation of municipal governments and the community […] that seeks to gradually guarantee for all the country's inhabitants, especially the impoverished and excluded population, a basic social support system through the implementation of specific policies and programs"; and that "keeps in mind the life cycle of individuals" (Government of El Salvador 2010, p. 66).

The Basic Universal Pension

From a conceptual and holistic point of view, the SPSU is made up of contributory and noncontributory social security pillars (figure 9.8). The government considers it "essential, on the one hand, to start actions that strengthen the country's social security, specifically the contributory scheme of the pension sector, and on the other, intervene in the noncontributory sector, in order to establish the Universal Social Protection System solidary pillar" (Government of El Salvador 2010, p. 65).

Figure 9.8 Comparison of the Characteristics of the Contributory and Noncontributory Pension Schemes

	Noncontributory System	Contributory Systems		
Program, system, or special regime	Universal Basic Pension	Public Pension System (SPP)	Pension Savings System (SAP)	Special Pension Regime for the Military
Target population	Eldery in targeted municipalities	Public and private sector workers	Public, municipal, and private sector workers	Military personel
Type of scheme	Noncontributory, monthly transfer of US$50	Contributory, benefit defined	Contributory, contribution defined	Contributory, benefit defined
Managing institution	Fondo de Inversión Social para el Desarrollo Local (FISDL)	Instituto Salvadoreño de Seguridad Social (ISSS) and INPEP	Pension fund management firms	Instituto de Previsión Social de la Fuerza Armada (IPSFA)
Main source of funding	National budget	Contributions and state support, plus special funds	Contributions and special funds	Contributions
Legal framework	Decree 56, creating the Solidarity Communities Program	Pension Savings System Law, ISSS Law, INPEP Law	Pension Savings System Law	Social Insurance Military Institute Law

Source: Based on Argueta 2011.
Note: INPEP = Instituto Nacional de Pensiones de los Empleados Públicos.

Within the SPSU strategy, the component for attention to the elderly population is incorporated in the Five-Year Plan around the Basic Universal Pension (Pensión Básica Universal [PBU]) through two government programs: Rural Solidary Communities (Comunidades Solidarias Rurales) and Urban Solidary Communities (Comunidades Solidarias Urbanas). It originally consisted of a US$50 monthly pension given to individuals aged 70 and older that do not receive any other type of pension and reside in any of the 32 extremely poor municipalities identified in the 2005 Poverty Map (Facultad Latinoamericana de Ciencias Sociales [FLACSO] 2005). The PBU was created before the government's Five-Year Plan was completely formulated, during the fourth quarter of 2009 as part of the new Solidary Community Program (Programa de Comunidades Solidarias). The PBU was subsequently reinforced as a government policy in the Global Anti-crisis Plan at the end of 2009.

The PBU program began operations in November 2009 within the framework of the Rural Solidary Communities Program, intervening in 32 municipalities. This program is the responsibility of the Social Investment for Local Development Fund (Fondo de Inversión Social para el Desarrollo Local [FISDL]), with the support and backing of the Secretariat of Social Inclusion (Secretaría de Inclusión Social), the Technical Secretariat of the Presidency (Secretaría Técnica de la Presidencia), and the Health Ministry (Ministerio de Salud). In addition municipal goverments, municipal coordination committees, and some NGOs are co-implementers of the program.

The process of targeting the program was implemented using the census performed for the Rural Solidary Communities program (previously the Solidarity Network, Red Solidaria), which was used to identify potential recipients, as well as their living conditions. Subsequently, according to the eligibility criteria, authorities determined if they qualified as recipients of the program or not. Finally, those that were deemed eligible were incorporated into the system through a process managed by a supporting NGO (FISDL 2009).

In order to receive the PBU, the eligibility criteria specified that an elderly person must be at least 70 years old, reside in any of the 32 municipalities of severely extreme poverty identified by the National Poverty Map of El Salvador, and not receive any type of individual pension. To be able to identify people who received individual pensions, the program combined information about the elderly from the validation affidavits from the Municipal Coordination Committees (Comités Municipales de Coordinación [CMCs]) with information from the Armed Forces Social Protection Institute (IPSFA), Educators' Well-being (Bienestar Magisterial), and Superintendent of Pensions. The individuals that were validated by the CMC but also identified as recipients of another pension were excluded from the PBU (FISDL 2010).

The PBU ends when the recipient passes away or moves out of poverty. In addition, it is the recipients' responsibility to attend periodic health checkups at the nearest health care facility. These checkups include a general periodic health exam, immunization, and comprehensive geriatric evaluation.

Coverage Levels and Benefits

Even though the PBU is called universal, the scheme is targeted according to geographic and demographic criteria associated with the characteristics of poverty in the municipalities (Argueta 2011). In the first phase of the program (from November 2009 until 2010) 8,014 people in 32 municipalities of severely extreme poverty joined the program, and in the second phase the program was expected to incorporate 68 municipalities with high extreme poverty levels. However, in 2011 only 21 municipalities with high extreme poverty were incorporated. By December 2011, the program covered 15,300 beneficiaries in 53 municipalities (table 9.6).

By December 2012 the number of municipalities had increased to 75, covering 25,396 elderly. According to data from the Technical Secretariat of

Table 9.6 Number of PBU Municipalities and Beneficiaries, 2010–14

Year	*Number of municipalities*	*Number of beneficiaries*
2010	32	8,014
2011	53	15,300
2012	75	25,396
2013[a]	75	29,085
2014[a]	75	29,085

Source: Technical Secretariat of the Presidency, February 2013.
Note: PBU = Pensión Básica Universal.
a. Projected.

the Presidency, the government planned to maintain the same 75 municipalities for 2013, but increase the number of beneficiaries to 29,085, and in 2014 continue in the same 75 municipalities with the same number of beneficiaries as 2013.

Based on the 2010 Multipurpose Household Survey (Encuesta de Hogares de Propósitos Múltiples [EHPM]), the percentage of persons 70 years and older that live in a situation of poverty was estimated at 38.34 percent, and this percentage was applied to the projected population for 2010, resulting in a total of 114,162 elderly aged 70 years and older that live in a situation of poverty. If we compare this with the 8,014 recipients of the PBU in 2010, the coverage of the elderly living in poverty was 7.02 percent. Considering the population aged 70 and older projected for 2011 (306,015) and applying the percentage of those aged 70 and older in poverty from the 2011 EHPM (42.02 percent) to this age group, we obtain a total of 128,588 elderly aged 70 and older in poverty. Comparing this total with the recipients of the PBU in 2011, we estimate that coverage of the elderly living in poverty increased to 11.9 percent. These calculations should be taken with caution because they are approximate for two reasons. First, they assume that the PBU targeting criteria coincide with the criteria used for the Basic Nutritional Basket of Goods. Second, the estimate has been performed for the entire country, including municipalities that because of eligibility criteria could not form part of the PBU because it is targeted at municipalities in extreme poverty from the National Poverty Map of El Salvador.

With regard to the PBU, Mesa-Lago (2011) points out that

> the PBU delivers $50 per month to those who are age 70 and older or are disabled regardless of their age, are poor, and do not receive a contributory pension. … If a contributory pension beneficiary receives less than $50 per month, the PBU pays the difference. … The amount of the PBU is below the poverty line, which in 2009 was $95 in urban areas and $61 in rural areas; but is above the basic nutritional basket per urban inhabitant of $45 and rural inhabitant of $29. A survey of PBU beneficiaries in 2010 showed that they used the money first to buy food, second for medicines, and third for clothing; 62 percent said the PBU allowed them to buy

> essential goods that they could not buy before and 18 percent said that they no longer had to ask family members or friends for money (FISDL 2010). The PBU is equal to one-third of the minimum pension, one-sixth of the average SPP pension and one-tenth of the SAP average, and as a result should not create disincentives for joining the contributory system.
>
> (Mesa-Lago 2011)

Estimated Cost of the Program

In the event that the PBU program sought to cover all elderly persons over aged 70, Mesa-Lago (2011) has calculated (based on information from the 2007 census and subtracting contributory pension beneficiaries) that there would be 131,870 eligible persons at a cost of US$79 million or 0.4 percent of GDP in that year: "Because the PBU is targeted at the poor, its cost is minor: the Five-Year Plan initially projected US$74.5 million during the five-year period or US$15 million per year; a review of the Plan in 2011 including operating costs increased the five-year cost to US$147 million or US$29 million per year" (Mesa-Lago 2011, p. 45).

Other Programs Aimed at Social Protection for the Elderly

Turning to other social protection initiatives for the elderly at the government level, the formulation of the residential program "Our Greatest Rights" ("Nuestros Mayores Derechos") is still in progress. In the design of this program, policy makers are considering a set of interventions; among them, the Ministry of Public Health and Social Assistance "will develop specific actions so that the elderly will receive promotion, prevention, diagnostic, recovery, and rehabilitation services, through the various levels of the health care system, and according to their needs, the elderly who cannot visit health care facilities because of disabilities will also be attended in their homes." Additionally, they propose to teach literacy "to the elderly, giving priority attention to women, using the literacy circles program from the Education Ministry as a model of action; it also includes training in new technologies specially designed for the elderly." Concurrently, they will develop "communications strategies to build awareness and share information through different communications media to promote the revaluation and social recognition of the elderly" and "fun, cultural, recreational, and physical activities directed to older persons." The government will invest "in the improvement of public spaces open to all for the elderly"; and the promotion of "economic autonomy," though the "promotion of entrepreneurship, based on the identification of products and services from the community with a potential market" and the "occupational orientation and mediation interfacing with public and private institutions open to hiring the elderly in dignified and decent conditions" (Secretariat of Social Inclusion 2012, pp. 2–3).

Conclusions and Future Challenges

Despite the structural reform that came into effect in 1998, the Salvadoran pension system continues to be segmented "although a partial and incomplete unification process has occurred" (Mesa-Lago 2011, p. 17), and the segmentation affects the principle of organization and unity of social security because of the lack of integration among the programs.

The various pension schemes in El Salvador "attend different populations and have very limited coverage. Up to the present, there are no consolidated numbers in the country regarding the coverage of the different pension schemes (social protection and contributory) with respect to the same population base (EAP or the elderly), although there are coverage estimates for contributory pension coverage relative to the EAP (between 23% and 33% of the EAP in recent years)" (Argueta 2011, p. 22).

This lack of integration and the absences of consolidated information for the different pension programs has not allowed analysts to estimate the level of resources that the country dedicates to social protection in terms of pensions. Because the PBU is relatively new, it lacks an external evaluation of the program's targeting.

In the future, one challenge is to improve the coordination among the contributory and noncontributory programs, but above all to ensure that both are a part of the SPSU, which is for now still a conceptual proposal in the design phase.

One of the main challenges for the pension system is to increase coverage. During the period 1998–2011, the contributory system stalled at around 23.6 percent coverage of the EAP according to institutional data, or 30.7 percent according to household surveys. These data show low coverage of active contributors in the pension system. According to data from the 2007 Census, among the elderly population just 20.5 percent of the economically inactive population receive pensions. This means that despite reaching retirement age, just a small percentage of the elderly population achieves access to a pension. This topic becomes more relevant in light of the analysis undertaken of the demographic transition that El Salvador has experienced in recent decades, and the significant process of population aging that is in progress.

The analysis presented of the social protection system (the PBU) for the elderly population shows low coverage of this recent program, begun at the end of 2009. During 2011 the PBU was estimated to have covered 11.9 percent of the elderly aged 70 and older living in poverty. With respect to this program, which despite being called "universal" is more of a targeted pension, we can identify two challenges. The legal basis that ensures the program's sustainability over time is one challenge, because this program is not supported "by a legislative decree that guarantees its permanence over the long term, nor is it part of a larger law (like the Comprehensive Service to the Elderly Law, Ley de Atención Integral para la Persona Adulta Mayor)" (Argueta 2011, p. 20). Another challenge is the need for coordination and articulation with the contributory pension system: "Nor do these schemes have legal frameworks that give their operations consistency as part of an integrated social protection system. The institutions that administer these schemes have traditionally operated under distinct laws, rules, and directors; they do not necessarily share information and do not have common indicators that allow for monitoring of the joint operations of social protection in the face of the eventualities of old age, disability, or death as a public policy" (Argueta 2011).

With respect to the contributory pension scheme (SAP), in recent years various diagnoses and proposals have been formulated that signal that the system faces the need for a comprehensive reform to meet various challenges. A basic agenda of topics of reform for SAP includes the following: (1) supervision of evasion and default, (2) diversification of the investment portfolio, (3) improvement of the pension funds' return on investment, (4) implementation of the annuity option and a combined option, (5) reduction of gender inequalities, (6) greater efficiency and reduction of administrative costs, (7) coverage expansion, especially in the informal sector of the economy, (8) improvement to the statistics system, (9) reinforcement of the financial and actuarial sustainability of the system, and (10) strengthening of the Superintendent of Pensions and the Ministry of Labor (Mesa-Lago 2011).

The demographic transition that the country is undergoing is characterized by a downward trend in the dependency ratio (increasing the relative weight of the population at potentially productive ages and decreasing that of persons at potentially inactive ages). This represents a window of opportunity for the country in the coming decades if it knows how to take advantage of it: "However, in order to take advantage of this potential it is necessary to create public policies aimed at improving the functioning and absorption capacity of the labor market to receive the growing working age population increases, and in job quality, such that jobs offer salaries and benefits related to social security; as well as invest in human capital, especially in youth" (Córdova et al. 2010, p. 44). If the country takes advantage of this window of opportunity, then there will be less need to invest resources in the social protection pension program in the future. But this opportunity presents a significant challenge in terms of coverage expansion, above all in the informal sector of the economy. In addition, the state fills the role of guaranteeing a minimum pension. If the contribution density does not improve as a result of labor market dynamics, in the future this could create new demands on public finances.

Notes

1. According to Salvadoran law, the elderly population consists of individuals aged 60 years and older.
2. Two limitations of this indicator should be considered. First, not all individuals stop being economically active automatically when they turn 60 years old, and, second, not all individuals between 15 and 59 years old are economically active.
3. This indicator is approximate; the category on the census questionnaire is for retiree, pensioner, or individual deriving income from personal investments.

4. Moreover, the Armed Forces Social Protection Institute's (Instituto de Previsión Social de la Fuerza Armada [IPSFA]) defined benefit system remained. For more information about the different pension programs in El Salvador, see Mesa-Lago (2011).
5. The five AFPs that began operations with the new system continue operating today.
6. Average monthly income based on contributions, which is one of the two highest in the region, and is adjusted by the Consumer Price Index (CPI).
7. Households in extreme poverty are those whose income does not exceed the cost of the basic nutritional basket of goods, whereas households in relative poverty receive income less than the cost of the expanded basket of basic goods. The cost of the expanded basket is estimated to be two times that of the nutritional basket.

Bibliography

Alvarenga, L. 2002. "A Cinco Años de la Reforma de Pensiones en El Salvador y su Impacto en la Equidad de Género." ECLAC, Santiago, Chile.

Argueta, N. 2011. "Entre el individuo y el Estado: condicionantes financieros del sistema de pensiones en El Salvador." Estudios sobre políticas públicas no. 2, FUNDAUNGO/Friedrich Ebert Stiftung, San Salvador.

CELADE (Centro Latinoamericano y Caribeño de Demografía—División de Población de la CEPAL). 2012. "Estimaciones y proyecciones de población a largo plazo. 1950–2100. Revisión 2012." CELADE, Santiago, Chile.

Córdova, R., D. Burgos, V. Tablas, and F. Rodríguez. 2010. "Las tendencias demográficas de la población adulta mayor y sus implicaciones para las políticas públicas en materia de seguridad social." Cuadernos Salvadoreños de Población 3, FUNDAUNGO/UNFPA, San Salvador.

Córdova, R., C. López, and C. Mesa-Lago. 1994. "El Salvador: Diagnóstico y Propuesta de Reforma de la Seguridad Social." FUNDAUNGO/CINDE/Friedrich Ebert Stiftung, San Salvador.

DGEC (Dirección General de Estadística y Censos). 2008. "VI Censo de Población y V de Vivienda 2007." DIGESTYC, San Salvador.

———. 2010. "Encuesta de Hogares de Propósitos Múltiples 2010." DIGESTYC, El Salvador.

———. 2011. "Encuesta de Hogares de Propósitos Múltiples 2011." DIGESTYC, El Salvador.

DGEC (Dirección General de Estadística y Censos), Fondo de Población de las Naciones Unidas y Centro Latinoamericano, and Caribeño de Demografía. 2010. "Estimaciones y Proyecciones Nacionales de Población 1950–2050." DIGESTYC/UN-FPA/CELADE, San Salvador.

ECLAC (Economic Commission for Latin America and the Caribbean). 2008. "Transformaciones demográficas y su influencia en el desarrollo de América Latina y el Caribe." Informe del trigésimo segundo período de sesiones, ECLAC, Santiago, Chile.

FISDL (Fondo de Inversión Social para el Desarrollo Local). 2009. "Programa de Atención Integral a la Persona Adulta Mayor." FISDL, San Salvador.

———. 2010. "Programa de Atención Integral a la Persona Adulta Mayor: Estudio base sobre las condiciones de vida de los y las beneficiarios de la Pensión Básica Universal." FISDL, San Salvador.

FLACSO (Facultad Latinoamericana de Ciencias Sociales). 2005. "Mapa de Pobreza: Política Social y Focalización." FLASCO Programa El Salvador. FISDL, El Salvador.

Fundación Dr. Guillermo Manuel Ungo. 2011. "La rentabilidad de los fondos del sistema de pensiones en El Salvador 1998–2011." Aportes al debate sobre las Políticas Públicas no. 1, FUNDAUNGO, San Salvador.

Gill, I., T. Packard, and J. Yermo. 2005. *Keeping the Promise of Social Security in Latin America*. Washington, DC: Stanford University Press and World Bank.

Government of El Salvador. 2010. "Plan Quinquenal de Desarrollo 2010–14." GOES, San Salvador.

Martínez de Ayala, M. 2008. "El Sistema de Pensiones Público a 10 años de la Reforma Previsional." Superintendent of Pensions, San Salvador.

Mesa-Lago, C. 2004. "Las reformas de pensiones en América Latina y su impacto en los principios de la seguridad social." Serie financiamiento del desarrollo no. 144, ECLAC, Santiago, Chile.

———. 2011. "Diagnóstico del Sistema de Pensiones en El Salvador (1998–2010)." Estudios sobre Políticas Públicas no. 1, FUNDAUNGO, San Salvador.

Secretariat of Social Inclusion. 2012. "Programa Presidencial Nuestros Mayores Derechos." El Salvador.

UNPF (United Nations Population Fund). 2010. "El Salvador: transformaciones demográficas y sus implicaciones en las políticas públicas." Cuadernos Salvadoreños de Población 2, UNFPA, San Salvador.

World Bank and Inter-American Development Bank. 2010. *El Salvador Public Expenditure Review: Enhancing the Efficiency and Targeting of Expenditures*, vols. 1 and 2. Washington, DC: World Bank and Inter-American Development Bank.

CHAPTER 10

Mexico

F. Alejandro Villagómez and Gabriel Darío Ramírez

History

Mexico is one of the Latin American countries with lowest coverage among its elderly population, particularly for retirement pensions. Despite having reformed its main pension programs, replacing them with fully funded, defined contribution and individual account systems, these actions were more a response to fiscal pressures and the need to stimulate financial savings and achieve greater coverage. Additionally, faced with significant labor informality and high mobility between the formal and informal sectors, even among workers that are registered with a contributory program, it is likely that many workers will not even obtain a minimum guaranteed pension because of the low levels of contribution density. As a result, during the last decade the government has resorted to implementing several noncontributory social protection programs, based on income transfers that guarantee a minimum income, with varied effects.

Profile of the Elderly Population

The elderly segment of the population has grown significantly in recent decades. This change in the population's demographic structure can be explained by a combination of diverse factors, among which several stand out: the increase in life expectancy and the reduction in the fertility rate due to improvements in the provision of health care services, nutrition, and hygiene habits, along with women's growing entry into the labor market. In Mexico, life expectancy has increased from 49.6 years in 1950 to 71.4 years in 1990 and 74 years in 2010. For its part, the fertility rate has fallen from 3.4 children per woman at the end of her fertile years in 1990 to 2.3 in 2010. As a consequence, the number of people older than 65 years as part of the total population has increased from 3.4 percent in 1950 to 6.2 percent in 2010 and is estimated to climb to 16.8 percent in 2050 (table 10.1).

Estimates show that in 2010 the population older than 65 years rose to 7.1 million, of which 62.5 percent resided in urban areas (table 10.2). Around 15.3 percent of the elderly live in areas of high or very high marginalization, according to the index constructed by the National Population Council

Table 10.1 Population Profile, Projection 1990–2050

	1990	*2000*	*2010*	*2020*	*2030*	*2040*	*2050*
Total population	87,064,847	100,895,811	114,289,406	125,016,451	131,478,659	135,671,370	137,477,524
Men	43,493,548	49,664,815	55,849,322	60,722,721	63,238,173	64,644,896	65,083,916
Women	43,571,299	51,230,996	58,440,084	64,293,730	68,240,486	71,026,474	72,393,608
Total growth rate (%)	1.72	1.22	1.20	0.6	0.41	0.22	0.05
Population 65 years and older	3,740,168	5,224,003	7,058,363	9,772,004	13,856,382	18,940,139	23,130,490
Percentage	4.3	5.2	6.2	7.8	10.5	14.0	16.8
Men	1,784,656	2,455,863	3,254,001	4,441,473	6,201,545	8,346,979	9,984,276
Percentage	47.7	47.0	46.1	45.5	44,8	44.1	43.2
Women	1,955,512	2,768,140	3,804,362	5,330,531	7,654,837	10,593,160	13,146,214
Percentage	52.3	53.0	53.9	54.5	55.2	55.9	56.8
Growth rate 65 years and older (%)	3.4	3.2	3.1	3.6	3.5	2.6	1.5
Gross birth rate (%)[a]	27.9	23.4	19.7	17.5	15.8	14.7	14.0
Gross mortality rate (%)[a]	5.6	5.1	5.6	6.0	6.9	8.0	9.2
Total fertility rate (%)	3.4	2.6	2.3	2.1	2.1	2.1	2.1
Life expectancy at birth total	71.4	73.6	74.0	75.7	77.0	78.2	79.4
Men	68.0	70.9	71.1	73.3	74.6	76.0	77.3
Women	75.0	76.4	77.0	78.3	79.4	80.5	81.6

Source: Based on Basic Demographic Indicators 1990–2010 and Population Projections 2010–50, National Population Council (Consejo Nacional de Población, CONAPO).
a. For every 1,000 inhabitants.

(Consejo Nacional de Población [CONAPO]). The index measures the total impact of deprivations that afflict this population as a result of the lack of access to primary education, precarious dwellings, low monetary income, and the challenges of living in small, scattered, and isolated localities.[1] However, this situation is even more marked considering just the elderly population in rural areas, in whose case 37.7 percent show a high or very high index of marginalization.

The distribution of the elderly by household type reveals that more than 85 percent live in nuclear or extended households, practically the same proportion in each in 2010. Just 11.9 percent live in one-person households. This pattern is basically the same throughout the country, regardless if we consider urban or rural areas. Another interesting aspect of the elderly population is the high level of illiteracy compared with the national average (12.1 percent). In 2010, 25.8 percent of the elderly population was illiterate, and this figure was substantially higher in rural areas, reaching 43.4 percent. In fact, 20.4 percent of rural elderly report that they speak an indigenous language, compared with 3.7 percent in urban areas.

In terms of socioeconomic and labor characteristics, it stands out that 19 percent of the elderly do not receive any type of income (table 10.3), with this situation significantly more prevalent among women (26.8 percent) than among men (9.8 percent). Among those that do receive income, 28.2 percent

Table 10.2 Marginalization, Illiteracy, and Living Arrangements among the Elderly, 2010

	National	*Urban*	*Rural*
Population 65 years and older	7,058,363	4,408,004	2,650,359
%	100.0	62.5	37.5
CONAPO Marginalization Index	100.0	100.0	100.0
Very high	3.8	0.0	9.8
High	11.5	1.4	27.9
Medium	10.8	2.3	24.7
Low	15.1	11.0	21.8
Very low	58.7	85.2	15.8
Speaker of indigenous language (%)	100.0	100.0	100.0
Yes	10.1	3.7	20.4
No	89.9	96.3	79.6
Literacy (%)	100.0	100.0	100.0
Yes	74.2	85.1	56.6
No	25.8	14.9	43.4
Household type (%)	100.0	100.0	100.0
One-person	11.9	11.3	13.0
Nuclear	43.3	42.5	44.4
Extended	43.4	44.8	41.1
Composed	1.0	0.6	1.5
Coresident	0.5	0.8	0.0

Source: Based on information from Population Projections 2010–50, National Population Council (Consejo Nacional de Población, CONAPO), and National Household Income and Expenditure Survey (Encuesta Nacional de Ingresos y Gastos de los Hogares, ENIGH), 2010, National Institute of Statistics and Geography (Instituto Nacional de Estadística y Geografía, INEGI).
Note: Rural includes populations up to 14,999 individuals, urban with 15,000 or more.

of the population supplements the transfers they receive (pensions and social assistance programs) with labor income; of them, 10.2 percent receive pensions and the rest receive cash transfers from social protection programs, with "70 y más" ("70 and older") being the most important at 10.3 percent (table 10.3). The distribution of income source by gender reveals disparities. Although great differences are not found by gender among those that receive just labor income (31.6 percent men, 30.0 percent women), the category of transfer income stands out with 47.3 percent of men receiving pension payments compared to just 28.1 percent of women. In contrast, 33.3 percent of women's transfer income comes from the "70 y más" program and 20.9 percent comes from the Opportunities (Oportunidades) program, whereas for men the respective proportions are 28.4 percent and 2.6 percent. It is important to point out that the payment mechanism of the latter program is directed to the women of the household.

In terms of labor participation, for those adults older than 65 that reported performing some type of activity, it stands out that 42.7 percent of the national total reported performing artisanal, livestock, and agricultural activities

Table 10.3 Socioeconomic and Labor Characteristics of the Elderly, 2010

	National	*Men*	*Women*
Population 65 years and older	7,058,363	3,254,001	3,804,362
%	100.0	46.1	53.9
Receive an income (%)	100.0	100.0	100.0
Yes	81.0	90.2	73.2
No	19.0	9.8	26.8
Type of income (%)	100.0	100.0	100.0
Single income	30.8	31.6	30.0
Income and pensions	10.2	12.5	7.7
Income and "70 y más"	10.3	10.2	10.5
Income and other transfers	7.7	7.0	8.4
Pensions	22.2	27.6	16.6
"70 y más"	12.3	8.9	15.9
Other transfers	6.5	2.2	10.9
Labor activity (%)	100.0	100.0	100.0
Artisanal, agricultural, and livestock	42.7	49.7	25.9
Shopkeepers and traders, employees, and sales	17.7	10.9	34.2
Domestic workers	15.8	13.8	20.9
Technicians and assistants	7.6	8.6	5.0
Mining, construction, manufacturing, transport	7.3	8.8	3.8
Street vendors and food sales	5.0	4.5	6.3
Civil servants, executives, and managers	3.8	3.8	3.8
Type of transfer (%)	100.0	100.0	100.0
Pensions	37.8	47.3	28.1
"70 y más"	30.8	28.4	33.3
Opportunities	11.7	2.6	20.9
Procampo	6.6	11.0	2.1
Other transfers	13.1	10.6	15.6
Receives medical attention (%)	100.0	100.0	100.0
Yes	75.0	74.1	75.7
No	25.0	25.9	24.3
Medical assistance institution (%)	100.0	100.0	100.0
Popular insurance (Seguro Popular)	31.9	32.3	31.6
IMSS	50.7	51.2	50.3
ISSSTE	13.7	12.8	14.5
PEMEX, Defense, Navy	1.7	1.7	1.6
Other	2.0	2.0	2.0

Source: Based on information from Population Projections 2010–50, National Population Council (Consejo Nacional de Población, CONAPO), and National Household Income and Expenditure Survey (Encuesta Nacional de Ingresos y Gastos de los Hogares, ENIGH), 2010, National Institute of Statistics and Geography (Instituto Nacional de Estadística y Geografía, INEGI).
Note: IMSS = Mexican Social Security Institute (Instituto Mexicano del Seguro Social); ISSSTE = Instituto de Seguridad y Servicios Sociales de los Trabajadores del Estado; PEMEX = Petróleos Mexicanos.

(49.7 percent in the case of men and 25.9 percent of women). In general, work as shopkeepers and traders, employees, and sales (34.2 percent) as well as domestic workers (20.9 percent) predominate among elderly women, but men's participation in these activities does not exceed 14 percent. Finally, just 3.8 percent report being civil servants, executives, and managers, independent of gender.

Examining this population's income by income quintiles and urban/rural area is another dimension on which to capture the situation in terms of levels and sources. In this case it stands out that 95.1 percent of the population aged 65 and older in the first quintile (I) that live in urban areas and 87.2 percent in rural areas reported not receiving any income. In the second quintile (II), the main source of income is from transfers (including pensions) that represent 45.7 percent of the urban population's income and 63.5 percent for the rural population. In the latter group, the combined income from both labor as well as that derived from transfers is the main source for the III, IV, and V quintiles with proportions between 45 percent and 55 percent.

In comparison, we observe that for the first two quintiles the incomes are below the minimum salary (MS), whereas for the third quintile, 87.6 percent of the urban population and 96.2 percent of the rural are in the same situation (table 10.4). More than 90 percent of the population of the fourth quintile receives income between one and two MS, and only 48.1 percent of the

Table 10.4 Income, Education, and Health of the Elderly, by Income Quintile, 2010

		Urban					
	National	*I*	*II*	*III*	*IV*	*V*	*Total*
Average monthly income (Mex$)	2,747	3	518	1,321	2,500	10,637	3,432
Average monthly income (US$)[a]	217	0.2	41	105	198	842	272
Receive income (%)	100.0	100.0	100.0	100.0	100.0	100.0	100.0
Transfers only	33.2	0.5	45.7	39.8	45.2	35.7	31.3
Income only	24.9	4.4	43.3	38.9	30.3	33.9	28.0
Income and transfers	22.8	0.0	8.2	20.5	24.4	30.1	17.6
Does not receive income	19.0	95.1	2.9	0.8	0	0.3	23.2
Income level (MS, %)	100.0	100.0	100.0	100.0	100.0	100.0	100.0
0–1	58.4	100.0	100.0	87.6	n.a.	n.a.	49.4
1–2	20.8	n.a.	n.a.	12.4	97.5	n.a.	24.0
2–3	8.3	n.a.	n.a.	n.a.	2.5	35.0	9.7
3–4	3.5	n.a.	n.a.	n.a.	n.a.	16.9	4.4
5 or more	9.1	n.a.	n.a.	n.a.	n.a.	48.1	12.5
Medical assistance institution (%)[b]	n.a.	n.a.	n.a.	n.a.	n.a.	n.a.	n.a.
Popular Insurance	25.3	14.8	29.2	14.6	12.6	5.5	13.6
IMSS	40.1	43.7	38.1	62.4	65.9	51.2	53.0
ISSSTE	10.8	10.4	8.6	8.7	11.0	22.9	13.3
PEMEX, Defense, Navy	1.3	2.0	0.5	1.0	1.2	3.8	1.9
Other	1.6	1.8	0.4	0.5	0.8	5.6	2.2
No coverage	25.0	31.7	27.0	17.6	13.7	16.2	20.8
Education (%)[c]	100.0	100.0	100.0	100.0	100.0	100.0	100.0
No education	28.6	26.6	31.1	21.4	16.5	6.9	18.9
Primary	53.8	54.0	60.5	65.2	66.3	36.3	54.7
Secondary	5.7	8.0	3.7	5.3	8.8	11.9	8.2
Technical	5.8	9.7	3.7	6.2	5.9	14.8	8.9
Higher	6.1	1.8	1.1	1.9	2.5	30.2	9.3

table continues next page

Table 10.4 Income, Education, and Health of the Elderly, by Income Quintile, 2010 *(continued)*

		Rural					
	National	*I*	*II*	*III*	*IV*	*V*	*Total*
Average monthly income (Mex$)	2,747	9	496	1,203	2,531	7,563	1,608
Average monthly income (US$)[a]	217	0.7	39	95	200	599	127
Receive income (%)	100.0	100.0	100.0	100.0	100.0	100.0	100.0
Transfers only	33.2	0.3	63.5	30.7	30.3	21.1	36.3
Income only	24.9	12.5	19.6	20.0	25.0	23.9	20.0
Income and transfers	22.8	0.0	16.5	49.1	44.7	55.0	31.4
Does not receive income	19.0	87.2	0.3	0.2	0.0	0.0	12.3
Income level (MS, %)	100.0	100.0	100.0	100.0	100.0	100.0	100.0
0–1	58.4	100.0	100.0	96.2	n.a.	n.a.	73.0
1–2	20.8	n.a.	n.a.	3.8	92.8	n.a.	15.6
2–3	8.3	n.a.	n.a.	n.a.	7.2	45.3	5.8
3–4	3.5	n.a.	n.a.	n.a.	n.a.	20.0	2.1
5 or more	9.1	n.a.	n.a.	n.a.	n.a.	34.7	3.6
Medical assistance institution (%)[b]	n.a.	n.a.	n.a.	n.a.	n.a.	n.a.	n.a.
Popular Insurance	25.3	35.0	49.1	56.3	30.5	30.7	44.2
IMSS	40.1	15.1	12.0	12.7	37.2	38.9	19.3
ISSSTE	10.8	5.3	4.5	5.4	10.1	15.2	6.8
PEMEX, Defense, Navy	1.3	0.0	0.3	0.4	0.4	0.5	0.3
Other	1.6	0.3	0.3	0.6	0.4	2.3	0.6
No coverage	25.0	46.5	35.8	27.8	26.5	18.2	31.9
Education (%)[c]	100.0	100.0	100.0	100.0	100.0	100.0	100.0
No education	28.6	43.3	55.8	47.4	31.9	20.0	44.3
Primary	53.8	54.0	43.1	51.4	60.5	69.1	52.2
Secondary	5.7	2.4	0.6	0.9	3.6	3.5	1.7
Technical	5.8	0.1	0.5	0.4	1.8	1.4	0.7
Higher	6.1	0.3	0.0	0.0	2.2	6.0	1.0

Source: Based on information from Population Projections 2010–50, National Population Council (Consejo Nacional de Población, CONAPO), and National Household Income and Expenditure Survey (Encuesta Nacional de Ingresos y Gastos de los Hogares, ENIGH), 2010, National Institute of Statistics and Geography (Instituto Nacional de Estadística y Geografía, INEGI).
Note: n.a. = not applicable.
IMSS = Instituto Mexicano del Seguro Social; ISSSTE = Instituto de Seguridad y Servicios Sociales de los Trabajadores del Estado; MS = minimum salary; PEMEX = Petróleos Mexicanos.
a. Exchange rate Mex$12.6303/US$ in 2010, Bank of Mexico, exchange rate pesos per U.S. dollar, determination date (FIX) average quotes.
b. The sum of the percentages of medical assistance is greater than 100 percent because of duplicated registrations in institutions.
c. Primary education includes preschool, higher education includes high school diploma, bachelor's degree, and postgraduate work.

population in urban areas in the last quintile receives income greater than five times the MS, whereas in rural areas this percentage is 34.7 percent.

When we look at access to health services, 75 percent of the population aged 65 years and older reported having received medical attention, and this percentage did not vary according to gender. Among those who are covered, approximately 50 percent receive coverage from the Instituto Mexicano del Seguro Social,, 17 percent from another social security institution, and 31.9 percent from Popular Insurance (Seguro Popular). The differences in access are relevant if we divide the population among those who live in urban and rural areas, respectively, and we consider the income quintile that they correspond to. For example, the urban population reports receiving more medical attention from social security institutions, mainly the IMSS, and in the case of those in the third and fourth quintiles this coverage exceeds 60 percent. As we might expect, the proportion using Popular Insurance decreases as income increases, representing just 5.5 percent of the fifth quintile. In contrast, the services provided by Popular Insurance are more important for the rural population, representing 44.2 percent of the total, and in the case of the third quintile reaching 56.3 percent. Finally, 32 percent of the rural population reported not receiving any type of service, a situation that is exacerbated for those in the first quintile, with 46.5 percent of the elderly population without coverage. Among the urban population, 20.8 percent reported not receiving any medical attention, with this proportion reaching 31.7 percent for those with incomes in the first quintile.

Finally, regarding the situation of the elderly in terms of poverty, the National Council of Social Development Policy Evaluation (Consejo Nacional de Evaluación de la Política de Desarrollo Social [CONEVAL]) reports figures do not differ much from the national average in 2010. According to this body, 45.8 percent of the population aged 65 years and older was living in poverty, compared with 46.3 percent of the population younger than 65 years. The same occurs with the population in extreme poverty, estimated at 11 percent for the elderly and 11.4 percent for those younger than 65.

Origins of Social Protection Systems for the Elderly

The origins of social protection programs in Mexico date to the end of the 19th century, linked to the incipient process of industrialization, which explains why these programs initially dealt mainly with the problem of on-the-job accidents. During those years mutual societies were created, precursors to the unions, whose function was exclusively welfare in cases of illness or death. This relief was gradually expanded to include pension programs. At the beginning of the 20th century some state laws included provisions requiring employers to attend to workers in cases of accidents or death. However, an important step forward was contained in the 1917 constitution in the context of the Mexican Revolution, which recognizes that "the Social Security Law (Ley de Seguro Social [LSS]) is of public utility, and will include insurance for disability, old age, life, unemployment, illness and accident, childcare services, and any other directed at the protection and wellbeing of workers, farmers, unsalaried workers, and other social sectors and their family members."

Some more generalized efforts were made during the postrevolutionary governments. Retirement and survivor's pension programs funded via payroll taxes were proposed by the Obregón and Calles administrations in the 1920s, with support from the Regional Mexican Workers Confederation (Confederación Regional Obrera Mexicana) but were unsuccessful because of employer opposition. During the Calles administration, plans were established for public servants (General Law of Civil Retirement Pensions, Ley General de Pensiones Civiles de Retiro) and for members of the military. Both programs were improved during the Cárdenas administration (1934–40) at the same time that retirement pension plans were included in the collective contracts for petroleum and railroad workers. However, efforts to extend these benefits to the rest of the working class did not prosper. Another important advance occurred during the administration of Ávila Camacho (1940–46), with the approval of an LSS that extended various benefits to salaried workers and their families, such as protection for orphans, widows, illness, unemployment, and old age.

This law created the Mexican Institute of Social Security (Instituto Mexicano del Seguro Social [IMSS]), which began operations on January 1, 1944. Article 123 of the constitution in section B establishes various social security regimes for government workers and members of the armed forces. In the case of the first group, the government issued the Institute of Social Security and Services for State Workers Law (Ley del Instituto de Seguridad y Servicios Sociales de los Trabajadores del Estado [ISSSTE]), created in 1959 to replace the General Directorate of Pensions and Retirement. The armed forces have the Social Security Institute for the Mexican Armed Forces (Instituto de Seguridad Social de las Fuerzas Armadas Mexicanas [ISSFAM]). Similar laws were also issued in the states of the republic, creating state institutes to deal with health care and pensions for workers in the state governments. For example, the Mexico State and Municipal Employees Pension Law was promulgated in 1951, and in 1957 in Nuevo León the State Public Servant Pension and Complementary Benefits Law was established. Finally, various public enterprises and decentralized organizations included diverse retirement benefits in their labor contracts. The most important cases, by size of entity, are the Retirement and Pension Regime (Régimen de Jubilación y Pensión [RJP]) for IMSS workers; the workers of Petróleos Mexicanos (PEMEX); the Federal Electricity Commission (Comisión Federal de Electricidad [CFE]); the development banks; National Railroads of Mexico (Ferrocariles Nacionales de México); and the Central Power and Light Company (Compañía de Luz y Fuerza de Centro); the last two entities have since disappeared, but their pension obligations have not. Similarly, the majority of public universities included similar benefits in their collective contracts. In the vast majority of cases they are supplementary programs to the benefits offered by the IMSS or ISSSTE (Solís Soberón and Villagómez 1999).

In the beginning these programs were conceived as pay-as-you-go schemes with defined benefits, funded for the most part by contributions from workers, the state, and employers. Some of the state and university programs were exceptions to this rule. However, because they did not set aside the necessary reserves, over time practically all of these programs required resource infusions form general revenue funds to meet their commitments to retirees and pensioners. The fiscal cost is one of the main reasons that has provoked reforms in the main programs during the past two decades, replacing the majority of them with fully funded schemes, defined contributions, and individual accounts—IMSS in 1995 and ISSSTE in 2007—although some of them have undergone only parametric reforms.

In the end, the way in which the pension system took shape led to a highly fragmented system that was enormously heterogeneous in terms of benefits and offered no portability. Additionally, the system showed significant inefficiencies due to the lack of adequate information on the different programs and the absence of an entity that could centralize this information hindered the elimination of duplication of benefit payments and provision of other services. But more importantly, the levels of coverage among the population remained low. In 2009 approximately 35 percent of the economically active population (EAP) was enrolled in a public pension program; 6.6 percent received a pension from one of these programs and a little less than 6 percent received some type of pension support from one of the main noncontributory programs, which meant that a little more than half of the population was not covered (Acosta and Villagómez 2012).[2]

Recent Reforms to the Contributory Pension System

Currently the pension system can be mostly characterized by its duality and fragmentation. The duality of the system is expressed in the existence of a contributory social security system with a package of defined benefits for formal workers in the private and public sectors, which coexists with a set of fragmented noncontributory services and benefits offered through diverse social protection programs to the population living in poverty, with low income, and in the informal sector of the economy.

In 1992 the government implemented an important reform with the introduction of the Savings System for Retirement (Sistema de Ahorro para el Retiro [SAR]), a complementary program to the IMSS and ISSSTE pay-as-you-go and defined benefit programs, which was designed as a fully funded scheme with individual accounts. An account was opened for each worker enrolled in the aforementioned programs with two subaccounts, retirement and housing, in which 2 percent of the base contribution salary (Salario Base de Contribución [SBC]) was deposited for retirement and 5 percent for housing, charged to the employer. The latter amount was channeled through the National Institute for Promotion of Workers' Housing (Instituto Nacional de Fomento a la Vivienda de los Trabajadores [INFONAVIT]), paying an annual return according to the obtained amounts from operations, while the retirement funds were deposited in the Bank of Mexico, which would invest them in public debt instruments, paying an annual real return of not less than 2 percent. The SAR was an important precursor to the IMSS and ISSSTE reforms that occurred in later years.

IMSS Reforms

With around 15.7 million active members, IMSS is the most significant program.[3] Originally it was a pay-as-you-go defined benefit program, but a reform was approved in 1995 that replaced it with a fully funded, defined contribution program with individual accounts,[4] beginning operations July 1, 1997. The change was mandatory for all members and the system counted 11.2 million accounts registered in December 1997, nearly tripling by November 2012 to reach a total of 31.8 million accounts (figure 10.1).[5] These accounts are part of the private financial intermediaries created to administer and invest these funds, the Retirement Funds Administrators (Administradoras de Fondos para el Retiro [AFOREs]).

However, not all these accounts are active because of a significant amount of mobility between the formal and informal markets. When a worker moves from the former to the latter, he or she stops contributing to the account. An estimate of how many of these accounts are active can be obtained from the number of active workers that the IMSS reports each month.[6] It is important to emphasize that this phenomenon among active and inactive workers is largely a product of the characteristics of the Mexican labor market, in which the informal component is large and has grown in recent years, while mobility is high.

In the new scheme, each worker has an account in his or her name, with three subaccounts: retirement, housing, and voluntary contributions. The contributions to the system are divided in three parts and include an additional contribution called the social charge (*cuota social*) from the government that was initially set at 5.5 percent of the MS in January 1997 and indexed to the consumer price index (índice nacional de precios al consumidor [INPC]). This charge was reformed in May 2009, increasing the amount by 21 percent in the case of the MS and 16 percent for higher salaries. Table 10.5 shows the social charge that corresponds to three MS.

Figure 10.1 Accounts Registered in AFOREs, 1997–2012

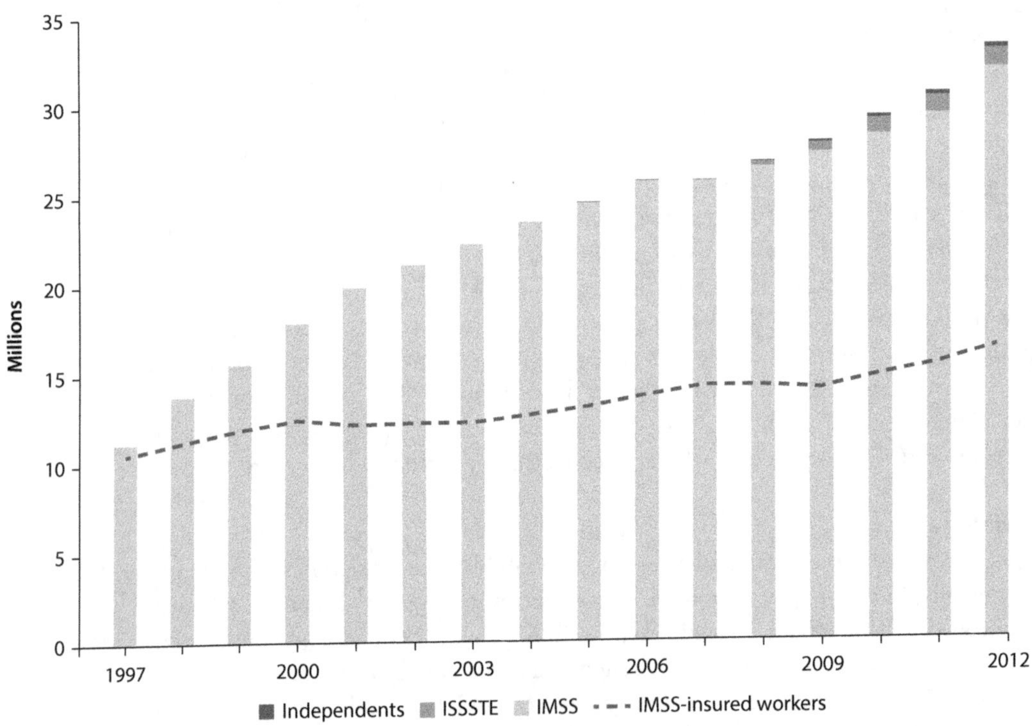

Source: Based on Comisión Nacional de los Sistemas de Ahorro para el Retiro (CONSAR) and Instituto Nacional de Estadística y Geografía (INEGI).
Note: IMSS = Instituto Mexicano del Seguro Social; ISSTE = Instituto de Seguridad y Servicios Sociales de los Trabajadores del Estado.

Table 10.5 Contributions to the IMSS Pension System
Percentage of the SBC

Concept	*Employer*	*Worker*	*Government*	*Total*
RCV				
Retirement[a]	2.00	n.a.	n.a.	2.00
Old age termination and retirement	3.15	1.13	0.23	4.50
Social charge[b]	n.a.	n.a.	2.30	2.30
IV				
Disability and life[c]	1.75	0.63	0.125	2.50
RT				
Occupational hazard	0.25–15	n.a.	n.a.	0.25–15

Source: Instituto Mexicano del Seguro Social (IMSS).
Note: n.a. = not applicable. IV = Invalidez y Vida; RCV = Retiro, Cesantía en Edad Avanzada y Vejez; RT = Riesgos de Trabajo.
a. This contribution went into effect in 1992.
b. This amount is contributed for each day of wages contributed and is updated quarterly based on inflation and forms part of the RCV insurance. In May 2009 this contribution increased.
c. The risk of illness and occupational hazards that result in disability or death are covered through the RT insurance, which is administered by the IMSS under a defined benefit scheme funded with employer contributions. Cases of disability or death outside of work are covered by the IV insurance. IV and RT insurance, when they cover an insured sum, are first funded with the individual retirement account.

The IMSS collects the contributions, transferring the housing funds to INFONAVIT and the retirement funds to the AFOREs. These entities record the funds linked to the system, but they administer only the retirement and voluntary contributions accounts. The National Commission of Savings for Retirement Systems (Comisión Nacional de los Sistemas de Ahorro para el Retiro [CONSAR]) is the authority that regulates and supervises the system. The AFOREs charge a commission for their services, which originally could be calculated based on the flow of contributions, the balance in the account, or the return on investment. As of 2008, it was decided that the commission could only be calculated based on the account balance.

The funds are invested in Specialized Retirement Funds Investment Companies (Sociedades de Inversión Especializadas en Fondos de Retiro [SIEFOREs]) with criteria of security and return on investment. The authority determines the criteria to create the investment portfolio, indicating the type and characteristics of financial instruments allowed and the limits accepted. The system began with just one SIEFORE, and currently there are four basic SIEFOREs whose risk level is linked to the worker's lifespan, such that the first fund (SB1) is designed for older members whereas the fourth (SB4) is for younger workers, with risk criteria adapted to each one of these groups.[7] The funds accumulated and recorded in the AFOREs include what the SIEFOREs invest, funds for housing (INFONAVIT and FOVISSSTE), social protection funds for some public and private entities, pension bonuses granted as a result of the ISSSTE reform, and SAR funds still deposited in the Bank of Mexico. These funds represented 17.5 percent of GDP in November 2012. The AFOREs administer the funds in the retirement (IMSS and ISSSTE) and voluntary savings subaccounts, the social protection funds, and their own capital, representing 11.9 percent of GDP.

The pension benefit for Retirement, Unemployment, and Old Age (Retiro, Cesantía, y Vejez) depends on the amount accumulated and capitalized in a worker's individual account, which is determined by the contribution level relative to the SBC, the worker's salary and salary growth, the investment and returns obtained by the SIEFOREs, commissions, and contribution density.[8] A minimum guaranteed pension (Pensión Mínima Garantizada [PMG]) is equal to one MS in July 1997 adjusted for inflation, which a worker receives if the accumulated balance does not guarantee a pension of at least the amount of the PMG. To be entitled to this benefit, the worker must contribute for at least 1,250 weeks. Retirement age is 65 years old or 60 for termination in older adults. Upon reaching retirement, the worker can opt for scheduled withdrawals from his or her AFORE or buy an annuity from an insurance company. "Transition workers," those that were already contributing to the system before the reform, can choose at retirement the benefits awarded by Law no. 1973 if these are greater than what they would receive from their individual account. In this case the accumulated funds are transferred to the government, which guarantees the payment of the worker's pension, according to the law. Finally, the reform did not affect the payment of pensions to workers who were already retired at the time of the reform.

ISSSTE Reforms

ISSSTE is the second most significant program by size and covers 2.7 million workers in the federal public sector. The initial pay-as-you-go defined benefit scheme was reformed in 2007 along the same lines as the IMSS. However, the change to a fully funded scheme with individual accounts was voluntary for workers who were already active, although it was mandatory for those who joined the workforce after the reform. The entitlements of pensioners who had already retired were not affected by the reform. The reform allowed the government to group the 21 insurance plans that had been offered in the previous scheme in four insurance plans analogous to the IMSS' offerings: (a) Retirement, Old Age Termination, and Old Age (Retiro, Cesantía en Edad Avanzada y Vejez [RCV]), (b) Disability and Life (Invalidez y Vida [IV]), (c) Occupational Hazards (Riesgos de Trabajo [RT]), and (d) Health (Salud). The worker and the employer (the government) make contributions. For the RCV, in the previous scheme the federal agency paid 3.5 percent of the SBC and the employee paid another 3.5 percent for a total of 7 percent. In the reformed program, after 2008 the contribution gradually increased to reach 6.125 percent from the federal agency and 5.175 percent from the employee (2 percent retirement and 3.175 percent old age termination and old age) for a total of 11.3 percent of the SBC. This includes a social contribution paid by the government equal to 5.5 percent of the MS in the Mexico City Federal District (Distrito Federal [DF]) as of July 1, 1997 and updated for inflation.

The transition workers are those that opted not to change to the new scheme and continue to be subject to the previous law, except for some modifications.

Their scheme does not include the social contribution proposed in the reform nor the option for solidary savings. To receive a retirement pension they must have 30 years or more of service and the same amount of time making contributions. Previously, age did not matter, but after the reform a minimum retirement age was established, beginning at 51 years old in 2010 for men and 49 for women, gradually increasing to 60 and 58 years respectively in 2028. To receive a pension for old age and time of service, a worker must be at least 55 years old and have at least 15 years of service with the same amount of time making contributions. For on old age termination pension the worker must be at least 60 years old and have contributed for 10 years. There is a minimum pension guarantee equal to two months of the Mexico City minimum salary at the time the law was enacted and adjusted based on the INPC. Finally, these workers also have the SAR created in 1992. For those workers that switched to the reformed scheme and for those who joined the workforce after the reform the program is based on defined contributions, fully funded, and individual accounts with three subaccounts: retirement, housing, and voluntary contributions.

Finally, reforms also took place in other programs involving changes to eligibility requirements as well as to the management of funds at the institutional level. The most important programs that underwent these reforms include the RJP for employees of IMSS, PEMEX, and CFE. However, there are many other programs in similar situations. Vásquez Colmenares (2012) reports that there are around 37 individual account pension systems and 68 pay-as-you-go public pension systems, which have no mechanisms for portability among them. According to the constitution, each state can determine the type of pension program and issue the laws that regulate it. The majority of these programs are pay-as-you-go with defined benefits, and few have the necessary funds to accomplish their commitments. Some states have undertaken reforms in recent years, although most of them have been parametric, just giving the systems a few more years of breathing room. According to Vásquez Colmenares (2012), systems in 15 of the 31 states and the federal district of Mexico City, face major problems that could seriously affect their viability.

Reforms to Expand Coverage

The main reasons that led to the reform of the IMSS' principal pension program were related to (1) stopping the explosive upward trend in fiscal spending and the creation of contingent liabilities that were provoking growing pressure on public finances, as well as (2) the need to stimulate greater domestic private savings and reduce the level of foreign savings, which had played an important role in the 1995 peso crisis. In terms of coverage, it was thought that as the effects of the structural reform took shape, along with the effects of other reforms undertaken at the beginning of the decade, the economy would create more formal jobs which result in greater coverage. However, this did not occur, and instead the existence of a growing informal sector along with the mobility between this sector and the formal sector is affecting the pension coverage effectiveness on the elderly population. This means not only lower individual contribution densities among those enrolled in the IMSS contributory program, but also that in many cases workers do not even make enough contributions to reach the PMG entitlement.

New Programs

The topic of coverage gained prominence in the discussions of social policy at the beginning of the 21st century in the framework of the fight against poverty, in this case among the elderly. As Rofman and Oliveri (2011) have documented, pension coverage among the adult population over 65 years did not reach 20 percent, and the situation was even more dramatic for women and the population in rural areas, reaching 14.9 percent and 6.3 percent, respectively, in 2000. As a response, a series of reforms and noncontributory programs were implemented.

Nutritional Pension for the Elderly in the Federal District

This program can be considered a pioneer in transfers to the elderly. In 2001 the government of the Federal District (DF) implemented the Nutritional Support, Medical Attention, and Free Medicines Program for the Elderly (Programa de Apoyo Alimentario, Atención Médica y Medicamentos Gratuitos para Adultos Mayores), covering elderly residents older than 70 in the DF under a scheme targeted at areas of high and very high level of marginalization. In 2003, along with the promulgation of the law that established the nutritional pension entitlement for elderly residents over 70 years old in the DF, the government modified the program with a universality rule, and in 2008 the benefit age was lowered to 68 years. The Institute for Elderly Services (Instituto para la Atención de los Adultos Mayores) in the DF operates the program. To receive benefits, participants must prove their age and residency in the DF for at least three years and sign a commitment letter. The benefit is equal to 50 percent of the current monthly MS in Mexico City, equal to Mex$897.30 in 2011, and is paid via an electronic card that can be used in commercial establishments and the main markets approved for the program. At the end of 2011, 480,000 individuals were registered in the program which had a budget of Mex$5,165,500,000 from general funds approved by the DF Legislative Assembly (table 10.6).

Table 10.6 Nutritional Pension for the Elderly in the DF Budget and Beneficiaries, 2006–12

Description	*2006*	*2007*	*2008*	*2009*	*2010*	*2011*	*2012*
Budget (millions Mex$)	2,764	3,708	3,823	4,341	4,625	5,165	5,165
Budget (millions US$)	253.6	339.3	342.8	321.4	366.2	415.4	392.5
Percentage of GDP	0.026	0.031	0.031	0.034	0.034	0.033	0.032
Beneficiaries	412,350	420,000	430,000	470,000	454,971	480,000	480,000
Pension amount (Mex$)	731	759	789	822	862	897	935
Pension amount (US$)	67.0	69.4	70.7	60.9	68.2	72.2	71.0

Source: Government of the Federal District.

Attention to the Elderly in Rural Areas

This federal program formed part of the National Agreement for the Countryside signed in 2003 and the first rules of operation were published in September of that year, under the direction of the Secretariat of Social Development (Secretaría de Desarrollo Social [SEDESOL]) through the General Directorate of Services to Priority Groups (Dirección General de Atención a Grupos Prioritarios). The target population was adults older than 60 years living in nutritional poverty (according to SEDESOL's own definition) and resident in highly and very highly marginalized rural communities with less than 2,500 inhabitants. The latter criterion was determined using information from INEGI and CONAPO. Additionally, the beneficiaries should not be participants in any other social protection program like Opportunities, the Social Provision of Liconsa Milk program (Abasto Social de Leche de Liconsa), or the Diconsa Nutritional Support program (Apoyo Alimentario de Diconsa). SEDESOL determined eligibility based on a socioeconomic survey. The initial benefit was Mex$2,100 per year. However, this program disappeared in 2007 when it was integrated into the "70 y más" program.

Opportunities Support to the Elderly Program

This program was created in 2006 as a complement to the Opportunities Program for those families that include adults older than 70. It is a targeted program for households in extreme poverty and is operated by the National Coordination of the Opportunities Program (Coordinación Nacional del Programa Oportunidades) in SEDESOL. The benefits include cash transfers conditioned on beneficiaries complying medical exams and children attending school. In 2012, if a household contained elderly family members, it received a supplementary benefit of Mex$335 per month for each elderly person with was paid bimonthly. This support is conditioned on the elderly family member's completion of a medical exam every six months. If the family is composed of only elderly members, a nutritional benefit (Mex$305) and a better living benefit (Mex$130) are added to the total amount. The payments are deposited in bank accounts or made in cash at specific centers.

From 2007 on, the benefit was provided to families living in communities of more than 2,500 inhabitants, while those living in communities up to 2,500 inhabitants and being part of the Opportunities program were supported through the "70 y más" program. This resulted in a decrease in beneficiaries of the Opportunities Support program from 950,000 elderly to 250,000 in 2007.

"70 y más" Program

The "70 y más" program was created in 2007 as part of the congressional budget negotiations (Rubio and Garfias 2010). In the beginning it replaced the Attention to the Elderly in Rural Areas program. As a result, the target population was individuals aged 70 years and over living in communities of up to 2,500 inhabitants. However, over the years the program was expanded until it became the flagship program of support for the elderly. At the beginning of 2012 individuals living in communities of up to 30,000 inhabitants were eligible, but this requirement was eliminated by the end of that year as the program moved toward universalization. Other eligibility criteria include age and a prohibition from receiving a pension from a contributory program or from the elderly supplement in the Opportunities program.

The program's coverage is national and the benefit consists of a 500 peso per month cash transfer paid every two months. Moreover, beneficiaries can access services from The National Institute of Older Persons (Instituto Nacional de las Personas Adultas Mayores [INAPAM]) and Popular Insurance for medical attention. The poverty criteria used is "asset poverty" defined by SEDESOL. SEDESOL operates the program through the General Directorate of Services to Priority Groups. The benefits are paid via a sheet of stamp vouchers or electronic transfer to a bank account. In 2012 2,847,836 beneficiaries were registered, and the budget spent so far during the year was Mex$18 billion (table 10.7).

With the beginning of the administration of President Enrique Peña Nieto on December 1, 2012, the government announced its intention to expand the "70 y más" program, lowering the age to receive benefits to 65 years and transforming it into a universal pension that guarantees a minimum income. The rules of operation have not been announced, but in the beginning there will not be substantial changes and the program will operate based on the "70 y más" infrastructure. The budget assigned for 2013 was Mex$26 billion.

State Noncontributory Pensions or Subsidies

During the last decade, following Mexico City's example, several states have created programs to support the elderly. According to a count performed by CONEVAL, there were 13 such programs in 2012 (table 10.8). The minimum eligibility age for these programs varies between 60 and 70 years; seven of them provide cash transfers, whereas the rest support the elderly with in-kind transfers. Chiapas' program is the largest, with 240,000 beneficiaries, a monthly benefit of Mex$550, and an approved budget of Mex$1.438 billion. Mexico state divides its support for the elderly in two programs: the first is for the population aged from 60 to 69 years old, and the second is for those older than 70 years. The benefits are delivered as in-kind food staples, and between both programs almost 281,000 beneficiaries are registered with a program budget of Mex$1.5 billion. As a whole, the state-administered programs reach 928,727 individuals. It is not possible to determine if there are individuals that benefit from both state-administered programs and the federal programs such as Opportunities and "70 y más."

Table 10.7 Budget and Beneficiaries of the "70 y más" Program, 2007–12

Description	*2007*	*2008*	*2009*	*2010*	*2011*	*2012*
Budget (millions Mex$)	6,550	9,916	11,976	13,101	13,127	18,068
Budget (millions US$)	599.3	889.2	886.6	1,037.3	1,055.6	1,372.8
Percentage of GDP	0.05	0.08	0.09	0.10	0.09	0.11
Beneficiaries	1,031,000	1,562,771	2,025,551	2,103,009	2,149,024	2,847,836

Source: Presidency of the Republic.

Table 10.8 State Programs to Support the Elderly, 2012

Entity	*Program*	*Minimum eligibility age (years)*	*Type of support*	*Monthly amount*	*Frequency*	*Benefi-ciaries*	*Approved budget (millions Mex$)*
Chiapas	Daybreak (Amanecer)	64	Cash transfer	550	Monthly	240,000	1,438.6
Chihuahua	Live in plenitude (Vive a plenitud)	65	In-kind	n.a.	n.a.	15,000	120.9
Colima	Nutritional pension for the elderly	65	n.a.	n.a.	n.a.	3,000	5.1
Jalisco	Strategy for attention to the elderly "Live Large" (Vive Grande)	70	Cash transfer	1,500	Quarterly	94,417	15
Mexico State	Nutritional pension for elderly from 60 to 69 years	60–69	In-kind	Staple goods	Monthly	120,000	299.7
	Nutritional Pension for the Elderly	70	In-kind	Staple goods	Monthly	160,912	1,150
Nayarit	Nutritional pensions for adults older than 70 years	70	In-kind	Staple goods	Monthly	47,988	40
Oaxaca	State nutritional pension for adults age "70 y más"	70	Cash transfer	1,000	Bimonthly	31,000	150.4
Puebla	Urban "70 y más"	70	Cash transfer	500	Monthly	n.a.	n.a.
Queretaro	Nutritional Support Program	60	In-kind	Staple goods	Bimonthly	96,600	9.9
Quintana Roo	Economic Support Program "I'm with you, grandparent" (Abuelito estoy contigo)	70	Cash transfer	850	Monthly	33,611	43.2
Sonora	"Creser" with the Elderly	65–69	Cash Transfer	1,000	Semiannual	50,500	50.5
Veracruz	Nutritional pension for adults over 70 years	70	Cash transfer	Half of 1 MS in Xalapa	Monthly	35,699	350

Source: Consejo Nacional de Evaluación de la Política de Desarrollo Social (CONEVAL) 2012.
Note: n.a. = not applicable.

The Political Economy behind the Reforms

The social security reforms are events whose political economy processes are very complex because of what is involved. This situation is exacerbated in the case of reforms to pension systems because by their nature they involve decisions that affect not just current generations, but also future ones. The importance of knowing and understanding the political economy of these processes lies in the fact that it affects the type of reform that can be achieved, its permanence, and future success.

An interesting exercise in this sense is the comparison of the reforms for the two principal contributory pension programs in Mexico: the IMSS program and the ISSSTE program. In both cases the government took a step toward fully funded schemes with defined benefits, individual accounts, and private administration, but the differences in the results are important. In the IMSS program, the change was mandatory for all active workers, whereas in the ISSSTE reform, the change was voluntary for active workers and mandatory only for those workers who started after the reform took effect. Although neither negotiation process was easy, in the case of the ISSSTE the process was much more complex and drawn out. We can find much of the explanation of these results in the differences in the institutions, policies, and actors involved along the process.

The IMSS reform was approved in 1995, during the first year of President Zedillo's administration. In that same year, Mexico experienced one of its worst economic and financial crises, which led to a broad bank and debtor rescue that precipitated a contraction of real GDP by more than 6 percent. However, it is in the context of severe economic crises when significant reforms are usually approved because it can be argued that they are necessary, although painful, measures to get back on the path to growth. Nonetheless, this situation alone is not enough to explain the approval of this reform because two key elements were present in the political negotiation process that was required for its approval.

First, the reform's target population did not constitute a homogenous, united group that could mount a solid opposition to the proposal. The negotiation was centered in the upper echelons of the main labor organizations, which, although they were already exhibiting reduced power compared to what they had displayed historically in past decades, were still a corporatist power integrated into the structure of the party in power, the Institutional Revolutionary Party (Partido Revolucionario Institucional [PRI]). Second, the PRI still maintained and absolute majority in Congress (this was the last legislative session in which this would be the case), which meant that there were not relevant complications in the negotiations with other political forces and this negotiation process took place via the traditional mechanisms within the party itself, where the labor organizations were represented and were part of the quota system for distributing different elected posts at both the federal and state levels.

In part, this explains why, despite having rescued important financial intermediaries that same year at a high cost to taxpayers, the reform still managed to create private pension fund administrators. Another interesting characteristic of this negotiation process is that the labor unions were allowed to form part of the governing board of the system's regulatory and oversight entity, CONSAR, even though this participation is not the norm in other commissions that oversee the banking and insurance sectors. This political process demonstrates one of the most important characteristics of the Mexican political system before 2000. Despite what Stein and Tommasi (2005) point out, the Mexican president is in constitutional terms one of the least powerful in Latin America, although as the head of state and of the PRI (the party that was in power for almost 70 years) he was very strong in legislative and partisan terms.

Similarly, the ISSSTE reform was approved during the first year of President Calderón's administration. In this case, however, the target population was much more unified and was a "closed population," as is the case with public sector workers. As a result of the political alternation of the presidency after 2000, the National Action Party's (Partido de Acción Nacional [PAN]) lack of a congressional majority, the fact that in the PAN the president is not also the head of his party, and considering his limited constitutional power, the executive had to learn how to maneuver in this context because the political negotiations were much more complex. But at the same time, this process appeared to favor the existence of positive characteristics in this public policy, such as the consistency and coordination and its possible stability. In fact, the reform proposal had been formulated since 2003 in President Fox's administration. As González Anaya (2012) describes, between 2003 and 2005 wide-ranging discussions with unions and legislators from all parties took place. Initially, the text of the bill was not revealed, but some elements of the reform were circulated sufficiently to be widely disseminated. A team from the Secretariat of the Treasury (Secretaría de Hacienda y Crédito Pública) made presentations in different national forums and it was widely disclosed in the news media. Finally, the bill was presented on December 13, 2005, by Senator Joel Ayala, director of the Federation of Unions of Public Service Employees (Federación de Sindicatos de Trabajadores al Servicio del Estado [FSTSE]). However, the electoral timeline did not allow the bill to continue forward and it was postponed for discussion in 2007. The negotiations included not only the FSTSE, but also the powerful National Union of Education Workers (Sindicato Nacional de Trabajadores de la Educación) and the bill was presented anew in Congress on March 15, 2007, and approved on the 31st of the same month with cross-party support, which reflected the significant lobbying and negotiating efforts undertaken. However, it is important to recognize the inclusion of other concessions to public employees, such as not making the switch to the new system mandatory for active workers, and including a solidary savings contribution from the government on top of the social charge contribution that also exists in the IMSS program.

Relative to the noncontributory or social protection programs, the political economy that frames their creation also reflects the changes that the Mexican institutional and political framework underwent after 2000 with the arrival of a new party, the PAN, to the presidency after 70 years of PRI domination. In large measure, many of the programs created in the past reflected the condition of a clientelistic party system, in which resources were directed to specific groups based on the government's own interests, as discussed in Rubio and Garfias (2010).[9] A large number of these programs eventually disappeared over time or were transformed. During the last decade, this situation began to change, in part because the PAN is not a clientelistic party that has corporatist groups at its base, and in part because since the end of the last century the governing party lost its majority in Congress, forcing it to achieve consensus or form alliances with other political forces or accept concessions to move its proposals forward. This is the history of the current flagship program of support for the elderly, "70 y más."

This program emerged in 2007 as part of that year's budget negotiations in Congress. It is important to remember that President Calderón's administration began in a context of political confrontation with a segment of the Mexican left led by the Democratic Revolution Party (Partido de la Revolución Democrática [PRD]) that did not recognize Calderón's victory. According to Rubio and Garfias (2010), the PRD proposed allocating Mex$6.5 billion to create a program for the elderly living in communities of up to 2,500 inhabitants. This proposal was approved with 257 votes from legislators from all parties in favor and 191 against plus one abstention from the PAN. It should be mentioned that this proposal was part of the campaign of the PRD's presidential candidate, in line with the program for the elderly that he implemented when he was the Head of Government of the DF in 2001. The new federal program replaced the existing program that covered rural areas and was part of the Agreement for the Countryside.

Impacts on Coverage

Despite government efforts during decades in expanding social protection and social security programs, the results in terms of coverage have been limited, at least until a decade ago. The problem is especially significant in the case of social security and its contributory programs. The main coverage gains among the elderly population have come from social protection programs and noncontributory transfers.

The significant increase in the number of registered accounts administered by the AFOREs is based on administrative data that do not do a good job of reflecting the actual situation of effective pension coverage. The high mobility between the formal and informal labor markets means that more than half of these accounts are inactive, negatively affecting the contribution density of members and replacement rates,[10] and even precipitating that many of them are not even entitled to the PMG. According to several studies, average contribution density among men fluctuates around 58 percent and around 49 percent among women Soto (2006). In the case of the ISSSTE the issue is clearer because it is a program for a "closed population." That is, coverage increases are determined by policy decisions depending on the program size desired by the government, which means the reform had no effect in terms of coverage.

Pension coverage in Mexico is low, and the broadest indicator, which is relative to the EAP, reached just 36 percent in 2010. Table 10.9 presents the coverage rates for active workers according to three definitions: contributors/EAP, contributors/employed, and contributors/salaried workers between 1984 and 2010.[11] This variable's behavior demonstrates a significant increase between 1984 and 2000, but during the last decade it has stalled, which can be observed in the first two indicators; and in the case of salaried workers it actually decreased slightly. The behavior of this indicator largely reflects the growth of labor informality in the country and the high mobility between the formal and informal labor markets.

One reaction to this situation has been the creation of transfer programs for the elderly, a group whose pension coverage did not reach 20 percent in 2000. Table 10.9 presents the total population older than 65 years that receives benefits, separated between pension income and income from the "70 y mas"

Table 10.9 Pension Coverage among Active Workers and the Elderly, 1984, 2000, and 2010
Percent

	Contributors/ EAP	*Contributors/ employed*	*Contributors/ salaried workers*	*Pensions/65+ population*	*"70 y más"/65+ population*	*Beneficiaries/65+ population*
1984	18.8	19.0	38.6	11.5	n.a.	n.a.
2000	36.1	26.6	56.0	19.0	n.a.	n.a.
2010	36.0	37.9	50.2	25.3	18.3	43.7

Source: Based on Rofman and Oliveri 2011 and National Household Income and Expenditure Survey (Encuesta Nacional de Ingresos y Gastos de los Hogares, ENIGH), 2010, National Institute of Statistics and Geography (Instituto Nacional de Estadística y Geografía, INEGI).
Note: EAP = economically active population; n.a. = not available.

program, and the impact is clearly visible during the past decade. Although the population that receives pensions increased 6 percentage points to reach 25.3 percent, those that receive noncontributory benefit transfers represent 18.3 percent. Even so, coverage of the elderly in 2010 is just 43.7 percent.

By separating the population according to educational achievement, we observe that coverage among those with low educational achievement is much lower than the level for individuals with more education (table 10.10). This situation reverses itself only in the case of the elderly enrolled in the "70 y más" program as a result of its targeting.

In the case of coverage by gender, the difference is less (except in 1984) among the active worker population. However, among the elderly population it is interesting to observe that the difference is pronounced. Men register greater coverage, which is explained by the pension component of income because in the case of benefits awarded by the "70 y más" program the coverage levels are similar between men and women (table 10.11).

Finally, another important distinction is evident if we separate the population by the area where they live, rural or urban. In this case, we observe an enormous divergence between these populations. Social security pension coverage for the active population is more than double in urban areas than in rural areas (table 10.12).

Fiscal Sustainability and Impacts on the Labor Market

One of the big problems that public pay-as-you-go pensions present around the world is their fiscal sustainability. The changes in the demographic structure of the population that lead to an increase in the ratio of pensioners to active workers, combined with the lack of adequate actuarial reserves in many cases, have meant growing transfers of general fiscal resources to meet their commitments with current pensioners and a growing contingent fiscal liability. This has been the case in Mexico among practically all of the existing public programs and has justified reforms in many of them. But even in the case of the reformed systems there are still significant requirements for fiscal resources to meet the commitments to "transition" workers, to those whose past contributions must be accounted for, as well as for the costs resulting from government contributions to these programs and the existence of the PMG.

Table 10.10 Pension Coverage, by Educational Achievement, 1984, 2000, and 2010

Percent

	Contributors/EAP			*Contributors/employed*			*Pensions/65+ population*			*"70 y más"/65+ population*			*Beneficiaries/65+ population*		
	Primary	*Secondary*	*Higher*	*Primary*	*Secondary*	*Higher*	*Primary*	*Secondary*	*Higher*	*Primary*	*Secondary*	*Higher*	*Primary*	*Secondary*	*Higher*
1984	11.4	50.2	59.7	10.7	70.6	77.3	9.7	48.7	33.8	n.a.	n.a.	n.a.	n.a.	n.a.	n.a.
2000	17.6	48.1	61.9	17.7	49.1	63.2	15.7	52.0	50.5	n.a.	n.a.	n.a.	n.a.	n.a.	n.a.
2010	16.8	40.6	60.1	17.5	42.8	63.6	20.0	45.4	60.4	21.8	3.0	0.6	41.8	48.4	61.0

Source: Based on information from Rofman and Oliveri 2011 and National Household Income and Expenditure Survey (Encuesta Nacional de Ingresos y Gastos de los Hogares, ENIGH), 2010, National Institute of Statistics and Geography (Instituto Nacional de Estadística y Geografía, INEGI).

Note: Primary includes No Education, Preschool, and Primary School; Secondary includes Secondary School, High School Diploma, Technical Degree; Higher includes Bachelor's, Master's, and Doctorate.
EAP = economically active population. n.a. = not applicable.

Table 10.11 Pension Coverage, by Gender, 1984, 2000, and 2010
Percent

	Contributor/EAP		*Contributor/ employed*		*Pensions/65+ population*		*"70 y más"/ 65+population*		*Beneficiaries/65+ population*	
	Men	*Women*	*Men*	*Women*	*Men*	*Women*	*Men*	*Women*	*Men*	*Women*
1984	16.2	32.6	16.3	34.0	13.2	10.1	n.a.	n.a.	n.a.	n.a.
2000	35.8	36.5	36.5	36.7	23.9	14.9	n.a.	n.a.	n.a.	n.a.
2010	35.5	36.9	37.7	38.2	34.9	17.2	17.2	19.3	52.1	36.6

Source: Based on information from Rofman and Oliveri 2011 and National Household Income and Expenditure Survey (Encuesta Nacional de Ingresos y Gastos de los Hogares, ENIGH), 2010, National Institute of Statistics and Geography (Instituto Nacional de Estadística y Geografía, INEGI).
Note: EAP = economically active population. n.a. = not applicable.

Table 10.12 Pension Coverage, by Area of Residence, 1984, 2000, and 2010
Percent

	Contributors/EAP		*Contributors/ employed*		*Pensions/65+ population*		*"70 y más"/65+ population*		*Beneficiaries/65+ population*	
	Rural	*Urban*	*Rural*	*Urban*	*Rural*	*Urban*	*Rural*	*Urban*	*Rural*	*Urban*
1984	8.1	35.9	8.3	40.2	1.9	17.4	n.a.	n.a.	n.a.	n.a.
2000	10.6	43.3	10.7	44.0	6.3	24.6	n.a.	n.a.	n.a.	n.a.
2010	16.4	46.9	18.3	47.8	9.7	34.9	40.0	5.0	49.7	40.0

Source: Based on information from Rofman and Oliveri 2011 and National Household Income and Expenditure Survey (Encuesta Nacional de Ingresos y Gastos de los Hogares, ENIGH), 2010, National Institute of Statistics and Geography (Instituto Nacional de Estadística y Geografía, INEGI).
Note: Rural-urban population: rural, with up to 14,999 inhabitants; urban, with 15,000 or more inhabitants. EAP = economically active population. n.a. = not applicable.

These costs can be examined from two perspectives, as annual public spending flows that affect the federal government's annual budget, or it can be estimated what the cost will be in future, known as the contingent fiscal liability. It is important to point out that a debate is ongoing regarding the usefulness of the latter indicator because even though it is a reference to future cost, estimating it is subject to serious problems with assumptions. We can lose sight of the fact that it is actually an estimate of future annual spending compared with the output of a single year.

In Mexico's case, there are some recent estimates of these costs,[12] using information reported in Vásquez Colmenares (2012). The IMSS's reformed program would have meant an expenditure of public resources in the amount of Mex$155.9 billion equivalent to 1 percent of GDP in 2012, for the payment of current pensions, government contributions, and the PMG. In the case of the ISSSTE program, this fiscal cost was estimated at Mex$146.8 billion for the same year, including current pensions, agencies' contributions, solidary savings,[13] the social charge, bond maturities during this year, and the PMG, equal to 0.9 percent of GDP. Finally, the group of RJP, PEMEX, CFE, Ferrocarriles, LyFC, ISSFAM, and Development Bank programs signified spending of Mex$117.6 billion, equal to 0.8 percent of GDP. If we consider the so-called contingent liability for the next 50 years from the IMSS programs (Law no. 73),

ISSSTE (insured members in transition), IMSS-RJP, decentralized organizations and enterprises, states, and universities, the fiscal liability adds up to 111.4 percent of 2010 GDP.[14] In an alternative estimate, Sinha (2012) suggests that this value would be 97.3 percent of 2010 GDP.

In the case of noncontributory social protection programs, the discussion references two elements: the fiscal cost associated with these programs as annual flows contained in the federal budget and the possibility that these programs could be fiscally sustainable in the future by guaranteeing a secure and permanent source of funding. In this sense the most important income transfer program for the elderly is "70 y más," which reported an allocated budget of Mex$18 billion, equivalent to 0.19 percent of GDP in 2012. The new administration's proposal is to expand the program by lowering the eligibility age to 65 years and more, for which a Mex$26 billion budget was approved for 2013. If we remove those who receive a contributory pension from the total population of this age group in the country and assume that the program will maintain the same transfer amount of Mex$500 per month, the fiscal cost of this program in 2012 would be 0.21 percent of GDP.[15] If this amount was adjusted to match the amount awarded by the DF's noncontributory pension, which is 50 percent of the MS, the cost would increase to 0.39 percent of GDP. The Centro de Estudios Espinosa Yglesias (CEEY) (2013) proposes another alternative: Introduce a universal pension through individual accounts payable to individuals aged 65 and older. The amount of the pension would be equal to one MS and the only requirement is residency. In this scheme, the government would have to deposit a certain quantity in these accounts after an individual turned 18 years old that would guarantee that he or she would receive the target pension amount. In this case it would be necessary to cover the amount that should be in the accounts for those individuals who are already older than 18 years (transition population) or supplement their accounts upon retirement. In the first case, the fiscal cost as an annual flow after the second year would be 1.25 percent because in the first year the government would have to pay recognition bonds, which would amount to 50 percent of GDP. This proposal has some similarities to the proposal advanced by Antón, Hernandez, and Levy (2012), but in the latter case the reform is to the health insurance system.

In any case, the important point in the different alternatives is to guarantee the source of future funding, which necessarily requires a fiscal reform that increases the government's fiscal income and, preferably, establishes one or more funds designed exclusively to finance these programs. Specifically, one proposal is to broaden the value-added tax (Impuesto de Valor Agregado), which is currently 16 percent but has many exceptions that result in low revenues from this tax.

The second aspect to highlight in the reforms to contributory pension systems and those that lead to the creation of noncontributory social protection programs and transfers is their impact on the labor market. This topic is not new, but it has gained growing importance because a serious problem of labor informality persists in the economy. As we have mentioned, the reforms to contributory pension systems did not include modifying labor market conditions to incentivize greater coverage as one of their principal objectives. As Sales, Solís, and Villagómez

(1998) point out, despite the fact that the IMSS program's reform did not include a reduction to the payroll tax rate on salaries, it was hoped that if benefits maintained a ratio more closely linked to contributions, this would make the system function less like a pure tax scheme and reduce labor market distortions. However, policy makers were conscious of possible negative effects resulting from the PMG because, on the margins, it could disincentivize participation in the formal labor market. Those workers that expected to receive the PMG would limit their participation in the formal market.

This problem appeared to grow with the expansion of noncontributory social protection programs, which, even though they deal with the problem of poverty, end up creating significant distortions in the economy, and especially in the labor market. Levy (2008) and Antón, Hernandez, and Levy (2012) have put forth and developed this thesis. These authors start from the premise that the low growth of the Mexican economy is the result of low productivity, which is in turn caused by the existence of a large informal sector that is in part incentivized by the introduction of noncontributory social protection programs. In other words, there is a segmented, dual social security system: contributory social security and noncontributory social protection. The first entails receiving a package of services for which a tax is paid on formal employment, and in the second workers receive a set of social security services that are not packaged and because they are not contributory they constitute a subsidy to informal employment. Antón, Hernandez, and Levy (2012) make estimates regarding these effects. They point out that the noncontributory social protection programs reduce salaried employment, push the overall makeup of employment toward illegality, and promote employment in family businesses and self-employment. In their model, the joint effect of these programs is to reduce salaried employment by 7 percent and increase the participation of illegal employment from 37 percent to 39 percent, as a result of the 5.3 percent increase in informal employment.

Implementation Challenges

One aspect that should be considered in the creation and/or reform of social protection programs deals with their implementation to ensure that benefits effectively reach the target population, as well as the administrative and operational costs that this entails. The current proposals to introduce universal social protection programs have the advantage that they can be built on top of existing infrastructure that has been tested by the programs implemented in the last decade, specifically Opportunities, "70 y más", and Popular Insurance. For example, this means using the infrastructure designed for payment of monetary benefits, both via banks and in cash.

The main challenge in the implementation of these universal programs is related to the information problem and the possibility of having a single registry that is trustworthy. Mexico still does not have an appropriate scheme that assigns a unique identification number to the entire population. The so-called Unique Population Registry Code (Clave Única de Registro de Población [CURP]) exists, which is supposed to be a national identification number, but it has not been possible to use it as a unique identifier. Consequently, each program, contributory and noncontributory, has its own registry without the possibility of cross-checking them, which means there are duplications in obtaining different benefits. Thus, a central challenge is the possibility of creating a Universal Registry and extending the use of the CURP as a unique identifier to gain access to the universal protection programs, both for health care as well as for pensions.

Territorial scope is another challenge. The geographic dispersion of many small communities represents another challenge to achieving effective access and the universalization of these services—this is particularly important in the case of health care services.

Finally, an important challenge for these programs is achieving integration of the existing programs and institutions such that duplications are eliminated and the government is able to standardize the quantity and quality of the services offered. In the case of pensions, the main point is achieving coordination between what would be a universal noncontributory minimum pension and the existing contributory programs, while seeking to eliminate possible incentives for informality. In the case of the health care system, the main idea in the integration of services is to maximize the use of existing infrastructure by guaranteeing the provision of a general and standardized basic package.

Other Services for the Elderly

The Organization of Health Care Services and Its Reforms

The history of health insurance and service provision goes hand in hand with the creation of programs for income protection through pensions. An important point in the drive to provide these services occurred at the beginning of the 1970s when the LSS was modified to expand the IMSS' services mainly to the marginalized rural population. In 1983 article 4 of the constitution was reformed to establish that "every person is entitled to health care protection" and that "the law will define the bases and modalities for access to health care services." In 1997 the Secretariat of Health was decentralized, creating the Public Decentralized Organizations (Organismos Públicos Descentralizados) charged with directing, administering, operating, and overseeing the health care service establishments transferred to the states (CEESES 2012). In 2003 the General Health Care Law (Ley General de la Salud) was reformed to introduce the Health Care Social Protection System (Sistema de Protección Social en Salud), known as Popular Insurance (Seguro Popular), which was the biggest step toward the universalization of health care services in the country. Popular Insurance allowed the government to extend these services to the population that was not entitled to services from the social security institutions, or that did not have any other social protection mechanism for health care.

Just as with the pension system, the health care system is highly fragmented, heterogeneously offering various services of differing quality to the population. The public component of the contributory system includes social security institutions that cover 65.4 million Mexicans,[16] the IMSS covers salaried workers in the private sector and their families, the ISSSTE covers federal public sector workers and their family members, and PEMEX and the armed forces offer medical services.

A second block that covers the uninsured population in the aforementioned programs includes services offered by the Secretariat of Health and the State Health Services (Servicios Estatales de Salud). Federal programs like IMSS Opportunities and Popular Insurance are included here. IMSS Opportunities emerged in 2002 when the name of the IMSS Clave Única de Registro de Población Solidarity program was changed, and although it is still administered by IMSS, its goal is to provide health care services to the uninsured population in vulnerable situations, principally in rural areas. In this way it connects with the Opportunities program, offering health care services to its beneficiaries. According to official figures, the list of beneficiaries of this program included 10.7 million in rural areas and 830,000 in urban areas for a total of 11.5 million in 2012.

As we have mentioned, the main reform in the last decade oriented toward expanding coverage was the introduction of so-called Popular Insurance. Its goal was to offer financial protection to Mexican families by avoiding catastrophic costs and seeking to reduce out-of-pocket expenses. The initial target population was those individuals in the first six deciles of the income distribution in certain states and regions of the country. Over time, these restrictions were loosened. The membership unit is the family, including children younger than 18 years of age. The membership criteria include living in an area where this insurance is available, not belonging to another social security health care system, and joining voluntarily. In 2006 the services were decentralized to the states as part of a national agreement between the federation and the states.

Membership is open to any Mexican or family that does not have social security and payment of a progressive premium is based on income level, such that those families in the first four deciles do not pay a premium. For individuals older than 18 years and individual members, the premium is 50 percent of the family premium. However, beyond the design of the premium system, in practice more than 98 percent of the member families are exempt from payment of the premium (CEESES 2012).

The introduction of the Medical Insurance for a New Generation (Seguro Médico para una Nueva Generación) program in 2006 also had the impact of expanding the coverage of this insurance program. The new program's goal was to include all Mexican children born after December 1, 2006, that did not have social security. It is important to note that upon enrolling the child, the family was automatically enrolled in the event that it was not already enrolled, which resulted in a large increase in coverage. Currently the program is operated by the National Commission of Health Protection (Comisión Nacional de Protección en Salud), which is a decentralized authority of the Secretariat of Health, with technical, administrative, and operational autonomy. This insurance offers medical/surgical, hospital, and pharmaceutical services, covering 284 procedures and around 1,500 illnesses described in the Universal Catalog of Health Care Services (Catálogo Universal de Servicios de Salud).

The national health care system has exhibited significant advances in the last two decades but still has serious problems. Two recent diagnostics, CEESES (2012) and FUNSALUD (2012), agree, pointing out the system's complexity and fragmentation, offering incomplete and unequal protection to the population enrolled in social security and the population enrolled in social protection. An important topic is the quality of services and infrastructure, which varies widely. Finally, the reports reference the aspects of effective coverage and effective access, which the system does not adequately measure. Despite the increases in membership and coverage, effective access, understood as the ratio between the community and the health care system, appears to show serious failings.

In table 10.13 we observe that the principal coverage increase, especially since 2000, occurred in the uninsured population. This is where the IMSS Opportunities and Popular Insurance programs have made an impact. Coverage among this population doubled between 1990 and 2000 and the biggest effect of the Popular Insurance program was registered between 2000 and 2005. Without a doubt, Popular Insurance has played an important role in closing the coverage gaps among the country's population in recent years, even though 19 percent of the population still reports that they do not receive any health care services.

Broad discussion has been underway in recent years that includes diverse reform proposals for the health care provision system. One common point among these proposals is the diagnosis of the current system, which is considered

Table 10.13 Health Care Services User Population[a] and Total Coverage, 1990–2012
Thousands of persons

Concept	*1990*	*2000*	*2005*	*2010*	*2012*[d]
Total	45,351	77,066	88,093	91,177	94,884
Percentage of total population[a]	49.5	79.1	84.5	81.2	81.2
Uninsured population	16,173	37,403	43,709	43,114	45,590
Secretariat of Health[b]	16,173	26,478	33,323	32,220	33,505
IMSS Opportunities	n.a.	10,925	10,049	10,499	11,800
Universities[c]	n.a.	n.a.	337	393	285
Insured population	29,178	39,663	44,384	48,063	49,293
IMSS	23,428	29,979	35,021	36,131	39,115
ISSSTE	4,489	7,203	7,209	8,211	8,538
PEMEX	872	647	708	743	760
SEDENA	225	489	n.a.	1,048	n.a.
SEMAR	164	155	172	240	264
States[c]	—	1,189	1,275	1,691	616

Source: Consejo Nacional de Población (CONAPO) and Secretariat of Health.
Note: Data for 2002 and 2003 are not included because there are only estimated figures for the total population constructed based on the sample from the XII General Population and Housing Census 2000. The sum of parts might not coincide with the total due to rounding. IMSS = Instituto Mexicano del Seguro Social; ISSSTE = Instituto de Seguridad y Servicios Sociales de los Trabajadores del Estado; PEMEX = Petróleos Mexicanos; SEDENA = Secretaría de Defensa Nacional; SEMAR = Secretaría de Marina-Armada. n.a. = not applicable; — = not available.
a. Population that demanded medical services at least once per year.
b. In 1990 the Secretariat of Health's population included the Federal District.
c. The data for 2010 differ from that published in previous years because for this year a higher university hospital user population was reported for Puebla and Nuevo Leon. Among the states, the Mexico state ISSEMyM reported information.
d. Estimations up to December.

to be highly fragmented, unequal, and unequitable, offering services of varying quality, with different coverage levels for different social groups. Along these lines, all of the proposals point toward universalization of services for the entire population regardless of age. Among these proposals are those formulated by the Mexican Foundation for Health (Fundación Mexicana para la Salud; FUNSALUD 2012); the Center for Economic and Social Studies in Health (Centro de Estudios Económicos y Sociales; CEESES 2012) of the Federico Gómez Children's Hospital and presented by CONEVAL; and the Espinosa Yglesias Center for Studies (Centro de Estudios Espinosa Yglesias; CEEY 2013). The last (CEEY) tries to organize the points of consensus among the other studies. Finally, it is clear that health care and insurance costs will continue to rise and it is necessary to guarantee a funding source, which means that the topic of fiscal reform mentioned earlier applies equally here.

Other Programs

Four services that form part of the "Services to Groups with Special Needs Program" (Servicios a Grupos con Necesidades Especiales) stand out. The first service is primary health care via medical appointments. Second, INAPAM cards are supposed to help the elderly obtain discounts and preferential rates on goods and services. Third, organizations offer a variety of services such as training for work, and activities in workshops to learn skills, crafts, and art at cultural centers and clubs for the elderly; laboratory studies and medical supplies; temporary and permanent housing with balanced meals; and art education classes in diverse disciplines. Fourth, clubs for the elderly promote the participation of the population aged 60 and older, encouraging organization and intervention to solve their problems, while also promoting community belonging.

Programs and activities also exist in the educational sector. The Adult-Demanded Education Services program (Atención a la Demanda de Educación para Adultos) offers technical advising, books, teaching materials, educational services, certifications, and achievement certificates.

Other types of programs can benefit the elderly as well, even though their target population is usually larger than just this group, such as those that target families. CONEVAL (2012) presents a list of programs and federal social development actions for 2011, including a total of 179 programs and 94 actions. The list categorizes the federal programs and actions according to stage of life, including 94 that serve the elderly, although not all are exclusive to this age group. Of these, 27 deal with health issues, 19 economic well-being, eight anti-discrimination, 10 work-related support, eight healthy environments, six social security, four nutrition, and four housing.

The Social Provision of Milk program (Programa de Abasto Social de Leche) in charge of Liconsa that offers fortified milk at a low price and the Rural Supply Program (Programa de Abasto Rural) managed by Diconsa that offers subsidized foodstuffs in marginalized areas are two examples. In some cases these programs do not just consider income, health, and nutrition. For example, the Support Program for Agricultural Income, PROCAMPO for better Living (Programa de Apoyo al Ingreso Agropecuario [PROCAMPO para Vivir major]), offers subsidies for machinery and equipment and infrastructure in highly and very highly marginalized rural areas. Although the beneficiary population of these subsidies is mostly adults, it should be remembered that a significant percentage of the elderly remain in the labor market, mainly in activities related to agriculture, as we detailed in the first section of this chapter. The Agricultural Day Laborer Services Program (Programa de Atención a Jornaleros Agrícolas), offers food, housing, and infrastructure promotion, among other services. The National Solidary Support Fund for Enterprises (Fondo Nacional de Apoyos para Empresas en Solidaridad), directed to rural and urban populations with scarce resources that demonstrate their organizational, productive, and entrepreneurial abilities to open a business, offers support services including loans and basic consulting.

Conclusions

The elderly population in Mexico is increasing significantly as a consequence of demographic change. However, this growing population may be poorly protected from various risks, including reduction in income, illnesses, or accidents. The contributory social security programs have demonstrated serious limitations in extending coverage to a significant portion of this population, a situation that has been exacerbated by the existence of a growing informal sector in the economy.

The solution that the authorities have implemented for this problem has been creating and expanding varied noncontributory social protection programs that offer transfers or expanded provision of diverse services. These actions have been reinforced during the last decade and have allowed the government to increase the protection of the elderly in areas such as income and health care. Programs such as Popular Insurance and "70 y más" (now "65 y másr") stand out because they have permitted significant coverage expansion among the elderly in the past decade, even though they have not yet achieved universality and they still have problems with effective access.

Nonetheless, these programs cannot be viewed as a permanent and stable solution to this predicament unless their design and operations are rethought in a comprehensive context of social security reform, because they represent increasing fiscal costs and unsustainable budget pressures in the future. Moreover, the design of some of these programs has ended up contributing to incentives for growing informality, which feeds back into and worsens the problem. This has led to the creation of a dual system of social security and social protection. Regardless of which part of the solution requires the government to correct the economy's structural problems, it is necessary to reconsider the design of the existing social protection programs to eliminate the segmentation and heterogeneity in the provision of their services. It is important to guarantee that these programs satisfy criteria regarding equality, solidarity, joint responsibility, pluralism, and sustainability without creating distortions that incentivize informality and affect the operation of the labor market.

Finally, it is necessary that these programs and actions are the result of combined, democratic effort from all those involved such that the most appropriate institutional design is achieved that guarantees the system's existence in the future. These are topics that are on the table for discussion and debate in our countries and should be central elements of the public policy agenda for our governments.

Notes

1. Such as lack of health care services, equipment, and adequate infrastructure, which creates a precarious framework of opportunities that hinders the full development of human potential.
2. These data come from the 2009 National Employment and Social Security Survey, published by INEGI.
3. This figure corresponds to workers registered with the IMSS in May 2012 that were active contributors to the system. This number differs from the number of registered accounts reported by CONSAR, because that number includes inactive accounts and accounts from ISSSTE workers who opted for an AFORE plan. In September 2001 there were a total of 42.3 million accounts.
4. For a discussion of the reform, see Sales, Solís, and Villagómez (1998).
5. Currently ISSSTE member accounts are also counted, after this system was reformed in 2007 to give these workers the option to change over to a scheme similar to the IMSS scheme, and which we will discuss later.
6. This variable does not include ISSSTE workers that participate in the AFOREs, which were slightly more than 990,000 in May 2012.
7. Up until the end of 2012 there were five SIEFOREs, but the authorities decided to merge the SB4 and SB5 SIEFOREs as of November 2012 because of the decrease in the relative size of the SB5 fund compared to the entire system, which is explained by the lower number of young workers that entered the formal labor market, which limits the investment policies of this type of SIEFORE in the long term. It is worth mentioning that the SB4 and SB5 investment regime is practically the same, except for the limit on exchange-trade instruments. Even so, the limit on these instruments is 1.14 percent for SB4 and 1.26 percent for SB5.
8. Contribution density expresses the proportion of time making contributions to social security (contribution) relative to the total time spent working. Essentially it refers to the effective contribution of a worker during his or her work life.
9. This work makes reference to the Díaz Cayeros and Magaloni (2003) and Díaz Cayeros, Magaloni, and Weingast (2005) studies, which document these clientelistic practices in Mexico during the 1990s and the public policies.
10. There are diverse estimates of contribution density in the IMSS program, but an approximate figure suggests that about 50 percent of members have contribution densities less than 60 percent.
11. We use the definitions proposed by Rofman and Oliveri (2011) to allow for comparability over time and with other countries. With the goal of preserving comparability with Rofman and Oliveri (2011), the definition of the EAP is 20 years and older. The data source used is the ENIGH, which after 2010 offers detailed information on the income that comes from the main transfer programs for the elderly such as "70 y más" and Opportunities.

12. The most recent estimates can be found in Vásquez Colmenares (2012), Aguirre Farías (2012), and Sinha (2012).
13. These estimates are based on Vásquez Colmenares (2012). For the solidary savings, we assume that 50 percent of workers opt for the maximum contribution percentage.
14. These values come from estimates from Vásquez Colmenares (2012) and Aguirre Farías (2012), the latter providing information on the states and universities.
15. See estimates in CEEY (2012).
16. Figures from the institutions' administrative records and taken from CEESES (2012).

References

Acosta, B., and A. Villagómez. 2012. "La cobertura de pensiones en México." In *Seguridad Social Universal*, Fausto Hernández, editor. CIDE.

Aguirre Farías, F. 2012. "Pensiones … ¿y con qué?" Fineo Editores, México.

Antón, A., F. Hernandez, and S. Levy. 2012. "The End of Informality in México?" Inter-American Development Bank, Washington, DC.

CEESES (Centro de Estudios Económicos y Sociales en Salud). 2012. "Propuesta de un sistema nacional de servicios de salud." Draft, October, Mexico.

CEEY (Centro de Estudios Espinosa Yglesias). 2012. "Construyendo un Sistema Nacional de Salud: una propuesta para alcanzar la cobertura universal." Draft, November, Mexico.

———. 2013. "Propuesta para una Pensión Universal." Draft, Mexico.

CONEVAL (Consejo Nacional de Evaluación de la Política de Desarrollo Social). 2012. "Inventario de Programas y Acciones Federales de Desarrollo Social." Mexico. http://www.coneval.gob.mx/evaluacion/ipfe/Paginas/default.aspx.

Díaz Cayeros, A., and B. Magaloni. 2003. "The Politics of Public Spending." Background paper for the *World Development Report 2004*, World Bank, Washington, DC.

Díaz Cayeros, A., B. Magaloni, and B. Weingast. 2005. "Tragic Brilliance: Equilibrium Party Hegemony in Mexico." Working paper, Hoover Institution, Stanford University.

FUNSALUD (Fundación Mexicana para la Salud A.C.). 2012. "Universalidad de los servicios de salud: Propuesta de FUNSALUD." Draft, September.

González Anaya, J. 2012. "Reforma de Pensiones en México." Draft presentation for "A 15 Años de la reforma del Sistema de Pensiones en México," AMAFORE, September 19.

Levy, S. 2008. *Good Intentions, Bad Outcomes.* Washington, DC: Brookings Institution Press.

Rofman, R., and M. Oliveri. 2011. *La Cobertura de los Sistemas Previsionales en América Latina: Conceptos e Indicadores*. Washington, DC: World Bank.

Rubio, G., and F. Garfias. 2010. "Análisis comparativo sobre los programas para adultos mayores en México." Serie Políticas Sociales 161, ECLAC.

Sales, C., F. Solís, and F. Villagómez. 1998. "Pension System Reform: The Mexican Case." In *Privatizing Social Security*, edited by Martin Feldstein. Chicago, IL: University of Chicago Press.

Sinha, T. 2012. "Estimating Future Pension Liability of the Mexican Government." Draft, Inter-American Development Bank, Washington DC.

Solís Soberón, F., and A. Villagómez. 1999. "Las Pensiones." In *La Seguridad Social en México, Lecturas del Trimestre Económico*, F. Solís and F. A. Villagómez, editors. No. 88, FCE-CIDE, Mexico.

Soto, C. 2006. "Movilidad Laboral: Impacto en la tasa de reemplazo, el caso de México." Presented at Comisión Americana de Actuaría y Financiamiento, Mexico.

Stein, E., and M. Tommasi. 2005. "Democratic Institutions and Policymaking Processes and the Quality of Policies in Latin America." Inter-American Development Bank, Washington, DC.

Vásquez Colmenares, P. 2012. *Pensiones en México: la próxima crisis.* Mexico City: Siglo XXI Editores.

CHAPTER 11

Panama

Gonzalo Reyes and Javier Bronfman

History

Demographic, Labor, and Macroeconomic Context

In a context of demographic dividend, the elderly represent one of every 10 inhabitants of the total population in Panama. The incorporation of groups at active ages into the labor force is continuous, and we have observed disparities in labor participation by gender, with women facing disadvantages in terms of access to the pension system. Meanwhile, the stability of macroeconomic variables suggests that fiscal space will continue to be available to consolidate the social protection system for the elderly.

Panama is a relatively small nation with a high proportion of the population under 14 years of age and sustained population growth rates. According to the last census, from May 2010, the total population amounted to 3,405,813 people with 9.6 percent of them older than 60 years. The trend during the last 30 years reflects a gradual increase in the proportion of the elderly, nearly doubling between 1985 and 2010. This is explained by the demographic transition, in which economic development is accompanied by lower mortality rates (and a higher life expectancy at birth) and lower fertility rates, as shown in figure 11.1. Panama's total fertility rate, which reached nearly six children per woman in 1960, fell to less than half that amount 30 years later and is expected to stabilize below the replacement rate around 2040. In addition, life expectancy at birth for both genders, which increased by almost 20 years during the second half of the last century, will continue increasing until it reaches 80 years in 2050 and 85 by the end of the century.

As a result of these trends, the population of Panama is expected to age drastically in the coming decades, with the elderly population representing almost one-quarter of the total population in 2050 and 35 percent in 2100, whereas the population under 15 years will fall from nearly one-third of the total at the beginning of this century to almost half that level 50 years later and to just 15 percent in 2100. In terms of the dependency ratio (the ratio between children and the elderly and the working age population), Panama is experiencing a process known as the demographic dividend, in which this ratio will temporarily

Figure 11.1 Evolution of and Projections for Life Expectancy at Birth and the Total Fertility Rate, 1950–2100

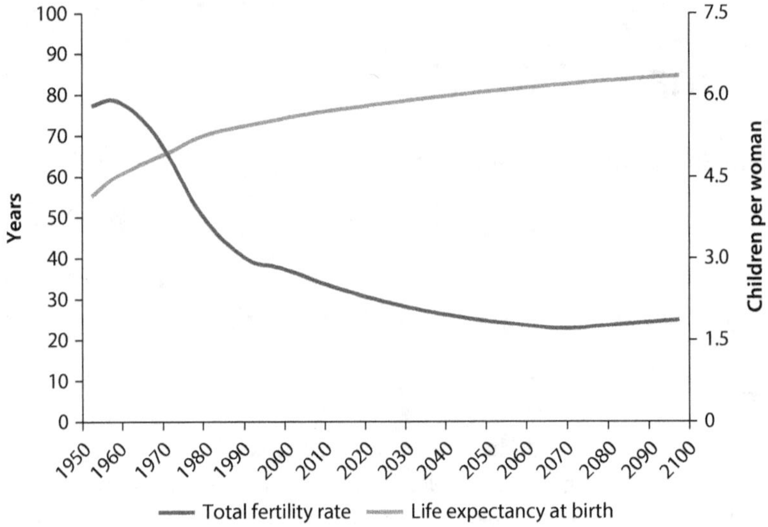

Source: Economic Commission for Latin America and the Caribbean (ECLAC) 2009.

Figure 11.2 Population by Age and Total Dependency Ratio, 1950–2010

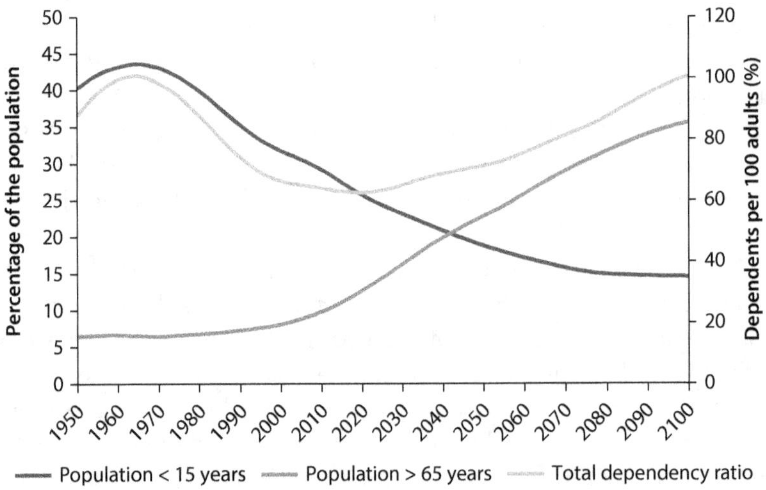

Source: Centro Latinoamericano y Caribeño de Demografía (CELADE) 2009.

decrease as a result of the transition (figure 11.2). The percentage of the population that is working age (15–59 years) will continue its growth trend and reach its peak around 2020. After that, the aging effect will become more pronounced, meaning that the "earnings" generated by the reduction of the youth population will be more than offset by the increase in the number of elderly persons, and the dependency ratio will begin to increase anew. These demographic changes will have substantial effects on the sustainability of the pension and social protection systems for the elderly.

Panamanian economic activity has increased in recent years, fundamentally as a consequence of greater participation among women in the workforce. Although at the beginning of the 1990s the female activity rate fluctuated around 39 percent, in the last two decades we have seen a major change. Women's participation has reached 50 percent, while the participation rate among men has been stable around 82 percent (figure 11.3).

Between 30 percent and 35 percent of Panamanian workers are self-employed, which means that they have more limited access to traditional social security systems. This proportion has remained very stable for most of the past two decades, but it appears to have begun to decline since 2005, especially among men (figure 11.4). Even though the proportion of independent workers continues to be higher among men than among women, the gap between both indicators has decreased significantly in the last 20 years.

Historical Profile of Social Protection for the Elderly

Panama's pension system is made up of multiple regimes with different characteristics in terms of administration, design, mandatory nature, and target population. The general regime is administered by the Social Security Bank (Caja de Seguro Social [CSS]) and obligatorily covers all private and public sector workers that perform activities in Panama, nationals and foreigners, including independent or self-employed workers. Since 2008, the system can be classified as mixed, maintaining a pay-as-you-go pillar and creating another individually funded pillar for private sector workers. The most recent innovation is the creation of the "100 a los 70" ("100 at 70") program in 2009.

Figure 11.3 Labor Participation of the Population Aged 15 Years and Older, by Gender, 1990–2012

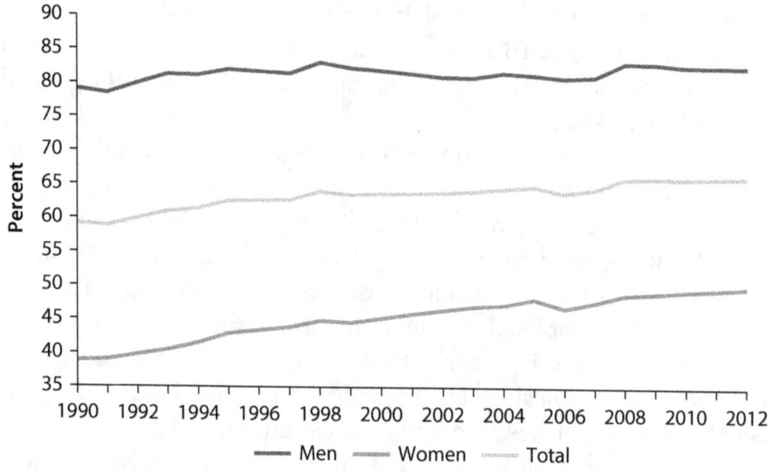

Source: International Labour Organization.

Figure 11.4 Evolution of the Proportion of Independent Workers by Gender, 1991–2010

Source: World Development Indicators and Global Development Finance, 2012 update, World Bank.

Panama's social security system can trace its formal roots back to 1941, and since then it has grown in terms of both coverage and scope. The system provides old age, disability, illness, and death pensions, as well as transfers to families. The benefits have historically been funded through a pay-as-you-go scheme, but since January 1, 2008, individual accounts have formed the second pillar of the system.

The first law that Panama promulgated on the subject of social protection legislated safeguards for workers relative to possible on-the-job accidents. In 1924 Law no. 9 was promulgated, establishing a special retirement system for telegraph operators, and in 1926 Law no. 65 created a retirement system for employees of the Postal Agency of Panama (Agencia Postal de Panamá), the National Bank of Panama (Banco Nacional de Panamá), and the Saint Thomas Hospital (Hospital Santo Tomás). In addition, in 1930 Law no. 78 legislated pensions for professors, and in 1935 Law no. 7 established public employees' right to a retirement based on their contributions that were registered in their individual accounts, establishing for the first time financing based on contributions and a uniform defined benefit regime for all public employees. Additionally, according to Law no. 8 employees in commerce and manufacturing participated in a retirement system that varied by ages and years of service, with benefits available for workers who had completed a minimum of 20 years of continuous work. Employees and workers in other activities, except domestic and agricultural workers, had access to health benefits and occupational hazard compensation because of a system that was managed by their employers.

Although the legislation prior to the creation of the Social Security Fund (Caja de Seguro Social) provided a social security system to Panamanian citizens, this system exhibited significant failings, mainly in terms of inequality and a lack of flexibility regarding benefits because they were linked to particular activities or jobs. Government employees enjoyed entitlements very different from those of employees and workers in private firms, and additionally a lack of medical benefits existed. As a whole, the majority of the existing social security systems for public employees relied on the availability of government funds, and the benefits provided by the private system did not offer additional guarantees to its beneficiaries. Thus in 1941 the Social Security Bank was created, which established a more ambitious, extensive, and harmonious social protection system than the one that had existed until then. In 1943 Law no. 134 was promulgated, supplementing Law no. 23 on the subject of the technical and organizational bases of the regime established in 1941.

During the following years, multiple reforms were introduced, tending toward coverage expansion to districts and communities that did not participate in the system. In the 1960s and 70s the government made progress in consolidating the services, especially focusing on expanding health coverage to insured members' families, as well as advances in the survivor's pension regime, family member allocations, temporary disability subsidy, and improvements to the pregnancy subsidy. This expansion, particularly in the area of health care, created financial difficulties because the CSS assumed a large part of the costs, replacing obligations that had previously been the responsibility of the Ministry of Health (Ministerio de Salud). The Supplementary Social Benefits Fund was also created during this period for public employees, and it increased the old age and disability pensions.

In the 1980s the CSS faced a serious crisis, originating from the country's macroeconomic difficulties, an internal financial crisis provoked by the collapse of a housing program, and the impact of the 1989 military invasion. The pension system (Disability, Old Age, and Death) suffered an actuarial deficit of grand proportions, which climbed above B 900 million, due to a major decrease in income as a result of the country's economic and productive recession and the increase in the number of pensioners, especially due to early retirements.

In that context, the authorities proposed a reform agenda, led by President Guillermo Endara Galimany, who asked citizens for their direct commitment to accept the need for reform. The fruits of this effort to reformulate the CSS finally became evident toward the end of 1991, with the approval of reforms to the CSS Enabling Law (Ley Orgánica de la CSS) that included an increase of two years in the retirement age after 1995 (to a minimum of 57 years for women and 62 for men to access a retirement pension), although the minimum contribution to the system to be entitled to a pension remained at 180 months. The pension amount also remained the same, at 60 percent of the monthly base salary, calculated as the average of the salaries of the best seven years of contributions.

At the beginning of the new millennium, the government focused its attention on reinforcing the solidary nature of the social protection system. Accordingly, it concentrated on improving access to benefits regardless of the amount contributed to the system, reducing contribution evasion and delay in payment, and optimizing the investment system to improve returns.

In that context in 2005 the Social Security Law no. 51 was approved and was later modified by Law no. 2 of January 8, 2007, which established a mixed system with pay-as-you-go and fully funded components. The new Social Security Law increased coverage to include all new and current workers under 35 years old (including independent workers), and those workers older than 35 could choose between the mixed two-pillar system or remain in the old pay-as-you-go system. Those workers whose monthly salary was less than B 500 would only have to contribute to the pay-as-you-go system (pillar I), and those who earned more than B 500 per month would contribute to both pillar I and to their individually funded account (pillar II).

The minimum pension ages remained at 57 for women and 62 for men and the possibility of retiring two years early was added if the retiree agreed to accept a lower pension. The minimum contribution requirements increased gradually from 180 months in 2007 to 240 for 2013 and beyond. The contribution rate for pensions, disability, and old age were gradually increased from 7.5 percent to 9.25 percent of a worker's salary and from 3.5 percent to 4.25 percent for employers. For those workers with individual accounts, their contributions were divided among both pillars, with the contributions for the first B 500 going to pillar I and the contributions for amounts above B 500 deposited in pillar II. The benefits from the individually funded accounts are calculated based on actuarial criteria, to guarantee income stability via scheduled withdrawals.

Panama's current social protection system is mixed, with publicly and privately managed components. The social protection system establishes that all workers from both the public and private sectors as well as voluntary or independent workers are eligible for benefits of the system. In the case of salaried workers, contributions to the system are shared; that is, both the employer and the employee contribute to the system. This contribution is calculated as a percentage of the monthly salary with no upper limit.

The monetary benefits of the government's elderly pension system are equal to 60 percent of the basic monthly salary (which corresponds to the average of the monthly salary from the best 10 years). A the system pays out 1.25 percent of the basic salary for each 12-month period of contributions that exceeds the required minimum. The minimum pension established by Law no. 51 from December 27, 2005, added up to B 175 per month in 2009, and this amount is readjusted by B 10 every five years. The maximum pension amount varies between B 1,500 and B 2,000 depending on the quantity of the member's contributions.

Public sector workers are also covered by a supplementary regime called the Public Servants' Pension Savings and Capitalization System (Sistema de Ahorro y Capitalización de Pensiones de los Servidores Públicos [SIACAP]), which awards benefits in addition to those provided by the CSS and is based on individual savings. Participation in this system is voluntary and includes a government subsidy.

After 11 years of operations, in 2011 SIACAP had more than 390,000 members, of which 20 percent were currently contributing to the system.

Private sector workers have access to a supplementary pension savings system managed by private entities overseen by the Superintendent of the Stock Market (Superintendencia del Mercado de Valores). In July 2012, 55,780 members were divided between two administrators that participated in the system. This system was implemented through Law no. 10 of 1993 "which establishes incentives for the formation of funds for retirees, pensioners, pensions, and other benefits."

In terms of health coverage, the insured members and their dependents whether active or retired have free access to health care services provided by CSS facilities. The government, in line with its constitutional commitments, should look out for the health of the population by guaranteeing these benefits. For their part, employers must collaborate contributing to the health care fund (Illness and Pregnancy Risk Fund, Fondo Riesgo de Enfermedad y Maternidad), currently equal to 0.25 percent of the salaries paid to employees.

Performance of the Contributory Pension System

In the last decade an expansion of social security coverage took place. The increase was greater among the active population, in which employment growth was accompanied by an increase in contributions. In turn, the inclusion of new elderly pension beneficiaries has kept inequalities in coverage by income levels.

Since 2000 the positive performance of the Panamanian economy has allowed the contributory pension system to increase coverage significantly. The total number of active contributors reported by the CSS increased from 55 percent of the total employed population in 2004 to 70 percent in 2010 (figure 11.5). We should keep in mind that although the number of active contributors counts all persons who made at least one contribution during the year, the number of employed persons corresponds to a measurement from the Labor Market Survey (Encuesta de Mercado Laboral) from March and August each year. Thus, counting the number of contributors at a point in time would be a more comparable

Figure 11.5 Evolution of CSS Coverage during Active and Retired Stages, 2004–10

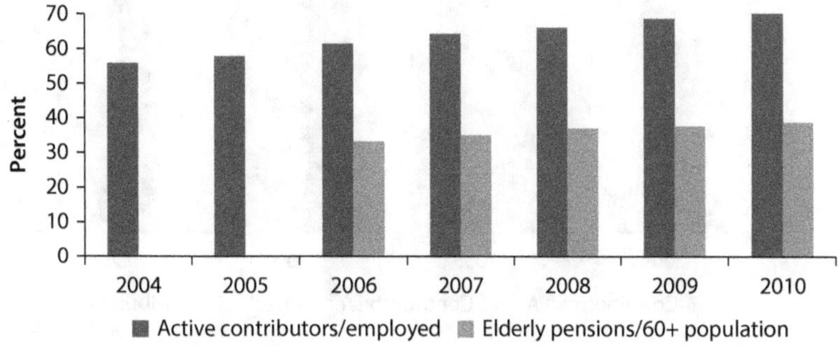

Source: Based on Social Security Statistics (Estadísticas de Seguridad Social) and Labor Market Statistics (Estadísticas de Mercado Laboral) published by Instituto Nacional de Estadística y Censo (INEC).

figure with the number of employed persons.[1] In any case, the figures show an upward trend for pension coverage among the population.

This same upward trend is confirmed if we use data from the Continuous Household Survey (Encuesta Continua de Hogares) as reported by Rofman and Oliveri (2012). This data source allows us to measure coverage at the time of each survey, although it is based on self-reported social security contributions made by those surveyed instead of the number of contributions recorded in administrative data. These data show that the total number of contributors as a percentage of the economically active population rose from 39 percent in 2004 to 49 percent in 2009 and the number of contributors as a proportion of employed persons increased from 47.1 percent in 2004 to 51.5 percent in 2009 (figure 11.6). Additionally, the data indicate that the private sector experienced the greatest growth in coverage, increasing from 37 percent in 2004 to 43 percent in 2009, and the percentage of covered employees in the public sector changed from 95.9 percent to 96.3 percent (figure 11.7). These data are consistent with the job creation experienced in the private sector and indicate that the majority of these new jobs belonged to the formal sector.

Additionally, the number of active elderly pensions for the population aged 60 and older increased from covering 33 percent in 2006 to 39 percent of the target population in 2010. Household survey data confirm this trend, reporting that 45 percent of the population aged 65 and older received a pension benefit in 2009. Moreover, household survey data allow us to identify inequalities in the distribution of pension benefits that have persisted over time. In 2009 benefit

Figure 11.6 Evolution of Pension Coverage during the Active Stage: Alternative Indicators, 2004–09

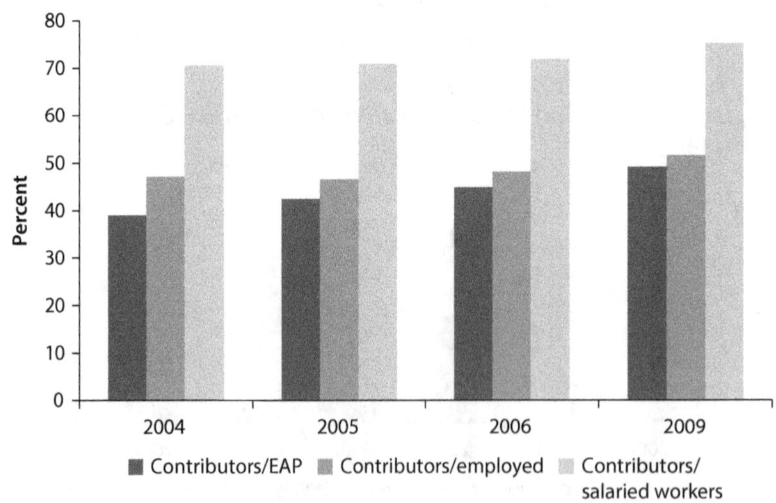

Source: Rofman and Oliveri 2012.
Note: EAP = economically active population.

coverage among the elderly that belonged to households in the first quintile of the income distribution was just 5 percent, whereas for the richest quintile it was 80.5 percent (figure 11.8). The coverage gap for the elderly in the poorest households is perhaps the greatest challenge that the government faces in expanding pension coverage.

Figure 11.7 Evolution of the Employed Persons Coverage, by Economic Sector, 2004–09

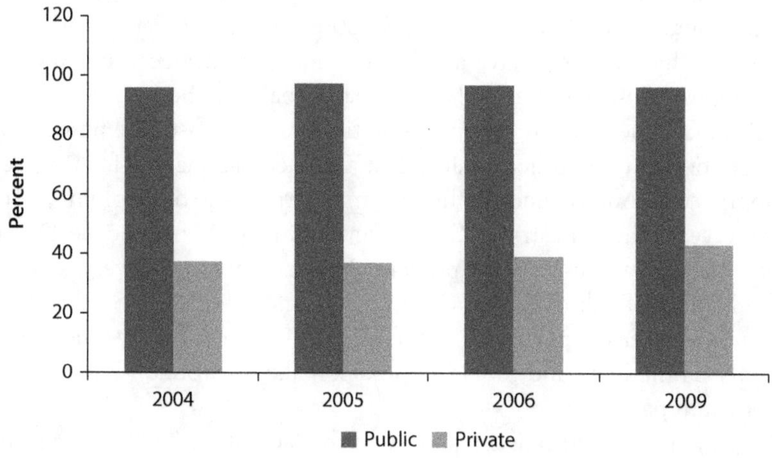

Source: Rofman and Oliveri 2012.

Figure 11.8 Evolution of the Elderly Coverage, by Per Capita Family Income Quintile, 1989–2009

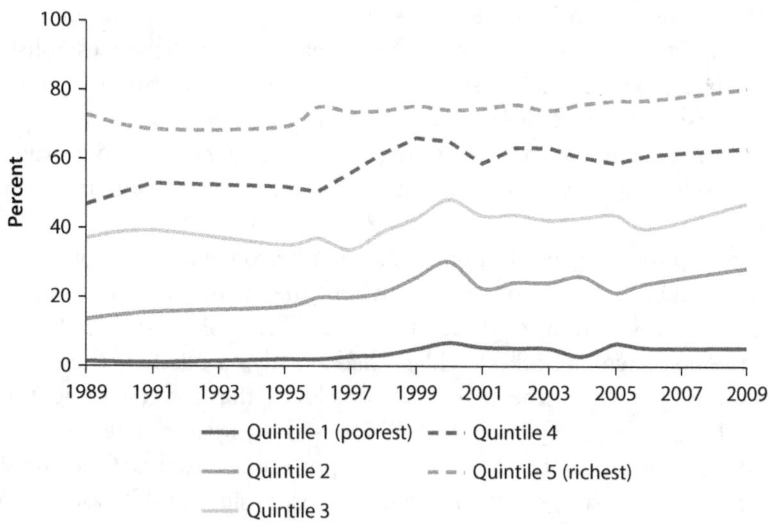

Source: Rofman and Oliveri 2012.

Coverage Expansion: The "100 a los 70" Program

In the face of the contributory system's coverage problems in offering protection to the elderly population, the government of Panama introduced a new monetary transfer program in 2009. In its implementation the program has surpassed its coverage goal and has experienced subsequent adjustments tending toward improving the targeting and giving predictability to the associated fiscal requirements.

The "100 a los 70" program was born in 2009 as a proposal during the presidential campaign of then-candidate Ricardo Martinelli. The program's design is extremely simple: It consists of giving B 100 per month to Panamanian citizens over age 70 that do not receive another pension benefit. Because it was a campaign proposal designated as an "unforgivable goal" for the first 90 days of the administration, the program's implementation was very fast. The new Martinelli administration entered office on July 1, 2009, the enabling law for the program was approved in August, and the first payment was made on September 16th of the same year. The Ministry of Social Development (Ministerio de Desarrollo Social [MIDES]) administers the program. Payments are made every two months via the National Bank of Panama and an agreement with the Savings Bank, in addition to in-person payments made by MIDES in difficult-to-access areas. Payments via the Bank and the Savings Bank make up around 82 percent of the total program payments.

The program was born as a response to the lack of pension coverage among the elderly. Information from the Living Conditions Survey (Encuesta de Nivel de Vida [ENV]) and the Population and Housing Census (Censo de Población y Vivienda) from 2010 showed that between 60 percent and 62 percent of the elderly over 65 did not receive pension income.[2] Thus, a coverage gap exists in the contributory system that the government is trying to close with a noncontributory benefit. Originally, the spirit of the initiative was to give a pension to the elderly population living in poverty that was not receiving another economic benefit. Law no. 44 of 2009 that created the program established as requirements that beneficiaries must have a valid identification card and not receive pension or retirement income, but did not include any socioeconomic targeting criteria.[3] In practice, the program was launched as a quasi-universal benefit, excluding only those that already received a pension from another source.

The program "100 a los 70" undertook an in-person enrollment process of the elderly in MIDES's service offices throughout the country and in dissemination activities in areas that were difficult to reach. As of August 1, 2009, that is, before the first payment, 58,000 elderly had already enrolled via these methods, which was 84 percent of the goal of 70,000 elderly that the government had set (figure 11.9). To process payments, MIDES used the system that was already in place for payments from the Network of Opportunities (Red de Oportunidades) program, a conditional cash transfer that has existed since 2006. Based on census data from 2000, the government estimated that 70,000 potential beneficiaries

Figure 11.9 Number of Benefits Paid, by Payment Method, 2009–12

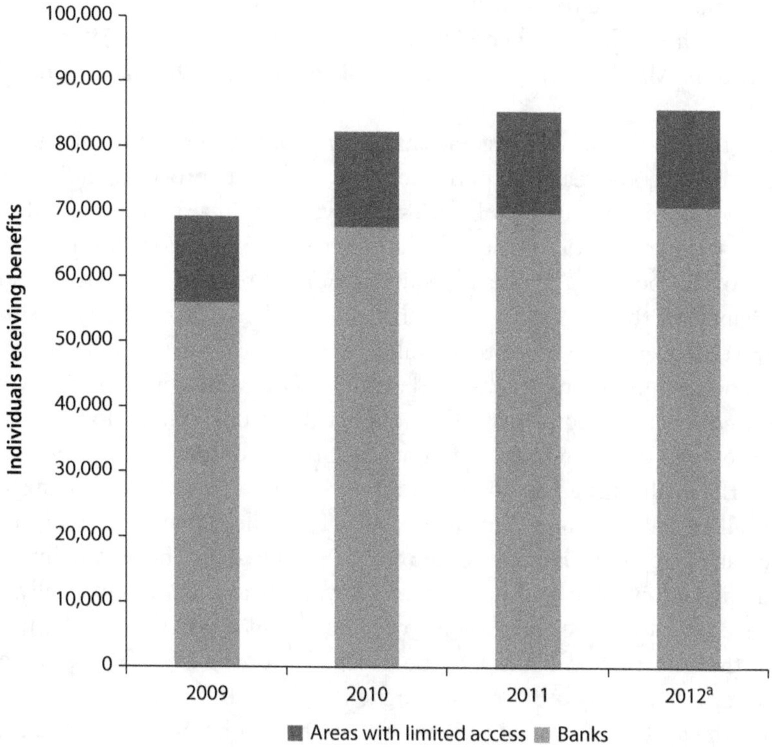

Source: Ministerio de Desarrollo Social (MIDES).
a. The last payment for each year, except for 2012, which is the third payment of that year.

existed, defining beneficiaries as elderly aged 70 and older that did not receive pension or retirement income. However, because the program did not include socioeconomic qualifying criteria, the number of individuals enrolled in the program increased rapidly, climbing to 82,000 by the time the first payment was made in 2010. This participation was greater than the expected and therefore the program exceeded its allocated budget (which had been based on the goal set by the government). In 2010 the effective spending on the "100 a los 70" program was 34 percent higher than the budgeted amount.[4]

Even though the lack of implementation of targeting criteria could have resulted in an oversized program, the total number of potential beneficiaries also could have been underestimated. Using figures from the 2010 Census, there are about 168,000 elderly over age 70, of which 42 percent state that they receive a pension. Among the remaining 98,000, about 6,000 claim to be insured as currently employed workers. Therefore, using the broad criteria of not receiving a pension, up to 92,000 elderly persons could eventually request the benefit.

Universality versus Targeting

The eligibility requirements at the program's launch established only, in addition to the age threshold, that beneficiaries not receive a pension. After reviewing these criteria, MIDES incorporated the verification of conditions of vulnerability as well.

Even though the initial expectations for program enrollment could have been underestimated, the early experiences operating the program indicated that there were cases in which beneficiaries that were not in a situation of vulnerability, even though they did not receive another type of pension, still received the "100 a los 70" benefit. As a result, the government pushed through a change to the original law that explicitly stated that the beneficiary should be in a situation of poverty, extreme poverty, vulnerability, or social risk to access the program.[5]

This new requirement also created new challenges. First, although Law no. 86 defined each of these concepts, it did not provide specific criteria for determining if a person was or was not living in one of these conditions. Thus, it was the job of MIDES, as the program implementer, to design a targeting mechanism that would allow it to evaluate the socioeconomic conditions of potential program beneficiaries. Second, this new requirement modified the benefit delivery process, adding a new step and potentially delaying its allocation. Originally, applicants had only to prove their identity and age upon enrollment in the program so that this information could later be checked with the CSS to make sure they were not receiving any other pension benefits. Now MIDES had to add a step to confirm the applicant's socioeconomic situation via a home visit from a MIDES social worker for each potential beneficiary. Finally, it was also necessary to evaluate the socioeconomic situations of current program beneficiaries as well to ensure that these individuals met the requirements to receive benefits.

Even though there has been no analysis of the quality of the "100 a los 70" program's targeting, it is possible to perform an approximate analysis using information on the number of payments by province and the geographic variation of poverty levels (figure 11.10). Using the data corresponding to the last payment of 2011 and comparing it to the population aged 70 and older from the 2010 Census, we can obtain an indicator of program coverage by province to compare to the percentage of the population in poverty in each province from the 2008 ENV. Although a correlation is found between the percentage of the population living in poverty and the coverage of the "100 a los 70" program in extreme cases, this association is not consistent. The provinces of Bocas del Toro, Darien, Veraguas, and Cocle exhibit similar levels of poverty, but the coverage of "100 a los 70" varies from 54 percent in Bocas del Toro to 78 percent in Veraguas. Something similar happens in the next group of provinces, where despite having significantly lower poverty levels, the program's coverage is between 60 percent and 70 percent. Only in the extreme cases of the indigenous regions, which exhibit poverty levels of 96 percent, and the provinces of Colon and Panama can we observe a marked difference in the program's coverage. This suggests that the targeting of the program can be improved if policy makers want to limit the program's size to ensure its long-term viability.

Figure 11.10 Poverty Rate and "100 a los 70" Coverage, by Province, 2008

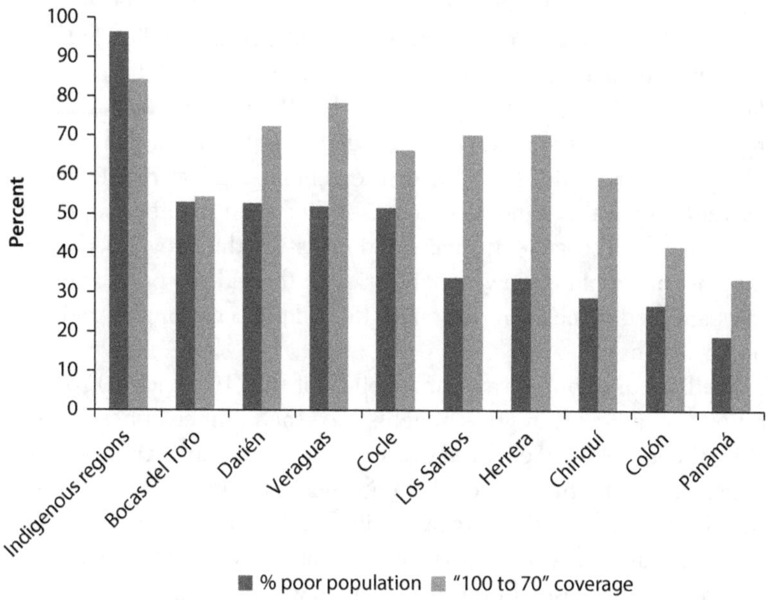

Source: Based on Ministerio de Desarrollo Social (MIDES), 2010 Census, and 2008 Encuesta de Nivel de Vida (ENV).

Costs and Sustainability

This program is funded by the "Special Fund for the Elderly without Retirement or Pension" ("Fondo Especial para los Adultos Mayores sin Jubilación ni Pensión"), created especially for this purpose and which receives financing from the National Treasury (Tesoro Nacional). In 2012 its spending reached 0.3 percent of GDP. Coverage expansion and the need to adjust benefits to preserve purchasing power lead analysts to forecast greater pressure on the budget in coming years.

Another challenge that the program faces is its sustainability over time. The demographic transition will cause the number of inhabitants over age 70 to continue increasing year after year. The funding for the "100 a los 70" program is charged to Panama's National Treasury, which created the Special Fund for the Elderly without Retirement or Pension in conditions of social risk, vulnerability, marginalization, or poverty. According to information available from the Ministry of Social Development, the budget allocated for fiscal year 2012 to deliver these transfers was B 100,999,200.[6] The budget available for delivering transfers would allow for the incorporation of 84,166 beneficiaries during the year. In February 2012 the program had exceeded this figure by 585 beneficiaries and in April 2012 by 1,790 beneficiaries. If the current trend continues, it could seriously compromise the short-term sustainability of the program, forcing it to request additional resources and reinforcing the need to improve beneficiary targeting.

If we consider benefits, the program faces the additional challenge of maintaining a level of adequacy capable of meeting the economic needs of the beneficiaries. Indeed, B 100 per month is equivalent to 106 percent of the poverty line and 15 percent of per capita income. This amount is probably adequate given the level of development and the country's different needs. However, although inflation is generally low in Panama because of its dollarization policy, in the medium and long term the B 100 amount will inevitably lose some of its value. Therefore, an adjustment policy will be necessary so that the benefit can preserve its purchasing power at a stable level. Accordingly, the government has recently announced an increase in the value of the benefit to B per month beginning in 2014. Even though this announcement is in line with maintaining the benefit's real value, it will also generate increased costs for the program on top of the ongoing cost of enrolling new beneficiaries as the elderly population increases and an established mechanism for rating the elderly according to their economic situation is lacking.

The medium and long-term sustainability of the "100 a los 70" program will depend on the increases in gross benefits (i.e., the number of beneficiaries multiplied by the average benefit) relative to the increases in fiscal resources or the economy in general. Thus, if gross benefits increase more rapidly than the economy, the fiscal needs of the program will continue to increase, and this could threaten its sustainability. This situation is possible, given that the elderly population will increase because of population aging, which means that if the improvements in the contributory system observed in recent years are not sustained, then fiscal pressure could grow rapidly.

Figure 11.11 shows the possible evolution of the program's cost under three alternative scenarios. The first ("constant nominal value") assumes that the benefit amount will remain at B 100 permanently over time, and coverage will remain constant as well (at 50 percent of the population aged 70 and older). In this case, the cost of the program, as well as its relevance in social terms, will tend to disappear in the medium term. In an alternative scenario we consider the recent announcement of an increase of B 20 per month beginning in 2014, and we project that over time the pension will increase in value by 20 percent every four years. In this case the cost of the program rises to 0.4 percent of GDP in 2026 and to 0.5 percent in 2038. A third scenario assumes that the program's coverage will also increase gradually until reaching 60 percent in 2020. This coverage level would close the coverage gap among elderly older than 70, complementing the 40 percent of this population that receive contributory pensions from other sources. This scenario adds another 0.09 percent of GDP to the cost of the program in 2020 and up to 0.13 percent in the long term.

Effects on Poverty

The transfer would result in a reduction of poverty indices not just for the elderly, but also for the households in which they reside. Even for those individuals and households that do not manage to exit poverty, a large number of them would exit extreme poverty. Among the elderly, extreme poverty would be reduced by at least six percentage points, and nonextreme poverty would fall by three percentage points. At the household level, the improvements would vary around less than one percentage point.

Figure 11.11 Projected Cost of the "100 a los 70" Program as a Percentage of GDP, 2012–50: Alternative Scenarios

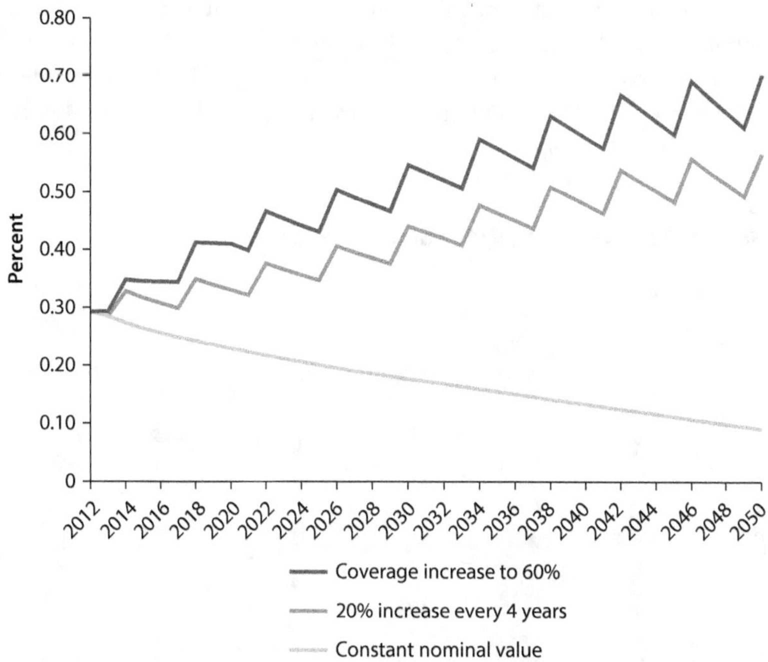

Source: Based on International Monetary Fund (IMF), United Nations Population Statistics, and Ministerio de Desarrollo Social (MIDES).

The 2008 ENV reveals that 33 percent of the Panamanian population was living below the poverty line (figure 11.12). According to the survey, the elderly over 60 years represented 11 percent of the population in 2008. In terms of poverty among the elderly population, 23 percent of those aged 60 and older were living in poverty, 24 percent of those aged 65 and older, and 23 percent of those aged 70 and older, lower than the average for the total population. However, for the 23 percent of the population older than 70 years living in a precarious situation below the poverty line, given their characteristics it is unlikely that they would have the tools necessary to exit this situation of poverty.

Because a more recent survey that would allow us to evaluate the impact of the program is not available, a simple simulation allows us to approximate the expected effect. Table 11.1 shows the results of this exercise, in which we simulate two scenarios, one where we assume that the entire population over age 70 participates in the program, and another where we exclude those who receive another benefit. These simulations were performed separately to analyze the effect of this monetary transfer on poverty among the elderly as well as on the levels of household poverty in Panama.

The new poverty levels, after the simulation performed on the elderly population, reflect a positive impact on poverty reduction. If the benefit were given to all elderly over age 70 with no restrictions, the effect on poverty reduction would be 11.2 percentage points on total poverty and 6.7 percentage points on extreme poverty. If we add the restriction on receiving other pension or retirement benefits, the impact's magnitude is lessened, but it continues to have a substantial effect. The analysis at the level of all household members demonstrates similar transitions, but of a lesser magnitude. Total poverty decreases from 32.7 percent to 31 percent and extreme poverty falls from 14.4 percent to 13.4 percent (table 11.2).

Figure 11.12 Poverty Rate, by Age Groups and Gender, 2008

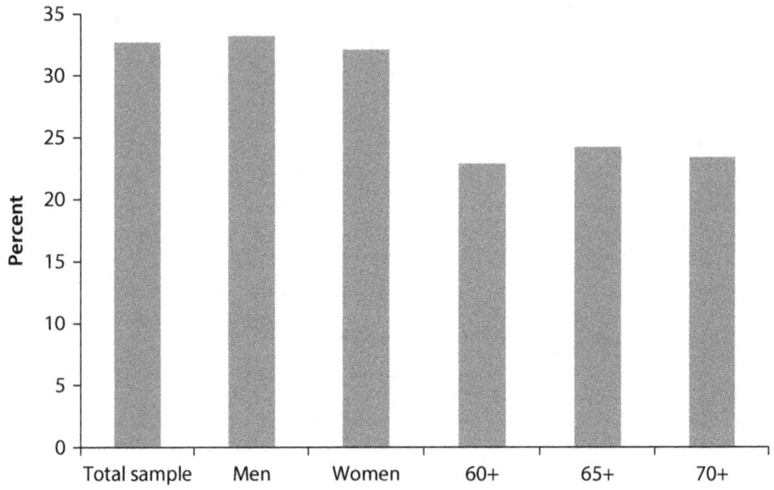

Source: 2008 Panama Encuesta de Nivel de Vida (ENV).

Table 11.1 Simulation of the Effect of "100 a los 70" on Poverty Rates: Population Aged 70 and Older

	Poverty level (%)		
	Original result (2008 ENV)	*Simulation with universal coverage*	*Simulation with incompatibility with other benefits*
Extreme poverty	9.41	2.70	3.23
Total poverty	23.42	12.19	13.89

Source: Simulation with data from the 2008 Encuesta de Nivel de Vida (ENV).

Table 11.2 Simulation of the Effect of "100 a los 70" on Household Poverty Rates

	Poverty level (%)		
	Original result (2008 ENV)	*Simulation with universal coverage*	*Simulation with incompatibility with other benefits*
Extreme poverty	14.43	13.38	13.44
Nonextreme poverty	32.70	30.97	31.30

Source: Simulation with data from the 2008 Encuesta de Nivel de Vida (ENV).

Services for the Elderly

The population insured by the CSS (including pensioners) has access to medical services. These services include hospital attention, medicines, dental attention, and radiology and laboratory services. Pensioners and retirees can also receive a reimbursement for the acquisition of glasses and dental prostheses equivalent to half of the cost incurred. These services can be provided in the CSS' own facilities or in facilities contracted by the CSS. Additionally, the law allows the Institution to create rules to expand the services it offers, through the guidelines on Medical Benefits. CSS pensioners and retirees can apply for a personal loan of up to B 25,000 payable in up to 18 years.

Furthermore, elderly beneficiaries of the "100 a los 70" program must have health checkups and participate in lectures, courses, and seminars on psychological and medical orientation. For both the checkups and the educational activities, beneficiaries should request attendance certificates that they can show to social workers in the supervisory visits.

Conclusions and Lessons

The Panamanian case illustrates the way in which a social security system's performance depends on the conditions in which it is implemented. Specifically, the pay-as-you-go pension system established in 1941 appears to have been particularly affected by the economic crises that the country experienced in the 1980s and the structure of the labor market. As a result, despite favorable demographic conditions, the system became insolvent. There followed a series of parametric reforms that increased retirement ages, minimum contribution requirements, and contribution rates. Then in 2008 the system underwent a structural reform, changing into a mixed scheme with defined benefits complemented by a defined contribution pillar.

In addition to sustainability problems, the system constantly faced a coverage gap. In its best moments, despite legal requirements to pay into the contributory system, the proportion of contributors reached only around 60 percent of total employed workers. Because of the mobility between the formal and informal markets, only some of these contributors were able to meet minimum contribution requirements to gain access to a pension. This partially explains why no more than 40 percent of the elderly population benefits from a pension in the country.

In 2009 the government made the important decision to implement a noncontributory pension system to close the coverage gap among the elderly. The design and implementation of this program illustrates many of the important decisions that must be made to ensure the success of a noncontributory pension scheme. First, the eligibility age was set at 70 years, which designated a target population with obvious characteristics in terms of their vulnerability, even though it is not the group most affected by poverty. Additionally, because the contributory system's retirement ages are 57 for women and 62 for men, this age is sufficiently distant to prevent effects on labor market incentives and participation in the contributory scheme.

The B 100 amount is a round number that is easy to remember, but it is also slightly above the poverty line, below the contributory scheme's minimum pension, and equivalent to about 15 percent of the country's per capita income. This amount appears adequate given the program's objectives, but it lacks an adjustment policy or mechanism to preserve its real value over time. The fact that the program includes the benefit amount in its name could create inflexibility in terms of changes. A simple and descriptive name for this type of program is a good idea, but in this case the name incorporates the amount and the eligibility age, potentially making it more difficult to change either of these parameters over time.

One of the main lessons that the Panamanian experience leaves us is the need to clearly define the target population that the program should cover. Although the original intention was to alleviate the conditions of poverty and vulnerability among the elderly, in practice the program was launched as a quasi-universal benefit in which the only criteria for socioeconomic exclusion consisted of a limitation on receiving another type of pension or retirement benefit. In addition to being imperfect because receiving a pension does not guarantee that an elderly person will avoid poverty, this criterion was not sufficiently strict to constrain the program's size within the limits expected by the authorities. This failure resulted in the need to change the original law to include the condition of poverty or vulnerability as a requirement to receive the benefit. This new requirement, in turn, created a new challenge with the practical implementation of a mechanism that would allow authorities to evaluate the socioeconomic conditions of beneficiaries. All of these considerations should ideally be part of the program's original design to give the population predictability regarding the conditions they must meet and the procedures they must follow to gain access to benefits.

The future evolution and sustainability of the program will depend heavily on the readjustment policy that is implemented regarding the benefit amount and the trends that are observed in the contributory pension system. An automatic indexation mechanism that allows beneficiaries to recuperate the costs of inflation would be the preferred policy to give predictability to changes in the benefit amount to both beneficiaries and the government. The program's funding should be in line with this future evolution.

Finally, as this analysis has shown, the Panamanian experience highlights the importance of adequate analysis and availability of information. Estimating the number of potential beneficiaries of a noncontributory benefit should be performed with the most recent available information and using conservative assumptions regarding beneficiaries' behavior and how they will react to the program's implementation. Additionally, it is necessary to adopt a long-term vision and put an actuarial value on the government's obligations to its citizens from the provision of noncontributory pensions.

Notes

1. For example, August of each year to be able to compare with the respective Labor Market Survey.
2. See Rofman and Oliveri (2012) and http://www.contraloria.gob.pa/inec/Redatam/index_censospma.htm.
3. Law no. 44, Digital Official Gazette form Tuesday, August 4, 2009, http://www.gacetaoficial.gob.pa/pdfTemp/26338_A/GacetaNo_26338a_20090804.pdf.
4. Budget Execution Report, December 2010, http://www.mides.gob.pa/wp-content/uploads/2011/02/informe-mensual-de-diciembre-2010.pdf.
5. Law no. 86, Digital Official Gazette from Thursday, November 18, 2010, http://www.gacetaoficial.gob.pa/pdfTemp/26663_E/GacetaNo_26663e_20101118.pdf.
6. Budget Execution Reports from January, February, March, April, and May 2012, http://www.mides.gob.pa/?page_id=45.

References

ECLAC (Economic Commission for Latin America and the Caribbean). 2011. "Long-Range Population Projections." Santiago: Demographic Observatory 11.

Rofman, R., and L. Oliveri. 2012. "La cobertura de los sistemas previsionales en América Latina: conceptos e indicadores." Serie de Documentos de Trabajo sobre Políticas Sociales 7, World Bank, Buenos Aires.

CHAPTER 12

Paraguay

Juan Martín Moreno

History

In line with the regional trend toward expansion of social protection coverage, Paraguay launched a noncontributory pension (NCP) program focused on the elderly over age 65, called the Pension Alimentaria para Adultos Mayores, and generally known as "Adultos Mayores" (or "Elderly"). The program's launch was more connected to the political dynamic than to demographic or socioeconomic motivations. Regardless of the young demographic profile of Paraguay's population, the existing programs' coverage has historically exhibited low coverage rates with redistribution effects that have not favored the poor. This NCP program supplements Paraguay's traditional social security coverage at the same time that it inverts the redistributive logic of the programs directed to elderly persons.

Sociodemographic Profile of the Population

As with the majority of countries in the region, Paraguay's population is passing through a demographic transition or ageing process. The base of Paraguay's population pyramid has decreased in size while the upper reaches have swelled as a product of the lesser relative importance of the younger population and the greater relative importance of the potentially active population (between 15 and 64 years). In 1950, 47 percent of the population was less than 15 years old, a percentage that shrank to 33 percent in 2010. At the same time, the population over age 65 grew from 3 percent to 5 percent of the total during the same period, somewhat less than the 7 percent observed in Latin America as a whole (figure 12.1).

Paraguay's population is in the "full"[1] transition stage of the demographic transition, with a declining natural growth rate around 2 percent per year. The total fertility rate was around 6.5 children per woman in 1950 and descended abruptly from 4.3 to 2.5 children per woman between 1998 and 2008.

The author thanks Sara Troiano for her helpful comments.

Figure 12.1 Population Pyramids for Paraguay and Latin America, 1950 and 2010

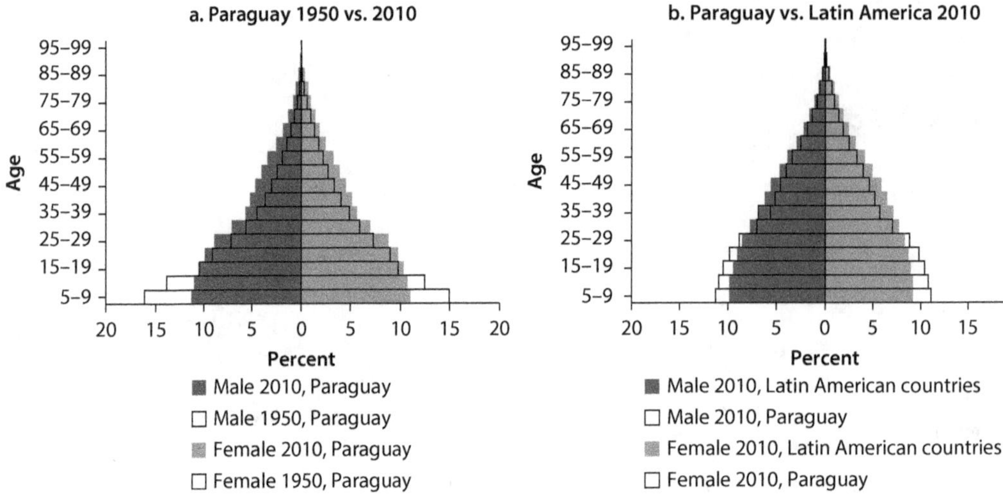

Source: Based on Centro Latinoamericano y Caribeño de Demografía (CELADE)

Life expectancy increased by four years during the period 1950–2000, growing from 60.7 to 64.7 years for men and from 67.2 to 71.7 years for women. These changes negatively impacted the ratio of active population to retired population in Paraguay. In 1950, for each person older than 65 there were 17 potentially active persons, but this ratio had decreased to 11 in 2010.

Even though we have observed an accelerated process of convergence in Paraguay's demographic transition, its population continues to be relatively "younger" than the region as a whole. Although in Paraguay 33 percent of the population was less than 15 years old in 2010, this proportion was 28 percent for Latin America in the aggregate. We can observe that Paraguay's population pyramid continues to be wider at the base than the corresponding pyramid for the region as a whole. CELADE projections estimate that the relative weight of each age group will be similar to the region as a whole in 2100, with elderly over age 65 representing around 29 percent of the total population.

Poverty among adults over age 65 is on the rise. The incidence of poverty among the elderly over age 65 is less than the population average, but it is increasing, contrary to what is occurring with the total rate. Although the incidence of poverty for the total population fell from 39 percent in 2008 to 32 percent in 2011, the percentage of persons over age 65 living in poverty increased from 26 percent to 28 percent during the same period. Even the percentage of the extremely poor increased, from 12 percent to 14 percent during these four years.

In summary, even though demography matters when designing targeted social protection programs for specific age groups, in Paraguay's case it does not appear to be the main reason justifying the launch of this program. Perhaps the incidence of poverty among this specific age group makes a more convincing argument. However, Paraguay has had a pension system since the middle of the

20th century, theoretically designed to address the contingent social risks for this age group. The capacity, effectiveness, and efficiency of the existing institutions explain the motives for expanding the noncontributory programs to care for the elderly.

The Evolution of Social Protection

The origin of social protection in Paraguay lies in schemes exclusively for public employees that were later institutionalized in the middle of the 20th century in centralized, autonomous, public systems. Mesa-Lago (1991) classifies countries such as Paraguay in the group of countries with "intermediate development." Paraguay's main pension fund, the Social Protection Institute (Instituto de Previsión Social [IPS]) dates to 1943. Even though this institution concentrates the greatest proportion of contributors and beneficiaries, social protection in Paraguay remains highly fragmented without a maximum authority that regulates, coordinates, and harmonizes these institutions. Although the contributory structure of these pay-as-you-go regimes could differentiate them from the social assistance schemes that round out the universe of social protection in Paraguay, the recurring deficits that the smaller banks incur result in permanent requirements for government assistance.

Thus, social security is composed of a heterogeneous set of contributory pension regimes that are characterized by low average coverage.[2] Other contributory social security schemes such as unemployment insurance or family allowances[3] do not exist in Paraguay. This unbalanced set of pension schemes comprises two large actors and a set of smaller regulated and nonregulated entities that provide insurance schemes for risks faced by the elderly. The IPS and the Directorate of Retirements and Pensions (Dirección de Jubilaciones y Pensiones) from the Treasury Ministry (Ministerio de Hacienda, Caja Fiscal, Fiscal Fund) gather more than 90 percent of the active and retired insured. Another six retirement and pension funds make up the rest of the universe of regulated social security entities. There are also Mutual Funds (Cajas Mutuales) that form the group of nonregulated entities, completing the universe of organizations offering insurance for the elderly.[4]

This level of heterogeneity and lack of coordination discourage the use of the term "system" to group the set of providers of social protection insurance for the elderly. The lack of contribution portability between regimes and the parametric variations that determine the operations of each fund reflect the lack of compatibility existing among them. Although the IPS is structured based on a pay-as-you-go or defined benefit system classically defined as Bismarckian and contributory, the Fiscal Fund provides coverage to the public sector through a scheme that is in practice noncontributory.[5] The Retirement Funds also exhibit a contributory scheme with defined benefits, and the Mutual Funds do the same through a fully funded or defined contribution system. Many providers of individually or collectively funded pension schemes have ceased functioning, whereas those with origins as mutual companies have survived.[6]

Beyond the coordination and institutional problems that exist for social protection in Paraguay, the problems of low coverage are associated with the combination of a highly informal labor market and a contributory social security scheme.[7] Even though Paraguay's labor market exhibits a low open unemployment rate (it fluctuates around 6 percent of the economically active population), informality is the norm (between 60 percent and 70 percent of the employed population). In addition to informality, migration to neighboring countries (Brazil and Argentina) basically functions as "unemployment insurance" in the face of insufficient labor demand to absorb the supply, as well as demand dips. It is not surprising that in this scenario the answer to low coverage has come from the assistance or noncontributory branch of social protection (figure 12.2).

Contributory Programs

The main social security fund in Paraguay is the IPS, organized via a pay-as-you-go or defined benefit system, which exhibits a surplus balance given the high active/retired ratio. In 2012 the system received contributions from 436,000 private-sector workers[8] and paid pension benefits to 39,600 retirees and pensioners, doubling levels from 2002. The average benefit paid by the IPS was approximately ₲2.8 million, equal to US$660 per month. The US$313 million spent on retirements and pensions in 2012 represents 1.5 percent of GDP. Employee and employer contribution levels vary by economic activity, but they do not exceed 23 percent of salary (9 percent from workers and 14 percent from employers). The system manages funds for old age and survivors pensions, illness, and maternity, which are funded with contributions of 12.5 percent, 9 percent, and 1.5 percent, respectively.

Private sector workers are overrepresented in the contributory social protection system, except for a set of retirement funds for workers from the public

Figure 12.2 Labor Market and Pension Coverage, 2008–11

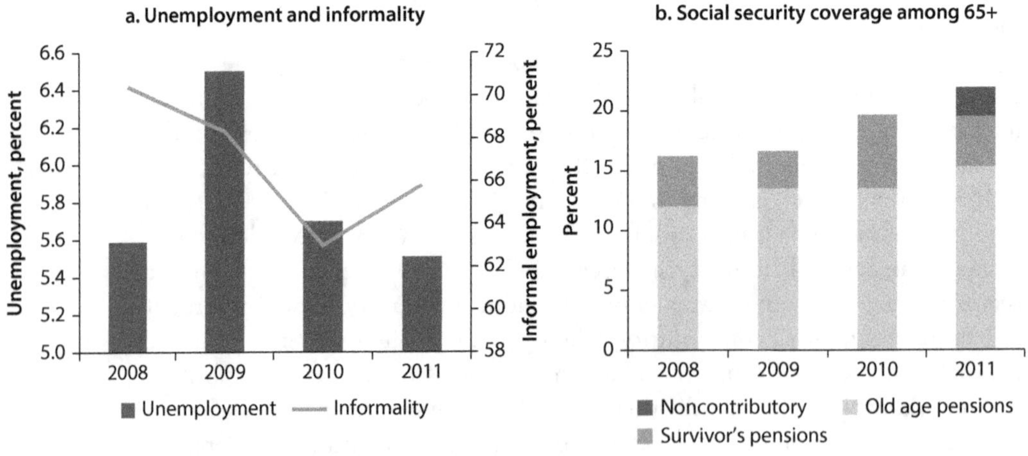

Source: Based on Permanent Household Survey (Encuesta Permanente de Hogares [EPH]).

Table 12.1 Active and Retired Workers, by Pension Fund, 2003, 2007, 2012

	Active		*Retired*	
	2003[a]	*2012*[b]	*2007*[c]	*2012*[d]
IPS[e]	180,000	436,000	23,000	39,858
Municipal fund	7,761	6,750	946	1,538
Banking fund	4,518	9,870	—	2,623
ANDE fund	3,000	5,200	841	1,290
Itaipu fund	1,800	1,896	738	—
Railroad fund	138	—	784	610
Parliamentary fund	125	124	159	—
Fiscal fund	151,056	172,856	55,504	107,630
Contributory	—	—	30,938	45,555
Noncontributory	n.a.	n.a.	24,566	13,393
Elderly	n.a.	n.a.	n.a.	48,682

Note: ANDE = National Electricity Administration; IPS = Instituto de Previsión Social; — = not available; n.a. = not applicable.
a. Rodríguez Silvero 2003.
b. Treasury Ministry 2012a.
c. World Bank 2009.
d. Ortiz Trepowski and Navarro Amarilla 2012.
e. Social Security Institute 2012.

sector or state enterprises (table 12.1). Eight providers make up the universe of contributory pension service providers: the IPS, the contributory regime of the Fiscal Fund, the retirement and pension funds for (a) municipal employees, (b) banking employees, (c) National Electricity Administration (ANDE), (d) Itaipu Bi-National, (e) railroad employees and workers, and (f) legislative branch members. The nonregulated entities that offer contributory systems with fully funded schemes consist of the following funds: (a) Cooperative Mutual, (b) Media and University Professionals, (c) UCA Educational Staff Mutual Company,[9] and (d) Chaco Social Security.

The IPS is the main retirement fund in terms of contributors and the second in terms of beneficiaries. The ratio of active workers to retired workers increased from 8 to 11 between 2003 and 2012, which helps explain the institution's surplus. The Fiscal Fund, the responsibility of the Treasury Ministry, administers retirements, pensions, and "payments" to beneficiaries, which are categorized in reports available for the contributory and noncontributory schemes. To better identify the relative importance of the Elderly program, table 12.1 shows the number of retired workers from these three groups of beneficiaries separately. We can observe that by the end of 2012, the Elderly program had become the program with the most beneficiaries in Paraguay. We can also observe that the numbers of active and retired workers in the other contributory funds are relatively lower with lower active to retired ratios that vary between 7 and 3.

The financial unsustainability of the smaller pension funds is evidence of the need for parametric reforms in the short term or the establishment of a homogenous and uniform social security system that would allow authorities to improve the administrative efficiency of social security management in Paraguay. The group of contributory pay-as-you-go pension providers demonstrates a wide variety of eligibility criteria. Contributions range from 5 percent to 18 percent for ANDE and the Parliamentary Fund, respectively. The retirement age varies from 40 (teachers) to 60 years (IPS, Banking Fund, and ANDE). The minimum period of contributions ranges from 10 years for the Itaipu Fund and legislative staff, to 30 years for the Fiscal, Banking, and IPS funds. The replacement rate varies from 100 percent in the case of the Railroad and Banking funds to 60 percent in the case of the Municipal Fund and the IPS (60 percent of the average of the last 36 salaries). Interestingly, workers' contributions to the IPS are portable among social security systems within MERCOSUR, but not to other Pension Funds or Mutual Companies in Paraguay. Benefits vary by pension fund and include social protection coverage for the elderly and disability insurance (for occupational hazards), survivor's benefits, and maternity benefits in some cases.

Noncontributory Regimes

The Fiscal Fund groups together the pension funds for public employees. The largest include the groups of workers in public administration, teachers, university professors, police, armed forces, and judicial employees. The Directorate of the Treasury Ministry that administers the Fiscal Fund does not manage the "notionally" contributory funds (14 percent of the salary of covered public employees) but instead makes payments based on the budgetary resources assigned to the Treasury Ministry. The benefits paid by the Fiscal Fund include elderly pensions, disability, and survivor's benefits. The system has almost 150,000 contributors and 30,000 pensioners. According to Holst (2003) the Fiscal Fund's deficit amounted to 1.8 percent of GDP in 2000.

Theoretically the Fiscal Fund is comprised of contributory and noncontributory regimes. In practice, the funds of the different public workers' groups operate only as "notionally" contributory schemes given that potential beneficiaries experience a salary reduction in the amount equivalent to their personal contributions. The Fiscal Fund makes the payments based on the funds that are allocated in the national budget to the directorates of contributory and NCPs, respectively. At the same time, the Fiscal Fund pays the benefits of the traditional noncontributory programs such as the war veterans pension regime and ex gratia pensions. A report from the World Bank (2004) pointed out that the number of benefits (equal to one minimum salary) appeared relatively high for the number of possible surviving participants from that war. Figure 12.3 presents the joint distribution of amounts and quantity of benefits paid for each program administered by the Treasury Ministry.

The Elderly program stands out from the rest, not only because of its higher coverage, but also because it is less "generous" based on the benefit amount that it provides. Although this program is still in a process of geographic expansion, and therefore coverage expansion as well, in 2012 it covered more people than the group of so-called contributory and noncontributory programs administered

Figure 12.3 Retirement Benefits and Pensions Paid by the Fiscal Fund (Treasury Ministry), 2012

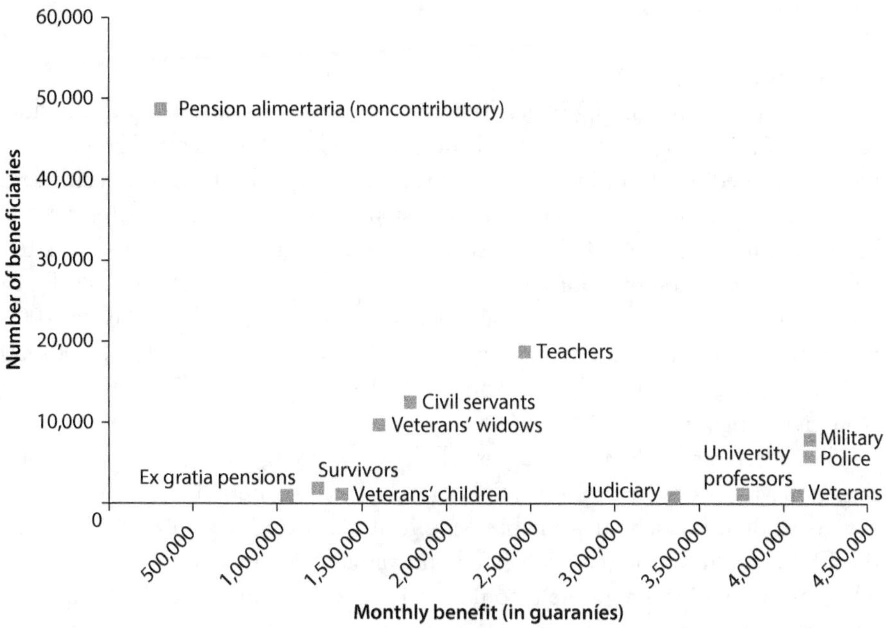

Source: Based on Treasury Ministry 2012b.

by the Fiscal Fund. By design, the Elderly program pays one-fourth of the current minimum salary.[10] All of the "contributory" or retirement programs administered by the Fiscal Fund paid average[11] benefits that were higher than the minimum salary in 2012. The majority of the "noncontributory" or pension programs paid benefits below the minimum salary, but above 1 million guaraníes, that is, more than double the Elderly benefit.

Reforms to Expand Coverage

Although NCP programs exist to transfer resources to the elderly, social protection increased the social inclusion of this population group after the expansion of the social assistance components. Since 2005 social protection in Paraguay has begun to fight against poverty and improve income distribution through the implementation of income transfer programs with noncontributory funding. Two excluding programs stand out among this group of initiatives: (1) Monetary Transfers with Coresponsibility (Transferencias Monetarias con Corresponsabilidad [TMC]) and (2) noncontributory pensions (Pensiones No Contributivas).

These programs show many similarities and overlaps that indicate the absence of a system of social protection that brings these interventions together and makes the public social spending more efficient. In contrast to the TMCs, the NCP programs do not include any elements of co-responsibility in their design[12] and are an indefinite-term income transfer. Because both programs directly or indirectly provide social inclusion to the elderly over age 65, they are discussed together in this section.

TMC Programs

The TMC programs, among which Tekopora stands out, aim to achieve the dual goal of alleviating income poverty in the short and medium term. The program focuses on medium-term intervention through a demand subsidy on health care and educational services. Using coresponsibility as a vehicle to improve the human capital of children in the household, these programs propose to break the intergenerational transmission of poverty. Initially launched in 2005 as a pilot in just a few municipalities, this program's coverage expanded quickly in 2009 under the direction of then president Lugo, increasing from 18,000 to 90,000 beneficiaries in 2010, including the TMC Pro-Country II (Pro-País II) and Ñopytivo programs.[13]

The elderly are indirectly and partially covered by the TMC programs. Even though TMC programs are not explicitly targeted to the elderly, they may be covered if their household is eligible. Modifications introduced in 2009 increased the TMC benefit amounts (both fixed and variable) and expanded the number of reasons for which a household could receive these variable amounts. Originally only the existence of children under 16 years old (later increased to 18 years old) up to a maximum of four children entitled the household to receive a variable, uniform amount for each of child. In addition, in 2009 households could also receive a variable amount in the event they contained persons with disabilities (up to one person), elderly (up to one person), or pregnant women.

The TMC Tekopora program suffered severe financial problems that impeded its implementation and distorted the initial objectives of fighting against poverty in the short and medium term. Although monitoring information is scarce, a World Bank report (2010) compiled separate publications and constructed a series that shows the evolution of the program. Between 2005 and 2008 the program increased from approximately 5,000 to18,000 beneficiaries. After 2009, the program began a process of rapid geographic expansion, reaching coverage of around 90,000 people by the end of 2010. From 2011 on, the budget projection included in the original projects was modified before its approval in Congress, delaying the periodic payment of benefits, forcing late retroactive benefit payments, and, more recently, preventing the payment of the program's six bimonthly disbursements. It is not surprising in this context that the households that have the ability to choose between the TMC Tekopora and Elderly programs lean toward the one that offers more certainty and foresight in terms of payments.

The NCP Program

The Elderly program, launched in 2010, consists of a monthly cash transfer to persons over age 65 living in poverty. According to estimates made at the time of the launch of the implementation strategy, the target population was around 100,000 people. The benefit amount is 25 percent of the minimum salary (about US$100). Once the goal is reached, this program will consume US$120 million annually, approximately 0.65 percent of GDP at current 2010 prices. The Directorate of Noncontributory Pensions from the Treasury Ministry administers benefit payments. This agency reported that in 2012 the program had reached 48,602 beneficiaries. Staff from the Secretariat of Social Action (Secretaría de Acción Social [SAS]) and the General Directorate of Statistics, Surveys, and Censuses (Dirección General de Estadística, Encuestas y Censos), and the Social Economy Unit (Unidad de Economía Social) oversee the use of the targeting tool. Beneficiaries receive their pensions directly through debit cards from the Development Bank (Banco de Fomento).

The implementation and expansion strategy was very similar to the one undertaken by the TMC Tekopora five years earlier. Based on a geographic prioritization index (combination of income poverty and unsatisfied basic needs), the municipalities were ranked, and the program began in the geographic areas with the greatest needs. In the selected municipalities implementers use a targeting tool or quality of life index (Índice de Calidad de Vida [ICV]) that indirectly approximates household poverty based on an algorithm that combines 29 variables (characteristics of the household, dwelling, and possession of consumption goods) and calculates a score from 1 to 100. Based on this mechanism, those that score below 40 are considered poor and therefore eligible to be included in the program.[14]

There are many overlaps between the TMC Tekopora and the Elderly programs. First, the coverage areas of both programs overlap, leaving areas without coverage, at least until the geographic expansion process is able to cover all of Paraguay. Second, both programs use the same outdated tool for targeting. Even though the existence of the ICV is a drastic improvement compared to the rest of social assistance programs, it was developed in 2002 and implemented for the first time in 2005.[15] Third, both programs include the elderly in poverty as a target population. In the case of the TMC Tekopora, they mean an additional benefit for being in the targeted household, whereas in the case of the Elderly program they are the only target population. Given the characteristics of the construction of the ICV, many of the variables require on-site observation (i.e., main material in roofing, floor, or walls) of characteristics of the dwelling. This strategy for registering potential beneficiaries, combined with the limited institutional capacity of the organization in charge of carrying out this process, does not result in a dynamic process for enrolling and dismissing beneficiaries. This is especially relevant for the Elderly program, both for verifying the dismissals as well as for future enrollments, as the younger age cohorts reach the minimum age and become eligible.

As poverty-fighting strategies, NCPs have some advantages over TMCs. First, NCPs feature automatic benefit indexation, based on the minimum salary. The institutionalization of indexation confers greater transparency and external validation to the program, at the same time that it makes budget planning less predictable because it depends on an external factor such as the minimum salary. Second, the absence of coresponsibility as a counterpart of the transfer simplifies the program's administration. Third, NCPs target a population segment for which it is difficult to argue that there are adverse incentives for economic activity. Conversely, the lower employability of the population in this age group makes the poverty reduction role of a program like the NCP more relevant and noticeable.

The Policy Behind the Reform

The expansion of social protection coverage in Paraguay has been the victim of political tensions between the government and the opposition, the executive branch and the legislative branch, and even within the governing coalition of ex-president Lugo. Raising the flags of redistribution, the former president prioritized, both as a matter of discourse and in fact, the expansion of the TMC programs. The SAS's budgetary expansion forced the institution to face an institutional challenge without precedent. In 2009 the external economic context helped to justify this redistributive and, especially, countercyclical expansion that also honored campaign promises.[16] Having learned how to implement the process, and achieved some of the geographic expansion and coverage goals, the administration flaunted its accomplishment, and the opposition reacted as a consequence. First, the legislature approved legislation that decentralized the resources and administration of the TMC Tekopora program to the municipalities. President Lugo vetoed this law. Later, budget cuts seriously affected the implementing institutions' capacity to face the payment obligations they had assumed with the beneficiaries,[17] distorting the concept of coresponsibility and of the program itself.

While the TMC programs expanded their coverage, the government was developing another profound modification to Paraguay's social protection system. In 2009 Law no. 3,728 was approved, which created the nutritional pension for the elderly living in poverty. The bill had been sent to the Congress during the administration of then president Nicanor Duarte Frutos, and vetoed by then president Fernando Lugo. Congress overrode the presidential veto, and the law was certified by Decrees no. 4,542 and no. 4,728 of 2010. Although the program must target the poor population, it does not have an a priori budget limitation, opening the debate about the universality of the entitlements and social inclusion for all. Regardless of the theoretical and conceptual debate, the passage of this law, on the one hand, forced the administration to rethink its budget priorities in the face of the need to incur unforeseen spending, or at least spending that was not the result of one of the projects from its own electoral platform. On the other hand, the need to veto a bill that Congress had originally passed represented a political cost for a leader that arrived in power based on discourse supported by income redistribution.

The budget limitation on projects pushed by the government along with the approval of other preexisting high-cost projects demonstrate that Paraguay was not facing a classic political economy problem in which redistribution creates winners and losers, but rather a political problem among the various participants in the separation of republican powers. Many of the overlaps of geographic coverage, beneficiary eligibility, and targeting instruments between TMC Tekopora and Elderly reflect the lack of institutional capacity to organize and coordinate social protection, but fundamentally, the lack of coordinated, consensus-based, and predictable decision making. In this context it would appear to be clear that the potential gains in social protection in Paraguay will not come from increased spending, but rather from an improvement in the efficiency of the system. It does not appear to be impossible, but it clearly requires political consensus, which was not guaranteed during the Lugo-Franco administration.

The Impact of the Elderly Program

Social security coverage in Paraguay decreased markedly in the 1990s and mainly affected men and the poorest sectors of income earners. Male social security coverage fell by more than than half in percentage terms between the 1980s and the first decade of the 21st century. In contrast to coverage of women, mostly made up of those entitled to pensions from previous retirees, the coverage of men fell from covering 55 percent of those over 65 to less than 20 percent two decades later (figure 12.4). This reduction in social security coverage affected the least advantaged sectors of the society differently. The social security coverage gap between the richest and poorest quintiles has doubled since the 1980s. Although social security coverage among the elderly over age 65 in the richest quintile remained stable or increased slightly, the proportion of persons in the poorest quintile of per capita income that received retirement or pension benefits was practically nonexistent during the last 15 years.

Contributory social security proved inadequate as a tool for combating poverty and improving income distribution in Paraguay. Even though the implementation of the government's actions aimed at improving the population's well-being

Figure 12.4 Social Security Coverage of Persons over Age 65, by Gender and Per Capita Income Quintile, 1983–2009

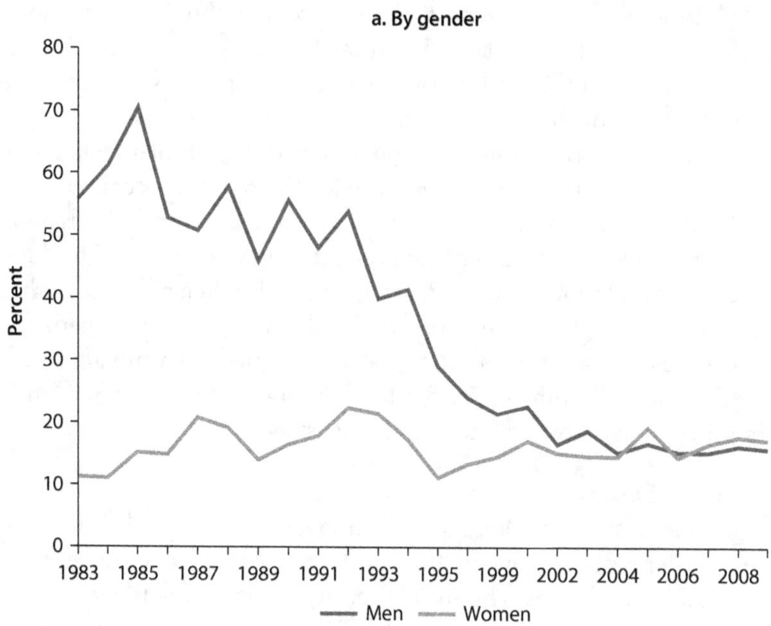

figure continues next page

Figure 12.4 Social Security Coverage of Persons over Age 65, by Gender and Per Capita Income Quintile, 1983–2009 *(continued)*

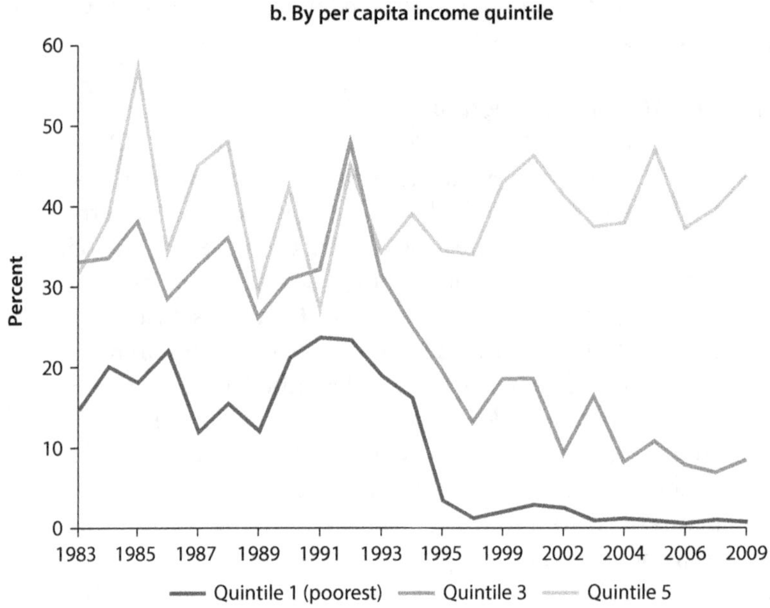

Source: Rofman and Oliveri 2012.

do not appear to have emerged from a consensus-based and planned strategy, the initiatives could be considered appropriate in virtue of the social protection framework in Paraguay until 2008. The initial expansion of TMC Tekopora, which by virtue of being a benefit for the entire household managed to extend coverage to some elderly over age 65, and the later expansion of the Elderly program were aimed at utilizing income transfer programs as supplements to the proven inefficiency of the social security funds. The consensus achieved around the need to target the programs to the poorest, and their implementation using a targeting mechanism, has been consistent with the previous scenario. Just as we have avoided referring to the set of contributory social security funds as a social security system, we also consider it appropriate to avoid referring to the recent innovations in social protection as a reform, especially when referring to the social security component. The recent process could possibly be categorized more appropriately as a maturation of social protection aimed at improving distributive equality and the opportunities for the less-advantaged through noncontributory transfer programs, also referred to as social assistance.

Redistributive Effects

The expansion of the social assistance components is clearly aimed at directing income transfer policies toward the most unprotected extreme that is also concentrated in rural areas. The social security components transfer income to the highest quintiles of the income distribution, which are overrepresented in urban areas. The noncontributory social assistance programs began their implementation in rural areas, including their expansion to the peripheral zones around the urban areas, such as the wetlands around the capital, Asunción. Figure 12.5b shows how much the TMC Tekopora and the Elderly programs have focused on the lowest percentiles of the income distribution, whereas the Retirement and Pension benefits do likewise in the highest percentiles of the same per capita income distribution.

The expansion of the Elderly program was carried out by transferring beneficiaries from the TMC Tekopora program. The population over age 65 adds up to about 430,000 people. In 2010 the TMC Tekopora covered 11,300 of this population (2.7 percent), but in 2011 the coverage had been reduced in absolute values to half that (5,100 people, equal to 1.2 percent); see figure 12.5a. According to the 2011 EPH, the number of persons covered by the Elderly program amounted to 13,700 (3.1 percent of the total over age 65 population). Given the geographic overlap between both programs, the incompatibility between the two forced beneficiaries to choose between these mutually exclusive programs.

These coverage expansion initiatives could have had greater impact if they had been considered complementary. The nature of the strategy that was chosen demonstrates that the public expenditure involved could improve its efficiency without the need to increase the amount of spending.

The Results of Existing Evaluations

The impact evaluations of the programs mentioned here are as numerous as the monitoring information that the programs themselves allow. Two impact

Figure 12.5 Social Security Coverage and Distributive Impact

a. Persons over age 65 covered by contributory pensions, TMC or NCP, 2010–11

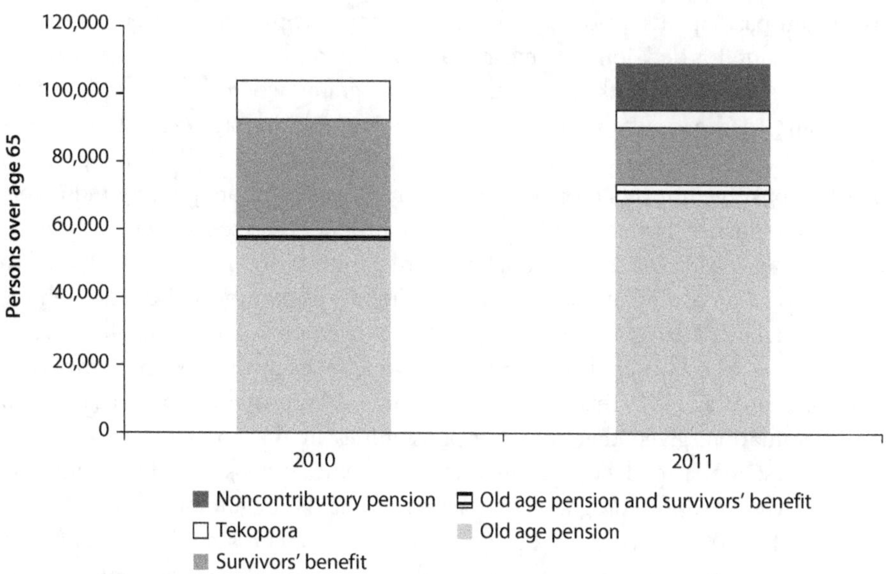

figure continues next page

Figure 12.5 Social Security Coverage and Distributive Impact *(continued)*

b. Distributive incidence curves: contributory pensions, TMC and NCP, 2011

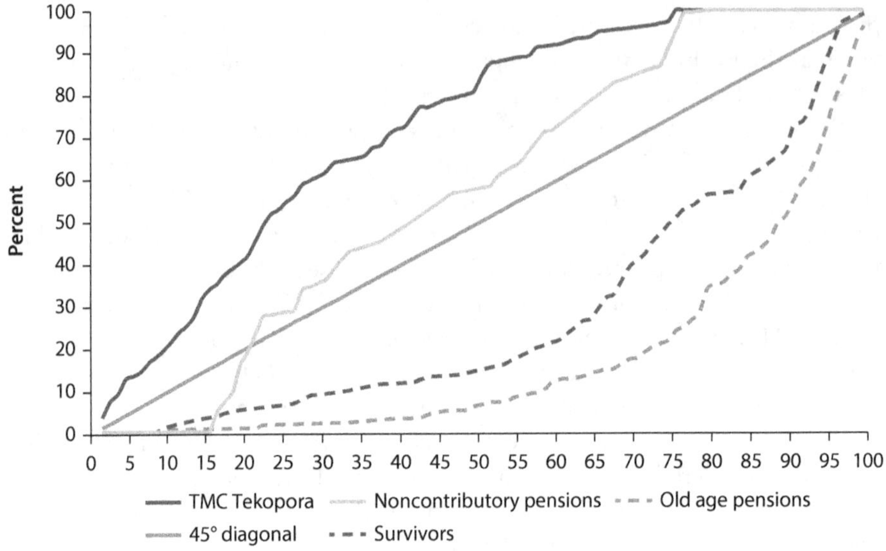

Source: Based on Permanent Household Survey (Encuesta Permanente de Hogares, EPH).
Note: NCP = noncontributory pension; TMC = Transferencias Monetarias con Corresponsabilidad.

evaluations of the TMC Tekopora and Elderly programs are available. In both cases they are pseudo-experimental designs based on small samples in the pilot or early stages of the programs. Even though both evaluations highlight the limitations and assumptions necessary for the interpretation and validity of the results, the introduction of comparisons of temporary changes between the experimental groups (program participants) and control groups (nonparticipants) represents a toolkit of great value for decision making, at least for the implementers themselves.

The expansion of both noncontributory programs would have been positive, according to the results obtained from the available impact evaluations. Veras Soares, Perez Ribas, and Hirata (2008) maintain that the TMC Tekopora program has had positive impacts on per capita income, consumption, poverty reduction, school attendance, investment in agricultural production, access to credit, savings, and social participation. Even though this program was not exclusively directed to the elderly over age 65, it included them indirectly as members of the household. The incidence of poverty among this population group is a result of the poverty reduction in the households where they live. However, the design elements of programs such as TMC Tekopora do not include actions that can be considered in their evaluation, given that the coresponsibilities in the program are aimed at children (school attendance, vaccination, and medical checkups). The evaluation of the TMC Tekopora program was carried out at the beginning of 2007 with a sample of 1,400 observations, using administrative records as the baseline, and taking two districts where the program had not yet expanded as the control group for comparison to the five districts where the program had already expanded.

The evaluation of the Elderly program reports that there had been a short-term impact on health, housing quality, and subjective perceptions of well-being. This evaluation was carried out in 2011, comprised 1,200 observations, and was limited to the waterfront area of Asunción. Using the registration information from the targeting instrument and through the difference-in-differences technique, this evaluation observed the behavior of beneficiaries and nonbeneficiaries in two moments in time, one year apart. The program appears to have had an immediate effect with respect to the chronic deficiencies such as open sewage or wells, health insurance, and incidence of illnesses. Given the original differences between the experimental and control groups, as a result of the application of a targeting tool, the program appears to have reduced the deficiencies of the beneficiaries with respect to those who registered but were not able to participate.[18]

The Elderly program reduced poverty among the elderly over age 65 by 1 or 2 percentage points. The effects of the income transfer programs are marginal in poverty reduction for the total poverty of Paraguay due to their coverage and "generosity." However, among adults over age 65 the effects of the Elderly program benefit are relatively more apparent. The poverty rate for this population group remained almost unchanged in the simulation without the TMC Tekopora program. Nonetheless, in the simulation without the Elderly program, the poverty rate increased by almost one percentage point (figure 12.6). Given that the

Figure 12.6 Total and Simulated Poverty Rates (without NCP, without TMC, and without Either), by Total Population, Population over Age 65, and Households, 2011

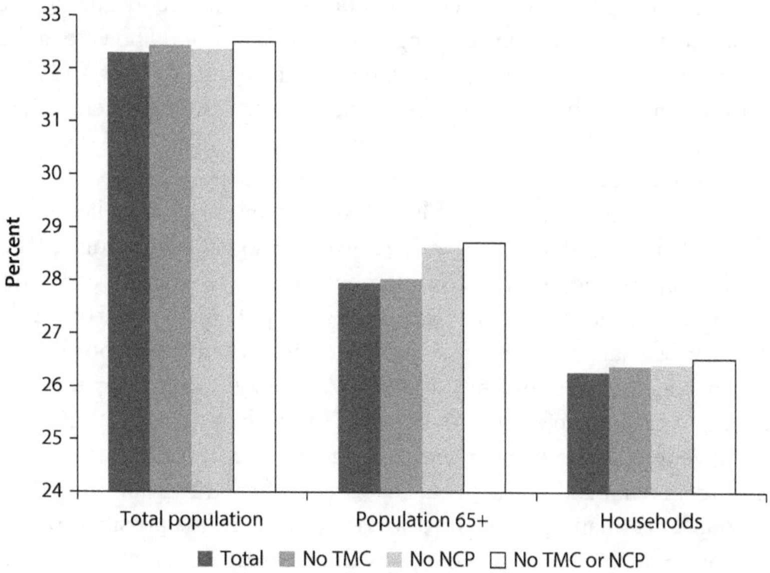

Source: Based on Permanent Household Survey (Encuesta Permanente de Hogares, EPH).
Note: NCP = noncontributory pension; TMC = Transferencias Monetarias con Corresponsabilidad.

program began its geographic expansion in 2011, this figure could double once the expansion goals are met. In the absence of appropriate sources of information, a World Bank report (2010) simulated the effects that these programs would have once their expansion was complete and forecasted a decrease in the poverty rate, ceteris paribus, of two percentage points.

Summary and Conclusions

In the last decade, Paraguay has expanded social protection coverage through noncontributory social assistance programs that transfer income to specific population groups. These programs aim to reduce poverty in the short and long term, provided that they improve income distribution. Coverage expansion occurred through two types of programs that directly and indirectly covered the elderly over age 65.

Neither demographics nor the socioeconomic conditions of the elderly appear to have been the fundamental causes to explain the launch of a social assistance program directed exclusively to the elderly population. Even though the effects and evolution of poverty specific to this age group could be used as an argument, an ideal instrument was at hand to remedy these problems: the TMC Tekopora program. In fact, this program changed its benefit structure to include a variable amount in the event that an adult over age 65 lived in the household.

In this chapter I argue that the principal reason that explains the expansion of social security coverage is Paraguay's own political process. The bill that was approved was not part of the electoral platform of then president Lugo; it had been presented but had not been dealt with by Congress during the government of his predecessor Nicanor Duarte Frutos. The bill's passage created a significant budget commitment for the executive branch, which had begun to increase social spending on another similar program, TMC Tekopora. The veto and subsequent congressional override speak to the different points of view and the internal political tension. The existing institutional capacity to implement this second social assistance program forced the implementers to replicate the strategy of the TMC Tekopora program.

Despite not having been developed with consensus, the launch of the Elderly program exhibits lessons and mistakes for social protection in Paraguay. Among the smart choices, the complementary role that social assistance can play in the face of social security's lack of ability to fight poverty stands out. Contributory social security comprises little more than an uncoordinated and fragmented pension regime that offers low coverage to the upper reaches of the income distribution, who live in urban areas. In this sense the strategy of beginning geographic expansion gradually in the neediest rural areas and using a targeting mechanism have been consistent with the prior diagnosis. The institutional and financial capacities will determine if it is possible to close the gap and provide "universal" coverage to the poorest in Paraguay. The criteria chosen to fight poverty and improve income distribution have been clearly propoor.

Among the mistakes, the lack of a social protection system that can strategically and rationally decide in a harmonious and coordinated manner the most efficient way to use resources destined for social spending and investment stands out. Social protection in Paraguay has not been characterized by coordination and comprehensiveness. The coexistence and incompatibility of pension regimes, and the multiplicity of TMC programs with nearly identical designs, are evidence of this lack of coordination. The duplication of the geographic expansion strategy of similar but supplementary programs, the use of the same targeting mechanism, and the lack of updates to this mechanism are proof of the institutional capacity limitations to orchestrate social protection and the lack of consensus to carry it out consistently. The coverage of social protection programs could be improved through a more rational and strategic use that avoids overlaps and coverage gaps throughout the process of geographic expansion.

The use of the same social spending targeting mechanism to prioritize the fight against poverty could be interpreted in two ways. The positive interpretation highlights the propoor nature of social spending and investment through the implementation of a tool designed to achieve that goal. In addition, this process legitimizes the use of funds as long as eligibility criteria are part of an objective, predefined mechanism. The negative interpretation expresses the overlap of the goals of similar programs. The rationale for using a targeting mechanism is to estimate the condition of poverty. If two similar programs (income transfer) can use the same tool to identify their target population, it is clear that they are focused on the same goal: reducing poverty and improving income distribution. The question then becomes: why duplicate (or multiply) the administrative structures and repeat the registration processes?

The biggest challenge in Paraguay for social protection in general and for social security in particular is putting together a system that allows authorities to more efficiently use social spending resources. The strategy for the fight against poverty requires that such a system work. The development and strengthening of institutional capacities is essential to implement it. Improvements in technical aspects also require political consensus, as we can see from the implementation of the Elderly program.

Notes

1. According to CELADE's classifications of demographic transitions, countries can be grouped into four stages according to the natural growth rate. The stages are Incipient (higher than 2.5 percent annual), Moderate (around 2.5 percent annual), Full (around 2 percent annual), and Advanced (around 1 percent annual).
2. Health coverage is only associated with pension coverage in four pension funds: the IPS, the Medical Fund, the Chaco Social Security for the Mennonites in Chaco Central, and university professionals.
3. Even though it is not a family allowance scheme, maternity benefits from the IPS can be similar to some of the benefits that these social security subsystems offer.

4. Note that we avoid mentioning the set of contributory schemes, given the noncontributory nature of the Fiscal Fund (Caja Fiscal).
5. For an explanation of this assertion, see the subsection on noncontributory regimes later in this chapter.
6. Holst (2003) mentions the following nonregulated entities that ceased operations: Private Retirements and Pensions (Jubilaciones y Pensiones Privadas), a mutual retirement fund that formed part of the Family Well-Being Group (Grupo Bienestar Familiar); the Union of Mutual Fund Administrators (Unión de Administradoras de Fondos Mutuos); and the Pension Program of the Union Bank Public Limited Investment and Development Company (Programa Previsional del Banco Unión Sociedad Anónima de Inversión y Fomento).
7. We define informality here as salaried or self-employed work without contributions to Social Security.
8. It is worth mentioning that the quantity of contributors has doubled since 2002 (see Social Security Institute 2012).
9. Catholic University of Asunción (Universidad Católica de Asunción).
10. At the time of this report, the minimum salary in Paraguay amounted to ₲1,658,232, approximately equivalent to US$370 at the current exchange rate. This minimum salary was most recently adjusted in April 2011.
11. The information available is not ideal in terms of frequency and quality. Here the paid amounts have been estimated based on the sums exercised for each budget line item, which in some cases can include the programs' administrative costs. As such, the author would like to clarify that the reported amounts are estimates of the average benefits received by beneficiaries.
12. The beneficiaries must present a Life and Residence Certificate issued by a justice of the peace or commissioner.
13. In the case of Pro-Country II, the expansion is explained by the existence of a program with minimal (if any) differences in design and implementation that had its own source of funding (loan from the Inter-American Development Bank). In the case of Ñopytivo, this TMC program exhibited very limited coverage of just about 500 households, whose main characteristic was the ethnic origin (hometowns) of its beneficiaries, in addition to in-kind instead of cash payments. The profusion of similar programs and the minimal levels of coverage that some of them have are further evidence of the need for a social protection system that would organize and coordinate the interventions, minimizing the multiple organizational structures that generate socially inefficient administrative spending relative to the covered population.
14. There is also a process of community validation to include beneficiaries.
15. A decade after its first estimate, many of the variables that were associated with poverty and helped in scoring it have changed and are no longer relevant predictors (among them, possession of a cell phone or motorcycle).
16. The international economic crisis that began in the real estate finance sector in the United States spread throughout the world and affected the prices of various primary products. Many countries in the region were affected by the triple F crisis: food, fuel, and financial crisis. However, the effects on the Paraguayan economy were minor, in part because the country was a "beneficiary" of an increase in the price of primary foodstuffs, especially soy.

17. In some cases the cuts forced payment delays that were later caught up retroactively. In other cases the delays stretched to six months, and the skipped payments were not paid retroactively.
18. By virtue of the use of the ICV targeting tool, the socioeconomic characteristics and possession of goods corresponding to the nonbeneficiaries is higher than that of the beneficiaries.

References

Holst, J. 2003. "La protección social en Paraguay Condiciones, problemas, desafíos y perspectivas de los sistemas de previsión." GTZ-PLANDES y Secretaria Técnica de Planificación, Asunción.

Mesa-Lagoa, C. 1991. *Social Security and Prospects for Equity in Latin America.* Washington, DC: World Bank.

Ortiz Trepowski, E., and B. Navarro Amarilla. 2012. "La protección de la población paraguaya por los sistemas jubilatorios." Instituto Paraguayo de Investigaciones Económicas, Asunción.

Rodríguez Silvero, R. 2003. "Seguridad Social Descripción del Sistema Vigente de Jubilaciones y Pensiones en Paraguay." Secretaria Técnica de Planificación, Proyecto PLANDES, Asunción.

Rofman, R., and M. L. Oliveri. 2012. "La cobertura de los sistemas previsionales en América Latina: conceptos e indicadores." Serie de Documentos de Trabajo sobre Políticas Sociales 7, World Bank, Buenos Aires.

Social Security Institute. 2012. "Informe de Gestión." Social Security Institute, Asunción.

Treasury Ministry. 2012a. "Balance Anual de Gestión Pública Dirección de Pensiones no Contributivas." Treasury Ministry, Asunción.

———. 2012b. "Informe Financiero 2012. Control Financiero y Evaluación Presupuestaria." Treasury Ministry, Asunción.

———. 2012c. "La Política de Pensión Alimentaria para Adultos Mayores en el Paraguay. Resultados y desafíos." Treasury Ministry, Asunción.

Veras Soares, F., R. Perez Ribas, and G. Hirata. 2008. "Achievements and Shortfalls of Conditional Cash Transfers: Impact Evaluation of Paraguay's Tekoporã Programme." Evaluation Note 3, International Poverty Centre, Asunción.

World Bank. 2004. *Paraguay. Definir una estrategia para la política de Protección Social.* Reporte 27352-PA, Social Protection Unit, Human Development Departament, Argentina, Chile, Paraguay, and Uruguay, World Bank, Regional Office for Latin America and the Caribbean.

———. 2009. "Notas de Politica." Nota 5, "Red de Proteccion y Seguridad Social." World Bank, Buenos Aires.

———. 2010. *Paraguay Poverty Assessment: Determinants and Challenges for Poverty Reduction.* Washington, DC: World Bank.

CHAPTER 13

Peru

Javier Olivera Angulo

History

The current situation of the elderly in Peru, a population showing continuous growth, reflects the extension of the living conditions they experience during their economically active periods to their elderly years. A significant portion of this population faces a situation of unmet needs and difficulties sustaining themselves economically, which limits their ability to retire from the labor market. The traditional pension system covers one-fourth of the population aged 65 and older, with even less coverage of those who live in rural areas and in the poorest regions of Peru.

Profile of the Elderly

Although Peru is currently classified as a country in the moderate stage of population aging, the continued increase in life expectancy and the fall in fertility (figure 13.1 and table 13.1) will accelerate its rate of aging. Currently the population aged 65 and older is about 6 percent of the total population, a percentage that is expected will increase to 17.1 percent in 2050 and to 29.9 percent in 2100 (CELADE 2011). Additionally, the share of the eldest individuals (persons age 80 and older) will grow substantially, from less than 1 percent of the population today to more than 12 percent in 2100.

On the one hand, the shift toward a lower fertility rate means that the elderly will have few children to support then, and on the other, the longer life expectancy will mean that adult children's cost of caring for their parents will stretch over a longer period. These two forces will necessarily reduce the value of the children as social insurance, which is more important as a substitute for social security for poor populations and of traditional values than in terms of parents' care.

The living conditions of the current generation of the elderly have been determined in good measure by the opportunities that they had in the past. Table 13.2 reveals the uncertainty surrounding these past opportunities for the elderly that today are between 65 and 80 years old. The high level of illiteracy and the low level of educational achievement among this generation, especially for women,

Figure 13.1 Population Structure, by Large Age Groups, 1950–2100

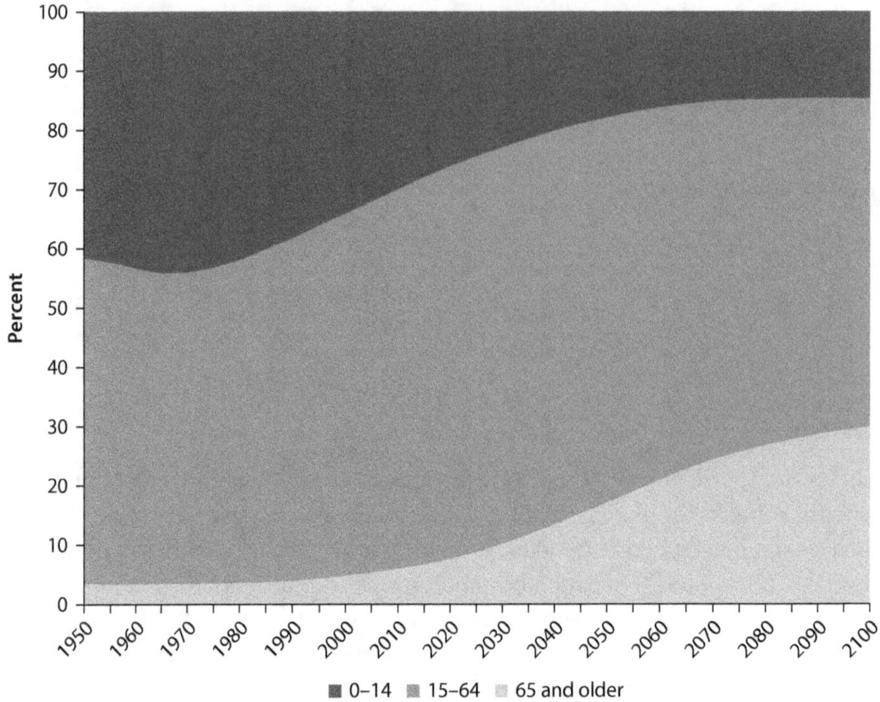

Source: Based on Centro Latinoamericano y Caribeño de Demografía (CELADE) 2011.

Table 13.1 Evolution of Demographic Indicators, 1950–2100

	1950	*1975*	*2000*	*2025*	*2050*	*2075*	*2100*
Total fertility rate	6.85	5.38	2.8	2.05	1.75	1.79	1.89
Life expectancy at birth	43.90	58.53	71.61	76.33	79.68	82.44	84.27
Percentage of population 65+	3.46	3.56	4.83	8.76	17.10	25.70	29.89
Percentage of population 80+	0.33	0.34	0.78	1.87	4.67	9.23	12.45

Source: Based on Centro Latinoamericano y Caribeño de Demografía (CELADE) 2011.

Table 13.2 Characteristics of Persons Aged 36–51 Years in the 1981 Census
Percent

Description	*Men*	*Women*	*Total*
Illiteracy	12	35	24
Primary education or less	67	77	72
Piped potable water within the dwelling	44	45	45
Piped sewer drainage within the dwelling	35	36	36
Dwelling walls made of good quality materials	37	36	37

Source: Based on 1981 Population Census, Instituto Nacional de Estadísticas (INEI).

stand out and have played a large part in determining their opportunities and current situations.

Additionally, we can observe the differences in education by region and level of poverty of the elderly. The literacy rate for individuals from 65 to 69 years old in urban areas is 86.2 percent, whereas in rural areas it is 49.3 percent. This indicates that the distribution of opportunities in the past has been noticeably unequal across the country (figure 13.2).

In terms of age group, the poverty rate among persons aged 65 and older is 28.4 percent, which is less than the national average of 30.8 percent. Children exhibit the highest poverty rate among all age groups. Until age 13, the poverty rate remains above 40 percent and then drops, only to increase again between 25 and 40 years old and after age 60 (figure 13.3).[1] Significant differences are seen between poverty measured in urban and rural areas: Levels are much higher in the latter. In 2010 the urban poverty rate was 20 percent, whereas the rate in rural areas was 61 percent. For persons aged 65 and older, the poverty rate was 16.7 percent in urban areas and 58.0 percent in rural areas.

Figure 13.4 shows rates for extreme poverty by age and by urban or rural area. The patterns by age and area are similar to those for the total poverty rate, but the incidence of extreme poverty in rural areas is much higher compared to urban areas. Essentially, extreme poverty affects the country's rural population much more. For persons aged 65 and older, the extreme poverty rate was 2.0 percent in urban areas and 24.5 percent in rural areas.

Figure 13.2 Literacy Rate, by Age Group and Area, 2007

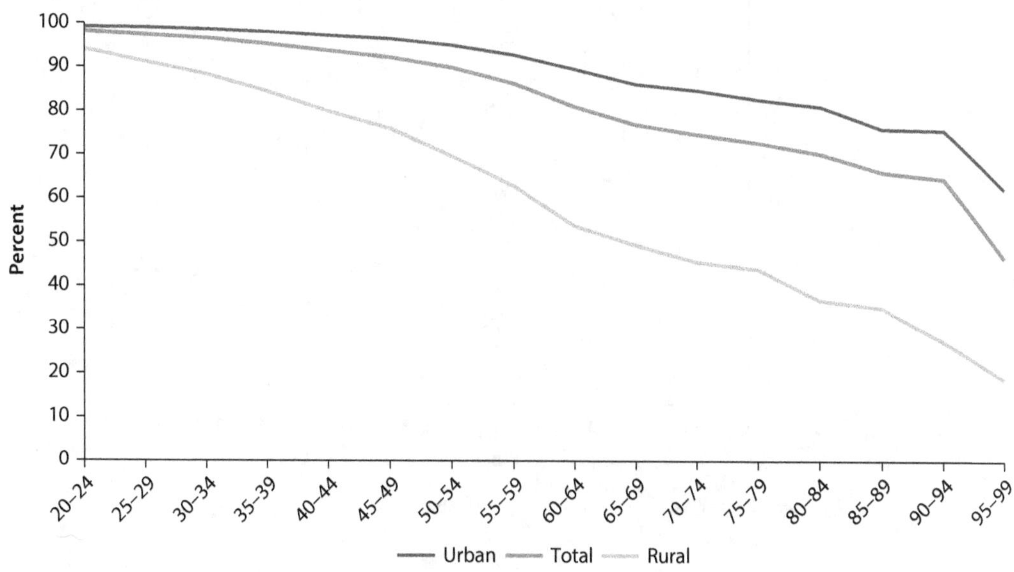

Source: Based on 2007 Population and Housing Census, Instituto Nacional de Estadísticas e Informática (INEI).

Figure 13.3 Poverty Rate, by Age and by Urban or Rural Area

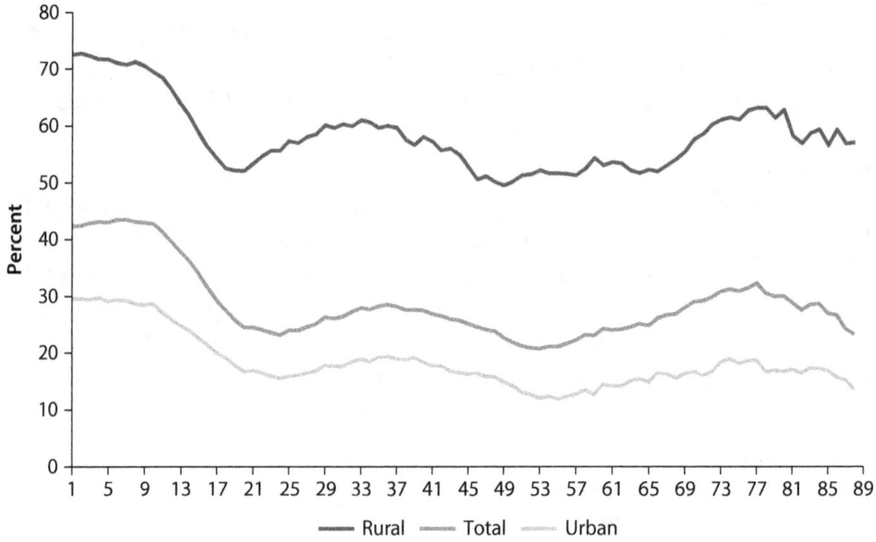

Source: Based on National Household Survey, Encuesta Nacional de Hogares (ENAHO) 2010.

Figure 13.4 Extreme Poverty Rate, by Age and by Urban or Rural Area, 2010

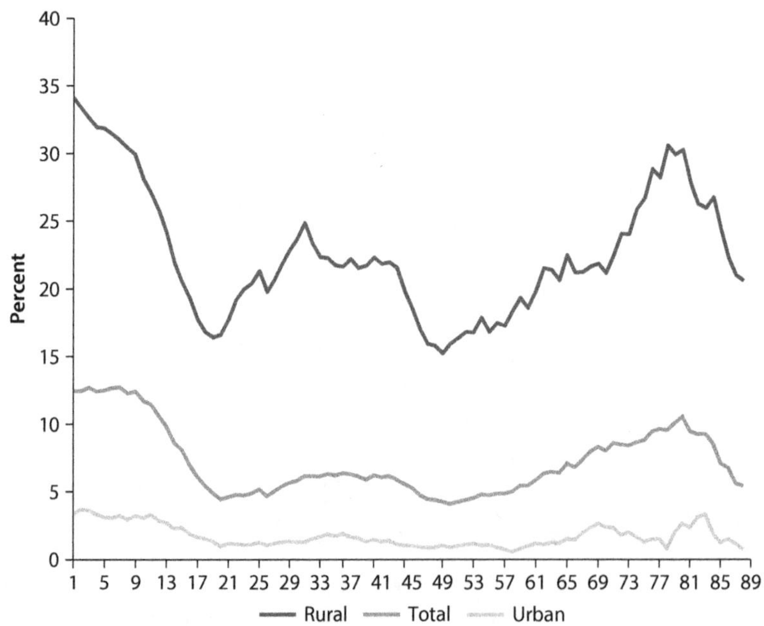

Source: Based on National Household Survey (ENAHO) 2010.

Similarly the differences among regions can be quite obvious. Although the incidence of poverty among individuals aged 65 and older exceeds 50 percent in Apurimac, Huancavelica, Puno, Huanuco, Cajamarca, and Ayacucho, it is below 13 percent in Lima, Tumbes, Ica, and Madre de Dios. Similarly, extreme poverty among the population as a whole can reach levels above 25 percent of the population (Apurimac and Huanuco) or less than 1 percent (Tumbes and Madre de Dios) (table 13.3).

Health is an important component of well-being, especially among the elderly, because their quality of life can deteriorate rapidly if their illnesses and discomforts are not treated adequately and opportunely. In particular, untreated illnesses can worsen and affect an elderly person's independence and autonomy. Peru faces a high percentage of the elderly that do not seek medical attention for their illnesses or they do so inadequately: They go to pharmacies or use

Table 13.3 Total Poverty Rate and among 65+ Population, by Region, 2010
Percent

	Total population			*Population age 65 and older*	
Region	*Poverty*	*Extreme poverty*	*Region*	*Poverty*	*Extreme poverty*
Huancavelica	63.0	21.8	Apurimac	64.0	30.2
Apurimac	62.0	24.1	Huancavelica	57.8	22.7
Cajamarca	55.2	23.0	Puno	56.3	23.3
Huanuco	54.7	22.1	Huanuco	51.0	25.5
Amazonas	50.5	18.6	Cajamarca	50.4	24.8
Loreto	49.8	19.5	Ayacucho	50.4	22.9
Puno	48.6	15.8	Loreto	44.8	15.4
Ayacucho	48.2	17.0	Pasco	42.1	17.1
Piura	44.3	9.6	Cusco	42.1	15.8
Cusco	42.7	12.4	Piura	41.9	8.1
Lambayeque	38.2	4.6	Lambayeque	41.2	7.5
San Martin	36.9	10.1	Amazonas	39.0	10.8
Pasco	36.3	8.5	San Martin	34.5	5.9
La Libertad	31.4	9.7	La Libertad	27.5	6.7
Junin	28.4	3.9	Junin	26.8	4.5
Ancasch	27.1	4.4	Ancash	24.6	5.6
Ucayali	21.7	4.2	Moquegua	19.6	3.4
Tumbes	19.7	0.2	Tacna	16.2	3.3
Lima	16.2	1.0	Ucayali	15.3	2.3
Moquegua	14.3	1.4	Arequipa	14.2	2.7
Tacna	14.2	1.1	Ica	12.6	0.5
Arequipa	13.6	1.9	Lima	11.9	1.1
Ica	12.4	0.2	Tumbes	11.3	0.3
Madre de Dios	5.0	0.5	Madre de Dios	3.1	0.0
Total	30.8	7.6	Total	28.4	8.3

Source: Based on National Household Survey (ENAHO) 2010.

traditional medicines. Indeed, 60 percent of the population aged 65 and older belongs to this category. However, significant differences are seen when the elderly population is categorized by poverty level: 82 percent, 72 percent, and 54 percent of the extremely poor, non-extreme poor, and non-poor, respectively, do not seek treatment for their illnesses or seek insufficient treatment. Differences also appear by geographic area; 54 percent of the elderly population does not seek medical attention for their illnesses or seeks insufficient attention in urban areas, and this percentage increases to 73 percent in rural areas.

With the help of population projections by region from the INEI (2010a) for 1995–2025, it is possible to estimate the survival rate for each age cohort for various years. Table 13.4 shows the probability of survival for the cohort of individuals that were 65 years old in 2012. For example, for each 100 people in Lima in 2012 that were aged 65, 74 would survive until 2025. In contrast, in Huancavelica, only 48 of 100 individuals would survive until 2025. The correlations between the survival rate until 2025 by region and the poverty rates are

Table 13.4 Probability of Survival to Age 65, Calculated in 2012
Percent

Region	*2012*	*2015*	*2020*	*2025*
Lima	100.0	95.4	86.3	73.6
Callao	100.0	94.5	85.1	72.5
Arequipa	100.0	94.7	84.7	72.1
Lambayeque	100.0	94.6	84.8	72.1
La Libertad	100.0	94.7	84.2	71.0
Ica	100.0	94.7	83.6	70.5
Moquegua	100.0	94.5	83.0	68.3
Tacna	100.0	93.7	82.3	68.0
Ucayali	100.0	93.0	78.9	63.4
Puno	100.0	93.6	80.0	64.0
Ancash	100.0	93.0	78.9	63.4
Tumbes	100.0	91.5	78.5	62.8
Huanuco	100.0	92.7	78.4	62.7
Piura	100.0	91.6	78.2	62.5
Madre de Dios	100.0	91.5	78.1	62.0
Junin	100.0	91.8	77.9	61.8
San Martin	100.0	91.4	76.8	60.6
Cusco	100.0	92.1	77.1	59.9
Cajamarca	100.0	92.0	76.1	58.8
Pasco	100.0	90.7	74.8	57.1
Loreto	100.0	90.9	74.8	56.9
Apurimac	100.0	91.5	74.5	56.6
Ayacucho	100.0	91.9	74.8	55.9
Amazonas	100.0	90.4	73.1	54.3
Huancavelica	100.0	89.1	69.9	48.2

Source: Based on Instituto Nacional de Estadísticas e Informática (INEI) 2010a.

negative and significant,[2] which means that higher poverty and elderly mortality are associated.

One especially interesting aspect of the difficulties facing the elderly population is that the lack of regular income, for example, from a pension, forces individuals to work until they have exhausted their abilities at the expense of their health and integrity, or for their entire lives. This has been defined as "ceaseless toil" by Benjamin, Brandt, and Fan (2003) when analyzing the labor supply of the elderly in rural China. Kassouf, Rodriguez, and Aquino (2011) confirm that without the noncontributory pension in Brazil, the elderly would not be able to retire from the labor market. In Peru the employment rate of the elderly is much higher in rural areas than in urban areas.[3] Figure 13.5 (with a three-unit moving average) shows that the difference between elderly men in a condition of extreme poverty in rural areas and men not living in poverty in urban areas grows with age up until about 78 years old. From 65 to 75 years of age the employment rate remains between 90 percent and 100 percent for men in rural areas, but it drops to between 70 percent and 40 percent for non-poor men in urban areas. This could indicate that individuals in rural areas cannot retire from the labor market like those living in urban areas are able to do and are forced to continue working.[4]

The figures from table 13.5 complement figure 13.5. Comparing the employment rates between the elderly population in extreme poverty and the population not living in poverty—without differentiating by area—we observe that 94 percent of extremely poor men between 65 and 69 years old are working

Figure 13.5 Male Population Aged 65 Years and Older, by Age, Area, and Condition of Poverty, 2010

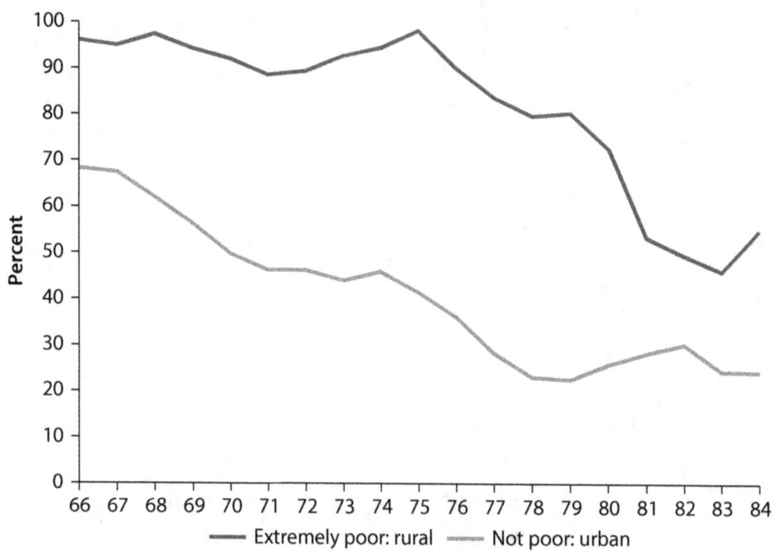

Source: Based on National Household Survey (ENAHO) 2010.

whereas the corresponding rate is 71.3 percent for men in the same age group that are not living in poverty. This means there is a gap of 22.7 percentage points between the two groups. This gap grows to 48.4 points if we compare the extremely poor and nonpoor in the 75–79 years old age group. If we analyze these gaps in rural and urban areas, we find that the gaps are more significant in urban areas than in rural areas.

The problem of low pension coverage among the elderly has its counterpart among persons who are almost old enough to join this age group (figure 13.6). Approximately two-thirds of the population between 44 and 64 years old is not enrolled in a contributory pension system. Even among those who are enrolled, not all of them will gain access to a pension because they do not

Table 13.5 Male Population Aged 65 and Older, by Age Group, Area, and Condition of Poverty, 2010
Percent

	Urban				*Rural*				*Total*			
Age	*Extreme poor*	*Non-extreme poor*	*Non-poor*	*Total*	*Extreme poor*	*Non-extreme poor*	*Non-poor*	*Total*	*Extreme poor*	*Non-extreme poor*	*Non-poor*	*Total*
65–69	78.3	73.0	65.7	67.1	96.6	94.2	95.4	95.3	94.0	81.6	71.3	74.9
70–74	66.0	56.8	45.9	47.8	89.9	96.8	91.4	93.0	84.4	78.0	55.1	61.6
75–79	92.0	51.3	32.4	36.4	87.9	89.1	84.6	87.1	88.4	68.1	40.0	50.7
80 and older	74.9	36.2	22.1	26.1	51.9	73.2	68.5	66.0	58.3	53.2	29.5	36.9

Source: Based on National Household Survey (ENAHO) 2010.

Figure 13.6 Population Not Enrolled in Any Pension System, by Age, Area, and Condition of Poverty, 2010

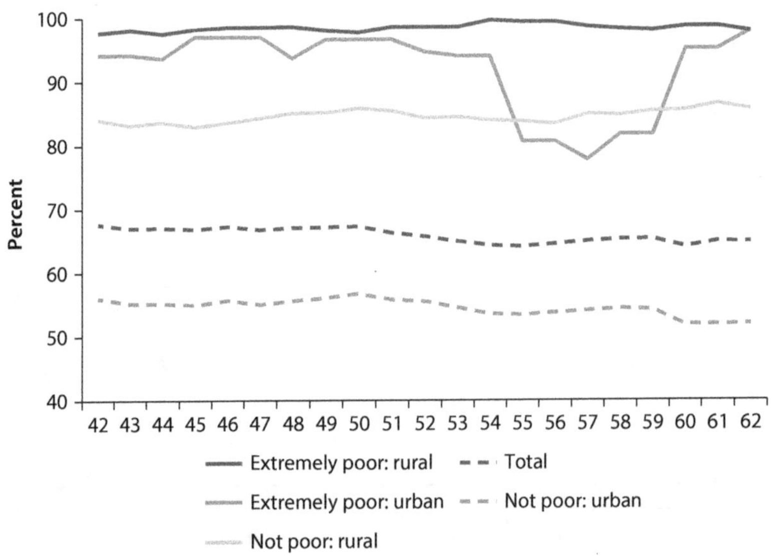

Source: Based on National Household Survey (ENAHO) 2010.

contribute regularly. Individuals younger than 65 years old that live in extreme poverty in rural areas are the most unlikely to be covered by a pension program, with percentages near 100 percent. The non-poor rural population exhibits a similar lack of coverage, with more than 80 percent not enrolled in a formal pension system. In total, this could indicate a social protection problem that affects both the current population of elderly as well as those who will soon form part of this group.

Development of Social Security

The structure of the current Peruvian pension system dates to 1993 when Decree-Law no. 25,897 created the Private Pension System (Sistema Privado de Pensiones [SPP]), which is based on individually funded accounts. Additionally, this system coexists and "competes" with the National Pension System (Sistema Nacional de Pensiones [SNP]), which was created in 1973 as the result of the merger of sectoral funds that had been created decades before and is organized as a public defined benefit system. There are also pension regimes designed to cover specific groups, such as the Military and Police Personnel Regime (Régimen del Personal Militar y Policial), and those that have already been closed to new workers but continue to pay pensions, such as the Social Benefits Fund for Fishers (Caja de Beneficios Sociales del Pescador) and the fund for government workers called Living Credential (Cédula Viva, Decree-Law no. 20,530).

The SNP offers pensions calculated based on its pension rules. These rules include a minimum contribution period of 20 years, minimum and maximum pension values, and a replacement rate that depends on the number of contributions made and the cohort of birth of the beneficiary. As with any defined benefit system, the financial sustainability of the SNP is mainly based on the ratio of contributors to pensioners.

Conversely, the SPP is a self-financing system because it is based on individually funded accounts. Each insured member has to choose from one of four existing Pension Fund Administrators (Administradoras de Fondos de Pensiones [AFPs]) that will manage and invest his or her contributions and the returns they generate. At retirement age, the member has access to the final balance of his or her account and must choose one of several pension options offered by different insurance companies in the market or from the AFP that administered the account. These options include scheduled withdrawals, full annuities, or annuities combined with withdrawals and different percentages for spousal pensions.

The retirement age for women and men is 65 years in both systems. The contribution rate is a fixed percentage of total monthly salary. Currently this rate is 13 percent for the SNP and 10 percent for the SPP. The AFP charges a commission and an insurance premium as a percentage of the insured's salary, which total about 3 percent. The SNP offers a minimum pension to all insured members as long as they meet certain requirements. In contrast, the SPP guarantees a minimum pension for individuals born before 1945 that have contributed on a salary base of at least one minimum salary for at least 20 years in any pension system.

Performance of the Pension System

At the end of 2010, the economically active population affiliated with any pension system was 7.2 million people, of which 4.6 million belonged to the SPP and 2.6 million to the SNP, equivalent to 29.6 percent and 16.3 percent of the labor force, respectively. This means that less than half of the labor force was insured by a pension system. However, if we consider only contributors, that is, those members that regularly contribute to the pension system, only 19.2 percent of the labor force effectively contributes and could access a pension in the future. This low regular participation of workers inside the pension system in Peru lays the foundation for the vulnerability that these individuals will suffer when they join the elderly population, because they will have fewer tools to face old age. The SPP pension fund added up to S/. 87.296 billion, equivalent to US$31.088 billion or 20.4 percent of GDP.

Given that social security generally follows the Bismarckian model, which is based on insurance through formal paid work, this system offers limited coverage in economies with a highly informal labor market, as is the case in Peru. This is one of the principal causes of the persistent low coverage of the pension system, even after the structural pension reform undertaken at the beginning of the 1990s. In 2010 just 26 percent of individuals aged 65 and older were receiving a pension (Rofman and Oliveri 2012). Although participation in the pension system increases along with the income quintile, we take note that the participation rate never reaches a very high level, even in the highest income quintiles. For example, in 2010 among the richest 20 percent of the population, only 58 percent of the elderly were covered by a pension system (table 13.6).

Table 13.6 Coverage Rates for the Elderly, by Per Capita Family Income Quintile, 1995–2010

Percent

Year	*Quintile 1*	*Quintile 2*	*Quintile 3*	*Quintile 4*	*Quintile 5*
1995	6.78	15.37	25.76	37.83	56.00
1998	4.02	10.69	29.75	43.94	61.86
1999	2.59	18.00	24.76	45.13	67.35
2000	2.58	15.39	26.78	34.43	61.32
2001	2.12	10.35	23.83	40.70	53.4
2002	0.85	8.27	23.32	40.42	56.49
2003	0.95	8.27	22.22	41.51	58.46
2004	2.14	10.30	24.09	42.21	55.95
2005	3.22	9.20	22.60	38.24	62.57
2006	1.98	9.16	25.90	40.20	61.50
2007	1.03	9.34	26.36	38.64	58.79
2008	1.43	9.62	25.45	40.84	56.67
2009	1.83	7.20	20.35	39.38	56.66
2010	1.50	7.88	23.65	38.32	58.43

Source: Rofman and Oliveri 2012.

Table 13.7 Evolution of the Coverage Rate among the EAP, Employed Persons, and the Elderly, by Region, 1995–2010
Percent

	Contributors/EAP			Contributors/employed			Beneficiaries/65 and older population		
Year	Total	Rural	Urban	Total	Rural	Urban	Total	Rural	Urban
1995	n.a.	n.a.	n.a.	n.a.	n.a.	n.a.	28.36	6.70	40.59
1996	n.a.	n.a.	n.a.	n.a.	n.a.	n.a.	24.50	5.34	36.59
1997	n.a.	n.a.	n.a.	n.a.	n.a.	n.a.	27.47	7.00	38.49
1998	n.a.	n.a.	n.a.	n.a.	n.a.	n.a.	29.85	6.73	41.97
1999	n.a.	n.a.	n.a.	n.a.	n.a.	n.a.	31.52	9.63	42.10
2000	n.a.	n.a.	n.a.	n.a.	n.a.	n.a.	28.40	5.09	40.67
2001	13.70	3.06	19.16	14.24	3.09	20.46	25.91	5.21	37.22
2002	13.88	3.73	19.07	14.41	3.79	20.32	25.74	4.74	37.01
2003	14.83	3.78	20.74	15.24	3.85	21.85	26.19	5.72	38.80
2004	14.68	3.93	20.24	15.21	4.02	21.57	26.91	5.44	40.06
2005	12.42	3.35	17.27	13.08	3.40	18.69	27.16	6.42	39.48
2006	13.96	3.34	19.40	14.61	3.38	20.81	27.67	5.69	40.15
2007	15.96	3.68	22.14	16.59	3.69	23.45	26.79	6.94	38.42
2008	16.82	3.98	23.30	17.37	4.00	24.48	26.65	5.93	38.75
2009	18.33	4.65	25.34	18.92	4.65	26.66	25.09	5.72	37.17
2010	18.48	4.65	25.41	19.05	4.66	26.64	25.93	5.60	38.05

Source: Rofman and Oliveri 2012.
Note: EAP = economically active population; n.a = not applicable.

Table 13.7 also shows very marked differences between pension coverage in urban and rural areas. In fact, 5.60 percent of the population aged 65 and older in rural areas received a pension in 2010, but this percentage reached 38.05 percent in urban areas. Similarly, contributors make up 4.65 percent of the economically active population (EAP) in rural areas and 25.4 percent in urban areas.

When we disaggregate the percentage of the elderly that receive a pension from the contributory system by region and age, we observe a marked asymmetry. Figure 13.7 shows that older individuals are those that are more likely to have a pension. Of the total of elderly from ages 65 to 69, only 22 percent receive a pension, whereas 39.7 percent of individuals aged 80 to 84 receive one.[5] The differences between regions are also very noticeable. For example, 28.8 percent of individuals aged 65–69 in urban areas receive a pension, but this percentage falls to 3.8 percent for the same group in rural areas.

The differences among the elderly in terms of having a pension disaggregated by condition of poverty and gender are also significant. Only 0.7 percent of the elderly in extreme poverty have a pension, but that percentage is 10.4 percent for the non-extreme poor and 36.6 percent for the non-poor (table 13.8). Only 0.5 percent of the elderly living in extreme poverty in rural areas have a contributory pension, meaning that there is an enormous social protection gap for this group. In contrast, 42.1 percent of the non-poor elderly that live in urban

Figure 13.7 Elderly with Any Contributory Pension, by Age, 2010

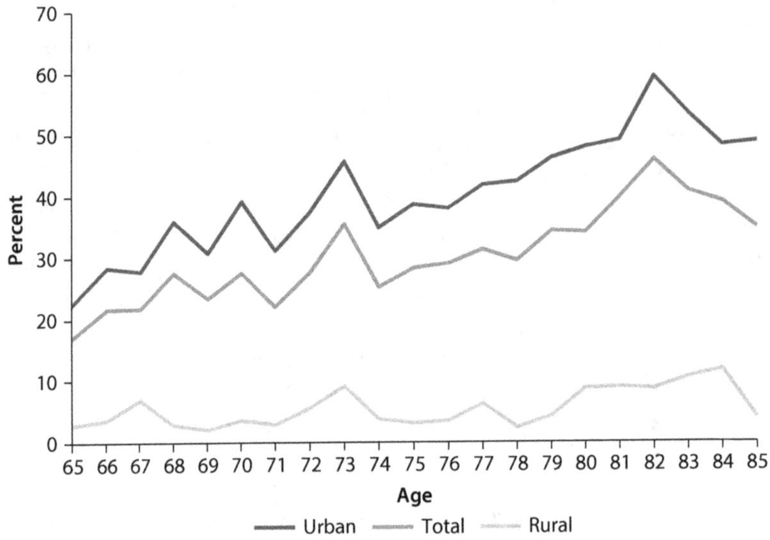

Source: Based on National Household Survey (ENAHO) 2010.

Table 13.8 Population Aged 65 and Older with Any Contributory Pension, by Gender, Area, and Poverty, 2010

Percent

	Total			*Men*			*Women*		
	Total	*Urban*	*Rural*	*Total*	*Urban*	*Rural*	*Total*	*Urban*	*Rural*
Extreme poverty	0.7	1.4	0.5	1.4	2.9	1.1	0.1	0	0.1
Non-extreme poverty	10.4	17.2	2.8	15.4	24.0	5.2	6.1	11.1	0.8
No poverty	36.6	42.1	9.0	45.6	52.7	12.7	28.7	33.0	5.3
Total	28.4	37.6	4.9	36.0	47.3	7.6	21.7	29.3	2.4

Source: Based on National Household Survey (ENAHO) 2010.

areas have a contributory pension. In terms of gender, we observe even more pronounced inequalities. Just 0.1 percent of women aged 65 and older living in extreme poverty in rural areas have a contributory pension, which is a negligible coverage rate. In contrast, 45.6 percent of non-poor elderly men living in urban areas have a pension. It is important to stress that, in terms of survival, there is a positive correlation (0.58 and significant) between the percentage of individuals aged 65 and over with a pension in each region and the probability of survival until 2025.

Even while recognizing some of the advantages of a regime like the SPP, it must be mentioned that its implementation has been very costly. On the one hand, the government has approximately S/. 13 billion in recognition bonds that have been delivered or are pending delivery to enrolled members that switched from the SNP to the SPP. On the other hand, the government Treasury must also transfer funds to pay SNP pensioners because the members who would be paying these pensions have transferred to the SPP. For the latter concept, the government has disbursed approximately S/. 26.4 billion since 1995, which is equal to about 6.2 percent of GDP. In recent years, the Treasury has paid on average the equivalent of about 0.5 percent of GDP annually. These transfers from the Treasury will continue and will even increase during the coming years because the SNP's contribution base, after being reduced by the creation of the SPP, is not sufficient to pay the pensions. The most recent calculation of the SNP's actuarial reserve—which is equivalent to how much the government should "save" today to pay future pensions—is S/. 100 billion, or 23.4 percent of GDP.

Recent Reforms Aimed at Improving Pension Coverage

Social security based on the Bismarckian model, that is, insurance through formal paid employment, has limited coverage in economies with highly informal labor markets,[6] as is the case in Peru. This is one of the principal causes behind the pension system's persistent low coverage levels. In recent years a series of proposed and implemented reforms have taken place with the goal of extending coverage to the elderly population. The launch of the Pension 65 program stands out among these reforms. This program offers coverage to the elderly that do not have a pension and live in extreme poverty.

The Reforms

Ley Mype

Since the SPP was created, the government has made various regulatory changes mainly focused on the system's efficiency, costs, and investments. Similarly, in 2004 the government made important changes to the public systems, especially with the closure to new workers of the Living Credential program that had covered public servants (Law no. 20,530), and a series of changes to the SNP's pension rules. In 2008 the government issued a regulation with the goal of expanding pension coverage via the SME Law (Ley Mype, D.S. no. 007-2008-TR), which created social pensions for workers in microenterprises.

The idea behind the law is that microenterprises and their workers should join the Social Pension System (Sistema de Pensiones Sociales)—based on individual accounts—and contribute an established minimum amount, on top of which the government would add another contribution. This was one interesting initiative and the first that sought to expand coverage, but it was not implemented, and it did not have the necessary political support.

SPP Reform Law of 2012

In November 2011 a technical group of experts was created to recommend reforms to the SPP with the goals of improving the system's efficiency and increasing pension coverage. This group was made up of academics and public servants. The closest counterpart to the formation of this commission is the Marcel Commission in Chile, which carried out a broad reform of the Chilean pension system in 2008. Up to now there has not been an official document produced by the Peruvian commission, and it stopped meeting in March 2012. Congress passed the reform bill sent by the Ministry of the Economy and Finances (Ministerio de Economía y Finanzas [MEF]), which among other things seeks to expand pension coverage in two main ways. On the one hand, the reform would make it mandatory for all self-employed workers under age 40 to join an AFP or the National System. On the other hand it would create social pensions for workers that earn up to 1.5 times the Minimum Living Wage (Remuneración Mínima Vital). These pensions are based on a matching contributions scheme, that is, the government would pay a subsidy for each contribution that a worker makes.

The pension reform bill has not been free of controversy given that its introduction to Congress and debate has followed an unusual path.[7] Much criticism has been seen in the news media of the virtues of the approved reform, both technical as well as legal, and the way in which it was carried out, which have eroded its legitimacy to some extent. Currently, the Constitutional Tribunal is evaluating a lawsuit alleging unconstitutionality due to the new form of paying funds management fees (based on the balance) and the bidding for the flow of new members.

Social Pensions

In July 2010 the Gratitude Bonus (Bono Gratitud) social pension pilot program was created, and it began to function in October of that year. Under this program, all elderly over age 75 and living in poverty receive a pension of S/. 100 per month, equal to about US$36. This was the first attempt to create noncontributory pensions in Peru, but the number of registered users was reduced and a series of accusations surrounded the delivery of benefits to individuals that did not meet the requirements. In August 2011 the Gratitude program had 21,783 beneficiaries nationally and was found in the following regions: Amazonas, Ancash, Apurimac, Ayacucho, Cajamarca, Cusco, Huancavelica, Huanuco, Junin, Puno, La Libertad, Lima, Callao, and Piura. The last four regions have a significant population living in urban areas and experiencing less poverty.

The Pension 65 program was created October 19, 2011, and began operations in November. Beneficiaries of the Gratitude program were absorbed into the Pension 65 program. To be a beneficiary of the Pension 65 program, an individual must fulfill a series of requirements, including being 65 years old and above; living in extreme poverty according to the Household Targeting System (Sistema de Focalización de Hogares [SISFOH]); and not receiving any pension or grant from any public or private entity, including Social Health Insurance (Seguro Social de Salud [ESSALUD]) as well as other social programs, except for Comprehensive Health Insurance (Seguro Integral de Salud [SIS]), the National Movement for Literacy Program (Programa Nacional de Movilización por la Alfabetización), and the Reparations Programs from Law no. 28,592 (for victims, and their family members, of the violence from 1980 to 2000). As of May 2012, the program had registered 126,787 beneficiaries.

The pension amount is low, but its relative weight varies depending on the region and the indicator for comparison. The transfer of S/. 125 (approximately US$46) represents 33 percent of the national per capita spending, but the relative weight of this transfer is much greater in rural areas (table 13.9). The transfer represents 53 percent of per capita spending for families in rural areas, whereas in urban areas this percentage is just 22 percent. Additionally, the pension amount represents 60 percent of the rural poverty line and 91 percent of the rural extreme poverty line.

Additionally, the program contemplates connecting existing health care services among the managing institutions (Ministry of Health, public health centers, posts, etc.) and the beneficiary elderly of the social pensions. Another component that comes with the program is the promotion and strengthening of the social support networks for the elderly.

The Political Economy of Pension Reforms

The policy debate on pensions in Peru is characterized by several distinct features. First, the country does not have many experts on the subject, and the variation in opinions on normative issues is minimal. Second, the topic is complex, but despite that thought leaders and authorities support specific social security policies without considering the effects they will have. In effect, there is not enough academic research on the subject of pensions in Peru, and society does not value the important efforts put forth by the institutions with significant roles dealing with the problems. Moreover, there is limited microeconomic and administrative information available on members and pensioners that could enable researchers to undertake better academic and independent research

Table 13.9 Monthly Poverty Lines in 2010 and the Pension 65 Benefit

	Urban	*Rural*	*National*
Amount in nuevos soles			
Poverty line	293	208	264
Extreme poverty line	155	137	149
Per capita expenditure	571	263	454
Minimum pension[a]	484	484	484
Minimum living wage[a]	750	750	750
Percentage that Pension 65 represents = S/. 125			
Poverty line	43	60	47
Extreme poverty line	81	91	84
Per capita expenditure	22	53	28
Minimum pension	26	26	26
Minimum living wage	17	17	17

Source: Based on Instituto Nacional de Estadísticas e Informática (INEI) 2011 and National Household Survey (ENAHO) 2010.
a. Values in 2012.

projects, nor are specialized surveys available on topics related to pensions. The regulations sent by the MEF and the Superintendent of Banking, Insurance, and AFP (SBS) to Congress are complex and are not completely explained. Outside the more specialized Economy Committee, congresspersons continue proposing regulations without considering the adverse effects they could create. At the same time, the more technical regulations are approved with little debate and without understanding their effects very well.

Third, the debate is emotional and is rooted in political positions and values. The public debate provoked as a result of the noncontributory Pension 65 proposal during the last electoral campaign from February to May 2011 is interesting. One persistent idea in the debate was that persons who had never contributed to a pension system did not deserve to receive a pension from the government. On the other hand, opinion makers and authorities estimated enormous costs for the noncontributory pension with the goal of weakening the proposal. However, it should also be mentioned that complete information was not available on the program's design. Three former Ministers of Economy expressed such views. The estimated costs that were published in the news media varied from S/. 3 billion to S/. 14 billion (from 0.7 percent to 3.3 percent of GDP). However, once the proposal is implemented, it is expected to cost around S/. 400 million, or 0.09 percent of GDP.

Perceptions of what is right on the subject of pensions are based on more general values about how society should be organized and the exchanges that take place within it. In some ways, it is not surprising that one of the most popular arguments against Pension 65 has been that those who have not contributed do not deserve a pension. Table 13.10 presents the results of the last version of the World Values Survey in selected Latin American countries. We observe that Peru is the country where most people believe that "each person should individually assume more responsibility in order to make his or her own living" in contrast to "the government should assume more responsibility for providing a living to everyone." Support for this value is the majority position in both lower and upper social classes.

Table 13.10 Percentage of People Who Think "Each Person Should Individually Assume More Responsibility in Order to Make His or Her Own Living"

	Brazil	*Colombia*	*Uruguay*	*Chile*	*Argentina*	*Guatemala*	*Mexico*	*Peru*
Upper middle class	43.0	n.a.	46.3	41.5	41.5	n.a.	n.a.	56.0
Lower middle class	30.3	n.a.	33.2	35.8	42.2	n.a.	n.a.	57.0
Working class	27.1	n.a.	37.6	37.6	38.1	n.a.	n.a.	54.6
Lower class	29.3	n.a.	29.5	34.9	32.7	n.a.	n.a.	53.3
Total	29.0	33.3	35.6	37.2	39.3	44.9	47.0	55.5

Source: Based on the World Values Survey, fifth wave (2004–08).
Note: For the survey question, the respondent should express his or her position on a scale of 1–10 between "The government should assume more responsibility for providing a living to everyone" (=1) and "each person should individually assume more responsibility in order to make his or her own living" (=10). The figures in the table indicate the percentage of people that expressed a score from 6 to 10. n.a. = not applicable.

Finally, in Peru we do not find a comprehensive vision for the pension system. This observation is validated by the way in which the social security institutions are organized. The SBS supervises the AFPs, the Office of Social Security Regulation (Oficina de Normalización Previsional) regulates and administers the SNP and other public systems, the MEF regulates the public systems and the SPP in terms of laws, the Central Bank (Banco Central de la Reserva del Perú) sets some operational investment limits for the AFPs and manages the Consolidated Reserves Fund (Fondo Consolidado de Reservas) for the public system, the Superintendent of Taxes Administration (Superintendencia de Administración Tributaria) collects contributions for the public systems, and the Ministry of Development and Social Inclusion (Ministerio de Desarrollo e Inclusión Social [MIDIS]) manages the noncontributory Pension 65 program.

As a result of this multiplicity of institutions, a comprehensive pension policy does not exist. Each institution defends its jurisdiction and regulates without a global vision. Even inside the MEF—an institution that could help unify the visions in some way—the section in charge of the private system is in a different vice ministry than the section in charge of the public systems.

Pension 65 Targeting

The Pension 65 program's targeting strategy has two stages. First, geographic targeting is applied (selection of districts) based on the 2009 poverty map from the National Statistics Institute (Instituto Nacional de Estadísticas [INEI]). Within these districts, a second stage uses the targeting system applied in other social programs (known as Sistema de Focalización de Hogares [SISFOH]), which maintains a General Household Registry (Padrón General de Hogares [PGH]) with information on all of the households considered eligible for social programs. SISFOH sends the program the list of potential users created based on the PGH and also sends the socioeconomic categorization of those potential users identified by the program. Based on this information, the program proceeds to verify compliance with the requirements and whether potential beneficiaries are alive. The verification that Pension 65 beneficiaries are still living is carried out in coordination with municipalities and other entities. This verification can also be performed by comparing the registry of users with the National Identification and Civil Status Registry (Registro Nacional de Identificación y Estado Civil). The program can also request that SISFOH reevaluate its users.

Nonetheless, we must specify that because the SISFOH system has not yet registered all households, there is an exception rule for individual targeting in those districts where the program has already begun to operate. This rule states that potential beneficiaries that live in urban districts with more than 50 percent extreme poverty or in rural districts with more than 30 percent are considered eligible without the need to verify their individual socioeconomic conditions. This rule will continue to be applied in those districts where implementation is already underway even if the SISFOH database is completed. In contrast, in the districts where implementation is not yet underway, individual targeting will apply. According to estimates from MIDIS, the number of potential users could reach 273,529 in 2012 and 323,672 in 2018.

Although the program began operations recently at the end of 2011, some information is available that allows us to see its fast growth. It reached 54,122 users in January, 78,657 in March, and finally 126,787 in May 2012. Additionally, the program has been able to establish links with geriatric health care services between users and the Ministry of Health, but no data are available regarding this service yet. In terms of the effects of the program, the authorities plan to carry out a baseline measurement in 2012 with the goal of obtaining an impact measurement in 2013.

In terms of targeting, with the data currently available, we can observe only the geographic targeting component, that is, at the district level. Based on the last user registry from May 2012 and the 2009 Poverty Map (INEI 2010b), it is possible to see the level of poverty in the districts where Pension 65 beneficiaries live. Figure 13.8 shows the cumulative number of beneficiaries on the vertical axis and the incidence of existing poverty (ordered from least to greatest) in the respective districts on the horizontal axis. Thus, it is easy to observe that approximately 20 percent of the program's beneficiaries live in districts with 50 percent or less of the population in a condition of poverty. This could indicate a certain level of leakages, but we must remember that Pension 65 inherited some beneficiaries from the old Gratitude program, who lived in urban districts with lower

Figure 13.8 District-Level Targeting of Pension 65 Beneficiaries, 2012

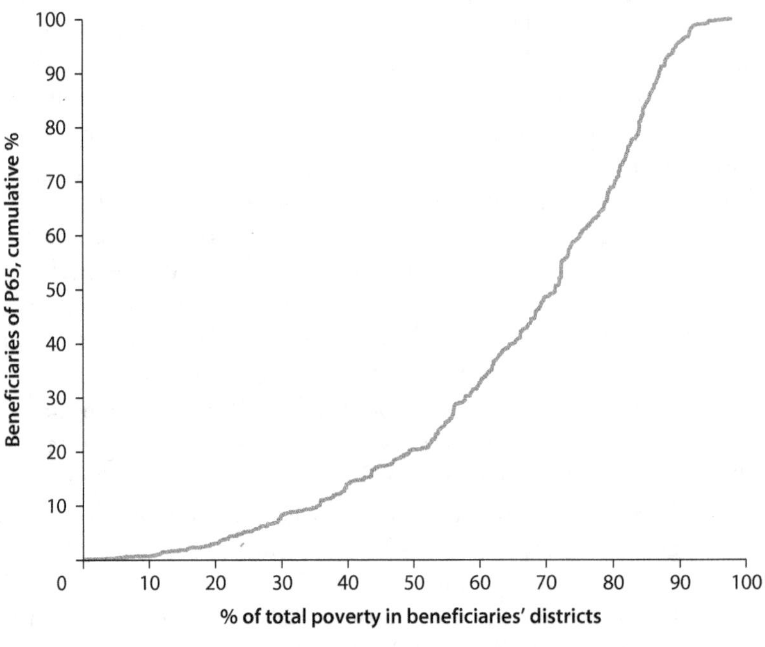

Source: Based on Instituto Nacional de Estadísticas e Informática (INEI) 2010b; Pension 65 user registry.
Note: Only districts with at least one beneficiary are considered.

poverty rates. Additionally, the analysis based on geographic targeting is limited because it does not account for the concentrations ("pockets") of poverty in urban cities, which are diminished by the statistical effects of measuring poverty for an entire district.

Figure 13.9 allows us to observe how the Gratitude program affects the targeting of the Pension 65 program and if the way in which the program operates has meant an improvement in terms of targeting. As before, we constructed the ratios between the cumulative number of beneficiaries and the level of poverty in the districts in which they live. The blue curve represents the beneficiaries of the Gratitude program, and the orange curve represents those of the Pension 65 program (i.e., the old Gratitude beneficiaries and the new enrollees). We can observe a clear improvement in targeting. After the curves intersect, which occurs approximately in the districts with 50 percent poverty, Pension 65 includes more beneficiaries in the poorest districts. It is also clear that before this intersection, the Gratitude program included more beneficiaries from the less poor districts.

In terms of the program's coverage, a total of 55.7 percent of districts do not have a single beneficiary. If we were to consider only the districts with an incidence of poverty of at least 50 percent, the district subcoverage rate would be

Figure 13.9 District-Level Beneficiary Targeting for Pension 65 and Gratitude

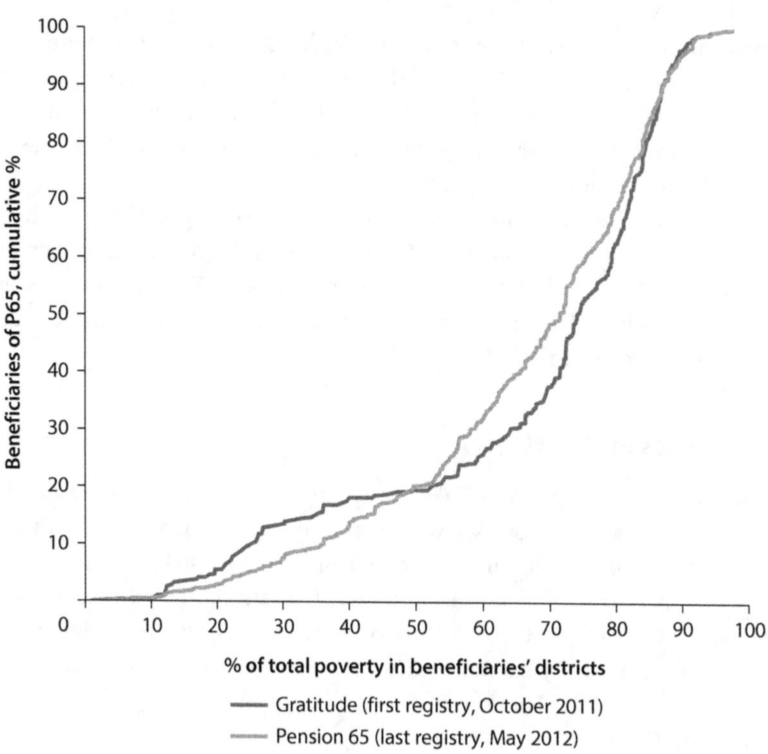

Source: Based on Instituto Nacional de Estadísticas e Informática (INEI) 2010b; Pension 65 user registry.
Note: Only districts with at least one beneficiary are considered.

Table 13.11 Districts with Pension 65 Beneficiaries, by Poverty Level, 2012

Incidence of poverty in the district	*Districts with no beneficiaries*	*Districts with beneficiaries*	*Total*	*Percentage of districts without beneficiaries*
Less than 10%	35	28	63	55.6
10–20%	109	40	149	73.2
20–30%	157	52	209	75.1
30–40%	159	62	221	71.9
40–50%	144	58	202	71.3
50–60%	147	90	237	62.0
60–70%	113	145	258	43.8
70–80%	110	163	273	40.3
80–90%	41	138	179	22.9
Greater than 90%	7	38	45	15.6
Total	1,022	814	1,836	55.7

Source: Based on Instituto Nacional de Estadísticas e Informática (INEI) 2010b, 2010c; Pension 65 beneficiary registry.

42.1 percent. An approximate measure of the penetration rate comes out to 28.3 percent, which indicates the percentage of districts with at least 50 percent poverty that have at least one program beneficiary. Table 13.11 presents further details.

Program Costs

The program is not costly in fiscal terms. With the data about potential beneficiaries it is possible to simply and rapidly obtain the cost of the program, at least of the portion corresponding to transfers to the elderly. It can be estimated that in 2012 Pension 65 will cost approximately S/. 410 million, or 0.09 percent of GDP, without including the program's administrative costs. If the pension amount remains the same and we assume a conservative GDP growth rate of 3 percent, then during the coming years the program's cost would remain around 0.08 percent of GDP. Additionally, the population aged 65 and older covered by the program will be 14.8 percent in 2012 and will decrease slightly in the coming years (to 14.2 percent in 2018).

Other Services for the Elderly

Contributory pensions provide links for access to health care services and other social programs. Furthermore, as we mentioned, Pension 65 has a component that connects with health care services from the Ministry of Health with an emphasis on geriatric care and a component to strengthen the social support networks for the elderly through the promotion of a greater priority for the elderly in the community agenda and the connection with social services.

Health Care Attention

Health is an important dimension of well-being for the elderly because their quality of life can deteriorate rapidly if their illnesses and discomforts are not treated adequately and in a timely manner. Because contributory pensions in Peru are generally accompanied by health insurance (ESSALUD), the limited coverage of pensions also results in low health insurance coverage. Nonetheless, although approximately two-thirds of the elderly are enrolled in the SIS, the data show that many of them do not visit health care facilities to treat their illnesses because they do not have enough money and the facilities are located too far from their homes. Additionally, the lack of health care coverage for one-third of the elderly is a serious problem because this group will have more difficulties facing the risks that come with old age.

Approximately one-third of the elderly do not have any health insurance, whether they are poor or not poor; and among those elderly that are covered differences are found in the type of insurance (table 13.12). About 67.5 percent of extremely poor adults are enrolled in the SIS and 0.9 percent in ESSALUD.[8] In contrast, 45.9 percent of the elderly that are not poor are covered by ESSALUD and 18.2 percent by the SIS. Additionally, according to insurance status by region, we observe that the SIS has greater coverage among the extremely poor in urban areas than those in rural areas.

The interesting element of Pension 65 is that by including a health care component the program resembles a social security scheme, which generally includes

Table 13.12 Health Insurance among the Population Aged 65 and Older, 2010
Percent

Type of insurance	Total				Urban				Rural			
	Extreme poor	Non-extreme poor	Non-poor	Total	Extreme poor	Non-extreme poor	Non-poor	Total	Extreme poor	Non-extreme poor	Non-poor	Total
ESSALUD	0.9	15.1	45.9	36.1	2.7	25.2	52.2	47.4	0.5	3.6	13.5	7.0
Private health insurance	0.0	0.0	3.2	2.3	0.0	0.0	3.7	3.1	0.0	0.0	0.3	0.1
Health care services entity	0.0	0.0	0.1	0.1	0.0	0.0	0.2	0.1	0.0	0.0	0.0	0.0
Armed forces/police insurance	0.0	0.8	3.2	2.4	0.0	1.5	3.6	3.2	0.0	0.0	0.9	0.4
Comprehensive health insurance (SIS)	67.5	52.2	18.2	29.0	76.4	40.5	11.9	17.3	65.7	65.4	50.8	59.3
University insurance	0.2	0.0	0.0	0.0	0.7	0.0	0.0	0.0	0.1	0.0	0.0	0.0
Private school insurance	0.0	0.0	0.0	0.0	0.0	0.0	0.0	0.0	0.0	0.0	0.0	0.0
Other	0.0	0.1	0.1	0.1	0.0	0.2	0.1	0.1	0.0	0.0	0.2	0.1
No insurance	31.4	31.8	29.3	29.9	20.2	32.6	28.3	28.7	33.7	31.0	34.3	33.0
Total	100.0	100.0	100.0	100.0	100.0	100.0	100.0	100.0	100.0	100.0	100.0	100.0

Source: Based on National Household Survey (ENAHO) 2010.
Note: ESSALUD = Seguro Social de Salud; SIS = Seguro Integral de Salud.

a pension and health insurance. Additionally, this scheme is justified as a way to alleviate the high levels of inequality of opportunity experienced in the past that were not corrected over time (Olivera 2011).

Social Support and Other Services

A series of initiatives and services for the elderly exist beyond income and health care protection. However, the elderly population's participation is not significant, and in some cases these services are directed to specific groups, such as pensioners or insured members of the public pension system.

In turn, the noncontributory pension programs are focused on providing economic security to the elderly, given the limitations that old age imposes on individuals. But another important process also takes place during aging: the weakening of social networks due to the loss of a spouse, groups of friends, and family members. The exchange of support is the basis of the existence of social networks. In a context of high informality and faced with minimal development of social security institutions, social support networks became an important element for individuals to gain protection and satisfy unmet needs (Lomnitz 1994). Additionally, apart from the economic aspect, emotional needs are also a motivation for belonging to a network.

Social support for the elderly has positive effects on their well-being through the reduction of feelings of isolation and indirectly through the promotion of healthy behaviors that provoke an increase in the resources and options related to health and well-being through direct emotional support (Pillemer et al. 2000). Additionally, according to Antonucci and Akiyama (1987), what really matters is the accumulation of communications from other individuals about how valuable, capable, and important a person is (or continues to be), and not so much the specific support. In this sense, the Barros (1991) study, with information from the elderly in Santiago de Chile, detected that belonging to an organization of elderly people contributed to the exchange of information on how to better take care of oneself, provided companionship and affection, and contributed to improving family relationships, as long as the elderly became more independent. In terms of health, it has been established that people that have more social support networks can face illnesses, depression, stress, and other difficulties better (Antonucci and Akiyama 1987). Some studies find a negative relationship between social support for the elderly and mortality and morbidity (Antonucci and Jackson 1990; Berkman 1984; Blazer 1982). In the Salinas, Manrique, and Téllez Rojo (2008) study on individuals that received the elderly component of the Opportunities program in Mexico, researchers found that the size of the network had a significant impact on the availability of support, and on economic, instrumental, and emotional support. Additionally, the authors point out that among the elderly population affiliated with the Opportunities program, having small and undiversified networks—which indicates excessive pressure on the network's members—the program's economic transfers and medical checkups become vitally important.

In this sense, the positive effects of a noncontributory pension program on the elderly's well-being could be strengthened if it were possible to incentivize the reinforcement of the elderly's social support networks in some way. In Peru the elderly can benefit from the following initiatives.

Comprehensive Centers for Attention to the Elderly (Centros Integrales de Atención al Adulto Mayor [CIAM])

These centers seek to increase the social inclusion of the elderly and their family members. They seek the elderly population's active and organized participation with other community members. They offer recreational, educational, and social activities, as well as health campaigns and the like. The Ministry of Women and Vulnerable Populations (Ministerio de la Mujer y Poblaciones Vulnerables [MIMDES]) promotes the creation of these centers, but it is the responsibility of provincial and district municipalities to create and operate them. Law no. 28,803 of 2006, the Law of the Peruvian Elderly (Ley del Adulto Mayor Peruano), mandates the creation of these centers. This law establishes that district and provincial municipalities, in coordination with the Directorate of Elderly People of MIMDES, should create the CIAMs. According to the most recent figures from MIMDES's portal, the creation of CIAMs in just 95 districts has been ordered, of the more than 1,800 districts that exist in Peru, which represents approximately 5 percent of districts.

Directorate of the Elderly (Dirección de Personas Adultas Mayores [DIPAM])

This MIMDES department is in charge of designing, monitoring, and following up on social policies directed at the elderly population. The DIPAM is responsible for promoting, coordinating, supervising, and evaluating the policies, plans, programs, and projects aimed at the elderly population, particularly for persons that suffer discrimination, social exclusion, poverty, and extreme poverty.

Center for the Elderly (Centro del Adulto Mayor [CAM])

The CAMs are centers where the elderly can receive educational workshops on emotional intelligence, art, productive activities, etc. They also organize elderly volunteers to help other elderly persons and offer prevention and treatment for illnesses, providing basic medicines. CAM services have no cost, but are directed only to the ESSALUD pensioner population (public system) that is elderly (older than 60 years). CAM offices are located in all regions throughout Peru, with a total of 121 centers in 2010. In 2010 the centers served 141,105 elderly persons.

Elderly Circles (Los Círculos del Adulto Mayor [CIRAM])

These are a social gerontological service offered by ESSALUD to insured elderly members, organized in associations in geographic areas where a CAM does not exist. The CIRAM's basic set of activities are occupational, artistic, physical, self-help, social tourism, and socio-cultural workshops. In 2010 the CIRAMs served 12,460 participants.

Elderly Club (Club del Adulto Mayor)

The Elderly Club is a department that exists within the Comprehensive Family Development Centers (Centros de Desarrollo Integral de la Familia [CEDIF]) that are administered by the National Comprehensive Family Well-Being Program (Programa Integral Nacional para el Bienestar Familiar). Twenty-three CEDIFs are located in the provinces and 13 in Lima. The clubs are directed to individuals over 60 years old that live in poverty, extreme poverty, or without contact from family members. The purpose of the club is to provide the elderly with a set of activities that allow them to share experiences and moments of recreation and relaxation, which help raise their self-esteem and improve their quality of life. According to figures from 2011, the CEDIFs served a monthly average of 33,350 people, of which 2,139 were age 60 or older.

Residential Attention Centers for the Elderly (Centros de Atención Residencial para Personas Adultas Mayores [CARPAM])

These centers serve as homes for the elderly and offer social, medical, and psychological support to their residents. MIMDES is in charge of supervising and regulating these centers. According to available figures, 21 of these centers are registered in Lima, and only six of them are public.

National Registry of Organizations for the Elderly (Registro Nacional de Organizaciones de Personas Adultas Mayores)

MIMDES promotes the registration of organizations for the elderly or that work with this population with the goal of developing collaboration among the members of this group and building social networks that offer emotional support. By enrolling in the Public Registries, these organizations can join in the Participatory Budget in their community. Additionally, this registry is a means to formalize the association and register it with the local government as part of the municipal organizations. According to the most recent figures, there are 240 organizations that have a total of 30,706 members, of which 20,853 are women and 9,853 are men.

Conclusions

The goal of increasing pension coverage is positive in and of itself because it allows the elderly to retire from the labor market and pay for their needs during old age. Achieving this vision with just a contributory social security model in a context of high labor informality is not possible. Peru has 1.8 million elderly, of which only one-fourth receive a pension, with around half a million elderly are poor.

The Pension 65 program seeks to cover the gap left open by the contributory systems to supply the elderly with secure incomes that allow them to retire from the labor market and improve their living conditions. This presupposes, therefore, that the elderly necessarily require this transfer to be able to retire from the market smoothly. Therefore, the program should identify the elderly that should be targeted, generally those that live in conditions of poverty.

Based on other experiences and the elderly population's specific needs, the creation of the health care and social network components is positive for Pension 65 beneficiaries. We have seen that very few of the elderly who live in poverty, and above all in rural areas, use health care services. Additionally, the initiatives that exist to promote social and health care services for this population group are scarce or limited to those insured by the public system. Therefore, connecting health care services and social networks as a part of Pension 65 is a positive step. Nonetheless, we need more evidence to understand the effects of the noncontributory pension on the elderly and their families. The baseline measurement and impact studies planned during 2013–14 will shed more light on the program's effects and allow policy makers to put in place the necessary changes.

Another alternative to the targeted pension would be the creation of a universal benefit, but that would require the government to evaluate its cost and fiscal sustainability. It is important to offer social protection to the elderly, but the generosity and scope of the program should be decided within the framework of fiscal sustainability. One option for the government would be to promote and reinforce formality in the labor market so that individuals can contribute to a pension system, but this policy can require an extended period of effort before it demonstrates results. However, it is necessary that such a measure be accompanied by social pensions for the elderly populations that had few opportunities to save for old age in the past.

Individual participation in a contributory pension system can definitively lessen the fiscal burden in the future. Without such participation, the government must face growing costs to attend to the needs of the elderly without coverage. This is particularly relevant in the current context of aging, in which the population aged 65 and older today represents 6 percent of the total population and in 2050 and 2100 will be 17.1 percent and 29.9 percent, respectively. These demographic changes will signify large movements in the population's consumption and productivity patterns, at the same time that it will exert pressure on the government to direct public spending toward older age groups.

Notes

1. Moving averages of five observations are used to adjust the series in the figure.
2. The correlations between the probability of survival until 2025 and the poverty rate, the extreme poverty rate, and the poverty rate among those age 65 and older and the extreme poverty rate of said group are –0.7205, –0.7058, –0.5738, and –0.5681, respectively, with 99 percent confidence.
3. The employment rate is defined as the number of employed persons of a certain age divided by the total population of the same age.
4. We use statistics only for men because the percentage of women who are unemployed or without paid work can be very high (because of the traditional division of labor in the household), especially in rural areas.

5. This is associated with the fact that individuals that receive a pension are in general richer than those that do not receive a pension. They also have a higher level of education and greater access to health care services. All of this greatly affects an individual's probability of survival. In this sense, it is likely that the people with a greater probability of surviving to older ages are pensioners.
6. Based on the legalistic definition (workers that in their jobs are not forced to join social security or pay contributions) of formality described in Chong, Galdo, and Saavedra (2008), approximately 70 percent of jobs would be informal.
7. See Valladares (2012) for a political analysis of this reform and the path it followed.
8. SIS is a health insurance program administered by the government that prioritizes enrolling vulnerable populations that are living in poverty. ESSALUD refers to employees' health insurance, which are mostly provided for those in formal salaried jobs.

Bibliography

Antonucci, T., and H. Akiyama. 1987. "Social Networks in Adult Life and Preliminary Examination of De Convoy Model." *Journal of Gerontology* 42 (5): 519–27.

Antonucci, T., and J. Jackson. 1990. "Apoyo social, eficacia interpersonal y salud: una perspectiva del transcurso de la vida." In *Intervención psicológica y social, Gerontología clínica*, 129–48. Biblioteca de psicología, psiquiatría y salud—Serie Universidad. Barcelona: Ediciones Martínez Roca.

Barros, C. 1991. "Viviendo el Envejecer." Cuadernos del Instituto de Sociología Pontificia Universidad Católica de Chile, December, Santiago.

Benjamin, D., L. Brandt, and J. Fan. 2003. "Ceaseless Toil? Health and Labor Supply of the Elderly in Rural China." Draft, University of Toronto.

Berkman, L. 1984. "Assessing the Physical Health Effects of Social Networks and Social Support." *Annual Review of the Public Health* 5: 413–32.

Blazer, D. G. 1982. "Social Support and Mortality in an Elderly Population." *American Journal of Epidemiology* 115: 684–89.

CELADE (Centro Latinoamericano y Caribeño de Demografía). 2011. *Estimaciones y proyecciones de población a largo plazo. Revisión 2011*. ECLAC, Santiago.

Chong, A., J. Galdo, and J. Saavedra. 2008. "Informality and Productivity in the Labor Market in Peru." *Journal of Economic Policy Reform* 11 (4): 229–45.

INEI (Instituto Nacional de Estadísticas). 2010a. "Perú: Estimaciones y Proyecciones de Población Departamental por Años Calendario y Edades Simples, 1995–2025." Boletín Especial 37, Lima.

———. 2010b. *Mapa de Pobreza Provincial y Distrital 2009. El enfoque de la pobreza monetaria*. INEI, Lima.

———. 2010c. "Perú: Estimaciones y Proyecciones de Población total y edades quinquenales, según Departamento, Provincia y Distrito, 2005–2015." Boletín Especial 21, Lima.

———. 2011. *Evolución de la pobreza al 2010*. INEI, Lima.

Kassouf, A. L., P. Rodriguez, and J. Aquino. 2011. *Impact Evaluation of the Brazilian Non-contributory Pension Program BPC (Beneficio da Prestação Continuada) on Family Welfare*. Final Report, University of São Paulo.

Lomnitz, C. 1994. *Redes Sociales, Cultura y Poder: ensayos de antropología latinoamericana.* Mexico City: Editorial Miguel Angel de Porrúa, FLACSO.

Olivera, J. 2011. "Estudio sobre el diseño y costo de una pensión no contributiva en Perú." Envejecimiento con dignidad, por una pensión no contributiva, International Labour Organization, and PUCP, Lima.

Pillemer, K., P. Moen, E. Wethington, and N. Glasgow. 2000. *Social Integration in the Second Half of Life.* Baltimore, MD: Johns Hopkins University Press.

Rofman, R., and M. L. Oliveri. 2012. "La cobertura de los sistemas previsionales en América Latina: conceptos e indicadores." Serie de Documentos de Trabajo sobre Políticas Sociales 7, World Bank, Buenos Aires.

Salinas, A., B. Manrique, and M. Téllez Rojo. 2008. "Redes de apoyo social en la vejez: adultos mayores y beneficiarios del componente para adultos mayores del programa Oportunidades." Sociedad y Adulto Mayor en América Latina, Estudios de Envejecimiento en la Región, Asociación Latinoamericana de Población.

Valladares, J. 2012. "Horror al vacío: un año de relaciones entre Ejecutivo y Congresos." *Revista Argumentos* 6 (3), Instituto de Estudios Peruanos.

CHAPTER 14

Trinidad and Tobago

Gonzalo Reyes and Javier Bronfman

Background

The country of Trinidad and Tobago is not an exception to the process of demographic transition. The proportion of working age population is close to its peak and the proportion of the old age population has been growing, and projections suggest it will be even higher in the near future. The participation of the old age population in the labor market has decreased in the last decade. In the country's economic situation, challenges are being felt to broad fiscal space after the international crises and the decreasing energy effects on public revenues.

The Demographic, Labor, and Economic Environment

Trinidad and Tobago is a relatively small and young country with steady population growth. The total population in 2010 was 1.34 million, and 10.6 percent was older than age 60. The trend for the past 50 years has been an increase in the proportion of the old age population, from 5.8 percent in 1960 (figure 14.1). It is common to observe a demographic transition pattern in many countries alongside their development path. As countries get richer, mortality rates decrease, increasing longevity in the population. At the same time, fertility rates also decrease, which translates into a lower proportion of young individuals in the population. In the case of Trinidad and Tobago, the total fertility rate has decreased from 5.3 children per women in the period 1950–55 to 1.64 in the period 2005–10 and is expected to slowly recover and stabilize around 2 by the end of this century (United Nations 2010). Mortality rates also have declined from 11.4 deaths per 1,000 people in 1950–55 to 8 in 2005–10. Life expectancy at birth has increased from 58.3 in 1955 to 69.4 in 2010 and should reach more than 80 by 2100. Population projections for the next 50 years show that the proportion of the population older than age 60 will increase to 31.6 percent by 2050.

The authors acknowledge the collaboration of the Ministry of Finance of Trinidad and Tobago, which has signed an Advisory Services Agreement with the World Bank for the analysis of its pension system. The authors also thank the National Insurance Board of Trinidad and Tobago, the Treasury Department, the Ministry of the People and Social Development, and the Central Statistical Office for providing valuable information and John Gubbels and William Price for their comments.

Figure 14.1 Composition of the Population, by Age Groups, 1950–2100

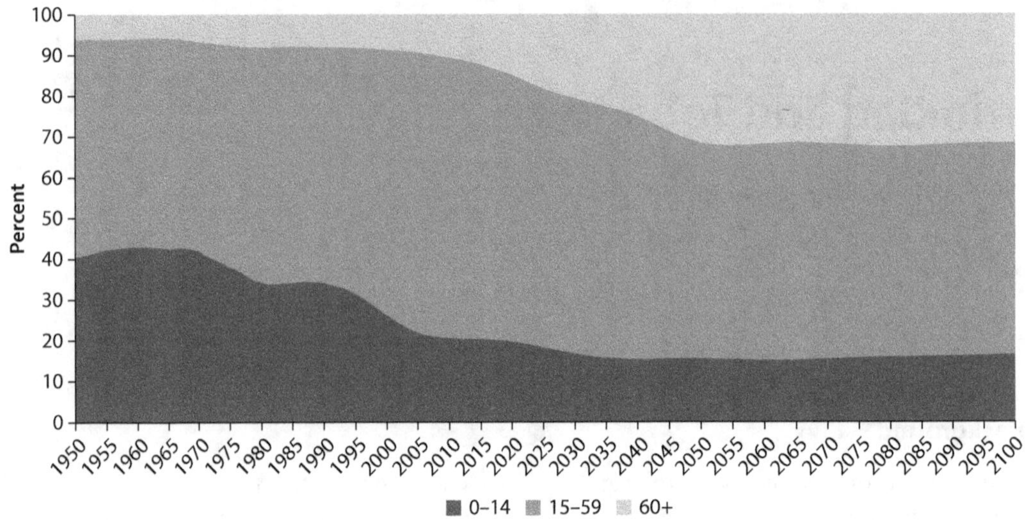

Source: United Nations Population projections for Trinidad and Tobago.

Demographic changes affect the ability of a pension system to provide adequate support in a sustainable manner. Pay-as-you-go and noncontributory benefits are especially affected since the decline in the working age population negatively affects the revenue side (through taxes or contributions) and the rise in the old age population increases the expenditure side. Until now, Trinidad and Tobago has benefited from the demographic transition because it has increased the proportion of the working age population. However, this trend is about to reverse its path. The proportion of the working age population (aged between 15 and 59) increased from 58 percent in 1985 to 69 percent in 2010. However, population projections show that it will decrease again to 61 percent by 2035 and will continue to fall until it reaches 51 percent around 2080. The demographic transition for the past 25 years has resulted in a maturing population, diminishing the proportion of children and increasing the proportion of the working age population, which gives rise to what has been labeled a "demographic dividend," but this process is usually accompanied by higher economic growth rates. In the future, demographic transition will translate into a diminishing proportion of the working age population and an increasing importance of the old age population. This will have implications for the economy as well as for the public policies intending to provide income protection for the elderly.

Since the beginning of the 1990s, Trinidad and Tobago's labor market has experienced favorable dynamics. The total labor force expanded by 32 percent from 1990 to 2010, and participation increased more than six percentage points. Unemployment, which affected 20 percent of all workers in 1990, has steadily declined and now is only 5.9 percent of the labor force (figure 14.2). This extraordinary reduction in unemployment has had a positive impact on the financial sustainability of the pension system, because more workers contributing to the

Figure 14.2 Unemployment Rate, by Gender, 1990–2010

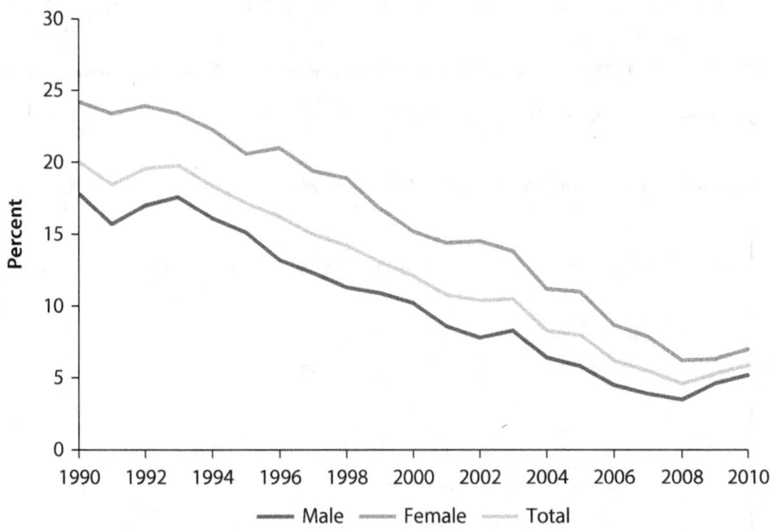

Source: Trinidad and Tobago Central Statistical Office, various years.

system increase funding for future pensions. Nevertheless, it is important to analyze the composition of the labor force in terms of employment status. Depending on what sector of the economy is absorbing previously unemployed workers, we can expect different effects on the pension system.

In terms of labor participation by gender, it is worth noticing that Trinidad and Tobago has followed the path of other countries when it comes to female activity. From 1990 onwards, male participation has been stationary at approximately 74 percent, whereas overall female participation increased by 13 percentage points from 38 percent to 51 percent (figure 14.3). Male participation has also been stable at different ages. At earlier stages of the life cycle male participation is high. However, when it comes to the group of male workers closer to retirement age the participation rate appears to be much lower (figure 14.4). On the other hand, female participation has experienced larger dynamism, because labor participation has increased for almost all age groups. Since 1990 Trinidad and Tobago's labor force participation of the female population increased rapidly, with great emphasis on the 55–64 age group, which grew its participation by 90 percent from 1990 to 2010 (figure 14.4).

In general, an increase in contributions made by new workers will benefit the financial sustainability of the system. Nonetheless, these newly incorporated workers also will become a liability to the system in the near future, particularly because the larger increase in participation seems to be happening in the age group nearest to retirement age. It is important to understand other possible effects of these labor dynamics and female incorporation on the country's pension system. For example, if female workers enter the labor market at later stages in life, they may be unable to contribute enough to qualify for contributory pensions.

In 1990, public sector workers (civil servants and government owned-enterprises employees) represented 45 percent of paid employment (excluding the self-employed). This participation has decreased in time, reaching 33.8 percent in 2010 (figure 14.5). On the other hand, the number of nongovernment-related employees increased from 41 percent to 51.8 percent of total employment

Figure 14.3 Labor Force Participation, by Sex, 1990–2010

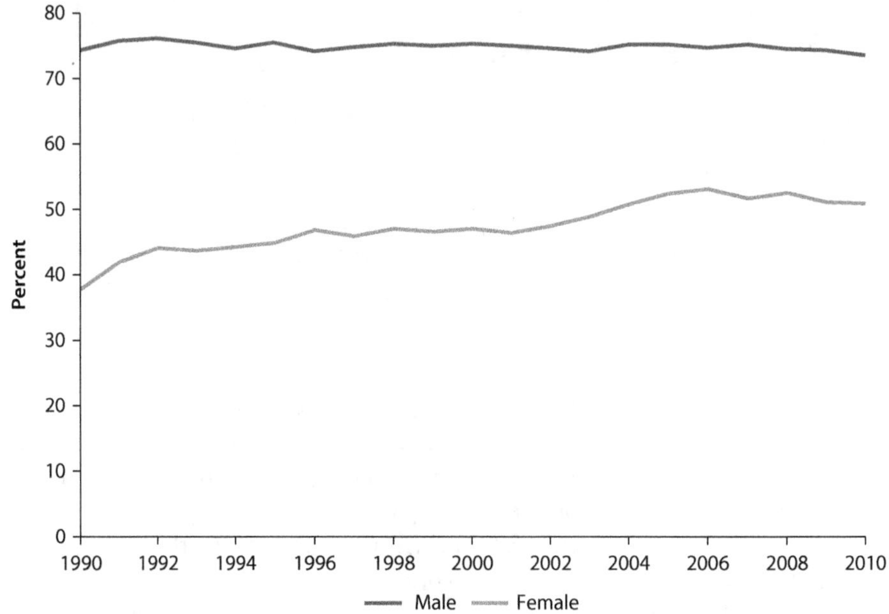

Source: Trinidad and Tobago Central Statistical Office, Labor Force Surveys.

Figure 14.4 Male and Female Labor Participation, by Age Group, 1990–2010

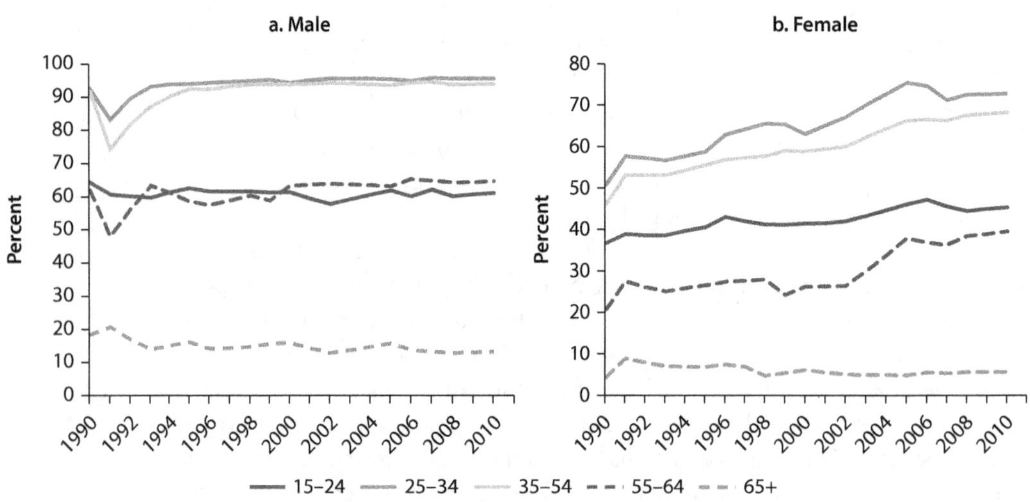

Source: International Labour Organization (ILO), Key Indicators of the Labour Market database.

Figure 14.5 Total Employment, by Type of Employment, 1990–2010

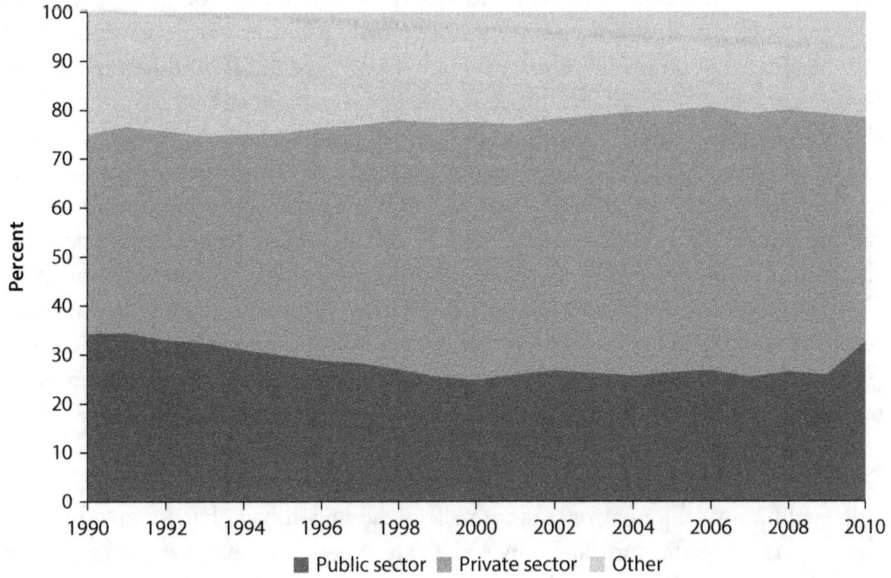

Source: Trinidad and Tobago Central Statistical Office.

between 1990 and 2010. Changes in the participation of government employment and the migration from government employment to the private sector might have a negative impact on the sustainability of the defined benefit government pension scheme. The available data show that the participation of self-employed in total employment has remained constant. These figures suggest that during the 1990–2010 period, when unemployment decreased from 20 percent to 6 percent, the private sector was the main source of job creation in the country. Informality in Trinidad and Tobago is relatively low (around 17–19 percent of the labor force) and does not seem to have changed significantly since the early 1990s.

Before the 2008 international financial crisis, Trinidad and Tobago's economy experienced uninterrupted growth for a period of 15 years. Furthermore, growth was rapid: Between 1996 and 2008, the economy grew at an average rate of 7.6 percent per year in real terms. GDP per capita reached US$19,252 in 2008 and then declined to US$15,543 in 2009. Government revenues increased from levels of approximately 25 percent of GDP in 2001 to 34 percent in 2008. The economic situation between the mid-1990s and 2008 was of prosperity, with increased income levels to sustain improved quality of life at the household level and more resources for the public sector for the provision of public goods and services. However, the 2008 international crisis underscored the vulnerabilities of a small open economy when facing external shocks. Alongside the drop in per capita income, government revenues decreased to 30 percent of GDP, and the fiscal deficit was 5.8 percent of GDP in 2009. The local economy is highly dependent on the production of oil and gas and related industries. The energy sector accounted for 44 percent of GDP in 2010 and 58 percent of government revenue in the fiscal year 2010–11. Because of its capital intensity, this sector employs only 3 percent of the labor force. Natural gas extraction has become the dominant activity within the sector, and currently its output is about eight times the magnitude of oil production. Although 43 percent of oil production is in the hands of the state-owned enterprise Petrotrin, 95 percent of natural gas production is in hands of three foreign companies. Oil production has been on a declining trend since the 1980s. Total output averaged 92,000 barrels per day (bpd) in 2011, compared to 145,000 bpd in 2005. On the other hand, natural gas production has increased, especially since 2001. Nevertheless, the prospect for the future seems worrying: As of 2007, proven oil reserves were equivalent to 14 years of production, and as of end-2010, proven gas reserves were equivalent to nine years of production. The sector faces a volatile external market and competition from shale gas production overseas, which reduce incentives to invest in exploration of new sources of natural gas in the country (IMF 2012).

Developments on the Provision of Social Protection for Elderly People

The evolution of the pension system in Trinidad and Tobago has followed a path that differs from the typical Latin American experience and is more similar to other former British overseas colonies, such as Australia, New Zealand, or South Africa. The first existing pension arrangements were those for public sector workers, with the first Pensions Act passed in 1934. Subsequent amendments to the act incorporated further categories of public sector workers, often under special rules, such as police, firefighters, prison workers, etc. This evolution resulted in a fragmented set of rules and provisions that provided coverage to public sector workers, depending on their category of work in the public sector. In general, pensions in the public sector are noncontributory with defined benefit salary schemes.

The second component of the old age income protection system came about in 1939, with the introduction of the Old Age Pension, a noncontributory benefit for the population aged 65 and older. This benefit was likely the response of the British rulers to a series of strikes and riots that affected the Caribbean colonies between 1934 and 1939. It originally established a relatively modest means-tested benefit for the elderly population, but available figures indicate that it already covered 80 percent of the population aged 65 or older by 1966.

Before establishing a national social security scheme, Trinidad and Tobago also had occupational pension plans in the private sector. In particular, well-established industrial firms set up private pension plans for their employees, in great part incentivized by tax concessions granted to employers under the Income Tax of 1963. Weise (1969) mentions that by the end of 1965 more than 220 approved plans were in operation covering over 30,000 workers in the private sector. These figures are of similar absolute magnitudes of what we observe today, which indicates that occupational pension plans have decreased their relative importance as pension providers throughout the years.

After becoming independent on August 31, 1962, Trinidad and Tobago engaged in plans to introduce a national system of social insurance. There was a recognition that the existing income protection provided through the Old Age

Pensions program along with specific plans for public sector and some private sector employees were not enough to ensure adequate living standards to the old age population. The development of the plan and rules took some years and benefited from the assistance of the International Labour Organization. In 1967 the government appointed a committee to make recommendations based on the existing situation and lessons from international experience, in particular the recently implemented systems of Jamaica and Barbados. This process resulted in the submission of a White Paper in September 1968 containing the basic characteristics of the proposed national insurance system, incorporating coverage for sickness, maternity, disability, work-related injuries, old age, and death. The National Insurance Act was finally enacted in 1971, with the new system being implemented on April 10, 1972. The system originally started with a contribution rate of around 8 percent, being paid two-thirds by the employer and one-third by the employee, based on eight earnings classes with a maximum weekly income of TT$80. The benefit schedule was similar to the one existing today, with a minimum requirement of 750 weekly contributions to access a retirement pension, benefits that are income related and provide higher replacement rates for lower earnings classes and a pension increment awarded for each block of 25 contributions paid in excess of the 750-week minimum.

The system experienced long periods during which no valorization of its parameters occurred. The original definition of earnings classes was in place until 1980, when the income ceiling was raised from TT$80 to TT$230 per week (TT$1,000 per month). This definition remained in place until May 1999, when the income ceiling had to be raised from TT$1,000 to TT$3,510 per month. This has meant that for a long portion of its existence, the National Insurance contributions and benefits have been relatively low compared with real wages in the economy. Even today, the real value of the income ceiling is approximately 25 percent lower than in 1980. This may partly explain the high compliance rate (85 percent of the employed population contribute to the National Insurance Board of Trinidad and Tobago [NIBTT]) and the concentration of contributions in the top earnings class (35 percent of contributors) that we observe today.

Perhaps the most relevant reshuffle of the benefit schedule for National Insurance retirement pensions was the introduction of a minimum pension in 2003. The minimum pension was originally set at TT$1,000 per month; it was increased to TT$2,000 in 2008 and again to TT$3,000 in February 2012. The evolution of the parameters of the system, coupled with the introduction of this minimum pension, has resulted in a system that effectively today pays out a flat benefit.

The Current Pensions System

The current pension system in Trinidad and Tobago has multiple components that can be categorized in at least three layers: a noncontributory pension for those old age people with a low income, a contributory pension for salaried workers, and occupational pension plans. The first layer, the noncontributory pension, benefits individuals who are 65 years of age or older and earn an income below a certain threshold. This benefit is currently called the Senior Citizens Pension (originally Old Age Pension) and is managed by the Ministry of the People and Social Development. The second layer is the contributory, mandatory, defined benefit system managed by the NIBTT. It covers all salaried workers, in both the public and private sector, and provides pensions for individuals who are 65 years of age or older, or 60 and older if retired from work. The third layer of benefits corresponds to occupational pension plans, offered by some employers in the private sector, and public sector pensions, which are available to all monthly-paid public sector employees.

The NIBTT is implementing a comprehensive plan to enforce compliance of contributions by self-employed individuals, for which the mechanism to pay contributions has not been implemented yet. The system is based on 16 earnings classes, defined as brackets with a minimum and maximum level of earnings, which determine the amount of weekly contributions to be paid, depending on the earnings of the individual, as can be seen in table 14.1. The number of earnings classes and their bounds have evolved over the years to adapt to the increase in real wages in the economy. The contribution rate is currently 11.4 percent (one-third employee, two-thirds employer) of earnings since January 2012. The contribution rate has increased from a level of 9.3 percent in 2006 to 10.5 percent in 2008 and 10.8 percent in 2010 following the recommendations of the seventh actuarial review. Employers collect and pay contributions to the NIBTT. The official retirement age is 65, but no penalty exists if the

Table 14.1 Earnings Classes and Contributions in Effect from January 2, 2012, to March 3, 2013, Based on a 11.4 Percent Contribution Rate

Earnings in TT$

Earnings classes	*Weekly earnings*	*Assumed average weekly earnings*	*Employee's weekly contribution*	*Employer's weekly contribution*	*Total weekly contribution*
I	120.00–199.99	160	6.08	12.16	18.24
II	200.00–269.99	235	8.93	17.86	26.79
III	270.00–359.99	315	11.97	23.94	35.91
IV	360.00–449.99	405	15.39	30.78	46.17
V	450.00–549.99	500	19.00	38.00	57.00
VI	550.00–659.99	605	22.99	45.98	68.97
VII	660.00–769.99	715	27.17	54.34	81.51
VIII	770.00–879.99	825	31.35	62.7	94.05
IX	880.00–1,009.99	945	35.91	71.82	107.73
X	1,010.00–1,129.99	1,070.00	40.66	81.32	121.98
XI	1,130.00–1,259.99	1,195.00	45.41	90.82	136.23
XII	1,260.00–1,399.99	1,330.00	50.54	101.08	151.62
XIII	1,400.00–1,549.99	1,475.00	56.05	112.1	168.15
XIV	1,550.00–1,719.99	1,635.00	62.13	124.26	186.39
XV	1,720.00–1,914.99	1,818.00	69.07	138.13	207.2
XVI	1,915.00 and over	1,915.00	72.77	145.54	218.31

Source: National Insurance Board of Trinidad and Tobago (NIBTT) 2010.

person retires at 60 or older for reasons of leaving work. This clause seems to exist to accommodate the initiation of benefit payments to public sector retirees, whose retirement age is 60.

On retirement a pension is calculated based on the average earnings class throughout the career. Given that earnings classes have been redefined over the years as the system evolved, each modification in the earnings classes was coupled with a retroactive definition of the categories. This redefinition of contributions paid, coupled with the instauration of a minimum pension that now reaches TT$3,000 per month (US$460 approximately), has translated into all retirees from the NIBTT receiving a monthly pension of TT$3,000. In other words, in practice the NIBTT is currently a contributory flat benefit system that coexists with a noncontributory flat benefit system (the Senior Citizens Pension). In principle, this gives little incentive to participate and make contributions into the system, although we will later see that coverage is relatively high.

Public sector employees are subject to special regimes that complement the pension obtained from the NIBTT, with different schemes for specific groups of workers.[1] The most common rule for monthly-paid civil servants and teachers is a pension calculated as 2 percent of the last salary before retirement per each year of service with a maximum of two-thirds. This means that after 33 and one-third years of service, the individual reaches the maximum pension level. The vesting period (minimum years of service to obtain a pension) is 10 years, and the compulsory retirement age is 60, with some exceptions for executive positions.

Workers in the private sector and in large publicly owned firms can access employer-sponsored private occupational plans that complement the pension received from NIBTT. These plans are generally defined benefit plans, financed by employer and employee contributions, and managed by trustees. The Board of Inland Revenue is responsible for registering the pension plans, because contributions are tax deductible. Regulation and supervision of these occupational plans is carried out by the Central Bank of Trinidad and Tobago (CBTT). According to information provided by CBTT, 199 employers offer pension plans covering 37,760 active members as of December 2010, which corresponds to 6.5 percent of the total number of persons with jobs in that period. Members of occupational plans enjoy adequate income protection given the defined benefit nature of these plans and the supplement they provide to NIBTT benefits. However, given the low coverage of this type of plans, members represent a privileged group of the population. In addition, defined benefit plans are subject to the potential economic pressures suffered by their sponsors. Occupational plans must be adequately supervised to ensure that the promise of income security during retirement can be fulfilled.

Figure 14.6 highlights three of the main characteristics of the pension system in Trinidad and Tobago. First, little income replacement is found in the system. The predominance of flat benefits such as the Senior Citizens Pension and the prevalence of minimum pensions in NIBTT and public sector pensions result in a benefits system that is mostly flat, with no relationship between income during retirement and earnings during work careers. This presents potential

Figure 14.6 Schematic Representation of the Trinidad and Tobago Pension System

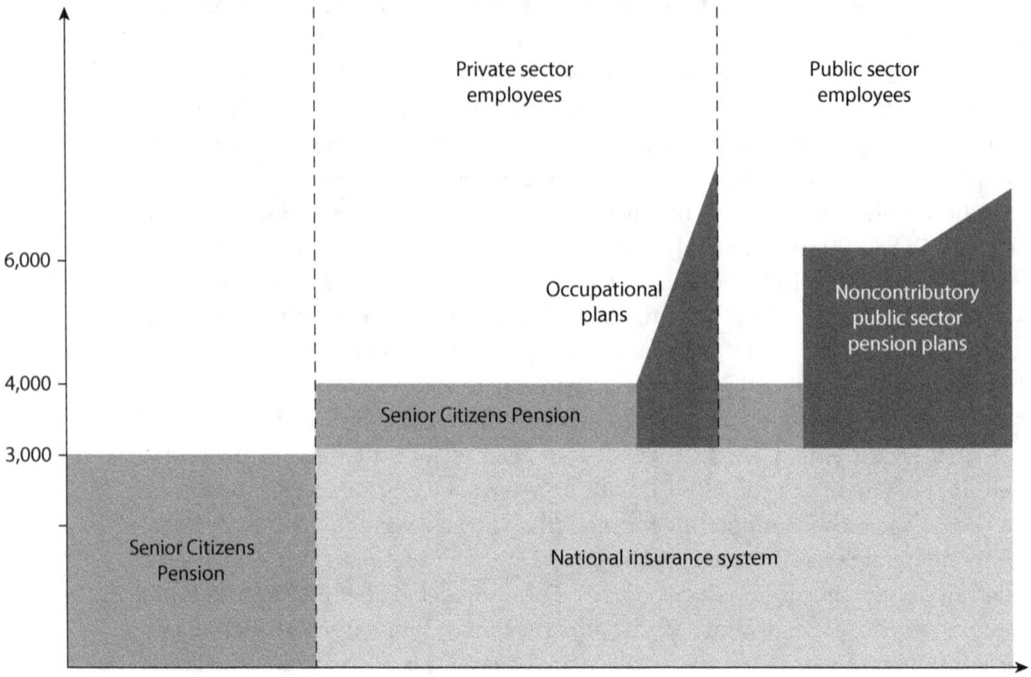

shortcomings in terms of adequacy for high-income groups and incentives to contribute in contributory schemes.

A second characteristic is its fragmentation. The system provides benefits depending on the sector in which the individual was employed. Although National Insurance covers everyone, different provisions apply for supplemental pensions whether the individual worked in the public or private sector, with no portability of benefits among them. Even within the public sector, several different provisions impose a cost in terms of pension entitlements whenever the individual moves from one position to another. Some public sector employees are not covered by any provision, particularly daily-paid and contract workers. These features do not adjust well to a mobile labor market, which is the characteristic of a competitive economy in the 21st century.

Finally, the system has universal coverage. At least in principle, anybody aged 65 and older is entitled to a benefit. Even if someone does not contribute for at least 750 weeks to National Insurance, the individual can rely on a Senior Citizens Pension from age 65, provided compliance with some residency criteria and an income threshold. This implies that the steps toward building a universal pension scheme do not require expanding coverage to uncovered parts of the population in the case of Trinidad and Tobago, but ensuring better integration between the different pieces of the pension system to cover the old age population in an effective way.

Table 14.2 summarizes the current system in Trinidad and Tobago according to this framework (developed by the Word Bank for classifying pension systems according to the different means of pension provisions that are used in different countries)[2] and sets out the key features of each element. A range of changes have been made to the minimum payout for the Senior Citizens Pension in recent years, from the National Insurance System and from the Civil Service schemes. The table aims to show the latest position. Since Civil Service pensions are often pay-as-you-go defined benefit schemes, they are formally in the first pillar, but for reform options it can be instructive to compare their schemes with comparable employer-sponsored schemes in the third pillar. There is no second pillar arrangement in the country.

Recent Trends in the Traditional Pensions System

One of the most relevant dimensions of coverage is the number of people in old age who receive income support in the form of a pension. To quantify this measure of coverage in the context of Trinidad and Tobago, we need to take into account the different pension arrangements that apply to diverse parts of the

Table 14.2 Pension Arrangements in Trinidad and Tobago, by World Bank Pillars Model

	Zero pillar	*First pillar: A*	*First pillar: B*	*Third pillar*
Program	Senior Citizens Pension	National Insurance Scheme (NIS)	Public service pensions (monthly paid workers)	Private sector occupational plans—defined benefit Personal defined contribution pensions
Legislation	Senior Citizens Pensions Act	National Insurance Act 1971 (with amendments)	11 main plans with more than 20 relevant acts	Insurance Act/Income Tax Act/1969 Draft Regulation/1939 Trust, Ordinance Income Tax Act (s134)
Managed by	Ministry of People and Social Development	NIBTT, Report to Ministry of Finance	Ministry of Finance/ relevant ministry	Trustees (IRB and Central Bank supervise) Financial services firms
Financing	General Budget	(11.4% salary 1/3 employee 2/3 employer) and asset returns	General Budget with small contributions for three plans	Employer and employee contributions (plan-specific for DB plans), variable for DC plans
Retirement age	65 and older	65, but retire at 60 without penalty	Varies: from 45 to 60 for unreduced pension	Based on plan (often 60) Based on "maturity date" chosen between 50 and 70
Benefits	Means tested, TT$3,000 for poorest and decreasing scale	TT$3,000 minimum after 750 week of contributions, effectively flat rate	DB rules vary by plan, new TT$3,000 minimum, maximum 2/3: 85% salary	Typically DB: no guaranteed indexation, some insurance benefits, DC: linked to returns
Coverage	All 65+, means tested	All employed, 85% coverage in 2009, self-employed to be added	Membership of relevant profession and plan rules	As per plan rules, 37–55,000 active members, 140,000 annuity policies

Note: DB = defined benefit; DC = defined contribution; NIBTT = National Insurance Board of Trinidad and Tobago; NIS = National Insurance Scheme.

population at distinct eligibility ages. This gives rise to different categories of beneficiaries. First, individuals with no income in old age are eligible for a full Senior Citizens Pension starting at age 65. Second, public and private sector workers who contributed for at least 750 weeks to NIBTT are eligible for a national insurance retirement pension starting at age 60. Third, national insurance beneficiaries covered by public sector pensions (monthly paid civil servants, armed forces, etc.) or by occupational plans in the private sector are eligible for a supplemental pension that complements the NIBTT retirement pension. Finally, National Insurance beneficiaries with no other income during retirement are entitled to a reduced Senior Citizens Pension starting at age 65.

Given this, the relevant figures for coverage are given by the recipients of NIBTT retirement pensions from 60 to 65 years old and by the combination of NIBTT recipients and Senior Citizens Pensions recipients for the population 65 and older. The number of recipients of long-term benefits from NIBTT represents 73 percent of the total population aged 60 or older, and the number of recipients of retirement benefits represents 48 percent (figure 14.7). Long-term benefits include survival benefits and some of them effectively go to elderly widows with no other form of income support, so the true coverage figure of NIBTT benefits among the older population lies between these two numbers. Retirement pensions that are paid to individuals between 60 and 64 years old cover 41 percent of the population in this age group, with significantly higher coverage for men (58.5 percent) than for women (27 percent).

Figure 14.7 Pensions Coverage, 2005–10

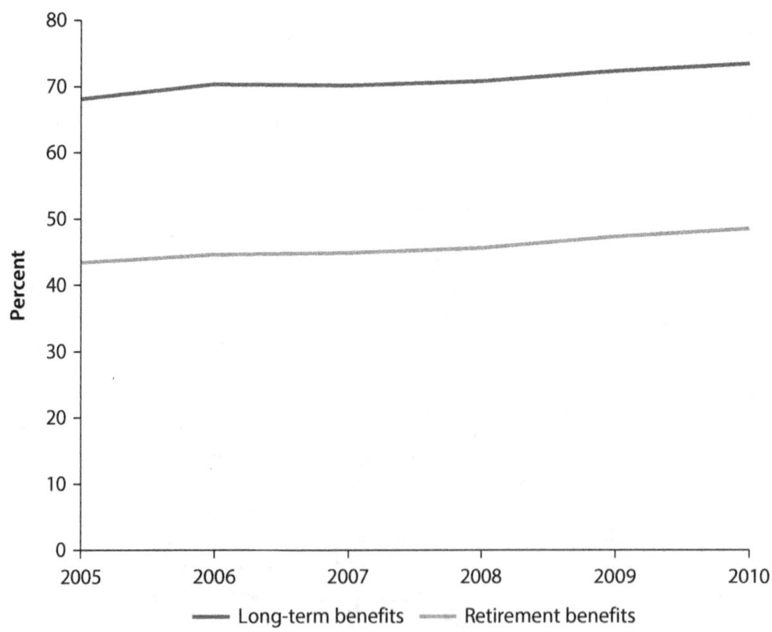

Source: Based on National Insurance Board of Trinidad and Tobago Annual Reports and Central Statistical Office.

In parallel, the number of beneficiaries of Senior Citizens Pensions corresponds to 80 percent of the population aged 65 and older, which is a high coverage rate by international standards. Because an overlap between Senior Citizens Pensions recipients and NIBTT recipients is seen, coverage in these age groups is even higher. However, the available information does not allow us to accurately measure this overlap.

Benefits Adequacy

The basic benefit of the contributory pensions reaches around 45 percent of the average income earned by workers. When beneficiaries receive the other pillar's components they recover the full average income. The adequacy of benefits is usually a measure that takes into account two dimensions: (1) Are the benefits enough to prevent poverty in old age (core adequacy) and (2) are benefits enough to maintain quality of life at a similar level as the one the individual had while working (broad adequacy).

In terms of broad adequacy it is relevant to compare the benefits obtained by retirees with the income levels they had while working. As an approximation, it is possible to compare the level of benefits with the average earnings of current workers in the economy. Table 14.3 shows that a minimum pension recipient from NIBTT received at the end of 2010 a benefit equivalent to almost 45 percent of the average earnings in the economy, and those who also received Senior Citizens Pension reached nearly 90 percent. On the other hand, a private sector retiree received a pension that was higher than the average economy-wide earnings by 12 percent. However, when compared with average earnings in the respective job category, both private sector retirees receiving NIBTT and Senior Citizens Pension benefits and public sector retirees received a total benefit that is close to 66 percent of the average earnings for paid employees and for public sector employees.

Affordability and Fiscal Costs

The amount of resources devoted to pension programs represent close to 4.35 percent of GDP. In 2010 expenditure on Senior Citizens Pensions represented 1.4 percent of GDP, the cost of public sector pensions ascended to 1.43 percent of GDP, and expenditure on long-term benefits for NIBTT beneficiaries (retirement, survivor's, and disability pensions) represented 1.53 percent of GDP.

Table 14.3 Value of Pension as a Percentage of Average Earnings, by Type of Worker, 2010
Percent

	All workers	*Private sector workers*	*Public sector workers*
Minimum pension (NIBTT)	44.9	33.1	n.a.
NIBTT + Senior Citizens	89.8	66.3	n.a.
Public sector plus NIBTT minimum	112.2	82.8	65.9

Source: Based on Central Statistical Office statistics.
Note: NIBTT = National Insurance Board of Trinidad and Tobago. n.a. = not applicable.

Although these figures represent the total public pension spending in Trinidad and Tobago, part of these expenditures are financed by general revenues (the Senior Citizens Pension and public sector pensions) and part by contributions and a reserve fund (the NIBTT). Expenditures on the three programs have rapidly grown between 2008 and 2009 but seem to have stabilized since then (figure 14.8).

Noncontributory pensions also represent an increasing proportion of government resources. In 2011, expenditure on public sector pensions and Senior Citizens Pensions combined represented more than 10 percent of government revenues, up from the 5.5 percent they represented in 2005 (figure 14.9).

The cost of public sector pensions is such that if a contribution would be imposed on all public sector employees to pay for the cost of pensions each year, such contribution would have to be higher than 27 percent of gross wages. In the case of public sector pensions, a contribution rate is just an accounting mechanism, because both gross salaries and pensions are paid from the same source of general revenues. Nevertheless, the level of this hypothetical "equilibrium" contribution rate suggests that public sector pensions are imposing increasing pressure on the fiscal budget (figure 14.10).

Profile of a Longstanding Noncontributory Pensions Program: The Senior Citizens Pension

Noncontributory pensions adjustments have a long history in Trinidad and Tobago, even longer than contributory transfers. These pensions experienced several reforms, the most important ones related to the eligible population. Since 2010 the program has been known as the Senior Citizens Pension.

Figure 14.8 Pension Expenditure as a Percentage of GDP, by Pension Program, 2005–10

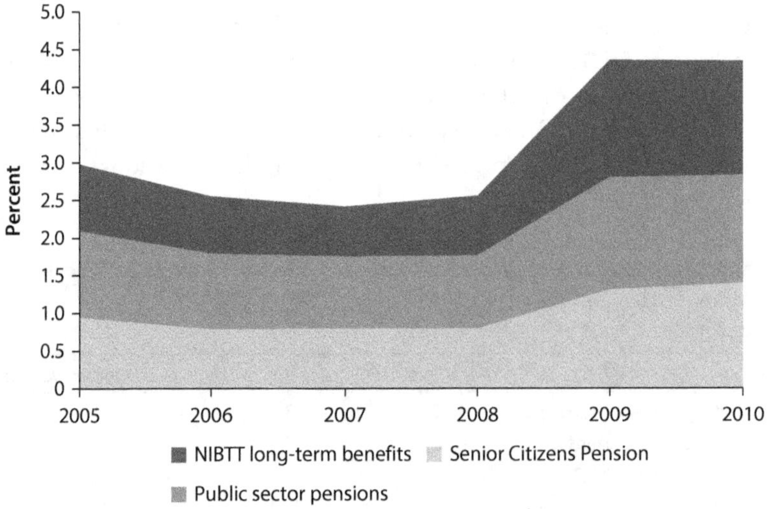

Source: Based on National Insurance Board of Trinidad and Tobago Annual Reports and Government of the Republic of Trinidad and Tobago Budget Reports, various years.
Note: NIB = National Insurance Board.

Figure 14.9 Pension Costs as a Percentage of Government Revenues, 2008–12

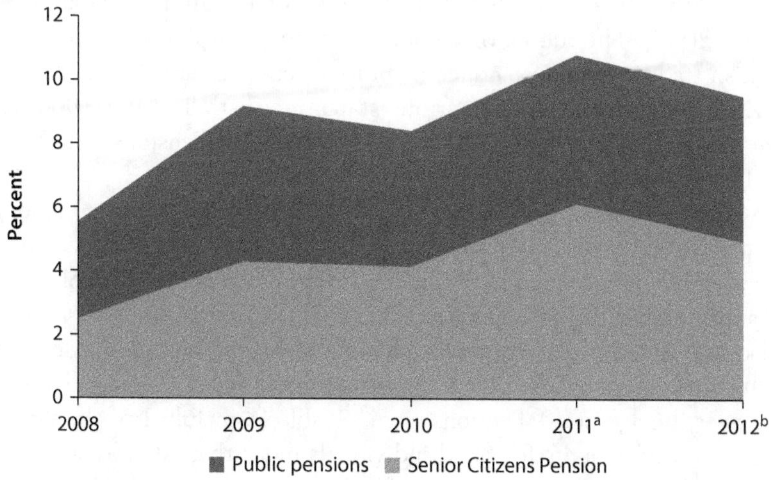

Source: Based on Government of the Republic of Trinidad and Tobago Budget Reports, various years.
a. Estimated.
b. Forecasted.

Figure 14.10 Pay-As-You-Go Equilibrium Contribution Rate: Public Sector Workers, 2008–12

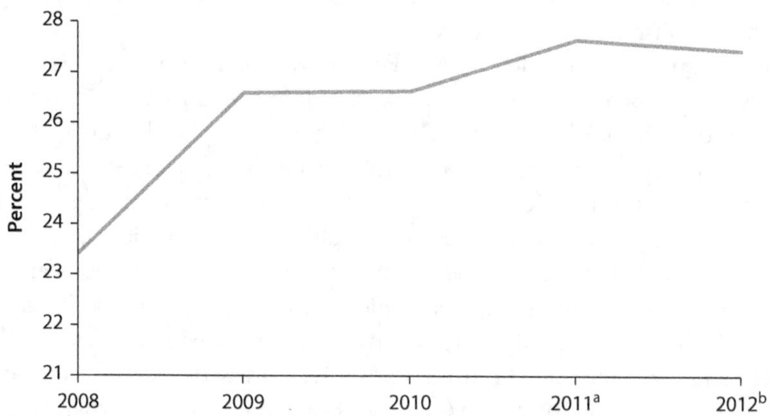

Source: Based on Government of the Republic of Trinidad and Tobago Budget Reports, various years.
a. Estimated.
b. Forecasted.

History of the Program

Trinidad and Tobago introduced a noncontributory pension for individuals aged 65 and older in 1939, while still under British colonial rule. The introduction of such a benefit followed the climate of social unrest that the colonies of the West Indies experienced in the period between 1934 and the eve of World War II as a result of the Great Depression, which included historic riots in Barbados and Trinidad in 1937. In fact, Barbados was the first colony to implement such a pension (at a modest level and for individuals aged 70 and older) in July 1937, and British Guiana followed after Trinidad in 1944 (Seekings 2006). The model of a noncontributory pension was adopted from the British tradition because noncontributory pensions had been introduced in New Zealand in 1898, in the various states in Australia from 1900, and in Britain (and Ireland) in 1909, under its 1908 Old Age Pensions Act (Macnicol 1998; Thane 1996).

The idea of a pension for old age individuals gained acceptance among the governors of the islands and in the case of Trinidad and Tobago was championed by key political figures, such as the Major of Port of Spain, founder of the Labor Party, and member of the Legislative Council, Mr. Arthur Andrew Cipriani. In Trinidad and Tobago a bill providing for old age pensions was passed in June 1939. It provided a small pension to people over the age of 65, as well as to blind people over the age of 40. Pensions were payable from July 1 of the same year. The provision of benefits for blind individuals older than 40 was subsequently transferred and complemented with other benefits in the Public Assistance Act of 1996, leaving the Old Age Pension purely as a cash transfer for the elderly.

The early adoption of a noncontributory pension places Trinidad and Tobago as one of the first countries in the world to introduce cash benefits for the elderly. The old age pension was the most important component of the pension system in Trinidad alongside the Civil Service Pensions that were operational since 1934. The contributory Social Insurance pensions did not come into effect until 1972, with the establishment of the NIBTT.

Throughout the years, the Old Age Pension was periodically revised to adjust the level of the benefits and income threshold, but no structural modifications were introduced, and the scheme seems to have gathered little public attention. The residence criteria was modified in 1996 from the original 20 years immediately preceding the claim for a benefit with maximum temporary absences summing up to two years in that period to a double criteria of residence during the last 20 years with a maximum absence of five years or a total of 60 years in the country. The benefit was renamed a "Senior Citizens' Grant" in 2007 and finally a "Senior Citizens Pension" in 2010. A dual schedule of benefits was introduced in 1996 and was maintained until 2009. Individuals with income close to zero receive the full benefit, and individuals with income below a certain threshold received a reduced benefit, generally TT$100 lower than the full pension. In 2009 a third category was introduced, and in 2010 the ladder schedule that is utilized today was implemented.

According to Weise (1969), there were 35,223 recipients of the Old Age Pension at the end of 1966, which represented 80 percent of the population aged 65 and over. By 1995, the first date for which modern administrative data are available, more than 59,000 people received this benefit, at a cost of TT$262 million. This represents more than 80 percent of the population older than 65 years of age and 0.83 percent of GDP for 1995. These figures show that the program has had high coverage for a long time and as a result is an important component of the pension policy.

One of the most radical changes that this program experienced was in 2010, around the early elections called that year by the government. As part of the campaign, the incumbent government promised to increase the minimum level of the Old Age Pension from TT$1,950 to TT$2,500 and did so in May 2010, before elections were held later that month. As a result, the benefit became much more generous, with significant increases in the amount of pensions received at each income bracket and on the income thresholds to qualify for such benefits. Additionally, for the first time the level of the noncontributory pension surpassed the level of the minimum pension for members of NIBTT, which requires 750 weeks of contributions and was set at TT$2,000 at the time.[3] However, the opposition coalition made a similar campaign bid and promised to increase the level of the pension to TT$3,000 per month. Since the opposition won this early election, the basic level of this pension reached this amount in September 2010. As a result, the basic Senior Citizens Pension grew by almost 40 percent in real terms between 2009 and 2010, whereas it had grown by 13 percent in real terms over the previous five years, between 2004 and 2009 (figure 14.11).

Coverage and Adequacy

As of December 2011 there were 77,897 recipients of Senior Citizens Pensions, which is equivalent to around 79 percent of the total population of individuals aged 65 and older in Trinidad and Tobago. As far back as 1995 and throughout the period, coverage of this program has been 80 percent of the eligible population or higher. Therefore the means test seems to have been operating in practice as an "affluence test" in the sense that instead of targeting the benefit to the very poor it is in essence impeding the 20 percent most affluent to access the benefit (table 14.4).

Figure 14.11 Real Value of Senior Citizens Pension, 1999–2011

Source: Based on Ministry of the People and Social development and Central Statistical Office.

Table 14.4 Coverage of the Senior Citizens Pension, by Age and Gender, 2011
Percent

Age	Male	Female	Total
65–69	66.1	67.8	67.1
70–74	80.9	75.9	77.9
75–79	97.4	83.1	88.1
80+	114.6[a]	92.3	98.7
Total	82	78	79.3

Source: Based on administrative records and United Nations Population projections by age groups.
a. The number of male recipients of Senior Citizens Pensions in the group aged 80 or above is higher than the estimated total population in that group according to the United Nations Population projections. This may indicate a problem of underestimation in those projections or may be due to administrative errors in the payments of Senior Citizens Pensions or in the recording of ages of beneficiaries. In any case it would require further investigation, and from these figures we just highlight the general trends that show that coverage increases with age and is somewhat higher for men (82 percent) than for women (78 percent).

It is interesting to notice that despite the complex benefit schedule introduced in 2010 with 10 income brackets, more than 90 percent of recipients obtain either the full TT$3,000 or the reduced TT$2,000. This indicates that the vast majority of applicants either declare no income or declare only the income from their NIBTT pension. This reflects that the capacity of detecting other sources of income is very limited for the Ministry of the People and Social Development.

The bimodal distribution of pensions has a gender component: Although 52 percent of males receive the full pension and 36 percent receive the reduced TT$2,000 pension, 82 percent of women receive the full pension and just 9 percent the TT$2,000 pension (figure 14.12). This is probably a result of women being less likely to qualify for a National Insurance pension because of lower labor force participation and higher incidence of partial careers among female workers.

The value of the full Senior Citizens Pensions of TT$3,000 per month, which is given to individuals with income lower than TT$500 per month, is equivalent to one-third of GDP per capita, around 1.36 times the value of the minimum wage, and 2.6 times the value of the poverty line, which was updated from 2005 to 2011 using the Retail Price Index variation between those years. These figures are comparatively high for a typical social pension, whose aim is to alleviate poverty in old age and serve those who otherwise would not have other sources of income.

Costs and Sustainability

In 2011 the total cost of the Senior Citizens Pension was TT$2.57 billion, or 1.8 percent of GDP. The cost of the program as a percentage of GDP increased rapidly in the last three years because of the increase in generosity, which increased the numerator, coupled with stagnation in growth, which lowers the denominator. The fact that recent increases in generosity have increased the cost of the program put in danger the long-term sustainability of the Senior Citizens Pension as currently designed.

Given the current distribution of Senior Citizens Pensions and the coverage of the program, we ran a simulation of the cost of this program for the future, based

Figure 14.12 Distribution of Senior Citizens Pension Amounts, by Gender, 2011

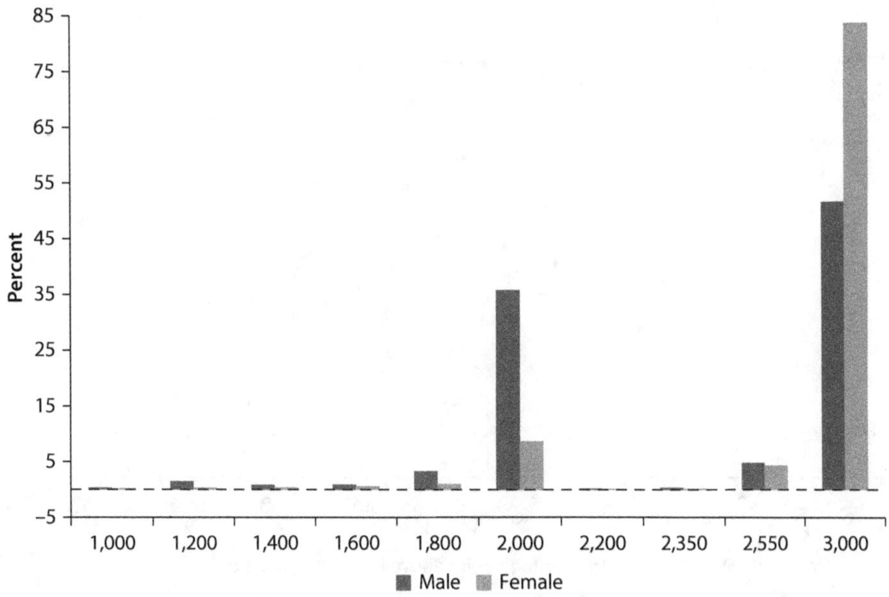

Source: Based on data provided by Ministry of the People and Social Development.

on demographic assumptions, under different alternative scenarios. If the current coverage and distribution of pensions were to be maintained, and their values adjusted with inflation, the cost of the Senior Citizens Pensions is projected to increase from the current 1.8 percent of GDP to 2 percent in 10 years, reaching 2.3 percent of GDP by 2030. Given the demographic projections and macroeconomic assumptions, the cost is expected to decrease starting in 2030, but would remain above 2 percent of GDP for the foreseeable future.

Although the coverage of the program is very high and the majority of beneficiaries receive the full pension, a universal pension that pays TT$3,000 per month to all citizens aged 65 and older would be considerably more expensive. The cost of such program would be 2.8 percent of GDP in 2012 and would increase to 3.6 percent of GDP by 2030, adding more than 1 percent of GDP to the cost of the current program (figure 14.13).

The most important parameter that will affect the cost of the program in the future is the indexation policy. If, for example, pension values were adjusted 1 percentage point above inflation each year (continuing the increasing rate between 1999 and 2011), this would mean a significant increase in the cost of the program, which would surpass 2.7 percent of GDP by 2030 and reach figures close to 3 percent of GDP in the long run.

Impacts on Poverty

The latest poverty figures in Trinidad and Tobago were obtained in 2005 and show that although the national poverty rate was estimated at 16.7 percent of total population, among individuals aged 65 or older, the poverty rate was just

Figure 14.13 Cost Projections for Senior Citizens Pensions, 2011–50

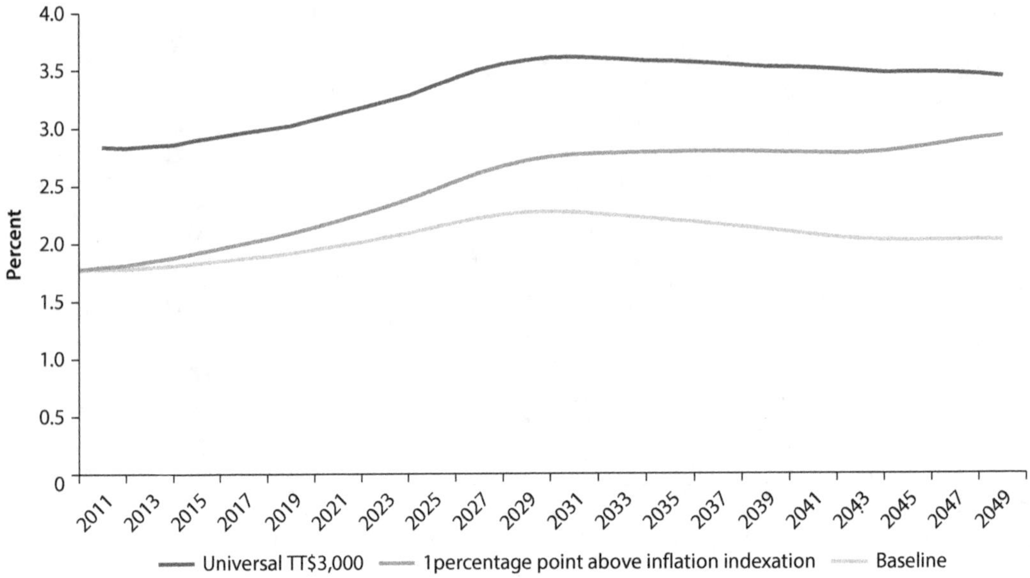

Source: Based on Ministry of the People and Social Development data.

6.7 percent. Poverty is much higher among the youth and tends to decrease with age. Poverty and inequality in Trinidad and Tobago are measured using the Survey of Living Conditions (figure 14.14). The last version of this survey is from 2005, before the dramatic increase in generosity of the program, but in a period where the pension reached almost 80 percent of the population 65 years old or older in the country.

Since these figures consider a Senior Citizens Pension whose real value was almost 50 percent lower than the current TT$3,000 per month, we ran a simulation to assess what the poverty incidence would have been in 2005 with the current value, in real terms, of the Senior Citizens Pension.[4] The results of this simulation show that the increase in Senior Citizens Pension (almost doubling it in real terms) would have had a limited impact on poverty incidence among the total population of Trinidad and Tobago (table 14.5). Overall poverty would fall 1 percentage point, with vulnerability falling another percentage point and no effect in extreme poverty, given that extreme poverty incidence is low and households receiving Senior Citizens Pensions are automatically above the extreme poverty line, at least in terms of income.

If we restrict our analysis to households with individuals older than 65 years old the effect is more meaningful. Although the initial poverty incidence is lower, the increase in the real value of the Senior Citizens Pension reduces the poverty rate by 1.5 percentage points and the population that is at least vulnerable by 3.75 percentage points, increasing the proportion of nonpoor/nonvulnerable among households with individuals 65 years of age or older from 87 percent to 90.7 percent (table 14.6).

Figure 14.14 Poverty Rates, by Age Group, 2005

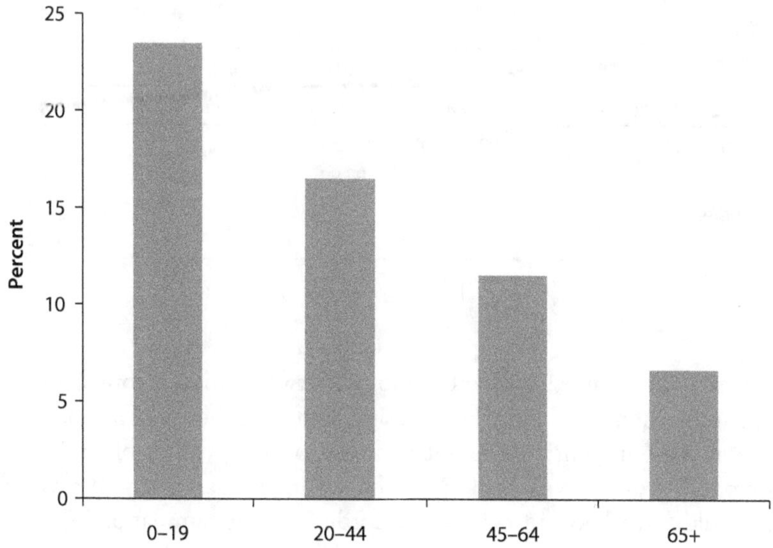

Source: Kairi Consultants 2007.

Table 14.5 Simulated Effects of Increasing the Senior Citizens Pension on Poverty Rates
Pension

Socioeconomic status	*Original results*	*New old age pension*
Extreme poor	1.2	1.2
Poor	15.9	15.0
Vulnerable	11.0	9.7
Nonpoor	71.9	74.1
Total	100	100

Source: Based on Survey of Living Conditions 2005.

Table 14.6 Simulated Effects of Increasing the Senior Citizens Pension on Poverty Rates for the Population Aged 65 and Older
Percent

Socioeconomic status	*Original results*	*New old age pension*
Extreme poor	0.3	0.2
Poor	6.4	4.9
Vulnerable	6.3	4.2
Nonpoor	87.0	90.7
Total	100	100

Source: Based on Survey of Living Conditions 2005.

Table 14.7 Transition Matrix across Poverty Status Following Increase in the Senior Citizens Pension
Percent

	After simulation			
Before simulation	*Extreme poor*	*Poor*	*Vulnerable*	*Nonpoor*
Extreme poor	98.02	1.39	0	0.59
Poor		92.99	5.70	1.30
Vulnerable			79.51	20.49
Nonpoor				100.00

Source: Based on Survey of Living Conditions 2005.

Analyzing the transition of households between these groups due to the increase in pension amount, it becomes evident that the most important effect that the increase in pension amount had was to move vulnerable individuals to the nonpoor category. Nearly 20.5 percent of individuals living in a vulnerable status would have become nonpoor according to the simulations. The second largest effect is that 5.7 percent of those initially categorized as poor would have become vulnerable, as shown in table 14.7.

Effects on the Labor Market

There is no evidence that the benefit provided by the Senior Citizens Pension generates adverse incentives in labor market participation for individuals aged 65 and older. The current design of the Senior Citizens Pension is a subsidy that effectively guarantees a minimum monthly income of TT$4,000 for anyone who earns between TT$1,450 and TT$3,000 per month (figure 14.15). This gives little incentive to earn or declare income higher than TT$1,450 and a big incentive to under declare income if the person earns more than TT$3,000. However, the two most common pension amounts indicate that people either declare no income or they declare the income coming from their NIBTT pension.

The level of generosity in the Senior Citizens Pension also gives raise to the potential effect that people who would otherwise participate in the labor market and work opt to retire and receive this pension. The labor force participation rate for individuals aged 65 or more is very low in Trinidad and Tobago, which could be a response to the existence of this noncontributory pension. It is interesting to notice that the lowest participation rates and the highest drops in labor force participation between the age group 55–64 and the age group 65 and above in the Caribbean occur in the only two countries that offer a noncontributory pension in old age: Barbados and Trinidad and Tobago.

However, when we analyze the rapid increase in the level of the Senior Citizens Pension in the period of May–September 2010 and compare labor force participation before and after that period, there does not seem to be a significant decrease in the employment rate of individuals 65 and older, compared with other age groups who were not affected by the increase in pensions (figure 14.16).

Figure 14.15 Total Income under Current Schedule of the Senior Citizens Pension

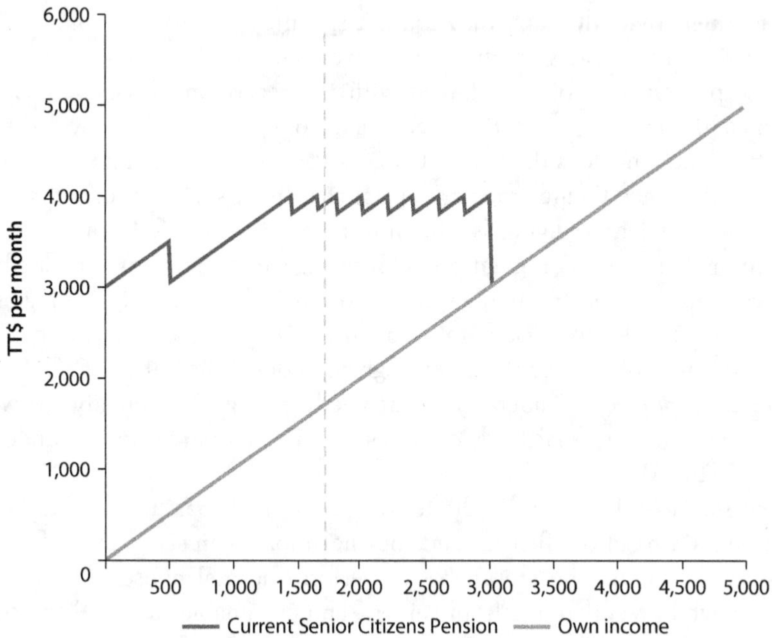

Figure 14.16 Labor Force Participation Rates, by Age Group, 55 and Older, 2008–11

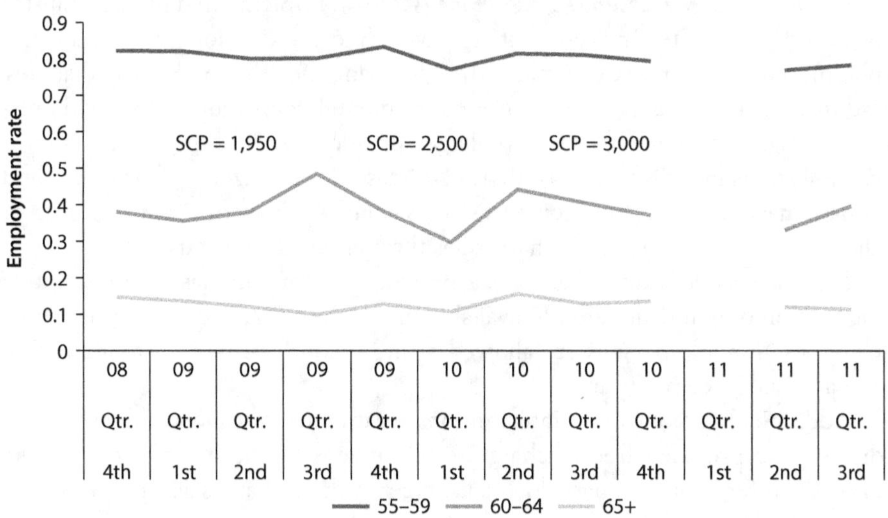

Source: Central Statistical Office Labor Force Bulletin, various issues.
Note: Data for first quarter 2011 is not available. SCP = Senior Citizens Pension.

Social Services to Elderly Population

Several programs are managed by the Ministry of the People and Social Development that, although they are not specifically aimed at senior citizens, given their characteristics, are more likely to benefit the elderly population. None of these programs is formally linked with the reception of a Senior Citizens Pension, although they primarily target clients of other services provided by the Ministry, which includes the Senior Citizens Pension. As an example, within the General Assistance Grant program, several triggers of social benefits may prove beneficial for elderly individuals. The most relevant are the following.

Housing Assistance. This grant provides assistance to clients to purchase building materials for construction or repair of their homes. A one-off grant of TT$15,000 is given to persons to access materials from a reputable hardware vendor. In times of disaster the amount given under this grant is TT$20,000.

Medical Equipment. Under this grant needy persons can qualify for wheelchairs, commodes, special beds, dentures etc. The amount allowed under this grant is TT$7,500.

Domestic Help. This grant facilitates the provision of part-time domestic help for three months in the first instance but not more than six months if deemed necessary to clients who are unable to perform normal household chores, for example, while recuperating from surgery, and are unable to afford the cost of domestic assistance. The amount paid to a caregiver is TT$1,800 per month.

Dietary Grant. This grant of TT$600 per month assists clients who suffer illnesses that require special diets, for example, renal patients and clients with uncontrolled diabetes.

Chronic Disease Assistance Programme (CDAP). Implemented by the Ministry of Health, the CDAP provides citizens with free prescription drugs and other pharmaceutical items to combat the following health conditions: diabetes, asthma, cardiac diseases, arthritis, glaucoma, mental depression, high blood pressure, benign prostatic hyperplasia (enlarged prostate), epilepsy, hypercholesterolemia, Parkinson's disease, and thyroid diseases. All citizens of Trinidad and Tobago have access to a specified list of around 47 prescription drugs free of charge at approximately 250 pharmacies throughout the country.

Pharmaceutical Grant. This grant is provided for the purchase of prescriptive medication only if drugs are not available under the CDAP or at the public dispensaries. Suitable persons are allowed a three-month supply up to TT$2,500 and are paid once per year.

Additionally, among other interventions, treatments for cancer and respiratory diseases are provided free of charge to all citizens at specific medical centers upon the referral of a primary doctor. Emergency dental care is also provided free of charge at specific dental centers.

The Ministry of the People and Social Development also includes a Division of Ageing, whose main objective is to educate the population on ageing issues and coordinate the implementation of the National Policy on Ageing, which was developed by a multidisciplinary committee and approved by the cabinet in 2006. This division holds regular dissemination and training events as well as managing the senior activity centers in Trinidad and Tobago where older persons can attend and take part in educational and recreational activities.

Citizens aged 65 and older and social welfare recipients can apply for a free bus pass, allowing them to travel free on the public transportation service. In addition, the Ministry of Community Development runs a program called the Geriatric Adolescent Partnership Program that aims at linking youth with older generations by providing training in geriatric care to the at-risk youth population. Although the aim of the program is developing basic job skills in vulnerable young people, it also serves as a source of affordable care for elderly individuals.

Lessons from the Experience in Trinidad and Tobago

The country has developed a comprehensive pension system with relatively high coverage. The pension system has multiple components that can be categorized in at least three layers. A first layer is a noncontributory pension that benefits individuals who are 65 years of age or older and who earn an income below a certain threshold. This benefit is currently called the Senior Citizens Pension and is managed by the Ministry of the People and Social Development. The second layer is the contributory, mandatory defined benefit system managed by the NIBTT. It covers all salaried workers, in both the public and private sector and provides pensions for individuals who are 65 years of age or older with no other requirement, or 60 and older if retired from work. The third layer of benefits corresponds to occupational pension plans, offered by some employers in the private sector, and public sector pensions, which are available to all monthly-paid public sector employees.

Currently, the country is not facing a severe shortfall in pension financing, although it has recently increased benefits in a way that may affect its finances in the near future.

One of the characteristics that stands out in the pension system is the lack of coordination between its different components. In some aspects the system is fragmented, because benefits depend greatly on the sector of employment and little portability is found among them. On the other hand, when benefits are compatible among each other, redundancy is seen in their objectives and their compatibility does not ensure better income protection. The latter is the case between the Senior Citizens Pension (managed by the Ministry of the People and Social Development) and the National Insurance pensions (managed by NIBTT).

To assess the effectiveness of the pension system, it is necessary to analyze the environment in which the pension system operates. This environment is affected by three primary factors: (1) the demographic conditions, which determine the composition and evolution of the population that will be subject to participation in the system; (2) the macroeconomic situation, which determines the availability of resources in the economy; and (3) the characteristics of the labor market, which determine the extent of coverage for a contributory system. The fact that these environmental factors differ from country to country is one of the reasons why one size does not fit all in pension policy. A policy that is appropriate in a high-growth, young, and flexible labor environment may not be adequate in a stagnant, highly indebted, highly informal, and aging economy.

The evolution of the pension system in Trinidad and Tobago differs from the typical cases in Latin America. For a long time, the main component of the pension system was the noncontributory benefits for individuals aged 65 and older, alongside the pension schemes for public sector workers. The contributory National Insurance scheme only started to operate in 1972. Given the modest benefits promised under the National Insurance system and the degree of formality and dynamism of the economy, the contributory defined benefit system looks solid with a high level of funding. However, policy decisions regarding the level of the minimum pension have transformed the contributory system into a relatively generous flat benefit system that overlaps with the noncontributory Senior Citizens Pension. This threatens the future health of the contributory system, both because it has increased the implicit promise made to participants in the system and because it has reduced the incentives to participate in the system.

The interaction between the Senior Citizens Pension and the National Insurance retirement pension generates important challenges for the pension policy in the country. It is worth questioning whether it is reasonable to have a flat benefit noncontributory scheme operating alongside a flat benefit contributory scheme. It seems more sensible to devote the task of providing an absolute minimum income level during retirement to the noncontributory benefit while pursuing adequate income replacement through the contributory scheme. This would require improving the income replacement features in the National Insurance scheme and revising the compatibility of Senior Citizens Pensions with NIB pensions.

The current legislation for the Senior Citizens Pension indicates that there is a means test and that the value of the pension depends on the individual's total income at the time of claim. However, in reality any other income different from a formal pension (provided by NIBTT or a public pension plan) is very difficult to verify. In addition, the means test is not particularly strict, because 80 percent of the population older than 65 receives a Senior Citizens Pension. Given these considerations, and consistent with the view that the Senior Citizens Pension is an essential component of the pension system in Trinidad and Tobago, it may be more practical to enforce just a pensions test, disregarding any other sources of income to qualify for a Senior Citizens Pension. This pension test would include retirement as well as disability or survivors pensions, as needed, and could easily be made based on the individual records held by NIBTT.

At the same time, despite the current design of the benefit schedule comprising 10 income brackets, in practice 90 percent of Senior Citizens Pension recipients receive either the full pension or the amount that corresponds to the complement of the NIB retirement pension. It may therefore be worthwhile to simplify again the benefit schedule and have only two benefits, consistent with checking just the pension income.

The experience also shows that when two programs are serving the same population, compatible with each other and managed by different agencies, the role of good registration and monitoring systems becomes critical. Inclusion errors are found in the Senior Citizens Pension because its record systems are not fully compatible with those of NIBTT. This problem would be easier to solve were both programs to be managed by one institution.

Political decisions also affect the evolution of the noncontributory system. As long as the benefit value can be modified discretionally, the program is subject to political pressures that may endanger its long-run sustainability. In this sense, adopting an automatic indexation rule could give more predictability to the program. Additionally, given the long-term impacts of the program, it would be advisable to subject the Senior Citizens Pensions to long-term actuarial reviews.

The eligibility age for the Senior Citizens Pension has remained at 65 since its introduction in 1939. However, the life expectancy at birth has changed from 58.3 in 1950 to 70.4 years in 2010 and is expected to reach 81 years by 2100. This means that the Senior Citizens Pension eligibility age has remained constant throughout a period when life expectancy has increased by at least 12 years, and is expected to further increase by 11 in the current century. Given the potential impact of noncontributory pensions on retirement decisions, it is advisable that the eligibility age for the Senior Citizens Pension be equal or higher than the retirement age for contributory pensions. If those retirement ages are somehow pegged to the evolution of life expectancies, it will eventually be necessary for the Senior Citizens Pension eligibility age to follow the same path.

These lessons highlight that although noncontributory pensions may play a relevant or even preponderant role in closing the coverage gap, their design and operation should be carefully articulated with that of the contributory pension systems. Any unbalance in their generosity may provide perverse incentives to participate or affect the sustainability of the system. Inadequate articulation may result in inefficiencies on public spending. The parameters of the system, such as the value of the pension and eligibility age, must be carefully reviewed alongside their counterparts in the contributory scheme. A permanent, careful, and comprehensive analysis with a long-term perspective will allow the noncontributory pension scheme in Trinidad and Tobago to continue playing a relevant role in the income provision in old age as it has done for more than 70 years.

Notes

1. There are special rules for teachers, assisted secondary school teachers, police, fire personnel, prison service staff, the military, judges, Industrial Court staff, Legislative Services staff, and Diplomatic Service staff.
2. See World Bank (2008). The pillars are (0) mandatory, public, focus on adequacy and coverage, income and in-kind transfers to support basic consumption; (1) mandatory, public, mainly income replacement, also redistributive minimum pension guarantee, sometimes partly backed by assets in public investment funds; (2) mandatory private, income replacement; (3) voluntary private for income replacement, pure

individual personal pensions and employer sponsored; (4) financial assets, family transfers, housing; and (5) labor income and own-consumption.

3. However, it is worth noticing that a person who contributes would still be better off than a noncontributor because the former would receive TT$1,550 *on top* of the minimum TT$2,000, provided that the National Insurance Pension is his or her only source of income at age 65.
4. The simulation was designed using data from the Survey of Living Conditions and adjusting the value of the pension for those households that report receiving an Old Age Pension, so that it would reach the equivalent of TT$3,000 in real terms in 2005. Notice that the impact of increasing the income threshold that defines eligibility was not simulated. Also, because poverty is measured according to expenditures, the simulated increase in households income was used to simulate an increase in expenditures using an estimated marginal propensity to consume, based on households' characteristics.

Bibliography

Bosch, M. 2012. "Labor Market Impacts of Non-contributory Pensions: The Cases of Brazil and Argentina." Mimeo, Inter-American Development Bank, Washington, DC.

IMF (International Monetary Fund). 2012. *Trinidad and Tobago: Staff Report for the 2011 Article IV Consultation*. IMF Country Report 12/127, IMF, Port of Spain.

Kairi Consultants. 2007. *Analysis of the Trinidad and Tobago Survey of Living Conditions 2005*. Kairi Consultants, Tunapuna.

Macnicol, J. 1998. *The Politics of Retirement in Britain, 1878–1948*. Cambridge, U.K.: Cambridge University Press.

NIBTT (National Insurance Board of Trinidad and Tobago). 2010. "Earnings Classes and Contributions from January 2, 2012." NIBTT, Port of Spain. http://www.nibtt.net/Contribution_Rates/cont_Jan02_2012.htm.

Seekings, J. 2006. "Pa's Pension: The Origins of Non-Contributory Old Age Pensions in Late Colonial Barbados." Center for Social Science Research Working Paper 164, August, University of Cape Town, Cape Town.

Thane, P. 1996. *Foundations of the Welfare State*. 2nd ed. Harlow: Pearson Longman.

United Nations. 2010. *World Population Prospects.* New York: United Nations.

Weise, R. 1969. "British Commonwealth Areas of the Caribbean." *Social Security Bulletin* 32 (4), U.S. Social Security Administration, Washington, DC.

World Bank. 2008. *The World Bank Pension Conceptual Framework*. World Bank Pension Reform Primer Series. Washington, DC: World Bank.

CHAPTER 15

Uruguay

Jorge Papadópulos

History

Social protection for the elderly in Uruguay is operationalized as a set of policies and programs divided into two categories: monetary transfers and differentiated goods and services, respectively. The monetary benefits are highly developed and structured policies that have evolved from the beginning and represent the country's largest social investment. In the case of goods and services, they are delivered via public sector programs that are more heterogeneous. Some are more or less structured policies (such as housing for retirees and pensioners), others are programs within other policies (as is the case for health care for the elderly). Still others are isolated programs offered by specific sectorial policies or local governments that offer a diverse set of programs.

Evolution and Profile of the Elderly Population

Uruguay faces a demographic reality that situates it as the country with the highest proportion of elderly citizens in the region and one of the highest in the world. According to the 2011 National Population Census (Censo Nacional de Población), 12 percent of the total population is over 65 years old, and the percentage of people over 60 years old is nearly 20 percent of the total population of the country. In addition, the country is experiencing "aging within aging," which means that the population aged 75 and older will increase more rapidly than the rest of the population. Moreover, estimates show that the population over age 60 will double between now and 2100, easily surpassing one million people (table 15.1).

In terms of the total demographic structure and the dependency ratio, the quantity of children aged 0–14 years will fall significantly between 2010 and 2100. Finally, a reduction of half a million people is expected in the population aged 15–59 by 2100. Because the system of funding social protection is essentially contributory, this age structure constitutes a limit to its growth. According to the aforementioned projections, by 2050 there will be a little more than two people in the economically active age group (15–60 years) for each elderly person, and in 2100 the ratio will be three elderly persons for every four in the economically active age group, which creates a major challenge for the social policy system.

These trends are connected, as in other countries, to the sustained drops in the levels of mortality and fertility. Uruguay is the country that most quickly began its demographic transition in the region. In 1950 the total fertility rate was less than three children per woman, during a period when the same rate for Latin America as a whole was double this value. In terms of mortality, life expectancy at birth exceeded 66 years in 1950 and has maintained a sustained improvement of approximately one more year of life every five years, currently exceeding 76 years (figure 15.1). The differences in these rates between Uruguay and other

Table 15.1 Evolution of the Population, by Age Group and Dependency Ratios, 1965–2100

Year	*0–14 years*	*15–59 years (1)*	*60 and older (2)*	*75 and older (2)*	*Elderly dependency ratio (2)/(1) (%)*
1965	756,321	1,606,699	331,724	49,103	20.6
2010	758,743	1,992,030	622,470	150,423	31.2
2050	582,853	2,027,541	1,006,767	257,200	49.7
2100	460,865	1,526,537	1,142,923	332,727	74.9
Index of age group size: base 1965 = 100					
1965	100.0	100.0	100.0	100.0	100.0
2010	100.3	124.0	187.6	306.3	151.3
2050	77.1	126.2	303.5	523.8	240.5
2100	60.9	95.0	344.5	677.6	362.6

Source: Centro Latinoamericano y Caribeño de Demografía (CELADE).

Figure 15.1 Evolution of Fertility and Mortality in Uruguay, 1950–2100

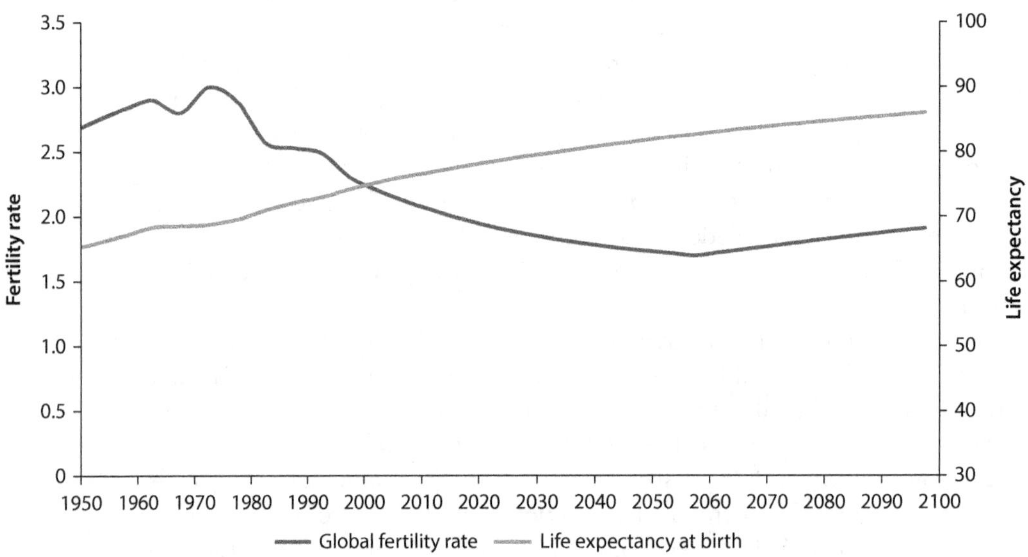

Source: Centro Latinoamericano y Caribeño de Demografía (CELADE).

Table 15.2 Population, by Type of Household Residency and Age, 2011
Percentage of the total

Population	*One-person*	*Nuclear without children*	*Others*
Total	5.1	8.0	86.9
60 years and older	18.1	23.8	58.1
75 years and older	26.3	24.8	49.0

Source: Based on the 2011 National Population Census.

countries in the region have been decreasing over time and are expected to continue on a path to convergence that, by the end of this century, will place the majority of the countries at approximately similar levels.

Slightly more than 40 percent of the elderly over age 60 live with a partner (without children) or alone, a percentage that increases to 51 percent among those older than 75 (table 15.2). In comparison, just 13.1 percent of the population age 20–59 years resides in this type of household. The percentage of the elderly living alone is three and a half times greater than that of the entire population: 18.1 percent versus 5.1 percent. This situation makes the elderly that live alone extremely dependent on their personal income, and therefore the adequacy of the benefits they receive if they are retired.

If the elderly, in addition to living alone, also have some kind of limitation that makes them partially or totally dependent, then those that live alone must turn to a market arrangement to ensure they receive the necessary care. The disability survey undertaken by the Institute of Statistics (Instituto de Estadística [INE]) shows that a little more than 8 percent of the population has some sort of disability. Among the population over age 65, the incidence is 25 percent, which makes them totally or relatively dependent.

The Labor Market

The labor market activity rate in Uruguay has grown constantly in the past two decades, increasing from nearly 70 percent of the population from 25 to 64 years to more than 80 percent between 1988 and 2010 (figure 15.2). Almost all of this increase is explained by greater participation among women, who increased their rate by almost 20 percentage points and reduced the difference between themselves and men to half of the level observed two decades ago.

This increase in women's labor participation has been observed among different age groups, but it is clear that the main improvement has been observed among middle-aged women, from 25 to 55 years old, who are reaching levels near those of their male counterparts (figure 15.3). This trend is important as it relates to the job and employment situation, it but also has significant effects on the social security system, both in the short term (contributing significantly to the increase in the number of potential and effective contributors) as well as in the long term. It implies that many elderly women (who currently receive social security through their spouses and survivor's benefits) will begin to receive retirement benefits for their own work.

Figure 15.2 Total Activity Rate, by Gender, Population 25–64 Years, 1989–2010

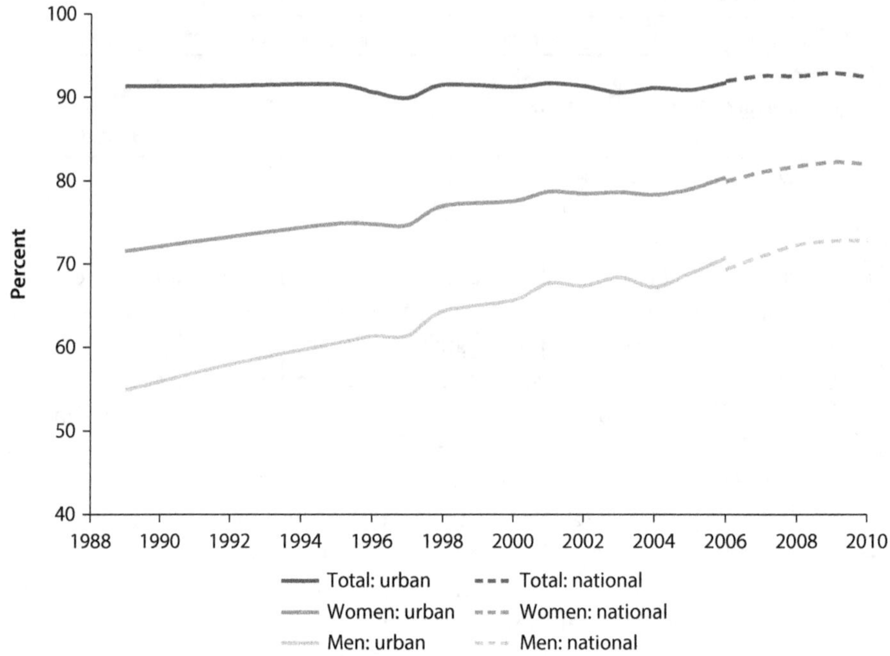

Source: Centro de Estudios Distributivos, Laborales y Sociales (CEDLAS).

Figure 15.3 Female Activity Rates, by Age, 1980–2010

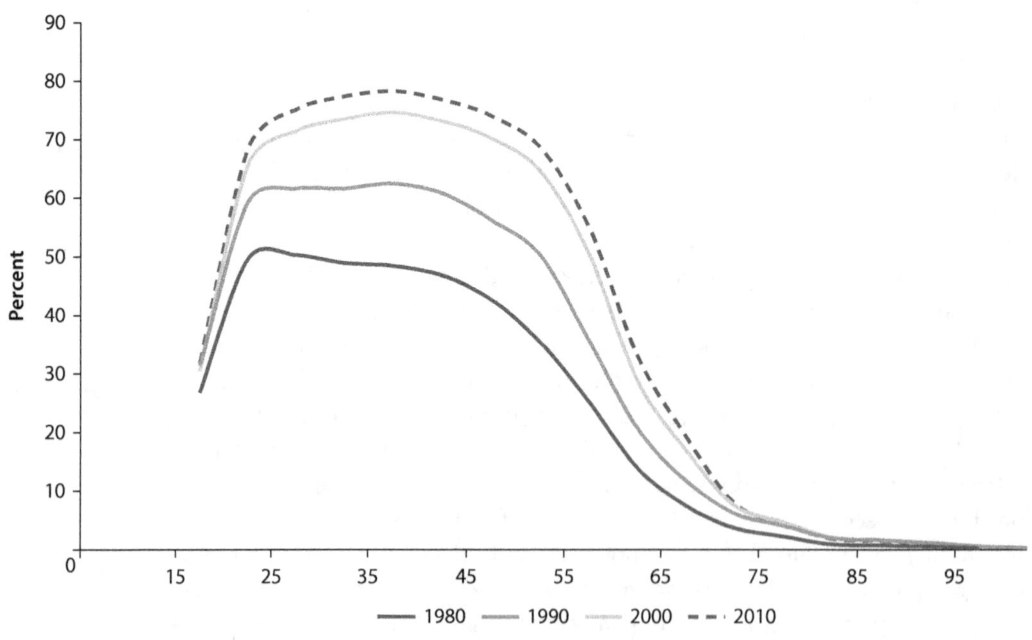

Source: Centro Latinoamericano y Caribeño de Demografía (CELADE).

Figure 15.4 Percentage of Employed Persons with a Formal Job, by Age Group, 1991–2010

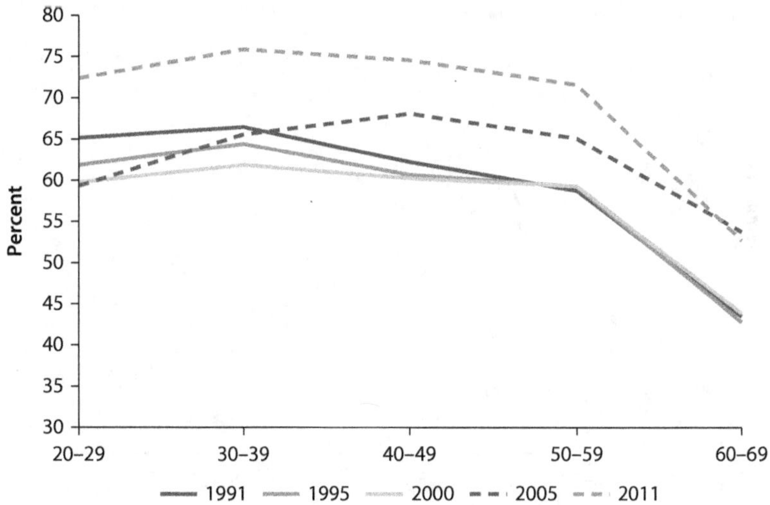

Source: Rofman and Oliveri 2012.

The sustained improvement in women's activity rates (and, as a result, of the whole population) was not directly accompanied by the evolution of labor formality. During the 1990s, while the activity rate was increasing, labor formality was decreasing, from 61.3 percent of employed persons in 1991 to 58 percent in 2000 (figure 15.4). This drop was mostly among younger age groups, that is, those less than 40 years old. In contrast, beginning in 2005 the trend reversed and has improved rapidly, first among older age groups and later expanding to the rest of the population.

An empirically verified reality stands out in Uruguay: The elderly population has a better income situation than other age groups. This ratio has not varied significantly in the last 20 years because, on average, per capita family income for the elderly is between 10 and 20 percent more than that for persons between 40 and 49 years old, and the per capita income for children is significantly less. The curves presented in figure 15.5 show that the fluctuations since 1990 have been minor, with some relative income loss for the elderly during the 1990s and an improvement in the last decade.

The Emergence and Evolution of the Social Security System

Social protection for the elderly began in Uruguay with the fragmented development of a system of disability insurance and survivor's benefits, and later moved toward protection during old age (Mesa-Lago 1978, 1985; Papadópulos 1992). The monetary coverage for the risks of Disability, Old Age, and Survivorship (Invalidez, Vejez, y Sobrevivencia [IVS]) is precisely what allows the elderly to take charge of their situations and enables them to use their income to face the various risks that they are exposed to in old age.

Figure 15.5 Per Capita Household Income, by Age, 1990–2010
base 40–49; years = 100

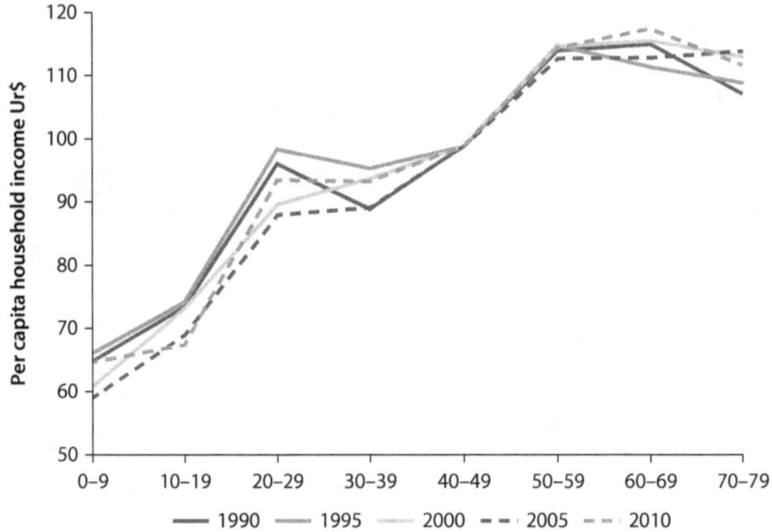

Source: Based on the Encuesta Continua de Hogares (ECH).

Turning the pension programs into a "system" required a long political process that created legislation marked by multiple "relative privileges" (Abranches 1982) for different employment categories. This legislation provided social security benefits by adding programs according to a "vertical logic" (many programs for a few select employment categories) instead of horizontal or citizen-based expansion. As in the rest of the region, in Uruguay initially one did not find an entitlement to protection from the risks associated with the elderly. In contrast, a gradual expansion of social protection occurred for groups of workers that, as a result of their relative power or their place in the structure of the labor market, obtained benefits in a sort of "regulated citizenship" (dos Santos 1979).

Social security—in the strict sense of retirement and pension programs—had several different stages. The first began in 1829, one year before the first constitution of the Eastern Republic of Uruguay was signed. That year the government awarded disability benefits for combatants in the independence wars and survivor's benefits to widows of combatants. Nine years later, in 1838, the government passed a law that awarded retirement benefits to civil servants. These public employees received retirement benefits (upon reaching old age), retirement from work (when for any reason the employee's services were considered surplus), and survivor's pensions. These benefits were funded by a percentage of the salary of the employees and were administered by general revenues. Gradually benefits to members of the military and civil servants became more complicated and grew throughout the 19th century until they accounted for 35 percent of all government spending in 1858.

Almost 70 years later, this first stage was followed by an important institutional innovation in the creation of the first social insurance scheme that followed the Bismarckian model. It was called the "Schools Retirement and Pension Fund." It was the first organization with a financing model in which workers and employers contributed (in this case the government because the members were public school employees). The fund was directed by an Autonomous Council made up of management personnel in public education. The fund was a decentralized organization of the Ministry of Development (Ministerio de Fomento) that was in charge of public education. The fund prepared the case files, but awarding retirement and pension benefits was the exclusive domain of the Executive Branch. Initially the fund awarded benefits to teachers and technical personnel in the schools, but nonprofessional employees were gradually added. This Bismarckian model later expanded to other groups of public workers. This process ended with the creation of the Civil Retirement Fund (Caja de Jubilaciones Civiles) in 1904, which included nonteacher public employees. Later, in 1933, these funds were merged to create the Institute of Retirement and Pensions of Uruguay (Instituto de Jubilaciones y Pensiones del Uruguay).

Elderly pensions were a very important social innovation introduced in 1919. The law created the Institute of Elderly Pensions (Jubilaciones a la Vejez). This legal institute is very important because it introduced noncontributory pensions for those individuals that had not been able to gain an entitlement to a contributory pension. These pensions were awarded to individuals who could prove insufficiency of means (extreme poverty) and were over 70 years old. Even though today it could be considered a residual policy, it was of great importance in a country with low levels of labor formality and high poverty rates.

In 1919, the Retirement and Pension Fund for Public Service Employees and Workers (Caja de Jubilaciones y Pensiones de Empleados y Obreros de los Servicios Públicos) was created, which incorporated private workers for the public services, such as telegraphs, railroads, streetcars, telephones, running water, and gas. The board of directors that was set up to direct this fund included representatives from three sectors: workers, the government, and businesspeople. Both the Civil Fund (Caja Civil) as well as the Public Service Employees and Workers Fund traced a path of gradual inclusion of professional categories from the private sector. The Public Services Fund included various categories of workers from the private sector, and the Civil Fund, in addition to merging with the Schools Fund in 1933, included workers from the departmental governments and other public entities (public bodies and decentralized services).

In 1954 when almost all the private sector workers had been incorporated into the Disability, Old Age, and Survivor's insurance regime, a law was passed that established that "the liabilities regime administered by the Retirement and Pension Fund for Manufacturing and Commerce" will incorporate "all persons that perform legal and remunerated activities and that are not covered by other pension regimes" (Law no. 12,138 of 1954). In this way, the government stopped creating public retirement funds that administered retirement and pension funds for public and private sector workers. This process "universalized privileges" in a highly stratified logic of vertical integration with deep internal inequalities in the value, quality, and type of benefits received by the different occupational groups. This process of incorporation created a stratified system that reflected the labor market's inequalities and exhibited high levels of institutional fragmentation. Other groups of high-income workers, such as university professionals, notaries, and banking employees, subsequently created their own "retirement funds." These institutions were (and still are) semiofficial, meaning that they are administered by their beneficiaries (active and retired) and supervised by the government.

During its first decades of existence (until the middle of the century) the young retirement system allowed the funds to generate surpluses, and they were organized as collectively funded regimes. As the system matured, the funds began to experience deficits and had to resort to financial support from the government. The system's maturation and the concurrent crisis, which was already noticeable in the 1960s, was not just a consequence of the demographic shift and population aging. The crisis was the result of the unorganized incorporation of occupational sectors, the irrational creation of new benefits, and the lack of technical expertise in managing the accumulated financial resources.

Up until 1967, when the constitution was reformed, the creation of retirement and pension benefits, as well as other benefits and benefit increases, were initiated by the legislative branch. Social security and its funds were a political resource at the service of political parties, which had developed a particular and clientelistic brand of politics (Filgueira 1970) that made the system completely irrational. Moreover, the system's directors adopted investment policies for the system's funds that in some cases were aimed at development (such as financing two large hydroelectric projects) and in other cases were aimed at satisfying their "clientele's" interests (loans to officials to buy residences and summer homes, their furnishings, and construction of rental properties for retirees and pensioners). In both cases the loans, both for public works as well as for properties for system officials, were offered with repayment periods of 30 years and interest rates fixed at 6 percent per year. The country's economic stagnation beginning in the mid-1950s, accompanied by growing inflation, completely wiped out the retirement system's reserves.

The constitution that took effect in 1967 equipped the executive branch with greater economic and financial management and planning abilities. It took the power to initiate retirement legislation away from the legislative branch and concentrated it in the executive branch and also created the Social Protection Bank (Banco de Previsión Social [BPS]). The BPS was created as an independent entity, with financial and administrative autonomy from the central administration organizations. It merged the various funds and advanced toward the unification of criteria for awarding benefits and their amounts, and it tried to streamline management. However, these measures were not sufficient to improve the economic and financial equations in a context of rising labor market informality and an institutional management style that continued to facilitate "informal" retirement mechanisms, with little proof of contributions from employers and workers.

A new stage for social security began with the civilian-military dictatorship that governed the country between 1973 and 1985. Using its complete control of the government, this dictatorship tried to deepen the administrative streamlining and advance the centralization of management. The BPS was replaced by the General Directorate of Social Security, an agency dependent on the Ministry of Labor and Social Security. The fragmented funds that covered the areas of health, family allowances, and maternal and child health care were centralized in various directorates (Mesa-Lago 1985).

The social protection model that the Uruguayan regime adopted differed radically from the Chilean model, despite the regime's liberal economic rhetoric. In Uruguay the pension system was not privatized, but rather the government sought to streamline it while maintaining the same economic and financial logic of the previous social protection model (Papadópulos 1992). The normative changes that made the access mechanisms for retirement and pension benefits more rigid also created indexation instruments for monetary benefits. However, instead of improving the value of the benefits that they indexed, these tools became—along with the real value of public sector salaries (according to Saldain 1987)—"adjustment variables" of the fiscal deficit. Thus, the average real value of benefits fell almost 30 percent between 1982 and 1985.

The period that began with the democratic opening in 1985 reinstated the BPS, but the regulations created by the dictatorial regime for system management as well as those regarding awarding pension benefits remained mostly unchanged. In the area of social security, democratization invigorated two large demands. The first was the incorporation of workers, retirees, and businesspeople into the BPS board of directors. These sectors had a longstanding desire (legitimized by the constitutional mandate) that the BPS board of directors should be made up of representatives from the executive branch as well of workers, retirees, and businesspeople. The second great aspiration was improving the value of the system's monetary benefits. This was a major battleground between the government on one side and the leftist opposition (the Frente Amplio coalition) and a vigorous and powerful retiree and pensioner movement on the other side. The dispute was settled in 1989 when, along with national elections, the retirees and pensioners achieved the approval of a constitutional change via popular vote that indexed benefits to the median salary. In this way, after 1989, the indexation mechanisms led to increases in spending on retirement and pensions benefits. This spending reached 15 percent of gross domestic product (GDP) in 1995 and represented 3 percent of the fiscal deficit.

As can be seen in figure 15.6, the political and legislative negotiations during the early years of the democratic opening led to an increase in the revaluation of benefits, which stagnated in 1989. This stagnation was the issue that drove the retiree and pensioner associations to push for the constitutional change. Its impact was immediate, and the value of retirement and pension benefits was linked to workers' salaries. Thus, benefits increased during boom periods and were affected by crises, as occurred in 1995, and more clearly in 2001–02.

Figure 15.6 Evolution of the Benefit Revaluation Index in Real Terms, 1985–2011

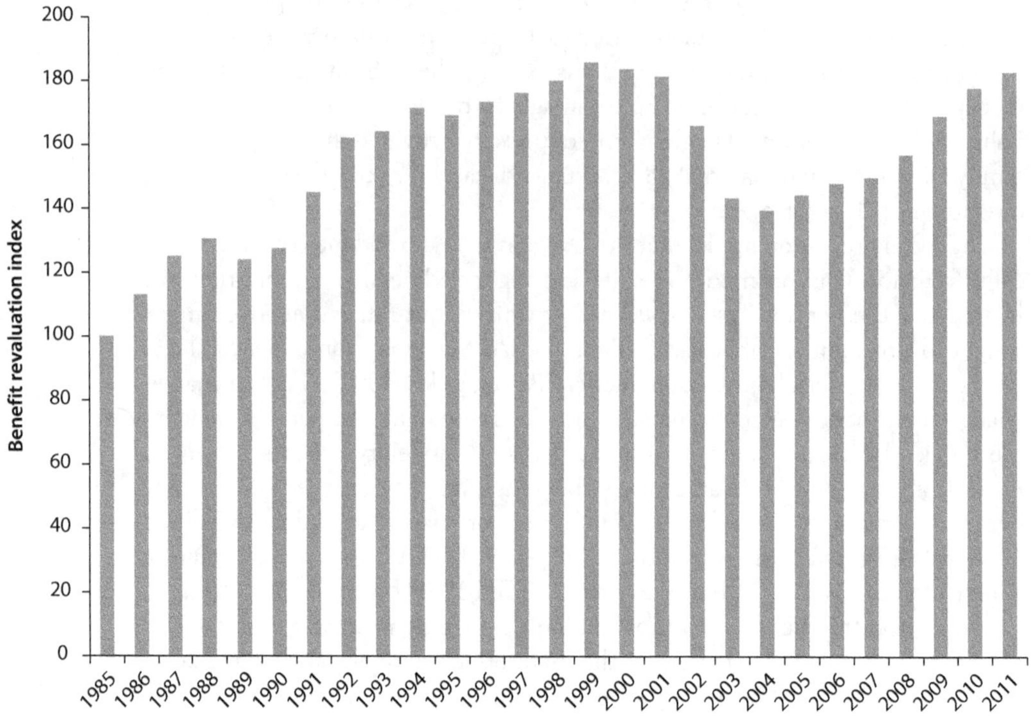

Source: Banco de Previsión Social (BPS), Statistical Bulletin 2005 and 2012.

In 2011 the benefit level neared its historical maximum from 1999 and was nearly 80 percent higher than in 1985 in real terms.

The 1995 Reform of the Retirement and Pension System: The Construction of a Mixed System

In 1995 Law no. 16,713 was approved, which took effect in April 1996. This law created a mixed retirement system (pay-as-you-go and individually funded) whose objective was to spread risk, improve benefits, and balance or reduce the pension system's accumulated deficit. The reform was preceded by a law five years earlier that made registering both salaried and independent workers' job histories mandatory, as well as business' employment histories. These employment histories were to be managed by the BPS and became the main means of proof of contributions to the system. Thus, Law no. 16,713 established that beginning in 1996 only the record of activity in a worker's employment history could be used as proof of employment. Alternatively, documentary proof would be accepted, and as a last resort, witness testimony. In the Uruguayan retirement system, testimony from witnesses has been used to evade responsibility for contributions to the system and receive benefits without contributing. The creation of a subsystem of individual accounts administered by private institutions would have been infeasible without an improvement in the registration systems that allow for efficient collections and benefits closely linked to individual contributions.

According to the classification system developed by Mesa-Lago and Bertranou (1998), the system is a mixed type.[1] This means that the intergenerational pay-as-you-go subsystem coexists with and is connected to the new individual savings subsystem.[2] It is common in specialized literature to speak of "pillars" when referring to the components of a system. Strictly speaking, the pillar metaphor does not exactly fit the Uruguayan case. It is more appropriate to maintain the overlapping components metaphor because one component complements the other.

The law established three income groups that determine how workers are included in the social security system. Low-income workers contribute only to the pay-as-you-go component. Middle-income workers contribute to the pay-as-you-go component until reaching the income limit and contribute to the individually funded component for the rest of their income. A third category of contributors, workers who have income levels above the secondary limit set by the law, contribute additional savings voluntarily. Essentially those workers with very high incomes contribute obligatorily to the first and second components of the system, and only voluntarily contribute based on the rest of their income to the individually funded system. In this way, upon retirement, the benefits are combined, with the portion returned by the pay-as-you-go component on the one hand, and the amount generated by the individually funded component on the other.

Nonetheless, the law gives low-income workers (those whose income is below the primary limit) the opportunity to contribute to the individually funded component. These workers contribute to the intergenerational pay-as-you-go system based on 50 percent of their income and to the individually funded component for the other 50 percent. When the base retirement salary is calculated, contributions made to the pay-as-you-go component are multiplied by 1.5. This option is a clear stimulus to promote membership of low-income workers in the mixed system.

In terms of workers' and employers' contributions, employers contribute 7.5 percent of salaries, and workers contribute 13 percent. One hundred percent of the employer contribution is paid into the pay-as-you-go system, and workers' contributions are distributed between the components according to the contribution percentage for each of them.

This structural reform was preceded by parametric adjustments that changed the retirement age, replacement rates, and number of years of work necessary before retirement. According to the regulations in force until 1996, the replacement rate varied from 60 to 80 percent of the worker's average salary during the last three years of employment. The retirement age was 55 years for women and 60 years for men. In either case a minimum of 30 years of economic activity was required, along with the corresponding contributions.[3] In the new legislation, the minimum retirement age was standardized at 60 years (for men and women), the required years of work and contributions increased to 35 years, and the replacement rate was calculated based on the last 10 years of employment or the best 20 years of the contributor's employment history. These parametric reforms made the conditions for retirement much stricter, which, as expected, reduced access to benefits and as a result lowered spending and the deficit.

The 1995 Reform of Traditional Noncontributory Programs: Defining Access

Noncontributory benefits have a long history in Uruguay. The first noncontributory pensions were created in 1919 with Law no. 6,874 and were for persons aged 60 and older. The legislation on this subject advanced and in 1934 was elevated to the constitutional level, which was ratified in the 1967 constitution, and is still in force. In it (article 67) the document states that "elderly pensions constitute an entitlement for anyone who reaches the limit of their productive age, after a long residence in the country and lacks resources to pay for his vital needs." Constitutional law does not regulate the entitlement to elderly and disability pensions as a subjective right, but rather it makes this entitlement conditional upon the economic capacity of the potential beneficiary's family. The regulations gradually changed targeting criteria, mainly in terms of defining age and "indigence and disability" until reaching the 1995 reform.

The 1995 reform established access requirements according to the type of benefit. In the case of elderly pensions, the reform established that the beneficiary must be an inhabitant of the republic (it does not require citizenship, but at least 15 years of continuous residence), at least 70 years old, and lacking economic resources to meet his or her basic needs. To this effect, the system considers the applicant's income along with that of family members that are legally obligated to sustain him or her, whether or not they live together. The BPS is in charge of analyzing and determining the situation of need. The regulations establish that to access the benefits, the beneficiary cannot receive income greater than the amount he or she would receive from the elderly pension (about US$360). If the beneficiary's income (from any source) is lower than this amount, he or she will be entitled to a benefit that covers the difference. Nonetheless, if the family that is obligated to meet the pensioner's needs exceeds certain income levels, the pensioner does not receive the benefit. Obligated family members include spouses, children, siblings, and parents. If the potential beneficiary lives with obligated family members, to access the benefit, family income cannot exceed US$240 or US$360 depending on the type of family member. In the event that the potential pensioner does not live with family members, his or her income should not exceed the value equivalent to US$1,000 or US$1,200 depending on the type of family member.

In relation to the noncontributory disability pension, persons of any age in a condition of absolute disability for any type of remunerated work without sufficient resources to cover their basic needs can be beneficiaries. Just as with elderly pensions, disability pensions are subject to means testing, both for the beneficiary and for obligated family members, although the maximum income amounts are different from the amounts for elderly pensions. The requirements are as follows: not to receive income above three Base Units for Benefits and Taxes (Base de Prestaciones y Contribuciones [BPCs]) (US$360); that the obligated family unit with whom the person with a disability lives does not receive income that exceeds two or three BPCs, that is, US$240 or US$360 (depending on which family members are the caretakers); and that the obligated family members that do not live with the pensioner do not receive income that exceeds US$1,200 if they are married and US$1,000 if they are unmarried.

The Effects of the Reform on Costs, Funding, and Coverage

The referendum passed in 1989 implied the indexation of the value of benefits to the variation of the median salary index. It was expected that this would make spending levels very inflexible and that they would increase continuously, pushing the system into a deficit. This concern was the primary motivation behind the 1996 reform. However, between 1996 and 2004 the growth of the government's contributions to spending were concomitant with the fall or the stabilization of collections from contributors, which indicates that the reforms aimed at greater effectiveness in collections (the so-called employment history) were not enough to increase them.

The system's total spending, which had increased from 10 percent of GDP in 1990 to almost 14 percent in 1996, began a slow process of reduction that allowed the total to stabilize around 10–11 percent of GDP after 2004 (figure 15.7). However, the "genuine" resources (i.e., the contributions) also

Figure 15.7 Total Resources and Expenditures of the BPS, 1990–2011

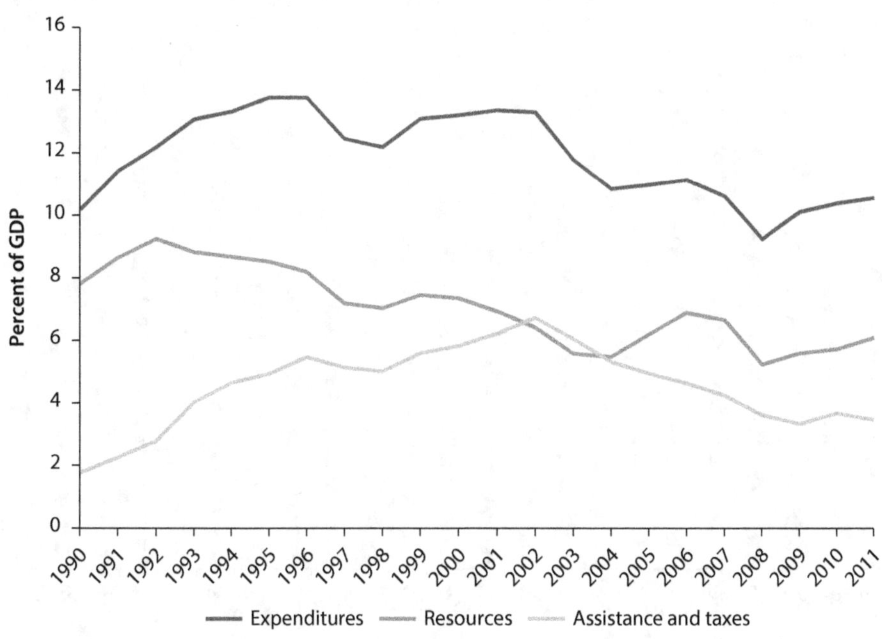

Source: Based on Banco de Previsión Social (BPS), 2012.

decreased, which caused the level of assistance from the national treasury (including connected taxes and direct transfers to the BPS) to continue increasing after the reform, until reaching a maximum level of 6.2 percent of GDP in 2002. After this point, better collections results allowed these transfers to decrease, falling to 3.5 percent of GDP in 2011.

One goal of the 1996 reform was to promote an increase in the formalization and registration of workers in the contributory system, along with the registration of employment histories. As figure 15.8 shows, after the reform took effect, the number of contributing jobs effectively increased between 1996 and 1998. However, this growth was affected by the economic difficulties that began in 1999 and by the severe crisis that the country suffered in 2002, whose impact on the formal labor market lasted until 2004. Strictly speaking, it would appear that economic growth has a very strong effect on labor formality regardless of the scheme that is adopted to manage the social security system.

According to data from the Continuous Survey of Households, in 1990 nearly 90 percent of individuals older than 65 years received contributory pension coverage.[4] The variation between 1990 and 2000 (among the same type of coverage) exhibits a slight downward trend, which continues until 2008. In the last

Figure 15.8 Evolution of the Number of Positions Contributing to the BPS, 1988–2011

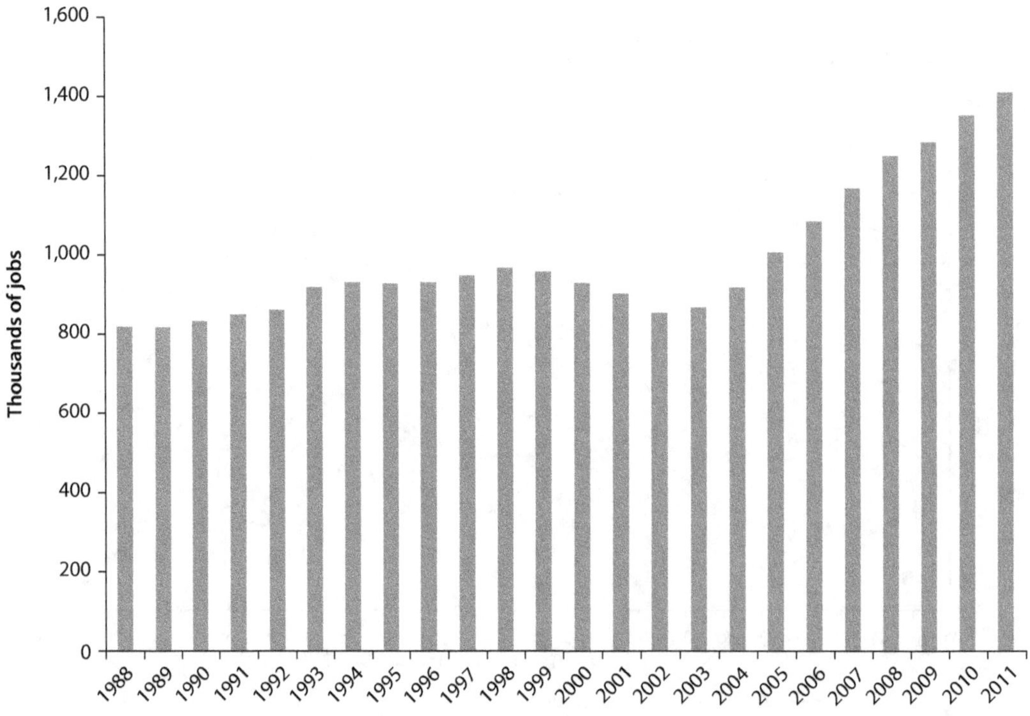

Source: Banco de Previsión Social (BPS), 2005, 2012.

Figure 15.9 Social Security Coverage among the Elderly, 1989–2010

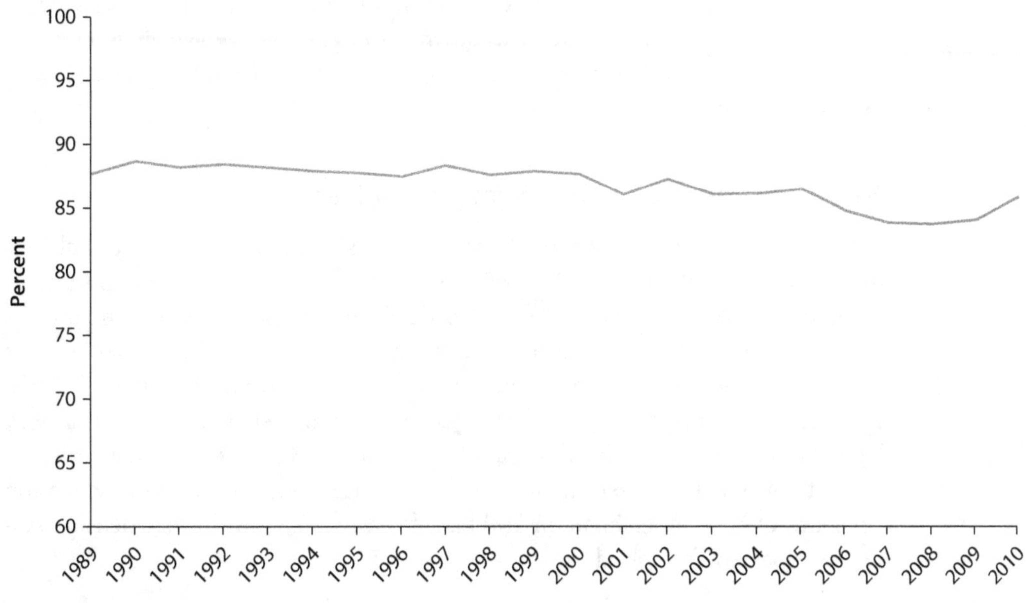

Source: Rofman and Oliveri 2012.

two years observed, the level began to rise again because of the reform implemented in 2008 (figure 15.9). These coverage levels are among the highest in the region. This information does not discriminate based on type of coverage (retirement, pension, contributory, or noncontributory benefits). The type of coverage determines the benefit amount because retirement benefits are higher than pensions, and contributory pensions are higher than their noncontributory counterparts. As we know, coverage is not equal to adequacy. Moreover, as long as the contributory retirement regime replicates the structure of labor market inequalities, it is likely that a significant percentage of retirement benefits will be for very low amounts. When the BPS registration information is analyzed, the image is somewhat different, with somewhat higher levels, possibly because of the differences in the base population considered.

The absolute number of BPS benefits showed a declining trend between 2001 and 2009, mainly because of the drop in the number of contributory retirement and pension benefits. Retirement benefits fell from 383,098 in 2000 to 358,492 in 2008, and contributory pensions from 277,406 to 271,029 during the same period. Noncontributory pensions, in contrast, grew from 65,486 to 71,999. We can suggest that as the registration of workers' employment histories was consolidated and the requirements for retirement increased (mainly in terms of age and number of years worked), access became more difficult, mostly affecting workers with lower contribution densities (women, harvest workers, and low-income workers).

After 2004 the improvement in the economic environment and the triumph of the Frente Amplio did not immediately translate in a change in the downward trend in the number of benefits. This downward trend in coverage did not reverse until 2009, with the beginning of the implementation of a reform that we will discuss in the next section.

New Programs and Reforms: Recent Initiatives

After 2005 the government sought to increase social protection for the elderly in two ways. On the one hand, in an innovative scheme, the government implemented the Social Equality Plan (Plan de Equidad Social), which included a series of structural social reforms such as the reform of the health system, the creation of the National Integrated Health Care System (Sistema Nacional Integrado de Salud [SNIS]), and other social programs such as noncontributory benefits for minors (family allowances) as well as for workers and the elderly. For the latter group, the government created a new noncontributory Elderly Pension program. On the other hand, in 2008 a reform to the contributory pension system was passed that eased access.

Noncontributory Pension Programs

The new noncontributory benefits did not seek to restructure the existing schemes, but rather were built as a complement to them, targeting their benefits at a more vulnerable population than the one cared for by the traditional programs. The programs began in 2005 with the National Plan for Attention to the Social Emergency (Plan Nacional de Atención a la Emergencia Social [PANES]), a shock program that sought to reduce the high levels of social vulnerability resulting from the 2001 crisis. The plan began at the beginning of the administration of President Tabaré Vázquez. Management of PANES was turned over to the Ministry of Social Development (Ministerio de Desarrollo Social [MIDES]) to be implemented as a short-term project with a limited budget. The noncontributory social benefits were tools to provide coverage to informal segments of the labor force as well as to vulnerable low-income families.

At the same time, the government advanced with changes to the regulations regarding the social security system. In December 2007 Law no. 18,241 was passed, which created a subsidy benefit for persons with insufficient resources between 65 and 70 years old. This benefit reached those individuals that did not qualify for elderly retirement (70 years old and 15 years of registered contributions—Law no. 16,713—or that did not meet the age requirements for the Elderly and Disability Pension—70 years and lacking resources to meet their basic needs). Strictly speaking, this reform eases access to the so-called elderly pensions by not requiring contributions such as the elderly retirement scheme and lowering the minimum age to access the benefit. The poverty and extreme poverty status required by the law to be eligible for the pension must be accredited and proven by technical test mechanisms whose parameters are determined by the Economics Department of the University of the Republic (Facultad de Economía de la Universidad de la República).

In contrast to access to traditional pensions, which are evaluated by the BPS, MIDES determines access for the assistance pensions. Once a potential beneficiary has satisfied all of the requirements, MIDES notifies BPS, which pays the benefit to the beneficiaries in an amount equal to the noncontributory assistance benefit established in Law no. 16,743 (older than 70 years without the ability to meet their basic needs). The funds used to pay these benefits do not correspond to the BPS, but rather are part of MIDES's budget and are transferred to the BPS.

Reforms to the Contributory Benefits Regime

Laws that eased access to the retirement system were also passed between 2007 and 2008. One of these laws had a general scope, and the other regulations were issued with the goal of easing access or improving benefits for specific professional categories. Law no. 18,395 (general scope) reformed Law no. 16,713 regarding access to retirement benefits and in the calculation of the years of work required for women who had children. This regulation states that workers (salaried or independent) that have registered a minimum of 30 years of employment with effective contributions to the retirement system (even when the minimum age is reached after the last date of employment) can retire. This regulation reduces by five years the required years of work with effective contributions to qualify for retirement (according to the 1996 law the requirement was 35 years).

Second, an important reform was introduced that recognized women's different role in the labor market. The same law established that for women with children the system will recognize one year of employment for each child born or adopted (up to a maximum of five) for effects of retirement calculations. With this regulation, for example, mothers with five adopted or biological children could retire at age 55.

The same law established a new triggering event called the Temporary Subsidy for Compensated Unemployment (Susidio Transitorio por Inactividad Compensada). Even though in legal terms it is not *sensu stricto* a triggering event, the situation arises in those cases in which a worker, who is at least 58 years old and has worked for 28 or more years, finds him- or herself in a situation of forced involuntary unemployment for a period equal to or greater than one year. Given these circumstances, the worker receives compensation from the BPS equal to 40 percent of his or her average income received during the six months prior to the termination of employment. The subsidy is available for a period not greater than two years or until the worker is eligible for retirement. Both the period and the subsidy amount are considered in the retirement calculation.

The law also eased access to retirement by creating a category called "advanced retirement." A mix of age and years of employment allows persons with as few as 15 years of registered employment that are at least 70 years old to retire. But the change also created a progressive scale that allows individuals to retire at younger ages, but with more years of registered employment. Thus, a person that is 65 years old, but has registered only 25 years of employment, can also retire. This scale continues in this way: 69 years old and 17 years of employment, 68 years old and 19 years of employment, 67 years old and 21 years of employment, 66 years old and 23 years of employment, 65 years old and 25 years of employment. It is clear that the replacement rate changes in these situations, resulting in less favorable calculations than if the worker had fulfilled the normal retirement requirements (60 years old and 30 years of employment).

Law no. 18,395 for Easing Access Conditions (Flexibilización de las Condiciones de Acceso) also eliminated some of the requirements for accessing Retirement for Total Disability (Jubilación por Incapacidad Total). Current regulations still require a worker to have worked for at least two years, but the law eliminated the requirement to have contributed during the six months before the disability if the event occurred while the worker was employed or on subsidized unemployment. Similarly, Law no. 16,713 required workers younger than 25 years to have registered at least six months of employment immediately before suffering a disability, but with the reform the requirement that these months of employment occur immediately before the disability was eliminated. In the case of the Temporary Subsidy for Partial Disability (Subsidio Transitorio por Incapacidad Parcial; disability that does not prevent the worker from preforming a different job), the law also eliminated the requirement for six months of contributions before the disability or termination of employment. This is a benefit that is provided for a maximum period of three years, and its amount is calculated based on the percentage of remaining ability and the worker's age.

Law no. 18,246 on cohabitation is an important regulation that has effects on the expansion of coverage of groups that were previously excluded from social security benefits. This law recognizes the rights of partners (men or women) that can prove cohabitation for a period of not fewer than five years. This union must be legally recognized, and either cohabitant can jointly or separately request recognition. Once the condition is proven, reciprocal aid obligations are established as in the case of a civil marriage. This recognition creates rights and obligations similar to those established in civil marriage, including the right to alimony in the case that one of the partners was eligible and also, of interest in the present study, to survivor's benefits. Widowers are entitled to pensions as long as they can prove their dependence on the deceased or a lack of sufficient resources. Widows are entitled to a pension if their annual income does not exceed $15,000.[5] This pension would be paid as an annuity if the widow were over 40 years old. If she were younger than 40 (between 30 and 39 years) she would receive the pension for five years, or for two years if she were younger than 30 years old.

Within this framework, Law no. 18,326 provides that in those cases in which there are collective agreements in cases of corporate restructuring, layoffs, and subsequent rehiring, the retirement system will count workers' unemployed periods as employment. The calculation of contributions will be based on the amount agreed to between workers and employers, which will create the corresponding tax obligations for employers.

Domestic employees represent a special case because they have historically had very low participation rates in the social security system. The lack of regulations and the essentially nonexistent enforcement made protecting this vulnerable group very difficult. As a result, Law no. 18,065 created very specific regulations for this activity and its relationship with the social security system in 2006. First, domestic workers were included in collective bargaining to promote their unionization. In addition, their working conditions were regulated and placed under the supervision of the General Labor and Social Security Inspectorate (Inspección General del Trabajo y la Seguridad Social) to monitor compliance with the regulations and workers' rights created by the law. Household inspections were authorized, and stiff penalties were established in the event of noncompliance with the new regulations.

The government also approved Law no. 18,095 at the beginning of 2007, establishing an income bonus by age for retirees that receive very low benefits. The government sought to improve benefits for the most vulnerable retirees because they receive an increase (bonus) on top of their benefit that is progressive based upon their age (at least in the beginning). To access the benefit, the retiree should be at least 70 years old and receive an income less than three BPCs, and in the retiree's household there must not be any income above the limit, including that of the retiree.

In 2008 a period of extensive legislative activity began in the area of social security, which gave way to the passage of regulations that dealt with the specific situations of some occupational categories facing various circumstances. In June Law no. 18,310 was passed, establishing the calculation of implicit employment for former workers in the refrigeration industry that had been kept from working for political reasons. The workers covered by this law had been idled for political, union, ideological, or merely arbitrary motives between 1973 and 1985 (from the beginning to the end of the civilian-military dictatorship). For effects of retirement, this law counted the time that these workers had not been able to work during their unemployment. The law specified that their implicit salary was to be seven BPCs[6] during the reference period.[7] Moreover, these workers were promised a minimum retirement of four BPCs (around US$400); and if they had not met the age requirement (60 years old for retirement age) and were at least 50 years old with 20 years of employment, they were promised a special retirement sum equal to four BPCs.

In October 2008 with Law no. 18,355 the retirement calculation was improved for workers in construction. The law established that the base retirement salary for these workers would be calculated based on the worker's salary, plus personal retirement contributions and contributions for health insurance. This represented a significant increase for the calculation of retirement contributions that, to be funded, were covered with funds transferred from general revenues to the BPS.

That same month Law no. 18,834 was passed, incorporating artists, who until then had faced many difficulties gaining recognition from the social security system. As a result, the law created a registry in the Ministry of Education and

Culture (Ministerio de Educación y Cultura) in which workers employed in the arts and related activities, whether salaried or independent, should register themselves. This registry also records contracts related to artistic activities that are undertaken by employees. For effects of retirement calculations, the system considers the time effectively worked and includes drafts, setup, execution, performance, and maintenance of the work. Other artistic activities are also considered, and the law created a Certification Commission (Comisión Certificadora) that must accredit activities presented as artistic or related to the arts. The commission is made up of representatives from the government and artists' associations.

The Effects on Spending, Funding, and Coverage

The period that began in 2005 with the electoral triumph of the Frente Amplio was characterized by an explicit political will to increase coverage and improve benefits and by a vigorous process of economic recovery. In this environment of parametric reforms that expanded contributory and noncontributory coverage and of very noticeable economic growth, an increase in expenditures took place. This is particularly true after 2009 when the effects of the new reforms introduced in the retirement and pension system began to be felt. These reforms impacted both the level of coverage as well as the amount of social security benefits. After expenditures reached a peak in 1996 (at almost 14 percent of GDP) they began to fall until 2008, when spending began to grow again, as is evident in figure 15.7.

On the other side, the series of reforms from the Frente Amplio government and the evolution of the macroeconomic situation contributed to the increase in collections, especially related to expenditures. In effect, the volume of the so-called net assistance (transfers from general revenues to cover the deficit) and the taxes allocated to the system have decreased continuously since 2002, when they represented 7 percent of GDP, to less than 4 percent in 2011. The total transfers from the treasury, which represented less than 10 percent of the BPS's expenditures in 1990, had been increasing until reaching 50 percent of spending in 2003 (figure 15.10). Since then, transfers' relative importance has begun to decrease, as the BPS's own resources (contributions) have increased. This is related to growth in the number of contributors (salaried and independent).

Transfers fell in 2011 despite growth in the number and amount of benefits. The reduction in the government's contributions was due to the marked growth of the economically active population that contributed to the BPS, indicating a significant increase in labor formality. Bene and Colombo (2012) analyze the evolution of potentially contributing jobs and effectively contributing jobs during the period 2004–11. They compare the number of formal workers with informal workers (understood to be noncontributors to the BPS), which produces a net balance of informality. The analysis of the difference between one variable and the other indicates a reduction of informality of more than 50 percent between 2004 and 2011, reaching the lowest percentage in history (for recorded history): 18.65 percent, falling from almost 40 percent in 2004 (table 15.3).

Figure 15.10 BPS Resources, 1990–2011

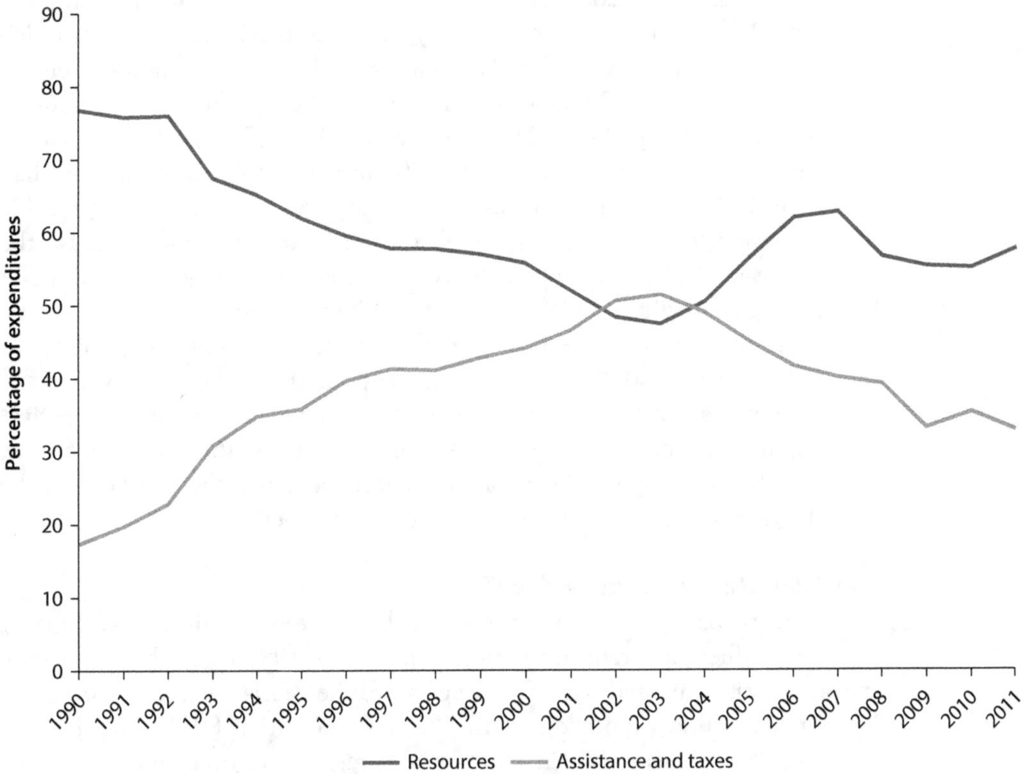

Source: Based on Banco de Previsión Social (BPS), 2005, 2012.

Table 15.3 Evolution of Contribution Evasion in Jobs, 2004–11

Year	*Potentially contributing jobs*[a]	*Contributing jobs*[a]	*Noncontributing jobs*	*Percentage of evasion (%)*
2004	1,244,619	751,762	492,857	39.60
2005	1,265,105	834,576	430,529	34.03
2006	1,285,255	899,442	385,813	30.02
2007	1,389,460	979,790	409,670	29.48
2008	1,448,482	1,056,155	392,327	27.09
2009	1,429,016	1,097,667	331,348	23.19
2010	1,454,020	1,161,222	292,798	20.14
2011	1,498,323	1,218,858	279,465	18.65

Source: Bene and Colombo 2012.
a. Does not include jobs in rural activities.

In 2009 the set of regulations that eased access to contributory retirement and pension benefits, as well as the new noncontributory pensions created, had an impact on the scale of retirees and pensioners in a relatively brief period because they modified the more restrictive aspects of access to benefits. The most evident result of this easing was the marked increase in noncontributory pension coverage. These benefits were stable around 64,000 from 1997 until 2005, increasing from 2005 until 2007 somewhat more than 8 percent, and between 2007 and 2011 they increased by almost 20 percent. As a result, during the first years of the Frente Amplio's administration noncontributory pension coverage increased by 29 percent. Meanwhile, the number of contributory pensions decreased by almost 11,000 between 2005 and 2011 and retirement benefits increased by approximately 30,000, surpassing the figure that they had reached in 1999. Looking at the fall in contributory pensions, it is very probable that many beneficiaries opted for the noncontributory pensions because the proof of years of employment for the contributory pensions was more difficult than proving eligibility based on necessity and low income.

In a recent work that does not cover all of 2012, Scardino (2012) points out that just between 2008 and 2012 an increase in the quantity of benefits of 6 percent is evident, considering contributory and noncontributory benefits.[8] Keeping in mind that this increase was produced in just three years, we must conclude that it is very significant, above all if it warns that the trend during the prior 10 years was one of a decreasing quantity of benefits.

The Political Economy Behind the Reforms

The social security system in Uruguay has been the object of intense debates, political conflicts, and radical transformations since 1985 when the democratic transition was cemented with the election of Julio María Sanguinetti from the Red Party (Partido Colorado). During his administration (1985–90) the BPS was reinstitutionalized, but in addition a fierce debate occurred around the readjustment of benefit values. Between 1985 and 1987 the Executive Branch applied a revaluation system from Institutional Act no. 9, which adjusted benefit values lower than what the organizations of retirees and pensioners thought was fair.

In this process, the topic of social security became central on the public agenda and catalyzed the formation of a powerful coalition of interests that was led by an incipient association of retirees and pensioners. The associations grew stronger during the conflict with the executive branch and in the same process strengthened the political left (the Frente Amplio), which at every opportunity acted to support their demands. The most salient point from this period is that it created the opportunity for the formation of powerful associations of retirees and pensioners that were able to impose their retirement demands first and later promote a referendum that led to the reform of the constitution of the republic in 1989, when increases in retirement and pension benefits were linked to salaries. The Associations of Retirees and Pensioners (Asociaciones de Jubilados y Pensionistas) emerged from this process as the most powerful social movement in the country (except for the Workers' Central, Plenario Intersindical de Trabajadores-Convención Nacional de Trabajadores—PIT-CNT), and were even capable of imposing a constitutional reform even against the will of almost all of the political forces, obtaining the support of 82 percent of the electorate in favor of their proposal.

In the same movement that ratified the constitutional reform, President Luis Alberto Lacalle, from the National Party (Partido Nacional), was elected, triumphing on a reformist platform that was characteristic of the liberal governments in the 1990s in Latin America. His agenda contained a clear series of stabilization and structural adjustment measures. In that scenario it was clear that the retirement and pension system required significant reform as a result of the predicted impact of the indexation mechanism created in the constitution. It was expected that the new mechanism would increase public spending on retirement and pension benefits significantly, something that went against the adjustment and stabilization policies of the new government. During the five-year period of Lacalle's administration, the Executive Branch sent to the parliament four reform bills, and all failed. These reforms could not be passed because some participants assumed they were too radical, while others thought they were lukewarm. Nonetheless, this period allowed for the accumulation of political and technical will that made the subsequent reform during President Sanguinetti's period viable.

In 1995 the new administration of Dr. Julio María Sanguinetti (who had been president during the first democratic period from 1985 to 1990 and was reelected in 1995) had the opportunity to introduce a structural reform to the social security system. The process of building consensus for the reform was carried out by first reaching technical agreements between the members of the National Party and the Red Party (Partido Colorado) and also with the Frente Amplio. The National Party (governing party) called for the creation of a technical commission and another political commission made up of representatives of all of Uruguay's political parties. The technical commission was supposed to come to an agreement on basic topics such as the reliability of the information supplied by the government, as well as other more complex topics such as the reform options. The work of the technical group achieved consensus on some aspects of the diagnosis and even on a reform option based on a model of creating a system of "notional accounts." This idea became a bill that the executive branch submitted to parliament for consideration, but it did not obtain the necessary majorities. The Frente Amplio, whose technical advisors had joined the consensus on the proposed model, opposed the reform in parliament along with legislators from the Red Party. During the final year of President Lacalle's term, the government hired a consultancy with support from the Inter-American Development Bank to analyze the financial and political viability of various reform models. The results of this work were delivered to the government as its term was ending and were inputs for decision making in the incoming government. One of the alternatives that the inputs contemplated was a system similar to the one that was finally approved and that had been presented by the National Party in the technical commission. The foreknowledge of the alternatives, and especially of the option that was finally approved, opened a window of opportunity for the Whites (Blancos) and the Reds (Colorados) to agree quickly, during the first year of Sanguinetti's term, finally approving the reform in 1995.

The process begun during the National Party's term in government, with the participation of political teams in the technical discussions, created a level of policy community that allowed policy makers to deepen the debate on alternative models and created the need to implement changes agreed to among all the participants. This reform was preceded by a process of consensus building in which all the political parties represented in parliament participated. Once the discussion reached advanced stages, the Frente Amplio withdrew from the negotiations, claiming that social organizations had not been invited to participate in the debate. This withdrawal ended up facilitating the agreement between the two traditional parties.

Once the law was approved, the Frente Amplio, the retiree and pensioner organizations, and the union movement opposed it very strongly. Thus, they converted repeal of the law into one of the central issues in the political conflicts that defined the following years until the Frente Amplio became the governing party 10 years after the social security system reform had been approved. However, when the Frente Amplio took over government, the proposal to revise the 1996 reforms lost momentum in the political agenda. Nonetheless, the fight to "remove profit" from the social security system is still a central demand of the union movement, the retiree and pensioner movement, and some sectors of the Frente Amplio that are waiting for an opportune moment to newly reform the system.

The Frente Amplio participated in the 2004 national elections in a coalition that included sectors that had previously not been included in this party. The leftist coalition structured a common platform that was managed by the so-called Integrated Platform Commission (Comisión Integrada de Programa). This commission created what was called the "Support for the Broad Programmatic Guidelines for the 2005–10 Government" ("Respaldo de Grandes Lineamientos Programáticos para el Gobierno 2005–10"). This document, on the subject of social security, recognized that radical changes to the system would face "multiple" difficulties because the system had already been in place for seven years and "the workers have already seen their contributions move" toward the AFAPs. However, it was proposed to move gradually toward the creation of a new system for which they would specify legislative and administrative measures.

The platform document is very brief in terms of what the alternative model to Law no. 16,713 should be. However, it does point out that it should have three pillars: a solidary noncontributory one, a second intergenerational pay-as-you-go pillar, and a third pillar, termed complementary, for high-income workers. The system is presented not as an individually funded scheme, but as a collectively funded one. The institutions that are in charge of administering the complementary subsystem should be state-owned, semiofficial, or social interest organizations but, in all cases, should be nonprofit. The Frente Amplio's set of proposals, as a whole, aimed at a gradual structural reform of the system that would essentially increase coverage and the quality of benefits.

The different improvement and coverage expansion measures proposed in the Frente Amplio platform were implemented. The required number of years of contributions was lowered from 35 to 30, and elderly retirement was relaxed. Even though access requirements for the Elderly Pension were not relaxed, a subsidy for needy individuals between 65 and 70 years old was created, which essentially had the same effect. Unemployment insurance was also relaxed, offering a subsidy to individuals close to retirement age who lost their jobs. In addition, the number of occupational categories covered was increased, and the terms for joining the system for workers from these categories were made more attractive (domestic employees, construction workers, and the refrigeration industry).

The government also made progress on the funded component of the system in the reduction of the AFAPs' commissions. The first measure was the passage of Law no. 18,356, which limited the administrators' options for choosing the base amount upon which to calculate commissions. Even though this was not a true reduction in commissions, it reduced the AFAPs' discretion in terms of the amount that would be considered when charging commissions. Moreover, the state-owned AFAP (Republic AFAP), which holds more than 50 percent of the deposits from members of the mixed regime (just 38 percent of total members), began a significant process of reducing its commissions.

The big achievement of the Frente Amplio administration was the spectacular increase in labor formalization and, consequently, the number of workers contributing to the system, which also resulted in an increase in coverage. The relaxation of retirement requirements implemented through the various laws mentioned earlier had a major impact on the expansion of coverage in recent years.

What explains this relative success in the Frente Amplio government's ability to carry out its plans regarding social security? Indeed, the programmatic agreement among political forces in the government was a key part of this achievement. The absolute majority of the Frente Amplio in both chambers of parliament was also important because it facilitated the passage of the laws in question. Another factor that must be mentioned is that the government began a National Dialogue for Social Security (Diálogo Nacional por la Seguridad Social) in 2007. In this dialogue policy makers made some important agreements that dealt with both supporting some measures already adopted by the government as well as the need to institute some reforms (box 15.1).

It is clear that the dialogue's strategy was in line with the proposals from the government's platform. The great success of the political handling of the reform was not just in making the programmatic measures a reality; it was also in ensuring that the reforms enjoyed broad consensus. As Busquets, Bucheli, and Setaro (2009) argue "the Dialogue allowed for the invigoration of a process of exchange between government, social, and business sector actors, that at the end translated in a series of important transformations to the social security system."

Providing Services to the Elderly

One of the incoming government's priorities in 2005 was the reform of the health care system. The reform's main objective was to make the system more inclusive by reducing the large access inequalities. Moreover, the reform sought

Box 15.1 National Dialogue for Social Security, 2007

Agreements Reached

- Facilitate access to retirement benefits by reducing requirements.
- Recognize the gains achieved by the law that acknowledge years of contributions when workers near retirement were not employed, through an agreement with the employer in cases of corporate restructuring.
- Promote measures that resolve the situation of women having fewer months of contributions (because of the time they spend caring for their families)—including the recognition of one year of employment for each biological or adopted child for working mothers.
- Recognize the gains in family allowance laws and elderly assistance laws for adults older than 65 years old in a situation of social emergency (Law no. 18,227 and Law no. 18,241).
- Propose that, in the medium term, the government review the elderly pension scheme to ease access for individuals living in poverty.
- Promote a decrease in management commissions charged by the AFAPs.

Source: Murro 2008.

to improve management on both micro and macro levels (strengthening the regulatory capacities of the Ministry of Public Health [Ministerio de Salud Pública, MSP] and improving the management of public and private institutions, as well as avoiding duplication of services and reducing costs) and strengthening the service model, placing a special emphasis on primary health care service.

Inclusive Reforms to Health Insurance

In Uruguay health service was provided by the public State Health Care Services Administration (Administración de los Servicios de Salud del Estado [ASSE]). ASSE served more than 50 percent of the population and was a dependency of the MSP—a direct provider via almost 50 Collective Medical Service Institutions (Instituciones de Atención Médica Colectiva [IAMCs]) and a few private insurance plans. As a result of this situation, the MSP had little regulatory capacity, the system was very fragmented, and quality depended on the subsector provider. The per capita budget of the public subsector was four times lower than that of the IAMCs and its quality was inferior. The IAMCs emerged as mutual associations and were widely accepted by a portion of the population because their service quality was good. The retirees and pensioners had to pay out-of-pocket fees to join an IAMC or be assisted by the ASSE. Low-income retirees were one exception, because they could receive mutual coverage by opting for an automatic deduction of a small percentage of their retirement benefits. The reform also sought to expand health insurance for all retirees and pensioners, a goal that was laid out gradually.

As part of the health care reform, the government decided to create the SNIS. This system included all of the comprehensive service providers in a system based on cooperation (public-private and among private providers).[9] This meant that the service, management, and funding models needed to be reformed. The government created a contributory insurance policy based on the social security model with contributions as a function of insured members' payment capacities and with similar benefits that were differentiated only by the comprehensive provider that insured members decided to join. The incorporation of beneficiaries has taken place gradually in sequential stages, with workers' children, public sector workers (and other occupational categories that have special coverage schemes), retirees and pensioners, and spouses entitled to benefits (box 15.2). Given the high fiscal cost of incorporating retirees and pensioners, their entrance into the SNIS was proposed as a gradual process over time. In January 2011 parliament passed Law no. 18,731, which began the process of incorporating all retirees and pensioners into the SNIS and which is supposed to be completed in 2016.

Box 15.2 Timeline for Incorporating Retirees and Pensioners into the SNIS

July 2011

- Retirees with complete disability and income less than four BPCs

July 2012

- Retirees and pensioners that were already paying for their own coverage in the private subsector since at least December 1, 2010
- Retirees and pensioners aged 74 and older whose benefits (retirement or pension) do not exceed three monthly BPCs

July 2013

- Retirees and pensioners over 70 years old, whose total income from retirement, pension, and other similar benefits does not exceed the sum of four monthly BPCs

July 2014

- Retirees and pensioners over 65 years old, whose total income from retirement, pension, and other similar benefits does not exceed the sum of five monthly BPCs

July 2015

- Retirees and pensioners over 60 years old, whose total income from retirement, pension, and other similar benefits does not exceed the sum of 10 monthly BPCs

July 2016

- All retirees and pensioners who have, for any reason, not been incorporated into the system yet
- All spouses and partners of retirees and pensioners

Table 15.4 Evolution of the Population Insured by National Health Insurance, 2007–12

	July 2007	July 2008	July 2009	July 2010	July 2011	July 2012	December 2012
Total workers	667,952	829,683	881,917	933,316	1,019,883	1,098,554	1,122,273
Minors	n.a.	405,831	451,557	477,732	537,424	585,765	593,926
Retirees and pensioners	50,644	68,926	77,844	101,699	127,124	278,910	319,530
Spouses and partners	n.a.	n.a.	n.a.	n.a.	26,486	69,641	73,007
Total	718,596	1,304,440	1,411,318	1,512,747	1,710,917	2,032,870	2,108,736

Source: Elaboration based on information provided by the Banco de Previsión Social (BPS).
Note: n.a. = not applicable

From a coverage point of view, the new Comprehensive Health Care System tripled insured coverage. It increased from 718,596 to 2,108,736 insured members in three and a half years (table 15.4). Children stand out among covered beneficiaries, increasing from zero to almost 600,000, and the number of retirees and pensioners increased from 50,644 insured members in 2007 to 319,530 in 2012.

In addition to the health care coverage expansion undertaken through the incorporation of retirees and pensioners into the National Health Insurance system, the management contracts that the Health Care System (the National Health Care Council, la Junta Nacional de Salud) signed in 2009 with health care service providers specified that "both parties agreed to meet a service goal of two free annual checkups (no copayment) for the elderly between 65 and 74 years old, and four annual visits for adults older than 75. This guideline was relaxed and in the end was fixed at one annual checkup for the elderly between 65 and 74 years old and two annual checkups for adults older than 75" (ROU 2012, p. 10).

Other Social Protection Programs for the Elderly

In Uruguay a large number of policies and programs are directed to social protection for the elderly. Some of them are made up of more or less stable policies, others are programs with national reach, and others have only local reach. The most important and significant are the Housing Solutions Program (Programa Soluciones Habitacionales) and Treatment for Ocular Illnesses (Tratamiento de Afecciones oculares).

Housing Solutions Program

The so-called Housing Solutions Program was created in 1987 by Law no. 15,900 and updated by subsequent legislation. The law originally established a 1 percent withholding on retirement and pension benefits for BPS beneficiaries, with the proceeds flowing into the National Housing Fund (Fondo Nacional de Viviendas). The money was collected by the BPS and transferred to the Ministry of Housing, Territorial Planning, and the Environment (Ministerio de Vivienda, Ordenamiento Territorial y Medioambiente [MVOTMA]). This ministry was responsible for managing tenders, construction, and maintenance. Meanwhile the BPS was responsible for receiving requests and allocating units using need-based criteria.

The law established that retirees and pensioners were entitled to housing if they received less than or equal to 12 Re-adjustable Units (Unidades Reajustables [URs]) as a monetary allowance or 24 URs if the request was from a region or community in the country that had a high level of housing availability.

After the Frente Amplio took over government, two changes took effect. First, the tax reform that created the Personal Income Tax (Impuesto a la Renta de las Personas Físicas [IRPF]) took effect and financed the program with general revenue, transferring the necessary funds to MVOTMA. At the same time, the administration of the program moved to the BPS, which now receives the funds from MVOTMA. The BPS maintains a registry of demand and allocates dwellings based on vulnerability criteria (that includes other variables in addition to income). The BPS also carries out tenders for the construction of housing complexes and their execution as well as taking care of maintenance and making administrative decisions regarding communal issues and the appropriate use of the dwellings.

The Housing Solutions Program began as a program that gave dwellings to low-income retirees and pensioners capable of living independently in usufruct. This means that the elderly that are no longer able to live independently cannot remain in this type of housing. To solve this problem, after 2007, because in some communities it was not efficient to construct dwellings, the government created a rental housing subsidy to offer housing solutions in a different way. In addition, the Bed Quota Program (Programa de Cupos Cama) was created. This program transfers a quantity of money to Elderly Residences (Residencias de Ancianos) that have agreements with the BPS for each beneficiary that moves from the dwellings to the Residences. Moreover, from these funds the Residence charges its beneficiaries 75 percent of their income from retirement or pension payments from the BPS.

Currently there are some 15,000 housing units, around 300 in the Bed Quota Program, and 500 rent subsidies. BPS authorities have determined that the fixed amount of funding that is paid for beds is not enough for elderly homes that have agreements with the institution to accept residents who are not self-sufficient. In addition, the cost of rents far exceeds the subsidy that the BPS offers, which limits the availability of dwellings under this program.

Treatment of Ocular Illnesses for Low-Income Elderly Persons

In 2007 the MSP, ASSE, and MIDES signed an agreement in which, with support from a team of Cuban surgeons, the government offered access to cataract and pterygium surgeries for the elderly. These ailments are causes of blindness, and the treatments' cost is inaccessible for the majority of the Uruguayan population, especially for low-income retirees. The agreement allowed low-income retirees that were users of the IAMC and ASSE systems to freely access the operations.

The unsatisfied demand resulted in 54,000 examinations and 23,000 operations during a seven-year period. The examinations are carried out with the collaboration of the National Organization of Retirees and Pensioners (Organización Nacional de Jubilados y Pensionistas), which schedules examination appointments before surgical interventions, and the BPS, which provides a vehicle and driver to the team of doctors that moves throughout the country carrying out these examinations. The surgeries take place in an ASSE hospital, and patients recover in what used to be a Jewish home for the elderly that was bought with funds from the BPS housing program and that is now managed by ASSE and MIDES.

Conclusions and Future Challenges

The economic recovery that began in 2004–05, the series of regulations that improved coverage of active workers (or labor formality), the health care reform that stimulated labor formalization, and the improvement in the BPS's collection mechanisms and the tax system's collections have had a major impact on improving the equilibrium calculation on the retirement and pension system. In this context, the increase in salaries as a product of economic growth generated a substantial improvement in retirement and pension benefits (due to Uruguay's indexation mechanisms). Additionally, mechanisms such as the age bonus and the differential revaluations that favored retirees and pensioners with lower incomes improved the adequacy of retirement and pension benefits. The mixed system created in 1995, although it is still far from maturity, will improve retirement amounts according to projections (Papadópulos 2007).

However, the aging of the population continues to be a challenge for the system's financial stability. It must be remembered that the dependency ratio will increase in the coming years, and unless productivity does not increase significantly, authorities will have to consider parametric reforms. The recent relaxation of access to retirement and pension benefits that has allowed coverage levels to increase since 2007 with a retirement age of 60 years and 30 years of working period creates doubts about whether the financial equation will be sustainable in the medium and long term without again changing retirement criteria. Benefit indexation cannot be modified unless it is changed in the constitution. As a result, the criteria that can be modified are the retirement age, number of contribution years, and replacement rates. To this, it must be added that even though the system is mixed, the pay-as-you-go component conceals very significant transfers from general revenues, whether through taxes allocated or transfers to cover the deficit (which together represent 40 percent of spending). As a result, a structural reform, which would be the most complex alternative but also the truest one, must move toward (1) a basic minimum funded from general revenues, and (2) a complementary system made up of a pay-as-you-go component and an individually funded component. Such a reform will help insure that the system's finances are transparent and that spending redistribution systems can operate according to need-based criteria.

Finally, it must be pointed out that the incorporation of retirees and pensioners into the health care system (to the health insurance system) corrects a structural inequality in the health care system and lowers health care costs for the elderly, which, as we know, tend to grow with age. However, while the health care system fills the role of attending to illnesses, it does not provide long-term eldercare.

Therefore, in the future, the government will need to combine monetary transfers from the IVS system with an eldercare system that accounts for demographic, family, and labor market transformations that are underway.

Notes

1. The new system created the class of Administrators of Retirement Savings Funds (Administradoras de Fondos de Ahorro Previsional [AFAP]) that are private entities responsible for investing workers' contributions. In exchange for managing the funds, the AFAPs are authorized to charge a commission on the individual savings account of each member, with this being the only payment they receive. Workers can join the AFAP that they choose. Collection of contributions continued to be a responsibility of the BPS, which retains a portion of the contributions (pay-as-you-go component) for its own funds and transfers the individual surpluses to the AFAPs. The law allowed the creation of one state-owned AFAP. The AFAPs invest in the instruments that they choose, subject to regulations on type and limits imposed by the AFAP regulator at the Central Bank. As the system has become more consolidated, regulations have become more permissive in terms of instruments and types of investments.
2. The pay-as-you-go system was not eliminated as it was in Chile ("replacement" model), nor does it compete with the individually funded system as in Peru and Colombia ("parallel" structural reform model).
3. Strictly speaking, this was the "general retirement" system. Alongside this system numerous special cases existed that, above all, established more advantageous retirement conditions, as is the case for teachers who can retire after just 25 years of work and without a minimum age requirement.
4. It is important to point out that the Uruguayan social security system, in addition to offering pension benefits from the BPS, includes the Military Fund, the Police Fund, the Banking Sector Fund, the University Professionals Fund, and the Notary Fund. Each of these so-called semiofficial funds covers professionals from the respective sectors and creates, at a certain level, "privileged" retirement systems. The funds cover only a minor percentage of Uruguayan social security beneficiaries (just a little more than 7 percent).
5. Equal to approximately US$700.
6. The Base de Prestaciones y Contribuciones (BPC) replaced the National Minimum Salary (Salario Mínimo Nacional [SMN]) as a base for readjusting various benefits. It took effect with Law no. 17,856 of 2004 as an amount equal to the SMN at that time. Its readjustment was fixed "as a function of the financial situation of the State and at the discretion of the Executive Branch, at the same time that general adjustments were made to salaries in the Central Administration, as a percentage equal to the variation in the consumer price index, or the variation of the median salary index, subject to the financial capacity of the Executive Branch to modify the rate of change chosen up or down by up to 20%."
7. US$800 as of October 2012.
8. Scardino presents an evolution of benefit figures that is different from the BPS's Statistical Bulletins (exhibiting a slightly higher record of benefits), although the recorded trend is similar.
9. Comprehensive Service Providers are the IAMCs (nonprofit institutions—mutuals and cooperatives—that offer services that cover all three levels of care), the ASSE, and

the health insurers that were recognized by the MSP (private insurers that offer the same type of benefits as the IAMCS or the ASSE). There are 48 IAMCs in the country and seven Comprehensive Insurers.

Bibliography

Abranches, S. 1982. "The Politics of Social Welfare Development in Latin America." Presentation at the XII World Congress of the International Political Science Association, Rio de Janeiro, August.

Bene, N., and C. Colombo. 2012. "Evasión en puestos de Trabajo." Comentarios de Seguridad Social, Tercer Trimestre 37, Edición Especial.

BPS (Banco de Previsión Social). 2005. "Boletín estadístico." BPS, Montevideo.

———. 2012. "Evolución de las Pasividades." BPS, Montevideo.

Busquets, J., M. Bucheli., and M. Setaro. 2009. "El Diálogo Nacional en Seguridad Social: Contenido y proceso." In *La seguridad social en Uruguay. Contribuciones a su historia*. Montevideo: RAFAP, ICP, FCS.

Dos Santos, G. 1979. *Cidadania e justica: a política social na orden brasileira*. Rio de Janeiro: Editora Campus.

Filgueira, C. 1970. "Burocracia y clientela: Una política de absorción de tensiones." *Cuadernos de Ciencias Sociales* 1 (1).

Mesa-Lago, C. 1978. *Social Security in Latin America: Pressure Groups, Stratification, and Inequality*. Pittsburgh: University of Pittsburgh Press.

———. 1985. "El desarrollo de la seguridad social en América Latina." Estudios e Informes de la ECLAC 43, ECLAC, Santiago.

Mesa-Lago, C., and F. Bertranou. 1998. *Manual de la economía de la seguridad social*. Montevideo: CLAEH.

Murro, E. 2008. "Diálogo Nacional en Seguridad Social en Uruguay, 2007–08." *Estudios de la Seguridad Social* 101.

Papadópulos, J. 1992. "Seguridad social y política en Uruguay. Orígenes, evolución y mediación de intereses en la restauración democrática." CIESU, Montevideo.

———. 2007. "Mercado de Trabajo, Género y Reforma del Sistema Pensionario en Uruguay: ¿Cuáles son las Perspectivas para los Adultos Mayores?" AISS, *Estudios de la Seguridad Social*.

Rofman, R., and M. Oliveri. 2012. "La cobertura de los sistemas previsionales en América Latina: conceptos e indicadores." Serie de Documentos de Trabajo sobre Políticas Sociales 7, World Bank, Buenos Aires.

ROU (República Oriental del Uruguay). 2012. "Informe nacional: Uruguay." Official report presented at the Tercera Conferencia regional intergubernamental sobre envejecimiento, San José, Costa Rica, May 8–11.

Saldain, R. 1987. "El 'social welfare en Uruguay'." Draft, Montevideo.

Scardino, A. 2012. "Evolución de las pasividades por sector. 1995–2012/s1." Comentarios de Seguridad Social 37, July, August, September.

Environmental Benefits Statement

The World Bank Group is committed to reducing its environmental footprint. In support of this commitment, the Publishing and Knowledge Division leverages electronic publishing options and print-on-demand technology, which is located in regional hubs worldwide. Together, these initiatives enable print runs to be lowered and shipping distances decreased, resulting in reduced paper consumption, chemical use, greenhouse gas emissions, and waste.

The Publishing and Knowledge Division follows the recommended standards for paper use set by the Green Press Initiative. Whenever possible, books are printed on 50 percent to 100 percent postconsumer recycled paper, and at least 50 percent of the fiber in our book paper is either unbleached or bleached using Totally Chlorine Free (TCF), Processed Chlorine Free (PCF), or Enhanced Elemental Chlorine Free (EECF) processes.

More information about the Bank's environmental philosophy can be found at http://crinfo.worldbank.org/wbcrinfo/node/4.

green press INITIATIVE

www.ingramcontent.com/pod-product-compliance
Lightning Source LLC
LaVergne TN
LVHW080007210926
848481LV00011B/2966